THE ENCYCLOPEDIA OF
CLASSIC CARS

THE ENCYCLOPEDIA OF

CLASSIC CARS

FROM 1890 TO THE PRESENT DAY

GENERAL EDITOR: CRAIG CHEETHAM

THUNDER BAY
P·R·E·S·S

San Diego, California

Thunder Bay Press
An imprint of the Advantage Publishers Group
5880 Oberlin Drive, San Diego, CA 92121-4794
www.thunderbaybooks.com

Library of Congress Cataloging-in-Publication Data

The encyclopedia of classic cars from 1890 to the present day / general editor, Craig
Cheetham.
      p. cm.
   Includes index.
   ISBN 978-1-59223-781-4
   1. Antique and classic cars--Encyclopedias. 2. Automobiles--History. I. Cheetham,
Craig
   TL9.E5236 2007
   629.222--dc22

                              2007011437

Project Editor: James Bennett
Copy Editor: Siobhan O'Connor
Additional Text: Richard Gunn
Picture Research: Terry Forshaw, Kate Green
Design: Hawes Design

Printed in China

1 2 3 4 5 11 10 09 08 07

CONTENTS

INTRODUCTION

It may seem hard to believe in today's automated world, but the motor car is still a relatively new invention. Its appearance in the late nineteenth century came fairly late in the industrial revolution, way behind the dawn of the railway and only a few years ahead of powered flight. Yet despite having been in existence for little more than twelve decades, the automobile has changed beyond recognition from its early days.

This book charts that progress, from the pioneering days of the 'horseless carriage' right through to the modern day and the introduction of supercars designed by, and sometimes reliant on, some of the most sophisticated computer systems ever developed.

While it would be impossible to catalogue every single car ever made, at least not in a book you'd be able to lift off the coffee table, this book features

Thanks to Henry Ford's innovative method of mass production and the car's low purchase cost, the Ford Model T was the first car to truly bring motoring to the masses.

the most significant cars throughout history, starting with Karl Benz's 1885 three-wheeler – the very first vehicle to be powered by an internal combustion engine, and by definition, the world's first motor car.

The story unfolds with a myriad of pioneering names like Benz, Cadillac, Peugeot, Opel, Renault and Vauxhall which are still with us today, and others such as Darracq, Oldsmobile and Panhard-Levassor, which were giants in their day but have since fallen by the wayside, as victims of incredible growth within the motor industry.

More than five million Italians fell in love with the Fiat Nuova 500 – its cute styling and tremendous handling made it a massive hit, and meant it stayed in production for over 20 years.

That growth, which moved motoring from the exclusive preserve of the seriously wealthy through to a means of transport for the masses was very much down to one man – Henry Ford.

Motoring for the Masses

Ford was the son of an Irish potato farmer, whose family had moved to America in the nineteenth century to capitalize on the growing farming economy of the time. But while his father made a modest income from his farming methods, it was his son that would finally realise the Ford family fortune.

Using methods employed on the family farm, in which one group of workers picked the crops, a second group sorted them and a third cleaned them for sale, Henry realised that applying a similar technique to automobile manufacturer would be more straightforward and less expensive than building one car at a time, as well as speeding up the whole process.

In 1906, he opened a factory in Dearborn, on the outskirts of Detroit, Michigan, building the now-famous Ford Model T – by far the cheapest car ever sold, and one that soon found itself in favour not just in the USA, but across the entire planet.

By the time the Model T ceased production in 1927, it was being built in four different factories in the USA, as well as plants in the UK and Europe. The motor industry had also changed significantly, as Ford had brought motoring to the masses, and other manufacturers had followed the company's lead towards mass production.

Economic Growth

By the 1940s, a car was no longer something that only a rich person could own, and even today car ownership is reaching those who have never previously been able to drive, spurred on by economic growth in China and the Middle East. This popularity led to the motor car becoming a much

Although the oil crises and political unrest meant the 1970s were times of turmoil for the motor industry, there was still room for the odd supercar, as the gorgeous Ferrari 308 would prove.

more common sight, but it also led to excessive demands from wealthy buyers, who realising that owning a car no longer held any distinction insisted on a much more extravagant vehicle.

Sweeping Changes

The 1920s saw some of the most extravagant and beautiful cars ever made, such as the Auburn Speedster, Duesenberg Model J, Mercedes 540K and Bugatti Royale. Indicative of a social phenomenon that would never be repeated, they swiftly disappeared.

The onset of the Great Depression, initially in the United States and then affecting most of the rest of the world, followed by the enormous upheavals of World War II, saw sweeping changes across the global motor industry, and while there was still a limited demand for handbuilt luxury vehicles, the 1940s and 1950s saw buyers opting for a more austere, humble type of vehicle.

The period wasn't without innovation, however. It was during this time that aerodynamics started to become more important, while unitary construction – where a car's bodyshell is built as one unit, rather than a separate body and chassis – was developed in the UK and quickly became the accepted construction method across the world.

Postwar Glitz and Muscle

With the war over and economic stability returning to the car industry's traditional heartlands of the USA, Europe and UK, the 1950s saw a decade of austerity giving way to glitz and glamour, as car design grew ever more adventurous. It was this period that saw some of the most dramatic – if occasionally impractical – cars ever built.

The Sixties saw the birth of the muscle car – a type of modified sedan or coupe which was very much the precursor to today's range of performance cars, and for a while the motor industry enjoyed a glorious heyday.

But it wasn't to last. While environmental developments and a commitment to reducing exhaust emissions may seem very much today's concern, it was the fuel crises of the 1970s that saw car makers initially making more efficient and compact vehicles – a theme which has continued ever since. Big, flashy cars became unpopular, with buyers favouring more compact, fuel efficient models – a move that not only saw the styles and shapes of cars changing, but which also opened the door for significant growth for car makers in Europe and Japan, both of which capitalized on selling vehicles in the American market before the US manufacturers were ready to respond to this shift in consumer demand.

Safety First

Driving today's cars is fundamentally little different to driving those of the 1970s or 1980s. A little faster, more refined and safer, perhaps, but whereas cars would change significantly every few years in the past, the cars of the late twentieth century and beyond differ in more subtle yet equally important ways.

Today's car, for example, has been designed to withstand several types of accident. It features thousands of miles of wiring, with computer controls for everything from the door locks to the brakes and air conditioning system.

Car manufacturers today face more challenges than ever before. Environmental legislation, higher taxation, a question mark over the future of fossil fuels, and increased demand from customers for comfort, reliability and value for money make building cars a tougher proposition than ever, yet it's a business that is still fuelled by, staffed by and powered by enthusiasts. Those with a passion for motoring have created some of the finest vehicles ever built, and there are enough fascinating cars out there to prove that they still do so. This book celebrates them all, and long may it continue!

The quest to build the world's fastest car is as earnest today as it ever was. The Mercedes-McLaren SLR was quickest in 2004, but has now been beaten by the awesome Bugatti Veyron.

CHAPTER ONE

THE PIONEERS

1890–1925

The early days of motoring were also some of the most fascinating, as manufacturers got to grips with the notion of building a 'horseless carriage', and the general public got used to seeing them on the road.

Don't forget that these were the days when there were no television or radio broadcasts, and those who hadn't read about the new self-propelled vehicles in the newspapers were taken somewhat by surprise, and were rather suspicious, on the rare occasion they encountered a vehicle that wasn't pulled along by a horse!

Some of the cars from the earliest days of motoring may seem curious or downright ridiculous today, but at the time each new idea was an interesting experiment, even if it was an engineering dead end. Perceptions changed in the early part of the twentieth century, however, with the debut of the Ford Model T and the dawn of mass production, which brought motoring within the reach of a new class of buyer.

This led to hundreds of fascinating vehicles appearing all over the world, as other manufacturers rapidly embraced the production line idea and created new cars of their own, from humble saloon cars and sports models to handbuilt upmarket grand tourers.

By the end of this pioneering period, the motor car had evolved from a rudimentary form of self-propelled transport to a fledgling version of the cars we know today, complete with luxury interior trim, enclosed cabins, multiple ratio gearboxes and pneumatic tyres. These may not sound like huge technical advances, but compared to the very first cars, they represented a significant move forwards.

Mercedes-Benz can lay claim to being the creator of the automobile with the 1885 Benz Cyclecar, but by the early twentieth century it had grown into a true luxury brand. The Mercedes 60 was a race-bred car for the seriously wealthy.

PANHARD ET LEVASSOR

ENGINE: 566cc (35cu in), V-twin
POWER: n/a
0–60MPH (96KM/H): n/a
TOP SPEED: about 32km/h (20mph)
PRODUCTION TOTAL: n/a

René Panhard and Emile Levassor were true pioneers of motoring and were already established as industrial engineers when they produced their first car in 1890. It featured a 566cc (35cu in) V-twin engine licensed through Edouard Sarazin in France from Gottlieb Daimler in Germany; the pair would build their own vertical-twin unit a year later. While the Daimler engine was mid-mounted, the next car established a drivetrain used by nearly every other carmaker thereafter, with a front radiator and engine, driving a pedal-operated clutch, gearbox and then a chain-driven rear axle. It was known as Système Panhard. However, the original machine was suspended on rudimentary cart springs, solid rubber tyres on wood rims and tiller steering. In 1892, their car became the first to prove itself in a drive from Paris to Versailles, followed by another excursion, from Paris to Etretat. At an average of 10km/h (6mph), it took nine days and included a break to rebuild the engine.

Development of the Panhard et Levassor continued apace, while the company's first four-cylinder engine appeared in 1898.

As basic as it may now seem, the first Panhard et Levassor car proved its worth right at the dawn of motoring, by successfully undertaking 'long distance' drives around Paris.

BENZ VIKTORIA

ENGINE: 1730–2915cc (106–178cu in), single-cylinder
POWER: up to 5bhp (3.7kW)
0–60MPH: n/a
TOP SPEED: up to 35km/h (21mph)
PRODUCTION TOTAL: 43

Son of a locomotive driver and often called the 'Father of the Motorcar', Karl Benz began making motorized transport with an unstable 'cyclecar' in Mannheim, Germany, in 1885. The Motorwagen three-wheeler was the first car to

The Viktoria was the first four-wheeler from 'Father of the Motor Car' Karl Benz and was the first car to complete a 1000km.

use an internal combustion engine based on Nikolaus Otto's four-stroke principles and quickly became a blueprint for other pioneers. Benz's wife Bertha is acknowledged as being the first long-distance driver, when she took it and her sons on a perilous 100km (62-mile) trek from Mannheim to Pforzheim. The initial sales of 25 examples were slow, so Benz introduced the four-wheeled Viktoria in 1893, featuring a king-pin steering system; pneumatic tyres and suspension were still to be developed.

An important part of motoring history, it was the first car to complete a documented 1000km (621-mile) journey. In 1893, Czech textiles millionaire Theodore von Gondorf drove it from Liberec to Koblenz without breaking down.

DAIMLER FOUR-WHEELER

ENGINE: two-cylinder, capacity unknown
POWER: 4hp (3kW)
0–60MPH (96KM/H): n/a
TOP SPEED: 32km/h (20mph)
PRODUCTION TOTAL: 89 (in first eight months)

In 1893, F.R. Simms, an Englishman born in Germany, established a Cheltenham-based company and invested in the failing business owned by motoring pioneer Gottlieb Daimler. By 1896, Harry J. Lawson's bicycle empire in Coventry acquired the licenses for Daimler's internal combustion engines, including those held by Simms. While Lawson recognized that motorized transport was the future, a hurdle of flag-wavers from the steam carriage days had to be overcome. With influential friends in government, Lawson achieved his aim, and vehicles could travel at up to 19km/h (12mph). The key to the Four-Wheeler's success had been the development of the atomizing carburettor. Also heavily influenced by the Panhard developments, the English Daimler had automatic inlet valves, tiller steering, tube ignition, four-speed and reverse gearboxes, chain drive and solid tyres.

Prices ranged from £398 for a phaeton, up to £418 for what was described as a 'private omnibus'. The Four-Wheeler became the first car made by Daimler in any significant numbers. Gottlieb Daimler remained a director of the English firm until his resignation in 1898, by which time the company was producing four-cylinder cars.

Daimler's Four-Wheeler pushed forward automobile development thanks to its use of an atomizing carburettor. For an early car, its production run of 89 in just eight months was an impressive output.

LANCHESTER TWIN-CYLINDER

ENGINE: 4035cc (246cu in),
two-cylinder
POWER: 8bhp (6kW)
0–60MPH (96KM/H): n/a
TOP SPEED: n/a
PRODUCTION TOTAL: n/a

In 1895, the Lanchester Motor Company was established at Armourer Mills, Montgomery Street, Birmingham, England, by brothers George and Frederick, whose reputation was to grow during the Edwardian period with a number of technical innovations.

Working alone, the brothers were responsible for their own engineering developments – from their complex and highly effective two-speed and reverse, pre-selector epicyclic gearbox to their low-tension magneto ignition and worm-drive rear axle. In fact, the Lanchester brothers' first car appeared in 1895 with a single-cylinder 5hp (3.5kW) engine. By 1900, however, it had been developed into a horizontally opposed twin-cylinder 8hp (6kW) unit. Strangely, the Lanchester was steered by side tiller, although the transmission was an innovation used recently, in a modern form, by the hybrid Toyota Prius of 1997.

The engine itself featured the fascinating invention of two superimposed crankshafts, each with its own flywheel, that rotated in opposite directions. These were subsequently geared together and linked to two pistons by six connecting rods. The engine remained perfectly balanced and vibration-free at all times because it was operating in complete reverse rotation. This was a ground-breaking achievement, one which has been used by various carmakers ever since. The engine was used in other Lanchester cars until 1905, by which time the company had developed cantilever suspension and pre-selector three-speed epicyclic gears.

MERCEDES 60

The Mercedes marque was named after the daughter of wealthy German entrepreneur and part owner of Daimler, Emil Jellinek, with the innovative, sporty and powerful 60 as its first model.

ENGINE: 9293cc (567cu in),
four-cylinder
POWER: 65bhp (48kW)
0–60MPH (96KM/H): n/a
TOP SPEED: 106km/h (66mph)
PRODUCTION TOTAL: n/a

In partnership with Gottlieb Daimler, Wilhelm Maybach produced the first petrol-powered internal combustion engine in 1883. By 1886, they had created the first Daimler car, with production starting in 1890. Daimler died in 1900, leaving control of the company in the hands of Maybach; however, the German Consul in Nice and motoring enthusiast Emil Jellinek joined the business in 1900, with the sole intention of persuading it to construct a high-performance machine. The car made its debut in 1901 and featured innumerable technical innovations. Jellinek ordered a fleet of 36 examples.

Using his daughter, Mercedes, as a pseudonym, Jellinek decided that he wanted to go racing. However, the brand name was first used for Daimlers sold in France to avoid licensing infringements, although it was later adopted for all Daimler cars built at Cannstatt from 1902. Based on the earlier Mercedes-Simplex cars, the 60 featured open two-seat or four-seat bodywork, a separate pressed steel chassis frame with semi-elliptic leaf spring suspension and wooden 'artillery'-type wheels.

The Mercedes Simplex 60 famously competed in the Gordon Bennett races at the Athy Circuit in Ireland and, following a fire at the factory, which destroyed all five of the competition cars, owners were encouraged to 'donate' their vehicles to the company for the event. One of them, loaned by an American, won a memorable victory in the hands of Camille Jenatzy at an average speed of 79.1km/h (49.2mph).

NAPIER 18HP

ENGINE: 4942cc (302cu in),
six-cylinder
POWER: n/a
0–60MPH (96KM/H): n/a
TOP SPEED: n/a
PRODUCTION TOTAL: n/a

The Napier company, which was established by Montague Napier, was a market-leading, precision engineering firm long before its association with motor cars. It was the foresight of Selwyn Francis Edge, however, that led to Napier's racing cars becoming the benchmark of an era. The 1900 prototype Napier was powered by a 2471cc (151cu in) vertical-twin that contested the 1000-Miles Trial. A one-piece aluminium engine block, with four pressed-in iron cylinder liners and three valves per cylinder (4942cc), arrived later that year. Painted Napier Green, (later known as British Racing Green), one of his cars won the Gordon Bennett Trophy in 1902, and in 1903 the 18HP 6-cylinder production model was launched.

Edge, an innovator who believed in progress through experiment, did whatever it took to fund his thirst for engineering knowledge. Many of his cars never appeared in mainstream production, but that didn't stop Edge introducing new ideas. The 4.9-litre 18HP was the first production six-cylinder unit, but was very unreliable. Serious vibrations often caused the crankshaft to break (Edge attempted to dismiss the noise to customers as 'power rattle'). Napier persisted with six-cylinder technology and later units set new standards for smoothness and dependability.

Although the Napier 18HP was the first production six-cylinder car, its inventiveness wasn't matched by reliability or smoothness, with broken components a common complaint on the early models.

DE DION BOUTON 6HP POPULAIRE

FRANCE 1903

ENGINE: single cylinder
POWER: 6hp (4kW) Types N and Q
0–60MPH (96KM/H): n/a
TOP SPEED: 64km/h (40mph)
PRODUCTION TOTAL: n/a

The company's history can be traced back to 1880, when Comte Albert de Dion produced a variety of steam vehicles ranging from a powered bicycle to an Omnibus. By 1883, de Dion had entered into partnership with Georges Bouton and his brother-in-law Charles Trepardoux. However, Trepardoux was unconvinced by the future of the internal combustion engine and departed the company in 1894, which was renamed De Dion, Bouton et Compagnie. The new firm developed petrol engines, then a three-wheeled petite voiture that remained in production until 1902.

The firm's first car arrived in 1900, and it became the biggest carmaker in the world, selling 400 examples. It also commenced manufacturing in North America. By 1903, 40,000 units had been made of their 700cc (43cu in) or 942cc (57cu in) engine, and it was increased in capacity and power output. An unusual control feature of the early cars, which lasted until World War I, was the decelerator pedal which progressively reduced the engine speed. The driver would then apply a transmission brake to stop. The model was also known for its outstanding reliability, which appealed to doctors, who found the cars invaluable in rural districts. Another feature of the unit was that it ran very smoothly and developed its full power at 1600rpm. The range of models available then started to grow as the company went on to develop twin-cylinder engines.

The 'Populaire' lived up to its name by being an extremely successful model, thanks to its small size, low cost and durability. It helped turn De Dion into the largest carmaker in the world.

ROLLS-ROYCE SILVER GHOST

UNITED KINGDOM 1906–25

ENGINE: 7428cc (453cu in),
    6-cylinder
POWER: n/a
TOP SPEED: n/a
0-60MPH (96KM/H): n/a
PRODUCTION TOTAL: 7876

Often called the 'Best Car in the World', the description relating to this model arose from a critical appraisal in the *Autocar* magazine in 1907. Registered AX201, it is actually the car that most people refer to as the (original) Silver Ghost because the then managing director of the firm, Claude Johnston (himself something of an icon, often referred to as the 'hyphen' in Rolls-Royce), wanted to have one of the four chassis built for the Olympia Motor Show, in London, finished in silver with silver-plated fittings.

Several bodies were fitted to various Rolls-Royce chassis and an open-topped version was built by Barker, which became the car used in the Scottish Reliability Trials 1907. It was sold in 1908, but recovered by the company in 1948, since when it has been used for publicity purposes and remains virtually priceless, even though it was comprehensively restored in 1989. Intriguingly, this same car has now covered more than 500,000 miles (800,000km) and still runs impeccably today.

The Rolls-Royce Motor Company started making petrol-engined cars in Manchester in 1904. Frederick Henry Royce, who preferred to be known as Henry, was a meticulous engineer, but he felt happier designing and improving his cars than he did trying to sell them. He needed an outgoing salesman to convince buyers of the engineering excellence he had built into his vehicles, and Charles Stewart Rolls, the youngest son of Lord Llangattock, was selling Panhard et Levassor cars to London's aristocracy from an exclusive dealership in Mayfair. They were a perfect match.

A well-known racing driver and aviation pioneer, Rolls was also an astute businessman. The engineering excellence of Henry Royce's motor cars appealed to

The Silver Ghost established Rolls-Royce as the maker of the best cars in the world.

him, as he believed it would become a major selling point among his upmarket customers.

The pair struck their deal in 1904, building initially in Manchester, later at Derby, then at Crewe (where Rolls-Royces were still produced until production transferred to Sussex in 2002, under new owner BMW, and Bentley, a subsequent partnership, was left at Crewe in Volkswagen's care). According to arrangement, Royce and his workforce would build the cars under Claude Johnston, who was also Royce's top engineer and designer. In fact, Johnston was more important in the shaping of the company than Charles Rolls himself, who was

killed in a flying accident in 1910 at the age of 32. Up to 1906, Rolls-Royce had built several different models with four- and six-cylinder engines, and even a V8. For 1907, a one-model policy was decided upon for the company. This would permit it to concentrate efforts on developing it, rather than wasting resources building several different models.

The Silver Ghost was a large car, weighing in at more than 1500kg (1.5 tons). Its power was derived from a 7.4-litre (453cu in) side-valve six-cylinder engine that possessed amazing refinement and smoothness, while tall gearing gave it a much higher top speed than most cars of the era. In 1911,

a special aero-bodied example was clocked at more than 163km/h (101mph) at Surrey's Brooklands race track. The 'Silver' part of the moniker came from the silver-plated metal trim parts of the car, while the 'Ghost' implied its quiet operation – a tradition that continues as the Rolls-Royce ethos to this day. The Silver Ghost models were officially known as the 40/50 Series, but the more common name, 'Ghost', is often used by enthusiasts.

To demonstrate the new model's quality, the original Ghost was taken on a 3200km (2000-mile) reliability run, which included driving from the south coast of England up to Scotland in top gear,

under the strict scrutiny of motoring organization, the RAC. The car completed the distance effortlessly. In order to prove its dependability further, the company immediately sent it out on a 24,000km (15,000-mile) test, with Charles Rolls as one of the drivers. This, too, was completed without involuntary stops (except for tyre changes), and it broke the world record for reliability and long-distance driving. The Ghost was then stripped down by engineers to determine how much wear it had suffered. Amazingly, there was no deterioration in the engine, transmission, brakes or steering, and the model quickly established itself as the finest car in the world.

FORD MODEL T

ENGINE: 2896cc (177cu in), four-cylinder
POWER: 20bhp (15kW)
0–60MPH (96KM/H): n/a
TOP SPEED: 72km/h (45mph)
PRODUCTION TOTAL: 15,000,000

Henry Ford's Model T is, arguably, the most important car ever, bringing cheap motoring to the masses thanks to its production techniques. 15-million examples also made it one of the biggest selling too.

History was made on 16 June 1903, when Henry Ford and 11 business associates signed the Articles of Incorporation and invested the $28,000 that led to the formation of the Ford Motor Company. It took five years before the Model T first appeared, and a further five years before Henry had spotted a meat worker on a production line, which gave him the idea of making motor cars in a similar way. The production time for each car dropped from 12 hours and 8 minutes to 1 hour and 33 minutes. By the time production ended in 1927, a Model T was rolling off the company's lines every 24 seconds. Nineteen years and 15 million Model Ts after its formative steps, Ford Motor Company was a multinational giant.

It is often attributed to Henry that he said, 'You can have any colour you like, so long as it is black ...' Yet the earliest Model Ts were red, grey and Brewster Green. Blue was among the initial colours, and black came along later. The first production Model T Ford was assembled at the Piquette Avenue Plant in Detroit, Michigan, on 1 October 1908. Production relocated to a brand new Highland Park plant in 1910, production starting on the fourth floor and winding downwards to road level. Amazingly, the old-fashioned car resulted in the longest run of any single model apart from the later Volkswagen Beetle, a figure more recently superseded by the Toyota Corolla. From 1908 to 1927, the

Model T had hardly changed, but Henry Ford had succeeded in his quest to build a car for the masses.

For $825, a Model T customer could take home a car that was light, at about 544kg (1200lb); was quite powerful, with a four-cylinder, 20hp (15kW) engine; and was fairly easy to drive, with a two-speed, foot-controlled 'planetary' transmission. In its first year, more than 10,000 'Tin Lizzies' were sold, which was a record. The success was not surprising because the T was a very good car. The simple ladder frame chassis was particularly robust, and the development of light but tough vanadium-steel alloys was crucial to achieving the company's aims. As there were hardly any significant changes during the T's long production run, components were interchangeable and cars

could keep on running. The transverse leaf spring suspension allowed the chassis and wheels to negotiate easily the unmade roads that made up most of the US road network at the time. A wide variety of bodystyles, from a sporty speedster to hard working pick-up or van, meant that there was a Model T for every type of car buyer, and Henry had the market to himself.

However, Ford was determined to continuously reduce the T's price. When it sold for $575 in 1912, the Model T cost less than the average annual wage in North America. Although profit margins fell as he slashed prices from $220 in 1909 to $99 in 1914, sales rose to an astounding 248,000 in 1913. In 1921, the Model T Ford held 60 per cent of the American new-car market. Plants around the world

turned out Model Ts at a furious rate, and Henry Ford's only problem 'was figuring out how to make enough of them'. This attitude led to problems, not least because the company was too reliant on one model.

Customers appreciated the cheapness of the Model T, but increasingly wanted something more sophisticated. Chevrolet, in particular, targeted the same customers with better designed and styled cars featuring important innovations such as smooth three-speed gearboxes. The company took sales from the Model T. On 25 May 1927, Ford abruptly announced the end of the Model T's production. Soon after, he closed the Highland Park factory for six months; incredibly, he had no replacement model ready and needed time to design one.

AUDI 10/22

ENGINE: 2612cc (159cu in),
four-cylinder
POWER: 22bhp (16kW)
0–60MPH (96KM/H): n/a
TOP SPEED: 75km/h (47mph)
PRODUCTION TOTAL: n/a

The first car to bear the Audi name was the Type A 10/22 Sport Phaeton. The name arose from the company's inventor, August Horch, whose German surname translates into Latin as 'Audi'. The company had actually been started in Zwickau, in 1909, by Horch and his partner Hermann Lange. The modern badge of four interlinked rings represents the auto union of Germany's four leading carmakers – DKW, Wanderer, NSU and Horch – in 1932. The high-quality Audi 10/22 adopted several Horch practices: the four cylinders of the engine were cast in pairs, and the unit used an overhead inlet valve (operated by small rocker arms) and a side exhaust valve, operated by a gear-driven camshaft. In 1914, the 10/22 gained a new pointed grille, which came to symbolize the Audi brand. Ironically, one of the companies to join Audi in 1932 was Horch's original eponymously named firm, which had started making prototypes, then high-quality production cars, in 1904.

ALFA 24HP

ENGINE: 4084cc (249cu in),
four-cylinder
POWER: 42bhp (31kW)
0–60MPH (96KM/H): n/a
TOP SPEED: 100km/h (62mph)
PRODUCTION TOTAL: 50

The origins of the Alfa company date back to 1906, when the French Darracq works was bought out by a group of Italian car enthusiasts known as Anonima Lombardo Fabbrica Automobili, which became abbreviated to ALFA. In fact, Nicola Romeo's name was not appended to the company until 1915, when the enthusiastic Milanese bought into the firm. The 24hp was the ALFA company's first car and featured a Giuseppe Morosi-developed four-cylinder 4084cc (249cu in) engine, possessing a peak power output of 42bhp (31kW). Mated to a four-speed gearbox, the motor was potent enough to propel the car's huge chassis, fitted initially with a six-seater body, at impressive speeds. Central to the model's success was its reliability, and, for this reason, a stripped-out racing version appeared in 1911 and was entered into the legendary Targa Florio race in Sicily.

The first ALFA was the 24HP. Initially a luxury model, ALFA soon made its reputation with a 'bare bones' racing version.

VAUXHALL PRINCE HENRY

ENGINE: 3054cc (186cu in),
four-cylinder
POWER: 60bhp (45kW)
0-60MPH (96KM/H): n/a
TOP SPEED: 120km/h (75mph)
PRODUCTION TOTAL: 58

Until 1908, Vauxhall had no sporting heritage at all, but, in that year, the engine from the company's 3-litre (186cu in) model was developed to produce 60bhp (45kW) (RAC-rated at 20hp). This engine was then installed in the three team cars entered for the 1910 Prince Henry of Prussia tour, which gifted the new model its name. The C-type, as it was originally called by the factory, was first shown at the 1910 London Motor Show and, in 1911, the car was officially listed as a Vauxhall model, fitted with four seats but no doors, the emphasis being on speed and handling. It sold for £600. Indeed, the Prince Henry soon gained a reputation for being one of the best sporting cars of its day, thanks to a top speed of 120km/h (75mph) and excellent engine flexibility. It had been designed by Laurence Pomeroy in 1907, when the company's design chief, F.W. Hodges, was on annual leave. Within two years of the car going into production, it received a larger, 3964cc (242cu in) engine, which developed 86bhp (64kW) and was RAC-rated at 25hp (19kW). This meant even better performance and, to cater for 'lady drivers', small doors were fitted to offer some degree of protection from the elements – a further 133 of these later cars were built.

The Prince Henry gained its name from the Prince Henry of Prussia tour, a sporting event for which the first examples – fitted with an uprated engine – were specially constructed.

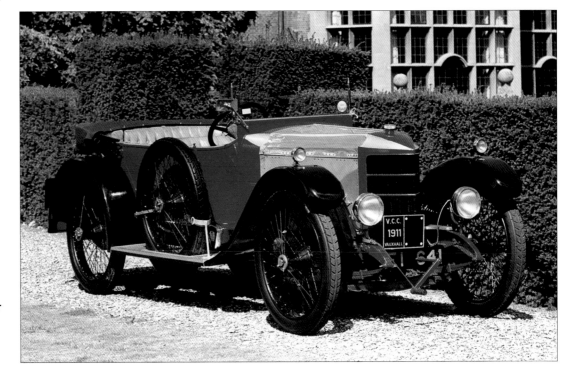

HISPANO-SUIZA TYPE 15T

UNITED KINGDOM SPAIN 1911–14

Although Spain is not renowned as a hub of the European motor industry, in 1904, Swiss engineer Marc Birkigt joined forces with Spanish engineers Damien Mateu and Javier Castro in Barcelona. The car pioneered the 'big flexible four' sports car cylinder type, long before the likes of Vauxhall and Bentley, and it is seen today as one of the very first 'production' sports cars. The surprisingly compact and lightweight Type 15T also featured other innovations, including a three-speed gearbox that was in unit with the engine, propeller shaft final drive instead of chain drive, and the use of semi-elliptic suspension. The model earned its nickname 'Alfonso' from royal motoring enthusiast King Alfonso XIII of Spain, who bought the first example to experience the T15's high top-gear flexibility and precise steering first-hand. The car was raced successfully in southern Europe. Several body styles were available, the most popular being a short, open two-seater with large diameter centre-lock wire wheels. In late 1911, Hispano-Suiza production moved from Barcelona in Spain, to Paris, France, where production of the T15 continued until the start of World War I.

ENGINE: 3620cc (221cu in), four-cylinder
POWER: 60bhp (45kW)
0–60MPH (96KM/H): n/a
TOP SPEED: 128km/h (80mph)
PRODUCTION TOTAL: n/a

LAGONDA 11

UNITED KINGDOM 1913–16

The British car company Lagonda actually owes its existence to an American would-be opera singer. Wilbur Gunn came to England at the end of the nineteenth century hoping to find success on the stage, but instead ventured into motor transport. He named his car company after a river near his home town of Springfield, Ohio. Starting in 1905, he manufactured motorcyles before moving on to three-wheelers, then four-wheeled motor cars in 1907. In fact, he won the Moscow to St Petersburg Trial in 1910 at the wheel of his six-cylinder Torpedo model. Prior to World War I, his factory in Staines, Middlesex, specialized in high-performance, big-engined cars. Soon after, the company revised its policy and began making lightweight cars, one of which was the 11, a two-seater 1.1-litre 11hp (8kW) roadster.

With its simple but effective longitudinal valve rockers operating the inlet valves, side exhaust valves and plunger-type oil pump, the car appeared in racing form at Brooklands many times, but was never officially categorized as a sports car despite being its success in competition. It was the first car to be equipped with a 'fly-off' handbrake.

ENGINE: 1100cc (67cu in), four-cylinder
POWER: 11hp (8kW)
0–60MPH (96KM/H): n/a
TOP SPEED: n/a
PRODUCTION TOTAL: n/a

RILEY 17/30

UNITED KINGDOM 1913–22

The origins of Riley, as with many British car makes, lie in the bicycle industry – and the Bonnick Cycle Company of Coventry. While William Riley bought the firm in 1890, it was his 16-year-old son Percy who dabbled in motor cars, building his first 'in secret' in 1898. It was not until 1905 that the young Riley made his first true car, a vee-twin Tourer. Percy and his three brothers, Victor, Stanley and Allan, established the Riley Motor Manufacturing Company in 1913 and unveiled their first model, the 17/30, at the London Motor Show that same year.

Riley quickly established itself as a maker of high-quality luxury vehicles and proclaimed that Riley cars were 'As old as the industry; as modern as the hour'. The claim was spurious, however, when applied to the 17/30 – its first offering following World War I. Effectively identical to the pre-war Riley, except for its oblong radiator grille and elaborately styled front mudguards, the 17/30 was almost obsolete at launch. Yet it was a reliable machine and also featured a clever three-speed gearbox, with a constant mesh top allowing quiet, refined cruising. It appeared in price lists as late as 1926, but no examples were built after 1922.

ENGINE: 2951cc (180cu in), four-cylinder
POWER: 21bhp (16kW)
0–60MPH (96KM/H): n/a
TOP SPEED: n/a
PRODUCTION TOTAL: n/a

FORD MODEL T

UNITED KINGDOM 1911–27

ENGINE: 2890cc (176cu in), four-cylinder
POWER: 20bhp (15kW)
0–60MPH (96KM/H): n/a
TOP SPEED: 68km/h (42mph)
PRODUCTION TOTAL: 300,000

The legendary Model T, also known as the 'Tin Lizzie', made sense in Britain because it was tough, inexpensive and reliable. Assembled in the United Kingdom from 1911 onwards, at Trafford Park in Manchester, parts were imported direct from the United States. Indeed, Trafford Park played a key role in Ford production before the advent of the moving production line. A moving line was introduced first for the assembly of the Model T's flywheel generator in 1913, at the main Ford plant in Detroit, Michigan, and line assembly began in Manchester a year later, culminating in around 94 per cent UK content by 1924.

The Model T was a reassuringly basic car with a sturdy four-cylinder side-valve engine. The 3-litre (176cu in) unit produced a dependable 20bhp (15kW) and had pedal operated epicyclic gears, making it exceedingly easy to drive. The gears, two forward and one reverse, worked efficiently, as did the transverse semi-elliptic suspension front and rear. There were brakes on only two wheels and, although effort was required to stop a Model T quickly, they worked well. Several bodystyles were available, including a Roadster, Tourer, Tudor, Fordor and Town Car. Many companies took advantage of the chassis to build their own coupés and convertibles based on the uncomplicated running gear. It is no surprise that, in 1919, 41 per cent of all vehicles registered in the United Kingdom were Fords. Car production in Manchester peaked at more than 150,000 in 1923; the light van version continued until 1927.

Three years after its American introduction, the Model T went into production in Great Britain, and was just as successful. Within eight years, almost half of UK cars were Fords.

VAUXHALL 30/98

ENGINE: 4525cc (276cu in),
four-cylinder
POWER: 90bhp (67kW)
0–60MPH (96KM/H): n/a
TOP SPEED: 136km/h (85mph)
PRODUCTION TOTAL: 598

Laurence Pomeroy had already created something of a stir within Vauxhall when he designed the C-Type, which became known as the 'Prince Henry'. The 30/98 was already well under way during the period after World War I and became known as the E-Type model in 1919. As a lighter and more potent development of the C-Type, it is regarded as one of the benchmarks for early sporting cars – a car that could compete initially on equal terms with the best that Bentley, Alvis, Talbot and Sunbeam could provide. Throughout much of its life it was overshadowed by Bentley's 3-litre (183cu in) model, although the 30/98 was significantly quicker. Amazingly, until 1926, the car had rear wheel brakes only, although this was the norm at the time of its introduction.

The 30/98 was essentially a development of the Trials Car which Vauxhall had built to compete in reliability events in 1908. Durability was more important than outright speed, yet the trials car was still able to attain 137km/h (85mph) and, in streamlined form, reached 174km/h (108mph) at Brooklands. For those customers desiring speed alone, a stripped-out version of the car was offered, which was guaranteed to reach 161km/h (100mph) – an exceptional turn of speed at the time. It was not until 1912, however, that the first versions

competed in motorsport, enjoying regular successes, and, by the summer of 1913, the first road models were being built for their wealthy owners. They needed to be so, with a chassis priced at £900, when a complete Prince Henry could be bought for £580. The 30/98 was too expensive for all but the richest car fans. Only a dozen chassis were produced before World War I.

In 1919, the 30/98 became a properly catalogued model, although it was still too expensive. At £1675, with Velox coachwork, 274 cars found owners, who were won over by its reputation as the finest sporting machine of the early 1920s. The post-war alternative gained from significant developments over the pre-war examples, with both electric

lighting and starting, as well as a stronger engine cylinder block.

Fast and heavy, but with excellent roadholding, the 30/98 suffered from its high price, so, in 1921, the price was reduced to £1300. While a substantial reduction, it was still expensive, and the 3-litre (183cu in) Bentleys were now competing directly against it. For 1922, a redesigned 30/98 appeared, with a shorter stroke engine and an overhead-valve layout allowing it to be more free-revving. With 115bhp (86kW) produced, combined with a more rigid chassis, the drive was improved further by introduction of cable-operated brakes on the front wheels for 1923. Vauxhall had been taken over by General Motors in 1925, and the American company's policy was to turn it

The tough construction of the Vauxhall 30/98 made it a winner in both racing and trials events, as well-demonstrated here.

into a mass-market carmaker. Nevertheless, in 1926 an updated 30/98 appeared, with hydraulic brakes all round and a 120bhp (89kW) engine – enough to take it to 152km/h (95mph) and give it a 120km/h (80mph) cruising speed. At £950 for the chassis alone, though, prices remained high. Worse still, the car was now well over a decade old, and Sunbeam and Bentley were offering price parity for newer models. By the time 30/98 production ceased in 1927, just 598 examples had been built, an unacceptable figure for the new General Motors management.

PACKARD TWIN-SIX

ENGINE: 6950cc (424cu in),
12-cylinder
POWER: n/a
0–60MPH (96KM/H): n/a
TOP SPEED: n/a
PRODUCTION TOTAL: 35,046

In 1898, James Ward Packard was so disappointed with his new Winton Phaeton that he returned it to the maker, who challenged him to design and develop a much

better car of his own. The first Packard appeared in 1899 in Ohio, and it was considered so well engineered that prominent Detroit businessman Henry B. Joy invested in the company, taking control of the relocated carmaker completely in 1903. Packard soon earned a reputation for technical innovation, and the company introduced the first commercially viable V12 engine in 1915. The Packard Twin-Six was a luxury model aimed at wealthy owners and was a huge

Produced between 1915 and 1923, the Packard's 'Twin-Six' title referred to the car's V12 engine, which was such a new and exciting innovation for the era that the luxury model soon found favour as a U.S. Presidential car.

success, earning itself a reputation for both image and build quality. When US President W.G. Harding decided to use a Twin-Six for official duties, his was the first presidential inauguration in which the newly elected head of state travelled to the ceremony by car.

The company's reputation grew overnight. Despite the labour-intensive build methods involved, Packard managed to construct over 35,000 expensive Twin-Sixes in eight years, before it replaced the model with the in-line Single Eight in 1923.

CADILLAC TYPE 57 UNITED STATES 1918–23

ENGINE: 5146cc (314cu in), eight-cylinder
POWER: 70bhp (52kW)
0–60MPH (96KM/H): n/a
TOP SPEED: 88km/h (55mph)
PRODUCTION TOTAL: 205,179

The word 'Cadillac' conjures an image of big, powerful, V8 and sophisticated. When the new Cadillac V8 engine was introduced in September 1914, it marked the future for North America's most prestigious brand. Supremely sophisticated, it would define the marque for generations to come.

The Type 51 was the model that introduced the innovative V8 unit; it put Cadillac on the automotive world map. For 1915, the company offered four open and four closed bodystyles, ranging in price from $1975 to $3600. The high prices did not hinder sales, and more than 20,000 examples found homes that year. Introduced in 1916, the Type 53 witnessed Touring bodies on a special 335cm (132in) chassis. One year later, the Type 55 served with distinction during World War 1, as more than 2000 versions were dispatched to Europe as staff cars. Finally, the Type 57, heralded in at the war's end, saw new Town limousine and Town Landaulet models that were 10cm (4in) narrower to cope with increasingly congested city streets. By 1920, the 57 had been deposed by the Type 59, which came with a restyled body, stiffer chassis and front wheels changed from 10- to 12-spoke. The V8 was continually developed throughout its life, including fitting detachable cylinder heads in 1918 and further changes that lasted until its demise in 1949.

BUICK 18/20 UNITED STATES 1918–22

ENGINE: 2786cc (170cu in), four-cylinder
POWER: 35bhp (26kW)
0–60MPH (96KM/H): n/a
TOP SPEED: 80km/h (50mph)
PRODUCTION TOTAL: 88,500

Buick Motors was started by a Scotsman, from Arbroath. Born in 1854, David Buick emigrated to the United States at the age of two, with his parents. As a young man, he invented a process that coated iron with enamel, which led to the development of the ultimate luxury item of the time, the white bath. At the turn of the century, he became fascinated by motor cars and established the company that bore his name. Sadly, passion and business acumen do not always run together, and Buick sold out his interests in 1906 to William C. Durant, who would later go on to form General Motors. In 1916, Buick sold an astonishing 124,834 cars, but, as material supplies became restricted because of World War I, sales fell back. Yet, the company pressed ahead with a new range in 1917. The previous D-54 and D-55 models were dropped, while the new D-34 and D-35 were heavily promoted.

The new four-cylinder engine in these cars developed a competent 35bhp (26kW) from a displacement of 2786cc (170cu in), although for taxation purposes the engine was rated at 18.2hp (13.6kW) – hence they are known as 18/20s. The engine also featured a detachable cylinder head as part of the design, and the chassis used semi-elliptic springs rather than the usual cantilever units. Roadsters were available, but the four-door touring cars sold in the largest numbers. The cars received new designations in 1918 as the E34, E35 and E37, and a two-door saloon was added to the line-up. In 1920, Buick switched to six-cylinder engines only, and it seemed that the four-cylinder option was at an end. In 1921, however, Buick reintroduced the four-cylinder unit for the following model year. A development of the original engine, it was now rated at 18.23hp (13.6kW), although the displacement was identical.

WOLSELEY STELLITE UNITED KINGDOM 1913–28

ENGINE: 1100cc (67cu in)
POWER: n/a
0–60MPH (96KM/H): n/a
TOP SPEED: n/a
PRODUCTION TOTAL: n/a

Wolseley's Stellite model of 1913 was a joint venture between Wolseley and Birmingham-based Electric and Ordnance Accessories, a Vickers subsidiary. A third partner, Crayford, was also involved in the project, with the aim to produce a cheaper, reduced specification Wolseley.

Although the previous 12/16 and 16/10 were both very popular, with 7500 sold in total, Wolseley wanted to expand its production volumes. In 1913, the Stellite was announced, with an 1100cc (67cu in) monobloc four-cylinder engine that featured overhead inlet valves, an armoured wood frame and a two-speed gearbox in unit with the driven rear axle. The company had also become the United Kingdom's largest manufacturer, employing 4000 people and building 3000 cars at Adderley Park. Within a year, 1500 Stellites had been built, but the outbreak of World War I in 1914 meant production was halted until 1919. A Vickers-owned factory at Drews Lane, Birmingham, also became home to Wolseley, to cope with increased demand. Although the original Stellite went out of production in 1920, the name was revived the following year and placed on a less costly version of the Wolseley 10. Able to cruise at 40km/h (25mph) while returning 6.3L/100km (45mpg), this later version competed directly with cars from Austin and Morris – an aspect that caused Wolseley major problems, as most buyers chose to purchase its rivals' models.

AC 10HP UNITED KINGDOM 1919–20

AC is actually the oldest name in British carmaking circles, with continuous production since 1901. These days, the AC name is normally associated with fire-breathing sports cars. Yet, in its early years, commencing in 1904, the company made compact three-wheelers, called AC Sociables, and cyclecars. The AC 10hp was one of the first cyclecars to take on the appearance of a full-size car. Its engine was a French-built four-cylinder unit, while the chassis was made cleverly from pressed sheet steel made into U-sections, providing tremendous strength and light weight – an idea that was soon adopted by many other carmakers. In fact, the AC 10hp was initially too heavy to qualify as a true cyclecar under the regulations of the period, although a redesign of the transmission soon reduced it below the 10cwt (500kg) threshold. It was readied in time to take part in the first cyclecar trial, a sporting event organized by the ACU (Auto Cycle Union), in which the new model won several classification awards.

The 10hp was followed by a 12hp version which ensured that the AC company, which had always been precariously financed, could look forward to a more certain future, despite World War I's intervention. During that period, AC designed its own four-cylinder power unit, but it was never quite as good as the French one. The company, however, set its sights on bigger machines and broader performance opportunities.

ENGINE: 1315cc (80cu in), four-cylinder
POWER: n/a
0–60MPH (96KM/H): n/a
TOP SPEED: n/a
PRODUCTION TOTAL: 62

MORRIS BULLNOSE

ENGINE: 1548cc (91cu in),
four-cylinder
POWER: 24bhp (18kW) at 2350rpm
0–60MPH (96KM/H): n/a
TOP SPEED: 89km/h (55mph)
PRODUCTION TOTAL: n/a

William Morris, later to become Lord Nuffield, started by making motorcycles in Oxford, England. By 1912, he had built his first car in nearby Cowley. Morris the eponymously named motor company was born. The first efforts had a distinctive curved radiator surround, the top section resembling the appearance of a bullet, which earned the cars the 'Bullnose' nickname. Two versions were available: the less costly Cowley and more upmarket Oxford. Both were intended to cater for the fast-growing mass market. Naturally, buying in components at keenly negotiated prices was a priority, which led to Morris acquiring the component manufacturers as the most effective way to develop the company. Gearbox, steering and axles all came from North America and were considerably cheaper than their British equivalents. World War I caused a hiatus in production and, when hostilities were over, supplies from across the Atlantic became unavailable. The last Anglo-American Bullnoses were made in 1919, with one solitary example in 1920.

Morris – eventually to become one of the most popular and best-loved of British marques – started out with the cheap Bullnose, built using components from the USA to keep its price low.

STANDARD 9.5HP

ENGINE: 1328cc (81cu in),
four-cylinder
POWER: n/a
0–60MPH (96KM/H): n/a
TOP SPEED: n/a
PRODUCTION TOTAL: 1750

Although a relative latecomer to the fast-developing British motor industry, the first Standard Model S was introduced in 1913 and proved an immediate success, thanks to its affordability. Prices started at £195, which meant that it was within the reach of more ordinary people than many other rival models. Both closed and open cars were offered and, powered by a 1087cc (66cu in) engine, the car was reliable and economical to operate. During World War I, the company's efforts were directed towards making aeroplanes (over 1000 produced) and, in 1916, business operations were relocated to Canley, Coventry, for the future.

After the war, however, it became clear that something new was needed to keep sales buoyant. The answer was an updated version of the earlier model, which was launched in 1919. Called the SLS, the new model used a longer stroke version of the original engine, this time displacing 1328cc (81cu in). Although the price of the two-seater escalated to £350, the car remained markedly less costly than many of its competitors. Still, it was not competitive in technical or style terms, and a replacement model was needed urgently to maintain customer interest. The result was the 11.6hp, launched in 1921, featuring overhead valves in place of the side valves seen on every Standard engine up to that time.

The 9.5HP was a low budget option compared to its rivals, but after World War I its looks and technology were considered old-fashioned, leading to it being quickly replaced.

STUTZ BEARCAT

ENGINE: 6388cc (390cu in),
four-cylinder
POWER: 60bhp (45kW)
0–60MPH (96KM/H): n/a
TOP SPEED: about 129km/h (80mph)
PRODUCTION TOTAL: about 4000

Harry C. Stutz was the man behind the Stutz Car Company; however, the first of his machines, produced from 1911, were actually made by the Ideal Motor Car Company of Indianapolis. At that time, the cars were built only as racers. Yet, when the first road cars appeared in 1913, the Ideal name was seen as overconfident and the company changed its name to Stutz. The first sports car built by the newly named operation was the Bearcat, which made its debut in 1914. The car offered nothing in the way of interior comforts, as it was simply a road-going racer. Conventionally engineered throughout, with the exception of its transmission, it drew its inspiration from the contemporary Mercer Raceabout.

The Bearcat even featured the same type of basic doorless bodywork that its major rival did. In fact, the car's bodywork was deliberately kept to a minimum because the key to maximum performance was keeping weight as low as possible. With only 60bhp (45kW) on offer from the 6388cc (390cu in) four-cylinder engine, any extra mass would upset the power-to-weight ratio very easily. The T-head engine was supplied by powerplant manufacturer Wisconsin and, thanks to its large capacity, was not built for high engine speeds. In fact, maximum power was generated at just 1500rpm. For those who wanted an engine with a greater rev range, the company

The Bearcat offered few creature comforts, but as a street-legal racing car there were few in its class that could surpass it. Even today, the type is still famous for its many sporting achievements.

also offered a 6.2-litre (378cu in) six-cylinder unit, although very few versions ever sold.

To make the Bearcat handle well, the chassis was low-slung and featured a beam axle at the front suspended by semi-elliptic springs. At the rear there was a live axle, also suspended on semi-elliptic springs. There were no brakes at the front, just drum brakes at the

rear. The three-speed manual transmission was mounted in unit with the rear axle, driving it via a propshaft, which was particularly innovative at the time. More conventional was the exposed right-hand gearchange. A monocle windscreen was provided for the driver, but there was no other weather protection. Two armchair-style bucket seats and a steeply

raked steering column poking through the scuttle comprised the car's total level of interior trim.

The Bearcat's popularity grew on the back of its outstanding motorsport successes. In 1915, the White Squadron racing team won all sorts of competitions in Bearcats, although the purpose-built racers featured 16-valve overhead-camshaft engines

displacing 4.8 litres (293cu in) that had nothing in common with those fitted to factory-supplied models. In 1916, 'Cannonball' Baker, driving a Bearcat, smashed the time record for driving across the United States, boosting sales further. Production grew to 2207 in 1917, but this was the last year for the model as buyers sought greater comfort from their sporting cars.

NAPIER 40/50

Napier was a fairly active carmaker prior to World War I, having been the first British manufacturer to concentrate heavily on racing. Its first post-war model, the 40/50, was responsible

for introducing a component that became one of the most common in almost every British motorcar of the next 70 years. Launched in 1919, it was the first car to feature SU carburettors – a design that

would net the company hundreds of thousands of pounds over the coming decades.

While the company seemed determined to concentrate on aero engines, its new 40/50 was an unremarkable machine. Powered by a six-cylinder engine, the 40/50 marked the company's new one-model strategy. It was designed by highly respected coachbuilder A.J. Rowledge, who left to work for Rolls-Royce in 1920, but it was a smart if unadventurous design, with steel hulls built, without a hint of irony, by shipbuilder Cunard.

Although the 40/50 introduced SU carburettors, there was little ground-breaking about the rest of its rather staid design.

The Napier was an expensive car and one which failed to fire buyers' imaginations, thereby falling well short of its intended 500 unit sales. This led the company to cease car production overall and concentrate instead on engineering developments. Napier's only four-wheeled device thereafter was the Mechanical Horse, which was designed as a light articulated tractor unit, put into production by Scammell and popularized by British Railways.

ENGINE: 6150cc (375cu in),
 six-cylinder
POWER: 39bhp (29kW)
0–60MPH (96KM/H): n/a
TOP SPEED: 96km/h (60mph)
PRODUCTION TOTAL: 187

SINGER TEN

ENGINE: 1096cc (67cu in),
 four-cylinder
POWER: n/a
0–60MPH (96KM/H): n/a
TOP SPEED: about 80km/h (50mph)
PRODUCTION TOTAL: about 6000

With most carmakers' efforts directed towards World War I, Singer had joined suit and, when it returned from directing its efforts towards the hostilities, there was little to distinguish the post-war Singer Ten from its pre-war counterpart. The 1919 model featured electric headlights as standard, and the major change lay in the car's appearance, as a new range of bodystyles was made available for the Coventry-built lightweight model, which was also capable of attaining around about 14km/litre (40mpg). The two-seater Sports Coupé offered

80km/h (50mph) capability, while the standard Phaeton configuration could manage just 72km/h (45mph). When *Autocar* tested the 10 Sports, it commented on how good the engine was, along with the amount of practicality the car offered – especially in Phaeton form, if a dickey seat was fitted.

For 1923, a cut-price version was offered called the Coventry Premier, with less equipment and a smaller choice of bodystyles, and the company saw an opportunity to introduce a free insurance package to owners, which further boosted sales. Mechanically the

Principal among the cheap 'n' cheerful Singer Ten's attributes were its basic but rugged construction and light weight and very good engine, which endeared this simple British car to many buyers.

car was very conventional, with a three-speed gearbox, semi-elliptic springs all round and brakes on the rear wheels only. Its four-cylinder engine featured combustion chambers cast in pairs, and the car's overall simplicity and light

weight meant it was ideally suited to privateer motorsport thanks to its ready ability to be tuned. As a result, Singer 10s were seen regularly in competitive hillclimbs, trials and at racing circuits around the United Kingdom.

DAIMLER 45

After World War I ended, Daimler got straight back to business by building the huge chassis and luxurious carriages for which it

had become famous. The 45 was sometimes known simply as the Special. It was powered by the 80bhp (60kW) 'Silent Knight'

sleeve-valve engine, which was acknowledged as being very refined, thereby adding credibility to the brand's royal patronage that

had started at the turn of the century. The cars were also renowned for being expensive, however, and the chassis alone cost between £850 and £1275. It featured semi-elliptic front and three-quarter elliptic rear suspension with an underslung worm axle. The large eight-cylinder engine worked initially through a cone clutch, then, from 1920, used a disc system to control the four-speed gearbox, which had a right-hand gearchange for the chauffeur. Putting a limousine body on top of the chassis meant that these Daimlers rarely left the works costing less than £2000.

Both Daimler and outside coachbuilders produced their own bodies, which were built on subframes, then attached to the chassis with rubber fixings, which also helped to maintain the image of refinement. Invariably a favourite with the aristocracy, the 45 chassis was also used to build some replica's of George V's 1924 official car, to which a massive 8500cc (519cu in) 57bhp (42kW) engine was fitted. There were countless body and chassis combinations, so there was no such thing as a standard 45, not least because all Daimler records were destroyed in the Blitz.

ENGINE: 4962cc (304cu in), eight-cylinder
POWER: 80bhp (60kW)
0–60MPH (96KM/H): n/a
TOP SPEED: 104km/h (65mph)
PRODUCTION TOTAL: n/a

With British Royal patronage to recommend them, Daimler 45s were exclusive and luxurious carriages, intended to appeal to the very rich...who were about the only customers who could afford them.

HILLMAN 11HP

Although World War I interrupted production, Hillman's 11HP model was brought back after the end of the conflict for a further seven years, albeit with a new engine to update the design.

ENGINE: 1593cc (97cu in), four-cylinder
POWER: 11hp (8kW)
0–60MPH (96KM/H): n/a
TOP SPEED: n/a
PRODUCTION TOTAL: n/a

From having been a cycle manufacturer, William Hillman founded the Hillman Motor Car Company in 1907, at Ryton-on-Dunsmore, near Coventry, and, in his first year, commissioned Frenchman Louis Coatalen to design his first car for the Tourist Trophy race. After the 24hp (18kW) four-cylinder Hillman was eliminated early in the race due to a crash, Coatalen left to join the Sunbeam company, and Hillman began making models that included a 9.7-litre (592cu in) six-cylinder unit and a 6.4-litre (391cu in) four, as well as the 1357cc (83cu in) monobloc (cast from a single block of metal) four-cylinder which grew to 1593cc

(97cu in) and 11hp (8kW), this unit being reduced subsequently to 1496cc (91cu in). This last version developed 18bhp (kW), or 25bhp (19kW) in its more sporting guise. The 1357cc engine powered the pre-war Hillman 11hp, but the model was reintroduced, as were so many of its rivals in the post-war period, powered by the punchier 1.6-litre unit. It sold strongly, as a result of keen pricing and a good reputation for reliability and low running costs.

A similar version of the car's side-valve engine was used in the Speed model of 1921, which featured diecast light alloy pistons and a lighter crankshaft and flywheel. Using the company's three-speed gearbox, ratios were changed to enable the car to reach speeds in excess of 96km/h (60mph). Production of the model was dropped to make way for the growing demand for the 11hp (8kW). These small Hillmans proved very successful, until they were discontinued in 1925.

ROVER EIGHT

ENGINE: 998cc (61cu in), two-cylinder
POWER: 13bhp (10kW) at 2800rpm
0–60MPH (96KM/H): n/a
TOP SPEED: 72km/h (45mph)
PRODUCTION TOTAL: 17,700

One of the United Kingdom's innovators in the field of car production, Rover started in 1884 as a bicycle manufacturer, turning to cars only in 1905. It made a variety of different models, with varying degrees of success, moving its cars gradually upmarket. It did appear strange, therefore, when, in the period immediately after World War I, the Rover Eight was reintroduced. The company had been making lorries, motorbikes and a version of a Sunbeam model during the war years. The first production versions hit the roads in 1919, and they were powered by a lively if small-capacity air-cooled horizontally opposed two-

Although not apparent in this photo, the narrow engine bay meant that the Eight's cylinder heads were projected from the side of the bonnet (hood) – not something to be touched when glowing hot.

cylinder engine purchased from designer Jack Sangster. Rover also bought a redundant factory in Birmingham to build it. It was an inexpensive model, but what it

lacked in creature comforts it made up for in character. An intriguing feature of the Eight was the way the cylinder heads stuck out of the side of the bonnet (hood), and

glowed red whenever the car was driven hard. It looked dramatic, but wasn't a very practical design.

In its day, the Eight was a successful light car. Its chassis was

re-engineered in 1924 to accept a four-cylinder engine with water-cooling, that model being launched as the 9/20hp. The original Eight was dropped a year later.

BEAN TWELVE

The Harper company, consisting of Absolom and his sons John and Edward, started producing fenders in 1826, until it was joined by a bank clerk from Lincolnshire, George Bean, who married John's daughter in 1884. Established in Dudley, in England's West Midlands, in 1907 and producing ammunition for the war effort, A. Harper, Sons and Bean began building motor cars in 1919.

Originally, the company was a component supplier to other makers, but it acquired the rights to build the pre-World War I Perry 11.9hp, sold in the United States by Willys Overland, under licence. The Bean Twelve was effectively this car, but as much as 90 per cent of its components were redesigned by Bean and produced in-house. The intention was to follow the mass-production example of Henry

Ford, at a rate of 10,000 Beans a year. The first car to be produced on a production line system in the United Kingdom, its best month's performance was 505 examples made in July 1920. The car offered superb value for money and was cheaper than its key rivals from Austin and Morris, but ultimately was too old-fashioned to appeal to a fast-maturing market. Still, It had gained a tremendous reputation

for reliability; many examples were in service for over two decades, thanks to tough construction and lack of mechanical complexity.

ENGINE: 1796cc (110cu in), four-cylinder
POWER: n/a
0–60MPH (96KM/H): n/a
TOP SPEED: n/a
PRODUCTION TOTAL: about 10,000

BENTLEY 3-LITRE

Not satisfied with any other motor cars on the market, London-based car salesman W.O. Bentley decided to build his own prestigious sports machine. The first Bentley 3-Litre was shown at the 1919 London Motor Show, although cars weren't available to the public until 1921. Two lengths of chassis were available, while the colour of the radiator badge clarified the particular model's purpose. Red Label versions were short-chassis speed-orientated machines. Blue Label alternatives were built with the longer chassis and were designed to have formal

coachwork added, which came from various high-class suppliers in the London area. Finally, the Green Label cars were those which were capable of speeds of at least 161km/h (100mph).

It was the latter designation versions that made Bentley famous, proving their reliability and performance at the Le Mans 24-hour race, winning outright in 1924 and 1927. The 3-Litre was very fast for a four-cylinder model, however, with its unusually long stroke, which was great for torque, and novel four valves per cylinder construction. Nonetheless, it was

notoriously difficult to drive, possessing an awkward gearchange, brakes on the rear wheels only (although a four-wheel system arrived in 1923), a sharp clutch and little in the way of cabin comforts. It was exceptionally heavy, which led Ettore Bugatti to describe the car as the 'fastest lorry in the world'. The 3-Litre model was not a huge commercial success and, were it not for the finances of millionnaire racer Woolf Barnato, who funded Bentley from 1925 until it merged with Rolls-Royce in 1931, the company could easily have gone bankrupt.

Cars such as the 3-Litre, and its circuit exploits, made Bentley famous throughout the world, although it took real skill from the driver to be able to pilot successfully these somewhat agricultural machines.

ENGINE: 2996cc (183cu in), four-cylinder
POWER: n/a
0–60MPH (96KM/H): n/a
TOP SPEED: 161km/h (100mph)
PRODUCTION TOTAL: 1622

ARMSTRONG-SIDDELEY THIRTY

Siddeley Autocars of Coventry was formed in 1902 by John Davenport Siddeley, to make Peugeot motor cars fitted with English bodies. The firm merged with Wolseley in 1905, but Siddeley resigned and took over the Deasy Motor Company, which in 1912 devised the Sphinx mascot for its cars because they were as 'quiet as the Sphinx'. At the time of the Armstrong-Siddeley Thirty's

introduction, aircraft engineering firm Armstrong-Whitworth had bought Siddeley Deasy. Yet it was not until 1927 that Siddeley bought out the company and went on to build aircraft, aero engines and agricultural machinery.

While Armstrong-Siddeley was to become famous for its aircraft, the company also made a range of quality saloon cars for almost four decades. The Thirty was a huge

saloon that was equally popular as a taxi carriage as it was with upper class buyers. It was mechanically straightforward, with a 4960cc (303cu in) six-cylinder engine developing 60bhp (45kW).

The Thirty was a sedate car to drive and its relaxed nature gave it a reputation for longevity – the engines were unstressed and suffered very little wear in normal use. Production lasted for 12

years, which was a significant achievement at a time when other carmakers were changing their styling in successive years.

ENGINE: 4960cc (303cu in),
six-cylinder
POWER: 60bhp (45kW)
0–60MPH (96KM/H): n/a
TOP SPEED: 110km/h (68mph)
PRODUCTION TOTAL: 2700

LANCHESTER 40

ENGINE: 6178cc (377cu in),
six-cylinder
POWER: 100bhp (75kW)
0–60MPH (96KM/H): n/a
TOP SPEED: 104km/h (65mph)
PRODUCTION TOTAL: n/a

The Lanchester 40 sold in small numbers to the gentry and rivalled the Rolls-Royce as being the finest car in the world in its

era. It was a favourite of the Duke of York, later King George VI. A most stately machine, with a long wheelbase and limousine-type coachwork, its top speed was a mere 104km/h (65mph) because of its size and weight; however, that didn't worry those people who wanted to travel with dignity in a high level of refinement. The Birmingham-based manufacturer was already renowned for its use of innovative technology and the

Lanchester brothers themselves were responsible for much of the car's mechanical integrity, making many of the complex mechanical items themselves and even producing all-round brakes in 1924. Although not entirely hydraulic, the brakes relied on servo-assisted mechanical linkages fed via the gearbox. A number of different body styles was available, and there was even a highly modified racer built in 1921,

which raced successfully at Brooklands, including winning a number of long-distance awards. The Lanchester 40 was available until 1931, when it was replaced by the Straight Eight model.

Although largely forgotten these days, during its heyday Lanchester was an extremely prestigious marque; the 40 model was the choice of Royals.

HISPANO-SUIZA H6

ENGINE: 6597cc (403cu in),
six-cylinder
POWER: 135bhp (101kW)
0–60MPH (96KM/H): n/a
TOP SPEED: 139km/h (87mph)
PRODUCTION TOTAL: n/a

Having manufactured aero engines during World War I, Hispano-Suiza had an expectant motoring public waiting keenly for the first of Marc Birkigt's post-war Hispano-Suiza cars. The H6, as it was known, did not disappoint them, when it was revealed at the

1919 Paris Salon, as it was one of the most technically advanced cars of its time. In fact, Swiss-born engineer Birkigt himself designed the mechanically operated servo-assisted four-wheel braking system, technology that was later copied by Rolls-Royce for its vehicles.

In other areas, the H6 represented the pinnacle of technical endeavour, with its beautifully finished engine components, a superb pressed steel chassis and coachwork that was virtually without equal. Indeed, so prestigious was the quality of build throughout that only the privileged few could afford the sporting four-seater's high asking price. The car was made at the firm's French plant in Paris, and the company effectively employed a 'one model' strategy, developing the H6 through experiences both on and off the racetrack. In 1924, Birkigt launched the H6C Sport and Boulogne models, with the engine capacity enlarged to almost 8 litres (488cu in), and both models later went on to enjoy several key competition successes.

Fabulously complicated, but also fabulously expensive, Hispano-Suiza's H6 has now become a legendary classic among collectors.

ALVIS 10/30

ENGINE: 1460cc (89cu in), four-cylinder
POWER: 30bhp (22kW)
0–60MPH (96KM/H): n/a
TOP SPEED: 97km/h (60mph)
PRODUCTION TOTAL: 770

One of the great names of British motoring, the name Alvis has no human reference and was a name that had been used to describe an aluminium piston designed by G.P.H. de Freville, who, along with T.G. John, designed the first 10/30 car in 1920, their Coventry-based company trading under the name of Alvis Car and Engineering Company Ltd. The word 'Alvis' was intended simply to be easily pronounceable in any language.

The car was ahead of its time when it appeared, with a four-speed gearbox and force-fed lubrication system. The lightweight two-seater used a 1.5-litre (89cu in) engine designed by de Freville, and the essentially simple bodies were built by outside coachbuilders. Most of the engines were side-valve, but a few more sporting examples were fitted with overhead valve engines and became known as Super Sports models. They were around 32km/h (20mph) faster than their side-valve sisters.

Despite a relatively high price tag of between £750 and £870, sales proved to be impressive, as many customers were attracted by the 10/30's willing performance and tidy appearance. Most cars came in two-tone blue and grey paintwork as standard, which was complemented by a matching leather interior.

A slightly modified version, the larger-engined 11/40, appeared in 1921, but this was made for only six months before being dropped. The 10/30, however, continued in production until 1925.

First ever Alvis was the 10/30, a trim two-seater design that was technically advanced for its era. Its four-speed transmission was advanced for the period, especially in a car of this size and power.

CHEVROLET 490

In a marketing decision intended to unsettle the hugely successful Henry Ford, Chevrolet named its new model after the dollar price that it intended to slap on the car's windscreen. Mind you, paying only an extra US$60 would see it equipped with electric lights and starter. It never stayed that way, and the price did climb. When Ford lowered his prices, Chevrolet could not compete – although the sales to a market that wanted a bit more choice than just a Model T were excellent, they could not match Ford's dominance.

Chevrolet had positioned itself as a maker of premium-priced economy cars with more refinement and technical merit. It believed that, even at the budget end of the scene, customers were still looking for something with style and quality. At the forefront of this theory, the Chevrolet 490 featured an entry-level four-cylinder range at its launch in 1918. Although it proved to be popular, for 1920, Chevrolet surprised everyone by offering a restyled version of the car. This was one of the first examples of a manufacturer trying to stimulate sales through a redesign. The straight wings were replaced with curved ones, and the headlights were mounted on steel brackets to eliminate the clumsy tie bar. Sales rocketed.

By 1922, Chevrolet had enhanced the 490's practicality by turning the saloon into a four-door model.

The engines now had easy valve adjustment on the rocker arms, larger king pins on the suspension and single pedal brakes. These cars were therefore easy and cheap to maintain, and as a result managed to steal some sales from the more basic and less comfortable Ford Model T.

ENGINE: 2803cc (171cu in), four cylinder
POWER: 26bhp (19kW)
0–60MPH (96KM/H): n/a
TOP SPEED: 80km/h (50mph)
PRODUCTION TOTAL: 356,406

Built as a competitor to the Ford Model T, the 490 of Chevrolet's budget car title referred to its $490 sales tag, although many paid more for electric lighting.

LEYLAND EIGHT (UK/AUSTRALIA)

The magnificent Leyland Eight, designed by J.G. Parry-Thomas during World War I, possessed the promise to become the best car in the world, and nothing in terms of cost was spared for it to become a serious rival to Rolls-Royce. Sadly, it was all just a dream that could have become reality had Leyland provided Parry-Thomas with the backing he deserved, instead of concentrating on the manufacture of trucks. Indeed, the car was dropped after post-war financial problems took hold at the firm.

Strong visually, the car had an upright rectangular radiator grille, a flat hinged windscreen and peculiar steel disc wheels with conical centre caps. The Eight was a masterpiece of technical detail, with leaf spring control of the valves and an unusual camshaft drive. It even featured an early form of vacuum servo-assisted rear drum brakes, although there were no brakes at all on the front axle. Some examples were given an increased stroke, which served to raise the capacity of the straight-eight cylinder engine to 7266cc (443cu in). Unfortunately, only one example of the Eight exists today, a short-chassis sports version which was built in 1927 from parts that had been held at Brooklands in Surrey.

ENGINE: 6987cc (426cu in), eight-cylinder
POWER: 200bhp (149kW)
0–60MPH (96KM/H): n/a
TOP SPEED: n/a
PRODUCTION TOTAL: 18

The huge, imposing Eight was a vain attempt by truck company Leyland to build the best car in the world.

BUGATTI TYPE 13

ENGINE: 1496cc (91cu in), 4-cylinder
POWER: 40bhp (30kW) approx
0-60MPH (96KM/H): n/a
TOP SPEED: 140km/h (87mph)
PRODUCTION TOTAL: 2500 (Types 13, 22 and 23) approx

Son of an Italian artist, Ettore Arco Isadoro Bugatti was born in 1881 and became one of the foremost designers and developers of early motorcars, introducing a level of style and presence that few of his contemporary rivals could approach. Although his early intention was to study art himself, he became fascinated by the internal combustion engine instead. He even made one of his own, in 1909, and the Bugatti marque and legend was born.

The Type 13 was Bugatti's first production model; a light car based on prototypes he had built at his home. It was manufactured at Molsheim, in the Alsace region of eastern France, and was fitted with an advanced 1326cc (81cu in) overhead camshaft engine, at a time when this configuration was still a novelty. The Type 13 also featured the first application of Bugatti's trademark 'horseshoe' radiator grille, Ettore having been influenced by his father, according to reports, who highlighted that the most perfect shape found in nature was the egg.

Production was halted during World War I, but restarted in the 1920s, using an enlarged single block 1496cc (91cu in) engine. Significantly, it featured a more powerful 16-valve head in place of the original eight-valve unit. The Type 13's trim, handling and performance brought it a wealth of successes in racing and endurance events. As well as the standard model, longer wheelbase Type 15s and 17s were offered.

Although the Type 13 would be overshadowed by its later sisters, it helped direct Bugatti towards sporting greatness.

BUGATTI TYPE 23/BRESCIA

ENGINE: 1496cc (91cu in), four-cylinder
POWER: about 30bhp (22kW)
0–60MPH (96KM/H): n/a
TOP SPEED: 105km/h (65mph)
PRODUCTION TOTAL: about 2500 (Types 13, 22 and 23)

Developing the Bugatti Type 13 resulted in the Type 23. Like the earlier model, it featured a 1326cc (81cu in) overhead camshaft eight-valve engine, later enlarged to a 16-valve 1496cc (91cu in) unit, when production restarted after World War I. The key difference between the two types was in the length of the wheelbases. The Type 13 was 2m (6.5ft) long, while the Type 23's wheelbase was stretched to 2.55m (8.3ft), which allowed different classes of bodywork to be fitted. Suspension was by reversed quarter-elliptic springs, a system that became a Bugatti standard. An unusual feature of the engine was

its elaborate lubrication system. The main pump took its oil from a reservoir located beneath the dashboard, feeding it to an oil box at the end of the camshaft. Two additional pumps then distributed it to the sump. Although very

complex, this innovative system ensured that different amounts of oil could be distributed to different components, depending on their requirements, which in turn meant that Bugatti engines could last longer and drive further than

many of the firm's rivals. The Brescia name was adopted for the Type 13, Type 22 and Type 23 after great success in the 1921 Italian Grand Prix at Brescia, when Bugatti took first, second, third and fourth overall.

Bugatti were at home on the circuit. The Brescia title reflected Bugatti's 1:2:3 victory in the 1921 Italian Grand Prix and sold the car on its high performance.

AC 12/24

ENGINE: 1496cc (91cu in), four-cylinder
POWER: 24bhp (18kW)
0–60MPH (96KM/H): n/a
TOP SPEED: 76km/h (47mph)
PRODUCTION TOTAL: n/a

After World War I, AC realized that it was unable to use the French engine that had powered the earlier 10hp model. To replace it, the company chose a British-built Anzani four-cylinder unit, which proved to be exceptionally reliable and powerful for its time. (Anzani had originated in Italy.) It

was also very light in weight. One of the three Anzani-engined models built was the 12/24, so named because the RAC taxation rating on the engine was 12hp, while the actual power was 24bhp (18kW). A more sophisticated model than the previous 10hp, it gained a modest sporting reputation; some owners

stripped them of running boards and windscreen to run them in as many competition classes as possible, mostly at Brooklands. In fact, the 12/24 claimed an accolade as the first 1.5-litre car to exceed 100mph (161km/h) in competition. From the mid-1920s, brakes on all four wheels became an option.

BUGATTI TYPE 22

Interestingly, the Bugatti Type 22 fitted in between the shorter Type 13 and the longer Type 23. So named, the twenty-second car to be designed by Ettore Bugatti since 1898 had a 2.4m (7.9ft) chassis, but in most other ways was the same car as the Type 13. It first appeared before the outbreak of World War I, and was reintroduced after hostilities ended, equipped with the larger

1496cc (91cu in) 16-valve overhead camshaft four-cylinder engine replacing the original 1326cc (81cu in) eight-valve unit.

The handbrake worked on the rear wheels, while the footbrake acted on the transmission, an unusual development at the time. Suspension was by reversed quarter–elliptic springs, which was known by the more complex term 'reversed demi-cantilever springs'.

This provided the car with good handling, while the 16-valve engine endowed it with strong performance. Most Type 22s were fitted with touring bodies, leaving the smaller, open-bodied Type 13s to compete for racing glory.

Production of the Type 22 was carried out under licence in the United Kingdom, by the Manchester firm Crossley, using parts sent out from the Molsheim

Bugatti factory in France. Diatto in Italy and Rabag in Germany also made the Type 22 under licence.

ENGINE: 1496cc (91cu in),
four-cylinder
POWER: about 30bhp (22kW)
0–60MPH (96KM/H): n/a
TOP SPEED: 113km/h (70mph)
PRODUCTION TOTAL: about 2500
(Types 13, 22 and 23)

BSA TEN

ENGINE: 1075cc (66cu in), V-twin cylinder
POWER: 18bhp (13kW)
0–60MPH (96KM/H): n/a
TOP SPEED: 84km/h (52mph)
PRODUCTION TOTAL: about 5000

Although BSA is a company now renowned for its motorcycles, it was originally formed to make guns and ammunition. The initials stood for Birmingham Small Arms and, in 1907, the company added cars to its manufacturing portfolio, building them in a new factory in the Sparkbrook area of Birmingham, England.

Interestingly, BSA was a most successful company and bought

the Daimler car business in 1910. Yet the 1921 Ten was BSA's most significant offering. A two-seater lightweight sports car, it featured a modest 1075cc (66cu in) V-twin engine that had been built on similar principles to the units used in the company's motorcycles, and it delivered a surprising top speed of 84km/h (52mph). It was also fun to drive, with light and direct steering, a moderately easy-to-operate three-speed gearbox and effective brakes.

The BSA Ten was to earn a deserved reputation as a great trials competition car, thanks to its eager engine and lightweight build. It later appeared in a more luxurious form as the Daimler Ten.

Although BSA also owned Daimler, it chose to make less prestigious machines under its own name. The diminutive Ten displayed great sporting prowess, with its engine closely related to BSA's motorcycle designs.

AC SIX

Emanating from one of the worst periods of AC Car's existence, the AC Six was an enduring model that was produced in several versions over the years, all of which were classified according to engine power. Adding complication to its history, the car was sold with a variety of bodystyles, including a drophead coupé called the Aceca, a name which was to be reused by AC many years later. Yet, the basic

design of the Six remained the same throughout, with a highly advanced overhead camshaft six-cylinder engine, which started out with a capacity of 1.5 litres (92cu in) unit, but was later changed to 2 litres (122cu in).

The engine was developed by AC and was often used in racing and record attempts. The gearbox was a three-speed unit, and the suspension was by quarter-elliptic

springs, providing the car with good handling. The standard brake set-up was for the rear wheels only, although front brakes did become available as an option and, from 1927, were fitted as standard equipment.

The first versions developed 35bhp (26kW); however, that was increased to 40bhp (30kW) for the 16/40 version. A 16/56 version followed, which itself was replaced

by the triple carburettor 16/66. The company went into voluntary liquidation in 1929, with production ceasing in 1930.

ENGINE: 1992cc (122cu in),
six-cylinder
POWER: 66bhp (49kW)
0–60MPH (96KM/H): n/a
TOP SPEED: 137km/h (85mph)
PRODUCTION TOTAL: n/a

ARIEL NINE

ENGINE: 996cc (61cu in),
twin-cylinder
POWER: about 20bhp (15kW)
0–60MPH (96KM/H): n/a
TOP SPEED: 85km/h (53mph)
PRODUCTION TOTAL: about 700

Based in Birmingham, Ariel was a cycle firm that was also one of the early British automobile pioneers, building its first car in 1902. During its short, turbulent history as a car manufacturer, it changed hands several times. One revival of the name, in 1922, saw the introduction of the Ariel Nine, designed to compete in the small

car sector. Its diminutive flat-twin engine had a capacity of 996cc (61cu in); however, it was not a particularly refined unit. Its coarseness and vibration led observers to believe that it was air-cooled, although the engine was actually cooled by water. With low-cost affordability firmly in mind, the Nine was available with only

one colour as standard, an austere grey. Despite the Ariel Nine's low price and impressive fuel economy, combined with energetic and surprisingly entertaining performance, only around 700 examples were sold before the model was dropped in 1925, and Ariel concentrated on motorcycle production instead.

CLYNO 10.8

ENGINE: 1368cc (83cu in),
four-cylinder
POWER: 14bhp (10kW)
0–60MPH (96KM/H): n/a
TOP SPEED: 80km/h (50mph)
PRODUCTION TOTAL: 35,000

The name is little known today, but Clyno was once the third largest carmaker in the United Kingdom after Austin and Morris. It boasted proudly that it offered a price level that was as low as any car of like rating in the world, but with a value that was vastly higher. The company was formed in 1908, by Frank and Ailwyn Smith in Northamptonshire, England. They had designed and manufactured a pulley with a variable drive ratio for belt-driven machines. It was called the 'inclined pulley', but this

was soon abbreviated to 'clined' and finally became the 'Clyno'. The company started by manufacturing motorcycles, but had to be relaunched after a collapse in the market bankrupted the firm. Its first car, designed by George Stanley and A.G. Booth, appeared in 1922. It featured a 14hp (10kW) 1368cc (83cu in) four-cylinder Coventry-Climax engine, a Clyno three-speed gearbox and electric lighting, and sold for a remarkable £250. It was designed to compete directly with the Morris Oxford. Orders were higher than expected; by 1923, all motorcycle production had ceased and the car's price was reduced to £238. Clyno continued to upgrade the specification and broaden the product range as the 10.8 Family Model. Clyno was liquidated again in 1929, and the 10.8 disappeared with it.

Few have heard of Clyno these days, but during the 10.8's heyday, it was one of Britain's biggest car firms. However, fierce Austin Seven completion saw Clyno go bankrupt before the end of the 1920s.

ROLLS-ROYCE TWENTY

ENGINE: 3127cc (191cu in),
six-cylinder
POWER: n/a
TOP SPEED: n/a
0–60MPH (96KM/H): n/a
PRODUCTION TOTAL: 2940

Never the quickest off the mark to introduce new models, Rolls-Royce brought in the Twenty in 1922 – it was the first entirely new Rolls-Royce model since 1907. A compact alternative to the Silver Ghost, it was a more economical ownership proposition thanks to its smaller, more fuel-efficient engine. Yet it was still very expensive compared to most cars of the era, although you would not hear Rolls-Royce customers complain, as they recognized that they were buying a supremely well-engineered and hand-crafted

motor car. The Twenty carried the traditional Rolls-Royce upright radiator grille with the Spirit of Ecstasy mascot mounted proudly on the filler cap, while the rest of the car featured a host of modern developments. Early cars had a centrally positioned gearchange,

although this was moved back to the right-hand side of the steering wheel in a seemingly retrograde move halfway through its production life, which had more to do with the expectations of chauffeurs than improving driving ease. Other innovations included

servo braking on all four wheels from 1924. Interior space was massive, especially in the rear, although the Twenty was designed primarily with owner-drivers in mind, not chauffeurs and passengers, unlike larger models in the company's line-up.

The Twenty was about as close as Rolls-Royce ever got to an economy model, although it still cost a small fortune and so wasn't for the Model T crowd.

ARGYLL TWELVE

One of Scotland's several homegrown car manufacturers was also one of Britain's biggest car firms before World War I, but went bankrupt in 1914. It was bought by its repair works manager, J.A. Brimlow, and from late 1918 recommended building cars that were based on pre-war designs. The Twelve, introduced in

1922, was available with a 1496cc (91cu in) engine and, from 1926, a 1640cc (100cu in) engine that employed single sleeve-valves. This was simpler than a conventional poppet-valve motor, as fewer moving parts could go wrong or break. The smaller engined Twelves could boast 30bhp (22kW), while the bigger 12/40s mustered

40bhp (30kW). They were large, impressive-looking motor cars, but came with a fairly high price tag, which ultimately led to the company's demise. When the Depression hit on both sides of the Atlantic, Argyll found few buyers for its cars, and the firm quickly faded away again at the beginning of the 1930s, even if the company

did remain in existence until it was finally wound up in 1963.

ENGINE: 1496cc (91cu in),
four-cylinder
POWER: 30bhp (22kW)
0–60MPH (96KM/H): n/a
TOP SPEED: n/a
PRODUCTION TOTAL: about 250

AUSTIN SEVEN

ENGINE: 747cc (46cu in),
  four-cylinder
POWER: 10bhp (7.5kW)
0–60MPH (96KM/H): n/a
TOP SPEED: 84km/h (52mph)
PRODUCTION TOTAL: 290,000

Emanating from a time at which the British motor industry was making its influence felt around the world, the Austin Seven transformed motoring in Britain and introduced several nations to the vehicle manufacturing business. It became the subject of both admiration and derision for its malnourished size and, as we enter the ninth decade since the start of production, it still attracts a fanatical following.

Naturally, the secret behind its success lay in its price. Motoring had initially been the preserve of rich pioneers, but, by the breakout of World War I, the middle classes were also flirting with motorcar ownership. The nation's working classes, however, were stuck with cyclecars and motorcycle with sidecar combinations. To Herbert

Austin, the founder of the Austin Motor Company, this was manna from heaven, and he wanted to make his 'baby' car even more affordable than the Ford Model T, which had sold over one million examples by that time, albeit mostly in North America.

Working from his home (because the Austin Motor Company had rejected the idea of the Seven), with the help of a young draughtsman, Stanley Edge, Herbert Austin developed the car. It would have a rudimentary chassis, with two main beams running the length of the car, and little else except for a basic suspension. Initially, the engine was a tiny four-cylinder side-valve unit of just 696cc (42cu in), although this was enlarged to 747cc (46cu in) soon afterwards. The bodywork was a mixture of steel panels and aluminium-over-ash frame. It was very light and very simple to produce.

The public's response to the new car was overwhelming, when it was launched in 1922, advertised as the 'motor for the millions'. At just £225, it was the price of a well-equipped motorcycle with

sidecar combination. As more Sevens were sold, the price was reduced, so that by 1926 it cost just £145. Three years later, more than 100,000 Sevens had been sold, giving the Austin Seven a 37 per cent share of the British car market, which virtually killed off sidecars and cyclecars for good.

An increased number of variants was introduced, including saloons, open-top tourers and even sports models, some with superchargers. Sevens were built for the army, to use as staff cars and wireless carriers, and for tradesmen, who used them as delivery vans. There were even special versions for milk deliveries, with the back adapted to carry milk churns. On the race track, the Seven collected speed records and irritated the drivers of larger, more powerful machines. At Brooklands, the Seven became the first 161km/h (100mph) 750cc (46cu in) car in England. It was even raced in the Le Mans 24-hour race, with a degree of success. Private owners started to compete in their Sevens, too. Trials (which involved trying to cajole a car up a muddy, slippery

slope), rallies, hillclimbs and circuit racing were all deemed appropriate for the little Austin. Remarkably, the car continues to be used in classic events even now.

The Seven was responsible for vehicle production starting for several overseas car manufacturers. The rights to produce a French-built Seven were bought by Rosengart. In Germany, the car became the Dixi, which went on to form the basis for BMW, and, in North America, it was bought by a new firm, the American Austin Car Company. Bizarrely, a version of the US-built Seven went on to influence the original Jeep. By 1939, however, and despite several face-lifts, most notably the Austin Seven Ruby, with its larger, more sophisticated bodywork, the car both looked and felt dated against its rivals. The Seven was replaced by the more powerful, more comfortable and markedly more expensive Big Seven. It never sold like the original Seven, and Austin had to wait until 1959 before it produced another truly revolutionary vehicle to carry the name, the Austin Seven Mini.

The Seven – a British 'people's car' – changed quite a bit during its 18 year production life, but always remained refreshingly simplistic and therefore very cheap. Compare this early open two seater...

...with this later, more sophisticated Ruby saloon, introduced in 1934 and available up until the Seven went out of production in 1939, by which time dozens of different body styles had appeared.

TATRA TYPE 11

Named after a mountain range in the former Czechoslovakia, Tatra is reputed to be the third oldest carmaker in the world, as it started car production in 1897 and was originally called Nesselsdorf, the name of the town in which the cars were built. When the town was renamed Koprivnice in 1918, the new company of Tatra was introduced a year later. By 1923 a radical new car was launched,

designed by the innovative Hans Ledwinka, whose future would link him to Porsche.

The Type 11 used a backbone chassis in place of the previously specified conventional ladder frame. The body was supported on outriggers from the central tube and, at the rear, there was fully independent suspension using swing axles. The front-end was supported by a transverse leaf

spring, another innovation that provided low cost independent springing that was excellent at absorbing the nastiest bumps on the country's poorly surfaced roads. Located beneath a Renault-like front bonnet (hood) was a 1036cc (63cu in) air-cooled flat-twin powerplant. The car was an instant success. Over the next three years, around 3500 examples of the Type 11 were produced, before

the T12 arrived. This car was essentially a T11, but incorporated brakes on all four wheels and a raft of other minor improvements.

ENGINE: 1036cc (63cu in),
  twin-cylinder
POWER: 13bhp (10kW)
0–60MPH (96KM/H): n/a
TOP SPEED: 90km/h (56mph)
PRODUCTION TOTAL: about 3500

ARMSTRONG-SIDDELEY FOUR-FOURTEEN

ENGINE: 1852cc (113cu in),
  four-cylinder
POWER: n/a
0–60MPH (96KM/H): n/a
TOP SPEED: about 81km/h (50mph)
PRODUCTION TOTAL: 13,365

Although it seemed like an odd marketing decision, the Four-Fourteen was a more downmarket car from Armstrong-Siddeley. The model was the first of the company's cars to feature a four-cylinder engine and the 1852cc (113cu in) unit was unimpressive. Its reliability was only average, while performance and fuel economy suffered badly, as the motor struggled to overcome the weight of a heavy car. Until 1925, simple six-volt electrics and front brakes distinguished the Four-Fourteen from more upmarket Armstrong-Siddeleys, and it was immediately identifiable by its plain flat radiator grille. From 1925, the model name was changed to 14/30, with the launch of the Mk II version, which featured brakes on all four wheels and improved fuel economy. Various bodystyles were offered, although most came with four-door saloon coachwork.

LANCHESTER TWENTY ONE

ENGINE: 2982cc (182cu in),
  six-cylinder
POWER: 21bhp (16kW)
0–60MPH (96KM/H): n/a
TOP SPEED: 104km/h (65mph)
PRODUCTION TOTAL: n/a

As its main rival, Rolls-Royce, had introduced a Model 20, there was a certain inevitability to Lanchester introducing the '21', as it became known. Featuring an overhead camshaft, six-cylinder 2982cc (182cu in) engine, it was sold alongside the Sporting Forty, which lasted until 1929. Sold as a direct rival to the 'baby' Rolls-Royce, which was only £50 more expensive at the time, it was nicknamed the 'pup'. Little more than a scaled-down version of the Forty, the 21 featured a four-speed sliding pinion gearbox, while the Rolls-Royce Twenty offered only a three-speed transmission. It was also equipped with front brakes that featured large diameter aluminium drums lined with cast iron and deeply ribbed for circumferential strength and heat dispersion. By 1931, financial troubles forced the Lanchester company to merge with Daimler to provide access to a more price-conscious market, and the factory was moved to Coventry. Lanchesters after that time were really little more than Daimlers wearing Lanchester badges, and even this differentiation finally disappeared in 1956. Frederick Lanchester went on to design electrical and mechanical inventions until his death in 1946. His brother George left the company to join Alvis, and died in 1970.

Rolls-Royce built the Twenty…so competitor Lanchester produced the 21 to go one better. In many ways, the 21 was a superior car.

CHRYSLER MODEL B

Walter Percy Chrysler managed to achieve what few others did in starting a motorcar company in the 1920s and making it survive into the 1930s. The date was January 1924, and the location was the Commodore Hotel, New York, where the first new Chrysler was presented. An attractively priced, innovative motor car, it had mass-market appeal. It came as no surprise when, by the end of that year, it was announced that 32,000 examples had been sold, a first-year sales record in the highly competitive motor industry.

At the heart of the model was an L-head engine with a very high compression ratio. This meant that it was powerful, producing 68bhp (51kW) at 3200rpm, and provided excellent performance and a comfortable 113km/h (70mph) top speed. The engine featured aluminium pistons and full-pressure lubrication, and its chassis was equipped with four-wheel hydraulic brakes; a tubular front axle was fitted. Both developments were unique on a volume production car of the period. The Model B also excelled at motorsport, setting national records, leading the way for Chrysler to become the first US manufacturer to compete in the legendary Le Mans 24-hour race.

ENGINE: 3294cc (201cu in),
  six-cylinder
POWER: 68bhp (51kW)
0–60MPH (96KM/H): n/a
TOP SPEED: 113km/h (70mph)
PRODUCTION TOTAL: 32,000

ASTER 20/55

Some people on hearing the name Aster might erroneously link it with the aristocratic British family Astor, who could have become patrons of the company, had they not been so enamoured of Daimler and Rolls-Royce. In its heyday, Aster was regarded as a maker of some of the finest cars in the world. Established in Wembley, London, in 1898, the firm originally started making engines for a French carmaker of the same name. UK Asters became independent designs in 1922, when the factory occupied 18 acres of industrial land that is today occupied by London's North Circular Road.

The first UK-designed and built car was the 18/50, a luxury saloon with a 113km/h (70mph) cruising capability. This was superseded in 1924 by the hand-built 20/55, described in Aster's corporate literature as 'transport for those that know most about motor cars and for the connoisseur', among whom was the Duke of York, who replaced his Armstrong-Siddeley Thirty with an Aster 20/55, in 1924. Powered by a six-cylinder engine unique to the model, it could be ordered as a saloon or an open-top tourer. The company merged with the Scottish Arrol-Johnston in 1927, with production relocating to Dumfriess. In 1929, the receivers were called in, but the new Arrol-Asters remained in limited production until 1931.

ENGINE: 2890cc (176 cu in),
  six-cylinder
POWER: n/a
0–60MPH (96KM/H): n/a
TOP SPEED: n/a
PRODUCTION TOTAL: 52

DODGE TYPE A

The reputation of Dodge cars had been falling and its model range was in dire need of upgrading by the early 1920s. The response from the Dodge brothers was to introduce one of the first pressed all-steel bodies, and the Type A was available as a two-door roadster or four-door saloon.

Constant innovation was a key feature, as the wheelbase was lengthened for more interior space, but a lower overall height stopped the vehicle from looking too bulky. Dodge replaced the quarter-elliptic springs with semi-elliptics and, inside, lowered the seats and moved the gear lever and foot pedals forward to provide more legroom. Customers could also order a deluxe model, which boasted a nickel-plated radiator, bumpers, windscreen wipers and bright metal step plates on the running boards. By 1924, the Type A had helped Dodge to regain its former position as the number three carmaker in North America.

The company had been expanding its production capacity and the Type A was built in Walkerville, Ontario. For 1925, technical changes were introduced to upgrade the engine, and 51cm (20in) wheels and a one-piece windscreen were fitted. Along with the already well established Chevrolet and Ford, Dodge was now a recognized maker of cheap mass-market cars.

ENGINE: 3480cc (212cu in), four-cylinder
POWER: 35bhp (26kW)
0–60MPH (96KM/H): n/a
TOP SPEED: 88km/h (55mph)
PRODUCTION TOTAL: 810,861

BUGATTI TYPE 35

ENGINE: 2262cc (138cu in), eight-cylinder
POWER: 130bhp (97kW)
0–60MPH (96KM/H): 7 seconds
TOP SPEED: 201km/h (125mph)
PRODUCTION TOTAL: 340

Bugatti's Type 35 was one of the most beautiful and successful racing cars ever built, and its appeal was not only skin deep.

Alloy wheels and brake drums may look the part, but, when attached to a hollow front axle, the unsprung weight is vastly reduced. Furthermore, the Type 35 fulfilled Ettore Bugatti's ambition by providing an exclusive racer at a modest price. Although the engine was derived from the earlier Type 30, the 1990cc (121cu in) straight-eight engine could rev to 6000rpm, considerable for its time. Later variants followed, the 35C was supercharged and the 35T had a larger 2262cc (138cu in) engine. The 35B was the ultimate version, combining both the bigger engine and the supercharger.

During its racing career, the car claimed many victories, including winning the Targa Florio race for five consecutive years, from 1925 to 1929, even though its open yet cramped cockpit demanded the most from any determined driver. From 1930, the Type 35 added to

The Type 35 was a real 'femme fatale' of vintage cars, beguilingly beautiful yet also deadly when used in anger for racing.

its list of victories, piloted by many amateur racers and enthusiasts. Now, more than 80 years since production started, the Type 35 is still remembered as one of the most captivating racing cars ever.

CHECKER MODEL E

Russian immigrant Morris Markin came to the United States in 1914. His success as a tailor saw him purchase a trouser factory, and this enabled him to buy Commonwealth Motors, a small taxi bodywork manufacturer. Being a shrewd businessman, Markin ultimately formed the Checker Cab Company, which enjoyed almost 60 years of taxi manufacture; the last model rolled off the production line in July 1982. Replacing Checker's first taxi, the Model E was typical of 1920s automobile design and was joined by an open-backed Landau version which sold for a US$100 premium. With its strong Buda engine and capacious body, it gave operators reliability and its passengers comfort. About 930 Model Es were built in just over a year, before being succeeded by the Model F. Checkers are still seen as iconic twentieth-century North American taxis. The Model E was used by Hergé's fictional character Tintin, in an adventure set in Chicago's gangster-ridden downtown in the late 1920s. A later model featured in Martin Scorsese's 1976 film *Taxi Driver*.

ENGINE: 2000cc (122cu in), four-cylinder
POWER: 22.5bhp (17kW)
0–60MPH (96KM/H): n/a
TOP SPEED: 80km/h (50mph)
PRODUCTION TOTAL: 930

ROLLS-ROYCE 40/50 NEW PHANTOM

ENGINE: 7668cc (468cu in),
 six-cylinder
POWER: n/a
TOP SPEED: n/a
0–60MPH (96KM/H): n/a
PRODUCTION TOTAL: United Kingdom:
 2212; United States: 2944

Expensive, sophisticated and large, the Rolls-Royce is summed up by the 40/50. By the 1920s, however, the competition was closing in on Rolls-Royce's performance lead. A new car was the answer. Despite sitting on its predecessor's chassis, the New Phantom, with its new overhead-valve 7.6-litre (468cu in) engine, was the aspirational car of the 1920s. Although it was capable of

achieving 129km/h (80mph), performance was often hampered by the size and weight of the bespoke coachwork fitted by wealthy owners. Complemented by power-assisted rod and cable brakes and rear oil-filled shock absorbers, the ride and handling were significantly ahead of its rivals, especially as Rolls-Royce went to considerable lengths to road test, mainly in France. Two chassis lengths were available: 190.25in (4.83m) and 196.75in (4.99m).

The New Phantom was the first of the company's models to feature vertical radiator slats, a fitting which has become a distinguishing feature of the brand. The New Phantom was also built in America, the US cars differing by having a central gearchange and left-hand

drive. Production ceased in Britain in 1929, but continued until 1931 in the United States. The car was replaced by the Phantom II, the last Rolls-Royce designed by Royce himself, before his death in 1933.

The Phantom – the name a reference to how silent it was – was a leviathan of a machine. Different, often extravagant, body styles were chosen by owners.

ARAB SPORTS

The rakish good looks of the Sports should have ensured its success, but the death of one of the partners in the Arab company doomed it to a tiny production run of just 18 cars.

ENGINE: 2000cc (122cu in),
 four-cylinder
POWER: 65bhp (48kW) at 4000rpm
0–60MPH (96KM/H): n/a
TOP SPEED: 145km/h (90mph)
PRODUCTION TOTAL: 12

Although its production life was short, the Arab Sports was a technically interesting and advanced car with distinguished connections. Formed in 1925 from an Alliance between Reid Railton and J.G. Parry-Thomas, the Sports demonstrated their passion for speed, but sadly became Arab's only model. Driving through a Moss four-speed gearbox, the 2-litre (122cu in) engine had its valves closed by leaf springs and featured an electric fuel pump, which was a

novel feature at the time. Both low and high chassis (touring) versions were offered. Sadly, Parry-Thomas was decapitated by the drive chain of 'Babs', his beloved Leyland racing car, while attempting a land speed record on Pendine Sands, West Wales, in 1927. As a result, Railton lost his enthusiasm for Arab and so he closed the Letchworth works. Coachbuilders Thomson and Taylor assembled a few cars from spare parts, but the Arab Sports was never brought back into full production. The Railton name appeared again from 1933 on cars which combined exceptional performance with a low price; however, very few were built after World War II. Reid Railton emigrated to the United States and died in California in 1977, at the age of 82.

SUNBEAM 3-LITRE

ENGINE: 2916cc (178cu in),
 six-cylinder
POWER: 93bhp (69kW)
0–60MPH: n/a
TOP SPEED: over 145km/h (over 90mph)
PRODUCTION TOTAL: about 315

Sunbeam was one of the premier marques of the British motor industry, a reputation attributed to its considerable motorsport successes. From 1909 to 1926, Sunbeam cars broke speed records regularly and won prestigious races. The 3-Litre (or 'Super Sport') continued the heritage. Riding on the 16/60's chassis, introduced a year previously, the 3-Litre was launched by Sunbeam in 1925. It

was one of the most sophisticated cars of its time, boasting not only double overhead camshafts (a first for a British car), but dry-sump lubrication as well. A supercharged version followed, upping the power output to 130bhp (97kW). Unfortunately, the chassis was criticized for being inadequate, but modifications were made to address the 3-Litre's shortcomings. Nonetheless, the 3-Litre continued to demonstrate Sunbeam's racing prowess, gaining second place in the 1925 Le Mans race.

Forget the square-cut and basic body of the 3-Litre here and consider the inventiveness that lay underneath the bonnet.

Unfortunately, the company had allocated funds to support its racing rather than its shareholders. The company was absorbed by STD motors later that year and

again, in 1935, by the Rootes Group. Thankfully, the name Sunbeam became reacquainted with motorsport success again in the 1940s and 1950s.

CHAPTER TWO

THE GOLDEN YEARS

1926–1950

The late 1920s and early 1930s are often referred to as the golden days of motoring – an era when cars were getting better year after year, the roads were clear and open, and speed and glamour prevailed. It was a time when cars such as the Auburn and Duesenberg were as much the stars of Hollywood as the first ever film actors, while the supercharged 'Blower' Bentleys were the kings of European race circuits.

The golden years rapidly lost their shine, however. The Great Depression saw the bottom drop out of the luxury car market in the USA, taking some of the finest names in motoring with it, while the onset of World War II saw an even more significant downturn in vehicle production.

By the time the war ended in 1945, motoring tastes had changed significantly. The car was once again a means of transport rather than a status symbol, and the first post-war models were old-fashioned 1930s designs, rapidly rehashed to suit the new era.

There were still some hidden gems, though. In the USA, the Willys Jeep not only made a contribution to the war effort, but became an icon in its own right, while in France the front-wheel-drive Citroën Traction Avant proved that a car didn't have to be conventional if it was to prove popular.

The era also saw the birth of the legendary VW Beetle, or Bug – a car conceived by Adolf Hitler, but which ironically went on to become a symbol for peace and free love.

By the 1920s, the car industry was spreading its tentacles across the world. Italy's national maker, Fiat, was established in 1899 and by the 1920s was selling the 514 – a luxury touring saloon.

BENTLEY 6.5-LITRE/SPEED SIX

ENGINE: 6597cc (403cu in),
  six-cylinder
POWER: 140bhp (104kW)
0–60MPH (96KM/H): n/a
TOP SPEED: n/a
PRODUCTION TOTAL: 545

By the time that the merger between Rolls-Royce and Bentley took place, the Crewe company's position as the best of the best had been severely tested by its sportier rival – in fact, plenty of well-heeled customers had already made the switch over to W.O. Bentley's more brutal cars.

The Bentley 6.5-Litre was unveiled in 1926 and was certainly an expensive option at £1450 – for the chassis only. Coachbuilt bodystyles were charged over and above that. The car used a brand-new 6597cc (403cu in) overhead camshaft engine with 24 valves – a very advanced feature at the time.

The new car was a more docile drive, thanks to its lighter single plate clutch and luxury right-hand gearchange. The sensational 180bhp (134kW) Speed Six joined the 140bhp (104kW) 6.5-Litre in 1928, defining the Bentley name in exclusive circles.

Unlike earlier Bentleys, most of the 6.5-Litre cars were sold as touring cars, although a few were stripped down and used for racing. The company took a brace of Le Mans victories in 1929 and 1930 with this car – and, as a result, the passage of time has seen many tourers turned into Le Mans replicas for hillclimb and endurance events.

The 6.5-Litre is still regarded by many as an all-time great Bentley.

Bentley's 6.5-Litre boasted an advanced specification and was available as a luxury car for well-heeled enthusiasts.

DAIMLER DOUBLE-SIX

ENGINE: 7136cc (435cu in),
  twelve-cylinder
POWER: 150bhp (112kW)
0–60MPH (96KM/H): n/a
TOP SPEED: 129km/h (80mph)
PRODUCTION TOTAL: 500

During the 1920s, there had been plenty of rivalry in the luxury car sector, and that led to plenty of choice for the super-rich motoring elite. One common factor demanded by all buyers at this elevated level was a smooth, strong and silent engine. It was here that Daimler's Double-Six scored so highly. World leaders and industrial plutocrats soon came to appreciate the 7.1-litre (435cu in) Double-Six – Britain's first V12 engine.

Designed by Laurence Pomeroy Senior, then Chief Engineer at Daimler, the new engine was based on the existing 25/85 six – although the Double-Six's cylinders were cast in four blocks of three, with detachable cylinder heads. The name came from the fact that, effectively, the power unit was two six-cylinder engines joined at the crank. It was advanced, too, featuring one distributor per bank, four-jet carburettor and eccentric shaft to drive its steel valve sleeves.

A smaller 3.7-litre (226cu in) V12 based on the Double-Six joined the range in 1928, and this version was dubbed the Double-Six-30. A leviathan 7.1-litre (435cu in) version then appeared, and it was to become known as the Double-Six-50.

These hugely dignified cars were genuine alternatives to contemporary Rolls-Royce products and remain well loved today.

MARENDAZ 1.5-LITRE

ENGINE: 1496cc (91cu in),
  four-cylinder
POWER: 11.8bhp (9kW)
0–60MPH (96KM/H): n/a
TOP SPEED: 128km/h (80mph)
PRODUCTION TOTAL: n/a

So-called because they were the creation of a Captain Marendaz, these cars, which were first built in Brixton, London, then later at Maidenhead in Berkshire, remain extremely rare to this day. The first Marendaz cars were largely based on a light car made by Marseal – another car company in which Captain Marendaz had an involvement. The Marseals might have been uninspiring sports cars produced in the early 1920s, but the later cars finally to bear the captain's name were attractive, and resembled scaled-down vintage

Captain Marendaz after beating the world 24-hour record – the car's rare specifications boasted dampers on all four wheels.

Bentley racers, powered by a gutsy side-valve Anzani engine.

The later cars were powered by a more fitting 6-litre (366cu in) engine of American origin, and could be identified by their flexible side exhaust pipes emerging from the side of the bonnet (hood), while retaining the Bentley-esque grille. Only the Anzani-engined cars sold in significant numbers.

They did well in competition, and drivers who scored impressive results included Sir Stirling Moss's mother and interestingly a certain Miss Dorothy Summers, who was employed as a secretary at the factory in Maidenhead.

Captain Marendaz was killed in World War II, and no further cars were built bearing his name.

TALBOT 14/45

Designed by Georges Roesch and powered by a 1665cc (102cu in) six-cylinder overhead-valve engine developing a generous 45bhp (34kW), the Talbot 14/45 came along at the right time effectively to turn around the fortunes of the Sunbeam-Talbot-Darraq Group – of which the Sunbeam part of the group was performing very badly. The 14/45 emerged to be a rather special car, with its reliability soon proved by a string of racing successes – amazing considering its gestation period was a mere six months.

The car was launched in 1926, and its touring abilities were what distinguished it from its rivals, even if it had an uncompetitive top speed of 96km/h (60mph). The Talbot 14/45 was superbly refined with excellent handling, thanks to its race-bred chassis, and was more comfortable than its rivals. Its excellent handling was due to the well set-up suspension using semi-elliptics at the front and quarter-elliptics at the rear.

A large range of bodystyles was available – and Talbot made sure that there was something available to suit all customers. Alongside the cabriolet and tourer versions were saloons, coupés and even a pretty landaulette.

ENGINE: 1665cc (102cu in), six-cylinder
POWER: 45bhp (34kW)
0–60MPH (96KM/H): n/a
TOP SPEED: 96km/h (60mph)
PRODUCTION TOTAL: 11,851

STANDARD NINE

The Standard Car Company's fortunes were not looking great at the time of the Nine's launch in 1927. Widespread industrial action typified by the 1926 General Strike in the United Kingdom had left carmakers in deep trouble. Still, it was not as if Standard's cars occupied the upper end of the market and, although the cars were relatively affordable, what the company really needed was an economy car to compete with the Austin Seven and Morris Eight.

When launched at the 1927 Olympia Motor Show, the Nine seemed to be the answer to these problems. Proven by only scant pre-production testing of two prototypes, the Nine went into production, and passed into the showrooms without hitch. This was an impressive achievement considering the car passed from drawing board to full production in a mere six months. Unsurprisingly, it was conventionally engineered, featuring a side-valve engine and simple chassis construction.

The four-seater fabric-bodied saloon cost just £198 at launch – and proved an immediate success in these austere times. A new range of bodystyles was offered the following year, along with the unusual option of a supercharger.

A year later, the Nine's engine was upgraded to produce 9.9hp from 8.9hp – and racing success at Brooklands soon followed.

ENGINE: 1155cc (70cu in), four-cylinder
POWER: n/a
0–60MPH (96KM/H): n/a
TOP SPEED: 80km/h (50mph)
PRODUCTION TOTAL: about 10,000

VAUXHALL 20/60

The 1928 Vauxhall 20/60 has the honour of being the first of the company's products to be produced under the stewardship of General Motors – following its purchase of the British carmaker in 1925. As this was the first US takeover of a British car company, there was a wide degree of suspicion throughout the United Kingdom from those who feared an American invasion – and many commentators reported that the 20/60 was rather transatlantic in design. The 20/60 featured a number of innovations: 12-volt electrics, central gearshift and a single-plate clutch were the American norm, and the styling seemed to reflect the mood of Detroit, aping contemporary Buicks. Vauxhall countered these criticisms, by claiming the car was designed before the takeover.

Not that it mattered, of course, because the final product was very good – and dynamics capabilities were well beyond much of the opposition. Its cable and rod brakes were more effective than those on its predecessors, and more modern Marles-gears steering was a step up from the traditional Vauxhall worm-and-wheel set-up. Another big innovation was the adoption of wooden artillery wheels instead of the previously fitted wire items, thus allowing for improved reliability and smoothness.

ENGINE: 2762cc (169cu in), six-cylinder
POWER: n/a
0–60MPH (96KM/H): n/a
TOP SPEED: 108km/h (67mph)
PRODUCTION TOTAL: 4228

BENTLEY 4.5-LITRE

ENGINE: 4398cc (268cu in), four-cylinder
POWER: 104bhp (77kW)
0–60MPH (96KM/H): n/a
TOP SPEED: 178km/h (110mph)
PRODUCTION TOTAL: 720

Although the Bentley 4.5-Litre was seen as the last in the line of four-cylinder Bentleys, its engine was actually closely related to that of the recent 6.5-Litre unit, sharing the same bore and stroke, as well as other components.

Said to have been heavier and less sporting than previous Bentley models, nonetheless the 4.5-Litre was a sales success, and more

The 'Blower' Bentley project came about after race driver Sir Henry Birkin decided that what these cars needed was a supercharger.

than justified the appearance of a smaller model in the Bentley range. At the height of its Le Mans successes, the 4.5-Litre did not go down a storm with the racing team, though – race driver Sir Henry Birkin was reported to have been disappointed with the car's performance and therefore went to W.O. Bentley try to get it improved. Bentley told him that this was not necessary, as the 6.5-Litre was the the quick one – and, besides, the 4.5-Litre had competed at Le Mans in 1928 and managed to win, so there was obviously no problem. Birkin, however, was not convinced by Bentley's argument, and he created a more powerful version by fitting a supercharger, thereby creating a motoring legend.

W.O. Bentley may have been against them, but 55 'Blower Bentleys' were built, and the resultant racing successes proved the success of Birkin's project. Despite that, W.O. refused to accept any part in the 'Blower' project.

FORD MODEL A

UNITED STATES 1928–31

ENGINE: 2043cc (125 cu in), 4-cylinder
POWER: 40bhp (30kW)
0–60MPH (96KM/H): N/A
TOP SPEED: 105km/h (65mph)
PRODUCTION TOTAL: 3,562,610

Ford's Model T had become a legend within its lifetime, being the first car in the world to go into volume production – and in doing so it motorized the USA. But like all extremely successful cars, replacing it was not the matter of a moment.

However, Henry Ford met the challenge with some verve, and in the process created an automotive legend. Although on first appearance the Model A with its similar transverse leaf suspension looked as if it was based on its forebear, it was, in fact, a much more advanced car. The four-cylinder 2-litre (125cu in) engine produced enough power to give the Model A a top speed of 105km/h (65mph), and the equipment tally was much more up to date – electrical systems, four wheel brakes and a more conventional three-speed gearbox.

But the Model A's biggest attraction to buyers was its competitive list price, which made it the value for money choice in its class – and allowed Ford to continue to outsell its biggest rival in the USA, Chevrolet.

Final sales may have been dwarfed by the Model T, but with over three million units sold, the Model A was undeniably a roaring success.

Replacing the Model T was never going to be easy, but Ford managed it with the Model A. However, sales never matched its illustrious forebear despite being available in a number of body styles.

BMW DIXI 3/15

GERMANY 1927–31

ENGINE: 747cc (46cu in),
    four-cylinder
POWER: 15bhp (11kW)
0–60MPH (96KM/H): n/a
TOP SPEED: 73km/h (45mph)
PRODUCTION TOTAL: about 25,000

Long before the BMW name actually appeared on the grille of the Dixie, cars were being built in its factory in Eisenach, in Eastern Germany. Car production started there in 1896 – making it one of the oldest car factories in Europe. By 1904, the company had adopted the name Dixi. For the majority of the first 30 years of its existence, it lived hand to mouth on the verge of bankruptcy.

That all changed when Dixi licensed production of the Austin Seven. Dixi's version, called the 3/15 DA-1, was introduced in 1927, and the car quickly proved its popularity. Dixi's founder had other business interests, though, and in order to finance those, he sold the operation to a motorcycle and aircraft engine manufacturer, known as Bayerische Motoren Werke – or BMW.

The BMW Dixi 3/15 DA-1 ('3' stood for the number of gears, '15' for the horsepower and 'DA' for German version) came with saloon, roadster, tourer and coupé bodies, and it was updated in 1929 to become the DA-2. That car featured four-wheel mechanical brakes, and was followed by the DA-3 – a tiny two-seater sportster. The final version was the DA-4, another well-built saloon.

By 1931, 25,000 3/15s had been produced, and the BMW was well and truly established.

The BMW Dixi looks almost identical to the Austin Seven, and that's because it was a licensed production of the British car. Originally known as the Dixi, it became a BMW after the company's founder sold it to the then little known motorcycle and aircraft engine manufacturer.

ROVER SIX

UNITED KINGDOM 1927–32

ENGINE: 2023cc (123cu in), six-cylinder
POWER: 45bhp (34kW) at 3600rpm
0-60MPH (96KM/H): n/a
TOP SPEED: 97km/h (60mph)
PRODUCTION TOTAL: about 8000

Six-cylinder Rovers had actually been around for quite some time, with the first appearing at the 1923 London Motor Show. Although it looked ready for production, and with three prototypes built, the experiment was nonetheless put on ice, and the 3.5-litre (214cu in) engine went with it.

Four years later, a new Rover Six was unveiled – and was called the Rover 2-Litre. The company's first production six-cylinder engine was an impressive effort. Even though it was smaller, at 2023cc (123cu in), than its predecessor, it did feature an advanced pushrod overhead-valve cylinder head, designed by Peter Poppe. The engine would go on to power other models in the Rover range in future years. Backing up the advanced engine design were the options of a four-speed gearbox (to supplant the three-speeder) in 1930, and servo-assisted brakes a year later.

As was the fashion of the day, the Six was offered in a variety of bodystyles and two different wheelbases. A traditionally expensive upright fabric-bodied Weymann saloon option was offered, but, for those customers who liked their Rovers more sporting, they had the choice of the Rover Light Six – an appealing option, especially when specified with the partially aerodynamically styled Sportsman's coupé body. The model gained fame in January 1930, when one of the cars raced the luxury high-speed Blue Train express across France – and won.

The Rover Six gained notoriety after it raced a luxury high-speed Blue Train express across France and won – the era of trans-continental motoring had begun.

TRIUMPH SUPER-SEVEN

UNITED KINGDOM 1927–32

ENGINE: 832cc (51cu in), four-cylinder
POWER: 21bhp (16kW) at 4000rpm
0–60MPH (96KM/H): n/a
TOP SPEED: 85km/h (53mph)
PRODUCTION TOTAL: about 17,000

Set up by a German, Siegfried Bettman, in 1890, the Triumph Company started life as a bicycle manufacturer – just like many of its contemporaries. From there, Triumph went into motorcycle production in 1902, and the company established itself as a leader in the field in very little time. Car production would have to wait for more than 20 years – and the first car, the 10/20 of 1923, represented a radical departure for the company. Four years later, the compact Super-Seven became Triumph's first model to appeal to a wider audience, finding itself up against the Austin Seven – although the Triumph was the more costly option.

Available in several different styles, such as the Popular Tourer, Tourer de Luxe, Two-Seater de Luxe, Fabric Saloon and the streamlined Gordon England Fabric Saloon, the 832cc (51cu in) Triumph Super-Seven soon became popular. The elegant Coachbuilt Saloon, which looked like a scaled-down large car, added class to the range. Independent coachbuilders began to offer their own bodies for the car.

In 1929, an aluminium-bodied Special Sports with a Cozette

During the late 1920s, rival UK manufacturers launched a raft of competitors to the Austin Seven – Triumph's effort stood out for its excellent engineering, range of models and the supercharger option.

supercharger was introduced, and enjoyed competition success, although the car was more suited to rallying. The Super Eight replaced it in 1933, and saw the Super-Seven's engine married to a larger body.

BUGATTI ROYALE

FRANCE 1927–33

By the late 1920s, Bugatti was arguably one of the biggest forces that motorsport had ever seen – so it seemed fitting for the company's creator, Ettore Bugatti, to reveal his latest and most ambitious project at a Grand prix meeting. The 1928 German Grand Prix saw 17 Bugattis taking part – but they were all overshadowed by Le Patron's unveiling of the prototype Type 41 Royale.

Created on a grander scale than any other car, the Bugatti Royale was designed to go head to head with Rolls-Royce, and it was the culmination of Ettore Bugatti's aspirations to build the ultimate passenger car. Featuring imposing bodywork, the Bugatti Royale was powered by an enormous 14,763cc (901cu in) straight-eight engine, which produced a healthy 300bhp (224kW). Rather aptly, the excessively long bonnet (hood) was topped off by an elephant mascot – although this did not really denote the scale of the car, but rather was in memory of Bugatti's dead brother Rembrandt,

who was a talented sculptor of animal models. Despite that, it seems a fitting figurehead for a vehicle that many considered to be one of the biggest white elephants in motoring history. During a six-year production run, only six examples rolled off the production line – and, of those, only three were actually sold.

Bugatti had felt compelled to build such a car after hearing an Englishman tell him that, 'If one desired to be fastest, one must choose a Bugatti, but it was evident that if one wanted the best, one must apply to Rolls-Royce.' Bugatti's response was stark: 'Not for much longer.'

The prototype Royale was enormous – it featured a 4.57m

When it was launched in 1927 the Bugatti Royale was the king of the road – and even today its scale is still breathtaking.

(15ft) wheelbase, although later cars had 4.27m (14ft) bases. The length was 6m (19.7ft), but much of that was down to the super-long bonnet that clothed the huge engine – later reduced to 12,763cc (779cu in). As with all Bugattis to that point, the mechanicals were precisely created, with the engine being almost perfectly rectangular – a work of minimalist art. The straight eight claimed to develop its maximum power at an extremely low 1700rpm. This figure has since been revised by historians, who peg it closer to 200bhp (149kW).

Be that as it may, the Royale was a thoroughly awe-inspiring machine – and one that had bags of power. Although four-speed gearboxes were taking off by this point, the Royale only ever needed three thanks to its powerplant having so much power and torque. Accordingly, first gear was only really necessary for hill starts, while third was a long-legged cruising gear. In all other driving, second was all that was needed.

Bugatti's original plans were rather optimistic – he thought he could make and sell 25 cars, but never came close to matching that

figure. Of the six Royales that were produced, all had different bodies – and, as sometimes happens with cars such as these, some were rebodied more than once. After the original prototype Torpedo (as driven to the German Grand Prix by Bugatti) came the Berline, Coupé Napoleon, Coach Weymann, Double Berline de Voyage, Cabriolet Weinberger, Coach Kellner, Roadster, Limousine Park Ward, Coupé de Ville and Coupé Binder. All shared the same epic sense of scale and proportion.

The Royale was the ultimate car of its day, but it boasted the

ultimate price tag, too – Fr500,000 for the basic chassis, and potential buyers ended up buying Duesenbergs instead. Bugatti's pride took a blow from this, and the project never really recovered once his interest in it waned – despite that, he kept four cars for his personal use.

ENGINE: 12,760cc (779cu in), eight-cylinder
POWER: 300bhp (224kW)
0–60MPH (96KM/H): n/a
TOP SPEED: 200km/h (124mph)
PRODUCTION TOTAL: 6

MORRIS COWLEY

ENGINE: 1550cc (95cu in), four-cylinder
POWER: 27bhp (20kW) at 3400rpm
0–60MPH (96KM/H): n/a
TOP SPEED: 92km/h (57mph)
PRODUCTION TOTAL: 256,236

Known by many as the Flatnose, the 1927 Morris Cowley took over from where the much-loved Bullnose Morris left off. By this time, the original Cowley design was well past its prime, but an updated chassis, suspension and brakes made the new car far more competitive. The well-known curved radiator surround disappeared, and the new, more contemporary style ushered in a new design era at Morris. Sadly, however, many buyers found the new face lacking the character found in the original.

Much of the mechanical package remained unchanged from previous models, but new bodies were rolled out. These included all-steel bodies built to an American design; however, despite the American influence, the Cowley was as British as roast beef and Yorkshire pudding.

The Flatnose enjoyed a much shorter run than the Bullnose, and was soon replaced by a more elaborate design in 1932. That traditional recipe was spiced up with the addition of new bodies and hydraulic brakes. Interest in the Cowley started to wane, however, and it became the 12/4 in 1935. Between 1934 and 1935, a six-cylinder 1938cc (118cu in) version called the Cowley Six was also available (renamed the 15/6 in 1935). It was not the end of the Cowley name, though – that would reappear briefly during the 1950s.

First there was the Bullnose, then came the Flatnose – the Morris Cowley was named after the factory in which it was built and did not gain the same level of popularity as its predecessor.

ARMSTRONG-SIDDELEY 20

ENGINE: 2872cc (175cu in), six-cylinder
POWER: n/a
0–60MPH (96KM/H): n/a
TOP SPEED: n/a
PRODUCTION TOTAL: 4997

During the 1920s and 1930s, Armstrong-Siddeley had become well established in the automotive scene. Mainstay of its range was the 20 – a conventionally engineered but very well built machine. The option of two chassis were offered: a short version with room for five people,

featuring excellent rear legroom, and the long wheelbase chassis, which had been stretched enough to offer room for seven. Offered as a saloon or limousine, the longer Armstrong-Siddeley 20 was still rather compact compared to rivals.

A further two models were offered on the 20's chassis: the

Fifteen, which was sold as a budget family model, and the Twelve, which was aimed at younger drivers. Built between 1929 and 1937, these cars featured a 1.2-litre (73cu in) six-cylinder side-valve engine in place of the 20's more advanced and costly overhead valve unit.

MINERVA AK

In one of the car industry's stranger tales, for a short while at least, Minerva became known for creating the finest European luxury cars – not bad for a company that made its name building bicycles in a small factory in Antwerp, Belgium. The enormous Minerva AK became the transport of choice for kings, queens and movie stars all over the world, with sales in the early 1930s mostly

going to Hollywood – even if the honeymoon lasted only a decade. The seeds of Minerva's destruction as a luxury car producer were actually sown in Tinsel Town. The stars of the silver screen needed enormous cars, but US producers were responding to demand, building their own and eventually squeezing out the Belgian car producer. Still, the AK remains the finest of all Minervas, with a choice

of luxury bodystyles, crushed-velvet interiors and a smooth, effortless 5.9-litre (363cu in) straight-six under the bonnet (hood).

Political unrest in Europe and flagging sales in the United States saw Minerva drop the AK in 1937. The company never recovered, building a mountain of debts. It merged with fellow Belgian manufacturer Imperia and managed to survive for another 20 years,

but finally went bankrupt in 1958. By this time it was building Land Rovers under contract from the British government.

ENGINE: 5954cc (363cu in), six-cylinder
POWER: 150bhp (112kW)
0–60MPH (96KM/H): n/a
TOP SPEED: 145km/h (90mph)
PRODUCTION TOTAL: n/a

DODGE VICTORY SIX

ENGINE: 3410cc (208cu in),
  six-cylinder
POWER: 58bhp (43kW)
0–60MPH (96KM/H): n/a
TOP SPEED: 103km/h (64mph)
PRODUCTION TOTAL: 58,500

The Victory Six helped to seal Dodge's reputation for decades to come. It offered performance, styling and plenty of value for money, and as a result became a sought-after car. Budd Manufacturing built the Victory Six bodies, which featured a distinctive moulding that went around the upper bodywork, wearing it rather like a belt.

Two models were available, the 130 and 13, the latter being differentiated mainly by its larger wheels for extra ground clearance. Standard equipment on all models was generous, and included internal hydraulic brakes, chassis lubrication and aluminium pistons. Bumpers, wire wheels and a side-mounted spare marked out the more opulent Deluxe version.

The Victory Six remained on sale in 1929 with relatively few changes, as unsold stock from 1928 piled

up. The difficult economic conditions produced by the Wall Street crash meant that prices needed to be lowered to stimulate buyer demand. Further body options were also added, including lower coachwork and wider

opening doors, but this was not nearly enough to counter the effects of the Great Depression and the eventual takeover of the company by Chrysler – meaning that the Dodge Brothers became known simply as Dodge.

Dodge's reputation for performance and value for money was built on the design of the Victory Six. Although it remained in production for only a short time today it's in demand with classic car enthusiasts.

MG 14/40

The first MGs produced at Cecil Kimber's 'Morris Garages' workshop in Oxford, England, during the 1920s might have been

nothing more than special-bodied Morris Oxfords. What they were, however, was the small beginning of what would go on to become

The 14/40 was the start of something big, being the first independently produced MG to emerge from Cecil Kimber's 'Morris Garages' workshop. What marked it out as something special was its fine handling and respectable performance.

one of the world's best known marques. Cecil Kimber's specials featured the now-famous octagon logo on their running boards, and they proved so popular that he was inspired to create his own sporting models, with factory support from Morris.

A new MG factory was built in 1927, near the Morris plant in Cowley, Oxfordshire, and the first series production MG was produced there soon after.

The 14/40 mostly used Morris mechanical components, and it was aimed firmly at enthusiastic drivers. Considering its humble roots, the 14/40 had a perhaps surprising top speed of 96km/h (60mph) and excellent roadholding capabilities. And while the old-fashioned side-valve engine might not have been lusty, the servo-assisted brakes meant that the car stopped much better than any of its contemporaries.

Capacity at the existing factory was soon used up, and that prompted Kimber to open a new factory in neighbouring Abingdon. The Pavlova Works opened in 1929, and this would remain the home of MG until 1980, when the iconic marque was put on ice, and the factory closed, marking the end of a legendary run.

ENGINE: 1802cc (110cu in), four-cylinder
POWER: n/a
0–60MPH (96KM/H): n/a
TOP SPEED: n/a
PRODUCTION TOTAL: about 900

ALVIS FD/FE

During the 1920s, Alvis had been a very early adopter of front-wheel drive technology. The company built an FWD sprint car in 1925, and followed that with an eight-cylinder racer in 1926 – but the fun began when the company tried to introduce the same technology on its road cars in 1928, following successes at Le Mans, where two Alvis front drivers finished sixth and ninth.

Chief engineer T.G. Smith-Clarke and chief designer W.M. Dunn created that year's introduction for Alvis, the FD/FE series, and they ensured that the car was a technical curiosity. Adding to the cutting-edge drivetrain were all-independent transverse leaf suspension, an overhead camshaft engine (although limited to just four cylinders), a four-speed gearbox, inboard front brakes and the option of a Roots-type supercharger. There was also the option of an eight-cylinder engine (with the same capacity as the four) for those who wanted more power. On top of all this, the car could be specified in two-seater sports, four-seater sports or sports saloon form.

Buyers were not ready for the quantum leap, however, and sales were disappointing. This dismal performance led to Alvis dropping the model after a scant two years' production, and returning to more conventional engineering principles.

ENGINE: 1482cc (90cu in), four-cylinder
POWER: 75bhp (56kW) at 5500rpm
0–60MPH (96KM/H): n/a
TOP SPEED: 137km/h (85mph)
PRODUCTION TOTAL: 155

BEARDMORE 15.6

Created by Sir William Beardmore, the company that bore his name made most of its money building ships and armaments prior to World War I. Sir William's vast wealth put the company in a very strong financial position, and that strength saw Beardmore gain a number of post-war contracts, including the construction of cars and taxis.

These first taxis entered service in 1919, and were freighted to London by rail – an innovation at the time. By the time the updated 15.6 appeared in 1928, more than 6000 Beardmore taxis were in regular use in the capital. The driver sat alone at the front of the cab, with seating for four in the enclosed rear cabin. The 15.6 cemented this success. Although no production records were kept, it is estimated that at least 4000 were licensed in London between 1928 and 1930 – while others were pressed into service in the United Kingdom's other big cities.

Essential to the Beardmore success story was that the cabs were easy to own and maintain, returned good fuel consumption and needed little servicing. Such was demand that a separate factory was built in London in 1930 to supply cabs to the city.

ENGINE: 1500cc (92cu in), four-cylinder
POWER: n/a
0–60MPH (96KM/H): n/a
TOP SPEED: n/a
PRODUCTION TOTAL: n/a

DE SOTO MODEL K

As new model launches go, DeSoto's stands as one of the most successful in history. The Chrysler Corporation unveiled the DeSoto marque in 1928 and sold a record 81,065 in the first year – an achievement which stood for 30 years until the Ford Falcon exceeded this. Named after the Spanish explorer Hernando DeSoto, who discovered the Mississippi River in 1541, the new car offered an exciting new alternative to rivals available from Pontiac and Oldsmobile. The Model K featured a smooth straight-six engine and a wide variety of bodystyles, including the obligatory roadsters and saloons.

The thing that set the DeSoto Model K apart was that it was a good-value package. The L-head engine delivered 55bhp (41kW), and the Lockheed hydraulic brakes, Lovejoy shock absorbers and Hotchkiss driveshafts delivered a smooth drive. For $845, buyers thought that they were getting a very good deal.

Introduced on the cusp of the Great Depression, the DeSoto enjoyed a strong start, and came out of this black period in pretty good shape – these were hard times for all carmakers, but Chrysler did well with the DeSoto and actually fared better than most during the Depression, thanks to its good-value ethos. Sales of the Model K remained strong, and, despite the wider financial turmoil, Chrysler was confident enough to add a bargain priced eight-cylinder car to the fledging range.

ENGINE: 2867cc (175cu in), six-cylinder
POWER: 55bhp (41kW)
0–60MPH (96KM/H): n/a
TOP SPEED: 97km/h (60mph)
PRODUCTION TOTAL: 100,000

FRAZER-NASH SUPER SPORTS

The Frazer-Nash Company was set up in 1924, after Archie Frazer-Nash left cyclecar manufacturers GN to go into business himself. Building on what he had learned at GN, he added a proper chassis and used water-cooled four-cylinder engines in his cars. The result was a basic but technically very effective racer, one which won many fans.

The 'Chain Gang' Frazer-Nash models provided little in the way of comfort, but with their unique transmission (with separate exposed chain and sprockets; dog clutches for each gear) and solid rear axle, they offered plenty of interest. They were also prized for their sharp handling, slick gearchange quality and superb traction. The Super Sports enjoyed an excellent power-weight ratio due to lightweight construction. Despite developing only 47bhp (35kW), it was more than a match for the more powerful competition.

Owners particularly loved the car's sensitive steering and lively handling, and forgave the Frazer-Nash for its extremely hard ride, dictated by that narrow track and solid rear axle. A HE (high-efficiency) engine producing 52bhp (39kW) was developed and introduced in subsequent years.

ENGINE: 1496cc (91cu in), four-cylinder
POWER: 47bhp (35kW)
0–60MPH (96KM/H): n/a
TOP SPEED: 109km/h (68mph)
PRODUCTION TOTAL: n/a

FORD MODEL A

Although it was a huge hit in the USA with over three million examples sold, the Model A did not travel too well. In the austere 1930s the large 2-litre engine meant that it was too expensive for many family car owners.

ENGINE: 2043cc (125cu in), 4 cylinder
POWER: 40bhp (30kW)
0–60MPH (96KM/H): n/a
TOP SPEED: 105km/h (65mph)
PRODUCTION TOTAL: 14,516

It might have been comfortably the world's best selling car to this point, but by the late 1920s, the Ford Model T was getting close to its sell-by date, and a replacement was needed. Despite Henry Ford's doubts, the Model became a sales sensation in the United States – however, it was not a car that worked so well in Europe, and that was because the A came with a lumpy four-cylinder side-valve 3285cc (200 cu in) engine.

This might have made it powerful and easy to drive, but in the tax conscious UK it had little future. In response, a smaller 2043cc (125 cu in) unit was fitted to what was known as the Model AF – and although it cost £5 more than the 3-litre it also used more petrol. However, well-proven transverse springs, high ground clearance and a smooth three-speed gearbox meant that the Model A was durable and rugged.

Like the Model T before it, the A came in a variety of body styles - a roadster, a two-door touring, a four-door touring, a fixed coupé, a cabriolet and various saloons – sadly few people in the UK wanted one, and when the newly opened Dagenham factory in Essex, England, opened, apparently built just five Model A cars were built in its first three months of operation in 1931.

LANCIA LAMBDA

ENGINE: 2569cc (157cu in), four-cylinder
POWER: 69bhp (51kW)
0–60MPH (96KM/H): n/a
TOP SPEED: 120km/h (75mph)
PRODUCTION TOTAL: 4403

The extra strength and rigidity that were provided paid dividends, and blessed the Lambda with superb roadholding – a real rarity in other road cars of the time. The compact V4 engine also meant that the car went as well as it handled. The series 8 and 9 Lambdas, built from 1928 to 1931, dropped the monocoque design to ease the lives of coachbuilders who were clamouring to fit their own bodies to the Lambda. It was, however, a technological step backwards, and, in order maintain performance, beefier engines were fitted.

Look at how low the driver is in relation to the car's bodywork – this is a result of the new construction method pioneered by Lancia. The one-piece monococque structure did away with a separate chassis, making the car lighter and more wieldy.

For many, the Lancia Lambda was one of the industry's first genuinely 'modern' cars. The Lambda's low stance came about as the result of the marque's creator, Vincenzo Lancia, and the happenstance of a sea trip. He became interested in the way the ship was built, and realized that the ship's single-piece hull was far more rigid than a car could ever be using the conventional separate chassis methods of construction.

Lancia worked out how to apply these marine principles of hull construction to motor engineering, and in 1919 he patented the idea – which later became known as 'unitary construction'. The first car to use this principle was the groundbreaking Lancia Lambda of 1923, and, although it looked quite conventional to the casual observer, the monocoque chassis and body structure of the vehicle was utterly revolutionary.

LEA-FRANCIS 1.5-LITRE TYPE S

UNITED KINGDOM 1928–31

ENGINE: 1496cc (91cu in),
four-cylinder
POWER: 12bhp (9kW)
0–60MPH (96KM/H): n/a
TOP SPEED: n/a
PRODUCTION TOTAL: n/a

Lea-Francis was another company to make its name producing high-quality motorcycles, and, rather like much of the fledgling British car industry, it was also based in Coventry. Following considerable success, the company moved into car production, majoring on small sporting vehicles with a light chassis. The Meadows-engined 11/22 model ended up being one of the company's first cars.

The company then moved to a larger 1.5-litre (91cu in) Meadows power unit, and with it came a sting of credible sporting cars. One was the Cozette-supercharged 'Hyper' model, which came with the option of a fabric- or metal-body with two seats.

The supercharged Type S proved a very quick car, no doubt helped by its light weight. It also handled well, despite the narrow width and tall construction of its two-seater body – and furthermore the 1.5-litre (91cu in) gained competition honours by winning the very first Ulster TT race, with driver Kaye Don at the wheel.

The company also offered four-seater and saloon versions, to sit alongside the more sporting two-seaters that were available in the range – as well as a more slender Brooklands sports version.

In 1935, the company folded, but reopened a mere two years later, surviving until 1963.

Called the Hyper, and looking individual due to its distinctive rearwards sloping grille, the Lea Francis 1.5-Litre Type S was one of the first British series production cars to feature supercharging in order to boost performance and boasted a top speed of 136km/h (85mph).

MG 18/80

UNITED KINGDOM 1928–31

The MG 18/80 came about because of the failure of the 1927 Morris Light Six to go as well as William Morris had first envisaged. Having been first shown at that year's Olympia Motor Show, the new Woollard and Pendrel-designed straight-six overhead camshaft engine of the Morris Light Six had been quick but not wieldy.

William Morris had been let down badly by his engineers on the Light Six project, and the car ended up being saddled with ponderous handling characteristics at odds with its rapid straight-line pace. Morris turned to MG to develop a new chassis for the car, and the 18/80, which made its debut at the 1928 London Motor Show, and was badged as the MG Six, was the result – a far superior package to the original Light Six. The 18/80 was an impressive car which looked good, thanks to striking coachwork, and also came with impeccable road manners. The Mark II version appeared on the scene in 1929 and featured twin carburettors and uprated brakes. Top speed was increased over the original car's 126km/h (78mph), and it could theoretically cruise at more than 130km/h (80mph).

Five racing 18/80s were also built in 1930 for the MG works team. They featured lightweight bodywork, and, allied with the smooth, torquey straight-six engine, were capable of an easy 161km/h (100mph), enjoying some competition success in the process.

ENGINE: 2468cc (151cu in),
six-cylinder
POWER: 60bhp (45kW)
0–60MPH (96KM/H): n/a
TOP SPEED: 126km/h (78mph)
PRODUCTION TOTAL: 736

Although it was bigger than the more traditional cars previously offered by MG, the 18/80 still enjoyed the handling and performance that marked out the sportscars as such fine driving machines. MG proved the car's worth in competition too.

PEUGEOT 190

FRANCE 1928–31

ENGINE: 719cc (44cu in),
four-cylinder
POWER: n/a
0–60MPH (96KM/H): n/a
TOP SPEED: 94km/h (58mph)
PRODUCTION TOTAL: 33,674

The Peugeot name goes right back to the dawn of the motoring age – and has a history of which other manufacturers can only dream. Continuous car production started in 1889 and, since then, has never shown any signs of stopping. Put that down to a policy of continued success.

Peugeots were considered eccentric, thanks in no small part to the unusual but inexpensive Quadrilette. The Quadrilette was a bizarre two-seater small car that seated the passenger directly behind the driver and was the company's most famous car in the period prior to World War I.

The Peugeot 190, which made its appearance in 1928, was a more sophisticated effort, with conventional flat-nosed styling, side-by-side seating position and disc wheels.

Although it was based on an improved version of the Quadrilette chassis, the 190 was a more grown-up effort, even if the original car's dimensions limited it.

It was a good car to drive by the standards of the era, and enjoyed the benefits of an effective gear linkage linked directly to the rear axle. The three-speed gearbox was surprisingly nice to use, but the archaic four-cylinder side-valve engine was not.

The Peugeot 190 may have been utterly conventional, but it was also perfectly judged for its market. French family men loved the 190, appreciating its fine gearbox, if not the car's overall performance.

MERCEDES-BENZ SSK

GERMANY 1928–32

The foundations of the German motor industry were being well and truly laid by the end of World War I – Daimler built aero engines, and from 1921 had been led by chief engineer Ferdinand Porsche. Following that, a slump in car sales forced Daimler into a cooperative arrangement with car manufacturer Karl Benz in 1924. The result was the formation of Mercedes-Benz in 1926. Regarded as one of the most valuable cars of all time now, the Mercedes-Benz SSK was originally derived from the supercharged Model K touring car – and went well because of its understressed engine and its relatively light but long and open touring body.

As with all offerings from Mercedes-Benz, the SSK evolved in a very logical way. First came the S (Sport) version with its mighty 6.8-litre (414cu in) engine and four-seater body. That was followed by the SS (Super Sport), then came the SSK version (the K denoting 'kurz' or 'short') – featuring a lighter, shorter wheelbase and uprated 225bhp (168kW) powerplant. The versatile and very capable engine was powerful and powered Mercedes-Benz to countless Grand Prix victories, including the 1930 Irish Grand Prix and the 1931 Belgian 24-hour event, as well as various European hillclimb events. Eventually the SSK was superseded by the even rarer SSKL (with the L standing for 'leicht' or 'light'), which possessed a lighter chassis and a larger supercharger giving 265bhp (197kW).

ENGINE: 6789cc (414cu in),
six-cylinder
POWER: 225bhp (168kW)
0–60MPH (96KM/H): n/a
TOP SPEED: 200km/h (125mph)
PRODUCTION TOTAL: n/a

AC ACEDES MAGNA

UNITED KINGDOM 1929–30

ENGINE: 1992cc (122cu in),
six-cylinder
POWER: 56bhp (42kW)
0–60MPH (96KM/H): n/a
TOP SPEED: n/a
PRODUCTION TOTAL: n/a

The AC Six might have been AC's bestselling car during the 1920s, but, as the decade wore on, rivals were increasingly leaving it behind. A new car was needed – but the company decided instead that the solution to the problem was to revamp the 16/56 version of the Six, thereby creating the Acedes Magna. Significantly larger than the previous Six models, the revised car was a mixed bag.

Although it was more refined and much better equipped than the Six, the extra weight meant that the Acedes Magna was significantly slower. Given that ACs of this period were famous for their race and speed record successes, this was a major marketing blunder. Despite this, the Acedes Magna was still a much more modern machine than many of its competitors. It was equipped with hydraulic brakes on all four wheels, and its ignition was by coil, rather than magneto.

STAR COMET

UNITED KINGDOM 1929–32

As the Great Depression took hold, many companies found themselves needing to look down-market – the Star Comet was one such car, produced following truck manufacturer Guy's takeover of Star in 1928. The Comet was an attempt by Guy to take Star into the market's lower end in order to pick up sales in a contracting pool.

Introduced in 1931, the Comet was competitively priced at just £345, and it was available in either saloon or coupé form. As the car was hand-built in relatively small numbers, however, its profitability was marginal. Technically, it was a good effort, featuring a four-speed gearbox (which was built in-house), Bendix

Although it was a fine-looking car and enjoyed an impressive technical specification, the Star Comet wasn't enough to keep the company afloat. The quality was there, as was the price, but in the end it was doomed because of the UK economy's poor state.

cable brakes and Marles steering – all high-quality equipment.

The addition of varying styles of coupé and saloon managed to bring more customers for the Comet, but the cars still did not make money – and that inevitably

led to crisis for the company. Star tried to counter this by introducing the Comet Fourteen in 1932, in order to take the car even further downmarket – with a smaller engine. Despite this, the story remained largely the same.

Although Star used quality components in the Comet, this was not enough to lift it above the opposition. When sales and profitability failed to take an upturn, the decision was made in 1932 to close the company.

ENGINE: 2470cc (151cu in), six-cylinder
POWER: 14hp (10kW)
0–60MPH (96KM/H): n/a
TOP SPEED: about 112km/h (70mph)
PRODUCTION TOTAL: n/a

STUTZ BLACKHAWK

UNITED STATES 1929–30

ENGINE: 3957cc (241cu in), six-cylinder
POWER: 85bhp (63kW)
0–60MPH (96KM/H): n/a
TOP SPEED: n/a
PRODUCTION TOTAL: 1590

During the 1920s, Stutz was one of the most respected names in the business. It was profitable, and demand for its cars was high – its Vertical Eight,

otherwise known as the Safety Stutz, was selling well – and all was well with the world.

The cars produced by Stutz were glamorous and in many ways summed up the era. The Black Hawk Speedster was introduced to maintain that impression – a highly exclusive car aimed at the company's high-profile clientele. In this most glitzy of eras, the new car became hot property with the young and the rich. Even before the effects of the Great Depression

started to bite, however, Stutz introduced another car – called the Blackhawk – in order to cash in on that prestigious name while going downmarket. Initially, it was marketed as a separate marque, to distance it slightly from the parent company, Stutz.

The Blackhawk was offered in six- or eight-cylinder versions (producing 85bhp (63kW) or 95bhp (71kW), respectively), and a choice of open or closed bodies. The Wall Street Crash in 1929,

however, soon put an end to production. Although the Blackhawk was cheaper than contemporary Stutz models, few people could afford to buy them any longer – and by 1935 the company had gone bankrupt.

To generate more sales, Stutz decided to go downmarket with the 1929 Blackhawk. However, its efforts were scuppered by the effects of the Wall Street Crash.

CITROËN C4

FRANCE 1929–31

Although Citroën's first road car did not come until 1919, the company had since become a well-established force in the marketplace when it announced the C4. Launched in 1926, the B14

was the result of a radical decision taken by the company to replace all the existing models with just a single car – although with 27 different bodystyles available, you could hardly accuse Citroën of

narrowing choice. It lasted three years before being replaced by the mechanically similar C4.

Despite becoming known as a producer of innovative cars, Citroën produced a rather unadventurous

offering in the C4, serving up only servo-assisted brakes as a point of interest. The car became available on two wheelbases, and 16 different passenger bodies were offered, as well as seven utility

versions – and the styling was distinctly transatlantic. The C4's side-valve 1628cc (99cu in) engine was all-new, designed by the ex-chief engineer of luxury French auto firm Delage.

The C4 and its bigger brother, the six-cylinder C6, were successes from the start, cementing Citroën's reputation in Europe. These cars were also built in Slough in the United Kingdom, and the British flavours were the fabric-bodied saloon and sportsman's coupé.

ENGINE: 1628cc (99cu in),
four-cylinder
POWER: 30bhp (22kW) at 3000rpm
0–60MPH (96KM/H): n/a
TOP SPEED: 90km/h (56mph)
PRODUCTION TOTAL: 243,068

During the 1920s, Citroën had become adept at offering cars that customers actually wanted, and as a result enjoyed considerable success with different versions of the C4.

CROSSLEY SPORTS 2-LITRE
UNITED KINGDOM 1929–31

Based in Manchester, England, Crossley originally made four-stroke engines in the nineteenth century, before progressing to car manufacturing in 1904. After making staff cars and aircraft engines during World War I, the company developed a range of robust quality cars in the following two decades. Its first six-cylinder model arrived in 1925. Three years later, the lighter-engined model, the 1990cc (121cu in) 15.7hp (11.7kW), was launched. A 2-litre (121cu in) sports version was also built on the same 15.7 chassis, but featured a modified engine. Revised camshaft and induction produced more than 60bhp (45kW), as opposed to the standard 45bhp (34kW), and performance was lifted appreciably. The radiator was styled to resemble that of the Bentley, and it looked like a thoroughbred British sports car.

Capable of 7.5km/L (21mpg), it cost a reasonable £625 for the open tourer model and £550 for the 15.7hp saloon version.

ENGINE: 1990cc (121cu in), six-cylinder
POWER: 60bhp (45kW)
0–60MPH (96KM/H): 17.5 secs
TOP SPEED: 124km/h (77mph)
PRODUCTION TOTAL: 700

HILLMAN 20 STRAIGHT EIGHT
UNITED KINGDOM 1929–31

ENGINE: 2597cc (158cu in),
eight-cylinder
POWER: 20bhp (15kW)
0–60MPH (96KM/H): n/a
TOP SPEED: 112km/h (70mph)
PRODUCTION TOTAL: n/a

One of Britain's more famous carmakers, Hillman became a one-car producer between 1926 and 1928, as it began to concentrate on production of the roomy Fourteen. The Fourteen was typical family-car fare, marked out by excellent build quality at a reasonable purchase price. The car featured a side-valve engine and four-speed gearbox, and won plenty of fans who appreciated its solid quality.

When the Hillman company came under the control of the Rootes Group by 1929, the picture quickly changed. A much larger model, with an uncharacteristically large engine, was launched. Called the Hillman 20 Straight Eight, the new car was a relaxed drive, thanks to the capricious torque developed by its 2.6-litre (158cu in) straight-eight engine.

Often referred to as the Vortic, the roomy four-door saloon was renowned for its smoothness and high flexibility at low speeds – and the Straight Eight was described in a contemporary *Autocar* road test as being: 'An interesting car with a good engine and comprehensive equipment ... and comparing most favourably in performance with transatlantic machines possessing much bigger engines.'

The magazine also reported that the car's roadholding was good and that it remained body roll-free in corners – thanks possibly to the vehicle having adjustable shock absorbers. Additional features of note to be found on the Hillman 20 Straight Eight were vacuum servo-assisted brakes, bolt-on wire wheels and the traditional Hillman three-piece bonnet (hood).

ASTON MARTIN INTERNATIONAL
UNITED KINGDOM 1929–30

ENGINE: 1495cc (91cu in),
four-cylinder
POWER: 56bhp (42kW)
0–60MPH (96KM/H): n/a
TOP SPEED: 129km/h (80mph)
PRODUCTION TOTAL: 81

It happened a lot during the life of Aston Martin in subsequent years, but by the time the International was introduced in 1929, the company had already endured a major financial crisis, even though it had only been in existence for little more than a decade. The rescuers this time had been a number of rich investors, including Lady Charnwood, and the company gained its name of Aston Martin Motors. Founded by Lionel Martin and Robert Bamford just before World War I, it drew its name from Lionel's surname and a hillclimb venue, Aston Clinton, near Aylesbury, England. It could so easily have been called Bamford Clinton instead ...

The Aston Martin International was one of the 1.5-litre (91cu in) models produced by the company, but what made it special were the bodies. Designed by Enrico Bertelli, they were available in a choice of a two-seater sports, a four-seater sports, a fixed-head coupé or a drophead coupé. The International featured Aston

Martin's chain-drive overhead camshaft four-cylinder engine, and sported a pump-cooled cylinder head relying on the less advanced thermo-syphon system of cooling for the engine block. Another oddity to the International was its separate gearbox and a worm-drive rear axle, which was located behind the engine, a feature which distinguished it from the following model, the International Le Mans.

Even in its formative years there were plenty of signs that Aston Martin understood the needs of enthusiastic drivers. The low-slung engine resided a long way back in the chassis, resulting in fine weight distribution.

CORD L-29

UNITED STATES 1929–32

ENGINE: 5275cc (322cu in), eight-cylinder
POWER: 125bhp (168kW)
0–60MPH (96KM/H): 14 seconds
TOP SPEED: 129km/h (80mph)
PRODUCTION TOTAL: 5000

Like so many automotive fans of his age, entrepreneur Errett Lobban Cord wanted to create his own company – the only difference was that he could already count Auburn and Duesenberg among his car businesses. Cord already owned the Lycoming engine business, and, through that, he commissioned racing car engineer Harry Miller to design a car, which he called the L-29. The straight-eight Lycoming engine he used needed modification because the L-29 was designed with front-wheel drive. The engine was turned around so that the clutch end faced forwards and connected to a three-speed front drive transaxle ahead of it.

This concept was almost unheard of in North America, and managed to pre-date the Citroën Traction Avant in Europe by a full five years, becoming the first front-wheel drive car built in the United States.

There was more, though. Miller had to use an advanced front suspension to cope with this complex new set-up in order to house the running gear – a de Dion layout meant that a solid cross tube was suspended on four forward-facing quarter-elliptic leaf springs. Although impressive technically, customers were not convinced because of the sheer complexity of the whole package and the fact that reliability was not the greatest. Performance was underwhelming, too, as the massive 2087kg (4600lb) L-29 struggled to reach 129km/h (80mph). Shortly afterwards, the Wall Street Crash occurred, killing demand for the beautiful car stone dead.

With front wheel drive and a low-slung chassis, the Cord L-29 was a remarkably advanced car for its time. It was also loved by contemporary coachbuilders, who created a number of wonderful looking bodies to clothe the interesting mechanicals.

FIAT 514

ITALY 1929–32

ENGINE: 1438cc (88cu in),
  four-cylinder
POWER: 34.5bhp (26kW)
0–60MPH (96KM/H): n/a
TOP SPEED: 88km/h (55mph)
PRODUCTION TOTAL: 36,970

The Fiat 514 was a logical updating of the previous 509 model, sitting on the same wheelbase, but featuring a new 1.4-litre (88cu in) engine. Although Fiat is regarded to have produced many cars with flair, the 514 is not one of them. It did, however, boast six-volt ignition, a four-speed gearbox and mechanical brakes with a four-wheel handbrake.

Subjected to a programme of gradual improvement during its life, the 514 ended up with hydraulic dampers to replace the original friction units, as well as other small improvements – and

the driving experience improved as a result. Body variations included Berlina, Coupé, Cabriolet Royal, Torpedo and Spider, as well as a longer wheelbase variant, the 514L – which was designed for taxi use – and also a van version. Coachbuilders Mulliner in the

United Kingdom also offered a fabric-bodied saloon. A 515 derivative with an X-braced frame and hydraulic brakes also entered the market. Wire wheels were usually standard.

Three sport versions were produced, and each could reach

113km/h (70mph). The 514S used a slightly tuned engine in the standard chassis, and the 514MM (Mille Miglia) used a more highly tuned engine in a longer van chassis. The 514CA (Coppa delle Alpi) used the more highly tuned engine and standard chassis.

The 514 became a mainstay of the Italian motoring scene during the 1920s and 1930s, and although it lacked the flair that marked out some of the more exuberant, later Fiats, it sold very well.

HUPMOBILE CENTURY

UNITED STATES 1929–32

Formed by Bobby Hupp and E.A. Nelson in 1908, the Hupmobile company introduced its first car, a 2.8-litre (171cu in) Detroit-built runabout with two-speed transmission, and enjoyed instant success. It lived a long life, too,

remaining in production until 1925, when it was joined by America's first budget-priced straight-eight cylinder car. It was replaced by a 3.2-litre (195cu in) six-cylinder side-valve-powered car a year later, and the new car with three

forward gears was also a success. In 1929, Hupmobile introduced another manufacturer, Chandler, and built these low-priced models in Chandler's Cleveland factory.

The Hupmobile Century followed the family line, and was

an elegant car with upright grille, wooden spoken wheels, large inset headlights and four doors. It would seat five passengers in comfort, and soon became known as the 'top gear' car, as it could easily accelerate in top gear from walking pace, and was renowned for its silent, smooth running.

Hupmobile's last automotive venture was a rear-wheel drive version of the Cord 810/812, which did nothing to revive the company's fading fortunes. The company finally decided to end car production altogether soon after, and moved into making car spares, electronics and kitchen products.

ENGINE: 3505cc (214cu in),
  six-cylinder
POWER: 25bhp (19kW)
0–60MPH (96KM/H): 37 seconds
TOP SPEED: 107km/h (67mph)
PRODUCTION TOTAL: 47,253

The Century very much followed in the family style that had been built up in Detroit since 1908, but this handsome 'top gear' car did not sell strongly in the aftermath of the Wall Street crash, and only remained in production for three years.

MORGAN SUPER SPORTS AERO

ENGINE: 1098cc (67cu in), V-twin
POWER: n/a
0–60MPH (96KM/H): n/a
TOP SPEED: about 153km/h (95mph)
PRODUCTION TOTAL: about 18,000

The Morgan Motor Company established itself as a producer of sporting cars in its formative years, and became well regarded when it came to building three-wheeled cars. In 1919, it moved from its founder H.F.S. Morgan's garage into a small factory in Malvern Link, Worcestershire, England, and that became a pivotal moment in the company's history, as the new premises finally provided H.F.S. Morgan with enough space to design and build a four-wheeled car.

Nothing is ever rushed at Morgan, however, and it took a further 17 years for the 4/4 to appear. To that point, the company continued building its range of three-wheelers – the most famous of which were the 'Aero-bodied' models announced in 1919.

The Aero-bodied models differed from the famous V-twin model, by featuring a streamlined cover over the rear wheel and a 'Bullnose' front end, which was the fashion of the time. Introduced in 1927, the Super Sports Aero featured excellent handling, and with a choice of JAP, Matchless, Ford and Blackburne motorcycle engines, it was popular with tuners and modifiers. Driving the car was

interesting – the accelerator was a simple lever on the steering wheel and the car had two-speed chain-driven transmission.

A one-make Morgan racing series was created and led the

company to competition success across the board.

Well known as an unusual cross between a car and a motorcycle, the Morgan qualified for lower-rate motorcycle tax.

The Super Sports Aero cemented Morgan's reputation for producing hugely entertaining three-wheel sportscars that were quick and fun to drive for those wanting to pay cheaper road tax.

MORRIS MINOR

If the Austin Seven mobilized the masses in the United Kingdom following its UK launch in 1923, the Minor was the direct answer to it, as produced by Morris Motors.

It took six years, however, for the Cowley rival to appear, but in doing so it became the first British car successfully to challenge Herbert Austin's important new baby car. The name chosen by Lord Nuffield for this car – Minor –

would end up living on for decades, and was to become one of the best known in British automotive history.

The 1929 car was, however, vastly different from the iconic Issigonis-created car of 1948. As an answer to the minimalist Austin, the original Morris baby was accordingly simply styled, but it did pick up an overhead-camshaft engine courtesy of the

company's takeover of Wolseley. In 1931, the 847cc (52cu in) overhead-camshaft-engined Minor was joined by a side-valve version with the same capacity, introduced to allow Morris to offer a £100 (US$150) two-seater tourer.

The purchase of Wolseley brought much-needed options to Morris, as greater production capacity was urgently required to build the new Minor.

The Minor came in a number of varieties – fabric saloons, two-seater tourers, sports coupés and a number of coachbuilt specials.

ENGINE: 847cc (52cu in), four-cylinder
POWER: 20bhp (15kW)
0–60MPH (96KM/H): n/a
TOP SPEED: 89km/h (55mph)
PRODUCTION TOTAL: 86,318

RILEY BROOKLANDS

By the introduction of the 1929 Brooklands, Riley had become a very successful producer of competition cars. The Brooklands is regarded as the most famous pre–World War II Riley, and, as a stripped-out racer based on the Nine, it was an exciting drive.

Featuring an all-new chassis, it was developed for racing by contemporary competition drivers

Reid Railton and Parry-Thomas. Shorter and lower than the Nine, the Brooklands boasted beautiful handling, and as a racer its enhanced performance was proved the icing on the cake in a winning mixture. The Brooklands featured high compression pistons, twin exhaust camshafts, a four-branch manifold, racing oil pump and dual carburettors. This was enough to

boost the top speed to something in the region of 145km/h (90mph); some cars were timed at much higher speeds in racing conditions.

In true racing style, the Brooklands featured minimalist bodywork, with little in the way of cabin protection, no roof and a tiny wind deflector in place of a front screen. The car enjoyed significant competition success,

the most notable of which was overall victory in the 1932 against faster, better backed opposition.

ENGINE: 1087cc (66cu in), four-cylinder
POWER: n/a
0–60MPH (96KM/H): n/a
TOP SPEED: 145km/h (90mph)
PRODUCTION TOTAL: n/a

AJS NINE

ENGINE: 1018cc (62cu in),
four-cylinder
POWER: 9bhp (7kW)
0–60MPH (96KM/H): n/a
TOP SPEED: n/a
PRODUCTION TOTAL: 3300

Created by A.J. Stevens, the Wolverhampton-based AJS company started out building motorcycles, and only entered car production in 1923 when Meadows-powered light cars were added to the mix. In a market dominated by big players such as Austin, Morris, Ford and Rootes, the small-scale operation did not enjoy much in the way of success on the market, and AJS quickly suspended production. Undaunted, the company tried again in 1929.

AJS offered a number of high-performance rolling chassis options, leaving the bodies a mix of coachbuilt saloons and tourers. The AJS Nine was one of this breed, and was available in two-seater or a fabric-hooded saloon. They were mainly powered by Coventry Climax engines. Technically, the car was standard fare. It featured a single dry plate clutch mated to a three-speed (later four-speed) gearbox and semi-elliptic suspension. The engines mainly came from Coventry Climax, and the general quality was good.

Most AJS cars were saloons fitted with the fabric bodywork, as was the fashion of the period, but this meant a low survival rate for these cars. Cars finished this way tended to look prematurely tatty.

The Nine was a high quality entrant into the UK's 9hp market, and although it was nothing special in terms of technical innovation, it was well received. Coventry Climax power was an added bonus.

ALFA ROMEO 6C1750

ENGINE: 1752cc (107cu in),
six-cylinder
POWER: 64bhp (48kW)
0–60MPH (96KM/H): n/a
TOP SPEED: 109km/h (68mph)
PRODUCTION TOTAL: n/a

The car company Alfa Romeo was formed during World War I, when Alfa was taken over by engineer and racing enthusiast Nicola Romeo – and, in doing so, he ensured that an Italian legend was born. The now iconic 6C was created by the gifted chief designer Vittorio Jano, after he was asked to develop a lighter version of the Alfa Romeo RL, which had been in production since 1923.

First in the new series of cars, the Alfa Romeo 6C1500 was originally specified with a massive six-seater body, but this was soon replaced by the far more appealing Sport version. This car featured an advanced twin-camshaft engine – and was later boosted with the introduction of the Super Sport in 1929. This Super Sport used a special lightweight alloy body built on a wooden frame, and was further enhanced by the option of a supercharger.

The 6C1750 also made an appearance in 1929. It was little different visually, but the bored-out engines resulted in a magical mix of speed and agility. Specialist bodies by coachbuilders Touring were a feauture, and a beautiful Zagato-built open-top two-seater version was offered. Run on a conventional chassis, the car was powered by an in-line six-cylinder engine with a cast-iron block and light-alloy crankcase. An optional Roots-type supercharger boosted power to a healthy 85bhp (63kW).

Well-proven in competition, the Alfa Romeo 6C has long since joined the ranks of the motoring greats.

LAGONDA 3-LITRE

ENGINE: 2931cc (179cu in),
six-cylinder
POWER: 20bhp (15kW)
0–60MPH (96KM/H): 40 seconds
TOP SPEED: 125km/h (78mph)
PRODUCTION TOTAL: n/a

Lagonda was well established by the time the 3-Litre was introduced in 1929, and had built its success on solid foundings.

After World War I, Lagonda revised its 1099cc (67cu in) '11' and subsequently installed a 1420cc (87cu in) engine in the car by 1921. Five years later, the company went upmarket with its new 14/60 – an advanced car that boasted a twin overhead camshaft, 2.0-litre (122cu in) engine and powerful Rubery brakes. Arguably this was over the top for a car aimed at the family car market, and the expensive car failed

commercially. Figuring life would be more profitable in the sportscar field instead, Lagonda launched a 3-litre (183cu in) six-cylinder car in 1929 – and, from that point, its fortunes changed.

Featuring traditional cycle mudguards, huge twin headlights set either side of the rounded grille and running boards, the Lagonda 3-Litre looked the part. The company wanted a large car without undue complexity and so

used a basic pushrod overhead-valve Meadows engine, with a massive seven bearing crankshaft and twin SU carburettors in the car. Suspension was similarly conventional, with half-elliptic springs, while the brakes were rods and cable-activated.

The 3-Litre was a worthy forerunner to the great pre-war 4 1/2-litre (275cu in) Rapide and V12 Lagondas, and was well equipped and easy to maintain.

MG MIDGET

ENGINE: 847cc (52cu in),
four-cylinder
POWER: 32bhp (24kW)
0–60MPH (96KM/H): n/a
TOP SPEED: 105km/h (65mph)
PRODUCTION TOTAL: 5992

Following its move to Abingdon, Oxfordshire, MG decided to embark on a small sportscar project, using the 847cc (52cu in) overhead camshaft engine developed for the Morris Minor. Until that point, MG specialized in large sporting saloons typified by the 18/18, but producing a smaller car opened up new options for the company – and boosted production in the new factory.

The new car's chassis also came from the Minor, but with lowered suspension. With weight pared to a

minimum by using fabric instead of metal for the body panels, the Midget was fun to drive.

With its appearance in 1929, the MG Midget became an instant success – its trump card was its low purchase cost, and, as a result, the MG company soon became known as a sportscar maker for the masses.

The original car was replaced in 1932 by the D-Type Midget, which lost some of the original's smart looks, but added an extra pair of seats, metal bodywork and a full folding hood.

The J-Type Midgets of 1932 saw the return of the two-seater layout on a car which again used the same engine and underpinnings. The J2 was a two-seater open top only, while a larger version, the J1, was offered with the option of four seats and a metal roof.

The first in a long line of great sporting roadsters, the Midget was so-called for one very obvious reason – it was tiny. With its highly tuneable engine, it soon became the darling of the tuning set.

INVICTA 4.5-LITRE

ENGINE: 4467cc (273cu in),
six-cylinder
POWER: 115bhp (86kW)
0–60MPH (96KM/H): n/a
TOP SPEED: 161km/h (100mph)
PRODUCTION TOTAL: 77

The Invicta car company was formed in 1924 by Noel Macklin and Oliver Lyle, of the British sugar-making company, its intention was to produce luxury vehicles combining British build standards and American-style performance. It grew from small beginnings: the Invicta factory was created from the three-car garage of Macklin's family home in Chobham, England.

One of the most famous Invictas was the 4.5-litre (273cu in) 'flat

iron' – identified by its trademark riveted bonnet (hood) and impressive performance. The chassis was supplied in two forms, 'high' and the 'lowered' S-type, but it was the latter that usually featured lightweight competition bodywork. Donald Healey helped to develop the car, then went on

to win the Monte Carlo rally in it in 1931. Despite being capable of only 144km/h (90mph) in standard form, the car became known as the '100mph' Invicta.

Later in its production run, power was increased to 140bhp (104kW), and, without doubt, the car would finally reach the magic

161km/h (100mph) mark. Still, the Great Depression affected Invicta – as it did with so many other companies producing upmarket cars – and production stopped after 77 4.5-litres were built. Macklin sold out to Earl Fitzwilliam after that, and the name was revived in 1946.

Not the fastest or most comfortable grand touring car, the Invicta 4.5-Litre offered excellent road manners.

DUESENBERG MODEL J

UNITED STATES 1929–37

ENGINE: 6882cc (420cu in),
eight-cylinder
POWER: 200bhp (149kW)
0–60MPH (96KM/H): 10 seconds
TOP SPEED: 193km/h (120mph)
PRODUCTION TOTAL: 470

Best known for its racing exploits, Duesenberg had been the creation of two men – Fred and August Duesenberg. Following financial trouble, E.L. Cord bought

the company, and immediately provided the finance for the brothers to build the ultimate Duesenberg, the Model J.

Christened the 'King of the Classics' by Cord when announced in 1928, there is no doubting that the Model J was an awesome car. Powered by a twin camshaft, 32-valve Lycoming straight-eight, with a nickel-plated crankshaft, the car produced at least 200bhp (149kW), and, despite its great weight, the Model J handled and performed

impressively. A plus point was that the Model J could be specified in any bodystyle.

The supercharged SJ topped the range for the 1928 season, and it developed a cool 320bhp (238kW), boosted to 400bhp (298kW) with the so-called 'ram's horn'. Top speed was a remarkable 225km/h (140mph), yet the SJ was still smooth enough to be driven like a limousine. The Hollywood glitterati queued up to buy a Duesenberg; famous owners included Gary

Cooper and Clark Gable, who ordered the only two short-chassis roadsters, designated SSJs.

The cheaper JN appeared in 1935, but this car and the Cord 800 series disappeared when E.L. Cord's business empire suffered losses in 1937.

Now celebrated as one of the most desirable classic cars, the Duesenberg was never a commercial success.

CADILLAC 353

UNITED STATES 1930–32

ENGINE: 5786cc (353cu in),
eight-cylinder
POWER: 95bhp (71kW)
0–60MPH (96KM/H): 45 seconds
TOP SPEED: 96km/h (60mph)
PRODUCTION TOTAL: 14,995

Vying with the likes of Cord, Rolls-Royce and Duesenberg, Cadillac was a genuine supercar

producer during the 1920s. The 353 was regarded as a high-water mark in the Cadillac story in the pre–World War II era.

A development of the previous Series 341-B, the 353 was offered with seven Fisher Custom closed bodies, to tempt affluent buyers. These included a convertible coupé, as well as a Fleetwood Special Custom line, which offered 11 basic bodywork combinations.

The 5786cc (353cu in) V8 was based on the previous (341cu in) flathead unit introduced in 1928, giving the stylish car all the power it needed. Cadillac understood its customers, and offered plenty of options, including wire wheels, demountable wooden wheels, heater and a boot (trunk) rack. You could even order a radio, for a cool $175.

Styling was gradually brought up to date from 1932, then

fashionably streamlined in 1934. Cadillac remained at the cutting edge, adding a synchromesh to its transmission, before adding a 'no-draft' ventilation system. Later came vacuum-assisted brakes, independent front suspension and all-steel bodies. The Cadillac 353 proved a major success, selling strongly in its first years before falling victim to the Wall Street Crash and Great Depression.

CHEVROLET AD UNIVERSAL

The Universal tag was applied to the Chevrolet model range in 1930, as part of the company's continuous programme of model updates. In its battle with the four-cylinder Ford Model A, Chevrolet had introduced the legendary six-cylinder engine to get one over its bitterest rival.

The Universal's engine was a robust overhead-valve unit and was eventually dubbed the 'Cast-Iron Wonder' during a production run that lasted into 1950s – and offered multi-cylinder motoring for a bargain price.

The Universal continued Chevrolet's penchant for upright styling, but combined it with a slanting non-glare windscreen. Other refinements included a dashboard-mounted fuel gauge, and circular instruments. A new manifold design improved the car's performance, while the chassis was beefed up with new hydraulic shock absorbers.

The huge 10-model line-up offered something for everyone. Many commentators claimed that it was every bit as responsible for motorizing the United States as the Ford Model A. Despite selling in huge numbers, some of the roadsters are very hard to find and have almost legendary status among collectors. The model range was renamed the Independence for 1931 with some minor stylistic and mechanical changes.

ENGINE: 3180cc (194cu in), six-cylinder
POWER: 50bhp (37kW)
0–60MPH (96KM/H): 40 seconds
TOP SPEED: 97km/h (60mph)
PRODUCTION TOTAL: 864,243

HUMBER 16/50

One of the oldest motor manufacturers in Britain, Humber had been doing good business since 1898, and boasted a two-factory operation – with plants in Coventry and Beeston in Warwickshire. It was also yet another motor company that had begun its life making bicycles.

The 1920s had been good to the company, and it had carved itself a reputation for producing good-quality and durable cars. Expansion inevitably followed success, and, in 1926, Humber entered into the commercial vehicle market by taking over Commer Cars, which was a Luton-based carmaker.

However, Humber had been under the microscope of garage owner, motor trade distributor and businessman Billy Rootes, and, in 1928, he planned to merge Humber and Hillman in order to create a more efficient carmaking operation at the factory in Humber Road, Coventry. The merger took place so quickly that, by the time the shareholders had agreed to it, the Rootes 1930 models were already on sale.

These included the stately Humber 16/50, which was also known as the 'medium' six. It officially superseded the 14/40 and was available in what was described as a 'dual purpose' bodystyle, which incorporated wind-down side screens. Further investment by Rootes resulted in the all-new 1.7-litre (104cu in) 12hp (9kW) model. and the side-valve engined 16/60. Production of the car with its aged inlet-over-exhaust engine ended as Humber became an integral part of the Rootes Group.

ENGINE: 2110cc (128cu in), six-cylinder
POWER: 50bhp (37kW)
0–60MPH (96KM/H): n/a
TOP SPEED: n/a
PRODUCTION TOTAL: 8183

RENAULT MONASIX

ENGINE: 1474cc (90cu in), six-cylinder
POWER: n/a
0–60MPH (96KM/H): n/a
TOP SPEED: n/a
PRODUCTION TOTAL: n/a

Pre–World War II Renaults are some of the most recognizable cars, and the Monasix featured typical styling – an angled radiator grille and Michelin disc wheels distinguished it from all of its rivals in the saloon-car class. Styling aside, it was totally conventional, featuring a side-valve small-capacity six-cylinder engine, which could summon up plenty of torque, but little in the way of performance.

Chassis wise, the Monasix was a simple steel affair, and featured transverse leaf springs on both axles. The layout made for a reasonably pliant ride, but the car's handling was very poor, badly affected as it was by vague steering and a tendency to drift if driven at speed.

The three-speed central control gearbox made down-changes difficult, but it was much the same as its rivals. What really marked down the uninspiring Renault was the poor performance from its mechanical braking layout. Dynamic ability was hardly the point, however, in an era when motivation was the key.

Ordinary motorists were well served by the best-selling Monasix, and it was built first and foremost to satisfy the needs of undemanding family buyers who needed an inexpensive means of transport. A variety of different bodystyles was offered, from two-door coupés and convertibles, up to seven-seater limousines – all very stylish indeed.

Considered to be one of the most reliable cars of its type in its era, the Renault Monasix sold well, despite being a little on the stodgy side to drive. Offered in several guises, for a time it was France's best-selling car.

VOISIN 32-140

In 1930, Gabriel Voisin introduced one of the most innovative designs to come out of France in the years preceding the outbreak of World War II. With swooping, wind-cheating lines, the Voisin 32-140 looked like nothing else that was available at the time – and it was certainly imposing.

At £1900, the limousine was hugely expensive, but there was also the option of a saloon, two-door coupé, four-door coupé and drophead coupé. Voisin's refined 5830cc (356cu in) overhead-valve straight-six engine powered the entire range, driven through a four-speed gearbox.

Voisin had a reputation for producing technically dazzling cars, and seemed unwilling to compromise the design or construction of any of his cars – no matter what it cost. This uncompromising approach led to a series of amazing cars, typified by the Laboratoire Grand Prix racer.

Like all of the era's best supercars, Voisins were incredible to look at and were suitably overengineered. Unfortunately, however, hardly anybody could afford to buy them – especially as the Great Depression spread through Europe, driving the cars even further out of buying range.

ENGINE: 5830cc (356cu in),
  six-cylinder
POWER: n/a
0–60MPH (96KM/H): n/a
TOP SPEED: n/a
PRODUCTION TOTAL: n/a

A prime example of Europe's great breed of Grand Routieres, the Voisin 32-140 looked distinctive and beautiful, and was refined to drive.

MORRIS OXFORD

UNITED KINGDOM 1930–35

Although Morris had been slowly moving upmarket – introducing its elegant six-cylinder Isis model in 1929, with a 2468cc (151cu in) overhead camshaft engine and very advanced styling – the company was not losing focus on where its major sales lay. In 1930, it launched a less powerful, more inexpensive side-valve six-powered version of the Isis called the Oxford. With its 1938cc (118cu in) engine, the Oxford Six did not skimp technically, and still featured hydraulic brakes – it was also very popular. Sales of the car were brisk in its first year, and 15,500 were sold.

The range was expanded with an attractive Sports Coupé in 1932, and, during that year, both the engine and chassis were modified – and a pleasant four-speed gearbox appeared. A bigger 2062cc (126cu in) engine was introduced in 1933, and that cured the overheating problems that had adversely affected the original car.

The Oxford Six drew further improvement in 1934, and another new chassis was introduced, even though it featured similar styling to the Cowley Six. An automatic clutch option was added to the car's all-synchromesh four-speed gearbox, although this was seen as a gimmick.

In 1935, the Oxford name was put on ice and the Six was renamed the Morris 16 – but it would return to live a long and prosperous life just over a decade later, when the Oxford MO made an appearance.

ENGINE: 1938cc (118cu in),
  six-cylinder
POWER: n/a
0–60MPH (96KM/H): n/a
TOP SPEED: 95km/h (59mph)
PRODUCTION TOTAL: 38,590

ROLLS-ROYCE 40/50 PHANTOM II

UNITED KINGDOM 1929–35

ENGINE: 7668cc (846cu in),
  six-cylinder
POWER: n/a
0–60MPH (96KM/H): n/a
TOP SPEED: n/a
PRODUCTION TOTAL: 1767

Although a few would argue that Rolls-Royce's self-proclaimed title of 'Best car in the world' was misplaced by the turn of the 1930s, the company's cars were still highlighted by their precision engineering. The New Phantom, however, came in for plenty of criticism for its long-in-the-tooth chassis, which, although offering compliant handling, was lumbered with heavy steering and poor lateral stability. This was corrected when the second-generation 40/50 Phantom II was unveiled in 1929 to replace the New Phantom.

The new suspension layout featured semi-elliptic leaf springs front and rear, and the result was far more rewarding roadholding, lighter steering and a more supple ride – something of a must with the company's clientele.

The earlier car's traditional right-hand gearchange remained and was not revised until 1932, when a synchromesh was added to the top three gears, making selection a far more restful affair. The New Phantom's powerful engine was retained, meaning the Phantom II was a suitably quick machine to drive. As the car shed weight over its predecessor, performance received a useful fillip.

With an improved power-to-weight ratio and improved gearing, the standard-bodied Phantom II had the ability to pass the 100mph (161km/h) barrier – making it a true supercar of its era.

Although debatable whether the Phantom II was 'the best car in the world', it was certainly a fine piece of precision engineering.

PACKARD STANDARD 8

UNITED STATES 1930–36

The Packard Standard 8 was a beautifully built, finely engineered and sumptuously equipped motor car, making it an iconic luxury car in the truest sense of the word. The 5.3-litre (326cu in) side-valve straight eight dished out gobs of power and torque, and that resulted in fine performance for its era.

The mechanical layout may have been utterly conventional, with the car being built on a separate chassis, but it was still an effective piece of kit. The Standard 8 used a spiral bevel final drive unit and semi-elliptic leaf springs all round.

The interior was laden with wood, and leather prevailed. Coupled with a vast rear seat, this meant that the Packard became the car of choice for those who preferred the chauffeur to take the strain of driving.

A bigger and more streamlined model replaced the successful original car in 1932, and the upright grille and individual mudguards were consigned to the history books. The new car also looked the part, featuring a longer wheelbase, split-folding roof, chrome-plated radiator mounting and wider running boards.

The final Standard 8 appeared in 1935 and was in production for just over a year. Featuring a more aerodynamic grille, it could be ordered with an elegant drophead coupé bodystyle for customers wanting to do their own driving.

ENGINE: 5342cc (326cu in),
  eight-cylinder
POWER: n/a
0–60MPH (96KM/H): n/a
TOP SPEED: 121km/h (75mph)
PRODUCTION TOTAL: 64,871

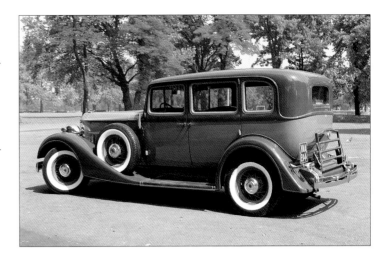

The Standard 8 was one of the finest cars during this era to be produced in the USA, and was favoured by those who preferred to be driven by chauffeur.

WOLSELEY HORNET

ENGINE: 1271cc (78cu in),
  six-cylinder
POWER: n/a
0–60MPH (96KM/H): n/a
TOP SPEED: 104km/h (65mph)
PRODUCTION TOTAL: about 32,000

William Morris bought the Wolseley Car Company in 1927 – and, as a direct result, all cars from that point on used a significant number of Morris components under the skin. The first product of the Morris-owned Wolseley was the 1930 Hornet, a car that featured a technically intriguing 1271cc (78cu in) six-cylinder engine. Although the Wolseley Hornet was more expensive than its bread-and-butter counterparts, it went on to sell in large numbers – within six years more than 30,000 were sold.

The Hornet was a mixed bag technically, with modern hydraulic dampers and brakes, but a terribly conventional chassis married with poor steering. The result of this combination was questionable handling and roadholding. However, Wolseley offered a chassis-only version of the Hornet with bespoke bodyshells in mind. That was good news for traditional coachbuilders, who had found themselves going out of business as mass-production became more widespread. By 1931, more than 2500 Hornets sold were specials, in up to 20 different variations.

An extra engine option (a 45bhp/34kW twin-carburettor power unit) meant that the options for potential buyers was increased still further. By 1936, when the car was phased out, 1378cc (84cu in) and 1604cc (98cu in) engines had been added to the line-up.

The Hornet was the first new car to be offered by Wolseley following its takeover by William Morris' Nuffield Group.

A Wolseley Hornet Special can still turn heads today. Here it is put through its paces at a classic car rally in the UK.

RILEY NINE

Riley Nines had been around since the late 1920s, but it was not until the launch of the second-generation car in 1930 that sales took off in a big way. Based in Coventry, England, Riley had found itself with a major sales success with its second-generation Nine.

The new car used a similar chassis to the original Nine, but possessed extra bracing and strengthened side members to offer more confident handling, thanks to a stiffer chassis. The introduction of cable-operated brakes also improved stopping power significantly when compared to the earlier cars.

The Nine was improved during the course of its production run, and 1933 saw a handy upgrade in the vehicle's engine power. Performance remained largely unchanged, however, as the larger, weightier bodywork, available in a variety of styles ranging from two-door convertibles to full four-seater saloons, gave the tiny engine more work to do.

The Nine was revised again in 1936, and the range usefully rationalized. A brand-new chassis frame that used tubular cross members to cut down on weight and thus improve performance was the main improvement on these last cars – unsurprisingly, they were the best Nines to drive. The top speed was a sprightly 96km/h (60mph), and the car's rod-type brakes gave the driver more confident stopping.

ENGINE: 1087cc (66cu in), four-cylinder
POWER: 24bhp (18 kW)
0–60MPH (96KM/H): n/a
TOP SPEED: 96km/h (60mph)
PRODUCTION TOTAL: n/a

The Nine was Riley's first truly sporting car, but it was perfectly judged and sold well. Sporting handling and a revvy four-cylinder engine meant that there was plenty to please the driver.

ROLLS-ROYCE 20/25

UNITED KINGDOM 1930–37

ENGINE: 3669cc (224cu in), six-cylinder
POWER: n/a
0–60MPH (96KM/H): n/a
TOP SPEED: n/a
PRODUCTION TOTAL: 3827

The Great Depression really hit the supercar manufacturers during the 1930s – either they were going out of business or producing smaller, cheaper cars in response. Even the mighty Rolls-Royce felt the pinch, and, in 1930, the company introduced its new 'baby' car – the 20/25.

History has not been kind to the 20/25, as it was viewed as a compromised product. However, it had a lot going for it – such as a compact, economical engine, flexible performance and a surprisingly agile chassis. The range of bodystyles seemed at odds with the fine quality of the engineering, particularly in later years, as the Rolls-Royce for the owner-driver became an absurd outdated idea. Once the economy picked up and buyers started returning to their old, extravagant ways, the compact and cramped 20/25 became undesirable.

The 20/25 seemed to grow more ostentatious with age – and it is the earliest cars, with Barker or Gurney-Nutting Coupé de Ville bodywork, that were the best. Rolls-Royce continued to stick with

the increasingly unpopular right-hand gearchange layout, despite most of its rivals opting for the more conventional solution. On the road, the 20/25 never inspired confidence, usually feeling big and unwieldy – with high-speed manoeuvres requiring careful forward planning.

Unrest in Europe in the lead-up to World War II killed demand for the 20/25, and, since then, Rolls-Royce has remained shy of entering the compact class again.

The 20/25 range was introduced to appeal to owner/drivers who were either downsizing in the wake of the Depression, or who could not afford its full-sized brother. Not a great seller, the 'baby' Rolls-Royce lacked appeal.

NASH EIGHT

UNITED STATES 1930–39

ENGINE: 4834cc (295cu in), eight-cylinder
POWER: 90bhp (67kW)
0–60MPH (96KM/H): n/a
TOP SPEED: n/a
PRODUCTION TOTAL: n/a

You certainly could never accuse Nash of not offering enough choice in its range – there were no fewer than 102 variants of Eight offered during the 1930s. It was possible to buy a car to suit all tastes, from the original upright-looking Town Sedan to the stylish 1939 Streamlined Roadster. Given the breadth of the range, all Nash Eights were built from the same platform – and all had something in common: they were fitted with huge and powerful straight-eight engines, and were built for comfort.

The Eight initially came with a side-valve engine when it was launched in 1930, but this unit was soon switched for an overhead-valve one in 1933. Smaller-engined Nash Sixes looked similar and used scaled-down styling from the bigger car.

The previous boxy shape was ditched in favour of a much more elegant, avant-garde design in 1934, and that featured a pointed 'shark-nose' bonnet (hood) and faired-in wings (fenders) with running boards – stylish indeed.

The Ambassador was the most common model in the Nash Eight range – and that was a six-seater saloon. Perhaps the most bizarre model was the 1935 Aeroform Fastback, with its stunning torpedo-shaped rear end with 'Speedstream' styling. Incorporating chrome flashes on the bonnet, a V-shaped windscreen, aggressive radiator grille and aerodynamic wheel spats, the Aeroform Fastback's aerodynamic credentials have never been tested.

Offered in an almost bewildering range of body styles, the Nash Eight shared its chassis with cars from Railton and Hudson. Huge and powerful straight-eight engines resulted in an effortless driving experience.

STUDEBAKER PRESIDENT

ENGINE: 5522cc (337cu in), eight-cylinder
POWER: 115bhp (86kW)
0–60MPH (96KM/H): n/a
TOP SPEED: n/a
PRODUCTION TOTAL: 67,372

Considering it was called the President, the 1927 Studebaker actually started out with quite a modest specification. Available with a six-cylinder engine at launch, it was not the opulent car it would later become. However, once the six-cylinder engine was dropped, a straight-eight powerplant slotted in its place, and a serious restyle unveiled, the President we have come to know and love began to emerge. Sleeker bodies and a longer wheelbase signified the car meant business.

Well priced compared with its rivals, the President was still Studebaker's most expensive car at the time, and it was aimed squarely at the rich. Buyers had plenty of choice in the bodystyle department, with a coupé, saloon, roadster or limousine on offer – needless to say, the latter option was the most expensive.

Equipment levels were lavish, and, by 1935, you could specify your President with a synchromesh gearbox, power-assisted brakes and an automatic choke.

Three years later, independent front suspension had arrived ... and you could even buy one with radio speakers incorporated into the car's headlining.

It may have looked a million dollars, with a glamorous style that rivalled anything from Cadillac or Lincoln, but the President was more affordable.

BUICK STRAIGHT EIGHT

ENGINE: 3617cc (221cu in), eight-cylinder
POWER: 77bhp (57kW)
0–60MPH (96KM/H): 25 seconds
TOP SPEED: 119km/h (74mph)
PRODUCTION TOTAL: 138,695

In a brave move, Buick's new straight-eight engines were launched across the entire range in July 1930 – setting the company apart from all of its competition. Despite its configuration, the smallest unit displaced a compact 3617cc (221cu in), and soon found its way into the 50- and 40-series.

The Buick 'Series' models were revised during 1930 – with a change of designations being run across the board: the 40 became the 60. The 60 featured the smooth 4457cc (272cu in) engine, and the largest straight-eight in 5637cc (344cu in) form found its way into the Series 80 and 90 Buicks. The cars caught the public's imagination, and sales of the straight-eights were dramatic in the first full year – in 1931, 138,695 cars were sold, but this performance soon tailed off as the Great Depression began to make its presence felt. Two years later, sales had fallen to 46,924 in 1933, and they picked up again only after 1936, when the restyled range hit the marketplace.

Smoothness and speed were the highlights of these cars, and they could cruise comfortably at around 110km/h (70mph) all day long – quite a feat for the 1930s. The straight-eights were also quite advanced, featuring an oil temperature system which cooled the oil at high engine revolutions and warmed it in the cold.

The most prestigious Series Buick were the convertible coupé and phaeton – especially desirable.

PLYMOUTH PA

Plymouth was conceived by Chrysler in an attempt to take the marque downmarket, appealing to buyers on a tighter budget. The name first appeared in 1931, on its first own design -- the PA. The car was offered in upright two-door saloon, coupé or convertible forms, and the PA was a genuine if spartan four-seater.

The PA was equipped with a three-speed floor-mounted gearbox, freewheel device and a Lockheed hydraulic braking system, making it surprisingly advanced for a budget car. Despite its downmarket roots, it was easy to drive and a lively performer – and unlike many other Americans, enjoyed limited success in the UK market. In the United States, it was altogether more popular – reaching third place in that country's sales charts.

The PA was replaced by the similar-looking PB for 1932; that car earned its new name through its stronger chassis, improved semi-elliptic leaf springs and higher price tag. The PA and PB were important landmarks in Plymouth history, and set the pattern for the marque's future models until well into the 1950s.

ENGINE: 3213cc (196cu in), four-cylinder
POWER: n/a
0–60MPH (96KM/H): n/a
TOP SPEED: n/a
PRODUCTION TOTAL: n/a

ALVIS 12/50

ENGINE: 1645cc (100cu in), four-cylinder
POWER: 52bhp (39kW)
0–60MPH (96KM/H): n/a
TOP SPEED: 115km/h (71mph)
PRODUCTION TOTAL: 642

The Alvis 12/50 remained well loved long after it went out of production – it first appeared in 1923 and was an evolution of the overhead-valve-engined 10/30 series, which had also proved popular. As the 1920s progressed it was continually developed, appearing in various forms until 1931, when it was replaced by the Series TJ 12/50.

Improved over its predecessors in a number of ways, the Series TJ 12/50 gained a coil ignition system (previous models had magnetos). The new car also used a separate radiator shell housing, where the original had a simpler one-piece block. Most importantly, though, the new 12/50 featured a new 1645cc (100cu in) overhead-valve engine, which replaced the original 1496cc (91cu in) unit. This was a big improvement in terms of power and refinement, and was coupled with a four-speed manual gearbox and hand- and foot-brakes working on all four

wheels. Bodystyles offered for the 12/50 were two-seater, tourer, drophead coupé and saloon.

The 12/50 was a significant model for Alvis, and it came to be regarded as one of the best of all British lightweight cars of the era. It racked up an excellent racing record, with its most impressive achievement being the victory it took in the 1923 Brooklands 200-mile (322km) race.

The 12/50 was well-loved, and is still considered to be one of the finest British sporting cars of its era. Its competition victories include the 1923 Brooklands 200 mile (322km) race.

REO ROYALE

Ransom Eli Olds formed REO in 1904 – and, if the name seems familiar, that is because he had previously created Oldsmobile. REO was formed to offer luxurious high-quality cars at a more accessible price – going head to head with the likes of Ford, Chevrolet and even Oldsmobile. Actually, most customers perceived an REO to be a higher quality alternative to these cars – without the price premium.

As large as many small trucks and considerably more luxurious, the REO Royale suffered after Wall Street Crash of 1929.

The REO Royale appeared on the scene in 1931, and with its torquey 5.9-litre (358cu in) eight-cylinder nine-bearing side-valve engine, smoothness and performance came as standard. That was if the driver did not push it – speed things up, and things got a lot noisier ...

The Royale certainly looked the part. It had a fluted aerodynamic radiator grille, rolled-edge wings (fenders) and a suitably plush interior. The 1932 model was the most desirable of the lot, with smoother styling and a vacuum-operated clutch. Later models became bulkier and less appealing.

In a familiar tale, REO suffered during the Great Depression, and sales were badly affected. Even when the US economy picked up in the late 1930s and the product improved drastically, the good times never returned. By 1936, the game was up – the company made its final car, a Flying Cloud.

ENGINE: 5866cc (358cu in), eight-cylinder
POWER: n/a
0–60MPH (96KM/H): n/a
TOP SPEED: n/a
PRODUCTION TOTAL: n/a

MG MAGNA

ENGINE: 1087cc (66cu in), six-cylinder
POWER: 37bhp (28kW)
0–60MPH (96KM/H): n/a
TOP SPEED: 113km/h (70mph)
PRODUCTION TOTAL: 1826

MG's Magna was a new venture for a company that until this point had been concentrating on sports and racing cars. It had been designed to appeal to a more mature clientele than the Midget –

and was therefore a more sedate, imposing car. Powered by a straight-six overhead camshaft engine that had been originally developed for the Wolseley Hornet, the Magna was an interesting beast. What set it apart from most of its rivals was that it offered two more cylinders than most of its rivals, despite being available in either a 1.1- (67cu in) or 1.3-litre (79cu in) forms.

The Magna suffered, however, in comparison with other MGs on the road. It had clumsy handling and a

fussy crash gearbox that required patience and concentration from the driver. The long wheelbase and narrow track did result in an acceptable ride, though.

The first MG Magna was called the F-Type, and it remained in production for just one year. The F-type was then supplanted by the L-Type. That car had wider bodywork and a more powerful engine, thanks to the addition of twin SU carburettors, and it proved slightly better to drive. Styling was improved, too – it had flared front

wings (fenders), a cutaway door line and a larger front scuttle.

The prettiest and rarest of all the Magna variants was the L-Type Continental Coupé – which, to many people, closely resembled the Bugatti Type 57.

Larger and more capable than the Midget, the MG Magna offered the benefits of six-cylinder motoring at a very reasonable price, as well as being popular in competition.

ROVER SPEED 20

The Rover Company had been around since the dawn of the motoring age, so, when the 1927 Rover Six appeared, it was the product of a confident car company.

Powered by Peter Poppe's 2023cc (123cu in) six-cylinder overhead-valve engine, the Six had plenty of development capacity, which it duly received. In 1927, it was enlarged to 2565cc (157cu in), and it was that engine that

formed the cornerstone of the Rover Meteor. This engine then found its way into the new Speed 20 model of 1931. The 'Speed 20' name came about because it was a combination of the company's biggest engine and smallest chassis, and that made it a fast, fun steer. Top speed was almost 137km/h (85mph), and handling was tidy.

Although fitted with Rover's most powerful engine, the power

output was compromised by the single down-draught carburettor, and that resulted in the adoption a triple SU set-up in 1934. This boosted power to 72bhp (54kW), and servo brakes complemented the higher power output.

Several body options were available, including a Weymann fabric body, a sportsman's coupé and the distinctive notchback Hastings coupé. The Speed 20

lasted until 1934, but the name was applied to a different model, fitted with the P2 body. That was in production from 1937 to 1940.

ENGINE: 2565cc (157cu in), six-cylinder
POWER: 72bhp (54kW)
0–60MPH (96KM/H): n/a
TOP SPEED: 134km/h (83mph)
PRODUCTION TOTAL: n/a

STUTZ SV16

ENGINE: 5277cc (322cu in),
eight-cylinder
POWER: 113bhp (84kW)
0–60MPH (96KM/H): n/a
TOP SPEED: n/a
PRODUCTION TOTAL: n/a

A derivative of the ill-fated Blackhawk, the SV16 featured a thumping 5277cc (322cu in) straight-eight engine, producing an impressive 113bhp (84kW). The price, however, was very high – US$5775 for the short-wheelbase car and $7495 for the long-wheelbase version – not good news during an economic downturn.

The Stutz SV16 was so-called because it featured an unusual 16-valve engine, with single valves arranged as one inlet, and one exhaust valve for each of its eight cylinders. Alongside this, Stutz offered the DV32, which drew its name from the fact that its power unit was a dual-valve 32 – making it a four-valves-per-cylinder design.

Sadly, however, the car was underdeveloped, and, although the option of a three-speed gearbox in place of the usual four-speed Warner unit was offered in 1933, allowing the price to be cut by $400, it was not enough to save the company. Six cars were sold in 1934, and, by 1937, the Stutz company was bankrupt.

BUICK SERIES 50

ENGINE: 3777cc (230cu in),
eight-cylinder
POWER: 86bhp (64kW)
0–60MPH (96KM/H): 19 seconds
TOP SPEED: 117km/h (72mph)
PRODUCTION TOTAL: 690,500

Buick's decision to build a range comprised exclusively of eight-cylinder cars – in the middle of a depression – was hitting sales hard. To counter the situation, the company introduced the Series 50, which was designed to ensure profitable mass-market sales.

With the new car came three new engines, but none of them had interchangeable parts with the larger eight-cylinder power units. The interior was still plush, with mohair or cloth upholstery, carpeting for the rear-seat floor area, dome lights and armrests. Mechanical refinement was improved by adding synchromesh transmission – previously a preserve of more upmarket Buicks.

The following year, more bodystyles were available: a two-door five-passenger Victoria coupé and a pretty convertible phaeton model. The styling and impressive engine were enough to attract all the right people. For 1934, a longer 302cm (119in) wheelbase was added, meaning a wider choice of bodies. In 1936, the styling took a distinctive turn to the art deco, marking Buick's design revival in the run-up to World War II, as the lighter series 40 took over from the heavy 50. In 1938, a novel semi-

automatic transmission option increased the refinement of the smallest Buick, ensuring the range's continued popularity.

The Series 50 was Buick's attempt to move its range down market in order to meet the demands of a changing market. Rapid sales success duly followed – thanks to a wide range of bodies and an interesting specification.

MAYBACH ZEPPELIN

ENGINE: 7995cc (488cu in),
12-cylinder
POWER: 200bhp (149kW)
0–60MPH (96KM/H): n/a
TOP SPEED: n/a
PRODUCTION TOTAL: n/a

Wilhelm Maybach had always been associated with famous engineers and products to the turn

of the nineteenth century. These included Gottlieb Daimler and Emil Jellinek (founder of Mercedes). He also became involved in the Zeppelin airships, developing the huge 21-litre (1282cu in) powerplants that propelled them across the skies of the world.

The Maybach automotive company was established in 1929 following Wilhelm's death, by his son Karl. His cars were exclusive,

imposing and incredibly expensive. These were luxury limousines bought by the super-rich. The Maybach W5 of 1927 was a confident beginning for Maybach, featuring a six-cylinder, 7-litre (488cu in) engine, and bodywork by German coachbuilders Spohn. It weighed an enormous 3500kg (7700lb) and seemed a fitting flagship for the German car industry. The Zeppelin continued

the grandiose theme, when it followed in 1931, and was equally huge – but powered by a far more suitable V12 engine.

In order to survive, the company moved into commercial vehicle production – an obvious decision when you are a producer of such large engines. In later years, Maybach also built heavy-duty diesel engines for marine and rail purposes, and, in 1960, Daimler-

Benz acquired a majority shareholder status. Six years later, Maybach-Motorenbau was merged with the heavy-duty engine arm of Daimler-Benz to form a new company, Maybach Mercedes-Benz Motorenbau GmbH. The name lives on today, adorning the flagship model in the Mercedes-Benz passenger-car range.

Named after the airships that the company's engines powered prior to World War One, the Maybach Zeppelin was a grandiose German touring car. After the Zeppelin went out of production, the company concentrated on commercial vehicles.

LINCOLN KB

ENGINE: 7340cc (448cu in), 12-cylinder
POWER: 150bhp (112kW)
0–60MPH (96KM/H): n/a
TOP SPEED: 150km/h (90mph)
PRODUCTION TOTAL: 2000

The Lincoln Company was founded in 1917 by Henry M. Leland. One of the founders of Cadillac, Leland left the Cadillac division of General Motors during World War I and formed the Lincoln Motor Company, to build Liberty aircraft engines. After the war ended, the company's factories were retooled to manufacture luxury automobiles. The company encountered severe financial troubles during the transition, however, and was bought by the Ford Motor Company in 1922. Ironically, Cadillac was bought out by arch rival General Motors – and the two companies created by the same man went head to head on the automobile market.

The huge Lincoln KB range of cars were seen by many as the archetypal large American car of the 1930s, and it soon became a firm favourite of the American establishment, becoming the choice of ride of presidents for years to come.

The KB was offered in four-door convertible form and featured a lengthy hood. A covered spare wheel was positioned in front of the driver's door – to become another Lincoln hallmark. It was not a technical marvel, however, featuring mechanical braking and non-independent suspension – but they did work well. The KB series ran until 1940, but lost the sales war with Chevrolet and Ford.

The Lincoln KB was considered by many to be the 'establishment' large American car, and in later years Lincolns became the car of choice for a number of presidents.

ASTON MARTIN LE MANS

ENGINE: 1495cc (91cu in),
　four-cylinder
POWER: 56bhp (75kW)
0–60MPH (96KM/H): n/a
TOP SPEED: 129km/h (80mph)
PRODUCTION TOTAL: 72

Aston Martin's Le Mans is arguably the finest of all the pre–World War II Aston Martins, challenged only by the more racer-like Short model that subsequently appeared. The car was based on the International, but featured a number of improvements over that car – and its sporting cousin, the International Le Mans.

The Aston Martin Le Mans built on the best bits of the previous car – the Moss gearbox, bevel back axle and sweet four-cylinder overhead camshaft engine – but on top of that added improved styling and a lighter body. The car's good looks were a result of the lower-slung radiator and a natty-looking outside exhaust pipe.

Three bodies were available in the line-up – a two-seater sports version, a four-seater sports and a long-wheelbase four-seater sports tourer. The Le Mans also sired the more useable 12/50 Standard model, which had the mechanical specification of the Le Mans, but with a more traditional-looking

four-door saloon bodystyle. A Short model closely related to the Le Mans was also introduced, and featured exhaust headers emerging from the sides of the bonnet (hood). This made it look even more purposeful than the car upon which it was based.

Tweaked styling over the International model dramatically improved the appeal of the Le Mans.

ALVIS SPEED 20

ENGINE: 2511cc (153cu in),
　six-cylinder
POWER: 87bhp (65kW) at 4200rpm
0–60MPH (96KM/H): 22 seconds
TOP SPEED: 143km/h (89mph)
PRODUCTION TOTAL: 1165

Regarded today as one of Britain's finest vintage racing cars, the Alvis Speed 20 was the product of an innovative company that continued to produce technically advanced cars. In terms of specification, performance and appearance, the Speed 20 fit well in this mould – it was comparable with far higher priced products from Bentley, Lagonda and SS (Jaguar), and could easily punch above its weight in terms of performance and handling. The Speed 20 had the pedigree and

The Speed 20 was the car of choice for gentleman racers in the 1920s, and proved that the company was on top form – with handsome styling, superb road manners and excellent performance.

style of a true racer, and its long-bonneted styling barely concealed its large six-cylinder triple-carburettor 2511cc (153cu in) overhead-valve engine. Bodystyles offered on the Speed 20 were the standard sports tourer, drophead coupé and sports saloon bodies, and several attractive special versions were produced, by notable coachbuilders such as Cross & Ellis and Vanden Plas.

The introduction of SB, SC and SD models from 1934 onwards cemented the car's reputation. In true Alvis style, they were real pioneers. Their all-new four-speed all-synchromesh gearboxes were a world first, and independent transverse-leaf suspension at the front was also cutting edge. As the name suggests, the Speed 20 was both a competition car and a luxurious grand tourer.

MG MAGNETTE

UNITED KINGDOM 1932–36

ENGINE: 1271cc (78cu in),
  six-cylinder
POWER: 48.5bhp (36kW)
0–60MPH (96KM/H): n/a
TOP SPEED: 121km/h (75mph)
PRODUCTION TOTAL: 1351

Rather like the MG Magna, the Magnette was produced in a huge number of model variations, offering all things to all men. The Magnette ended up being offered as a four-seater, a four-door saloon, a two-door saloon, a four-seat open tourer, or a two-door sports body. A number of power and capacity options were also available on the car, all based on the existing small-block six-cylinder Magna engine.

The most attractive of all these variants was the Magnette K2, a pretty two-seater sports car with separate mudguards and a neatly stowed roof. In 1933, the entire range was given a facelift, and it became known as the KN Magnette. Boasting increased equipment levels, more streamlined bodywork and a power boost to 56bhp (42kW), this was a most desirable car. The Magna was a fine car to drive, with sharp steering and strong brakes, and all that held it back was an awkward gearbox.

The more modern-looking N-Type Magnette appeared at the 1935 Olympia Motor Show in London. The styling became more sculpted, and the roadholding benefited from stiffer chassis and a firmer ride. The Magnette was also the basis for the record-

breaking K3. Tazio Nuvolari won the 1933 Tourist Trophy at the wheel of a supercharged competition special.

That car also won the 1933 British Racing Drivers' Club 500 mile (800km) challenge, averaging more than 171km/h (106mph).

The Magnette became best known for being the car in which Tazio Nuvolari won the 1933 Tourist Trophy.

SS1

UNITED KINGDOM 1932–36

ENGINE: 2054cc (125cu in),
  six-cylinder
POWER: 45bhp (34kW)
0–60MPH (96KM/H): 31 seconds
TOP SPEED: 112km/h (70mph)
PRODUCTION TOTAL: 4254

When William Lyons and William Walmsley teamed up to form a small coachbuilding company in Blackpool, few would have suspected it was going to be the start of something very special. From small beginnings, producing motorcycle sidecars, the Swallow Sidecar and Coachbuilding Company was building special car bodies by the end of the 1920s. The car-producing offshoot of the company became known as SS Cars Ltd in 1928, and the Jaguar legend was born.

The name change also saw a move to Coventry – and within 10 years of the formation of Swallow Sidecars, the company introduced its hugely influential SS1 model.

Up to that point, the company had been rebodying Austin Sevens, but, with the help of the Standard Motor Company, Lyons was able to secure a ready supply of six-cylinder side-valve engines of either 2054cc (125cu in) or 2552cc (156cu in) and chassis to match. These engines' four-speed manual gearboxes were strong, and the semi-elliptic suspension meant the handling was good.

When the first Standard based SS was launched at the 1931 Olympia Motor Show in London, it caused a storm. It looked more flamboyant than most rival offerings – which was an important point to consider in a crowded marketplace. The major talking point of the car, though, was the price tag – just £310. That made it far more affordable than any of its rivals – although in truth that was because the engineering quality was not as high as the fantastically designed body hinted at.

It was soon clear that the car had not properly been developed, despite the rave reviews, so the company returned the following year with an entirely new car.

The new SS1 was quite different from the original car – it remained dramatically styled, but this time the car was better engineered, featuring running boards, more flowing front wings (fenders), a lower roofline to make it look even sleeker, and more power from its better breathing engine.

The performance of the new SS1 was improved appreciably, and the first car's top speed of 112km/h (70mph) was easily improved upon. Build quality was improved markedly, too, as William Lyons pushed the boat out with the car – and this time, there was enough room for four people to travel in comfort. On top of that, it was a delight to drive, thanks to its excellent handling and roadholding. An extra 18cm (7in) added to the wheelbase helped with that, giving the car a much more sure-footed feel on the road. The result was a sales smash. Whereas just 502 examples of the first SS1 were built, the second-generation car was far more popular, with 1249 cars built in the first year. No doubt adding a tourer to the range helped.

The SS1's final development came in 1934, when an all-new chassis was introduced. Sitting on the existing wheelbase, and boosted by the arrival of the Airline saloon, the SS had come of age. The Airline was controversial, though, and its streamlined styling won many detractors, even if it was a shape of things to come. The more traditional saloon and drophead coupé were for more conservative buyers.

Technically, the final model was on the ball. It had a synchromesh gearbox and larger 2143cc (133cu in) or 2663cc (163cu in) engines. Although the side-valve straight-sixes might have been conventional, they were lusty – and reprofiled camshafts helped to add that final sparkle.

In truth, the SS1 had always looked much faster than it really was, but that was compensated for by the keen price which was part of the car's appeal. The last SS1s redressed the balance.

The exquisitely styled SS1 may be one of the most desirable classic cars ever, but the Jaguar didn't actually offer much performance. However its keen price brought the exotic to a new market area.

TERRAPLANE SIX

UNITED STATES 1932–37

ENGINE: 3162cc (193cu in), six-cylinder
POWER: 70bhp (52kW)
0–60MPH (96KM/H): n/a
TOP SPEED: 144km/h (90mph)
PRODUCTION TOTAL: n/a

Terraplane was a lower-priced marque and model created by the Hudson Motor Car Company in order to boost production. In its maiden year, the car was branded as the Essex-Terraplane, but in 1933 the car became known simply as the Terraplane – until 1936, when it was brought fully into the Hudson line-up.

Powered by a 70bhp (52kW) six-cylinder side-valve 3162cc (193cu in) engine, the Terraplane-Six was a quick performer, thanks to a lightweight chassis. Hudson claimed that this endowed the car with the greatest power-to-weight ratio of any car in its class, although that remains debatable. When the Essex-Terraplane was launched, it was cheaper than the Essex, but it was nonetheless a significant step forward. In light of the dire economic conditions of the early 1930s, it was essential for Hudson's survival that it took this course of action – buyers could no longer afford the more expensive cars the company traditionally offered at the time.

FRAZER-NASH TT REPLICA

UNITED KINGDOM 1932–38

Cashing in on its success in the Tourist Trophy of the early 1930s, Frazer-Nash offered a replica racing car known as the T Replica. The car ended up being a huge success and became one of the most popular of all Nash cars during the company's golden years of the 1920s and 1930s. Like other 'Chain Gang' Nashes it had the famed unique transmission with separate and exposed chain and sprockets for each gear.

Lookswise, the car was a true thoroughbred in every sense of the word. It boasted stark lines, set-back radiator, cycle wings

An example of road car sales benefiting from competition success – the TT replica drew its name from the marque's British Tourist trophy successes.

(fenders) and squared-off rear fuel tank – and looked magnificent. Its racing pedigree meant that it also handled well – high-geared rack-and-pinion steering and a solid rear axle allowed on-the-limit cornering and controlled drifting.

Model designations such as Shelsey, Boulogne, Exeter, Colmore and Nurburg hinted at the car's competition roots.

The majority of cars had the four-cylinder Meadows engine with two overhead valves per cylinder,

but a few had the superb twin-camshaft Blackburn engine, which was capable of producing an impressive 150bhp (112kW) when supercharged. As always, the customer had the last say on the final car's specification.

ENGINE: 1496cc (91cu in), four-cylinder
POWER: 62bhp (46kW)
0–60MPH (96KM/H): 8.8 seconds
TOP SPEED: 130km/h (80mph)
PRODUCTION TOTAL: 85

HISPANO-SUIZA J12 FRANCE 1932–38

Here was a car of truly epic proportions. The Hispano-Suiza J12 boasted a massive 9424cc (575cu in) V12 powerplant – which was really a refined Birkigt wartime aero engine. That fact simply adds to the car's sheer impressive scale.

That actually made the J12 one of the most powerful and most technically advanced saloons of its time, and it could easily cruise at

161km/h (100mph) all day long – fuel economy permitting. In fact, such was the scale of this supercar, it directly rivalled that great 'white elephant' the Bugatti Royale, in terms of prestige and sheer inefficiency.

Although it was a huge car – and it had an enormous wheelbase of 4.01m (13.3ft) – the size of the engine and gearbox meant that there was little room in the

passenger compartment for more than two people – and that made it a car of sheer decadence. The three-speed gearbox had ill-judged ratios, though, and frequent gearchanges were demanded when driving in hilly terrain.

A number of bespoke bodystyles exist, thanks to the efforts of European coachbuilders. The most elegant of these was the Saoutchick two-seater touring, which boasted

incredibly beautiful flowing lines. Hispano-Suiza later developed the Type 68-Bis, which boasted an 11.3-litre (690cu in) V12 engine.

ENGINE: 9424cc (575cu in), 12-cylinder
POWER: 190bhp (142kW)
0–60MPH (96KM/H): n/a
TOP SPEED: 161km/h (100mph)
PRODUCTION TOTAL: n/a

FORD UK MODEL Y UNITED KINGDOM 1932–39

ENGINE: 933cc (57cu in), four-cylinder
POWER: 23.4bhp (17kW)
0–60MPH (96KM/H): n/a
TOP SPEED: 96km/h (60mph)
PRODUCTION TOTAL: 157,668

By the 1930s, the fastest growing sector in the United Kingdom was the 8hp market. The Austin Seven and Morris Eight were mainstays here; Ford wanted a slice of the cake, but it had to move fast. The Model A's imminent demise meant that the Y needed to be developed in record time.

Ford duly delivered, going from drawing board to UK production line within a year. The Model Y's arrival sealed the future of Ford's Dagenham factory – without it, the plant would have closed. Within months of its introduction, the new car gave Ford half of the crucial UK 8hp (6kW) market. Part of its appeal was the bargain price. The Model Y Popular sold for just £100.

By 1933, the Model Y's styling had evolved. The radiator shell was lengthened and the bumpers

dipped attractively in the middle. Instruments were moved from the middle of the dash to directly in front of the driver. A top speed of

96km/h (60mph) was no great shakes, but, importantly, the Model Y gave many UK residents their first taste of motoring.

The Model Y's keen price and enticing specification meant that it became a huge success for Ford.

CITROËN 10CV FRANCE 1933–34

Consider the 10CV as the calm before the storm – it was one of the last conventional Citroëns before the Traction Avant arrived in a flourish of style panache.

The 10CV was the last of the old guard – a conservative product through and through, the C4-based car offered no surprises whatsoever. It shared the C4's rear-wheel drive layout, and boasted a four-cylinder side-valve engine.

Styling was old-school upright and right for its day, although the sloping front grille hinted at things to come and demonstrated that Citroën was at least considering aerodynamics.

The most noteworthy aspect of the 10CV was its one-piece body, built using American equipment, and the first appearance of the famous double chevron motif on the grille. There were no shortages

of options, and, with the range including the 8CV and the 15CV, that opened out the number of model permutations available to a staggering 69 in all.

Two distinct versions of the 10CV were available, known as the Light 12, which used a shortened wheelbase, and the Big 12. There was even the option to accommodate up to seven passengers in some versions.

There were Slough-built cars for the United Kingdom, and they featured synchromesh four-speed gearboxes and 12-volt electrics.

ENGINE: 1767cc (108cu in), four-cylinder
POWER: 36bhp (27kW) at 3200rpm
0–60MPH (96KM/H): n/a
TOP SPEED: 100km/h (62mph)
PRODUCTION TOTAL: 49,249

FORD 40 SERIES

ENGINE: 3622cc (221cu in),
eight-cylinder
POWER: 75bhp (56kW)
0–60MPH (96KM/H): 18 seconds
TOP SPEED: 140km/h (87mph)
PRODUCTION TOTAL: 485,700

When Henry Ford announced the V8 in 1932 he made history. The engine may not have been anything too special, but, when combined with typical Ford value pricing, it emerged as a truly remarkable product. For the following year, Ford combined that engine with the new Model 40 Series range, to offer V8 motoring in a huge range of bodystyles – in a competitively priced package.

The 40 Series had a stretched wheelbase – 284.5cm (112in) – and a well-engineered X-member double-drop chassis. Ford had cottoned on to the value of styling,

and this car was no different. It had sweeping front and rear wings (fenders), a new radiator design with vertical bars slanted back to match the inclined windscreen, and appealing acorn-shaped headlight shells. The one-piece bumpers with a centre 'V' dip were striking.

The new dashboard design featured an attractive machine-turned panel – and all the instruments were lined up directly in the driver's line of sight. A new ignition system meant that the V8 ran better than ever, and improved cooling, as well as a higher compression ratio and aluminium cylinder head, boosted the power output to 75bhp (56kW).

The 40 Series may not have looked all that exciting, but thanks to the addition of that V8 engine, it proved to be a remarkably successful product.

SINGER NINE

ENGINE: 972cc (59cu in),
four-cylinder
POWER: 9hp (7kW)
0–60MPH (96KM/H): n/a
TOP SPEED: n/a
PRODUCTION TOTAL: n/a

The Singer Junior was easily one of the most popular small cars in Britain during the 1930s, but, towards the end of its life, the Junior's sales began to wane as smaller cars grew less fashionable. When it came to producing a replacement, Singer successfully made its new car, the Nine, look visually very similar, in order to maintain that popularity.

Small car sales had been dropping at the beginning of the 1930s, and larger cars were the order of the day. As a result, the company upscaled the new car in order to meet demand. When the Nine was launched, in 1933, it was powered by the same overhead camshaft engine used in the Junior Special, but its coachbuilt saloon body was larger than its predecessor. A good-value product, the Nine was well equipped for the money and boasted opening windows all round, ashtrays in the front, a clock, a fuel gauge and leather seat trim.

In 1933 an all-new engine arrived. It shared the 972cc (59cu in) capacity of the original, but was built more sturdily. A face-lift also saw the introduction of a lengthened and widened chassis, improving handling and stability.

In a market that was rapidly becoming more affluent, the Singer Nine proved to be a well-judged product. It offered an advanced overhead camshaft engine and a good-looking design for a remarkably low price.

RAILTON TERRAPLANE

In an early example of platform sharing, both the US car company Hudson and the British carmaker Railton produced their own cars based on the US-developed Terraplane chassis. The companies would eventually move closer together to design and produce a new range of straight-eight engines. However, the US and UK cars built on the Terraplane chassis had a very different feel.

Hudsons were elegant touring machines, while Railtons were a far more exciting proposition. They were marketed as lower cost alternatives to cars built by Lagonda, Alvis and Bentley.

The Terraplane was available in a wide range of bodies: tourers, saloons, convertibles, limousines and even racing specials. The car's strong point was its performance. In standard form, the Railton could accelerate from 0–60mph (96km/h) in just 13 seconds, and it went on to a top speed of 161km/h (100mph). Race-tuned examples were even faster.

The imposing straight-eight engines were very strong and sweet, but used plenty of fuel on the way to achieving their results. The best figure an owner could expect was 17L/100km (16mpg), even if the car were driven gently.

Despite the success of the Terraplane, Railton would not restart car production once World War II was over.

ENGINE: 4010cc (245cu in), eight-cylinder
POWER: 124bhp (92kW)
0–60MPH (96KM/H): 13 seconds
TOP SPEED: 161km/h (100mph)
PRODUCTION TOTAL: 1379

BUGATTI TYPE 57

ENGINE: 3257cc (199cu in), eight-cylinder
POWER: 135bhp (101kW)
0–60MPH (96KM/H): n/a
TOP SPEED: 153km/h (95mph)
PRODUCTION TOTAL: 683

For many, the Type 57 was the last of the great Bugattis; however, it was actually Ettore Bugatti's son Jean who was mostly responsible for its introduction. A final flowering of the great marque, the Type 57 was an effort to build an exotic-looking, luxurious and fast grand tourer – and in those aims it succeeded.

An advanced 3257cc (199cu in) double-overhead camshaft eight-cylinder engine (featuring a one-piece cast-iron block with an integral cylinder head) powered the car, and it was suspended by semi-elliptic springs, with reversed quarter elliptics at the rear. Created by Jean Bugatti, the touring, saloon, coach, coupé and cabriolet bodies were exquisite, and the remarkable Atlantic coupé was stunning, It was a curvaceous, futuristic-looking design featuring a fin running down its centre, and remains a design icon to this day.

The Type 57C could be had with a supercharged 160bhp (119kW) engine, but that was trumped by the 175bhp (130kW) 57S. The last hurrah was the 57SC, though, which was powered by a supercharged version of the 57S engine, boosted to 200bhp (149kW). It was capable of around 200km/h (124mph).

Jean Bugatti died while testing a 57C-based racing car in 1939 – ironically for a race that never took place due to the outbreak of World War II.

The last Bugatti to be built when creators Ettore and Jean were in control, the Type 57 is regarded as being the last great Bugatti.

PIERCE-ARROW SILVER ARROW

Pierce-Arrow had endured a tough time during the recession-torn 1920s. First bought by Studebaker in 1928, it found itself sold to a conglomerate of Buffalo, New York, businessmen in 1933. These were sad times for the once great company. Under new management, the company's first project was to create a car that would star at the 1933 Chicago Exposition – a feat it comfortably achieved with the Silver Arrow. Designed by stylist Philip Wright, a close friend of Pierce-Arrow vice president Roy Faulkner, the Silver Arrow was quite simply stunning. It featured handcrafted teardrop-shaped bodywork, an odd raised rear 'dormer' window and a pair of spare wheels stashed behind secret panels in the front wings (fenders).

The interior was also suitably opulent – plush velour seats were complemented by lashings of maple veneer, and rear seat passengers enjoyed their own set of instruments. Amusingly, this was so that passengers could ensure the chauffeur was obeying the law. It also had a radio set built into a floor-mounted pod. The Silver Arrow never made it into full-scale production – although 10 cars were built and sold for $7500 to buyers who loved the prototype.

ENGINE: 7030cc (429cu in), 12-cylinder
POWER: 235bhp (175kW)
0–60MPH (96KM/H): n/a
TOP SPEED: 185km/h (115mph)
PRODUCTION TOTAL: 10

RILEY IMP

The Riley Nine may have donated its engine, but there was precious little else shared between it and the new Imp sports car. The larger family would have struggled to form the basis for a stunningly low-slung sports car with styling considered by many to be even more effective than that of the MG TC. Featuring flowing wings (fenders), upright headlights and a pretty chrome radiator grille, the Riley Imp seemed to have it all.

An all-new short chassis that provided great handling resulted in a car that was fun to drive, and there was a transmission choice between either an effective ENV pre-selector arrangement or a racier four-speed close-ratio 'box.

The ubiquitous Riley 1087cc (66cu in) side-valve four was a tight fit under the narrow bonnet (hood), and that meant access for servicing was difficult. A pair of twin SU carburettors gave it a useful boost in the power department over the Riley Nine.

On the road, it was all about fun, not speed – the Imp struggled to top 115km/h (70mph). The balanced chassis and sharp steering, however, meant that it could be driven with great gusto. This was a car that was all about having fun in the bends.

ENGINE: 1087cc (66cu in), four-cylinder
POWER: n/a
0–60MPH (96KM/H): n/a
TOP SPEED: 121km/h (75mph)
PRODUCTION TOTAL: n/a

RILEY MPH

ENGINE: 1726cc (105cu in), six-cylinder
POWER: n/a
0–60MPH (96KM/H): n/a
TOP SPEED: 145km/h (90mph)
PRODUCTION TOTAL: n/a

Slotting in the range above the impressive Imp, the Riley MPH was another attempt by the company to impress enthusiast drivers. The six-cylinder MPH was another Riley with impeccable performance car credentials.

The styling was a masterpiece of well-considered and tasteful design, and featured a racing-style rounded rear end and flowing wings (fenders) that evoked those on the Imp. On top of that, it featured the same ornate grille and large dished headlights.

With a chassis based on Riley's 1933 Tourist Trophy racer, the MPH was bound to be good. Underslung at the rear, the chassis sloped upwards to the front of the car and offered plenty of grip and masses of driver feedback from its communicative rear end.

For the MPH, the choice of overhead-valve straight-sixes developed for the 12/6 and 15/6 saloon models were suitably uprated in line with the new car's sporting aspirations. Upgrades included magneto ignition, twin SU carburettors and a six-branch exhaust – the end result was a glorious engine note.

The MPH proved that Riley was adept at producing quick and appealing, but rather expensive, open-topped sportscars.

The extras did not stop there, though, because the MPH could be specified with more performance updates. These included fitting massive brake drums with built-in cooling fins, and a choice of a close-ratio three-speed gearbox or pre-select transmission.

SUNBEAM TWENTY-FIVE

From successful car maker in the 1920s, Sunbeam struggled to maintain its momentum into the next decade – the problem seemed to be maintaining profitability. With very little finance available for investment in new models, Sunbeam's only option for developing new cars was to revise existing models. Therefore, the Sunbeam Twenty-Five had its roots firmly laid in the earlier 1929

Sixteen – but with the addition of a hefty price tag of £875.

The Sixteen was upgraded to become the Twenty in 1933, and that in turn was upgraded to become the Twenty-Five in 1934. Despite their long-in-the-tooth underpinnings, the cars retained their elegantly styled bodywork, and engines and suspension set-ups, which were up to the standards of the opposition. Still,

that problem of failing profitability continued – Sunbeam made no money building these cars.

The car was very pleasant to drive, and, although it weighed more than 2000kg (4400lb), the Twenty-Five had a 3317cc (202cu in) straight-six engine and a four-speed all-synchromesh gearbox that delivered a top speed of 128km/h (80mph). Sharp steering added to the driver's enjoyment.

In the end, poor finances weakened the company to such an extent that, in 1935, it fell into the ownership of the Rootes Group.

ENGINE: 3317cc (202cu in), six-cylinder
POWER: n/a
0–60MPH (96KM/H): n/a
TOP SPEED: 128km/h (80mph)
PRODUCTION TOTAL: n/a

TRIUMPH DOLOMITE STRAIGHT EIGHT

ENGINE: 1990cc (121cu in), eight-cylinder
POWER: 120bhp (89kW) at 5500rpm
0–60MPH (96KM/H): n/a
TOP SPEED: 177km/h (110mph)
PRODUCTION TOTAL: 3

Despite being the most technically advanced car built by Triumph until that time, the supercharged Dolomite Straight Eight failed spectacularly on the marketplace. Its amazing technical specification meant that it would end up becoming one of the most recognized and notable models ever produced by the company.

The mastermind behind the Dolomite Straight Eight was Donald Healey, who had joined Triumph in 1933 as experimental manager. He saw the need for a large-engined British sports car to compete against the best of the foreign opposition in international competition – and drew on the

Alfa Romeo 2300 for the basis of the Straight Eight.

Apparently flattered by the imitation, Alfa Romeo gave Healey its full approval for the Dolomite's development. Triumph began working on a project that would end up creating a near identical copy of the eight-cylinder Alfa Romeo, engine and all – although with a smaller capacity. The Alfa's supercharger was even retained, complemented by a beautiful Italianate open sports body.

Considering the company was in financial peril during the car's development, it was a brave move. Despite Healey's laudable ambitions for the car, only three examples were sold, and production was halted in April 1935.

Despite being a technical tour de force with its supercharged straight-eight engine, the Dolomite was a sales disaster with only three built.

ASTON MARTIN ULSTER

ENGINE: 1495cc (91cu in), four-cylinder
POWER: n/a
0–60MPH (96KM/H): n/a
TOP SPEED: 161km/h (100mph)
PRODUCTION TOTAL: 24

The mid-1930s were a torrid time for the Aston Martin Car Company – as it lurched through yet another financial crisis. Aston Martin financial backers, the Bertelli brothers, had a serious disagreement with one of the company founders, Lionel Martin. As a result, Martin left the company. This had a serious impact on the company, as it had now lost a figure crucial to the

The Aston Martin Ulster was the perfect embodiment of 1930s competition cars, including fold-down screens and bonnet straps.

design of the best Aston models. The Ulster was born amid these problems, and actually emerged as the last good Aston Martin before production of the DB range commenced after World War II.

The Ulster was extremely fast and born out of the the factory's racing efforts. Its engine was Aston's standard 1.5-litre (91cu in) four-cylinder unit, but with big valves and heavy-duty springs

fitted. A Laystall crankshaft, high compression ratio and large SU carburettors, added to the mix and resulted in a significant power boost for the compact engine. At the time of its appearance, the

Ulster was the most powerful Aston Martin. In the right conditions, it could top out at more than 161km/h (100mph), and that makes it as desirable now as it was in the 1930s.

BMW 303
GERMANY 1933–34

ENGINE: 1175cc (72cu in), six-cylinder
POWER: 30bhp (22kW)
0–60MPH (96KM/H): n/a
TOP SPEED: 105km/h (65mph)
PRODUCTION TOTAL: n/a

BMW's car-building reputation might have been established by the Austin Seven-clone 3/15, but the company realized the real money lay with the middle classes. The 1933 BMW 303 was the first car produced by the company to emphasize the ambitions of this young carmaker.

It was the first car to wear the now-famous BMW kidney-shaped grille, which has been incorporated into every BMW since,

After enjoying considerable success with the Dixi, BMW went upmarket with the 303. It was marketed as: 'the smallest big car in the world.'

and the 303 was the first in a very long line of straight-six-powered cars built by the Bavarian motor company. The new 1175cc (72cu in) power unit was an expansion of the four-cylinder unit already used in an earlier BMW, the AM-4.

The interior was commodious, which prompted BMW to promote the 303 as the 'smallest big car in the world'.

A good-looking car, the 303 was available in a choice of two-door saloon, cabriolet or a two-seater sports car. BMW's downward expansion of the range saw the introduction of the cheaper four-cylinder 309 version – and the more expensive 1500cc (92cu in) 315 and 319 both signalled the company's move upwards.

After that came the 315/1 and the 319/1, a pair of exclusive, expensive two-seater sports roadsters which were built in very low numbers. It was these cars that really made the motoring world take notice of BMW.

MG P-TYPE
UNITED KINGDOM 1934–36

It was a tough task to take on, and in the end MG decided to replace its famous Midget by playing it safe. The new MG PA sported a marginally longer wheelbase – and its engine was boosted by a stronger, three-bearing crankshaft. Other than that, however, only the unusual airline coupé bodywork stood out as a major step forwards.

Dynamically, the PA was better. Its steering was sharper, which made all the difference in terms of response. The best bits of the Midget were retained – notably, its appealing exhaust note.

The P-Type gained a very unusual feature – a combined rev counter and speedometer, which loaded a single gauge with a pair of needles and two sets of

numbers. It was a great idea, but ended up annoying drivers, who found the display rather confusing.

It was a short-lived car – and the PA was soon replaced by the PB in 1935. That made a further step forwards thanks to a larger-capacity engine offering more performance. The 939cc (57cu in) engine produced 43bhp (32kW), and fun was given a major boost.

The PP was also equipped with a conventional speedometer and rev counter, and a smoother gearbox.

ENGINE: 847cc (52cu in), four-cylinder
POWER: 40bhp (30kW)
0–60MPH (96KM/H): n/a
TOP SPEED: 121km/h (75mph)
PRODUCTION TOTAL: 2526

DE SOTO AIRFLOW
UNITED STATES 1934–37

ENGINE: 3958cc (242cu in), six-cylinder
POWER: 100bhp (75kW)
0–60MPH (96KM/H): 20 secs
TOP SPEED: 121km/h (75mph)
PRODUCTION TOTAL: 31,797

De Soto was living on borrowed time during the 1930s – times were tough and its owner, Chrysler, found that De Soto and Dodge were too close on the marketplace; they had effectively become in-house rivals. This was no wise state of affairs, and Chrysler figured that it would need

to reposition De Soto in relation to Dodge in order to ensure the company's survival. As a result, DeSoto was pushed upmarket into a higher price bracket than Dodge, but still somewhere below that of Chrysler. To further highlight the differences, from 1934, all DeSotos received Chrysler's streamlined Airflow styling.

Well ahead of its time, the De Soto Airflow's wings (fenders) were

The De Soto Airflow was a startling attempt at introducing aerodynamic styling to an unconvinced US public.

faired into the bodywork, and the headlights became part of the car. The bonnet (hood) extended down to the front axle and had horizontal louvres – just like a modern car. The underpinnings were advanced, too, and the Airflow boasted a monocoque bodyshell. The buying public baulked, however, at the new-wave style. Consequently, sales were disappointing. De Soto sold more Airflows than Chrysler – some 15,000 units compared to 11,000 for the parent company.

Sales tailed off the following two years, and De Soto, spooked by the market flop, dropped the Airflow model and replaced it with the more conventional Airstream range in 1935. Minor styling changes heralded the final two seasons, but these changes were not enough to stop the rot.

SINGER LE MANS

UNITED KINGDOM 1934–37

Singer competed successfully in the 1933 Le Mans 24-hour race with a Works Nine, and the obvious next step was to market a road car that capitalized on the good result. It launched a road car based on 9hp (7kW) and named after the famous French circuit a mere three months after the race. The Singer Le Mans therefore possessed the right name and the sporting credentials to compete with the MG TA.

Although the front end had a familiar look, the rear end was completely new, sporting stylish twin spare wheels, which were fixed behind a slab fuel tank. Befitting the name, the car's engine was more highly tuned, receiving a high-lift camshaft, raised compression ratio, a higher capacity aluminium sump and a counter-balanced crankshaft. The changes combined with the close ratio gearbox meant that the Le Mans drove as well as it looked.

It originally featured rear-hinged doors, but the design was quickly revised following a spate of failures that saw the doors fly open on corners – not a good feature on a competition car.

Needless to say, many owners of the earlier cars retro-fitted the modified doors to their own cars.

ENGINE: 972cc (59cu in), four-cylinder
POWER: 40bhp (30kW)
0–60MPH (96KM/H): 27 seconds
TOP SPEED: 120km/h (75mph)
PRODUCTION TOTAL: 500

TRIUMPH GLORIA

UNITED KINGDOM 1934–37

ENGINE: 1991cc (121cu in), six-cylinder
POWER: 55bhp (41kW) at 4500rpm
0–60MPH (96KM/H): 22 seconds
TOP SPEED: 120km/h (75mph)
PRODUCTION TOTAL: about 6000

The Dolomite might have been a glorious failure, but it did not prevent Triumph continuing its plan to move upmarket. The new Gloria model marked the point where the new direction gained momentum – and the company was proud of its new car, marketing it as the 'smartest car in the land' or the 'queen of cars'.

The creation of competition driver Donald Healey, the Gloria was offered with four- and six-cylinder Coventry Climax engines of 1087cc (66cu in) and 1476cc (90cu in), respectively, and with a variety of saloon and open bodies. These included the sporting Monte Carlo Tourer, which had its own special 1232cc (75cu in) twin carburettor engine.

In 1935, the company focused all its efforts on the Gloria, dropping all other models from the range. New bodystyles and engine options were offered, including the exotic-looking Flow-free model with fashionable aerodynamic, art deco styling. The Gloria Six was the most developed of the lot, featuring a 1991cc (121cu in) engine. Triumph emphasized its upmarket ambitions for the car by adding a new Gloria radiator mascot – a winged lady that was reminiscent of the Rolls-Royce Spirit of Ecstasy. Sales were not great, though, and production ceased in 1937.

The open-topped Triumph was well priced and a big success in the UK, but it wasn't enough to guarantee the success of the company that built it.

CITROËN TRACTION AVANT

FRANCE 1934–57

ENGINE: 1911cc (117cu in), four-cylinder
POWER: 56bhp (42kW) at 4250rpm
0–60MPH (96KM/H): 22.1 seconds
TOP SPEED: 122km/h (76mph)
PRODUCTION TOTAL: 806,793

Despite being one of the most advanced cars to hit the market, in a sad irony, the Traction Avant is also the car that hastened the Citroën company's descent into bankruptcy – and, indirectly, the death of André Citroën himself. It was certainly a revolutionary car for the mid-1930s, and the Traction Avant can be heralded as the first mass-produced front-wheel drive car to be built by a major car manufacturer. Sadly, however, it cost so much to develop that the money ran out and the tyre company, Michelin, ended up bailing out the company in 1934. Shortly after that, André Citroën died from cancer.

Unitary construction and independent suspension were other Traction Avant innovations apart from front-wheel drive, and this mechanical combination

73

resulted in a car that raised the bar for all other manufacturers of saloon cars in terms of ride and handling. There were problems initially, but the long-lived 1911cc (117cu in) engine that appeared in 1935 was not one of them.

The range included the practical Commerciale, with its hatchback door, and the Big Six, which married smooth power to that sensational dynamic package. It was, however, the Light 15 and its longer wheelbase Big 15 brother that were always the big sellers.

The Citroën Traction Avant was front wheel drive and built using a unitary construction method. Sadly this costly car hastened Citroën's descent into bankruptcy.

CHEVROLET EC STANDARD

ENGINE: 3409cc (208cu in), six-cylinder
POWER: 74bhp (55kW)
0–60MPH (96KM/H): 25 seconds
TOP SPEED: 112km/h (70 mph)
PRODUCTION TOTAL: 202,773

In the 1930s, the Detroit-based car manufacturer Chevrolet embarked on a programme that would give its cars a technological advantage over all of its immediate opposition. In 1934, the company introduced independent 'Knee Action' front suspension, and that put it well ahead of its rival Ford, which stuck to old-fashioned transverse leaf springs.

This move was reason enough for Chevrolet to overtake Ford as the bestselling car manufacturer in the United States, as it found customers clamouring for these exciting new cars.

The EA Master Deluxe series was the new model that was to spearhead that technical push, even though there was a price. To fight Ford's more value-for-money products, the company offered the more basic transverse leaf sprung ED and EC Standard models as well – and sold them at a competitive price.

The styling broke new ground, being similar to the previous DA, but the EC now had body-coloured headlight shells and, inside, the instruments were moved to a position in front of the driver's eyes, following Ford's lead. Under the bonnet (hood), the 'Blue Flame' six-cylinder engine was further updated to enhance appeal.

The interior specification may have been spartan, but there were plenty of extras that could be ordered. These included bumper overriders, a radio, a heater, a cigar lighter, spot lights, wire wheels and a rear-view mirror. In terms of bodystyles, the two-door sports roadsters, coupés and a phaeton were joined by four-door saloons.

SS SS90

The SS90 was a derivative of the groundbreaking SS1, with modifications to make it more responsive. The existing car's chassis had 38cm (15in) removed from the wheelbase, and the effective beam front axle on semi-elliptic springs was retained. The SS1's 2.7-litre (163cu in) side-valve six-cylinder engine was tuned slightly – and that pushed the SS90's top speed to around 144km/h (90mph), which was a very competitive figure.

By the time the SS90 went on sale, SS Cars Ltd was already riding high – and it should have scored a huge hit with its new car. The price was right at £395, and SS should have been struggling to cope with demand – but the reality was that a mere 23 examples of the SS90 were produced in 1936. The reason was simple – its six-cylinder engine was developed to incorporate an overhead-valve cylinder head, its displacement rose to 3.5 litres (214cu in) and, in doing so, it became the SS100.

The result is that the SS100 remains one of the most sought-after pre–World War II cars, whereas its all but identical-looking if slightly less powerful cousin that came a year earlier has been practically forgotten. The truth is, however, that the SS90 of 1935 possesses just as much charisma as its more widely recognized younger brother.

ENGINE: 2663cc (163cu in), six-cylinder
POWER: 70bhp (52kW)
0–60MPH (96KM/H): 17.5 seconds
TOP SPEED: 144km/h (90mph)
PRODUCTION TOTAL: 23

AUBURN 851 SPEEDSTER

ENGINE: 4596cc (280cu in),
  eight-cylinder
POWER: 130bhp (97kW)
0–60MPH (96KM/H): n/a
TOP SPEED: 170km/h (105mph)
PRODUCTION TOTAL: 500

In 1903, the Eckhardt Carriage Company set up an independent operation to make exclusive motor cars in Auburn, Indiana. From this factory, an offshoot brand known as Auburn was created – to build luxury cars for the super-rich. Like so many supercars of the era, the Auburns were handsome yet imposing, and usually were powered by huge eight- or 12-cylinder engines.

Although the Great Depression of the 1930s did its best to deplete the complement of producers of exclusive cars, Auburn managed to survive under Erret Cord, founder of Cord cars. He had joined the company in 1924, and kept its head above water until the mid-1930s. The company found itself in trouble by 1934, however, and as a last throw of the dice, Auburn developed the beautiful 851 Speedster, hoping that the innovative car would entice buyers back into the fold.

When it was launched, it was indeed an exclusive car, and it actually became the United States' most expensive car, which was hardly the medicine needed for a car company to survive a period of belt tightening. Still, there was no arguing about its beautiful boat-tail styling and sumptuous cabin – it was a wonderful car.

The 4.6-litre (280cu in) supercharged side-valve straight-eight engine pushed the 851 Speedster up to at least 161km/h (100mph), so its performance credentials were spot-on. The car never made money, however, and the company was forced into liquidation in 1937.

The 851 Speedster remains one of the most famous cars ever produced in America, and its swooping boat-tailed styling and advanced technical specification meant that it was adored by well-heeled customers.

TATRA TYPE 77

ENGINE: 2970cc (181cu in),
  eight-cylinder
POWER: 60bhp (45kW)
0–60MPH (96KM/H): n/a
TOP SPEED: 137km/h (85mph)
PRODUCTION TOTAL: n/a

Designed by Hans Ledwinka, the Tatra Type 77 was unlike anything else available on the market at the time – in terms of both styling and engineering. The backbone chassis was a standard Ledwinka design, but it was a pioneer because it featured a rear-mounted air-cooled 2970cc (181cu in) V8 engine.

The swing-axle suspension and unconventional engine layout led to 'interesting' handling, but the car's efficient aerodynamics were clearly demonstrated by a top speed of 137km/h (85mph), in spite of its not-inconsiderable bulk of 1678kg (3700lb). Specifying the optional 3400cc (207cu in) powerplant which became available in 1935, that tally was lifted by a further 8km/h (5mph). According to contemporary road tests, heavy weight resulted in poor acceleration, and the car also suffered from front-end lift at speed.

If one compares the Tatra Type 77 with any of its contemporaries, however, the car's unashamedly advanced design shines through – and in many ways it was years ahead of its time. Although the Citroën Traction Avant boasts a layout that does not look unusual in the twenty-first century, it was the Tatra that was most widely mimicked in the coming decades.

Full-width styling and a commodious interior were also Type 77 trademarks, and it is a pity that it was not recognized as an engineering marvel in the Western Hemisphere.

WOLSELEY WASP

ENGINE: 1069cc (65cu in),
   four-cylinder
POWER: n/a
0–60MPH (96KM/H): n/a
TOP SPEED: 96km/h (60mph)
PRODUCTION TOTAL: 5815

During the 1930s, Wolseley had a rapid model turnaround. In 1934, the Nine was introduced – a car for people who wanted a Wolseley, but did not need six-cylinder in their life. The overhead camshaft four-cylinder Nine proved popular, but lasted only one year, to be replaced by a new model called the Wasp in 1935. That also lasted only one year, but, unlike the previous Hornet, only closed saloon versions of the Wasp were offered – and it was clear that this was no sports car.

While the new name promised much, in reality, the Wasp was little different from the car that it replaced. The main changes were centred on the bigger engine, which had been increased to 1069cc (65cu in) from the earlier car's 1018cc (62cu in).

Other changes – all minor – included the adoption of Easiclean wheels in place of the Nine's spoked items, and 12-volt electrics and coil ignition were also welcome new additions to the specification sheet.

The new car's powerplant retained the pervious car's advanced overhead-camshaft layout, and the four-speed synchromesh gearbox was also carried over into the Wasp. What's more, the Wasp retained the previous car's all-round hydraulic brakes and semi-elliptic suspension – front and rear.

The deliberately conservative Wolseley Wasp was aimed at customers who wanted unchallenging but high quality motoring. It lasted one year.

HRG 1.5-LITRE

ENGINE: 1497cc (91cu in),
   four-cylinder
POWER: 58bhp (43kW)
0–60MPH (96KM/H): 18.4 seconds
TOP SPEED: 145km/h (90mph)
PRODUCTION TOTAL: 26

in true classic style, revealing the tubular front axle, reversed quarter-elliptical front springs and huge cable-operated drum brakes. At the rear of the car, suspension was by semi-elliptic leaves sliding in trunnions.

The HRG 1.5-Litre was a pleasure to drive, though. It was flexible, and soon became one of the mainstays of the club racing scene. It seemed most at home when being driven on fast roads and in hillclimbs, trials or rallying.

As a back-to-basics motoring experience, enthusiasts adored the HRG 1.5-Litre when it was new. With a Meadows four-cylinder engine and twin SU carburettors it was quick and had handling to match.

Named after its three founders, E.A. Halford, G.H. Robins and H.R. Godfrey, HRG produced cars that were not exactly state of the art technically, but were both well liked by enthusiasts and successful in competition.

The 1.5 two-seater sports cars were produced at the Tolworth works in Surrey, England, and were very purposeful in their design. There was little in the way of styling, with running boards and cutaway doors.

A Meadows four-cylinder engine was fitted, usually equipped with twin SU carburettors and a Scintilla magneto. The gearbox was a Moss unit that did not have the luxury of synchromesh – but was sweet and accurate enough for competition drivers. The upright chromed radiator was set back

PONTIAC EIGHT

ENGINE: 3801cc (232cu in),
  eight-cylinder
POWER: n/a
0–60MPH (96KM/H): n/a
TOP SPEED: 137km/h (85mph)
PRODUCTION TOTAL: n/a

The Pontiac Eight formed the mainstay of the Michigan-based company's line-up during the 1930s, and it is easy to see why. It was a pleasantly styled and comfortable car that customers found rewarding to drive. The 3.8-litre (232cu in) side-valve V8 that had a distinctive exhaust note never delivered particularly quick performance, but was well suited to the car's loyal customer base.

The Eight boasted a vast model range which included standard and long wheelbase saloons, two- and four-seater soft tops and a sports coupé bodystyle. The conventional chassis featured independent front suspension and a live rear axle, while all versions came with hydraulic brakes – and this resulted in pleasant dynamics which suited the car.

Light steering and supple ride made the Eight a good touring machine, but these positive points were countered by a gearbox that lacked a synchromesh on the lower ratios, and made driving in heavy traffic a bit of a chore.

The 1937 models featured more rounded frontal styling, a new radiator grille and repositioned headlights, and a larger 4.1-litre (250cu in) engine was added to the range. These cars also gained that much-needed but previously missing all-synchromesh gearbox.

The Pontiac Eight was one of America's most popular cars – and with its tuneful side-valve V8 engine and pleasant styling, it's easy to understand why.

ALFA ROMEO 8C2900

Alfa Romeo remained right at the forefront of automotive technology in the 1930s. When designing a replacement for the successful 6C, Jano ensured that the new range would build on that car's strengths. The legendary straight-eight twin-camshaft engine with its two four-cylinder blocks and twin-cylinder heads joined to a common crank, with camshaft drive up the centre of the unit was retained. And that glorious engine was installed in chassis of two different lengths to suit enthusiastic drivers' needs.

The shortest (Corto) was used for Grand Prix racing in a car fitting called the Monza, and the longer (Lungo), formed the basis of a rakish two-seater sports car. The racing 8C2300 demonstrated its prowess by displacing Britain's big Bentleys at Le Mans, winning the classic 24-hour event from 1931 to 1934 – achieved through its admirable lightness and agility.

The engine progressively grew through 2.6 litres (159cu in) and 2.9 litres (177cu in) before the ultimate version appeared sporting twin-superchargers in 1935. An all-new chassis with Grand Prix-type fully independent suspension was required to harness the power of that beast. This was the world's fastest pre–World War II production sports machine, and came with a selection of beautiful handcrafted bodies from Touring and Pininfarina.

ENGINE: 2905cc (177cu in),
  eight-cylinder
POWER: 180bhp (134kW)
0–60MPH (96KM/H): n/a
TOP SPEED: 184km/h (115mph)
PRODUCTION TOTAL: 30

HUDSON EIGHT

ENGINE: 4162cc (254cu in),
  eight-cylinder
POWER: 113bhp (84kW)
0–60MPH (96KM/H): n/a
TOP SPEED: 128km/h (80mph)
PRODUCTION TOTAL: n/a

The Hudson Company was founded by Detroit department store entrepreneur Joseph J. Hudson, and offered its first cars for sale in 1909. Early offerings such as the 20hp (15kW) Model 20 were underpowered, but became bestsellers in the United States.

The company lived on after Hudson's death in 1912 – and, in that same year, it launched its first six-cylinder car, the Model 6-54,

The Eight was Hudson's popular pre-war saloon offering, and featured a distinctive 'Waterfall' grille.

and the Hudson car company came of age. The Model 6-54 produced 54bhp (40kW) and was available in a number of different bodystyles. It was not long before the company proclaimed itself to be the world's largest manufacturer of six-cylinder cars.

The company had a number of firsts, including dual circuit brakes, dashboard oil-pressure and generator warning lights, and a balanced crankshaft – allowing it to rev more smoothly. However, in 1916, the four-cylinder engines were dropped altogether from the

range, and Hudson concentrated on what it knew best, adopting a one-model policy.

The 4739cc (289cu in) Super Six remained in production unchanged until the 1930s, when it was finally replaced by the straight-eight cars. The Eight was easily

identified by its exaggerated 'waterfall' chrome grille, and 'Electric Hand' electric gearshift – which became optional in 1935. The Eight also featured a 'safety engineered chassis' with hydraulic brakes and a secondary mechanical system for emergencies.

OLDSMOBILE EIGHT

UNITED STATES 1935–39

ENGINE: 3936cc (240cu in),
eight-cylinder
POWER: 80bhp (60kW)
0–60MPH (96KM/H): n/a
TOP SPEED: 137km/h (85mph)
PRODUCTION TOTAL: 155,618

Oldsmobile is one of the oldest manufacturers in the US car industry, and, although the man after whom the company was named, Ransom Eli Olds, left in 1904 to set up his own carmaking company known as REO, it continued on its successful way. Oldsmobile became a constituent company of the General Motors (GM) alliance and, like all GM's mainstream products, Oldsmobile's cars were touted as value-for-money competitors to Ford.

The Eight offered elegant styling and excellent levels of passenger space, for a modest price, and that emphasized the value-for-money ethos of the marque. Offered with two side-valve straight-eight

engines of 3.9-litre (238cu in) and 4.2-litre (256cu in) capacities, the Eight was quick. The larger version was capable of reaching a top speed of 145km/h (90mph). One major innovation of the Eight was that both versions were offered with a fully automatic gearbox – an industry first.

In 1938, the car was radically restyled and gained a new front end, with stylish streamlined looks, while the 3.9-litre (238cu in) engine was dropped. GM badge engineering entered the equation here – the later car shared its bodywork with the Pontiac De Luxe and Buick Special.

General Motors was truly coming of age during the 1930s, and the Oldsmobile Eight was a fine example of the company's badge engineering practices – sharing its body with the Pontiac De Luxe and Buick Special.

STUDEBAKER COMMANDER

UNITED STATES 1935–39

Studebaker cars occupied an interesting position in the market – they had premium levels of quality and equipment, but were offered at competitive prices. When the 1935 Studebaker Commander was introduced, it occupied the mid-slot in the range below the range-topping President and above the entry-level Dictator. The Commander was initially offered with the six- rather than

eight-cylinder engine, and this merely added to the massive total of 50 different variations in the company's range for sale.

Offered as a roadster, saloon or coupé, and in a variety of constantly changing specifications, the Commander found a willing public. Wheelbase changed twice during the production run – it was introduced with a 305cm (120in) wheelbase in 1930, then the eight-

cylinder Commander version received a shorter wheelbase of 297cm (117in) in 1932, before being stretched again in 1934 to 302cm (119in).

In 1935, the Commander was dropped from Studebaker's product line, only to be reinstated in 1937 when the name was applied to Studebaker's least expensive range, which was formerly known as the Studebaker Dictator.

In 1939, Studebaker introduced the Champion, and once again the Commander line was positioned as the mid-range vehicle.

ENGINE: 4064cc (248cu in),
six-cylinder
POWER: 75bhp (56kW)
0–60MPH (96KM/H): n/a
TOP SPEED: n/a
PRODUCTION TOTAL: n/a

MORRIS EIGHT

UNITED KINGDOM 1935–48

Much of Morris's success in the 1930s came from its Eight model, which was one of the most popular cars of the 1930s in the United Kingdom. Until the Eight's launch in 1935, Morris had been struggling financially, and it was only the outstanding sales figures of the Eight that helped to save the company from feeling the full effects of the economic depression which was to see off several of its competitors.

The car was influenced by Ford's products of the time – both in terms of styling (which looked like Ford's Model Y) and because of its side-valve engine design. Morris offered a further body variation, though – there was the choice of two- and four-seater tourer versions, and that added interest to the model range.

In 1938, the Eight was updated, with a slight restyle to match the other cars available in the Morris

range. The Series II changes included painted rather than plated radiator surrounds and disc (Easiclean) wheels to replace the previous wire-spoked ones. The engine and running gear, however, remained unchanged from the previous series.

For Morris, this new look was actually quite revolutionary, and the introduction of a four-speed gearbox was a step forwards. Following the end of World War II,

production of the Eight restarted and was to continue until 1948, when the new Issigonis-penned Minor replaced the (by-then) long-in-the-tooth Eight.

ENGINE: 918cc (56cu in),
four-cylinder
POWER: 29.5bhp (22kW) at 4400rpm
0–60MPH (96KM/H): n/a
TOP SPEED: 93km/h (58mph)
PRODUCTION TOTAL: 120,434

The Morris Eight was a very popular car in the UK during the late-1930s, and thanks to its sculpted radiator grille and wing mounted headlamps, buyers considered it cutting edge.

JAGUAR 1.5-LITRE

UNITED KINGDOM 1935–49

ENGINE: 1776cc (108cu in),
four-cylinder
POWER: 66bhp (49kW)
0–60MPH (96KM/H): 25.1 seconds
TOP SPEED: 112km/h (70mph)
PRODUCTION TOTAL: 13,046

The fantastic success story of William Lyon's car company, SS, was just about to take a massive step forwards. Although he had started out producing motorcycle sidecars in Blackpool in the early 1920s, with the creation of the SS1, SS90 and SS100, Lyons demonstrated that the company was going places.

The Jaguar 1.5 litre was launched four years before the start of World War II, and the car's name would go on to live a great deal longer than perhaps even William Lyons had suspected. The new saloon car featured a conventional four-cylinder engine with overhead valves, but in the context of its size and price, was actually considered to be advanced – especially when lined up against domestic competition. Retention of the fixed front axle and the rod-operated drum brakes, however, was an unwelcome throwback to a bygone era.

Despite being touted as a 1.5-litre car, the Jaguar had an engine

capacity that was actually significantly larger, rated at 1776cc (108cu in). However, the car's huge body meant that it was seriously underendowed in the engine stakes, and performance was seriously lacking, even in the larger engined version. Poor aerodynamics did not help, and

the top speed of the 1.5-Litre was limited to just 112km/h (70mph). Despite the lack of horses, the Jaguar was incredibly attractive and it found many friends, especially overseas.

Following World War II, all William Lyons-produced cars would adopt the Jaguar marque.

The legend begins here – the Jaguar 1.5-litre majored on value for money and fantastic styling to impress buyers into choosing a Browns Lane product. Four-cylinder powered, it wasn't as quick as it looked.

CHEVROLET SUBURBAN CARRYALL

UNITED STATES 1937–

ENGINE: 3548cc (217 cu in) 6-cylinder
POWER: 63kW (85bhp)
0–60MPH (96KM/H): 20 secs
TOP SPEED: 130km/h (81mph)
PRODUCTION TOTAL: n/a

The Suburban tag is one of the longest-lived in the automotive industry, as Chevrolet still produces a car carrying this moniker today. Although the first Suburban Carry-all was clearly truck-based, it rapidly found favour with large families as what we would term a Sport Utility Vehicle (SUV), thanks to its vast passenger eight-seat compartment and huge luggage area. Other family-friendly features included a drop down tailgate, although the three-door layout was a disadvantage.

Chevrolet's all steel Carryall-Suburban was sold alongside General Motors' sister brand, GMC's, version from 1937 – and these vehicles became known as the Suburban Carryall.

Although the Suburban tag was a generic name to indicate a windowed station wagon body mounted on a commercial frame, it was the Chevrolet example which remained in production for the longest period of time, selling against rivals produced by Dodge, Plymouth, Studebaker and GMC.

In 1966, only the Chevrolet Suburban was left standing, and in 1988 the company was awarded an exclusive trademark on the name following the 1980s boom in large Multi Purpose Vehicles (MPV).

The Suburban, still popular with large families, has always been one of the largest cars offered in America, and has traditionally featured three rows of seats in all examples sold.

CORD 812

UNITED STATES 1936–37

ENGINE: 4729cc (289cu in), eight-cylinder
POWER: 190bhp (142kW)
0–60MPH (96KM/H): n/a
TOP SPEED: 177km/h (110mph)
PRODUCTION TOTAL: 2320

After the adventurous L-29, Cord did it again, a mere three years later, with the 812. The supercharged 812 and its normally aspirated counterpart, the 810, were conceived to challenge conventional production cars, and they both featured Gordon Buehrig-penned styling.

The look was unique, with its pop-up headlights and smooth, futuristic lines, and the car looked every bit the sophisticated tourer. The vehicle was first conceived in 1933 as a Duesenberg; however, company management decided to put a Cord badge on the project to create the 810.

The costly monocoque body was a combined body/chassis unit, and beneath its so-called 'coffin-nose' bonnet was a new V8 engine. Like the L-29, the 810 and 812 were front-wheel drive, although the suspension did receive a number of modifications – transverse leaf springs and large trailing lower links. The four-speed gearbox featured an innovative selector system, which used electro-vacuum operation, and this meant that only a small steering column stalk was needed to change the gears. From 1936, a Schwitzer-Cummins supercharger boosted output to 190bhp (142kW) to create the 812, and it was easily spotted with its chrome-plated external exhaust pipes.

Sadly, both cars turned out to be glorious failures and ceased production less than two years after they were launched.

The 812 was another brave attempt by Cord to move the automotive industry forwards, but despite its supercharger, pop-up headlamps and unitary construction it flopped.

WANDERER W50

GERMANY 1936–37

Thanks to significant state funding, the Auto Union group had become a powerful force in the German car industry. Comprising of the marques Audi, Horch and DKW, the company offered cars in just about every area of the prestige market sector. DKW sat at the bottom of the range, then Wanderer, then Audi and Horch. The image they carried at the time was for a portfolio of cars seen as workmanlike and solid, but lacking in flair and panache – conventional albeit dependable.

The W50 fit the company profile perfectly with its high-quality engineering but rather predictable design. Buyers could specify the W50 in Pullman limousine form, as well as a four-door saloon, a four-seat cabriolet or a two-seat cabriolet. All models were powered by a Ferdinand Porsche-designed straight-six engine.

The engine was interesting. It had pushrod-operated overhead valves and a seven-bearing crank, but also featured an alloy block with cast-iron wet cylinder liners. The four-speed gearbox was teed up with a full synchromesh. The W50 also boasted independent suspension all round, with swing axles at the rear and a transverse leaf spring at the front.

ENGINE: 2255cc (138cu in), six-cylinder
POWER: n/a
0–60MPH (96KM/H): n/a
TOP SPEED: n/a
PRODUCTION TOTAL: n/a

BMW 328

ENGINE: 1971cc (120cu in),
  six-cylinder
POWER: 80bhp (60kW)
0–60MPH (96KM/H): 8 seconds
TOP SPEED: 150km/h (93mph)
PRODUCTION TOTAL: 461

BMW was a company on the move in the 1930s. Just eight years after the launch of the diminutive Dixi, it revealed perhaps one of the finest sports cars ever built – the 328.

The car's first public appearance was at the annual Eifelrennen motor race, held at the fabled Nurburgring – which it promptly won. The 328's styling was beguiling, and featured a curvaceous open-topped two-seater body that was further enhanced by the use of small running boards and no side windows – just cut-down doors.

Powered by a completely redesigned 2-litre (120cu in) version of the 303's six-cylinder engine, the 328 was quick, thanks to a power output of 80bhp (60kW). Lightness and agility were the name of the game. The engine sat high in its bay because of the three bulky Solex downdraught carburettors and the large new aluminium cylinder head. The body was mounted on a tubular frame and brakes were hydraulic front and rear.

Speed was impressive – with a top speed of 150km/h (93mph) in

road trim, and, for many, this was the ultimate evolution of the established 315/1 and 319/1 line of sports cars. The 328 cemented its reputation on the racetrack. In competition form, it produced

135bhp (101kW) and could crack 200km/h (124mph).

The 328's finest hour came in the 1940 Mille Miglia, where special-bodied versions finished first, third, fifth and sixth.

BMW's product range moved on leaps and bounds in the 1930s and with the launch of the 328 in 1936, it had finally joined the ranks of the world's finest sportscar producers.

BUICK ROADMASTER

ENGINE: 4070cc (248cu in),
  eight-cylinder
POWER: 107bhp (80kW)
0–60MPH (96KM/H): 16.4 seconds
TOP SPEED: 137km/h (85mph)
PRODUCTION TOTAL: 70,000

Roadmaster by name, road-master by nature – Buick's aptly named big car appeared in 1936 following a redesign of the entire range. At the time of its launch, it became the most prestigious model in the owner-driver class. With a 333cm (131in) wheelbase, it was cleanly styled and well engineered. It was also big, luxurious transport for the United States' affluent middle classes. The Roadmaster initially came in just

One of Buick's landmark cars, the Roadmaster proved a popular addition to the range and appealed directly to the USA's affluent middle classes.

two bodystyles: a four-door saloon and a convertible phaeton. In 1937, a six-passenger formal saloon was added.

It was 1938 that saw the big changes, when all Buicks received coil springs for their rear suspension – and the chassis also received a crossmember of channel construction. On top of this, the batteries were moved the front of the car. These changes transformed the way in which the Roadmaster drove – thanks to its improved handling and additional power of 141bhp (105kW).

The range was rejigged in 1940, and the Roadmaster Series 70 designation was introduced to make room for a new high-specification Series 80 Limited. The two cars shared the same bodyshell, with the new Super line models offering smoother styling and availability in four bodystyles. Sealed beam headlights and engine oil filters were important innovations.

The year 1941 was the existing bodystyle Roadmaster's swansong. They were now fitted with a revised 165bhp (123kW) engine.

DARRACQ 4-LITRE

FRANCE 1936–39

ENGINE: 3996cc (244cu in), six-cylinder
POWER: 140bhp (104kW)
0–60MPH (96KM/H): 15.4 seconds
TOP SPEED: 161km/h (100mph)
PRODUCTION TOTAL: n/a

After an initial flourish of models, Darracq had fallen on hard times. In 1920, it joined the English Sunbeam and Talbot group, and the company became known as STD. Although all three companies produced some great cars, by 1935 the group had declined so much it had fallen into the hands of the Rootes Group. Darracq, however, would make a comeback – Antonio Lago, a Rootes employee, was placed in charge of Darracq, and he managed to transform the company's products and image.

The Darracq 4-Litre (244cu in) was powered by an overhead-valve straight-six designed by Walter Becchia. It featured a hemispherical cylinder head and a higher compression ratio. Maximum power was a bountiful 140bhp (104kW), and that was allied to a short 294cm (115in) chassis. Suspension was independent at the front, and the chassis frame was cross-braced.

Both the two-door saloons and the drophead coupés looked sensational, especially when they were specified with coachbuilt bodies by Figoni and Falaschi.

The 4-Litre was a sporty car and, because it was so good on the road, it was inevitably modified for the track.

Using the very short 264cm (104in) chassis, it notched up significant victories in the French Grand Prix – where the cars finished first, second and third – and Tourist Trophy races. These cars were badged as Darracqs or Talbot-Darracqs in the United Kingdom, but in France they were always known as Talbots.

HANSA 3500 PRIVAT

GERMANY 1936–39

The brainchild of August Sparkhorst and Dr Robert Allmers, the Hansa company was founded in 1913. From their workshop in the Westphalia town of Bielefeld, Allmers and Sparkhorst quickly moved to merge with Lloyd of Bremen, to become Hansa-Lloyd. The name of Hansa would end up living on independently.

The early Hansas were clearly influenced by the French models of the time, including the Alcyon voiturette, and, before World War I, the company even built vehicles under licence for the British Royal Air Force.

Along with a number of other carmaking ventures, Hansa helped to create a new consortium of companies known as GDA (Gemeinschaft Deutscher Automobilfabriken) and, between the wars, the company offered a variety of four-, six- and eight-cylinder engined cars.

The Privat featured an overhead valve six-cylinder engine with a four-bearing crankshaft and twin SU carburettors, mounted on a pressed-steel platform chassis with cruciform side members and independent all-round suspension. An interesting feature of the Privat was the Vogal system of centralized chassis lubrication – and it was ahead of the game for featuring hydraulic brakes on all four wheels.

In 1939, the last of the Hansa cars, called Borgward, appeared.

ENGINE: 3485cc (213cu in), six-cylinder
POWER: 90bhp (67kW)
0–60MPH (96KM/H): 24 seconds
TOP SPEED: 120km/h (75mph)
PRODUCTION TOTAL: n/a

HORCH TYPE 853

GERMANY 1936–39

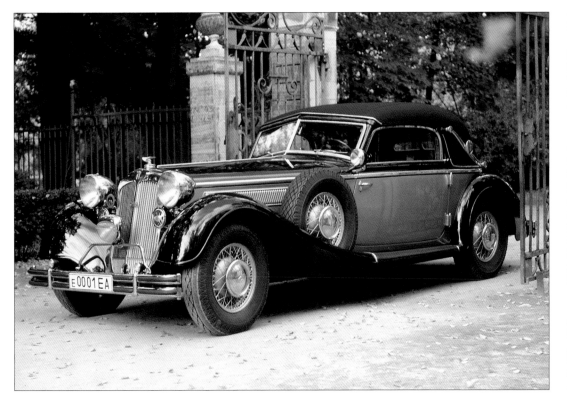

ENGINE: 4946cc (302cu in), eight-cylinder
POWER: 100bhp (75kW)
0–60MPH (96KM/H): n/a
TOP SPEED: 160km/h (100mph)
PRODUCTION TOTAL: n/a

August Horch was a pioneer of Germany's motor industry, first working for Karl Benz before selling his own prestige motor cars from as early as 1900. These were quiet, steady years, though, and it was not until the 1920s that Horch gained his reputation as a quality carmaker. However, in 1932, he had an argument with fellow company directors, left and formed the Audi marque in 1932.

Alongside Mercedes-Benz and Maybach, Horch represented the pinnacle of German engineering in the immediate pre-war period. Elegant styling and powerful engines mean it remains popular.

In 1923, Paul Daimler joined Horch, and his first designs were the straight-eight twin camshaft engines of 1926. He subsequently developed these throughout the 1930s, later adopting a single camshaft layout, which formed the basis of the 853.

The car was considered to be a mere second-division Mercedes, and it ended up being sold in large numbers to the Nazi Party hierarchy for use as staff cars. Some of the cars had rigid axles, while others had independent front suspension. The later 950 and 951 models were fitted with De Dion rear suspension.

Both the V8 and straight-eight models continued to the outbreak of World War II, but the Horch name disappeared for good after that – in 1945, its factory was in Russian-occupied East Germany.

JAGUAR 3.5-LITRE 'SS100'

UNITED KINGDOM 1936–39

ENGINE: 3485cc (213cu in),
  six-cylinder
POWER: 125bhp (93kW)
0–60MPH (96KM/H): n/a
TOP SPEED: 161km/h (100mph)
PRODUCTION TOTAL: 118

The SS Jaguars were one of those strange breeds of cars that always seemed to be a bigger hit in hindsight. Advertised originally as 'The Car with the £1,000 Look', despite costing only £325, the charismatic SS Jaguars were seen by many enthusiasts as cheap and shoddy, and it was not until later years, when the company had attained respectability, that their astonishing virtues were truly realized.

The SS100 was introduced in 1935 and used a shortened version of the chassis developed for the new SS generation of saloon cars. The ravishingly good-looking car featured a side-valve 2663cc (162cu in) Standard six-cylinder engine. For the introduction of the 3.5-Litre, however, an all-new and very powerful 3485cc (213cu in) engine was installed. That allowed the SS100 to finally reach the magical 161km/h (100mph) figure, making it an exceedingly fast car for the era – and especially when the price was taken into consideration.

The SS100 concentrated on style and performance, and made few concessions to comfort. Styling was a priority, in fact, and with sweeping front wings (fenders) and hugely charismatic twin headlights, the car remains a design icon to this day.

The company's reputation was massively enhanced by the SS100 in the run-up to World War II, and because the final production tally remained small at 118, original cars command high prices today.

With beautiful styling and excellent performance, the SS100 occupies a major place in Jaguar's history, as it was one of the fastest cars of its era.

LINCOLN ZEPHYR

UNITED STATES 1936–39

The Lincoln Zephyr has one major point of historical significance: it was seen as the first successfully designed streamlined car available in the United States. The Zephyr was introduced in late 1935, and it hit the market in early 1936, taking up a slot at the lower priced end of the Lincoln family.

The Zephyr was powered by a water-cooled 4784cc (292cu in) 75-degree V12 engine and sat on a 317.5cm (125in) wheelbase. Although the car was large, it could stop well – vacuum-assisted brakes were fitted as standard. A three-speed gearbox with steering column gearchange was fitted and, along with the Columbia two-speed rear axle, these features were linked with the Lincoln name.

A number of standard body options were offered by the company, and these were enhanced by the sheer variety of custom designs available from the likes of Le Baron, Brunn (who, in 1939, made a town car used by the wife of Edsel Ford, the man behind the later Lincoln Continental), Judkin, Dietrich and Willoughby.

Lincoln Zephyrs were conservative cars, and the later cars to bear the name carried over many design and styling cues that first appeared on the pre–World War II cars. All Zephyrs were imposing machines, and remained so until the 1942 facelift.

ENGINE: 4784cc (292cu in),
  12-cylinder
POWER: 110bhp (82kW)
0–60MPH (96KM/H): n/a
TOP SPEED: n/a
PRODUCTION TOTAL: n/a

Zephyrs were streamlined from day one, and that marked them out as looking more expensive than they actually were. This made them extremely successful and they would later form the basis of the Continental model.

MERCEDES-BENZ 260D

GERMANY 1936–39

Codenamed the W138, the Mercedes-Benz 260D was the world's first diesel-powered production car – and gained a certain notoriety for being the favoured transport of the dreaded German Gestapo during World War II. Widely used by the German naval and air forces, too, many 260Ds ended up featuring adopted specialized bodies with no doors and fabric hoods. Such was their

adaptability, some 260Ds were even modified for commercial use, appearing as ambulances and light artillery tractors. Quite a few did fall into civilian hands, though.

Mercedes-Benz's reputation for building great taxis was formed here, and, as the chassis and all-round independent suspension system was the same as the 230 model, the 260 combined comfort with low running costs.

The car's diesel engine was competitive with its petrol-powered rivals, though, and the innovative 260's engine was free-revving up to 3000rpm – a rare feat for a diesel. Road testers of the day suggested that the 260D's acceleration was competitive with its 3-litre (183cu in) petrol-engined rivals. The transmission was a three-speed manual, but after 1937 that was upgraded to a four-

speeder. Like the 230, the Mercedes-Benz 260 was available for general sale in tourer, saloon or folding-hood landaulette forms.

ENGINE: 2545cc (155cu in), four-cylinder
POWER: 45bhp (34kW)
0–60MPH (96KM/H): n/a
TOP SPEED: 109km/h (68mph)
PRODUCTION TOTAL: 1967

MERCEDES-BENZ 540K

GERMANY 1936–39

Very few carmakers have been completely transformed by the arrival of one man – but, when Hans Nibel replaced Ferdinand Porsche as its chief engineer in 1928, that is exactly what happened at Mercedes-Benz. His appointment marked the introduction of an entirely revised range of more refined sporting machines, and the supercharged 380 of 1933 was an excellent starting point for change. From

With its straight-eight supercharged engine, the 540K was a magnificent car produced by a confident Mercedes-Benz. A long bonnet and graceful curves disguised the car's vast bulk.

that car came the magnificent 500 of 1934. That finally transformed into the elegant supercharged 540K (K for 'kompressor', or 'supercharger') of 1936.

Considered by many as the ultimate car of its age, the 540K is seen as the epitome of the classic car shape, where at least half its length is bonnet (hood). The formidable 540K featured a straight-eight engine set well back from the car's front, followed by cabin space for two with room behind the seats, and further boot (trunk) space at the rear for luggage. Key features were the long folding bonnet, sweeping front wings (fenders), front-opening 'suicide' doors, twin spare wheels stowed forward of the A-post on each side of the car, and the imposing upright chrome grille with the famous three-pointed star emblem atop.

ENGINE: 5401cc (330cu in), eight-cylinder
POWER: 180bhp (134kW)
0–60MPH (96KM/H): n/a
TOP SPEED: 161km/h (100mph)
PRODUCTION TOTAL: 444

MG SA

ENGINE: 2288cc (140cu in), six-cylinder
POWER: 62bhp (46kW)
0–60MPH (96KM/H): n/a
TOP SPEED: 129km/h (80mph)
PRODUCTION TOTAL: 2738

Introduced in 1936, the MG SA was actually a step back into a bygone era for MG – it was an elegant grand-touring coupé that was not trying to be an out-and-out sports car. In usual MG style, the SA came in a range of different bodies, and was available in a variety of four-seat options. All featured good legroom and rear access, and the open tourer was offered in time for the summer of 1937. All were elegant designs graced with sweeping curves and a low bonnet (hood) and roofline. As with the smaller MGs, the SA was powered by a Wolseley pushrod engine with low-down torque and in-gear flexibility. The smooth ride and excellent steering made it a pleasant machine to drive, and the late 1937 addition of a synchromesh gearbox sweetened the deal.

Committee thinking led to the SA possessing an engine that was originally too tall for the car's engine bay. The unsuitability of the 2.3-litre (140cu in) straight-six power unit was down to the engineers and stylists not talking to each other, and the only solution was to design horizontal dashpots for the twin downdraught carburettors. This ingenious solution allowed the bonnet to close – just – with less than 2.5cm (1in) clearance to spare.

Marketed as a touring car, the MG SA occupied a lonely place in the pre-war MG range. It wasn't without its problems, but with such styling it could be forgiven for pretty much anything.

FIAT TOPOLINO

ENGINE: 569cc (35cu in), four-cylinder
POWER: 13bhp (10kW)
0–60MPH (96KM/H): n/a
TOP SPEED: 84km/h (52mph)
PRODUCTION TOTAL: 131,000

Best known as the 'Topolino' (or 'little mouse'), the 'baby' Fiat 500 was easily the smallest mass-produced car of its time – and one of the most recognizable. The two-seater car was powered by a 13bhp (10kW) 569cc (35cu in) engine and was conceived to bring motoring to the Italian masses. The tiny car was, surprisingly, an incredible success in Italy, leading to a long life – it remained in production until 1948 in its original form.

During that long production run, more than 110,000 had been sold with relatively few changes made,

somewhat against the fashion of the time. When production restarted after the war, it became known as the 500B – and it looked identical to the old car. However, the engine received an extra 3.5bhp (2.5kW), and the brakes, suspension and electrical equipment were upgraded. The 500 Giardiniera-Belvedere estate (station-wagon) version was launched in 1948, adding plenty of extra practicality, as it meant the 500 could finally hold four people in its longer body.

More changes were made in 1949 when the 500C arrived, with new frontal styling and aluminium-headed engines. These were the first Fiats with an interior heater.

The Baby Topolino was considered cute enough to eat by many buyers, and it proved a significant success for Fiat.

DELAHAYE 135M

ENGINE: 3227cc (197cu in),
 six-cylinder
POWER: 120bhp (89kW)
0–60MPH (96KM/H): 14 seconds
TOP SPEED: 161km/h (100mph)
PRODUCTION TOTAL: 2000

It is amazing what a change of powerplant will do to a company's fortunes. Until 1935, Delahaye would have appeared to be just another small manufacturer making fairly ordinary well-made family touring cars. That changed when the company's engineers took one of its truck engines and installed it in one of its car's chassis.

This powerful combination created the 135. The four-bearing six-cylinder engine was available in various states of tune – from a 95bhp (71kW) single carburettor entry-level version to a triple-Solex carburettor unit capable of producing 110bhp (82kW).

Available as a two-door saloon, a cabriolet and countless specials, the 135 looked good. The Coupé des Alpes model featured transverse-leaf independent front suspension, Bendix brakes, centre-lock wire wheels and a choice of non-synchromesh four-speed, or electric Cortal, transmissions. The

bigger-engined 3557cc (217cu in) 135MS produced at least 130bhp (97kW), and moved the company firmly into the competition arena two-seater form. The 135 had many competition achievements,

most notably winning the 1937 and 1939 Monte Carlo rallies and taking a victory in the Le Mans 24-hour race in 1938. The 135MS returned after the war, but never achieved the same level of success.

The road-going version of the Delahaye 135 was endowed with racing car levels of performance and handling. With 120bhp on tap, it could top the magic 'ton' (100mph or 161km/h).

MG T-SERIES

ENGINE: 1250cc (76cu in),
 four-cylinder
POWER: 54bhp (40kW)
0–60MPH (96KM/H): 22.7 seconds
TOP SPEED: 126km/h (78mph)
PRODUCTION TOTAL: about 51,000

The first of the legendary MG T-Series cars appeared in 1936, but without doubt its biggest achievements came during the 1940s and 1950s. Initial production was halted in 1939, due to the start of World War II, but the car came back with a vengeance in 1945.

This was more by accident than design. MG had no funds to spare and needed to restart production as quickly as possible after the conflict. In order to achieve this, and to revive the company, MG resurrected its old model. The TC featured minor improvements such

as a bigger cabin and partial synchromesh on the gearbox, but nonetheless was really a reheat of the pre-War TB.

The car's archaic ash-frame construction and semi-elliptic leaf suspension system were retained, but that did not blunt the TC's popularity, especially with American servicemen stationed in the United Kingdom. The distinctive engine note and fun handling were very sporting, and a firm ride and heavy steering made it an involving machine to drive. It was not perfect – the gearbox was tough, and the brakes were still lacking in stopping power.

In post-war Britain, it was export or die, and that meant most TCs went to the United States – despite being right-hand drive. MG knew it needed to evolve the T-Series if it wanted to enjoy sustained success, and, with limited funds,

the TD was introduced onto the market in 1949.

It retained the old chassis and XPAG engine, but with independent front suspension, uprated braking system and rack-and-pinion steering from the Y-Type saloon. The TD was a much easier car to drive, with lighter steering than its predecessors. Styling was tweaked, but, under the bonnet (hood), things looked better. A higher compression engine appeared in 1952 and pushed the TD's top speed to 137km/h (85mph), making it an even more fun proposition.

The final incarnation of the T-Series appeared a little later. The 1953 TF still retained much of the original car's styling, but did begin to reflect the shift towards more streamlined styling in the motor industry. The TF featured headlights that were faired into the bodywork, and the front end was smoothed

out by the addition of a sloping radiator grille and longer, lower and more elegant flanks. Inside, individual front seats replaced the TC and TD's benches, and wire wheels made a return after being omitted from the TD.

The TF's extra weight resulted in a drop-off in performance, and that meant that it was actually slower than the car it replaced – with a power output of 57.5bhp (43kW), its top speed fell to 127km/h (79mph).

A new 1500cc (92cu in) engine, fitted from 1954, improved things, and the performance finally lived up to the looks and dynamics. Only 3400 were built before the range was replaced by the MGA, and objectively that makes the TF 1500 probably the most desirable of the lot. Still, diehard MG fans will always prefer the purity of the original pre-War TA and TB.

MORGAN 4/4

The Morgan 4/4's claim to fame is that it has enjoyed the longest production run of any car ever made, with production continuing well into the twenty-

first century. Of course, the earliest cars were quite different to their more modern counterparts.

The new model was the culmination of HFS Morgan's dream

to produce a four-wheeled car. The 1936 car featured traditional Morgan features – the ash-frame construction and live rear axle with semi-elliptic leaf springs were

all there from the beginning, as was the tubular chassis on which all subsequent 4/4s have been built. Production ceased in 1939 to make way for World War II, but restarted in 1945 in an almost identical form. The only major change was a switch to 1.3-litre (79cu in) power as supplied by the Standard Motor Company.

The 4/4 continued in this form until 1950, when production was put on ice so that Morgan could concentrate on satisfying demand for the new Plus 4 (detailed below). The model returned in 1955, with a few a visual changes to denote the five-year rest. The 1955 cars featured wider, more flared wings (fenders) and running boards, and

Proving that a winning formula can be one that doesn't change, the Morgan 4/4 has, with a plethora of engine changes, remained in production since 1936.

a more aerodynamic grille. Even by then, the Morgan was old hat compared with its rivals.

The new 1955 models received a new engine – the 1172cc (72cu in) Ford side-valve engine, lifted from the Popular 100E. Performance was embarrassingly slow, and remained so until 1959 when the far livelier 997cc (61cu in) Ford Anglia overhead-valve four was shoehorned in. After that came the 1340cc (82cu in) and 1498cc (91cu in) Ford engines, developed for the Ford Classic and Cortina throughout the 1960s.The 4/4s remained Ford-powered save for a brief flirtation with Fiat Twin Cam power in the 1980s.

The 4/4 became a proper sports car in 1968, with the launch of Ford's Crossflow series of engines, as these offered plenty of tuning

potential and a potential of up to 95bhp (71kW). So powered, the 4/4 was able to hit 160km/h (100mph) for the first time. These crossflow engines remained the 4/4's motive power until the early 1980s, when they were replaced by Ford's new CVH (Compound Valve Hemi) engine. Initially, these Escort engines were fitted with carburettors, but later fuel injection – which was lifted from the Escort XR3i – was added.

A four-seater version was added in 1969, but that lacks the visual purity of the original car – and its sales were never in the same league as the two-seater 4/4 and the later Plus-8.

The latest cars, with their modern engines, remain true to the Morgan ideal – they are built on the same tubular chassis and

ash frame as their forebears, and remain demanding to drive. In objective terms, though, they are uncomfortable, with a somewhat boneshaking ride, and are cold and miserable to sit in during the winter. But it would seem that Morgan's buyers like it that way – and would like it to remain that way. For many, the 4/4 remains a loveable motoring anachronism, as it flies in the face of modern thinking. Customers are loyal, too, and the company remains healthy to this day as a result.

ENGINE: 1498cc (91cu in),
four-cylinder
POWER: 78bhp (58kW)
0–60MPH (96KM/H): n/a
TOP SPEED: 163km/h (101mph)
PRODUCTION TOTAL: about 8000

PHANTOM CORSAIR

ENGINE: 4729cc (289 cu in), V8 cylinder
POWER: n/a
0-60MPH (0–96KM/H): n/a
TOP SPEED: n/a
PRODUCTION TOTAL: 1

There's only one Phantom Corsair – literally. With genuinely advanced styling and engineering, the Phantom Corsair was off-the-scale amazing, although it remains an unfulfilled dream. The car is on display at the National Automobile Museum in Reno, Nevada.

Without doubt, the Phantom Corsair was one of the most amazing vehicle prototypes to emerge from the USA during the 1930s. Rust Heinz and Maurice Schwartz of the Bohman & Schwartz coachbuilding company jointly designed the unusual six-passenger coupe.

The steel and aluminum body did away with running boards, bumpers and door handles, and the styling was dramatically aerodynamic.

The advanced design was underpinned by an equally cutting edge chassis – that of the magnificent Cord 810. The Corsair retained that car's V8 engine and front wheel drive with electrically operated four-speed gearbox, along with fully independent suspension and adjustable shock absorbers. The 2000 kg (4500 lb) Phantom Corsair needed plenty of power – and the Cord 810's Lycoming engine was supercharged by Andy Granatelli to produce about 190bhp. Top speed was an equally impressive 185km/h (115mph).

Other prescient features included thermostatically controlled climate control and copious sound deadening inside.

With a padded leather dashbood it was also built to be safe.

Heinz planned to put the Phantom Corsair (which in 1938 cost approximately $24,000 to produce) into limited production at an estimated selling price of $12,500. However, his death shortly after the car was completed, scuppered those plans, leaving this car a fascinating might-have-been.

CHEVROLET MASTER GA

UNITED STATES 1937

ENGINE: 3548cc (217cu in),
  six-cylinder
POWER: 85bhp (63kW)
0–60MPH (96KM/H): 20 seconds
TOP SPEED: 135km/h (84mph)
PRODUCTION TOTAL: 519,024

In the year the Master GA was launched, Chevrolet finally bested Ford in the battle to become the bestselling marque in the United States. Conceived during that fight to boost sales, the new range did what its maker set out to do in helping Chevrolet become US favourite – and two years later made its 15 millionth car.

The Master series was an all-new model and featured a revised version of the powerful 85bhp (63kW) 'Cast Iron Wonder' six-cylinder engine. It had received a larger bore and shorter stroke, and four main bearings which helped to improve smoothness. A stiffened box girder frame and hypoid rear axle were used across the range.

The Unisteel body had a fresh contemporary 'Diamond Crown' look, and all the windows boasted safety glass. Straight wings (fenders) were new, the grille was swept in on each side, and the headlight surrounds were painted body colour.

The six-cylinder engines were very smooth and performance was quick. Inside, the car had plenty of equipment and high-quality trim, including a dashboard temperature gauge, front passenger armrest, twin tail lamps, double windscreen wipers, twin sun visors and more ornate bumpers with overriders.

It was a striking car, but one to which the middle-class working man could realistically aspire.

PANHARD DYNA

FRANCE 1946–54

To many observers, the Dyna had ugly, bug-eyed looks, but, despite that, it was a fascinating and truly innovative car. Although it did not appear until 1946, it was actually designed well before World War II. Soon after its launch. the Dyna became a popular choice for motorists on a budget.

The front-mounted 610cc (37cu in) flat-twin provided the motive force, and the engine was so easy to take in and out that most repairs ended up seeing a new engine fitted. Specialists loved it for that; it was cheaper and less labour-intensive to replace the engine, so many of them offered exchanges on reconditioned units taken from other cars.

Modern features included a four-speed overdrive gearbox (when most rivals made do with a non-synchromesh three-speeder), hydraulic braking system, lightweight unitary construction bodywork with alloy panels, and fully independent suspension.

Later cars gained the power they deserved, and the Dyna was offered with a choice of 745cc (45cu in) or 850cc (52cu in) flat-twin engines. In its most powerful form, it could reach 130km/h (80mph). A true French engineering marvel, it never sold as well as it deserved.

ENGINE: 610cc (37cu in),
  two-cylinder
POWER: 24bhp (18kW)
0–60MPH (96KM/H): n/a
TOP SPEED: 100km/h (62mph)
PRODUCTION TOTAL: 55,000

STEYR 50 AND 55

AUSTRIA 1936–40

Easily mistaken for the Fiat 500, the 50 was actually the last car to be designed and conceived by Steyr's brilliant engineer Karl Jenschke, before he left for rival carmaker Adler. Jenschke had worked for the company since the early 1920s, and his final car proved to be the smallest engined vehicle to leave the Steyr factory. Powered by a 984cc (60cu in) side-valve flat-four, the car was a remarkable move downmarket for a company that concentrated on more exclusive models.

With only 22bhp (16kW) on offer, performance was not a reason to buy this car, and the cable-operated brakes were not too helpful. They were a disappointment considering Steyr had used hydraulic systems in previous cars. On the upside, the 50 had all-round independent suspension and a monocoque construction for its two-door coupé bodyshell.

It was a popular choice, but was always crying out for more power. Buyer's prayers were answered in 1938, when an 1158cc (71cu in) engine was fitted, and, although it added only 3bhp (2kW), it helped performance. Following a face-lift, the model was rebadged Typ 55, but there were no further changes to engine capacity.

ENGINE: 984cc (60cu in),
  four-cylinder
POWER: 22bhp (16kW)
0–60MPH (96KM/H): n/a
TOP SPEED: 97km/h (60mph)
PRODUCTION TOTAL: 13,000

LA SALLE V8

UNITED STATES 1937–39

In the 1930s, General Motors was not short of brands – but being the number-one producer in the United States was hard work, and the company keenly looked for sales opportunities. Californian designer Harley J. Earl set up La Salle under the wing of General Motors, in a bid to win more sales, running side by side with Cadillac. The La Salle V8 had a lot to offer, though. It had supreme flexibility in top gear, and its excellent column-mounted three-speed transmission with synchromesh on second and top gear was another significant plus for choosy buyers.

It was an agile car, too – no mean feat for one so big. That was down to its big externally mounted independent coil springs at the front, and, although they resulted in a soft ride with lots of body roll, roadholding was surprisingly good. The car's excellent hydraulically operated brakes also received favourable comment from the press, and featured self-servo shoes that worked progressively with the amount of pressure applied to the pedal by the driver.

Two spare wheels were placed alongside the bonnet (hood), and the car was equipped with a large boot (trunk). Towards the end of the V8's lifespan, rationalization crept in, and the bodyshell was shared with Buick and Oldsmobile before production finally ceased in 1939.

ENGINE: 5277cc (322cu in),
  eight-cylinder
POWER: 37bhp (28kW)
0–60MPH (96KM/H): n/a
TOP SPEED: 149km/h (93mph)
PRODUCTION TOTAL: n/a

Part of the lexicon of brands that General Motors owned, the La Salle V8 fitted in the small niche beneath Cadillac in the model range. Marque values were eroded when the body shell was shared with Buick and Oldsmobile.

MG VA

ENGINE: 1548cc (94cu in),
four-cylinder
POWER: 53bhp (39kW)
0–60MPH (96KM/H): n/a
TOP SPEED: 129km/h (80mph)
PRODUCTION TOTAL: 2407

In the 1930s, MG could do little wrong – and, to cash in on the popularity of the SA, the company offered a smaller engined and cheaper variant that was based on the same chassis. The VA was available as an open or closed tourer, with plenty of room for four. Unlike with the SA, however, you could not specify exclusive coachbuilt bodywork. Despite that, the extremely keen asking price of £280 made the VA an appealing proposition over similarly priced but less capable rivals.

Built-in hydraulic jacks were a neat feature, but essential to avoid drivers jacking the car up in the wrong place – the VA's long and heavy bodywork and wood-framed panels meant that such a practice could prove costly. Body flex was a criticism often levelled at the SA and VA series, as well as heavy steering, thanks to the weighty coachwork and sliding trunnion suspension. The 1548cc (95cu in) engine was shared with the

Wolseley 12. Although not quite the cutting-edge fare of the rest of the MG range, raw performance was still almost as good as the SA's.

Despite these faults, however, the VA was one of the finest cars in its class and proved popular with buyers.

Considered by many to be a retrograde step over its predecessor, the MG VA featured a heavy ash frame.

89

TRIUMPH DOLOMITE

The 1937 Dolomite range was a drink in the Last Chance Saloon for a company that was rapidly heading for failure. Styled by Walter Belgrove, the Dolomite's new bodies updated the Gloria look, and were complemented by the first Triumph-designed and built engines.

As with the Gloria, the new Dolomite could be specified with Donald Healey masterminded four-cylinder engines of 1496cc (91cu in) or 1767cc (108cu in), or a bigger six-cylinder unit with 1991cc (121cu in). The new engines were a big improvement on their forebears, featuring an overhead-valve cylinder head with a crossflow design.

The cars were modern to look at, too, featuring a stylized 'waterfall' grille which mirrored what was happening in the United States. Many of Triumph's traditional buyers were shocked by the new style – despite the shapely grille – and so a conventional front end was offered on the later Dolomite Continental model to appease them.

To attract more customers, an increasingly desperate Triumph expanded the Dolomite range in 1938, introducing drophead and open versions. The extremely luxurious Dolomite Royal followed in 1939. It was not enough to save the company, however, and Triumph declared itself bankrupt on 7 June 1939, and all car production stopped.

ENGINE: 1767cc (108cu in), four-cylinder
POWER: 62bhp (46kW) at 4500rpm
0–60MPH (96KM/H): 32.2 seconds
TOP SPEED: 117km/h (73mph)
PRODUCTION TOTAL: about 7200

This two-seater roadster with a distinctly transatlantic-looking grille was Triumph's last throw of the dice at saving the company. It was a brave effort, but ultimately futile.

JOWETT 8HP

Benjamin and William Jowett's Car Company was set up in Bradford, England, and started production in 1906. Always regarded as producers of interesting cars, Jowett managed to keep its 816cc (50cu in) flat-twin-powered light two-seater in production for a very long time. The basic layout of this 1910 car remained in production until 1954. A remarkable achievement.

The hard-working twin-cylinder engine gained a reputation for good performance and solid reliability, and its capacity was increased to 907cc (55cu in) after World War I to keep it in line with customer expectations. The extremely economical engine evolved over its long life; during the 1920s, it received an electric starter. That coincided with the arrival of a four-seater saloon model in 1929.

The cars produced by Jowett in the early 1930s retained the proven twin-cylinder configuration, and were often named after various forms of wildlife – that including the sporty Kestrel of 1934 and the interestingly named twin-carburettor Weasel. From 1935, the cars gained a four-speed transmission and an intriguing centrifugal clutch mechanism. The range was improved with the arrival of four-cylinder versions in 1936. Twin-cylinder production continued, lifted by an increase in capacity to 946cc (58cu in), and 8hp (6kW).

ENGINE: 946cc (58cu in), two-cylinder
POWER: 8hp (6kW)
0–60MPH (96KM/H): n/a
TOP SPEED: 80km/h (50mph)
PRODUCTION TOTAL: n/a

FIAT 508

The Balilla range was a Fiat mainstay for several years, and, although it looked like an enlarged Topolino, it was a model in its own right. Also known as the 1100 or 508C, the car received a new 1089cc (66cu in) good for 32bhp (24kW). In terms of looks, it also shared many details with the larger 1500, including the same recessed door handles and pillarless doors.

The range was soon expanded with longer wheelbase 508L and cabriolet versions, and they broadened appeal. For the Mille Miglia race of 1938, Fiat even developed the MM in coupé form with an uprated 42bhp (31kW) engine, and it went on to win its class in the legendary event.

The 508C served through the war; from 1939 to 1945 it was produced in 'Militare' form, as Italy's answer to the Jeep. A much larger 'Coloniale' model was also produced until 1943, and that became the heavier duty staff car. Both models were powered by the venerable 30bhp (22kW) 1089cc (66cu in) engine with the four-speed transmission.

Following World War II, both the 508C and 508L were reintroduced, in almost pre-war form. Closely related to the 1100, the 508 continued to provide Italy with family transportation, while the 1100 became the upmarket choice for buyers.

ENGINE: 1089cc (66cu in), four-cylinder
POWER: 32bhp (24kW)
0–60MPH (96KM/H): 40 seconds
TOP SPEED: 116km/h (72mph)
PRODUCTION TOTAL: 11,947

TATRA TYPE 87

ENGINE: 2968cc (181cu in),
eight-cylinder
POWER: 75bhp (56kW)
0–60MPH (96KM/H): n/a
TOP SPEED: 161km/h (100mph)
PRODUCTION TOTAL: n/a

Tatra's reputation for producing technologically advanced cars was maintained with the Type 87. Learning lessons from the Type 77, the new Type 87 gained an aluminium engine which was both lighter and quieter than the unit it replaced – evening out weight distribution considerably. The car ended up being 24 per cent lighter than its predecessor because of that engine, and this improved the driving experience considerably. Corners were no longer something to be feared.

The car's designer, Hans Ledwinka, simply fine-tuned the lines of the Type 77 to produce the Type 87; as curved glass was still not a possibility at the time, it featured a three-piece windscreen

with small windows where the A-posts would usually be.

Compression ratio was just 5.6:1 to cope with poor-quality Eastern European fuel; however, despite this, the Type 87 could still manage an impressive 161km/h (100mph) on the 75bhp (56kW). Aerodynamics were sensational – a drag coefficient of just 0.36cd remains better than many of today's cars.

The handling, though improved, remained unpredictable. During World War II, many German Army officers were banned from driving the T87, as too many were being put through hedges backwards.

Featuring startling styling and equally arresting handling, the Tatra Type 87 was a rare treat that few in the west ever experienced.

DELAHAYE 148

ENGINE: 3557cc (217cu in),
six-cylinder
POWER: 90bhp (67kW)
0–60MPH (96KM/H): 21 seconds
TOP SPEED: 129km/h (80mph)
PRODUCTION TOTAL: n/a

In essence, the Delahaye 148 was a lower powered version of the Delahaye 135 and essentially shared the same mechanical and structural configuration. Given the drop in power, the 148 was a much less sporting derivative, and one aimed at different customers.

The 148 shared the same 3557cc (217cu in) straight-six engine, and sat on a longer 335cm (132in) wheelbase than the 135.

To achieve the cut in power, the 135's engine received a low compression ratio and single carburettor, and as a result the

power output was 90bhp (67kW). Given the more sober brief of the 148, it was mainly built with formal saloon and limousine bodywork, and it was never to see the extravagant sporting styles of the 135.

An interesting variation on the 148 theme appeared in 1939. The 168 used a Renault Viva Grand Sport body mounted on the 148 chassis, and was considered to be less than attractive. The car was only ever available in France.

After World War II, production of the 148 resumed, and a rather interesting range of body designs was offered – replacing the stately pre-1939 limousines. A range of fabulous art deco creations appeared, especially those by Henri Chaperon, whose convertibles featured voluptuous rounded wings (fenders) and long bonnets (hoods) patterned with louvres.

Although it was essentially a lower powered version of the 135, the Delahaye 148 was in no way an economy car – and some of the coachbuilt bodies offered were absolutely magnificent.

RENAULT JUVAQUATRE

The Renault Juvaquatre is a good example of solid French pre-war engineering at its best. Available in four-door saloon, van or commercial-based shooting brake forms, it proved popular with buyers. A plus point was its impressive interior space, and, although the 1.0-litre (61cu in) side-valve engine was nothing to write home about, it was economical and simple to maintain, exactly what was needed at the time. The specification sheet was up to date, with transverse leaf springs at the rear, independent front suspension, hydraulic brakes and a smooth gearbox.

It also had a big post-war advantage. It entered production so soon before World War II's outbreak that it was still relatively modern when the conflict ended in 1945. Renault was thus able to relaunch the car at the cessation of hostilities and offer a car that was cheap and significantly more advanced than many of its rivals.

It was a long-lived car as a result. The saloon models were dropped in 1950 because they were no longer needed following the seminal 4CV's launch, but the van and estate (station-wagon) models continued up to 1960, using engines from the 4CV and Dauphine. The Juvaquatre was an important and successful model for Renault when the French car industry needed it most.

ENGINE: 1003cc (61cu in), four-cylinder
POWER: 24bhp (18kW)
0–60MPH (96KM/H): n/a
TOP SPEED: 90km/h (56mph)
PRODUCTION TOTAL: 40,681

DODGE D-8

ENGINE: 3568cc (218cu in), six-cylinder
POWER: 87bhp (65kW)
0–60MPH (96KM/H): 26 seconds
TOP SPEED: 124km/h (77mph)
PRODUCTION TOTAL: 109,747

The 1930s were a glorious era of six-cylinder power for Dodge. The so-called 'Beauty Winner' range of six-cylinder engines entered production in 1935, and became the cornerstone of a multi-cylinder era for Dodge. At the time of the D8's launch in 1935, the company sat comfortably in the top five US manufacturers – and the new car cemented that position.

Called the D-8 for 1938, the new Dodge was actually only mildly redesigned for that model year. A new-style radiator grille featured narrower stripes down the centre and narrower horizontal bars on either side. The headlights were repositioned at the top of the wings, and, for the very last time, the Dodge Brothers emblem was used on the grille.

The all-steel 'silent-safety' body incorporated insulated roofs, rear quarters and door panels for extra refinement, and the front seats were newly adjustable. Standard equipment on the car included Autolite ignition, hydraulic brakes, single windscreen wipers and dual rear lights. The D8 was offered with 10 bodystyles that included a seven-seat limousine with longer wheelbase and a divider window between passenger and driver.

Reliable, sophisticated and comfortable, the car was a big seller at an accessible price.

Called the 'Beauty Winner', the D8 was a sure-fire success for Dodge following its launch in 1935. The 1938 version was actually a carry-over.

GRAHAM 97

The Paige-Detroit company went into decline during the Depression years, only to be saved in 1927 by the intervention of the charismatic Graham brothers Robert, Joseph and Ray. Until then, it had been a producer of cars for the American middle classes in the late 1920s, but, following the rescue, it was renamed Graham Paige until 1930, when the name was shortened to Graham.

The 1938 'Sharknose' range was ugly, and, despite being good to drive and entirely reliable, it was seen as a publicity stunt. Today these cars remain popular with collectors, especially in the United States, where they have become popular with customizers.

The company was already heading for demise when the Sharknose was launched, and, despite the introduction of the 'twin top' four-speed gearbox, the Blue-Streak of 1932 and the blown straight-eights of 1934, the company's death was postponed only by World War II. In 1945, the carmaking side of Graham Paige was absorbed by Kaiser, and the brothers moved on.

ENGINE: 3560cc (217cu in), six-cylinder
POWER: 25bhp (19kW)
0–60MPH (96KM/H): 19 seconds
TOP SPEED: 139km/h (87mph)
PRODUCTION TOTAL: n/a

MG WA

ENGINE: 2561cc (156cu in),
  six-cylinder
POWER: 70bhp (52kW)
0–60MPH (96KM/H): n/a
TOP SPEED: 137km/h (85mph)
PRODUCTION TOTAL: 369

Although the MG WA was an updated and improved SA, with all of the earlier car's problems ironed out – thanks to some intelligent engineering – it could not have been launched at a worse time.

The previous car's sluggish performance had been partially rectified by increasing the engine's compression ratio, and the brakes had been overhauled to incorporate a dual-circuit hydraulic system that rivalled most racing cars of its day. That made the WA an enjoyable car to drive – it retained all that was good about its predecessor and eliminated many of its bad points.

A familiar range of stylish coachbuilt bodies was offered and all were elegant and spacious inside. Equipment was lavish, with leather trim, thick carpets and wooden door cappings; the WA was a relaxing car in which to travel. The unusual octagonal ivory-backed dials were neat, and the comprehensively equipped toolkit was jewel-like.

Had it not been for World War II, the WA might have gone on to become one of the finest touring cars of its day, but, as it appeared in 1938, only 369 were built before the Abingdon factory ceased car production in order to assist with the war effort.

MG's large car range, the WA, was cruelly interrupted by the war before production could really gain momentum. With only 369 built, this handsome car remains highly sought after.

WILLYS MODEL 38

In its home market of the United States, the Willys Model 38 had one key selling point: its incredibly competitive price. The new car was a direct descendant of the Willys Model 77, but it did not look quite so competitive once exported to Europe, where it was overshadowed by its good-value opposition.

Willys had spent the 1930s in almost constant crisis and hoped that the Model 38 would attract serious sales and turn around the company's fortunes. But it did not happen. For example, in 1938, the company planned to build 125,000, but only 12,000 rolled off the production lines, despite various bodystyles being available. The 77 was outdated at its launch in 1933, so trying to reincarnate it five years later with a new name and face, and by adding servo-assisted brakes and a synchromesh gearbox, was never going to work.

The side-valve four-cylinder engine was harsh and gutless, but one innovation was the 'floating power' rubber engine mount system.

ENGINE: 2200cc (134cu in), four-cylinder
POWER: 48bhp (36kW)
0–60MPH (96KM/H): n/a
TOP SPEED: 112km/h (70mph)
PRODUCTION TOTAL: n/a

CADILLAC 90

As with so many producers of luxury cars, the 1930s were a lean time for Cadillac. In order to survive, the company needed to cut costs – and a first step was the introduction of a new flathead V16 to replace its range of overhead-valve V16 and V12 engines. The new power unit generated the same 185bhp (138kW) as before, but was lighter, easier and cheaper to build, and far more reliable.

The high wear rates that the earlier engines suffered were lessened by the advent of precision con rod bearings, eliminating the knock. Installing the engine into the bodywork of the V8 Series 75 created the Cadillac 90. Passenger room was never a problem – although the wheelbase was 33cm (13in) shorter than the old V16-powered limousines, the bodies remained equal in size and often larger. Most Cadillac 90s were spacious Imperial limousines, and only a few were coachbuilt as open models.

However, economies of scale were not in favour of Cadillac. The company found it uneconomic to produce this V16 unit past 1940, even when sharing so many parts and bodystyles with the V8 75 series. The last appearance of anything other than a V8 engine in a Cadillac was in 1940, and it was the last model year for this car. The end of the 90 marked the end of an era for Cadillac.

ENGINE: 7064cc (430cu in),
  16-cylinder
POWER: 185bhp (138kW)
0–60MPH (96KM/H): 15 seconds
TOP SPEED: 145km/h (90mph)
PRODUCTION TOTAL: 514

LEA FRANCIS 12HP

The Le Francis 12hp (9kW) was an elegant car available in three bodystyles – a four-seater saloon, a six-light saloon (where the rear quarterlights hinged open vertically) and an attractive two-door drophead coupé with forward-opening 'suicide' doors.

The sophisticated four-cylinder engine featured twin camshafts. It was unusual, however, as it had both camshafts located close to the top of the cylinder block, as opposed to the head itself – the conventional overhead arrangement is generally recognized to aid cooling. There was a single-plate clutch, four-speed gearbox and a divided propshaft and spinal bevel rear axle.

The 12hp was overshadowed by the company's struggles. Having closed temporarily in 1935, Lea Francis reopened for business in 1937, only to face stunted demand through a high purchase tax, then major shortage of raw materials due to the onset of World War II.

By the 1950s, the company was in trouble again, and closed. A third appearance was made in 1960, with the Ford Zephyr-engined Leaf-Lynx. The firm was moribund until the 1980s, when a brief alliance with Jaguar resulted in production of an unsuccessful roadster.

ENGINE: 1489cc (91cu in), four-cylinder
POWER: 12bhp (9kW)
0–60MPH (96KM/H): n/a
TOP SPEED: n/a
PRODUCTION TOTAL: n/a

With a sophisticated double overhead camshaft engine and three body styles, the Lea Francis 12hp should have been a genuine success. However, the company was struggling, and demand for the car was stifled by its high price.

SINGER SUPER TEN

The Singer Ten was a mid-range saloon that featured a spacious and airy interior, thanks to its four-door, six-light saloon body. Announced in August 1938, the new Ten and its upmarket brother, the Super Ten, featured a bored-out version of the engine fitted to the updated Bantam, the Ten's smaller sister. Isolated on rubber mountings for added refinement, the engine clearly demonstrated the Singer's high-quality engineering.

Two versions of the Ten were available, the cheaper Popular model and the De Luxe, or Super Ten. The difference between the two was marked. The Popular had a basic three-speed synchromesh gearbox, whereas the De Luxe made do with an extra ratio, which bridged the gap to the more expensive Twelve, the next car up in the Singer range. The De Luxe was also equipped with a sliding sunroof and two windscreen wipers; the Popular made do with just a single wiper. A minor 1933 face-lift saw changes to the radiator grille, dashboard and interior trim, but the car was dropped in 1940 to make way for the war effort.

ENGINE: 1194cc (73cu in), four-cylinder
POWER: 37bhp (27.5kW)
0–60MPH (96KM/H): n/a
TOP SPEED: 100km/h (62mph)
PRODUCTION TOTAL: 11,595

PEUGEOT 202

ENGINE: 1133cc (69 cu in) 4-cylinder
POWER: 22kW (30bhp)
0-60MPH (96KM/H): n/a
TOP SPEED: 96km/h (60mph)
PRODUCTION TOTAL: 104,126

The Peugeot 202 was launched as a downmarket version of the 402. Powered by an all-new overhead valve engine with 30bhp (22kW) and suspended by quarter elliptic leaf springs, this was not a car to set the pulses racing.

The 202's styling was adventurous (not always a Peugeot strong point), and the lean-back nose and integrated headlamps hinted at the more progressive styling that would sweep through the industry in the aftermath of World War II.

Production would stop for the conflict, but luckily for Peugeot its factory and production tooling for the car survived relatively intact, meaning a swift restart of production after the war.

The Peugeot proved to be a nice car to drive thanks to the pleasant three-speed all-synchromesh gearbox, if you weren't looking for electrifying performance.

TATRA T57B

CZECHOSLOVAKIA 1938–49

Being the first of the marque to be imported into the United Kingdom, the Tatra T57 was a mild introduction into the marketplace. At a price of £260, however, it was simply too expensive to compete successfully against its domestic rivals. When introduced in 1931, the Tatra T57B featured an 1150cc (70cu in) front-mounted air-cooled overhead-valve engine that generated a mere 18bhp (13kW). As was traditional with Tatra at the time, it also had a tubular chassis with swing axles at the rear; as a result, handling was 'interesting'.

As well as the standard cars, a special Fitzmaurice version was created. Costing a hefty £595, the upgunned model was powered by a 1484cc (91cu in) engine, and boasted extra instrumentation and a more luxurious interior. It became the T57A in 1936, when the power output was increased to 20bhp (15kW); further changes made in 1938 resulted in it becoming the T57B. Now powered by a 1256cc (77cu in) version of the same engine, maximum power was raised to 25bhp (19kW). T57B models included a closed saloon and an open tourer. They all had a ride quality far ahead of anything else available in the car's market.

ENGINE: 1256cc (77cu in), four-cylinder
POWER: 25bhp (19kW)
0–60MPH (96KM/H): n/a
TOP SPEED: n/a
PRODUCTION TOTAL: 22,000 (of all T57 types)

PACKARD EIGHT/120

UNITED STATES 1938–39

ENGINE: 4620cc (282cu in), eight-cylinder
POWER: n/a
0–60MPH (96KM/H): n/a
TOP SPEED: 135km/h (84mph)
PRODUCTION TOTAL: 40,271

Towards the end of the 1930s, Packard decided it was time to move downmarket. The 120 was the car with which to meet that aim and, as a result, it was a successful and desirable vehicle.

Originally called the Eight, its name was changed to Packard 120 after a mere six months in order to put clear blue water between this and Packard's more luxury-oriented cars. Styling was typically neat, with faired-in mudguards, a sloping grille and V-shaped windscreen.

The Eight/120 majored on typically impressive build quality, and the technical supremacy associated with the marque proved a big hit with the middle classes. It was keenly priced, and that made it a strong seller compared with more mainstream Oldsmobiles, Chevrolets and Fords – cars that were similarly priced, but were far more ordinary.

Available with several coachbuilt bodystyles, the Eight/120 was most popular in four-door touring saloon form. Buyers could also choose a two-door sporting coupé, a drophead convertible saloon, a shorter coupé-shaped convertible or a stretched limousine. All were good, solid cars to drive, while the addition of overdrive for the 1939 model year made them less thirsty than many of their contemporaries.

The 8/120 marked a move downmarket for the once mighty Packard, and although the price was more enticing, the quality remained as impressive as ever and it sold 40,000 in two years.

PEUGEOT 402

FRANCE 1939

The Peugeot 402 took streamlining to another level, with headlights concealed inside an art deco radiator grille, horizontal bonnet (hood) cooling fins and stylized rear wheel spats. It was obviously an answer to the technologically innovative Citroën Traction Avant, but the differences were stark – underneath the futuristic skin was a conventional machine. It featured cantilever suspension (independent at the

Peugeot's styling took an adventurous twist with the 202 and 402 ranges. Art deco streamlining and concealed headlamps looked excellent, but production ceased prematurely.

front) rear-wheel drive and a three-speed synchromesh gearbox, and was powered by an extremely conventional four-cylinder overhead-valve engine.

Interesting variants of the 402 included the 402L, which used the smaller bodyshell of the 302 coupled to the 402's engine and transmission, as well as the stunning 402DS racing coupé, of which 200 were built. It could top 150km/h (95mph) and had styling reminiscent of contemporary coachbuilt Delahayes. Still, conservative Peugeot buyers were not quite ready for the 402 when it appeared in 1939, and lifetime sales were correspondingly disappointing. The 402 could have been a massive success, though. Almost 80,000 were sold in its first year, but then World War II broke out and production was shelved.

ENGINE: 1991cc (121cu in), four-cylinder
POWER: n/a
0–60MPH (96KM/H): n/a
TOP SPEED: 129km/h (80mph)
PRODUCTION TOTAL: 79,862

HILLMAN MINX PHASE I

UNITED KINGDOM 1939–47

ENGINE: 1185cc (72cu in), four-cylinder
POWER: 35bhp (26kW)
0–60MPH (96KM/H): n/a
TOP SPEED: 104km/h (65mph)
PRODUCTION TOTAL: n/a

The year 1939 saw the beginning of one of the longer running family car names in British automotive history. The Hillman Minx was a conservative car, though – and, as with many cars designed immediately prior to World War II, the running gear was dated by the time the car went into production. With side-valve engine, semi-elliptic springs and Bendix brakes, only the floor gearchange felt modern.

The Minx Phase I was commonly used for military service and featured in many old war films. At the time, its half-unitary construction was something of a novelty, and the car-buying public wanted to buy the Minx in numbers once the war ended.

As well as the four-door saloon with its front suicide doors, there was an elegant two-door coupé from 1946 and an estate (station wagon) based on the Commer van, and a convertible. In terms of body engineering, an interesting

point of the Minx was that it was one of the first British cars to feature a one-piece 'alligator' bonnet (hood), where the sides lift up simultaneously with the grille.

The Phase II that replaced it was not a massive step forwards, but it did have integral headlights and hydraulic brakes, and went back to a column change.

Considered a conservative choice for family buyers when it was launched in 1939, the Minx Phase I did feature the then advanced semi-unitary construction.

DAIMLER DB18

UNITED KINGDOM 1939–50

In the late 1930s, Daimler's cars had acquired a reputation for being too large, heavy and unwieldy to deliver any real driving pleasure. No one knew this more than Laurence Pomeroy Senior, chief engineer at the company, and he signalled a major change in thinking.

The new car to reflect Pomeroy's new approach was the Light Straight Eight, a car that in four-door saloon form could reach an impressive 137km/h (85mph) top speed. The momentum was gained with the introduction of the smaller 'Fifteen' in 1935. This car featured Daimler's first independent

Although it might have looked sporting, DB18 majored on typical solid Daimler construction.

suspension set-up and was an altogether lighter drive. When the Fifteen's engine grew from 2.1 litres (128cu in) to 2.5 litres (154cu in) in 1938, it was renamed the DB18.

A sporting version known as the 'Dolphin' was launched. It was the sporting DB18 and had wedge-shaped combustion chambers, twin carburettors, a raised compression ratio and modified exhaust to produce 90bhp (67kW) from an engine that previously managed just 64bhp (48kW). It was in this form that the car became successful in domestic rally competitions.

World War II interrupted further development, but the DB 18 appeared almost immediately after with a production Dolphin cylinder head. The Special Sports, a focused performance model with drophead bodywork by coachbuilders Tickford, joined the standard four-door saloon and pretty two-door convertible in 1948.

ENGINE: 2522cc (154cu in), six-cylinder
POWER: 90bhp (67kW)
0–60MPH (96KM/H): 28 seconds
TOP SPEED: 115km/h (72mph)
PRODUCTION TOTAL: 3390

LANCIA APRILIA
ITALY 1936–49

Lancia's Aprilia was light years ahead of its time. Compared to the standard vehicles mass-produced by other European firms, its specification sheet read like that of a car built in the late 1950s, not the 1930s.

Like its more expensive cutting-edge counterpart, the Citroën Traction Avant, the Lancia Aprilia featured monocoque construction, all-round independent suspension and hydraulic brakes – in addition to that it also had neat, pillarless styling and an aerodynamically styled body that had obviously been designed in the wind tunnel. Powered by a small V4 overhead camshaft engine, the 1352cc (83cu in) engine was adequately powerful, but it was exceptionally lively. A well-driven Aprilia could outperform many supposedly superior sports cars.

The Aprilia was available in three different wheelbases and two conventional chassis configurations so that customers who wanted to could fit their own coachbuilt special bodies. At the end of World War II, production of the Aprilia restarted, except with an uprated 1486cc (91cu in) V4 engine. The last example was built in October 1949. When it came out of the factory, a handwritten note by an unknown employee was found in the boot (trunk), paying tribute to what was possibly Lancia's most influential car.

ENGINE: 1352cc (83cu in), four-cylinder
POWER: 48bhp (36kW) at 4300rpm
0–60MPH (96KM/H): 22.8 seconds
TOP SPEED: 132km/h (82mph)
PRODUCTION TOTAL: 27,642

FIAT 1100
ITALY 1939–53

Introduced in 1939, the Fiat 1100 was basically a 508C with a new grille – however, it went on to become the quintessential Italian family car. Its major qualities included a spacious, practical interior and excellent reliability. In fact, the entire Balilla/508/1100 family of models succeeded in providing all the essential transportation requirements for a generation of Italians, and its legacy lived on with subsequent mid-sized Fiats. Various versions were produced including a Berlina saloon, a Berlina saloon with opening canvas roof, a cabriolet, a long-wheelbase and a taxi version.

The range continued to grow, and, in 1947, a touch of glamour was added with introduction of the 1100S, a two-seat coupé with a 51bhp (38kW) version of the 1089cc (66cu in) engine.

A coupé designed by Pininfarina, the 1100ES, was equally striking and used the mechanicals of the 1947 1100S to great effect – and coachbuilders Cisitalia stunned the world with the beautiful GS version.

In 1949, the Fiat 1100 was brought up to date and badged as the 1100E, or the long-wheelbase EL, and the only major change made was that the spare wheel was moved from the boot (trunk) lid to the inside of the luggage compartment. The gear lever became a column shifter (all the rage on the continent), and the transmission was uprated. Synchromesh was now on second, third and fourth gears.

ENGINE: 1089cc (66cu in), four-cylinder
POWER: 32bhp (24kW)
0–60MPH (96KM/H): 40 seconds
TOP SPEED: 116km/h (72mph)
PRODUCTION TOTAL: 327,496

HRG 1500
UNITED KINGDOM 1939–56

ENGINE: 1496cc (91cu in), four-cylinder
POWER: 61bhp (45kW)
0–60MPH (96KM/H): n/a
TOP SPEED: 152km/h (95mph)
PRODUCTION TOTAL: 173

When it was launched, the HRG 1500 looked nigh on identical to the outgoing 1.5 model. But there were plenty of changes under the skin, not least adoption of a more refined three-bearing Singer engine with synchromesh gearbox to replace the ageing Meadows engine of the older car.

Specification and levels of tune could be determined by the owner; as a result, no two cars ever left the factory the same. The last dozen or so 1500s were given the suffix 'WS' and were fitted with hotter Singer SM engines. A smaller 1.1-litre (67cu in) version shared the same bodystyle, but had a slightly shorter wheelbase and was even more agile.

After World War II, the company produced a more modern, low-drag closed body design called the Aerodynamic. It featured a full-width body and was driven by a 65bhp (48kW) engine. Alas the car was not a success, and only 35 were made. Today, HRG is a very desirable marque with high asking prices particularly liked by purists.

The 1500 was typical of the HRG breed. It was a quick car which handled well and could be specified in a variety of engine power outputs.

STUDEBAKER CHAMPION

ENGINE: 2692cc (164cu in),
    six-cylinder
POWER: 80bhp (60kW)
0–60MPH (96KM/H): n/a
TOP SPEED: n/a
PRODUCTION TOTAL: about 450,000

Just as other rivals were rushing to introduce more affordable cars, Studebaker joined in the game in 1939. Launched to appeal to a mass-market customer, the Champion was offered in a number of bodystyles, including a saloon, a three-passenger coupé and a five-passenger coupé.

Although the Champion was more expensive than its direct competitors, the company could never build enough cars to meet the strong demand from its customers – so Studebaker sold every car it could build. Sales were also helped by the fact that Studebaker launched an all-new Champion in 1946, whereas its competitors did not have their new designs ready until part way through 1948.

The model lasted until 1947 with relatively little development, and was subsequently replaced with an all-new model featuring modern styling. Both the pre-war car and its 1947 post-war successor were powered by an

80bhp (60kW) six-cylinder engine, with the option of an 85bhp (63kW) unit in the later car. Like its predecessor, the 1947 Champion was styled by famed designer Raymond Loewy. By the time Studebaker launched its 1953 range, the Champion name had been reduced to the status of trim level, rather than a distinct model. By this point, the Commander and President were now the same car, but possessing higher levels of specification.

Further evidence if any were needed, that the American industry was more than capable of producing advanced cars. The Studebaker Champion was light, economical and featured a monocoque body.

FORD UK ANGLIA/PREFECT/POPULAR

ENGINE: 933cc (57cu in),
    four-cylinder
POWER: 30bhp (22kW)
0–60MPH (96KM/H): n/a
TOP SPEED: 97km/h (60mph)
PRODUCTION TOTAL: 701,553

The famous Ford Anglia started out in 1939, when a restyled version of the old 7Y was launched bearing the name. War punctuated production until 1945, when cars were produced again in almost identical form. In 1948, Ford took the unusual step of effectively reintroducing the pre-war 7Y, with a new grille and more pronounced boot (trunk). The more luxurious four-door Prefect arrived in 1938, based on the 7W. Like the Anglia, it was reintroduced after the war and updated in 1948. From 1953, the Ford Popular took over from the Anglia and Prefect as the most basic car in the Ford range.

A long lived favourite with buyers on a budget, these cost conscious Fords proved exceptionally popular.

CHRYSLER NEW YORKER

UNITED STATES 1940–62

ENGINE: 6425cc (392cu in),
  eight-cylinder
POWER: 325bhp (242kW)
0–60MPH (96KM/H): 10 seconds
TOP SPEED: 193km/h (120mph)
PRODUCTION TOTAL: 400,000

The Chrysler New Yorker was part of the company's 1939 C-23 series. Three distinct models were offered with the same engine/chassis platform, with the Imperial and Saratoga being the other two. The New Yorker sat at the top of the tree, and featured distinctive two-tone upholstery complemented by high-quality interior trim.

War interrupted production in 1942. When the conflict was over, the pre-war car was reintroduced, then not updated until 1949. During its production run, the specification was tweaked, and, by 1951, the wheelbase had been lengthened and a V8 was standard.

When Chrysler developed Imperial into a stand-alone premium brand in 1955, the New Yorker went to the top of the range. Under the bonnet (hood) was the largest production engine of its kind, at 6425cc (392cu in), producing 325bhp (242kW).

Available as a saloon, two-door, convertible and estate (station wagon), the next evolution came in 1957 when fins were added. By 1959, that huge engine was no longer available, as production

The top of the range New Yorker was a suitable flagship for the Chrysler range, and cars bearing the name remained in production for a very long time. Annual improvements kept it fresh.

costs were being slashed. A minor face-ift in 1961 saw less garish trim being used. This was also the last year for the once-fashionable fins, as Chrysler adjusted to the simpler styles of the 1960s.

LINCOLN CONTINENTAL

UNITED STATES 1941–69

ENGINE: 7045cc (430cu in),
  eight-cylinder
POWER: 300bhp (224kW)
0–60MPH (96KM/H): 11 seconds
TOP SPEED: 192km/h (120mph)
PRODUCTION TOTAL: 384,230

When it was launched in 1941, the Lincoln Continental took the already imposing Zephyr and lifted it to another level entirely. The new car was quite literally elephantine, and the motoring public was left quite literally agog by the new vehicle.

The Continental was the responsibility of Edsel Ford, who decided to undo much of Ford's shoddy treatment of the once-great marque during the 1920s and build an impressive new flagship car that would restore the

A long lived name and one that became synonymous with the American establishment, the Lincoln Continental was a spectacular car.

fortunes of the Lincoln name. It was aimed squarely at the rich and famous – and the name was long running as a result, lasting well into late 1960s.

Funds were tight for the initial project, however, and virtually all of Edsel's investment was put into the body at the expense of the engineering of the car, which was mostly carried over from the Zephyr. Production of the Continental stopped due to World War II, but continued straight after before being replaced in 1948.

Focusing on styling had been a good move because it was certainly an imposing vehicle, and the Continental featured a huge bull-nosed bonnet (hood) and a wheelbase that put many commercial vehicles to shame. And there was no forgetting also that liberal sprinkling of chrome.

In 1956, the Continental name made a return as the Mk II coupé. Designed by John M. Reinhardt, it sold well for such an expensive hand-built car, and it was more than obvious that customers loved its exclusivity. A convertible prototype was shown in 1957, although it never went into commercial production.

The Mk III Continental of 1957 was – again – an off-the-scale enormous car. It measured 572cm (18.8ft) in length and did nothing to hide its bulk, instead rather conspicuously celebrating the fact with lashings of chrome. The car's pricing was dropped, though, and this was a definite move in the right direction because the Continental was now competing directly with its size rivals. Many bodystyles were offered, including saloon, hardtop saloon, coupé,

convertible and limousine. The Mk IV and V models of the car that ran from 1958 to 1960 incorporated detail changes only.

It is the final version of the Continental that is possibly the most famous of the lot. In production from 1961 to 1969, the smaller car was far more discreetly styled than previous Continentals, and it was sold in saloon, four-door convertible (with electric hood and rear hinged 'clap-doors') and coupé form.

The Continental's greatest claim to fame, or infamy, was that it was the car that US President John F. Kennedy was travelling in when he was assassinated in November 1963. Despite its being fitted with two-way radio and thick bulletproof steel plating along the side, there was scant protection for its rear-seat passengers.

The MkVI Continental's opulent interior is a sight to behold, with its quilted leather seats, power-assistance on every control and fake wood veneer trim. Air conditioning, power steering, electrically operated windows and locks that operated as soon as the car began to move all marked this out as a seriously well-stacked car.

The 1964 Continental gained a longer wheelbase, while the two-door coupé and the bigger 7565cc (462cu in) engine, which was capable of producing 365bhp (272kW), appeared two years later.

The Continental name continued into the 1970s, featuring a Rolls-Royce-inspired grille, shuttered headlights and 'opera' windows. Today, the Continental continues, and remains the car of choice for Americans who appreciate a bit of glitz in their lives.

HUMBER SUPER SNIPE I

UNITED KINGDOM 1945–48

The Humber Super Snipe traditionally evokes images of solid middle-class British motoring, and underneath that straitlaced exterior beat the heart of a Hillman. The first post-war Super Snipe I was a light revamp of the 1938-style Snipe, a car which could trace its underpinnings to the pre-war Hillman 14. This was badge engineering Rootes-style (the Rootes Group had taken over Humber in the 1930s).

The Super Snipe's exterior was suitably restrained, with an upright chrome grille, individual chromed front headlights, a long bonnet (hood), flat windscreen and 'suicide' front doors. Humbers were a step ahead of their Hillman cousins technologically, though, featuring hydraulic brakes, modern independent front suspension, luggage compartments that extended beyond the rear body line, and a sliding metal sunroof.

Despite the impressive size of its engine at just over four litres (249cu in) and six cylinders, the Super Snipe's performance could never really be described as anything other than stately. Its excessive body weight and brick outhouse-like aerodynamics meant top speed was limited to a mere 130km/h (81mph). Still, in 1952, a Snipe was driven from London to Cape Town in a record 13 days and 9 hours. The Super Snipe was

to sire a Pullman version, which sported a wheelbase stretch of 30cm (12in), but only around 500 of these limousines were built between 1945 and 1948.

ENGINE: 4086cc (249cu in), six-cylinder
POWER: 100bhp (75kW)
0–60MPH (96KM/H): 24.5 seconds
TOP SPEED: 130km/h (81mph)
PRODUCTION TOTAL: 3909

ARMSTRONG-SIDDELEY LANCASTER

UNITED KINGDOM 1945–52

Like nearly all British cars that were produced between 1945 and 1948, the Armstrong-Siddeley Lancaster was actually a pre-war design. Although this one did not actually enter production until the end of World War II, to become Britain's first all-new post-war car, the Lancaster was conceived and designed in the run-up to the conflict. Armstrong-Siddeley was quick to launch it – the car

appeared in May 1945 – and that allowed it to enter the record books as a car to enter production on the same week that the war in Europe officially ended.

Named after the famous bomber aircraft, the Lancaster was the first of a number of the company's products to take their names from the aviation industry. Power and performance, however, were hardly fighter-like. Its engine was a 2-litre

(121cu in) unit developing 70bhp (52kW); a 2.3-litre (140cu in) 75bhp (56kW) unit replaced this engine in 1949.

The Lancaster was a solid car to drive, with a good ride thanks to torsion bar front suspension, hydromechanical brakes and a four-speed all-synchromesh gearbox. The interior of the car was spacious and well equipped, while rear legroom was on a par

with many much larger vehicles of the time. Armstrong-Siddeley replaced the Lancaster in 1952 with the all-new Sapphire.

ENGINE: 1991cc (121cu in), six-cylinder
POWER: 70bhp (52kW)
0–60MPH (96KM/H): n/a
TOP SPEED: 113km/h (70mph)
PRODUCTION TOTAL: 12,470

SKODA 1101

CZECHOSLOVAKIA 1945–52

The Czechoslovakian car manufacturer Skoda was a post–World War II success story and very much a testament to the determination of its management and workers – because, although the company's factory was all but destroyed in the last few weeks of the conflict, car production had resumed within just months of the cessation of hostilities.

Following the nationalization of the company in 1945, the first car

to be built by Skoda in the post-war era was the 1101. Pre-war in conception, it was based on the 1933 420 Popular, although the new car was longer, wider and more powerful, as well as being better equipped. The 1101 reached the marketplace in the autumn of 1945, and was only available in one bodystyle – a two-door four-seater saloon. It was known as the 1101 Tudor (for 'two-door'). An estate (station

wagon) and four-door saloon were launched in 1949, then in 1952, and the 1101 was replaced by the 1200 (available from 1949), which differed from the 1101 in only a few minor modifications.

The 1101 featured a four-speed gearbox mated to a 1089cc (66cu in) overhead-valve engine. More bodystyles were offered soon after the car's introduction, although they were not for general consumption, as they were mostly

ambulances and vans. The most interesting derivative was the 1101P, which was an all-terrain version built specially for military and police use.

ENGINE: 1089cc (66cu in), four-cylinder
POWER: 32bhp (24kW)
0–60MPH (96KM/H): n/a
TOP SPEED: n/a
PRODUCTION TOTAL: n/a

ARMSTRONG-SIDDELEY HURRICANE

UNITED KINGDOM 1945–53

Alongside the Lancaster, the Armstrong-Siddeley Hurricane was the first new British car to be launched after World War II.

Armstrong-Siddeley's range in the 1940s used a fair bit of component sharing. When the Hurricane was launched, it went alongside the Lancaster and shared the same chassis, although it was a two-door drophead only. The Hurricane's front-end styling was identical to the saloon, with flush-fitting headlights and faired-in front wings (fenders), plus wide-opening backward-hinged doors, giving it an appealing sporting look.

Extending the range was the budget Typhoon, and it had a cheaper fabric hood and a more spartan interior. Like the Lancaster, the Hurricane and Typhoon received a larger 2.3-litre (140cu in) engine in 1949, but the Typhoon version was dropped shortly after this engine was introduced, so only a handful of cars was equipped with the larger unit. The Hurricane and Typhoon were not great cars to drive, but they were comfortable touring machines.

ENGINE: 1991cc (121cu in), six-cylinder
POWER: 70bhp (52kW)
0–60MPH (96KM/H): n/a
TOP SPEED: 121km/h (75mph)
PRODUCTION TOTAL: n/a

RILEY RM

UNITED KINGDOM 1945–54

The first post–World War II model to be produced by Riley was the RMA. It was an elegant-looking saloon, which featured streamlined styling, and a torsion bar independent front suspension system and semi-elliptic leaf springs at the back. As a result the car looked good and handled well.

Despite a takeover by the Lord Morris's Nuffield organization, Riley cars had remained traditionally produced following World War II, and employed the same separate chassis and ash-frame construction that had graced the company's earlier cars.

The RMA was an impressive car for its era, featuring a 1.5-litre (91cu in) twin-camshaft that was

It might have boasted fairly staid styling, but a double overhead camshaft engine delivered the Riley RM with plenty of power.

way ahead of its time, offering an impressive power output for such a small-capacity unit. It was the basis for a host of other RM-type Rileys, right up to the RMF. The Rily RME, which replaced the RMB in 1952, used the same engine,

but had hydraulic brakes and better all-round visibility, while the RMB (another four-door saloon), RMC (two-door convertible), RMD (drophead coupé) and RMF came with a long-stroke four-cylinder 2443cc (149cu in) engine, a two-

door convertible option and the ability to reach 161km/h (100mph) in full 100bhp (75kW) tune.

This was a true and traditional British touring saloon that has often been overlooked by collectors in more recent years.

ENGINE: 1496cc (91cu in), four-cylinder
POWER: 54bhp (40kW)
0–60MPH (96KM/H): 25.1 seconds
TOP SPEED: 121km/h (75mph)
PRODUCTION TOTAL: 22,909

VOLKSWAGEN BEETLE

GERMANY 1945–2003

ENGINE: 1131cc (69cu in), four-cylinder
POWER: 25bhp (19kW)
0–60MPH (96KM/H): n/a
TOP SPEED: 101km/h (63mph)
PRODUCTION TOTAL: 22,000,000

Arguably the most popular car of all time and certainly the most recognizable, the Volkswagen Beetle was close to never actually entering production. In its 58-year production run, this car has engaged so many people like no other. Even today, long after its popularity as a humdrum mode of transport has faded away, it demands a cultish following that is sometimes difficult to explain rationally. Interestingly, although more than 22 million Beetles left production lines across the globe, not a single one ever wore that name badge – it was a nickname picked up because of its rounded and individual styling.

The Beetle started out as a pet project of Ferdinand Porsche, who set up a design studio in the early

1930s. He designed rear-engined cars for Zundapp and NSU, but neither could afford to tool up for production. In 1934, however, the German Nazi administration requested that a people's car (the German translation is *Volkswagen*) be designed and built. By 1937, 30 prototypes had been made by Mercedes-Benz, and the following year its car was ready for production until the outbreak of World War II delayed manufacture.

The first examples of the Beetle, which at the time were simply called the Volkswagen, were built in 1945. The first year of the car's manufacture produced just 1785 units, with each car fitted with an 1131cc (69cu in) four-cylinder engine, cable-operated brakes and a transmission with no synchromesh.

In spite of its basic specification, however, the Beetle proved popular, as it was cheap and reliable, and post-war Germans needed new cars. Production continued throughout the 1940s and, by the start of the 1950s, the major export drive began. The funny

little car caught the imagination of people all across the world, and this led to continuous development. The Beetle's sheer affordability and reliability were always major selling points, but roadholding was tail-happy, and performance lacking.

Because the Beetle was Volkswagen's sole product, it received considerable internal development until the beginning of the 1960s. The most significant external change was probably the move from a split rear window to a single unit in 1953; although under the skin changes were introduced on an almost annual basis – such as an improved transmission and better brakes.

In 1954, the engine grew to 1192cc (73cu in) and, in 1960, the car received a full-synchromesh gearbox, along with a small but welcome power increase to 34bhp (25kW). Similarly, the move in 1962 to hydraulic brakes in place of the previous cable-operated system made the car more faithful – although such a change was well overdue in its home

market, as export models had been equipped with the new brakes since 1950.

A 1285cc (78cu in) powerplant was installed In 1965, and the arrival of the 1500 Beetle the following year meant that the car was finally able to compete on equal terms with many of its competitors – especially as disc brakes were also now part of the mechanical package. In 1968, the bumpers grew in size, along with the rear light clusters, and, in 1972, the 1300cc (79cu in) 1302 and 1600cc (98cu in) 1302S were launched with MacPherson strut front suspension. These models were superseded by the curved windscreen 1303 and 1303S a year later. Production in Volkswagen's Wolfsburg factory was phased out in 1977, but continued in Mexico, where Beetles were made until 2003.

The Beetle remained in production for a remarkable run – it had great charm, legendary reliability and good build quality.

VAUXHALL 10

ENGINE: 1203cc (73cu in),
four-cylinder
POWER: 31bhp (23kW)
0–60MPH (96KM/H): n/a
TOP SPEED: 97km/h (60mph)
PRODUCTION TOTAL: n/a

Vauxhall's 1946 version of its family car, the 10, was little different from the car that had first been seen on the marketplace in 1938. However, because of the shortage of new cars in the immediate post-war period, this really did not matter – buyers were clamouring for cars, and every car that rolled out of UK factories found a buyer easily.

The Vauxhall 10 was not disadvantaged anyway, as it was perfectly capable when it hit the market in 1938 and, added to this, it was up against opposition that had been introduced long before that – as car design had been largely frozen by World War II.

The low-quality petrol that was available in the immediate post-war years meant that the 1203cc (73cu in) engine was detuned slightly, to allow it to run on the low-octane fuel, making it affordable to run.

The Vauxhall 10hp (7.5kW) was actually pretty advanced, thanks to its innovative semi-monocoque construction, a rare feature in its market sector at the time; most rivals still sat squarely on separate chassis. This, along with a longer wheelbase than its predecessor, meant that there was much more interior space than any of its rivals. The fact that four side windows ensured the cabin had a more spacious and airy feel also placed it ahead of the opposition.

Vauxhall's first new post-war car may have differed little from its pre-war counterpart, but thanks to semi-monocoque construction and roomy interior, it remained technically up to date.

WOLSELEY EIGHT

With World War II over, it was clear that the Nuffield Group's two main car companies would be doing a considerable amount of component sharing in the coming years. The process was already under way before the war, but, with the company needing to run as cost effectively as possible, this would be an agreeable way of helping to make ends meet.

When the post-war Wolseley Eight appeared it was no surprise to see that it was essentially a Morris Eight with a more distinctive Wolseley front end grafted on – something that would happen for a good number of years to come. With a 33bhp (25kW) overhead-valve engine displacing 918cc (56cu in) (derived from the side-valve unit seen in the Morris Eight), the

Wolseley Eight was fitted with a four-speed gearbox and hydraulic brakes, along with a beam front axle. The powerplant was noteworthy for being far smoother than the side-valve version.

A higher level of interior trim also distanced the Wolseley from its lesser sibling. The car was much nicer to drive than its Morris counterpart, but sales told a

different story – just over 5000 Wolseleys were made, compared with 120,000 Morris Eights.

ENGINE: 918cc (56cu in),
four-cylinder
POWER: 33bhp (25kW)
0–60MPH (96KM/H): n/a
TOP SPEED: 96km/h (60mph)
PRODUCTION TOTAL: 5344

TRIUMPH ROADSTER

In 1944, the Triumph Motor Company was purchased by Standard, which was looking for a way to give its model range a bit of a sporting lift. Although much of Triumph's physical assets were

badly damaged during bombing raids on Coventry during World War II, the name and enthusiasm for the old company remained intact. Standard oversaw the development of a new Triumph

tubular chassis – a set-up intended to be capable of taking two different bodies, a luxury saloon and a sporting open tourer.

The 1800/2000 Roadster made its debut in 1946, and a new era

for Triumph began. The Standard-Triumph concern designed the car in-house, producing a curvaceous and elegant but unconventional design. The Roadster could seat three abreast up front, making it an almost practical proposition – and, if the passengers were on speaking terms, another two could be tightly squeezed in the car's rear dickey seat.

A pre-war Standard 1776cc (108cu in) side-valve engine initially powered the Triumph Roadster, but a much more potent 2088cc (127cu in) unit replaced it in 1948. The Roadster was discontinued in 1949, after it found itself unable to compete strongly enough in the vital export market – although it holds claim to being the final British car to be sold with a dickey seat.

ENGINE: 1776cc (108cu in),
 four-cylinder
POWER: 65bhp (48kW) at 4500rpm
0–60MPH (96KM/H): 34.4 seconds
TOP SPEED: 121km/h (80mph)
PRODUCTION TOTAL: 4501

The Triumph Roadster was the first product to be launched by the re-invented Triumph, now owned by the Standard Motor Company.

HEALEY 2.4 WESTLAND

UNITED KINGDOM 1946–50

The Warwick-built Healey was one of the fastest British four-seaters of the post-war era, and is rare and highly sought after in any form. Its appeal came from its light alloy-over-wood body, which weighed around 1000kg (one ton), combined with a stiff box-section chassis and an accomplished high-camshaft Riley engine.

The Westland was the roadster version, and the most desirable of

With a top speed of 168km/h (105mph), the 2.4 Westland was one of the fastest four-seaters available in the post-war years.

the models, but there was also an Elliot saloon (which was one of the fastest closed cars produced in Britain at the time) and a slab-sided drophead coupé called the Sportsmobile. Despite its powerful 104bhp (77kW) engine, however,

it proved unpopular with the British car buyer.

With coil springs all round, and trailing arms at the front, handling of the Westland was predictable and neat – and the car also featured hydraulic brakes. This

was an advanced set-up for British cars of the 1940s. There were also some special-bodied cars made by Duncan and even Italian stylist Bertone, but these examples are rare and fetch high premiums on the classic car market.

ENGINE: 2443cc (379cu in), four-cylinder
POWER: 90bhp (67kW)
0–60MPH: 12.3 seconds
TOP SPEED: 168km/h (105mph)
PRODUCTION TOTAL: 64

INVICTA BLACK PRINCE

UNITED KINGDOM 1946–50

ENGINE: 2997cc (183cu in),
six-cylinder
POWER: 24bhp (18kW)
0–60MPH (96KM/H): n/a
TOP SPEED: n/a
PRODUCTION TOTAL: n/a

W.G. Watson, who had been responsible for the original Invicta of the 1920s, designed the Invicta Black Prince. When launched, the Black Prince cost a hefty £3000, although, by the time production had finally drawn to a close in 1950, that had increased to an eye-watering £4000. Needless to say, despite the financial investment and brave use of previously untried technology, very few examples sold.

The Invicta Company died just four years after World War II, when AFN Ltd took over its assets. The blame for this collapse can be pinned squarely on the door of the car – and not just on that high price. The Black Prince, with its

Meadows-based double-overhead camshaft straight-six 3-litre (183cu in) engine and semi-automatic transmission, was not exactly exciting – despite the novelty of built-in hydraulic jacks.

As there was no gearbox as such on the Black Prince, power was transmitted via a Brockhouse

hydraulic torque converter. The suspension was fully independent with torsion bars at the front.

As a goodwill gesture, rather than for commercial gain, the remaining cars, as well as all the company's spare parts, were bought by AFN Ltd, manufacturers of the Frazer-Nash.

With its Meadows-based double overhead camshaft, straight-six 3-litre (183 cu in) engine, the Black prince promised a lot, but failed to deliver excitement for its wealthy buyers.

DAIMLER DE 27

UNITED KINGDOM 1946–51

In a busy year, two new Daimler models were launched in 1946, the DE 27 and the 4.6-litre (281cu in) straight-eight DE 36. The 4.1-litre (250cu in) six-cylinder DE 27 was regarded as the poor driver's alternative to the bigger car, but it was still a magnificent machine in its own right.

The DE 27 had several advantages over its older brethren, which had made do with worm

drive. The DE 27 and DE 36's chassis were equipped with Daimler's first hypoid differential – quite a step forwards. Although the DE 27 was a large car, it was really well proportioned – because the engine was set well back on the chassis, there was no ugly overhang at the front.

Up to that point, Daimler had been buying other companies and had acquired some of the country's

longest established and most respected coachbuilders – including Barker and also Hooper. Those companies could then use their magic on this impressive new chassis to create limousines and a 381cm (150in) wheelbase for Daimler's own hire service. In fact, the DE 27 became one of the more versatile models. Hooper built an ambulance body on the DE 27 chassis, but, to ensure that there

was a low, flat floor, the whole drivetrain had to be offset so that the propshaft ran down the side rather than the centre of the body.

ENGINE: 4095cc (250cu in),
six-cylinder
POWER: 110bhp (82kW)
0–60MPH (96KM/H): 29 seconds
TOP SPEED: 127km/h (79mph)
PRODUCTION TOTAL: 255

BENTLEY MK VI

UNITED KINGDOM 1946–52

Bentley finally returned to an individual design for the Mk VI, its first post-war model launch after a decade of being Rolls-Royce's sporting arm. Using a modified Rolls-Royce chassis for the new car, the Bentley Mk VI parent company Rolls-Royce ensured that the new Bentley's compact body styling was used in the Silver Dawn. This was an export-only model which was built to satisfy demand for compact luxury cars in overseas markets. Launched in 1946, the Bentley

Mk VI featured a standard and rather predictable separate chassis construction. In other respects, however, the car was very modern, featuring industry standard servo-assisted brakes, a smooth four-speed gearbox and independent

Designed as an individual Bentley, the Mk VI was badge engineered to become the Rolls-Royce Silver Dawn. It was pretty to look at, though, and available with off-the-shelf coachwork.

front suspension. The car was also another first for Bentley in another way: it was the first Bentley to be sold as a finished product. This was because the Mk VI was an off-the-shelf bodystyle, rather than simply a chassis on which buyers would need to specify their own coachbuilt design.

Aluminium-bodied Park Ward, H.J. Mulliner and James Young styles were very much a symbol of wealth, costing more than twice the price of a standard car. So the bespoke option was there for customers, at a price. Reliable and comfortable, even if not as exciting as the Bentleys of old, the Bentley Mk VI was an exquisitely well-made vehicle that remains a classic to this day.

ENGINE: 4257cc (260cu in), six-cylinder
POWER: 137bhp (102kW)
0–60MPH (96KM/H): 16.3 seconds
TOP SPEED: 152km/h (94mph)
PRODUCTION TOTAL: 5201

DELAHAYE 175

FRANCE 1946–52

The Delahaye 175 and its sister the 180 may have been commercial and dynamic failures, but there's no denying their fine styling and pace: they had a top speed of 177km/h (110mph).

cylinder unit, and the car's seven-bearing motor had been bored out to a mighty 4.5 litres (272cu in). Depending on the state of tune (with up to three carburettors), it was capable of producing from 125bhp (93kW) to 140bhp (104kW). The unit was linked to a Cotal electromagnetic gearbox, and the axle tube passed through the side members of the chassis and hydraulic brakes were fitted.

The 175 was indisputably a very fast car, but the chassis design was an unsatisfactory combination of Dubonnet independent suspension and a rear de Dion set-up. There was a variety of bodystyles on offer, some of which were more successful than others, but all were amazing to look at. Sadly, the 175 and the companion Type 180 were both commercial and dynamic failures.

W hile most manufacturers were content to reintroduce their pre-war cars or present austerity models, the Delahaye 175 caused a sensation by being unashamedly glamorous and expensive.

Delahaye was unreservedly a star of the Paris Motor Show in 1946, but the company was firmly aiming the 175 at the lucrative export markets rather than the home one. The car was available in both left- and right-hand drive, and added to that as further enticement was even a choice of wheelbase lengths.

The 175's engine was a development of the old 135 six-

ENGINE: 4455cc (272cu in), six-cylinder
POWER: 125–140bhp (93–104kW)
0–60MPH (96KM/H): 12 seconds
TOP SPEED: 177km/h (110mph)
PRODUCTION TOTAL: 150

JENSEN PW

UNITED KINGDOM 1946–52

A llan and Richard Jensen were coachbuilders who set up their own company in 1934, and they launched the first car to carry their name, the 3.6-litre (220cu in) Ford V8-engined tourer, in 1935. The Jensen company survived the war and launched its elegant PW model (which stood, appropriately, for Post-War) despite a financially turbulent post-war period.

The PW was available in two bodystyles – a four-door saloon and, from 1948, a drophead coupé. The expansive and expensive body featured a number of technical innovations, and was mounted on a tubular-braced chassis from the pre-war HC model. It included independent coil-sprung suspension at the front and the luxury of all-round

hydraulic brakes. A straight-eight Meadows engine powered the opulent PW; however, vibration problems hastened a switch to a far smoother pre-war 4.2-litre (256cu in) Nash unit after a mere 15 cars had been built. From 1949, Austin A135 engines were offered instead.

Despite a production lifespan of six years, only a few of these

handbuilt cars were made at the West Bromwich factory, and only one convertible survives today.

ENGINE: 3993cc (244cu in), six-cylinder
POWER: 130bhp (97kW)
0–60MPH (96KM/H): n/a
TOP SPEED: 152km/h (95mph)
PRODUCTION TOTAL: 7

SALMSON S4

FRANCE 1946–52

D uring the 1920s, the first Salmson S4s were popular with people who needed budget mobility – and were cyclecars, based on the well-known GN

models. By the 1930s, a demand for more sophisticated transport meant that cyclecars were a dying breed, so Salmson moved upmarket through necessity.

The company's cars proved popular, and Salmson even set up a factory in Britain for a while; however, during the post–World War II period, all its cars were built

in France. In 1946, the S4 was launched and became Salmson's first post-war model.

With a 2218cc (135cu in) four-cylinder twin-camshaft engine, the car was aimed at the upper middle-class end of the market, and there was no shortage of innovation to be found under the car's bonnet (hood).

The conrods were made from Duralumin, the aluminium cylinder heads incorporated hemispherical combustion chambers, the crankshaft was nitrided to make it last longer, the valves incorporated chrome and the valve springs featured vanadium to increase their lifespan. The choice of materials sounds advanced even today. The most innovative engineering to be found on the car was in the Cotal pre-selector transmission. This allowed gearchanges to be made as quickly as the driver could execute them, without the need to use the clutch once the car was on the move – a system that proved very effective.

ENGINE: 2218cc (135cu in), four-cylinder
POWER: 68bhp (51kW)
0–60MPH (96KM/H): n/a
TOP SPEED: 130km/h (81mph)
PRODUCTION TOTAL: n/a

LAGONDA 2.6-LITRE

UNITED KINGDOM 1946–53

The new Lagonda 2.6-litre (157cu in) saloon had been introduced by 1935, designed by none other than the company's technical director at the time, W.O. Bentley. Still, the company's fortunes continued to look shaky. Lagonda had been rescued from receivership in 1935 by Alan Good (who paid just £67,000 for the company), but its fate continued to look uncertain until David Brown's revitalized Aston Martin company bought it out in 1947.

Two body types were available: a two-door saloon and a sleek-looking four-seater convertible. Each had semi-faired headlights, curving rearward chrome grille and sweeping front wings (fenders).

The new car was much smaller than the previous 1930s Lagondas, but it featured a traditional sturdy channel-section cruciform chassis and an all-independent suspension. The swing axles and torsion bars at the rear, rack-and-pinion steering and rear wheel in-board brakes were very effective.

The 1952 Mk II version of the Lagonda 2.6-litre had a variety of minor changes both inside and out, the majority of which were cosmetic. Only 550 of these luxurious cars were made during its seven-year production lifespan.

ENGINE: 2580cc (157cu in), six-cylinder
POWER: 105bhp (78kW)
0–60MPH (96KM/H): 17.6 seconds
TOP SPEED: 144km/h (90mph)
PRODUCTION TOTAL: 550

DELAGE D6 3-LITRE

FRANCE 1946–54

ENGINE: 2988cc (182cu in)
POWER: 130bhp (97kW)
0–60MPH (96KM/H): 14 seconds
TOP SPEED: 137km/h (85mph)
PRODUCTION TOTAL: 250

Like so many early post-war cars, the lineage of the 1946 Delage D6 can be directly traced to the pre-war cars such as the D6-70 and D6-75 models. These traditional tourers, saloons and specials were mated with Delage short-stroke 2729cc (167cu in) and 2800cc (171cu in) engines, and were essentially Delahaye designs.

The link between the two companies was close – Delage had been owned by Delahaye since 1935. The D6 was powered by a 3-litre (182cu in) engine with an innovative Cotal electric gearbox featuring four forward ratios and one reverse. Braking was hydraulically assisted, as was rapidly becoming the norm. The majority of D6s were supplied in rolling chassis form so that the buyer could then choose their favoured coachbuilder for a bespoke style.

Like many pre-war European cars, the D6 was available only in right-hand drive form, as it was seen as being safer when negotiating Alpine passes.

Although Delage could have continued producing reworked versions of Delahayes, the French government effectively wiped out its indigenous bespoke car industry by favouring mass production and penalizing the specialist manufacturers. Delage responded by merging with Hotchkiss in 1954, and this meant the end of the marque the following year.

This fussy-looking 1947 D6 drophead coupe may well have lacked the ultimate elegance of other Delage offerings, but with the option of going to various coachbuilders, buyers could avoid this problem.

JOWETT BRADFORD

UNITED KINGDOM 1946–54

ENGINE: 1005cc (61cu in), two-cylinder
POWER: 25bhp (19kW)
0–60MPH (96KM/H): n/a
TOP SPEED: 85km/h (53mph)
PRODUCTION TOTAL: 40,995

In the immediate aftermath of World War II, Jowett was very much a technically backward carmaker. The Jowett Bradford, for instance, featured an archaic flat-twin engine, cart springs and cable brakes – and these attributes linked it directly with the dawn of the motoring age. It was the same with the alloy-over-ash body and agricultural three-speed gearbox.

The car's performance was poor and the ride was boneshaking, but that did not slow sales at all. The Bradford won many plaudits because of its sheer invincibility – it never wore out and rarely let down its owner, no matter how badly it was treated. That led to a long life, and demand remained strong right up until the end of its production in the mid-1950s.

Despite the Bradford being available in a number of different bodystyles, including four- and six-light (window) forms (seating four and six people, respectively), it was as a lightweight commercial vehicle that it found most favour. Indeed, in this role – where a lack of refinement was no problem – the Bradford proved ideal, and it gained an excellent reputation as a reliable work tool.

Today, the Bradford retains its strong following among vintage commercial enthusiasts, and there is a very high survival rate among the 40,995 examples that were originally built.

TALBOT TALBOT-LAGO

FRANCE 1946–55

ENGINE: 2491cc (152cu in),
four-cylinder
POWER: 120bhp (89kW)
0–60MPH (96KM/H): n/a
TOP SPEED: 174km/h (109mph)
PRODUCTION TOTAL: about 80

Founded by Anthony Lago, Talbot-Lago was created to produce a range of exclusive and expensive sports cars. It was one of the companies that came about following the collapse of Sunbeam-Talbot-Darracq in 1935, when Lago bought the French portion of the group, Talbot, and its products remain highly desired today.

Initially, all Talbot-Lagos were six-cylinder machines, including the 1947 Grand Sport, which had a 4482cc (274cu in) engine – and that earned the company a reputation for smoothness and performance. The car was one of the era's ultimate grand tourers, and it had three carburettors, centre-lock wire wheels and independent front suspension.

Whereas the immediate post-war period and the return to austerity led to the downfall of other manufacturer's exotic designs, Talbot-Lagos remained admired by all – and were incredibly stylish with designs by flamboyant designer Saoutchik.

In 1950, the cheaper 2.7-litre (165cu in) Talbot-Lago Baby appeared, but even following a complete redesign in 1952 buyers stayed away. The company's last throw of the dice was the 1957 America model, which was powered by a 2.6-litre (159cu in) BMW engine. The company continued to struggle, and, in 1959, Simca absorbed the once-great marque.

Glorious to look at but financially devastating to its manufacturer, the Talbot-Lago had many admirers.

MOSKVICH 400

USSR 1946–56

ENGINE: 1074cc (66cu in),
four-cylinder
POWER: n/a
0–60MPH (96KM/H): n/a
TOP SPEED: n/a
PRODUCTION TOTAL: n/a

Moskvich, which means 'Muscovite', is a nickname for the cars produced by the Moscow-based company – but it was one that stuck, in much the same way as Beetle did for a certain small Volkswagen. Of course, Moskvich is a lot easier to pronounce than the company's official name, Avtomobilny Zavod Imeni Leninskogo Komsomola ('Youth Communist League Automobiles').

The company's first car, the Moskvich 10, was closely based on a 1920s Opel. This connection with the respected German carmaker continued for the 1946 400-Series cars and also with subsequent models, although not quite so directly. Based on the 1937 Opel Kadett, the 400 was ideal for the Russian market – it was ruggedly built and was powered by basic side-valve engines. Low maintenance and running costs were prime factors in such a vast, empty country. Joseph Stalin ordered that a four-seater model was produced, but this model – dubbed the 420 – was poorly built and best remembered for its huge panel gaps and scary body flex over rough surfaces.

During its 10-year production run, Moskvich sold more than half a million 400s. With technology firmly rooted in the 1930s, however, it was completely out of date by this time. In a market closed to imports, this was no great problem – which was just as well, as Moskvich had little money to develop a more modern replacement.

The classically styled Moskvich 400 was actually closely related to the Opel Kadett, and it was because of the good relationship between the two companies that the car could be launched in the Soviet Union.

ZIS 110

USSR 1946–56

ENGINE: 6-litre (366cu in),
eight-cylinder
POWER: 140bhp (104kW)
0–60MPH (96KM/H): n/a
TOP SPEED: 139km/h (87mph)
PRODUCTION TOTAL: about 1500

With looks that plagiarized the upmarket US Packards and Cadillacs of the early 1940s, the ZIS 110 was a limousine completely unaffordable for almost all Russians – remaining transport for the Communist elite.

Developed as World War II was coming to a close, the ZIS 110 went into production in August 1945, and was a clear statement of intent for the Russian industry. Powered by a huge 6-litre (366cu in) V8 engine generating 140bhp (104kW), the 110 could whisk its occupants to nearly 145km/h (90mph) and boasted up-to-the-minute features such as hydraulic valves, electric windows and independent front suspension.

Despite the fact that the car was an imposing limousine, its large dimensions lent it perfectly to the task of patients on stretchers. As a result, many were used as ambulances – without body modifications. Patients were simply loaded into the huge car

through the boot (trunk) opening. In 1966, when Stalin fell out of favour, a politically expedient move saw the ZIS 110 become the ZIL 110 – a return to the company's original nomenclature. When Lenin's popularity faded in the aftermath of his death, however, the company was renamed ZIS ('S' for Stalin) in 1933.

Although it looked like one, the ZIS 110 was no pre-war American luxury car. Beautifully built and finished in the USSR, only the elite could afford such a car.

ROLLS-ROYCE SILVER WRAITH

UNITED KINGDOM 1946–59

ENGINE: 4527cc (276cu in),
 six-cylinder
POWER: n/a
0–60MPH (96KM/H): 24 seconds
TOP SPEED: 137km/h (85mph)
PRODUCTION TOTAL: 1783

Rolls-Royce's first post–World War II car took over exactly from where the company left off before the conflict – the Silver Wraith was actually based on the short-lived 1939 car bearing the same name. Initially produced for export sales only, in a bid to boost Britain's shattered economy ('Export or Die'), most cars ended up going to the United States. In the end, the car was offered on the UK market from 1948 – and it was perfect for meeting pent-up demand.

Very few Silver Wraiths looked the same because no standard bodystyle was offered by Rolls-Royce, and it was up to the buyer to select a coachbuilder's design from those offered by dealerships. Many chose to have a car tailored to specific requirements – at a price, of course. The Silver Wraith's power came from a smooth new inlet-over-exhaust valve six-cylinder engine, and, although official power output was 'not stated' in line with Rolls-Royce tradition, most experts reckon it put out a healthy 130bhp (97kW).

In keeping with the marque's core values, the Silver Wraith was a supremely refined, beautifully engineered car, although it was no performance vehicle – and it was not bought for handling. Despite

Rolls-Royce's Silver Wraith had its roots planted firmly in the pre-war era, but its classic and timeless styling helped it become a major export seller.

this, the elegant and spacious long wheelbase variants became popular with the ruling classes – and that position was only further cemented when automatic gearboxes were offered from 1952. From that point in, these became a standard Rolls-Royce feature.

RENAULT 4CV

FRANCE 1946–61

ENGINE: 747cc (46cu in),
 four-cylinder
POWER: 42bhp (31kW)
0–60MPH (96KM/H): n/a
TOP SPEED: 140km/h (87mph)
PRODUCTION TOTAL: 1,105,543

Rather like Citroën's 2CV, the Renault 4CV was largely responsible for mobilizing the French masses. Considered by many to be the French Volkswagen Beetle, Regie's car had a lot in common with its German rival. It was powered by a four-cylinder engine that was mounted aft of the rear axle, it featured curvaceous styling and it also sported a distinctive engine note.

Early cars were hard to drive smoothly, with a clunky three-speed constant mesh gearbox, hard-to-fathom floor-mounted mixture control and an underpowered 18bhp (13kW) engine. As the industry embraced new technology, however, Renault would flow them into the 4CV – following a policy of constant improvement, just like the Beetle.

The Renault 4CV sold like hot cakes, and soon became a common

The 4CV was an interestingly styled car with close attention paid to its aerodynamics. Rear mounted engine and curvaceous looks meant that it was often compared to the Beetle.

sight on European roads. And when the car gained extra power from a new 747cc (46cu in) engine (which replaced the earlier cars' 760cc (46cu in) unit), sales were

significantly boosted. Despite Renault using idiosyncratic styling, rear engine layout and front 'suicide' doors on the 4CV, the French firm trod a different path

with the car's successor, the R4. Although it was a very different beast, it nonetheless enjoyed enormous success and sealed Renault's future.

For many, the most desirable version was the R1052 Sport variant, which boasted 42bhp (31kW) and the ability to cruise at more than 130km/h (80mph).

WILLYS STATION WAGON

UNITED STATES 1946–65

ENGINE: 2199cc (134cu in),
four-cylinder
POWER: 63bhp (47kW)
0–60MPH (96KM/H): n/a
TOP SPEED: 104km/h (65mph)
PRODUCTION TOTAL: about 350,000

With its reputation made by the World War II Jeep, Willys needed to follow up with a suitable replacement aimed squarely at the civilian market. The Station Wagon was certainly up to the task, becoming the United States' first estate car (station wagon) to feature an all-steel bodyshell.

The Willys Station Wagon was launched in 1946, and, although the initial proposal had been to produce a two-door family saloon to catapult the company into a period of post-war prosperity, that was soon changed in order to build on the Jeep's successes. With the Jeep's reputation as a trusty workhorse, it made more sense to build a more functional vehicle carved in the same niche.

The result was a two-door estate car (and later a two-door van). Although the Jeep was available only with four-wheel drive, the first Station Wagons (also designated Model 463) were rear-wheel drive, and it was not until 1949 that an all-wheel drive version was offered. The first cars looked good, boasting two-tone paintwork that

hinted at the 'woody' look, which was then popular. By the end of 1946, more than 6000 had been sold; by the end of the following year, the sales figures were more than five times this.

After World War II, Willys needed to find something other than the Jeep to build and its first effort at a car that was palatable to civilians was the rear wheel drive Station Wagon. The two-door model proved particularly popular.

WOLSELEY 25

UNITED KINGDOM 1947–48

Introduced just before the start of World War II, the largest of all the pre-war Wolseleys, the 25, was a seven-seater limousine that had been conceived as a Wolseley flagship. Following the end of hostilities, the model was reintroduced in 1946 and went back in to low-volume production.

Based on a cruciform chassis with an enormous 358cm (141in) wheelbase – one of the longest in

production anywhere in the world – this Wolseley limousine was an imposing beast. The bodyshell was traditionally made from steel panels over a wooden frame. The car was one of the most comfortable on the market, and the spacious cabin was befitting its limousine status. Obviously there was seating for five, and the passengers' surroundings were suitably plush,

with deep-pile carpets and wood trim all round.

The 3.5-litre straight-six under the bonnet (hood) was suitably smooth for the task of pushing the car along – a fact born out in competition. Before the car was even officially available, it had proved itself with a win in the 1939 Monte Carlo Rally Concours de Confort, and, thanks to a price of £2568, it did not really matter

that the 25 was offered only to government officials – as few private individuals in post-war Britain could afford it.

ENGINE: 3485cc (213cu in),
six-cylinder
POWER: 104bhp (77kW)
0–60MPH (96KM/H): 20.4 seconds
TOP SPEED: 136km/h (85mph)
PRODUCTION TOTAL: 75

BRISTOL 400

UNITED KINGDOM 1947–50

Following the end of World War II, the Bristol Aeroplane Company found demand for its aircraft dropping off, and decided to turn its hand to making cars in an attempt to move the business

forward. Bristol's thoughts initially turned to sports cars, but the project was soon knocked back when its first prototype was destroyed during testing on the company airfield.

Due to war reparations, Bristol ended up with several options from BMW, and the company then even managed to secure the release of a former BMW designer from military detention – and so

the Bristol 400 was born. The new car had a BMW 326-type chassis, with a body based on the BMW 327, and the engine was a development of BMW's 328 six-cylinder unit. The steel-bodied

It's no coincidence that the 400 looked similar to BMW's pre-war sportscars, as it was developed with the assistance of one of the company's former designers. Quality was extremely high.

wood-framed 400 was built to aircraft industry standards, and, in fact, the company soon developed a reputation for high-quality products that was to breed fierce loyalty from its owners.

Early examples of the 400 had a single carburettor and low

compression ratio to cope with the poor-quality 'pool' fuel available in the United Kingdom after the war. Triple carburettors were introduced later, but performance was never a key selling point – something that remained true for all of Bristol's products to the current day.

ENGINE: 1971cc (120cu in), six-cylinder
POWER: 80bhp (60kW)
0-60MPH (96KM/H): 14.7 secs
TOP SPEED: 152km/h (94mph)
PRODUCTION TOTAL: 700

FORD UK V8 PILOT

UNITED KINGDOM 1947–51

Ford UK's first post-war model, the Pilot, soon became very popular with buyers. It was launched into an expectant market full of pent-up demand for something new. Although the V8 Pilot had a familiar look, using the body of a pre-war V8-62 with a few front-end modifications, the all-new 2.5-litre (152cu in) engine was certainly food for thought.

Unfortunately, the new V8 was underpowered, and Ford was forced to quickly switch the car onto the classic 221 flathead 30hp (22kW) V8 that had earned a reputation for ability and longevity

Although it was mechanically simple and rugged, the Ford V8 Pilot was a taste of the exotic thanks to its thirsty V8 engine and easy to drive nature.

in military vehicles during World War II. The Pilot was a thirsty car, which was not good news during petrol rationing, but, for those who were guaranteed regular fuel supplies, such as doctors, it was a refined, robust and likeable choice.

It was not sophisticated – rod-operated Girling brakes were a throwback and the column gearshift was not popular with UK buyers, who favoured floor-shifters. Interestingly, the Pilot had built-in hydraulic jacks, something

that was never featured on any other UK Ford. The car proved very popular as a saloon for police forces (which favoured its easy performance), but its adaptable chassis also lent itself to other commercial applications.

ENGINE: 3622cc (221cu in), eight-cylinder
POWER: 85bhp (63kW)
0–60MPH (96KM/H): n/a
TOP SPEED: 133km/h (83mph)
PRODUCTION TOTAL: 35,618

CISITALIA 202 ITALY 1947–52

Regarded as one of the most beautiful cars of all time, the Cisitalia 202 remains a legend even to this day. The 202 was born as a result of the company's entrepreneur boss Piero Dusio's decision to concentrate his company's efforts in the post-war era on racing.

His first Cisitalia single-seaters were based on Fiats. With their 1100cc (66cu in) engines tuned to

produce more than 60bhp (45kW), 50 examples were built and duly went on to dominate their class. In 1947, racing Cisitalias finished second, third and fourth at the famed Mille Miglia.

With the company's reputation sealed, Dusio decided that it was time to capitalize by building road versions. Based on Fiat 1100 running gear, a multi-tubular chassis was designed by Fiat's

design genius Dr Dante Giacosa. If the engines were standard fare, the bodywork was fabulous and the finished car very expensive indeed, as the car was hand-built.

The Cisitalia 202 is now more closely associated with the success of Pininfarina's design than with the achievements of the car, and the Gran Sport coupé model is so beautiful that one is now enshrined at New York's renowned

Museum of Modern Art. This accolade unfortunately came too late to save Cisitalia, however, which lost money on the car.

ENGINE: 1089cc (66cu in), four-cylinder
POWER: 50bhp (37kW)
0–60MPH (96KM/H): 17 seconds
TOP SPEED: 129km/h (80mph)
PRODUCTION TOTAL: 170

OPEL OLYMPIA GERMANY 1947–52

The aftermath of World War II was a tough time for Germany's struggling economy. Its once successful carmaker Opel was in such dire straits that it was forced to reintroduce archaic pre-war designs in order to make enough money to develop a range of new models. It could not even boast the reasonably modern small Kadett in its armoury, as it had been sold to the Russians, in order

to become the new Moskvich. That left Opel with only the pre-war Olympia to sell in vitally important export markets.

Rather fortuitously, that car was rather advanced for its era, lessening the impact of going to the market with a 10-year-old new car. For a late 1930s car, with a monocoque body, overhead-valve engine, aerodynamic styling and surprisingly effective independent

suspension, the Olympia was well stocked. It was not a great car to drive, though, with lazy power delivery and vague steering.

Nonetheless, the Olympia performed an important job for Opel, and the German economy, because it had low production costs and therefore could be sold cheaply. By the time the Olympia ended production in 1952, it had served its purpose honourably,

and Opel was happily on its way to developing new and exciting models, with financial backing from General Motors.

ENGINE: 1488cc (91cu in), four-cylinder
POWER: 37bhp (28kW)
0–60MPH (96KM/H): 31.4 seconds
TOP SPEED: 110km/h (68mph)
PRODUCTION TOTAL: 187,055

TATRA T600 TATRAPLAN CZECHOSLOVAKIA 1948–54

Enjoying one of the faster development periods of its day, the Tatra T600 Tatraplan maintained the Tatra company's reputation for producing amazing and futuristic designs. Work on the car began during the winter of 1945 and, by early 1946, the first prototype was already complete.

Dubbed Ambroz, the T600 Tatraplan had a design which was predictably uncompromising, with a highly aerodynamic shape, a tailfin, enclosed rear wheels and a split windscreen. The company worked hard on the new car and had the first six models on display in the 1947 Prague Auto Salon. For its launch, the car carried the T107 nameplate, but was then renamed T600 Tatraplan as it went into production.

Launched in 1948, the T600 went on sale alongside the T57, T87 and T97, and the company's

range looked amazing. When first announced, it must have shocked traditional car buyers – much in the same way the Citroën DS would less than a decade later.

By the time production was halted in 1954, a vast number of

special versions had been created, with examples including the diesel-engined T600D, the aluminium-bodied Monte Carlo T601 and ambulance and pick-up models. Sadly, the car was rarely seen in the West.

ENGINE: 1950cc (119cu in), four-cylinder
POWER: 52bhp (39kW)
0–50MPH (80KM/H): 25 seconds
TOP SPEED: 130km/h (81mph)
PRODUCTION TOTAL: n/a

The T600 Tatraplan showed that the war didn't curb the styling of the Czechoslovakian company, though the car's performance was weaker.

FERRARI 166

The first true production Ferrari showed that it was possible to build a racing car, albeit with basic construction, for the road.

ENGINE: 1995cc (122cu in), 12-cylinder
POWER: 140bhp (104kW)
0–60MPH (96KM/H): 10 seconds
TOP SPEED: 201km/h (125mph)
PRODUCTION TOTAL: 75

Ferrari's indoctrination into road car manufacture was a steady process. Its first models were the Type 125, 159 and 166, which had evolved during 1947. Designed by Gioacchino Colombo, those cars were Type 125s with 1.5-litre (92cu in) V12s. When enlarged to 1900cc (116cu in), they became the Type 159 in late 1947, and, in even more potent 1995cc (122cu in) form, the Type 166 went on to win the Grand Prix of Turin. Producing around 140bhp (104kW),

the car's major advancement was its five-speed gearbox. Construction, on the other hand, was very basic, consisting of a tubular chassis with coil spring and double wishbone front suspension and a well-located live rear axle on semi-elliptic springs.

The 166 emerged as a dominant force in racing, despite its basic specification, because in 1949 the car notched up victories at Le Mans and the Mille Miglia. From this point on, the tuned 160bhp 166 had an MM suffix. Indeed, those 166 models intended for competition were designated Sport, and all other roadgoing 166s were known simply as Inter.

By the end of 1950, 40 Type 166 road cars had been built, with a wide variety of coachbuilders, including Ghia, Vignale and Bertone, producing a number of beautiful designs. The 166 was the car that firmly established Ferrari as a marque in the automotive elite, and prompted Enzo to establish a new factory in Maranello, near Modena.

JOWETT JAVELIN

ENGINE: 1485cc (91cu in),
  four-cylinder
POWER: 50bhp (37kW)
0–60MPH (96KM/H): 22.2 seconds
TOP SPEED: 133km/h (83mph)
PRODUCTION TOTAL: 22,799

In an era which is considered by many to be littered with boring British family car designs, the Jowett Javelin came as a breath of fresh air. It was an exciting new car that featured an exciting all-new aerodynamic profile, penned by the up-and-coming designer Gerald Palmer.

As well as its individual look, a flat-four engine, advanced torsion-bar independent front suspension and rack-and-pinion steering marked the Javelin out as a truly modern car. The vehicle's unitary construction by local firm Briggs

Clearly inspired by the styling of contemporary American cars, it was what lay under the skin that made the Jowett Javelin so interesting. Its flat-four engine resulted in a low centre of gravity and fine roadholding.

Motor Bodies of Doncaster, England, was also avant-garde.

The Javelin not only looked different to its opposition, but also was capable of carrying a family of six (thanks to the unusual engine configuration, which meant that it sat well forward of the cabin), handled well and was fast enough to cruise at 80mph (128km/h).

Sadly, the Javelin never enjoyed the success it should have. This was down to a high price (being far more expensive to run than more ordinary 12hp/9kW Austins) and early reliability problems which sullied its reputation. With fading fortunes, plans to build a bulky two-door drophead with three-abreast seating and a dickey seat (an extra row of seating extending from the boot/trunk), were shelved, despite a prototype appearing in 1948.

MG Y-TYPE

ENGINE: 1250cc (76cu in),
four-cylinder
POWER: 48bhp (36kW)
0–60MPH (96KM/H): 27.7 seconds
TOP SPEED: 115km/h (71mph)
PRODUCTION TOTAL: 7459

When it appeared in 1947, the MG Y-Type was the marque's first new post-war car – and, in the spirit of economizing, it used several parts already available from the Nuffield group's stable. This would be a running theme in future MGs. The body, rear panels and doors were all taken straight from the Morris 8, and the Y-Type's engine was the familiar 1250 XPAG unit which had first been seen in the T-Series sports car. In many ways, it was a less impressive car than its pre-war counterparts.

There were plenty of new developments underneath, signalling the Y-Type's intention of being an effective sporting saloon.

Independent front suspension using coil springs, as well as positive rack-and-pinion steering, marked this out as a driver's car. The steering system was designed by Alec Issigonis, who would later go on to create the Morris Minor, the Mini and BMC (British Motor Corporation) 1100/1300 Series.

All Y-Types were luxuriously equipped, with wood and leather interiors and comprehensive instrumentation. Later YB models had a more powerful engine and simpler rear axle layout. Despite claiming to be sporting saloons, the Y-Types were not very fast; the YB, for instance, had a top speed of 114km/h (71mph). It was, however, a pleasure to drive.

Although the first new post-war MG saloon dipped heavily into the Nuffield Group parts bin, it was still an advanced, individual car with independent front suspension that was good to drive.

VERITAS COMET

The Veritas Comet first made its appearance at the 1949 Paris Salon, and it was one of a family of three cars from the company which had made their debuts there. The other two were the Saturn and the Scorpion – and, although all three used the same mechanicals, the different names signified alternative bodystyles.

The Saturn was the most glamorous. It was a two-door coupé, while the Scorpion was a cabriolet version of the same car. It was the Comet that was the bread-and-butter model of the trio – the all-purpose model.

Each of the trio of Veritas cars was powered by the same seven-bearing 1988cc (121cu in) straight-six unit. This engine's sophistication made the cars very expensive in relation to their rivals, but it was possible for buyers to specify a short-stroke 1.5-litre (92cu in) engine taken from the BMW stable.

It was also possible to have the impressive BMW 328 engine fitted, and that meant power outputs which ranged between 98bhp (73kW) and 147bhp (110kW). All were fed through a five-speed manual gearbox – an esoteric feature which was shared with Ferrari at the time. All the cars were based on a BMW chassis; however, a de Dion rear axle fitted along with uprated brakes were individual features.

ENGINE: 1988cc (121cu in),
six-cylinder
POWER: 100bhp (75kW)
0–60MPH (96KM/H): n/a
TOP SPEED: n/a
PRODUCTION TOTAL: n/a

AUSTIN SHEERLINE

ENGINE: 3993cc (244cu in),
six-cylinder
POWER: 125bhp (93kW)
0–60MPH (96KM/H): 19.4 seconds
TOP SPEED: 134km/h (83mph)
PRODUCTION TOTAL: 8700

Back in the 1940s, Austin was prestigious enough as a marque to carry a range of upmarket models without the need for later style badge engineering and marque swapping. Irrefutable evidence of this fact was the first appearance of the imposing A110 Sheerline in 1947.

Made impressive by its sheer scale, the Sheerline was heavy engineering at its finest. The car certainly looked imposing, and it was heavily engineered on a box-section chassis, with large cross-bracing sections. The body was styled by Dick Burzi and featured razor-edge styling that evoked Bentleys and some Triumphs of the era.

A hefty six-cylinder overhead-valve engine that previously had used in pre-war trucks was chosen to power it – and the 3.5-litre (214cu in), 110bhp (82kW) unit was up to the task, also lending the car its A110 designation. Within the first year of production, the

engine was bored out to a more hefty 4 litres (244cu in), and power accordingly rose to 125bhp (93kW), leaving the car to become the A125. Alongside the Sheerline, Austin sold an upmarket version called

the Princess, featuring a more elegant bodystyle, as produced in aluminium by Vanden Plas.

The Princess was designated the A120, then the A135, both named after their power outputs.

The Sheerline and its Vanden Plas derivative really did look like Bentleys and because of their reasonable price and oodles of prestige, they were bought by many small-time dignitaries.

AC 2-LITRE

One of the oldest carmakers in the world, AC had been struggling to keep its costs low enough to stay in business during 1920s and 1930s. The cessation of hostilities at the end of World War II meant that the company desperately needed a new model to cash in on the unprecedented demand for new cars – without the all-out investment required for an all-new car.

The chassis that AC had used to good effect in the 1930s was to gain a new lease of life for the 1947 2-litre model. The engine had an even longer history, stretching back to the 1920s, as it was essentially the six-cylinder long-stroke pre-war AC engine.

AC designed a stylish two-door saloon body, and used the traditional construction of aluminium over an ash frame, with

little in the way of styling embellishment. A wide range of labour-intensive coachbuilt designs would have been desirable, but were out of the question for reasons of finance.

The interior, too, was pretty basic compared with its pre-war forebears, although the 2-litre later received higher specification trim and a four-door option. The 2-Litre was an unexpected hit for AC –

and the company would go on to greater things as a result of the sensible design approaches employed in this car.

ENGINE: 1991cc (121cu in),
six-cylinder
POWER: 74bhp (55kW)
0–60MPH (96KM/H): 19.9 seconds
TOP SPEED: 132km/h (82mph)
PRODUCTION TOTAL: 1284

VOLVO PV444

ENGINE: 1414cc (86cu in), four-cylinder
POWER: 40bhp (30kW)
0–60MPH (96KM/H): 24.9 seconds
TOP SPEED: 118km/h (74mph)
PRODUCTION TOTAL: 196,004

The Beetle-backed PV444 earned Volvo an enviable reputation abroad thanks to its tough build quality and excellent reliability. With styling clearly inspired by Detroit, there's no wonder it travelled well.

Developed during World War II, the Volvo PV444 did not go on sale until 1947 – but, without question, it was the car that put Volvo very much on the global map. Beyond that, the PV444 became a Swedish icon, as it was the country's first model to be exported in significant numbers.

Until the 1930s, Volvo had focused on side-valve six-cylinder engines, but fuel shortages and the need for affordable cars led the company to concentrate its efforts on four-cylinder cars. The car's unitary construction was inspired by the 1939 Hanomag, but the styling was far more transatlantic in

inspiration, featuring US aeroback-style detailing. The integrated front wings (fenders) also mimicked American thinking, as did the coil and wishbone suspension layout and hydraulic brakes.

The four-cylinder overhead-valve engine was just 1.4 litres (86cu in) in capacity, but the reasonably light

kerb weight of 968kg (2128lb) allowed a favourable power-to-weight ratio and a top speed of more than 115km/h (70mph). When the Amazon's 1582cc (97cu in) engine was later fitted, from 1957, the car improved markedly, before being replaced by the broadly similar PV544 in 1958.

STANGUELLINI

ITALY 1947–66

Stanguellini was one of those Italian concerns that litter automotive history, its legacy a handful of beautiful sporting cars. Between 1947 and 1966, it produced very small quantities of hand-built sports cars, based mainly on contemporary Fiats.

Having been in the business of producing racing cars since 1938, the company's post-war effort was

refocused on building road cars. The shift in thinking was based on a successful racing campaign in 1947, and the company decided to translate the results into success on the road. Stanguellini's first car was a four-seater berlinetta with an 1100cc (67cu in) engine – although it could be specified with a 1500cc (92cu in) Fiat engine in a Bertone-designed body mounted

on a tubular chassis. Contemporary Italian roads were poor, so the suspension was built for solidity, rather than ultimate handling.

Stanguellini developed its own 750cc (46cu in) engine for the 1950 Bialbero Sport, and, in 1954, the 1100 Berlinetta made its debut; however, only nine were built. A 750cc (46cu in) Formula Junior car arrived in 1958, but,

from that point, one failed project followed another and, in 1966, the company went bankrupt.

ENGINE: 750cc (46cu in),
   four-cylinder
POWER: 36bhp (27kW)
0–60MPH (96KM/H): n/a
TOP SPEED: 180km/h (112mph)
PRODUCTION TOTAL: n/a

TUCKER TORPEDO '48'

UNITED STATES 1948

ENGINE: 5491cc (335cu in),
   six-cylinder
POWER: 166bhp (124kW)
0–60MPH (96KM/H): 10.1 seconds
TOP SPEED: 193km/h (120mph)
PRODUCTION TOTAL: 51

The 1948 Tucker Torpedo was a glorious failure – and if ever a car deserved to succeed, it was this car. With so much in its favour, such as imaginative styling and engineering, there was every reason to expect that Tucker was going on to greatness, and, when

it was first shown in 1948, and alongside the predictable offerings from the more familiar American carmakers, it made a huge impact.

With a generous budget at the disposal of the talents of a forward-thinking designer, and Alex Tremulis on board to design

One of the world's greatest cars never to make it into full series production – the Tucker Torpedo was a startling car. In terms of engineering, it rendered the rest of Detroit obsolete overnight...

the car, it bristled with innovations such as a curved front windscreen, with disc brakes and rubber springing promised for later.

There was neither the time nor the money to deliver all these promises, but the 48 was still packed with fresh ideas. A central headlight, which turned with the front wheels, was something not seen before, and doors which were cut into the roof to ease entry and exit were also fresh – and were well ahead of their time.

The interior featured seat cushions that were interchangeable between the front and rear, so that wear could be evened out. Safety was also inherent in the 48's design, with recessed or protected controls inside the car, huge bumpers to protect the bodywork, windscreen glass that popped out on impact and a safety chamber

which front-seat passengers could dive into if a collision was imminent.

The engine was positioned below the rear seat line to ensure noise, heat and fumes inside the cabin were kept to a minimum, and the aerodynamic design (the drag coefficient was just 0.30cd) allowed the car to travel incredibly quietly. It was positioned at the back of the car rather than the front, and it was not like any powerplant fitted to any other car.

At launch, it was planned to be a 9.7-litre (592cu in) engine developed from a helicopter unit, and, although the original powerplant in helicopter guise was air-cooled, a sealed water-cooling system was devised for the powerplant's new application. This was another Tucker first. A Tuckermatic bespoke automatic transmission was promised – and,

within no time at all, the advanced specification had attracted 300,000 orders from customers eager to get their hands on the car.

Making everything work, however, was a major challenge – and Tucker was caught unawares by the scope of the development needed to make it all work. In the end, he needed to substitute the 9.7-litre (592cu in) engine with a 166bhp (124kW) 5491cc (335cu in) flat-six unit sourced from Air Cooled Motors. Not only that, but the Tuckermatic transmission was replaced by an off-the-shelf Cord gearbox as well.

The weight piled on, and in production form the Tucker '48' tipped the scales at a portly 1909kg (4200lb). Despite this, it was still quick – and took a mere 10 seconds to accelerate from 0–60mph (96km/h) – before going

on to a top speed of 193km/h (120mph). This was the application of aerodynamics at their very best. Fuel consumption was not that bad either – it could better 20mpg (14.2L/100km) at a steady 89km/h (55mph) – which was a far better figure than the established opposition.

However effective it was, the Tucker '48' was not the car its creator had promised his investors or customers, and the whole project was brought to a halt when fraud charges were brought against him. Eventually acquitted, Tucker's moment had already passed – his investors had lost confidence, as had most of his potential customers.

The final tally of 37 cars made (with a further 14 were built from remaining parts) was scant reward for this forward-thinking saloon.

ROVER P3

ENGINE: 2103cc (128cu in), six-cylinder
POWER: 72bhp (54kW) at 4000rpm
0–60MPH (96KM/H): 29.4 seconds
TOP SPEED: 121km/h (75mph)
PRODUCTION TOTAL: 9111

Like so many other British carmakers, Rover restarted production after World War II with a car that relied heavily on its pre-war predecessors. The pre-war 10,

12, 14 and 16hp P2 models were good solid fare, and their reappearance demonstrated the company's determination to succeed – Rover was required to move to Solihull after its old factory in Coventry was destroyed by the Luftwaffe.

Its first 'new' post-war model appeared in 1948, although it looked largely identical to its ancestors. The Rover P3 had been improved, though – it was wider and built on a new, shorter chassis

with an all-steel body. Two new inlet-over-exhaust engines – one a four-cylinder and the other a six-cylinder – were fitted, along with independent front suspension. The P3's front end with styling followed US fashions – something that Rover would continue to do with its next two important cars, the P4 and P5.

Two different bodies were offered, four- and six-light saloons. There was also a number of pretty special models, including those

made by coachbuilders including Tickford and Graber, who built a stylish tourer on the same chassis.

The P3 remained in production for a mere 18 months before it was replaced by the altogether fresher Rover P4.

Bridging pre- and post-war: the Rover P3's roots lay in the 10, 12, 14 and 16hp P2 models and as a result they were solidly built cars.

AUSTIN A70 HAMPSHIRE AND HEREFORD

ENGINE: 2191cc (134cu in),
 six-cylinder
POWER: 67bhp (50kW)
0–60MPH (96KM/H): 21.5 seconds
TOP SPEED: 132km/h (82mph)
PRODUCTION TOTAL: 85,882

Austin's 1940s and 1950s fare was definitely typified by the bulbous-looking Counties range of cars. The Austin A40 Dorset and Devon were the first proponents of this new Dick Burzi school of styling, but the A70 Hampshire that followed within a year moved it all up a gear.

The bigger cars boasted better styling and a healthy six-cylinder engine, whereas the smaller cars were powered by the four-cylinder overhead-vale unit, which went on to become the famous B-series, used in the MGB and saloon car counterparts. Bench seats front and rear were supposed to seat six adults, but, because of the car's compact dimensions (the A70 was only 10cm/4in longer than the A40), it was actually quite a squeeze. The more curvaceous and longer Hereford rectified the situation, replacing the Hampshire after two years in production.

While neither model handled with confidence, at least the brakes utilized in the Hereford were fully hydraulic, instead of the part-hydraulic, part-mechanical system used in the Hampshire. Both models were also offered in pick-up and Countryman estate

(station-wagon) forms, with US-style wood panelling down the sides of the latter, while the Hereford also came as a handsome convertible.

Known as the Austin Counties, these cars sold well and offered customers what they wanted – even if the handling wasn't as sharp as it could have been. Their six-cylinder engines were smooth and powerful.

HUMBER HAWK III

ENGINE: 1944cc (119cu in),
 four-cylinder
POWER: 56bhp (kW)
0–60MPH (96KM/H): 30.7 seconds
TOP SPEED: 110km/h (69mph)
PRODUCTION TOTAL: 10,040

The post-war styling of the Rootes Group was epitomized by Raymond Loewy's efforts – stylish, smooth and classy. The designer was responsible for the all-new Humber Hawk's design and was almost certainly influenced by the current US styling efforts. That meant flush-mounted headlights in the front wings (fenders), a deep screen and bulbous front nose – and they would influence Rootes' design until well into the 1950s.

The Humber Hawk story was not all about style. It boasted a new, shorter chassis, which meant less bulk at 1250kg (2756lb). Still, the mechanical layout remained curiously antiquated underneath, with old-fashioned channel section side members and the same side-valve four-cylinder engine under the bonnet (hood) that had powered Humbers since the early 1930s. The Hawk also retained the archaic column gearchange.

If the body engineering was passé, the suspension was modern. The car featured a new coil spring independent suspension system instead of the old transverse leaf type, helping to give an altogether more refined ride to match the car's contemporary looks.

The Hawk was priced at £799 when new, and became a steady seller throughout its nine-year lifetime. Its immediate successor, the Hawk Mk IV launched in 1950, was upgraded with a much-needed 2267cc (138cu in) engine, higher gearing and wider tyres, improving the driving experience considerably.

CHAMPION 250

Designed in 1946, the Champion 250 entered production in 1948 – and it was essentially a cyclecar right down to the spoked wire wheels. A cogwheel company based in Friedrichshafen which sold the rights to a former BMW engineer, Herman Holbein, owned this two-seater roadster's design. Small and perfectly formed, the 250 looked similar to the Triumph TR2, but did not have the British car's power.

A rear-mounted 250cc (15cu in) motorcycle engine made by TWN provided the power, but performance was poor because of the body weight. The 1950 coupé version, however, benefited from a larger 400cc (24cu in) engine, and that lifted things. The company was bought by two brothers, Otto and Wilhelm Maisch, in 1955, who renamed the Champion the Maico. They even fitted a larger 500cc (31cu in) engine to broaden the car's appeal. The cars proved expensive to build, however, with more than 200 suppliers providing parts, and, following a run of 8000 models, the company went bankrupt in 1958.

ENGINE: 250cc (15cu in),
 two-cylinder
POWER: 15bhp (11kW)
0–60MPH (96KM/H): n/a
TOP SPEED: 80km/h (50mph)
PRODUCTION TOTAL: 8000

JAGUAR MK V

ENGINE: 2664cc (163cu in),
six-cylinder
POWER: 104bhp (77kW)
0–60MPH (96KM/H): 17.0 seconds
TOP SPEED: 139km/h (87mph)
PRODUCTION TOTAL: 10,466

The Jaguar Mk V was a stopgap model launched shortly after World War II, and which was destined to last just two years in production before being replaced by the Mk VII. The Mk V was an interesting missing link between the post- and pre-war Jaguar models, and featured a mix of styling, incorporating both old and modern design elements.

New to Jaguar were the integrated headlights, which had been set into the inner edge of the front wings (fenders), so that they looked as if they were standalone items. The curvy roofline and modern-looking rear wheel spats added a contemporary feel, while the narrow screen and old-fashioned running boards were a strong link with the past. It has been suggested that Jaguar's approach was deliberately conservative in order to test public opinion, while not offending the traditionalists – something the company would return to in later years.

The Mk V's all-new chassis formed the underpinnings of all Jaguar's 1950s big saloons, and other innovations were the independent front suspension and hydraulic brakes. The car was fitted with either a 2664cc (163cu in) or 3485cc (213cu in) engine, both of which were straight-sixes. In terms of refinement, Jaguar raised its game with the Mk V and clearly signalled future ambitions.

An exotic drophead model was also offered, of which just 1001 examples were made.

WILLYS JEEPSTER

ENGINE: 2199cc (134cu in),
four-cylinder
POWER: 63bhp (47kW)
0–60MPH (96KM/H): n/a
TOP SPEED: 112km/h (70mph)
PRODUCTION TOTAL: 19,132

Hard on the heels of the Station Wagon, Willys launched a further addition to the range that would play heavily on the company's World War II origins. As its Jeep had proved such a roaring success, the company decided to cross it over into the civilian market with a car that was clearly related to the military version, but was a little more comfortable to use on a daily basis.

The intention had been to build an open-topped car which was immediately recognizable as a Jeep, but with a few more creature comforts that would make it more saleable. The Jeepster's ridiculously high price should have proved a stumbling block to sales. Willys had decided to recoup its development costs as quickly as possible, and therefore priced the Jeepster to be made in small numbers. Despite that, more than 20,000 cars were sold in just three years – an acceptable figure considering the Jeepster's price. If the price had been set at a more affordable level, however, this figure could easily have been much, much larger. The Jeepster was available with a 2433cc (148cu in) six-cylinder engine from 1940; up to this point it had been available only with the four-cylinder powerplant that was found under the bonnet (hood) of the Station Wagon.

It may have cost a fortune and looked like a pastiche of the famous World War II jeep, but the Willys Jeepster proved a success. It was offered with four- and six-cylinder engines.

AUSTIN A90 ATLANTIC

Unashamedly built for export markets, the A90 Atlantic dropped the safe styling of its saloon cousins and went for a glamorous transatlantic look. It didn't sell well abroad – or at home...

ENGINE: 2660cc (162cu in), four-cylinder
POWER: 88bhp (66kW)
0–60MPH (96KM/H): 16.6 seconds
TOP SPEED: 147km/h (91mph)
PRODUCTION TOTAL: 7981

British manufacturers were desperate to crack the American market during the late 1940s and into the 1950s – none more so than Austin. Certainly, the country provided great fascination for the company's chief stylist, Dick Burzi, who penned the A90 Atlantic.

Selling in the United States meant profits, and Dick Burzi worked hard – perhaps too hard – to emulate the glitzy US models of the time. The Atlantic sported three headlights, the third in the middle of the grille, an excess of chrome, a sweeping line from the top of the front wings (fenders) right to the back of the car, rear wheel spats and gold-faced gauges.

Under all the ostentatious bodywork was nothing more than the underpinnings of the humble A70, although the four-cylinder engine was bored out to 2660cc (162cu in) and was later used to power the Austin-Healey 100.

Initially, the A90 Atlantic was available only as a convertible, with power hood and electric windows (a first for a British mass-produced car) as options. A saloon version emerged a year after the convertible. Not surprisingly, the Atlantic flopped, selling a mere 350 in the market for which it was designed.

STANDARD VANGUARD

ENGINE: 2088cc (127cu in), four-cylinder
POWER: 68bhp (51kW)
0–60MPH (96KM/H): 22 seconds
TOP SPEED: 123km/h (77mph)
PRODUCTION TOTAL: 184,799

Vitally important, the Standard Vanguard was Britain's first post-war all-new car when it was announced in July 1947. Government regulations meant that the majority of cars produced in the immediate post-war years needed to be exported – hence the car's importance. Powered by a 68bhp (51kW) 2088cc (127cu in) four-cylinder engine and a three-speed gearbox, the Vanguard was capable of 120km/h (75mph) and 26mpg (10.9l/100km), while carrying five people in comfort.

Many Vanguards found their way to the United States, and the export-or-die ethos of the time meant that the car was designed specifically with that country in mind. So, it had a US-influenced exterior and a column-change gearshift, which was all the rage at the time. Despite massive steel shortages, between 1000 and 2000 Vanguards were produced each week, and few of them stayed in the United Kingdom.

In 1948, an estate (station wagon) and pick-up joined the range; in May 1950, coachbuilder Tickford began offering a full-length sunroof. The car was not developed any further until the end of 1951, once it became clear that it was not the massive export hit its maker hoped. The Phase II Vanguard eventually replaced the Phase Ia version in March 1953.

Another car designed to sell overseas, the Standard Vanguard should have sold well – however, its basic specification and lack of performance meant that it was an unappealing proposition.

BRISTOL 401

The BMW-based 400 established its maker as a producer of high-quality, exclusive machinery, but the company's first all-new car – and the one that was the making of Bristol Motors – was the 401, a far more sophisticated car.

The 401 was to mark the establishment of a change in direction for Bristol in terms of body construction – it adopted the Superleggera principle of using alloy body panels wrapped around a labyrinth of small-diameter tubing.

Inspired by aero thinking, the Bristol 401 used an aluminium skin wrapped around fine tubing to make a highly streamlined car.

Italian coachbuilders Touring, whose designs also inspired the 401's teardrop shape, pioneered this construction technique. Aerodynamics played a big part in the new Bristol's design, however, and this is where the company's aviation experience paid large dividends. Bristol developed the shape of the 401 on the company's runway; the new car was so far ahead of its time aerodynamically that the subsequent reduction in wind noise and increase in top speed clearly marked this out as a design for the future. With 2 litres and 85bhp (63kW), the 401 came tantalizingly close to breaking 100mph (161km/h).

The 401 also spawned the convertible 402 and the more powerful 403 – Bristol's first 161km/h (100mph) car – both based on the same body shape.

ENGINE: 1971cc (120cu in), six-cylinder
POWER: 85bhp (63kW)
0–60MPH (96KM/H): 15.1 seconds
TOP SPEED: 156km/h (97mph)
PRODUCTION TOTAL: 650

EMW 327

ENGINE: 1971cc (120cu in), six-cylinder
POWER: 55bhp (41kW)
0–60MPH (96KM/H): 30 seconds
TOP SPEED: 125km/h (78mph)
PRODUCTION TOTAL: n/a

After the war and the division of Germany, BMW's factory was located behind the Iron Curtain. The East Germans therefore set about building the first BMWs from the remaining stock of parts that remained in the Eisenach factory.

The first post-war cars produced by the newly formed EMW company were three Type 321s, hand-assembled from leftover parts; by Christmas 1945 another 68 cars had been completed. The following year Autovelo, the state car company, began to reorganize all car and motorcycle operations in the Soviet-controlled sector – giving the impression that the old BMW concern was back in business.

Around 2000 of these cars left the production line in 1947 and the tally grew by a further 4600 by mid-1948, when the company reintroduced the pre-war BMW 327 coupé and convertible under its own banner. The 327 later received modifications – big clumsy grilles and upright lights – that did nothing for the original car's elegance. The company was eventually forced to modify its badge to read EMW (Eisenach Motoren Werke).

The EMW 327 looked similar to the pre-war BMW 328 because it was essentially the same car now built behind the Iron Curtain.

FRAZER-NASH LE MANS REPLICA

ENGINE: 1971cc (120cu in), six-cylinder
POWER: 120bhp (89kW)
0–60MPH (96KM/H): 8.9 seconds
TOP SPEED: 185km/h (115mph)
PRODUCTION TOTAL: 34

Frazer-Nash developed a Bristol-BMW powered lightweight racing car that would be suitable for fast road use as well as being competitive on the racetrack – and it was chosen to accompany its successful chain-driven models,

With responsive rack-and-pinion steering, and powered by 120bhp (89kW) from its three-carburettor engine, the 690kg (1520lb) Frazer-

The Bristol-BMW powered racing car was a delight to use on the road thanks to its responsive rack-and-pinion steering and fine handling.

Nash very much lived up to its original 'High Speed' name. When a privateer took his car to Le Mans in 1949, and finished in third place overall, the model name was changed to 'Le Mans Replica' in honour of the achievement.

Thanks to transverse leaf independent front suspension, handling was taut and predictable, and the car stormed to various victories on racetracks in domestic and overseas events. As its cars were completely hand-built, no

two machines produced at the Isleworth factory in Middlesex, England, were the same and, as usual with Frazer-Nash, buyers could specify the exact set-up of both engine and suspension, along with colour and body details.

In 1952, a Le Mans Replica Mk II appeared, and it was even lighter and slimmer than the original; in 1953, its last year of production, the car was further improved by the fitting of a de Dion-type rear axle.

WOLSELEY 4/50

UNITED KINGDOM 1948–53

ENGINE: 1476cc (90cu in),
four-cylinder
POWER: 51bhp (38kW)
0–60MPH (96KM/H): 31.6 seconds
TOP SPEED: 118km/h (74mph)
PRODUCTION TOTAL: 8925

The Nuffield Organization unveiled four post-war family saloons in 1948, and the 4/50 was the last of the quartet to hit the market. Unlike its top-of-the-range brother, the 6/80, the mid-range 4/50 did not prove popular with buyers. Most customers preferred to take the more rational Morris

Oxford over the 4/50 despite its being less prestigious, opting to go for the space the Morris offered rather than the higher level of refinement that was boasted by the Wolseley.

The 4/50 was effectively a four-cylinder version of the 6/80 which also featured a plush interior – it

was not an upmarket version of the Oxford as many people assumed. It used an overhead camshaft engine, and had a shorter wheelbase than its bigger brother. When the Wolseley 4/44 arrived in the autumn of 1952, sales of the 4/50 dried up, and the model was dropped.

CONNAUGHT L2

UNITED KINGDOM 1948–54

ENGINE: 1767cc (108cu in),
four-cylinder
POWER: 98bhp (73kW)
0–60MPH (96KM/H): 12 seconds
TOP SPEED: 161km/h (100mph)
PRODUCTION TOTAL: 27

Specializing in sports and high-performance cars, Connaught was a firm well established in Surrey, England. Rodney Clarke and Kenneth McAlpine, who were considered to be among the best of the Bugatti-driving amateur racers, ran the company.

They decided to build their own competition car, called the L-type, and the first Connaught was a sports racing two-seater which used many components from the 1767cc (108cu in) Lea-Francis. The engine, a four-cylinder unit with short pushrods and hemispherical combustion chambers, was chosen because it was highly tuneable.

The car's chassis, with beam axle front and rear, could be set up for track handling and clearly showed its racing pedigree. Two cars were built, and they went on to dominate club racing. This success encouraged the company to divert into Formula Two and Grand Prix racing.

As a result, Connaught set about building a road-going version of the L2. The street-legal car was closely based on the racer, with the Lea-Francis engine tuned to produce an output of 98bhp (73kW). It featured a magnificent forward tilting bonnet (hood) and swooping wings (fenders) that

made the car look like a real racer. From 1951, a stripped-down L3R model was offered, featuring cycle wings and torsion bar suspension.

The L3R was not a sales success, however, and, all in all, just 27 road-going Connaughts were built before the company went bankrupt in 1959.

Essentially a road-going version of the L2 racecar, the street legal version was the car of choice for enthusiastic drivers. Lively performance was only part of the picture, as the handling was also first class.

HUMBER IMPERIAL II

UNITED KINGDOM 1948–54

The Raymond Loewy–inspired range of post-war Humbers was an interesting breed. They took a number of styling cues from their pre-war designs, but with a modern overall theme. The big new Humbers of the late 1940s and early 1950s had traditional 'alligator'-style bonnets (hoods), pillbox windscreens and narrow running boards, but featured more

modern influences such as the full-width body and integral headlights in the front wings (fenders).

The Imperial was based on the Pullman limousine version, which sat on a massive 330cm (131in) wheelbase, and was identical apart from the lack of division in the passenger compartment. This was essentially an old car, though, with column gearchange and dated

side-valve engine. The 'Evenkeel' transverse leaf independent front suspension was the car's only real attempt at modernity. It was in production until 1954, by which time it had gained an overhead-valve engine, improved ride and better braking. The model shared much of its running gear with the 1948–1952 Super Snipe II and III. Imperial models included a touring

limousine and an elegant but heavy-looking Tickford two-door convertible from 1949.

ENGINE: 4138cc (252cu in),
six-cylinder
POWER: 113bhp (84kW)
0–60MPH (96KM/H): 26.2 seconds
TOP SPEED: 131km/h (82mph)
PRODUCTION TOTAL: 4140

JAGUAR XK120

ENGINE: 3442cc (210cu in),
  six-cylinder
POWER: 160bhp (119kW)
0–60MPH (96KM/H): 12.0 seconds
TOP SPEED: 196km/h (122mph)
PRODUCTION TOTAL: 12,055

When the stunning Jaguar XK120 appeared at the 1948 Earls Court Motor Show in London, it became the darling of the show, representing the hopes and dreams of a new generation of drivers who were keen to put the hardships of World War II very definitely behind them.

In terms of design, the two-seater roadster, with its classically simple flowing lines, slender tail and deliciously exotic flush-sided body, was a massive leap forwards for sportscar design at the times. In many ways, its styling was unparalleled. Not only that, but the car also set new standards in terms of performance.

An all-new twin overhead camshaft straight-six with twin SU carburettors powered the XK and gave it supercar performance. The powerful 3.4-litre (210cu in) XK engine survived until the 1990s under the bonnets (hoods) of numerous Jaguar saloons and sports cars. The engine came at a time when no other company was making mass-produced twin-camshaft engines, and it transformed the way in which engines were looked at.

So called because it was easily capable of 120mph (192km/h), the XK120 would be later upgraded to SE (Special Equipment) status, and these versions had high-lift camshafts, twin exhausts and 180bhp (134kW) on tap.

Jaguar took an XK120 to Belgium's Jabbeke straight test road, to demonstrate the car's awesome abilities, fitted it with an undershield and a racing-type windscreen, and achieved a spectacular 213.32km/h (132.56mph) over a flying mile, and 203km/h (126mph) with the standard windscreen, hood and sidescreens fitted. That result marked it as one of the fastest production cars in the world.

Autocar magazine was duly impressed: 'In trying to convey in a word-picture of the supreme position which the XK120 two-seater occupies, there is a temptation to draw from the motoring vocabulary every adjective in the superlative concerning the performance, and to call upon the devices of italics and even the capital letter!'

The XK was not all about speed, and it could be trickled along a quiet country road just as happily as a high-speed one, while behaving impeccably amid traffic all traffic conditions. Light steering and taut yet comfortable suspension allowed the car to be hurled around bends with extreme confidence, and accompanied its tenacious grip and perfect handling.

Not as impressive, however, were the drum brakes, which were prone to fade (unless special linings were fitted) due to poor cooling – the car's modern enclosed bodywork contributed to this. Despite its diminutive size, the XK120 was also a practical car, with a useful luggage compartment which was obstructed only by the spare wheel.

William Lyons saw the XK120 as a limited-edition machine, originally envisaging a production

The shape of things to come: the Jaguar XK120 with its twin-cam straight-six engine, aerodynamic styling and ample performance.

run of just 200 cars, which is perhaps why the first examples used a wooden ash body frame and aluminium skin panels. Lyons was caught off-guard, however, by demand for the vehicle. As that demand accelerated, he switched to steel mass production in 1950, by which time only 240 cars had left the Coventry factory.

An elegant fixed-head version appeared in 1951 with a bulbous roofline, deeper windscreen and wind-up windows. A drophead coupé was offered in 1953, and it featured a more luxurious interior and walnut-veneer dashboard.

MORRIS OXFORD MO

ENGINE: 1476cc (90cu in),
  four-cylinder
POWER: 40.5bhp (30kW) at 4200rpm
0–60MPH (96KM/H): 41.4 seconds
TOP SPEED: 113km/h (70mph)
PRODUCTION TOTAL: 282

The Morris Oxford MO was quite simply a Minor for the family man who also wanted more power, luxury and space. In terms of styling, there was little to differentiate the two cars, despite there being little shared componentry between the two.

The Oxford's grille was slightly more elaborate than that of the Minor, but, other than that, the Oxford was almost an exact enlarged facsimile of its smaller relation. It was far less technically interesting, though, and went on to live a far shorter production life – only six years compared to the Minor's 23.

The 1476cc (90cu in) side-valve engine delivered barely adequate power, and was only just able get the car up to 113km/h (70mph).

It may have looked like little more than a pumped-up Minor, but the Morris Oxford NO lacked much of the smaller car's charm, handling and performance.

This was clearly no performance car, and the column-mounted gearchange was further dissuasion for spirited drivers. Independent front suspension (by torsion bars) was on the spec sheet, but it was not that great, with Morris needing to fit telescopic shock absorbers to it in 1950. Changes to the Oxford MO were minimal. In 1952, a two-door Traveller estate (station wagon) was introduced, with a wood-timbered rear end. A new grille was fitted on both models, and van and pick-up versions were made from 1950 to 1956.

MORRIS SIX

UNITED KINGDOM 1948–54

ENGINE: 2215cc (135cu in),
  six-cylinder
POWER: 66bhp (49kW) at 4800rpm
0–60MPH (96KM/H): 22.4 seconds
TOP SPEED: 138km/h (86mph)
PRODUCTION TOTAL: 12,464

With Morris and Wolseley sharing the family car duties within the Nuffield Group, it was inevitable that they would end up sharing components, while being pitched at largely similar markets. Morris appealed to the family man, while his bosses would buy the more upmarket Wolseleys.

In the late 1940s, a policy of standardization was introduced, which included sharing bodystyles between Morris and Wolseley. When the Wolseley 6/80 appeared

in 1948, it sired a very similar-looking Morris, known as the Six. The curvaceous body, from the long nose back to the rear of the car, was the same as the Oxford MO – which itself was just a bigger version of the Minor.

The Morris would feature a less comfortable interior, a distinctive Morris grille and a detuned version of the Wolseley 2215cc (135cu in) six-cylinder engine. That overhead-camshaft power unit was fitted with just one carburettor (the Wolseley had two); the result was a smooth but uninspiring performance and doubts over reliability.

While the Wolseley became popular with police forces, the Morris Six found few fans – it sold poorly, overshadowed by its more luxurious sibling, and finally went out of production in 1954.

Visually very similar to the Minor and Oxford MO, the Morris Six needed a nose job in order to accommodate the bulk of its six-cylinder engine. It was overshadowed by the plusher Wolseley 6/80.

SUNBEAM-TALBOT 90

UNITED KINGDOM 1948–54

ENGINE: 1944cc (119cu in),
  four-cylinder
POWER: 64bhp (48kW)
0–60MPH (96KM/H): 22.5 seconds
TOP SPEED: 128km/h (80mph)
PRODUCTION TOTAL: 20,381

When the Sunbeam-Talbot 90 went on sale in July 1948, it was not cutting-edge design, but it did have a beam front axle and half-elliptic springs all round, and a 1944cc (119cu in) overhead-valve engine that produced enough power to endow the car with respectable performance.

The range comprised a saloon and a drophead coupé, and both cars represented the start of a new line of faster smarter Sunbeam-Talbots. The cars were so capable that, when the Mk II was launched in 1950, the factory made a

concerted effort to compete in motorsport and demonstrate the revised car's abilities.

Sunbeam-Talbot's 90 Mk II featured an all-new chassis with coil spring and wishbone front suspension, and it was therefore a major development. Also, the engine was upgraded to a larger version of the four-cylinder powerplant fitted to the Mk I – this time with 2267cc (138cu in).

At the same time, the inset driving lights were abandoned in favour of extra cooling grilles and, when the Mk IIa arrived in 1952, the rear wheel spats were also dropped, to help cool the now larger rear brake drums.

Blessed with respectable road manners and performance, the Sunbeam-Talbot 90 was a popular choice from the Rootes Group.

WOLSELEY 6/80

UNITED KINGDOM 1948–54

Wolseley's post-war saloon range of 1948 offered a choice of wheelbase lengths and four- or six-cylinder engines, and the result was a pair of new Wolseleys – the 4/50 and 6/80. The logically named cars were formerly based on the Morris Oxford MO and latterly the unpopular but capable Morris Six. With monocoque construction,

independent front suspension and single overhead camshaft engine, the 6/80 was modern in conception. It was a much more upmarket affair than its Morris sibling, thanks to extra power from its twin-carburettor 2.2-litre (135cu in) powerplant. Finally, it also had a much more desirable interior. Standard equipment ran to leather trim and a heater/demister

unit. Build quality was high, as befitting the 6/80's status.

Sales were also brisk, and the car's speed and reliability meant that it was adopted by a number of police forces, which used 6/80s throughout the late 1940s and into the 1950s. There was little development of the car throughout its six-year lifespan, with only minor engine and suspension

modifications made. In 1954, the car went out of production and was replaced by the desirable 6/90.

ENGINE: 2215cc (135cu in),
  six-cylinder
POWER: 72bhp (54kW)
0–60MPH (96KM/H): 24.4 seconds
TOP SPEED: 125km/h (78mph)
PRODUCTION TOTAL: 25,281

PORSCHE 356

ENGINE: 1582cc (97cu in),
four-cylinder
POWER: 75bhp (56kW)
TOP SPEED: 169km/h (105mph)
0–60MPH (96KM/H): 11.2 seconds
PRODUCTION TOTAL: 77,509

While Porsche's first project was to design the Volkswagen before World War II, it was the 356 that ended up being the first machine to bear the company's name. Launched in 1948, the 356 was powered by an 1131cc (69cu in) flat-four VW engine, and was coupled to utterly distinctive styling to create a car that lives on today in the shape of the company's current output.

The 356 was not a cheap car, thanks to aluminium construction and Porsche's patented all-independent torsion bar suspension, but it still proved popular with those who could afford one. For its era, the 356 was dynamically brilliant – its low weight and advanced suspension

made it fun to drive, as the car boasted compliant handling and superb balance. Performance in 44bhp (33kW) form was fairly ordinary, but a variety of different performance upgrades meant most were fast, fun machines to drive.

From 1950, production moved from Austria to a new factory in Stuttgart, Germany, where the company remains today, and bodies were made out of steel in order to cut costs. To cope with the extra weight of the bodywork, the engine was given more grunt, first to 1286cc (78cu in), then to 1488cc (91cu in) for 1952.

A year later, Porsche unveiled the 356 Speedster, which was designed primarily for the booming American market – and buyers in hot-weather 'dry' states such as California lapped it up. They wanted open-topped cars, so Porsche removed the roof, fitted a rudimentary hood and sports seats, and called the new car 'Speedster'. Brilliant.

Although it was an attractive car, the Speedster suffered from

poor quality and, in 1958, Porsche commissioned coachbuilders Drauz of Heillbronn to create a better finished cabriolet with improved visibility.

The launch of the 356A saw the first significant change for the 356 in 1955, and, while it was still obviously a 356, the A had a higher ride height, new front indicator lenses, larger rear lights, different hubcaps and a one-piece panoramic windscreen, while the interior was made more user-friendly. Two new engines were offered – both air-cooled flat-fours, with a choice of 1290cc (79cu in) and 1582cc (97cu in) capacities. The same year also saw the launch of the 356 Carrera, which came with an 112bhp (83kW) race-tuned 1498cc (91cu in) engine, with four overhead camshafts and a top speed of more than 190km/h (120mph). The 356A and Carrera continued until 1959.

When the updated 356B was launched, using only the 1582cc (97cu in) engine from the A, it remained in production for three

years until the more modern 356C took over, again using the same engine, but with a new suspension set-up and four-wheel disc brakes.

The Carrera's successor, the Carrera 2, appeared in 1960 and boasted 155bhp (115kW) from its 1966cc (120cu in) four-camshaft race-tuned engine. Top speed was now over 193km/h (130mph).

Also noteworthy is the 356-based 550 Speedster, developed by Porsche to compete at Le Mans in 1953. It used an early version of the Carrera's 1.6-litre (98cu in) engine and was available as a road-legal machine, with thrilling but tricky handling characteristics. Despite its many competition successes, the 550 Speedster is best remembered as being the car movie icon James Dean was driving when he crashed and died.

Thanks to elegant styling, fine handling and excellent performance, the Porsche 356 led a long, fruitful life, contributing much to the 911.

FORD AG TAUNUS

ENGINE: 1698cc (104cu in),
four-cylinder
POWER: 75bhp (56kW)
0–60MPH (96KM/H): 15 seconds
TOP SPEED: 161km/h (100mph)
PRODUCTION TOTAL: 2,500,000

Established in 1925, Uncle Henry's German arm, known as Ford AG, was set up to import vehicles and build them under licence. Following World War II, Ford's German production did not restart until 1948, and, when it did, it was with the 1930s models,

including the Taunus Standard, Special and De Luxe.

The Taunus was a German middle-class stalwart, and, from 1952, when a new generation of no-frills cars was launched, they all carried the M designation, which stood for 'Masterpiece'.

The new 12M sported more contemporary styling and was powered by a 1.2-litre (73cu in) engine, producing 38bhp (28kW). That model was revamped in 1955, and the 15M was added to the range, now sporting 1.5-litre (92cu in) power and 55bhp

(41kW). These cars were given face-lifts in 1955 and 1957, and a 15M and 17M were also added; a 1.7-litre (104cu in) engine now topped the range. From 1960, a new body had been introduced, and, by 1962, the 12M was powered by a compact V4 engine, taking it to the top of Germany's bestseller list.

In 1966, the final German-only Taunus appeared, and smooth 2.3-litre (140cu in) and 2.6-litre (159cu in) V6 engines were added to the range. The UK-built Cortina took over from the smaller four-cylinder models in 1970, when the model became pan-European, and the bigger V-engined versions became Consuls and Granadas from 1972.

MORRIS MINOR

UNITED KINGDOM 1948–71

ENGINE: 1098cc (67cu in),
four-cylinder
POWER: 48bhp (36kW) at 5100rpm
0–60MPH (96KM/H): 24.8 seconds
TOP SPEED: 124km/h (77mph)
PRODUCTION TOTAL: 1,293,331

America had the Model T Ford, France had the Citroën 2CV, Germany had the Volkswagen, and Italy had the Fiat 500. All these cars were bought by the masses – and Britain's entry into that 'people's car' hall of fame must be a toss-up between the Mini and the ubiquitous Morris Minor.

The curvaceous, friendly-looking Minor stayed in production for almost a quarter of a century, and became a British icon. Plans for a new, post-war small Morris were drawn up during World War II, although it had to be done in secret, as development was against wartime rules. The car was the creation of Alec Issigonis, a gifted young engineer born in Greece.

The new Morris took shape rapidly and, by 1943, was already looking a lot like the final production version. Code-named Mosquito, after a British combat aircraft, the car had a curvaceous shape and boasted a monocoque bodyshell (a rarity in the United Kingdom at the time), and plans were afoot to power it by a new range of flat-four engines.

However, a lack of money meant that the tried and tested side-valve Morris Eight engine was used instead – something that Issigonis was dead against. In typical Issigonis style, development was quick, and continued right to the car's October 1948 launch date. Towards the end of the development programme, the entire car was widened (resulting in the strip down the centre of the bonnet/hood and split bumpers), and the Mosquito name was dropped, in favour of the Minor name, as used in the 1920s.

When the Minor was launched at the 1948 London Motor Show, it was just one of a line-up of three new Morris models. It was the one that attracted all the attention, however, eclipsing its bigger Oxford and Six. For many people, it outshone the star of the show, too – the new Jaguar XK120. The public and the press alike loved the Minor, with one magazine going so far as to proudly declare that it 'approached perfection'.

The only person that was not won over by the new Minor, it seemed, was the company's boss William Morris, by now Lord Nuffield. His reference to it as the 'poached egg' rather disparagingly if succintly summed up his feelings on the matter. Buyers, however, disagreed. During its production life, the Minor went on to sell well over 1.2 million vehicles (making it the first British car to reach the magic million mark) during its 23-year production life.

It was available from launch as a two-door saloon and a convertible tourer, and the four-door saloon followed in 1950. A running series of changes included the headlights being moved to the top of the front wings (fenders) in 1951, and, following the merger of Austin and Morris in 1952, the 803cc (49cu in) A-Series engine took over the job of powering the Minor. In 1953,

The Morris Minor remains the darling of the classic car set in the UK. Designed by Sir Alec Issigonis, it was as good to drive as to look at.

a Traveller estate (station wagon), van and pick-up were added, extending the range's appeal.

The 1956 update saw the A-Series engine expanded to 948cc (58cu in), denoted by a name change to Morris 1000 – and the dropping of the split windscreen – and another capacity increase to 1098cc (67cu in) followed in 1962. The car remained pretty much in that form until being replaced by the Morris Marina in 1971.

CITROËN 2CV

FRANCE 1948–90

ENGINE: 602cc (37cu in),
twin-cylinder
POWER: 28.5bhp (21kW) at 5750rpm
0–60MPH (96KM/H): 32.7 seconds
TOP SPEED: 114km/h (71mph)
PRODUCTION TOTAL: 3,873,294

Citroën's managing director Pierre Boulanger dictated that the company's new people's car should be able to carry two farmers, 50kg (110lb) of potatoes and a box of eggs, and return a fuel consumption of 30km/L (86mpg). It was a tall order – especially considering the rutted roads in rural France. Not only that, but he also added the challenge, 'If a box of eggs were placed in the car and it was driven over a ploughed field, not a single egg would be broken.'

Given the strict dictat, it seems almost impossible to believe that Citroën's engineers could actually produce a car to meet those demands. For one, the ideas were freakishly simple – and yet completely in tune with the demands of those buyers at which the car was aimed. As was said at the time, the 2CV's main rival was not another car – it was the horse and cart.

Despite dismissive nicknames such as 'Tin Snail', the 2CV was almost solely responsible for motorizing the rural French.

The end result was a car that would go on to become one of the greatest designs of all time, incredibly simple, practical and more capable than a glance at its spec sheet would have you believe. Design work began immediately after Boulanger issued guidelines, with the vehicle taking shape in complete secrecy. The 2CV was front-wheel drive, like that other great Citroën, the Traction Avant, but other than that everything else was to be as simple as possible, with the body made out of corrugated aluminium. Launch was scheduled for late 1939, but World War II meant that the car was put on ice, and the 2CV prototypes were hidden from the Germans when France was invaded.

Development work continued after war had ended, and the 2CV was refined for production, with the aluminium body being dropped in favour of steel. When the car did eventually hit the market, in 1948, it met with criticism from the press. But those who mattered – the customers – proved the commentators wrong. The masses it was intended to motorize took the car into their hearts, and the company was inundated with thousands of orders only days after the car's debut at the Paris Motor Show.

The 2CV was powered by a tough 375cc (23cu in) air-cooled flat-twin engine driving the front wheels, and the suspension was simple but effective – a single shock absorber on each wheel was interconnected front to rear. It was soft, and that meant roll in corners, but grip levels were astonishingly high. The roof was canvas, and could be rolled right back to the rear window.

The basic car was improved during its life – a 425cc (26cu in) engine came in 1954, and a bigger rear window was installed in 1956. From 1958 to 1966, the Sahara 4x4 version was available, powered by two engines and transmissions.

A face-lift to the car ironed out the creases in 1960, and, in 1963, a more powerful 602cc (37cu in) engine was installed. The final major addition came in 1982 – disc brakes.

Production of the 2CV lasted 42 years, and nearly four million were sold – proof if ever there was any needed that sometimes the people know what they want more than the press ...

ROVER LAND ROVER

UNITED KINGDOM 1948–PRESENT

ENGINE: 1997cc (122cu in), four-cylinder
POWER: 52bhp (39kW) at 4000rpm
0-60MPH (96KM/H): n/a
TOP SPEED: 97km/h (60mph)
PRODUCTION TOTAL: n/a

Maurice Wilks, Rover's chief engineer, picked up an ex-military Willys Jeep in the immediate aftermath of World War II and set about using it on his Welsh estate. He ended up being so impressed by it that, when it began to wear out and there was nothing else on the market to replace it, he set about building a British version, to sell to the public.

Wilks reasoned that the new car would find a willing band of

It's one of the automotive industry's longest-lived and most endearing shapes – and it was fashioned by function.

agricultural users, but it would also provide badly needed revenue for Rover. The 'temporary' vehicle became the 4x4 Land Rover, and, although it certainly never set out to do so, Rover created one of the automotive industry's most enduring success stories. Wilks's stopgap, basic and austere Jeep copy became a surprise legend, with its descendants remaining in production today.

From conception to production, it took a year to get the Land Rover onto the market, and, in order to speed up the process, it was decided to build the body out of readily available aluminium, as opposed to steel, which was hard to come by at the time. Also, as many standard car parts as

possible were incorporated to keep costs down, including the 1595cc (97cu in) inlet-over-exhaust petrol engine and gearbox from the P3 saloon. Four-wheel drive was permanently engaged.

The body design was primitive, with simple alloy panels mounted on a basic box-section chassis – but it all worked.

Despite that, the car received a sensational reception when it appeared at the 1948 Amsterdam Motor Show, with the press and public falling for this practical 'go anywhere' vehicle. Many customers also believed that the corrosion-proof aluminium body would be tougher than steel and easier to repair. Orders from all over the world started to flood in

within a few weeks – and the Rover company was soon churning out more Land Rovers than saloons at the Solihull factory.

Having rushed the Land Rover into production, the company set about a programme of steady improvement in order to keep the orders rolling in. In 1950, the provision to engage two-wheel drive in top gears was introduced and the headlights were moved to the wings (fenders) in 1951. The engine grew to 1997cc (122cu in) the same year, and two longer wheelbases became available in 1953, and again in 1956, in time for the introduction of Rover's new 2052cc (125cu in) diesel engine.

The Series II appeared in 1958, which made the vehicle look a lot

more habitable, but that only lasted until 1961, when the mostly unchanged IIa replaced it. By this time, 250,000 vehicles had been sold worldwide, with military buyers particularly keen. In 1970, the Series III, which featured an all-synchromesh gearbox, new grille and updated interior, arrived, and a long overdue overdrive gear was added just in time for the worldwide energy crisis in 1974.

Perhaps the most significant development to the Land Rover took place in 1979, when the Range Rover's 3.5-litre (214cu in) V8 engine was fitted in its less glamorous ancestor. The original Land Rover lives on today as the Defender, featuring Ford and Land Rover diesel and petrol engines.

HEALEY SILVERSTONE

UNITED KINGDOM 1949–51

ENGINE: 2443cc (149cu in), four-cylinder
POWER: 104bhp (77kW)
0–60MPH (96KM/H): 11.0 seconds
TOP SPEED: 180km/h (112mph)
PRODUCTION TOTAL: 105

It might have looked old hat when it was launched in 1949, but the no-nonsense Healey-Silverstone D Series was still an effective competition machine. Sporting cycle wings (fenders), the car possessed a number of unusual design features that included a windscreen that retracted into the scuttle – apart from a section of the top which remained proud to act as a wind deflector – twin headlights within the deep, sloped grille and a spare tyre that stowed horizontally at the back which also acted as a rear bumper.

The stressed skin alloy body ensured lightness, and the 104bhp (77kW) engine gave it a high top speed of 180km/h (112mph). In early 1950, the E Series, which had a slightly wider body, larger cockpit and better luggage stowing capacity, was launched, and could be distinguished from its predecessor by its front

bumper and air intake on top of the bonnet (hood).

Despite its relatively low production volume, the stunning-looking Silverstone gained many competition successes throughout

the 1950s, and was finally replaced by the Nash-Healey in 1951.

Today, examples of the car are highly prized and inevitably fetch high prices on the market when genuine ones do surface.

With its headlights concealed behind the radiator grille, retractable windscreen and spare wheel that also acts as a rear bumper, there's no chance of mistaking the Healey Silverstone.

MASERATI A6

ITALY 1947–51

ENGINE: 1488cc (91cu in), six-cylinder
POWER: 65bhp (48kW) at 4700rpm
0–60MPH (96KM/H): n/a
TOP SPEED: 145km/h (90mph)
PRODUCTION TOTAL: 61

Diversification was definitely the name of the game in the immediate post-war years. The

Maserati brothers – Carlo, Bindo, Alfieri, Ettore and Ernesto – had started building racing cars in 1926, but realized that in order to survive into the 1950s under its new owner, Omar Orsi, they would need to start producing road cars.

The new Maserati A6 was that road car, and it made its debut at the 1947 Turin Motor Show, with production starting the following year. Still, it was not a complete

production car; Maserati supplied the tubular steel frame chassis, fitted with wishbone front suspension and a live rear axle, and it was up to customers to put individual bodies on. Many were penned by Pininfarina or Zagato, but a few customers specified Vignale, Frua, Guglielmo and Allemano bodies, which add extra exclusivity to the range. Most A6s were coupés.

The engine was an all-aluminium 1488cc (91cu in) six-cylinder unit based on the pre-war racer. It was detuned using a single-carburettor set-up as standard, but three could be supplied as an option, to regain power. A competition version, the A6G of 1951, had a bigger cast-iron 1954cc (119cu in) engine, and was followed in 1956 by the A6G/2000, which used a twin-camshaft Formula 2 engine.

Its reputation had been built on the world's racing circuits, but Maserati's A6 road car also featured plenty of competition magic. Some of Italy's best design houses provided the bodywork options.

ALLARD P1

UNITED KINGDOM 1949–52

Set up during the 1930s by motor trader Sydney Allard, the cars that bore his name emerged from Adlards Motors (taking the Adlards name from his father's building firm) in Putney, South London. The first cars were a series of specials for motorsport, but, after World War II, he started a new company called Allard Motor Co Ltd – the intention to build

production cars using mostly Ford running gear. The two-door Allard P1 was an evoltion of these first post-war cars and took their distinctive curved grille, with fitted full-width bodywork and seating for at least four people.

Lighter aluminium bodywork meant that the underpowered car was still adequately quick, but the lugubrious column-mounted

gearchange did little to encourage sporting driving. This rather unsatisfactory state of affairs was put right with the launch of the M2X drophead coupé version, with its bizarre A-shaped grille. Power came from either a Ford 3622cc (221cu in) unit or a modified Mercury 4375cc (267cu in) V8.

The P1 was possibly the most popular of all the Allard cars, and

it went on to race successfully in the 1952 Monte Carlo rally, driven by Sydney Allard himself.

ENGINE: 3622cc (221cu in), eight-cylinder
POWER: 85bhp (63kW)
0–60MPH (96KM/H): n/a
TOP SPEED: 144km/h (90mph)
PRODUCTION TOTAL: 559

ASTON MARTIN DB2

UNITED KINGDOM 1950–53

David Brown bought Aston Martin and merged it with Lagonda in 1948 – and it looked like the company's troubles would at last be over. The DB Series cars soon followed, and Aston Martin Lagonda's future looked bright from that point on.

The Aston Martin 2-litre (122cu in) Sports was the first of the new cars to appear shortly after the merger, which then became known

as the DB1, simply because it acted as a testbed for so many of the models that followed it. The DB1 was not the best-made car produced by the company, however, and in all only 14 examples were produced.

The real Aston Martin Lagonda story began in 1950, with the launch of the DB2. This really was a special machine, and its bulbous but elegant styling was the work

of Frank Feeley. Feeley's styling set it apart from the crowd. Married to a well-sorted chassis that came from Claude Hill's DB1 design, the car was designed to use his engine, too, but this was dropped in favour of an unproven 2.6-litre (157cu in) engine design. The reason for its choice – it was better looking than Hill's engine.

The cars had good performance and beautiful build quality when it

came to their bodies. The DB2's stylish interior was also an object lesson in the use of wood, leather and Wilton carpeting.

ENGINE: 2580cc (157cu in), six-cylinder
POWER: 105bhp (78kW)
0–60MPH (96KM/H): 11.2 seconds
TOP SPEED: 187km/h (116mph)
PRODUCTION TOTAL: 411

The Aston Martin DB2 was a landmark car that shaped the future of the iconic sportscar company. Featuring beautiful exterior styling, as well as a well appointed interior and excellent performance, the DB2 remains in demand today.

TRIUMPH MAYFLOWER

UNITED KINGDOM 1949–53

Now under the control of the Standard Motor Company at this point in its history, Triumph's car production was moving in exciting new directions. No one, however, expected the controversy that surrounded the 1949 Mayflower, and no model since – apart from the TR7 – has come close to exciting the same response. Just why opinion was divided over the Mayflower is open to debate,

especially as the razor-edged look of the larger Triumph saloons was pleasing to the eye.

Conceived as an economy model for the US market, the Mayflower was a good idea, but what let the vehicle down was its poor execution. The individual style did not translate well on the smaller car, and that led to odd proportions. It did not help that Leslie Moore styled the basic body,

while Walter Belgrove oversaw the design at the front.

Unsurprisingly, the unitary construction Mayflower was not a big seller at home or abroad. It was worthy enough, with plenty of room and good build quality, but the challenging styling of the car proved a barrier to sales. Also, the underpowered 1247cc (76cu in) side-valve engine and three-speed gearbox were not up to the job,

and the wayward handling finished the picture. The car lasted only four years in production and was phased out in 1953.

ENGINE: 1247cc (76cu in), four-cylinder
POWER: 38bhp (28kW) at 4200rpm
0–60MPH (96KM/H): 30 seconds
TOP SPEED: 101km/h (63mph)
PRODUCTION TOTAL: 35,000

VOLKSWAGEN BEETLE HEBMULLER

GERMANY 1949–53

ENGINE: 1131cc (69cu in), four-cylinder
POWER: 25bhp (19kW)
0–60MPH (96KM/H): n/a
TOP SPEED: 101km/h (63mph)
PRODUCTION TOTAL: about 700

The Hebmuller name had been around a long time – the small coachbuilder had been formed in 1889 and, in 1919, when the founder died, it was taken over by his four sons. In the late 1940s, they decided to produce a roadster version of the Volkswagen – and it

should have been a recipe for success. Rather like the Karmann-built Beetle, the Hebmuller was a full convertible, but it had a flush-fitting stowed hood, which lead to much cleaner styling. The Hebmuller conversion always carried VW badges, and it was sold

through the official dealer network as the Volkswagen Cabriolet.

Following extensive testing, the VW management was so impressed with the car's quality that it ordered 2000 to be sold through its agents. The first cars were ordered at the beginning of July 1949, but by the end of that month disaster had struck, with fire destroying almost the whole Hebmuller factory.

Hardly anything survived the fire, and, although a few more cars trickled out of the factory in 1950 and 1951, it was clear that the company would never survive. By the middle of 1952, it was bankrupt, and the planned coupé died alongside the roadster.

The Hebmuller Beetle looked a lot cleaner than its contemporary, the Karmann-built convertible. However, a disaster at the factory meant an early end.

AC BUCKLAND TOURER

Although the AC 2-litre saloon remained the core product in the AC business in the years following World War II, the company's management readily accepted that in order to remain healthy, it would need to diversiFy by offering more specialized versions of the car. It needed to offer as many options as possible in order to attract buyers. That lead to a pre-war-like selection of

body options on the basic car, including a variety of four-door saloons, drophead saloon versions (which were almost unchanged from the waistline down), estates (station wagons) (to exploit a loophole in the tax laws) and a proper four-seater sports tourer, the Buckland.

So-called because the body was built by the Buckland Body Works in Cambridgeshire (well away from

AC's Thames Ditton factory), the chassis were sent to its workshops and married to the exciting new body. It was swooping but slightly bulky-looking, and constructed in the same aluminium-over-ash frame as the saloon.

The doors were much smaller than those on the saloon version, with curvy cutaways along their top edges, and the windscreen was designed to fold flat. The

idea was to enhance the sporty feel of the standard car, but its weight and slightly antiquated feel negated the effect of the styling.

ENGINE: 1991cc (121cu in), six-cylinder
POWER: 74bhp (55kW)
0–60MPH (96KM/H): n/a
TOP SPEED: 136km/h (84mph)
PRODUCTION TOTAL: 70

ALLARD J2

The J2 was the archetypal Allard and motoring at its most extreme. The new design featured a rigid tubular-braced ladder chassis and minimalist alloy bodywork that incorporated cycle wings at the front. The J2's performance was stunning, and it was a focused driver's car, offering little in the way of creature comforts – an aero was all the driver got.

Suspension was a split-axle independent suspension up front and a De Dion axle at the rear, and power came mostly from a bored-out Mercury V8 unit that rocketed the J2 to 96km/h (60mph) in a fraction under six seconds – quick by modern standards.

The Ford V8 could be tuned further, however, with an Ardun

overhead-valve conversion, which resulted in devastating performance at the expense of reliability. The majority of J2s sold to the United States were supplied without engines, to give the customer a choice of a number of V8 powerplants. The lairiest of the lot

were the Cad-Allards, which used 300bhp (223kW) Cadillac units. One such car, fitted with a 5.4-litre (331 cu in) Cadillac engine, scored a third place at Le Mans in 1950.

A number of J2 replicas have been built in recent times – and it is easy to see why.

ENGINE: 4375cc (267cu in), eight-cylinder
POWER: 110bhp (82kW)
0–60MPH (96KM/H): 5.9 seconds
TOP SPEED: 175km/h (110mph)
PRODUCTION TOTAL: 90

Powered by a bored and stroked Mercury V8, the Allard J2 was exceptionally quick for its day – and that was in standard form. Many went to the USA to have their engines fitted.

ARMSTRONG-SIDDELEY WHITLEY

ENGINE: 2309cc (141cu in), six-cylinder
POWER: 75bhp (56kW)
0–60MPH (96KM/H): n/a
TOP SPEED: 121km/h (75mph)
PRODUCTION TOTAL: n/a

The Armstrong-Siddeley Whitley featured more extravagant styling than the standard Lancaster saloon, with a wider, more angular nose and a taller rear roofline

Longer, wider and more extravagant than the standard Lancaster saloon, the Armstrong-Siddeley Whitley was a fast and capacious long distance cruiser designed with export markets in mind.

which allowed for extra headroom and leg space for rear-seat passengers. It was obvious that the company was thinking of export markets when it devised the car.

Only offered with the 2.3-litre (141cu in) engine used in later versions of the Lancaster, the Whitley possessed reasonable performance for the era. Available as a five-seater saloon, it was a comfortable and spacious car, and a good long-distance cruiser. It was offered as long wheelbase limousine, a Station Coupé and a utility pick-up, and all versions were built in very limited numbers and were seldom seen from the end of the 1950s. Production of the Whitley ceased in 1954.

FORD VEDETTE

FRANCE 1947–54

ENGINE: 2158cc (132cu in),
 eight-cylinder
POWER: 66bhp (49kW)
0–60MPH (96KM/H): n/a
TOP SPEED: 144km/h (90mph)
PRODUCTION TOTAL: 100,000

Ford was a global player after the end of World War II, and it had factories wherever there was a market for its cars. The purpose-built factory in Poissy in France was a pre-war effort, but it resumed Ford production in 1947 with a US-focused car previously launched in 1944.

With its US-influenced full-width grille, two-piece windscreen and fastback styling, it was quite unlike any of its European rivals – especially when considering the 2158cc (132cu in) V8 engine under the bonnet (hood). Sadly, the side-valve engine was not a paragon of reliability, and sales suffered even further.

Initially, the Vedette was available as a four-door saloon, but coupé's and convertibles appeared in 1949, and Facel even built a sporting coupé version called the Comte. For 1953, the Vedette received a face-lift with a single-piece windscreen, and a rear end with a proper boot (trunk) – not a great styling success. The engine was increased to 2355cc

(144cu in), and power went up from 66 to 80bhp (49 to 60kW).

A 4-litre (244cu in) 95bhp (71kW) version was also offered, but did not sell. The replacement Ford had in mind was shelved when the company was sold to Simca in November 1954, and production switched to Versailles, where these cars carried the French marque.

The French car market was in its infancy when the Ford Vedette was launched, but despite that it did pretty well and was later renamed a Simca.

SINGER SM1500

UNITED KINGDOM 1949–54

ENGINE: 1506cc (92cu in),
 four-cylinder
POWER: 48bhp (36kW)
0–60MPH (96KM/H): 33.7 seconds
TOP SPEED: 114km/h (71mph)
PRODUCTION TOTAL: 17,382

When the Singer SM1500 went on sale in October 1948, it was only for export – but, by the summer of the following year, cars began trickling onto the UK market. The SM1500 was the first true post-war Singer, and was heavily influenced by American thinking on styling.

Competing with cars such as the Jowett Javelin and Standard Vanguard, the Singer struggled against these rivals, although a face-lift in 1954, when it became the Hunter, did gain it considerable

character. The four-door saloon offered seating for six, and the column-mounted gearshift and independent coil spring front suspension were pure US thinking. Indeed, the suspension design was licensed directly from Packard.

There was a four-speed three-synchromesh gearbox mated to a 1506cc (92cu in) four-cylinder overhead-camshaft engine. Features such as a variable-speed fan heater and spring-loaded door check links to hold the doors open were typical Singer touches and ahead of their time – as was the viewing chamber on the side of the engine negating the need for a dipstick for checking engine oil levels.

Not the most inspiring post-war car, the Singer SM1500 still had some neat touches.

TRIUMPH RENOWN

ENGINE: 2088cc (127cu in),
 four-cylinder
POWER: 68bhp (51kW) at 4200rpm
0–60MPH (96KM/H): 28.4 seconds
TOP SPEED: 120km/h (75mph)
PRODUCTION TOTAL: 12,000

The Triumph Renown shared the same engine and mechanics as the rather sportier Roadster, and evolved from the 1800/2000 Saloon. It looked different and was designed for a very different kind of buyer, but the slightly altered chassis meant that it could be produced economically.

Triumph initially asked coachbuilders Mulliners of Birmingham to produce a design, but the new head of the Standard-Triumph body engineering department, Walter Belgrove, devised his own scheme, and inevitably these were chosen for the new car. The 1800/2000 ended up being a grand and stately-looking saloon, with elegant razor-edged styling, a design theme that company boss Sir John Black wanted to carry throughout the range.

Launched at the same time as the Roadster, the 1800/2000 Saloon went on to have a longer and more successful life than the Roadster, and the bigger 2088cc (127cu in) Vanguard engine was fitted in 1949, and very soon afterwards the car was renamed the Renown. It was at this point

Razor edged styling was the order of the day for Triumph in the post-war years, and the Renown saloon and limousines shared much with the Roadster.

that the car received the Vanguard's chassis and independent front suspension as well.

A longer wheelbase was introduced for 1951, which became the standard a year later. Production ended in 1954.

EMW 340

The EMW 340's appearance coincided with the company having to change its name from BMW. The East German state car company Autovelo had been infringing trademarks by continuing to badge its models as BMWs, despite that company having been re-formed in Munich. Following legal pressure, the Eisenach branch of BMW AG was dissolved on 28 September 1949, so that the Munich-based company could become the sole owner of the famous trademark.

This was important because at least half of the Eisenach's factory output was exported to the West. Without modifying the cars, Autovelo simply renamed them EMWs, which stood for Eisenach Motoren Werke, and changed the blue sectors in the propeller badge to Bolshevik red.

Like the 327, the power unit was the pre-war 1971cc (120cu in) six-cylinder engine, and the saloon was based on the equally pre-war 326. Rather than being elegant and stylish, the 340 had terrible US-influenced grilles that did not suit the car at all.

ENGINE: 1971cc (120cu in),
 six-cylinder
POWER: 50bhp (37kW)
0–60MPH (96KM/H): 32 seconds
TOP SPEED: 124km/h (71mph)
PRODUCTION TOTAL: n/a

ROLLS-ROYCE SILVER DAWN

Based on the Bentley Mk VI, the Silver Dawn was not so much a Rolls-Royce as a badge-engineered Bentley. It was a quality car nonetheless, with a well-equipped wood- and leather-trimmed interior, plus a larger version of the engine from the Silver Wraith. Still, it was not a great success.

Aimed primarily at European export markets, the Silver Dawn should have succeeded – it had compact dimensions and a Euro-friendly column-change Hydramatic gearbox. It was a simple car to drive and was more of a driver's car, belying its Bentley roots. Performance was adequate and handling reasonable, but that was not what the company's customers were looking for at the time. This was especially the case in the United Kingdom, where Rolls-Royce's customers were primarily interested in the larger cars. Of the 761 Silver Dawns produced, only a handful was sold in the company's home market. Most of the production run was reserved for left-hand drive.

The Silver Dawn was not as solid as other Rolls-Royces, and the pressed steel bodywork was prone to rust, making the Dawn a rarity today – and therefore desirable among collectors.

ENGINE: 4566cc (279cu in),
 six-cylinder
POWER: n/a
0–60MPH (96KM/H): 16.2 seconds
TOP SPEED: 140km/h (87mph)
PRODUCTION TOTAL: 761

THE ENCYCLOPEDIA OF CLASSIC CARS

A badge-engineered Bentley it may have been, but the Rolls-Royce Silver Dawn was still a luxuriously appointed car that just happens to have been scaled down a little. Never inspiring to drive, though.

JENSEN INTERCEPTOR

Undeterred by the relative lack of sales of its PW, Jensen pushed ahead with its new model plans. The Interceptor range was launched in 1949 and was a follow-up model to the JW. It also opened up new markets for the company. Production of the Interceptor started as a two-door drophead coupé, which was mounted on a modified Austin

chassis – only later to become available as a four-door saloon.

It was a grand tourer, and its looks were not to everyone's taste – and the bug-eyed headlights proved challenging for most people. It was a large car, and passenger comfort on the bench front seat was excellent, and there was also a generous amount of rear legroom.

Just like the PW, the Interceptor's power came from Austin's lumpy straight-six 3993cc (244cu in) A135 engine. That was enough to push the streamlined but somewhat slab-sided car to a top speed of 161km/h (100mph), an important selling point in 1949. Evolution of the Interceptor was straightforward. A hardtop version appeared in 1951, with a full fabric-covered

roof; overdrive became standard from 1952; and the bonnet (hood) was lowered after 1953.

ENGINE: 3993cc (244cu in),
 six-cylinder
POWER: 130bhp (97kW)
0–60MPH (96KM/H): 13.7 seconds
TOP SPEED: 161km/h (100mph)
PRODUCTION TOTAL: 88

ZIM (12)

Modelled on contemporary American designs, the ZIM (12) was one of Russia's flagship cars. It was built by Gaz and was known officially as the 12, and unofficially as the ZIM. The car was huge, with a length of 5.5m (18ft). It remained in production between 1950 and 1959.

Given its price, the ZIM (12) was completely unobtainable to all but

the richest Russians, but in many ways it was similar to the cars that many Americans were using as everyday transport. Despite that, the ZIM was not the top-of-the-line Russian car. That title was reserved for the prestigious ZIL limousine, transport of choice for the most important VIPs.

The 3.5-litre (214cu in) six-cylinder engine was not that

powerful, and the top speed was limited to 120km/h (75mph). The chassis was contemporary enough, however, with independent suspension at the front and a live axle at the rear.

The ZIM successfully rivalled the best the Americans could offer at the time of its launch, but a lack of development meant that, by the end of its run, it was an archaic

throwback. The problem was that modern automotive technology was closed to Russia in the 1950s.

ENGINE: 3.5-litre (214cu in),
 six-cylinder
POWER: 89bhp (66kW)
0–60MPH (96KM/H): n/a
TOP SPEED: 120km/h (75mph)
PRODUCTION TOTAL: n/a

BORGWARD HANSA

With a claim to fame of being the first all-new German car to be introduced after World War II, the Borgward Hansa should be better known today than it is. However, the future events of the

ill-fated company would come to overshadow it. Originally made by Carl Borgward, who had earlier produced Goliath and Hansa-Lloyd vehicles, the Hansa had an interesting evolution.

Once the hostilities were over, Borgward's plan to maximize his allocation of raw materials was to form three separate car companies: Lloyd, Goliath and Borgward. Borward's own Hansa

1500 was released in 1949, and immediately set a new technical precedent for the German car industry. It featured streamlined full-width bodywork, which was inspired by the American Kaisers,

and was also in possession of a modern mechanical specification.

Powered by an overhead-valve engine, the Hansa boasted an all-synchromesh gearbox and independent front and rear suspension – and as a result, looked set fair to find success on the marketplace. The range was expanded – a diesel and an 1800 petrol version were launched before the car evolved into the

Isabella. The Hansa remained, but it was exclusively six-cylinder-powered, and it was eventually phased out in 1958.

ENGINE: 1498cc (91cu in), four-cylinder
POWER: 48bhp (36kW)
0–60MPH (96KM/H): n/a
TOP SPEED: 105km/h (65mph)
PRODUCTION TOTAL: 35,229

Being the first all-new German car to be introduced after World War II, the Borgward Hansa had the weight of a nation's expectations on its shoulders. A modern specification and elegant styling aided its success.

ROVER P4

UNITED KINGDOM 1949–64

ENGINE: 2230cc (136cu in), six-cylinder
POWER: 80bhp (60kW) at 4500rpm
0-60MPH (96KM/H): 20.8 secs
TOP SPEED: 140km/h (87mph)
PRODUCTION TOTAL: 114,746

The launch of the Rover P4 in 1949 saw the long-lived company take a confident step into the modern age. The completely new saloon may have been underpinned by a chassis that had been developed from the P3, but the bold new styling of the solid new car was altogether more modern, strongly influenced as it was by the Studebaker designs of Raymond Loewy and Virgil Exner.

Another P3 carry over was its 2103cc (128cu in) engine, but it was not particularly exciting – unlike the rest of the car. The Rover 75 (as the first cars were called) earned the nickname 'Cyclops' because of its single auxiliary driving light mounted in the centre of the grille. The distinctive feature was dropped in 1952, however, when the front end was restyled.

The original Rover 75 was joined by the 2.6-litre (159cu in) Rover 90 in 1953 and the four-cylinder 1997cc (122cu in) Rover

60 and 2286cc (140cu in) Rover 80 the same year. A further face-lift in 1954 saw the 75 receive a 2.2-litre (136cu in) engine before the Rover 105 appeared two years later. The final P4s produced were

the 95, 100 and 110, which were fitted with an improved 2625cc (160cu in) engine.

The P4 lasted for 15 years and cemented Rover's solid 'Auntie' image.

It may be nicknamed the 'Auntie' Rover, but the P4 was actually a radical design when it was launched, and enjoyed the benefits of high build quality and mechanical refinement.

DODGE CORONET

UNITED STATES 1949–73

Remembered as a muscle car, the Dodge Coronet actually started as a luxury vehicle. The long-lived family of cars was constantly developed; as early as 1953 it was completely restyled. The newly downsized chassis was available in two sizes, and there were several bodystyles – saloons, estates (station wagons) and a convertible, as well as a so-called 'Red Ram V8', which produced 140bhp (104kW). In 1956, the company qualified for NASCAR

racing and the Coronet D-500 was the basis of the competition programme. It used a 5162cc (315cu in) V8 producing 260bhp (194kW), but retained unaltered styling. The 340bhp (253kW) D501

It started out as a luxury car, but by the 1950s, it had become a muscle car. Large engines and prodigious performance were the order of the day during its 24-year production run.

was added a year later, but the car was discontinued after 1959.

The name was revived in 1965. Now Dodge's midsize car, it was available with a full race 426 Hemi engine rated at 425bhp (317kW), but which actually produced a phenomenal 600bhp (447kW). As before, a full range of bodies was offered, and, in 1967, the car received a face-lift front and rear with fake vents and stripes. The legendary Coronet R/T was an important addition to the line-up, before the range was further changed in 1968 with the introduction of fashionable 'Coke bottle' curvy lines.

After the 1970 new-look face-lift, the Coronet faded away as muscle car sales imploded.

ENGINE: V8 7210cc (440cu in)
POWER: 375bhp (279kW)
0–60MPH (96KM/H): 6.6 seconds
TOP SPEED: 197km/h (123mph)
PRODUCTION TOTAL: about 2,500,000

OLDSMOBILE 88

UNITED STATES 1949–99

ENGINE: 6551cc (400cu in),
  eight-cylinder
POWER: 345bhp (257kW)
0–60MPH (96KM/H): 8.5 seconds
TOP SPEED: 181km/h (112mph)
PRODUCTION TOTAL: about 10,000,000

The Oldsmobile 88 lasted 50 years in production, so it is no surprise that it is an American automotive icon. During its life, the car changed beyond all recognition, and the original 1949 cars, which featured 1930s-style styling, was a far cry from the 1999 car that wore the same name. However, the model's target market remained the same throughout its production life.

The 88 retained a recipe of a compact body mated to powerful engines, and that meant that the final product was usually quicker than the opposition. During the 1950s and 1960s, it became the dominant force on the NASCAR racing scene, and perhaps the car's greatest achievement was winning the first-ever Daytona 500 in 1959, piloted by the stock-car legend Lee Petty.

By the mid-1970s, however, the 88 had become nothing more than a name applied to powerful versions of standard Oldsmobiles, and the saloons could not match the stylish cars of the first two decades of production. The 88 name died with Oldsmobile in 1999.

One particularly memorable 88, however, was the 1953 Starfire concept car. This model stunned visitors to GM's travelling Motorama, with its styling inspired by the Lockheed fighter jet, wraparound windscreen and sinister-looking wheel spinners.

Spanning a lifetime of 50 years, the Oldsmobile 88 name was an American institution. The early models were retro designed.

VOLKSWAGEN BEETLE KARMANN

GERMANY 1949–80

ENGINE: 1131cc (69cu in),
  four-cylinder
POWER: 25bhp (19kW)
0–60MPH (96KM/H): n/a
TOP SPEED: 101km/h (63mph)
PRODUCTION TOTAL: 331,847

Of all Volkswagens, one of the most sought-after to this day is arguably the Karmann-built Cabriolet. The German coachbuilder unveiled the production version of its Beetle Cabriolet in 1949, after producing its first drophead prototypes in 1946. Impressed with what it saw, Volkswagen ordered an initial batch of 2000, following a strenuous testing programme encompassing thousands of miles. (Company policy was to ensure that any product sold from its dealers was up to scratch in terms of quality and durability.)

During its 30-year lifespan, the Karmann Beetle received changes mirroring those of the standard car. Engine, brake and suspension upgrades were introduced through the years, as well as improvements to the interior and electrical systems – essential considering the car's high price. The Karmann's roof was also upgraded, as initially it offered almost no rear visibility when raised, thanks to its tiny rear window. The car's styling remains

Although the Karmann Beetle looks as if it's carrying a rucksack when the hood is folded, it enjoyed huge sales and has a cult following.

interesting today, and the bulky hood which stands proud of the rear deck when folded is a well-known styling cue.

Although visibility was never good, the quality of the multi-layered hood made the car refined, and it remains special today.

PLYMOUTH P-19

The P19 was the last of the famous P-Series Plymouths, and it could trace its roots back to the company's beginnings in 1928. In many ways, the P-19 symbolized all that was conventional about the Plymouth marque; despite being more advanced than previous P-Series models, it was Plymouth through and through. A notable point was its electric windscreen

wipers in place of vacuum-operated units, but the ordinary albeit curvaceous styling and the company's by-now familiar bull-nose radiator grille did little to update the company's image.

Other innovations in the P-Series evident on the P-19 were an interior light that came on and off when the doors were opened and closed (a first), plus an ignition

that worked by simply turning the key, which Plymouth falsely claimed it had invented. The P19 was the last car to feature Plymouth's award-winning 'Safety Signal' speedometer. This flashed a green light on the dashboard at speeds of up to 48km/h (30mph), then flashed amber up to 80km/h (50mph), before flashing red at speeds over that.

Restyled and renamed Plymouths appeared for 1951, and the P designations were dropped.

ENGINE: 4260cc (260cu in), eight-cylinder
POWER: 167bhp (124kW)
0–60MPH (96KM/H): n/a
TOP SPEED: n/a
PRODUCTION TOTAL: n/a

FERRARI 195

ENGINE: 2341cc (143cu in), 12-cylinder
POWER: 130bhp (97kW)
0–60MPH (96KM/H): 11 seconds
TOP SPEED: 177km/h (110mph)
PRODUCTION TOTAL: 25

The Ferrari 195 was a straightforward evolution of the 166, and early models were built specifically for racing. The car itself was not terribly successful as a competition car, which must have come as a crushing disappointment to Enzo, as he was strongly focused on beating Alfa Romeo in Grand Prix racing.

As a road car, however, it set the company well on the way to superstardom. The 195's enlarged 2.3-litre (143cu in) engine produced around 130bhp (97kW) in the Inter, or road, version, using a single Weber carburettor. The competition Sport engine was

boosted to 160bhp (119kW) using triple Webers, and this put the top speed up to 177km/h (110mph). For improved high-speed stability, the 195 Inter had a longer 250cm (98in) wheelbase.

The 195 chassis provided the basis for a number of coachbuilders to create their own designs. Two-seat touring, sports-racer berlinetta coupés and convertibles were the most numerous, with the majority of work carried out by either Pininfarina or Vignale.

Production of the 195 was limited at around 25 units. The cars seen at the 1952 Paris Motor Show were among the very first Ferraris to be built as left-hand drive models – much to the relief of potential owners.

Although it was a straightforward evolution of the 166, the Ferrari 195 was even quicker and more desirable.

VERITAS DYNA-VERITAS

In the late 1940s, Lorenz Dietrich of specialist carmaker Veritas was offered the chance to distribute the Panhard Dyna in Germany, with a view to using the chassis and engine from the car in a special of his own . The Dyna-Veritas was the result, and it was produced in tiny numbers between 1950 and 1952 – and it was a hand-built special which very few

Germans could actually afford. The choice was between coupé and cabriolet bodystyles, with most being the open-topped car.

The pretty bodies were designed by Veritas and built to order by Stuttgart-based coachbuilder, Baur. The conventional hand-made bodyshell was mounted on a tubular steel chassis, but that clothed an interesting Panhard-

sourced 744cc (45cu in) flat-twin engine which drove the front wheels through a gearbox also from the same company. With only 33bhp (25kW) on tap, performance surprised, thanks to a low kerb weight, and handling was sharp.

While the car was technically interesting and fun to drive, the company's finances were weak and had been an ongoing problem. The

cars' high cost and tiny sales took their toll, therefore, forcing Veritas out of business in 1952.

ENGINE: 744cc (45cu in), twin-cylinder
POWER: 33bhp (25kW)
0–60MPH (96KM/H): n/a
TOP SPEED: n/a
PRODUCTION TOTAL: about 200

ALVIS TA21 3-LITRE

Alvis had been producing some of the world's most advanced cars in the 1920s and 1930s, but things had been tough following World War II. The trouble was that the company's factory had been almost completely destroyed in the Blitz and that meant practically starting from scratch.

The first post-war car offered by Alvis was the TA14, based on the pre-war 12/70, and it was not until

the March 1950 Geneva Motor Show that the brand-new TA21 made an appearance. Retaining the traditional and aristocratic Alvis look, the TA21 attracted new customers to the marque. Styling was more modern and streamlined, with headlights incorporated into the wings (fenders) and the rear wheels partially concealed behind spats. Saloon bodies were produced by the Mulliner coachbuilding firm,

and Tickford supplied the coachwork for the drophead coupé versions of the TA21, of which only 302 examples were built.

The interior was typically British – wood and leather abounded. Power was provided by a new 2993cc (183cu in) six-cylinder engine, leading to the car's widely used public designation as the Alvis 3-Litre. Hydraulic brakes were a big

improvement over those used on previous Alvis models and the TA21 also boasted coil sprung independent front suspension.

ENGINE: 2993cc (183cu in), six-cylinder
POWER: 90bhp (67kW) at 4000rpm
0–60MPH (96KM/H): 19.8 seconds
TOP SPEED: 138km/h (86mph)
PRODUCTION TOTAL: 1313

AUSTIN A40 SPORTS

ENGINE: 1200cc (73cu in),
  four-cylinder
POWER: 46bhp (34kW)
0–60MPH (96KM/H): 25.6 seconds
TOP SPEED: 127km/h (79mph)
PRODUCTION TOTAL: 4011

Despite being named the Austin A40 Sports, the new open-topped car from Longbridge lacked the dynamic prowess to wear that tag convincingly. The root of the misnomer was obvious – Austin's products lacked glamour in the 1940s and, despite the appearance of the Atlantic and Metropolitan, the company's cars were still considered slightly dull if worthy by the buying public.

In 1949, Austin approached the Jensen car company, which had been using Austin engines in its sports cars, and asked Jensen for assistance in producing an upscale open-topped car. If it ended up producing a car that looked similar to the original Interceptor, Jensen can be forgiven – as there is no doubt that it evoked the more upmarket car.

With a decent folding hood and four seats, the Jensen design was a cruiser rather than a sportscar, but it was an attractive machine nevertheless – and won a number of admirers. It was based on an unmodified A40 Devon chassis, however, and the only performance additions were twin carburettors fitted to the humble four-cylinder engine – and that meant it lacked the go to match the show, with a top speed of 127km/h (79mph).

Sales were disappointing, and most of the A40 Sports built ended up in the United States.

It may have been open topped and called 'Sports' but the A40 derivative didn't capture the heart of the enthusiastic driver. Co-developed by the Jensen car company, it was an appealing cruiser.

DKW MEISTERKLASSE

ENGINE: 684cc (42cu in),
  two-cylinder
POWER: 23bhp (17kW)
0–60MPH (96KM/H): 45 seconds
TOP SPEED: 100km/h (62mph)
PRODUCTION TOTAL: 59,475

The Meisterklasse was the first DKW passenger car of the post-war era, and the story of its journey into production is almost as intriguing as the car itself. Featuring the modern aerodynamic steel body of the pre-war F 9, it was unclear whether the car would ever be made, as its blueprints were stranded on the wrong side of the Iron Curtain. It actually took a lot of clever espionage to get them to the West.

When the Meisterklasse finally entered production in mid-1950, it left the production line in a new Düsseldorf plant. Underneath the streamlined styling lay old technology. The chassis came from Auto Union and a twin-cylinder two-stroke engine from the pre-war F 8 powered the new car.

Given the model designation F 89 P, the Meisterklasse was initially offered in saloon form, and helped to get the German people on the road again. As buyers became more prosperous, a four-seat convertible with Karmann coachwork and a Hebmuller-supplied convertible and coupé versions were offered. A 'Universal' estate car (station wagon) featured a combined timber and steel 'woody' bodywork, and, later, an-all steel version appeared.

The modern aerodynamic body design was the definitive DKW look until the early 1960s; underneath, however, the car was still powered by noisy, polluting and slow two-stroke engines.

GUTBROD SUPERIOR

The agricultural machinery manufacturers Gutbrod founded the Standard motorcycle factory in 1926 and went on to build the rear-engined Standard Superior in 1933. In 1950, that became the Gutbrod Superior.

Like many cars from the post-war era, the Gutbrod featured an antiquated two-stroke twin-cylinder engine powering the front wheels and offering limited performance. Considering its economy intentions, much of the chassis technology was more up to date. The front suspension featured a double-wishbone coil combination layout; at the back was a more traditional swing-axle suspension layout. An ingredient for interesting handling, it was all bolted to a platform chassis. A larger 663cc (40cu in) engine option was added after 1951, and that endowed the Superior, which was always very well made, with a far more respectable performance.

The Superior was essentially a two-door coupé with bulbous front wings (fenders), a virtually flat front windscreen, and oval-shaped headlights set each side of an unconventional-looking slatted chrome grille. The coupé also featured a roll-back fabric roof. However, the company also offered saloon, estate (station wagon) and convertible versions of the Superior, as well as a very rare Wendler-built sports roadster.

ENGINE: 593cc (36cu in),
  two-cylinder
POWER: 20bhp (15kW)
0–60MPH (96KM/H): n/a
TOP SPEED: 96km/h (60mph)
PRODUCTION TOTAL: 7726

HOTCHKISS 2050

Another of those great pre–World War II producers of luxury cars, the French company Hotchkiss found itself in dire straits by the turn of the 1950s. Dwindling markets and lack of new product development left the company on the brink of bankruptcy.

The 2050 was available as an Anjou four-door saloon, limousine, Chapron-bodied Antheor convertible or a magnificent two-door 130bhp (97kW) Grand Sport. All remain sought after today, especially the latter version, which commands the highest prices.

Powered by a straight-six cylinder powerplant, the elegant 2050 was effectively a pre-war design – starting out initially in the 686 (from 1946) and later as the 686 S49. Further evolution took place, and coil-sprung independent front suspension and twin Zenith carburettors were added in 1950, and the 2050 was born. A four-cylinder version called the 1350 was also available.

The later model received a face-lift and featured a 'V' screen and recessed headlights – and a more contemporary look was fashioned.

The Hotchkiss company went on to waste a lot of money developing a flat-four part aluminium-chassis car called the Grégoire (of which just 180 were made), before merging with Delahaye and venturing into truck manufacture.

ENGINE: 3485cc (213cu in), six-cylinder
POWER: 100bhp (75kW)
0–60MPH (96KM/H): n/a
TOP SPEED: 141km/h (88mph)
PRODUCTION TOTAL: n/a

Available in a number of styles, it was the Chapron-bodied Antheor convertible that had the most appeal in the Hotchkiss 2050 range.

JAGUAR MK VII

UNITED KINGDOM 1950–54

ENGINE: 3442cc (210cu in), six-cylinder
POWER: 162bhp (121kW)
0–60MPH (96KM/H): 14.3 seconds
TOP SPEED: 61km/h (100mph)
PRODUCTION TOTAL: 37,181

The 1950s were an exciting decade for Jaguar – and it all started with the Mk VII, a rather effective full-sized saloon. Although the six-cylinder, twin overhead-camshaft XK engine had already been seen in the XK120 sports car, and the chassis was little more than a modified version of the Mk V, which the Mk VII replaced (there was no Mk VI, as Bentley had already used the name), the overall effect of the Mk VII's appearance on the market was spectacular.

The hefty saloon was not only spacious, plush and elegant, but was also easily capable of topping 161km/h (100mph), and all for a very modest price of £1276. At last, the Jaguar saloon had entered the modern age. The new car featured a totally new rounded shape with a full-width body, spats to cover the rear wheels and fully integrated headlights. A two-speed automatic option was added in 1953, but was soon dropped in favour of an overdrive option.

The Mk VIIM from 1954 had more power and wraparound chrome bumpers, and the 1956 Mk VIII sported a face-lifted grille, duotone paint, cut-away rear wheel spats, chrome side trim and a one-piece windscreen.

It may have looked huge and cumbersome, but the Jaguar Mk VII performed and handled rather well, with a top speed of over 161km/h (100mph).

JOWETT JUPITER

ENGINE: 1485cc (91cu in),
 four-cylinder
POWER: 60bhp (45kW)
0–60MPH (96KM/H): 16.8 seconds
TOP SPEED: 134km/h (84mph)
PRODUCTION TOTAL: 899

Jowett was one of the unsung British motoring heroes of the 1950s, producing interesting and very capable cars. The Jupiter was a perfect example of Jowett's ingenuity. Having developed an advanced tubular chassis, the company built an open roadster around it. While the running gear pure Javelin, the body was made of aluminium pressings on a tubular framework and was almost completely hand-built.

A memorable feature of the Jupiter was its innovative one-piece lift-up nose section; this was a feature made famous eight years later on the Austin-Healey Sprite. Like the Jowett, the Sprite also dropped the separate opening boot (trunk) lid, and luggage needed to be stowed in its compartment, accessible via the folding seats in the cabin. Good for structural integrity, this idea

was not practical, and by 1952, the Jupiter MK IA had a full boot lid, along with reshaped wings (fenders) and more power.

The Jupiter scored notable successes at Le Mans between 1950 and 1952, and encouraged a push in that direction. In late 1953, and despite the company suffering financial problems, the R4, a prototype competition Jupiter, was shown. The car featured a shortened wheelbase, new chassis and stubby two-seater body, but plans to produce the vehicle died with the company in 1955.

Because of its widespread competition success, including a class win at the 1950 Le Mans 24 Hour, the technologically advanced Jowett Jupiter enjoyed a strong following with enthusiasts.

LANCHESTER FOURTEEN/LEDA

The BSA-Daimler alliance added Lanchester to the company portfolio in 1931, and the Lanchester Fourteen was the first product as a result. The car was a taster of what would become the Daimler Conquest (which followed in 1953), but featuring a Lanchester grille and new four-cylinder 60bhp (45kW) engine instead of the Conquest's fabulous six-cylinder unit.

The car was built from pressed steel; the body was mostly hand-built. Cars for the UK market had a wooden frame, while those for the export market (called the Leda) used steel. Underneath the uninspiring styling was a box-section chassis. To that, a torsion bar and wishbone independent front suspension was attached. A fluid flywheel, hydromechanical brakes, and Bijur automated

lubrication to the central parts of the chassis were other fascinating features. Three body types were available – a saloon, drophead and coupé – and there were also plans to introduce two other bodystyles, the Dauphin and Sprite, although they never came to be.

The fact is that the Fourteen was an unremarkable car, and the Lanchester name fell into misuse when it was phased out in 1954.

Daimler-Lanchester was purchased by Jaguar in 1960, and the once-proud marque was buried for ever with regards to car production.

ENGINE: 1968cc (120cu in),
 four-cylinder
POWER: 60bhp (45kW)
0–60MPH (96KM/H): n/a
TOP SPEED: 120km/h (75mph)
PRODUCTION TOTAL: 2100

MUNTZ JET

ENGINE: 5424cc (331cu in),
 eight-cylinder
POWER: 160bhp (119kW)
0–60MPH (96KM/H): n/a
TOP SPEED: 180km/h (112mph)
PRODUCTION TOTAL: 394

When the American engineer Frank Kurtis decided that he wanted to build his own car in 1948, he knuckled down and produced a rather interesting prototype – especially when viewed as a production possibility. With curvaceous and streamlined styling, it was a complete and welcome contrast to some of the excesses of the rest of the United

States' carmakers, but it was practical and featured a huge four-seater interior.

Despite this, the bug-like styling found on Kurtis's car was deemed too strange-looking to attract any significant attention from the US car industry's major manufacturers, and, instead, Kurtis sold the project to wealthy car dealer Earl Muntz on the understanding that the prototype would make it into production.

With its love-it-or-loathe-it-looks, the Muntz Jet has divided opinion for years. However, it was fast, practical and was only let down by its high price.

Launched in 1950, the Muntz Jet was powered by a Cadillac 5.4-litre (330cu in) overhead-valve V8, and later models were to gain a slightly less powerful (and much cheaper) 5.5-litre (336cu in) Lincoln-derived side-valve V8. Weight was kept low by aluminium body panels and a glass fibre bonnet (hood), but this meant that the car was expensive to build and labour-intensive.

Sales were respectable enough, but with almost 400 Jets sold Muntz lost interest and went back to selling other people's cars in 1954.

FERRARI 340 AMERICA
ITALY 1950–55

ENGINE: 4101cc (250cu in),
12-cylinder
POWER: 220bhp (164kW)
0–60MPH (96KM/H): 8 seconds
TOP SPEED: 193km/h (120mph)
PRODUCTION TOTAL: 22

Only a tiny number of 340 Americas were built, but it was the start of something big for the prancing horse marque in the world's largest car market. A whole succession of Ferraris had already been developed from the original 166/195/212, but the 340 was the first to be powered by a larger, long-block V12 engine.

Designed by engine legend Aurelio Lampredi, the 4101cc (250cu in) engine was first used in racing, initially as a 3.3-litre (201cu in) unit, but was later enlarged to 4.1, then 4.5 litres (275cu in).

Like the original Colombo-designed Ferrari V12, the 340 had two inclined valves per cylinder and hairpin-type springs, and a much larger displacement was possible. Other innovations included roller camshaft followers and separate valve ports, all of which all raised the output to 220bhp (164kW). The single disc clutch channelled the power to the Ferrari five-speed gearbox.

Coachbuilt coupé bodies were elegant and had typically stunning styling associated with Ferraris. A racing version known as the Mexico also appeared, named because it had been conceived for the Carrera Panamericana race.

This model had a coupé body styled by Michelotti with a longer 260cm (102.4in) wheelbase and an engine that produced a sensational 280bhp (209kW).

KAISER MANHATTAN
UNITED STATES 1950–55

Although it was blessed with good performance and pleasant road manners, the Kaiser Manhattan was handicapped by its straight-six engine in an industry that had become dominated by V8s.

ENGINE: 3707cc (226cu in),
six-cylinder
POWER: 115bhp (86kW)
0–60MPH (96KM/H): n/a
TOP SPEED: 138km/h (86mph)
PRODUCTION TOTAL: 202,856

Sometimes money is not everything – and nowhere is this more apparent than in the misguided automotive adventures of American multimillionaire Henry J. Kaiser. Having made his fortune mass-producing ships and houses, Kaiser hoped to use his entrepreneurial skills to make even more money – by creating his own car company. However, the plan never reached fruition and none of his projects was successful.

The Manhattan was the first of a new series of cars which celebrated Kaiser's collaboration with the Dutch car designer Howard 'Dutch' Darrin, and featured a striking bodystyle with a low waistline and the use of vivid colour schemes. Well styled and technically advanced, it featured a number of safety features and sharp responsive steering – a novelty in the United States.

The interior was a work of art and included plastic that was made to look like alligator skin in the Manhattan 'Dragon' model, and the 1953 Manhattan even had a bamboo effect roof lining. Despite being a success in its own right, the Manhattan's long-term prospects were scuppered by the lack of a powerful V8 engine option. The final models were fitted with a supercharger, but it was not enough to convince the buying public.

SAAB 92
SWEDEN 1949–56

ENGINE: 764cc (47cu in),
two-stroke, two-cylinder
POWER: 25bhp (19kW)
0–60MPH (96KM/H): n/a
TOP SPEED: 105km/h (65mph)
PRODUCTION TOTAL: 20,128

With the 92, Saab made a suitably impressive debut as a carmaker – for a first production effort, it was startlingly brave and showed that there was genuinely innovative thinking in Sweden in the 1940s. The 92 flouted all conventional engineering and design principles, and, when the first prototypes were shown, the car looked like nothing else on the market – its exterior design majored on well-considered aerodynamics.

When it became Sweden's second car producer in 1950, Saab ensured it made a big splash with the 92. With aero industry-inspired streamlined styling and monocoque construction it was ahead of the game.

By employing all-round independent suspension and a strong monocoque, Saab acquired a reputation from the outset for quality and safety – even though there were a few shortcomings with the earliest cars. This was no sports car, and yet there was no boot (trunk) lid until 1953; to that point, the luggage area needed accessing from the rear seats. That face-lift also saw the arrival of a full-size rear window to replace the tiny split screen. An amusing option entered the price lists. Saab decided the car could be used for overnight accommodation, and a bed unit was then advertised to tell buyers that the car was more than just transport. It was a sales tactic also used later on the 900.

A year later, a further face-lift was greeted with the production of the company's 10,000th car, which demonstrated popularity. Two years later, the car was replaced by the 93 – and the Saab company was on its way.

CHEVROLET BEL AIR

ENGINE: 4639cc (283cu in), six-cylinder
POWER: 285bhp (212kW)
0–60MPH (96KM/H): 8 seconds
TOP SPEED: 193km/h (120mph)
PRODUCTION TOTAL: 3,293,543

One of the undoubted US classics of its era, the Chevrolet Bel Air was announced in 1950 as a sporting two-door hardtop coupé. Powered by a six-cylinder engine and using a smooth Powerglide automatic transmission, the Bel Air soon picked up a loyal following.

The Bel Air range was expanded in 1953, and, by that time, the name was extended to cover all four-door saloons and it was applied to a pretty new convertible. The following year, an estate (station-wagon) Bel Air was launched, badged as the Nomad.

Evolution continued, and, following a comprehensive restyle in 1955, and a mild face-lift the following year, Chevrolet arrived at the definitive classic shape – subtle fins and relatively clean lines were now the order of the day.

At the time, the Bel Air became Chevrolet's flagship, available as a two- and four-door saloon and a convertible with optional power hood. The three-door Nomad sported an individual style, and remains highly sought after on the classic-car market to this day. The Bel Air was powered by both

Perched at the top of the Chevrolet 'One Fifty' series range, the Bel Air was an imposing and desirable beast offered at an affordable price.

six-cylinder and V8 engines, but it was the bigger 285bhp (212kW) fuel-injected unit that delivered real performance. Sadly, that engine/body combination lasted one year, and from then on the Bel Air's importance declined.

GOLIATH GP 700

Part of the three-marque Borgward line-up, the Goliath products are best summed up by saying that they looked modern on the outside, but were underpinned by pre-war engineering.

Powered by an ancient two-stroke twin, mounted transversely and driving the front wheels via an antiquated power chain, and sitting on a tubular chassis, it was never going to be an engaging drive. Despite this, the car sold well, and served its purpose of providing Germans with budget transport well.

The original Goliaths were underpowered, but with the introduction of a fuel injection system, performance and reliability were boosted usefully – and the use of such technology was cutting-edge stuff at the time of the car's launch in 1950.

From 1955, engine capacity was increased yet again to 886cc (54cu in), and, all of a sudden, the Goliath had enough performance to keep up with the rest of the traffic. Being a two-stroke and having to mix oil with petrol to power the two-stroke engine was still a chore for most owners, though. The Goliath was offered in three bodystyles; a two-door saloon, an estate (station wagon)

and a convertible, the last of which was made only in very small numbers and is worth real money to collectors today.

ENGINE: 688cc (42cu in), two-cylinder
POWER: 24bhp (18kW)
0–60MPH (96KM/H): n/a
TOP SPEED: 94km/h (59mph)
PRODUCTION TOTAL: 36,270

ALFA ROMEO 1900

ENGINE: 1884cc (115cu in),
  four-cylinder
POWER: 90bhp (67kW)
0–60MPH (96KM/H): 17.8 seconds
TOP SPEED: 149km/h (93mph)
PRODUCTION TOTAL: 17,423

Regarded by many as Alfa Romeo's first fully modern post-war design, the 1900 certainly allowed the Turin company to compete with the cream of the European opposition. Compared with the 6C2500, which was largely a pre-war design, the 1900, with its unitary body and twin-camshaft was a product of the 1950s. Conceived by the brilliant Dr Orazio Satta Puliga, known universally as 'Satta', a new member of Alfa's design team, the 1900 was first true mass-market Alfa Romeo.

The car featured a simple monocoque body with four doors and understated styling. For the first time, it adopted aerodynamic styling, developed using Satta's aeronautical engineering knowledge. The 1900 was also roomy and could seat five people, thanks to its front and rear bench

seats and column gearchange. While pre-war production Alfa's borrowed fully independent suspension from their racing cars, the 1900 reverted to coils at the front and a solid rear axle at the rear to provide safe, controlled handling – which was necessary considering the power available.

The little Alfa possessed fantastic dynamics and a responsive engine, characteristics that were quite out of keeping with its mundane four-door saloon styling and reasonable price tag.

The 1900 Super from 1953 boasted a 1975cc (121cu in) engine and 115bhp (86kW).

Alfa Romeo may well have been regarded as a manufacturer of fine racing cars, but the introduction of the 1900 proved that it could also do the business in the saloon car market, too.

LANCIA AURELIA

Lancia had a hard act to follow to replace its amazing Aprilia, yet it managed it with an equally advanced and dynamic car. The main innovation in the Aurelia was the all-alloy V6 engine, which had

been designed during World War II. Smoothness was guaranteed, as the cylinder banks were mounted at a 60-degree angle to each other.

The Aurelia retained the unitary construction and effective all-

independent suspension layout of the Aprilia, but the more aerodynamic body was penned by Pininfarina. Despite the larger and more powerful engine, the new car was slower than the

Aprilia because it had put on considerable weight. Model designations were the B10 for the saloon, B15 for the limousine and B20 GT for the glamorous and beautiful coupé version. The sporting car boasted a twin-carburettor set-up for its 2-litre (121cu in) V6, and an even more elegant Pininfarina body.

The incredibly valuable B25 Spider convertible was also penned by Pininfarina, and it stunned buyers when it appeared in 1955. It was also powered by a new 2451cc (150cu in) V6, which delivered rapid acceleration. The following year, the design was updated – where it lost the original wraparound windscreen – and was renamed the GT 2500 Convertible.

ENGINE: 1991cc (121cu in),
  six-cylinder
POWER: 70bhp (52kW) at 4500rpm
0–60MPH (96KM/H): 18 seconds
TOP SPEED: 148km/h (92mph)
PRODUCTION TOTAL: 16,897

The Lancia Aurelia B20 Gran Turismo is an all-time classic. With its impressive aerodynamics, brisk performance and beautiful styling the Pininfarina penned car proved a great all-rounder.

SIATA DAINA

Siata officially linked up with Fiat in 1950 to put the Daina into production, having used Fiat parts extensively for many years. The arrangement had side benefits for both manufacturers, as it allowed Fiat to offer niche vehicles, while Siata's development burden was significantly lightened.

The Daina model appeared in 1950 and extensively used Fiat 1400 running gear – it was one of a breed of small Italian sports cars that extended the choice for enthusiastic drivers. The pretty car came in two forms, a closed coupé and an open-topped roadster. For all those who felt that the 1.4-litre (85cu in) did not deliver enough performance, the company also offered a more potent 1.5-litre (92cu in) option. All models boasted a five-speed gearbox, and the bodywork was constructed by Stabilimenti Farina.

From 1951, the Rallye 1400 received an MG TD-inspired rebody, and the range increased with the addition of a six-seater limousine and an estate (station wagon), thanks to the introduction of a longer chassis. The following year the Daina Sport (coupé) and Gran Sport (cabriolet) were launched, the former fitted with a 1500cc (92cu in) 75bhp (56kW) engine.

ENGINE: 1393cc (85cu in), four-cylinder
POWER: 65bhp (48kW)
0-60MPH (96KM/H): n/a
TOP SPEED: n/a
PRODUCTION TOTAL: 200 approx

FORD UK CONSUL/ZEPHYR/ZODIAC

ENGINE: 2553cc (156cu in), six-cylinder
POWER: 109bhp (81kW)
0-60MPH (96KM/H): 13.4 secs
TOP SPEED: 166km/h (103mph)
PRODUCTION TOTAL: 942,217

Launched at London's Olympia Motor Show in 1950, the Ford Consul/Zephyr range made quite a splash – after all, it was one of the most advanced designs of the era. The combined monocoque bodyshell, overhead-valve engine and innovative MacPherson independent suspension were all firsts for Ford, and the suspension system is still in use today. Ford also switched from six-volt to 12-volt electrics, still the industry standard. The Consul and Zephyr's main differences were limited to differing front end designs and a slightly longer wheelbase (10.2cm/4in) in the Zephyr's favour. This change was adopted in order to accommodate its larger six-cylinder engine. Above that, a higher specification Zephyr Zodiac variant was introduced in 1953.

The car was rebodied in 1956 and given more interior space, as well as Americanized styling. Convertible models were available, and a thorough face-lift in 1959 introduced a lower roofline and better interiors.

In 1966, the whole range repositioned upmarket and they were badged simply Zephyr and Zodiac. The Zephyr 4 replaced the Consul, and the six-cylinder models were the first Fords to officially beat 161km/h (100mph). In 1965, a top of the range Zodiac Executive was introduced.

For many it will always be known as the car that introduced MacPherson strut suspension to modern motoring, but the multi-car range proved a major hit with British drivers.

MORGAN PLUS 4

ENGINE: 1991cc (121cu in), four-cylinder
POWER: 90bhp (76kW)
0-60MPH (96KM/H): 17.9 seconds
TOP SPEED: 155km/h (96mph)
PRODUCTION TOTAL: 4542

Introduced in 1950, the Standard Vanguard-engined Plus 4 was Morgan's first attempt to try to replace the evergreen 4/4. Sales fell, however, and the lower priced 4/4 was reintroduced after a five-year hiatus. Although it looked similar to the 4/4, the Plus 4 had separate mudguards with bolt-on headlights, and a slightly longer wheelbase and roomier cabin.

Apart from the 2088cc (127cu in) four-cylinder engine, mechanical differences in the Plus 4 included a full synchromesh gearbox and hydraulic brakes; both became standard fitment to the 4/4 when it returned from its suspended production.

In 1951, a four-seater version was launched, and from 1953 onwards all cars received the more stylish 4/4-style curved radiator grille. In 1958, the Vanguard engine was replaced by the smaller and livelier Triumph TR2 2.0-litre engine (it had been an option since 1954), and in 1960 disc brakes were offered.

In 1961, the 104bhp (77kW) 2138cc (130cu in) unit from the new Triumph TR4 replaced the previous power unit, and that gave the Plus 4 a top speed of 196km/h (105mph). A Super Sports version of the car was built between 1962 and 1968, and, thanks to the adoption of twin Webers, it was able to reach a scarcely credible 193km/h (120mph). In total, 101 examples were made.

In many ways, the Standard Vanguard engined roadster was always dated, but it looked good and proved fun to drive.

Chapter Three

The Rock'n'Roll Era

1951–1964

As World War II was slowly forgotten and prosperity returned, the motor industry moved to reflect a shift in society. This shift in culture, fuelled by movies and the rapidly expanding music scene, led to car manufacturers producing ever more extravagant designs, bedecked in fins and chrome and growing in size each year.

The decade that introduced us to Elvis Presley, Marilyn Monroe and Buddy Holly also introduced us to classic cars such as the 1957 Chevy Bel Air, the legendary Cadillac Series 62, and America's first sports car, in the form of the Corvette. Over in Europe, Detroit-inspired styling was evident, too. Fins started to appear on the back of Mercedes-Benzs, Peugeots, and even Britain's humble Austins and Morrises.

But while glitz and glamour were all the rage in the USA, it was in Europe where the innovations were truly taking place. By the end of the 1950s, American pastiche had given way to a new generation of thinking, which saw cars like the Citroen DS showing off its swivelling headlamps and hydraulic suspension, and the Fiat Nuova 500 showing that a small city car could have just as much character as a chrome-draped dinosaur.

In the UK, the original Mini took the world by storm as the swinging Sixties began, while cars such as the cleverly-constructed Rover P6 showed that it wasn't just luxury models that were beautiful to drive.

But the US hadn't lost its way. Realizing that big, bold and brash may have been the way of the 1950s, but would not necessarily go down so well in the image-conscious 1960s, Ford introduced the Mustang in 1964. Compact, affordable and brilliantly styled, it was an unprecedented success.

By the 1950s, styling was what sold a car, and many of the major manufacturers turned to other countries to influence the look of their cars. The British-built Triumph TR4 was styled in Italy, by Giovanni Michelotti.

SALMSON RANDONNÉE

After a long career building a series of cars powered by the same basic long-stroke twin-camshaft engine, Salmson went for something more exclusive for the 1950 Randonée. Cast from light alloy and with a raft of lightweight components, the new engine allowed 50kg (110lb) to be shed from the car – and that benefited handling. The Randonnée was not entirely new, but rather a rework of the previous range-topping Salmson S4E launched in 1937.

Under the skin, besides that new engine, the engineering was a complete carry-over. The chassis was a simple ladder frame, and, just like its predecessor, had a torque tube located on the rear axle and a pair of diagonal radius arms suspended on cantilevered semi-elliptic springs. Independent front suspension by longitudinal torsion bars, telescopic front dampers and rack-and-pinion steering, along with hydraulic brakes, were nice contemporary touches, though.

There was a choice of ZF manual or Cotal electromagnetic transmissions, but, as the engine developed just 71bhp (53kW), performance was mainly irrelevant. This lack of performance was disappointing, especially given the car's relatively high price tag.

ENGINE: 2218cc (135cu in), four-cylinder
POWER: 71bhp (53kW)
0–60MPH (96KM/H): n/a
TOP SPEED: n/a
PRODUCTION TOTAL: 539

FERRARI 212

Ferrari's rapid rise to stardom as a car manufacturer continued with the 212. It was yet another variation on the 166/195 theme, except with an even larger, more powerful engine. Bored to 68mm (2.7in) to create a displacement of 2562cc (156cu in), the V12 retained the same stroke as the final version of the 166, which resulted in the same maximum power, but a higher top speed. As before, a single Weber carburettor on the road-going Inter version produced 130bhp (97kW), but, in racing tune, triple Weber set-up resulted in a power output of at least 150bhp (112kW).

The most impressive model was the Export. Its engine was rated at 170bhp (127kW), pushing the top speed up to 242km/h (150mph). The 212 Export model had a short wheelbase chassis, too – 223cm (87.6in) – which was quite a feat considering the 166 was not exactly long, at 241cm (95in).

There was no such thing as a standard 212; customers could specify the bespoke car exactly how they wanted it. So, the 212 Inter had three different suffixes after the chassis numbers – E, EL and EU – which designated long or short chassis lengths. In addition, Export engines could be fitted to Inter cars. With the 212, however, it was now clear that Pininfarina was Ferrari's favoured coachbuilder.

ENGINE: V12 2562cc (156cu in)
POWER: 130bhp (97kW)
0-60MPH (96KM/H): 11 secs
TOP SPEED: 177km/h (110mph)
PRODUCTION TOTAL: 80

Ferrari's 212 was a variation on the 166/195 and established Ferrari as a big name in the USA. The bodywork was supported by tubular steel framework.

DELAHAYE 235

Delahaye was reaching the end of the road – and, when it released the Type 235 in 1951, it was clear that this was the company's drink in the Last Chance Saloon. Delahaye looked as though it had finally replaced the old 135, but, under the new skin, the chassis was exactly the same. That meant that it retained the original mechanically operated drum brakes which, by the early 1950s, were proving inadequate, especially on what turned out to be a high-performance car. At least the styling was all-new, with

This 1953 Delahaye 235M featured elegant coachwork by Henri Chapron. Fewer than 400 235s were built.

a standard and very handsome body built by coachbuilders Antem and also Letoumeur.

A large, US-influenced grille, long bonnet (hood) and two-door coupé body were contemporary and striking. The engine had been upgraded as well, and now produced 152bhp (113kW). This helped to make the 235 a very fast car indeed. In a straight line, the 235's top speed was an impressive 193km/h (120mph). So it was no surprise when the Delahaye 235 had its moment of competition glory in 1953, when it set a record for crossing Africa from Cape Town to Algiers.

No one was fooled by the old 135 underpinnings, however, or convinced enough to pay the high asking price. Fewer than 400 235s were made before Delahaye finally went out of business.

ENGINE: 4455cc (272cu in), six-cylinder
POWER: 152bhp (113kW)
0–60MPH (96KM/H): 10 seconds
TOP SPEED: 193km/h (120mph)
PRODUCTION TOTAL: 400

HEALEY G-TYPE

Officially known as the 3-litre (183cu in) Sports Convertible, Healey's own version of the Nash-Healey was aimed directly at the American market. More often referred to as the Alvis-Healey, or G-Type, the car remains a rare classic today. The Healey had more conservative and slightly austere styling than the Nash – and the front grille of the Healey was smaller and neater. Other styling touches unique to the Healey were the front and rear bumpers, and more restrained use of chrome throughout. The walnut dash and leather upholstery gave it an appealing traditionally British feel. The front-end styling was cleaner, too – the Alvis TB21 engine meant that there was no need for Nash-style bonnet (hood) bulges.

Power to weight ratio was not good, though, and the wide and heavy body resulted in the G-Type having performance that was underwhelming – especially when compared with the faster and much prettier Jaguar XK120.

Only 25 examples were produced in total, making the Healey G-Type a rare sight today. For this reason, it has become much sought after and a desirable acquisition among enthusiasts for 1950s British sports cars.

ENGINE: 2993cc (183cu in), six-cylinder
POWER: 106bhp (79kW)
0–60MPH (96KM/H): 11.4 seconds
TOP SPEED: 160km/h (99mph)
PRODUCTION TOTAL: 25

JAGUAR C-TYPE

The C-type was the sports racing car that finally catapulted Jaguar into the big time. Also known as the XK120C, the curvaceous two-seater with aero screens and aluminium bodywork was developed to win Le Mans 24 Hour Race, which it duly did in 1951.

Underneath, the C-type featured a new tubular steel chassis, rack-and-pinion steering, strengthened front suspension and transverse torsion bar rear suspension. An uprated cylinder head, a new camshaft and a higher compression ratio of 9:1 boosted the twin-camshaft XK engine, and that resulted in a maximum power output of 204bhp (152kW). Aside from that, it was pure XK120.

After its Le Mans win, the C-type was further enhanced by a number of improvements, which included adding twin carburettors to the engine and a Panhard rod to the suspension, to aid stability – and that further improved the car's competitiveness. It also gained more powerful servo-assisted braking on all four wheels.

Only 54 cars were produced, although some examples did fall into the hands of private owners who relished their C-types as an exciting road car.

Few examples of the C-type survive today – although genuine competition cars fetch astronomical amounts of money. As a result of this rarity, more than a few replicas have been produced.

Proof if ever it were needed that racing improves the breed, the Jaguar C-type was one of the fastest and most desirable road cars ever built.

ENGINE: 3442cc (210cu in), six-cylinder
POWER: 204bhp (152kW)
0–60MPH (96KM/H): n/a
TOP SPEED: 230km/h (144mph)
PRODUCTION TOTAL: 54

NASH-HEALEY

If you think that Donald Healey cut his teeth building sports cars in association with Austin, you would be overlooking an association with the American car company Nash – and that resulted in a sporting car primarily destined for the American market.

The engine and chassis were pure Nash Ambassador, and that choice resulted in a lively performance, although the heavy steering and unresponsive brakes made the Nash-Healey a chore to drive with verve. The styling was unsportscar-like, too, but Nash commissioned a Pininfarina restyle in 1952, and that transformed the car. Curvaceous wings (fenders), bulbous rear arches and a notchback rear end were features. Although it might not have been one of the Italian designer's best creations, it was stylish enough.

While most Nash-Healeys sold in the United States were powered by a 3.8-litre (235cu in) engine of US origin, a few were built and marketed in Britain with the less powerful 2-litre (122cu in) Alvis engine (that had some tuning potential) under the bonnet (hood).

Sales were consistently slow, and the car died following Donald Healey's decision to sign a contract

with Austin to build his next sports car at the 1953 Motor Show in England. The Austin-Healey was to gain almost legendary status, while the Nash-Healey became little more than a footnote in motoring history.

ENGINE: 3848cc (235cu in), six-cylinder
POWER: 125bhp (93kW)
0–60MPH (96KM/H): 14.6 seconds
TOP SPEED: 168km/h (104mph)
PRODUCTION TOTAL: 506

This Anglo-American crossbreed was pretty and quick on the road, although poor steering and brakes meant that true greatness eluded it. Most were sold in the United States; Alvis provided engines for the UK version.

MERCEDES-BENZ 220

Set back by World War II bombing campaigns, and the subsequent damage to its factory, Mercedes-Benz took a considerable amount of time to get back on its feet. When it finally resumed production, it was with the pre-war 170 series. The later 220 was a variation on the existing theme, but powered by a new six-cylinder overhead camshaft engine.

The 170 and 220 Series cars looked almost identical – apart from the integrated headlights, and fixed bonnet (hood) sides. In addition to four-door saloons, the 220 series came in cabriolet and two-door closed-coupé bodystyles (after 1954), although only around 85 of the latter type were built – and as a result are very desirable today. The chassis were also

offered in bare form for coachbuilders wishing to convert the cars into light commercials.

Despite its old-fashioned styling – a flat, letterbox screen was passé in the 1950s – the 220 series was fundamental in the revival of the company during this potentially rocky period. The car offered buyers reasonable performance and economy from its

six-cylinder 80bhp (60kW) engine, as well as traditionally solid Mercedes-Benz build quality.

ENGINE: 2195cc (134cu in), six-cylinder
POWER: 80bhp (60kW)
0–60MPH (96KM/H): 19.5 seconds
TOP SPEED: 147km/h (92mph)
PRODUCTION TOTAL: 18,514

RENAULT COLARE PRAIRIE

The Renault Colare Prairie might have sounded exciting, but it was actually rather mundane. Introduced in 1951 to fill a gap in the Renault range, it was a stopgap estate (station wagon) cobbled together from components in the Renault parts bin to sit alongside the large Fregate saloon until an estate version of that car subsequently appeared in 1955.

From the windscreen pillars back, the Colare Prairie's humble

The Renault Colare Prairie's commercial origins weren't hard to spot – its huge load carrying capability was a boon, but it lacked style and verve.

commercial vehicle underpinnings were obvious, despite its smooth almost Austin-esque styling upfront. The standard Colare model was offered as either a panel van or pick-up truck; as a result, the Prairie's styling looked rather awkward. The rear body panels

had been hastily updated in order to squeeze in an extra pair of rear doors, and the car's commercial origins were no more apparent than in its considerable girth.

The suspension was set up for load lugging, rather than comfort, and the noisy 2.4-litre (146cu in)

side-valve engine, which could trace its roots back to 1936, was not good enough for its market aspirations. In 1952, the Colare Prairie received the Fregate's 2.0-litre (131cu in) overhead valve engine, but even this was not man enough to shift the car's bulk.

ENGINE: 2383cc (145cu in), four-cylinder
POWER: 56bhp (42kW)
0–60MPH (96KM/H): 43.8 seconds
TOP SPEED: 100km/h (62mph)
PRODUCTION TOTAL: n/a

SINGER SM ROADSTER

Launched in 1951 as a rival to the all-conquering MG TD, the Singer SM Roadster (also known as the 1500 Roadster) remains a popular choice with classic car enthusiasts today. However, the SM Roadster was essentially a revamped version of the Nine

Like many of its compatriots at the time, the Singer SM Roadster wasn't new at all, but a facelift of the pre-war Nine Roadster.

Roadster, and that had been first unveiled in 1939, meaning that the overall package was disappointing, as well as dated.

Independent front suspension with telescopic dampers was a technological leap over the Nine's set-up, but the worm-and-peg steering was imprecise and was no match for its rival from Abingdon. Fitted with hydromechanical brakes and a gemlike short-stroke single-overhead camshaft engine displacing 1497cc (91cu in), the

SM Roadster was certainly not without its merits.

In 1953, a twin-carburettor option was introduced to boost power from 48bhp (36kW) to a more impressive 58bhp (43kW). This engine's impressive specification lent the company further credibility and was able to bolster Singer's competition successes with the Nine Le Mans.

These days, the MG TD remains the preferred roadster on the classic car scene, but the Singer's

rarity is a major asset – and the best of all are the Bertone-bodied examples, which were constructed on behalf of the American Singer importer. Sadly, these particular cars rarely come up for sale.

ENGINE: 1497cc (91cu in), four-cylinder
POWER: 48bhp (35.8kW)
0–60MPH (96KM/H): 23.6 seconds
TOP SPEED: 117km/h (73mph)
PRODUCTION TOTAL: 3440

BUGATTI TYPE 101

'Le Patron' Ettore Bugatti cast a long shadow over the company he formed, and, following his death in 1947, keeping the marque alive was always going to be a challenge. The brave Type 101 of 1951 tried to relive those pre-war glories, but failed to ignite the imagination of the well-heeled buyers who bought the company's cars in such large numbers in the pre-war years.

The Type 101, styled by the Gangloff coachbuilding firm, close to Bugatti's Molsheim plant, bore a resemblance to the Jaguar XK120 – especially around the front end. Every effort was made to retain the traditional horseshoe grille.

However good it looked, though, the Type 101 was a major disappointment technically, where a Type 57 chassis could be found – technologically almost two

decades out of date. Rigid front and rear axles did the car no favours, and it was far behind what other luxury sportscar manufacturers were making. However, the Type 57's 3.3-litre (199cu in) engine endowed the car with sparkling performance, and the addition of a Supercharger meant that power boosted from 135bhp (101kW) to a very impressive 188bhp (140kW).

Only right-hand drive models were built, and the stunning looks did not lead to string sales, with only seven built in five years.

ENGINE: 3257cc (199cu in), eight-cylinder
POWER: 135bhp (101kW)
0–60MPH (96KM/H): n/a
TOP SPEED: 169km/h (105mph)
PRODUCTION TOTAL: 7

PEGASO Z102

ENGINE: 3178cc (194cu in),
eight-cylinder
POWER: 275bhp (205kW)
0–60MPH (96KM/H): 7.0 seconds
TOP SPEED: 258km/h (160mph)
PRODUCTION TOTAL: 112 (inc Z103)

Some of the best cars in history have been built as a response to challenges laid down by rivals – or perhaps as the single-minded ambition of its creator. This was certainly the case with the Pegaso Z102, as its creation was a direct response to an insult Enzo Ferrari had made to Pegaso chief Don Wilfredo Ricart. In the late 1940s, the 'Commendatore' had said that Ricart wore thick rubber-soled shoes to 'stop his brain from getting any shocks'.

Pegaso's response was direct, and the Spanish truck maker decided to make a very fast coupé that would beat Ferrari at its own game. The Pegaso Z102 duly appeared in 1951 and in many ways achieved what it set out to do. It was powered by a specially designed state-of-the-art quad camshaft V8 engine, available in a number of states of tunes, ranging from an impressive 190bhp (142kW) to as much as 360bhp (268kW).

Built entirely at the Pegaso factory in Barcelona, Spain, this stylish-looking car also boasted a

From the manufacturer of a number of fine lorries, came this amazing supercar, which had been conceived as a direct response to Ferrari.

five-speed gearbox, a state-of-the-art pressed platform chassis and a very complicated steering linkage – all Ferrari-style features. Brutally fast yet surprisingly agile to drive, the Z102 is a prized classic today.

HUDSON HORNET

Hudson was one of the more forward-looking US carmakers, and, following World War II, the company developed an all-new unitary construction process for its cars. It was called the 'Step Down' because you literally had to step down over the structural body sills to get into the car, and the 1951 Hornet was built around this principle which now underpins most modern cars.

The styling of the Hornet was contemporary, too – it featured smooth flanks, bright new interior fabrics and one-piece windscreen. Power for the Hornet, however, came from the company's old 5047cc (308cu in) L-head six-cylinder engine, which might have been traditional, but was still effective stock-car racing.

Although Detroit was rapidly moving towards V8 power, Hudson refused to shift from its traditional six-cylinder arrangement, and that

decision would eventually stunt sales growth. In 1954, the Hudson company answered back with the option of a Twin-H power option with a 'hot' camshaft and an alloy head, and increased compression ratio that pushed power up to 170bhp (127kW).

Hudson sales had already peaked before the launch of the Hornet, in 1950, and, as a result, the company was forced to merge with Nash to form American Motors in 1954, abandoning its future projects. The Hudson name was dropped in 1957.

ENGINE: 5047cc (308cu in),
six-cylinder
POWER: 160bhp (119kW)
0–60MPH (96KM/H): 12 seconds
TOP SPEED: 177km/h (110mph)
PRODUCTION TOTAL: n/a

The fastback styling of the 1951 Hudson Hornet was considered avant-garde when it first appeared on the scene.

VAUXHALL VELOX E-TYPE

In the United Kingdom, the years of post-war austerity were coming to a close at the turn of the 1950s, and car buyers were expecting increasingly more from vehicles. Companies responded by adding more comfort and equipment to their cars, making the driving experience more enjoyable.

US-owned Vauxhall was already on the case. When the Wyvern and Velox E-Type appeared in 1951, Vauxhall's links with its parent country seemed to get a little closer. Styling was based on a 1949 Chevrolet, and it featured a large grille, full-width and fluted bonnet (hood), and was dripping in chrome – very American.

With the larger E-type Velox, extra cabin space was a key selling point, and the car was big enough to carry six passengers in comfort – a major improvement over its predecessor, the Velox LIP, offered between 1948 and 1951.

The four- and six-cylinder Velox E-Type was also much more comfortable than its predecessor, thanks to independent coil-sprung suspension at the front. Developed throughout its life, with upgrades to the exterior and interior trim, as well as an increase in the window size to make the cabin airier, the Velox was a popular choice.

ENGINE: 2275cc (139cu in), six-cylinder
POWER: 55bhp (41kW)
0–60MPH (96KM/H): 20.9 seconds
TOP SPEED: 129km/h (80mph)
PRODUCTION TOTAL: 545,388
(including Wyvern)

RENAULT FREGATE

ENGINE: 2141cc (131cu in), four-cylinder
POWER: 60bhp (45kW)
TOP SPEED: 145km/h (90mph)
0–60MPH (96KM/H): 18.5 seconds
PRODUCTION TOTAL: 177,686

Demand for larger, prestige cars started to pick up in France during the early 1950s, as the country began to recover fully from the effects of World War II. Renault's offering in this market was the Fregate, a large unitary construction car with plenty of interior space and reasonable levels of luxury. All that put it back was build quality that was not up to class standards.

The Fregate was good to drive, though, offering a typically Gallic soft ride, thanks to all-round fully independent suspension. It also featured an all-synchromesh four-speed gearbox with a sweet-shifting column-mounted remote change. Two-pedal transmission was offered on the options list, initially as a full automatic and subsequently as Renault's patented 'Transfluide' semi-automatic set-up. In 1955, a new, more flexible 2.1-litre (131cu in) engine replaced the original 2.0-litre (122cu in) power unit, and an estate (station wagon) called the Domaine (seeing off the Colare Prairie) also appeared that offered a choice of six or eight seats, plus an enormous load bay.

Like many large saloons of its era, the Fregate suffered badly from rust and survivors are rare.

There was a definite family resemblance with the Dauphine, but the Renault Fregate was a larger and more capable car. However, it was overshadowed by more capable rivals.

SIMCA ARONDE

Simca took a very unconventional route into car manufacture – it reconstituted Fiat's spare parts into France's largest and most successful privately owned carmaker of its day, and, in doing so, bravely offered a range of cars heavily inspired by contemporary American designs. The Aronde was the first Simca car designed from scratch, and enjoyed substantial success in its home market in subsequent years.

First launched in May 1951, with conventional engineering under the skin, the Aronde seemed to catch the public's imagination. It had a unitary construction body and was suspended by coils and wishbones at the front and semi-elliptic springs at the rear. Initially, build quality was poor, denting early sales, but, by 1953, an estate (station wagon) (Chatelaine) and a two-door pillarless coupé (Grand Large) were added, widening the range's appeal. A small van (Commerciale) was added, followed up by a panel van (Messagère) and pick-up (Intendante).

In 1954, a one-off convertible came along. From then until production ended in 1962, running changes were incorporated on an almost annual basis – which ensured strong sales to the end.

ENGINE: 1221cc (75 cu in), four-cylinder
POWER: 45bhp (34kW)
0–60MPH (96KM/H): 28.6 seconds
TOP SPEED: 118km/h (74mph)
PRODUCTION TOTAL: 1,274, 859

AUSTIN A30 AND A35

For many, the A30 of 1951 was the spiritual successor to the bestselling baby Seven of the pre-war era. Certainly, it marked the happy reappearance of a baby Austin on UK price lists, and strong sales predictably followed. In fact, Austin initially named the new car the Seven, a reminder of those past glories for the company.

The A30's cute rounded styling and prominent grille hinted at US styling influences, but the size was exactly right for Europe. Extremely narrow it may have been, but there was still room for four adults seated in relative comfort, thanks to its height. The 803cc (49cu in) four-cylinder engine was the first chance to see what became BMC's A-series – an engine that would remain in production until 2000.

In 1956, the engine was enlarged to 948cc (58cu in), the

grille was changed from chrome to body colour and the rear window was made bigger. In doing so, it became the A35. The gearshift was also changed, using remote linkage instead of the A30's long gearstick direct from the gearbox.

The Morris Minor overshadowed the A30 and A35, but they sold well anyway – and, just like their rival from Cowley, remained in production for a very long time. In fact, the van version remained in production until 1968.

ENGINE: 948cc (58cu in),
 four-cylinder
POWER: 34bhp (25kW)
0–60MPH (96KM/H): n/a
TOP SPEED: 102km/h (63mph)
PRODUCTION TOTAL: 527,000

Austin's first all-new post-war car was an extremely important addition. Its chassisless construction and A-Series engine would leave a lasting legacy.

MERCEDES-BENZ 300

GERMANY 1951–62

ENGINE: 2996cc (183cu in),
 six-cylinder
POWER: 115bhp (86kW)
0–60MPH (96KM/H): n/a
TOP SPEED: 161km/h (100mph)
PRODUCTION TOTAL: 12,221

Despite the slow start after World War II, Mercedes-Benz soon got back into its stride, with the introduction of the 300. Aimed directly at established competition

such as the BMW 501, it became one of the most opulent prestige cars of the decade. Featuring a smooth alloy overhead-camshaft straight-six engine, all-synchromesh four-speed gearbox and cossetting independent rear suspension, the car established Mercedes-Benz as a major force in the prestige market once more. The face-lifted 300B of 1954 received more power and servo-assisted brakes, while the 300C of 1955 gained an automatic transmission as an option.

An elegant four-door Cabriolet was built between 1952 and 1956, and it has many admirers today. The fabulous two-door 300S of 1951 featured a shortened chassis and three bodystyles – a fixed-head coupé, a convertible and a roadster. The SC version of 1955 had direct fuel injection and dry sump lubrication.

Completing the range, the 300D from 1957 had a longer wheelbase and a restyled body with a more upright stance, wraparound rear

screen and fully wind-down windows, making the sides totally pillarless. The car was made in limited numbers (just 3008 were built), but even rarer were the Cabriolets – only 65 were produced.

Favoured by heads of state and industry leaders, the Mercedes-Benz 300 was a vitally important car for the German manufacturer. The Cabriolet version was offered between 1952 and 1956.

RELIANT REGAL

Thanks to the British comedy TV series *Only Fools and Horses*, the three-wheel Reliant Regal became a national institution, but the first generation of the car was a very different-looking beast. The beauty of Reliant's Regal was that it could be driven on a motorcycle licence, as it was classed as a tricycle, yet it offered car- and van-like passenger- and load-carrying capabilities. The bubble-shaped Regal appeared in 1951 and was crudely built using a pressed-steel chassis, with semi-elliptic leaf springs at the rear; the single front wheel had a single torsion bar and stub axle arrangement. Powered by a 747cc (46cu in) Austin Seven engine, it was surprisingly nippy, thanks to its low weight.

Effective hydraulic brakes and a four-speed gearbox added some modernity to the package, and early models of the Regal had aluminium bodywork attached to an ash frame, only gaining glassfibre bodywork for the second series, launched in 1962.

When that car appeared, it was powered by an all-new 592cc (36cu in) alloy engine, designed by Reliant and loosely based on the old Austin Seven unit. Saloon versions featured a Ford Anglia 105E-style reverse-rake rear window.

The Regal stayed in production until 1973, when the Robin (in production until 2001, despite a 1980s rename to Rialto) replaced it.

ENGINE: 747cc (46cu in), four-cylinder
POWER: 16bhp (12kW)
0–60MPH (96KM/H): n/a
TOP SPEED: 96km/h (60mph)
PRODUCTION TOTAL: n/a

WARSZAWA M20

When it was launched in 1951, the Warszawa M20 was nothing more than a redundant Soviet car, known as the Pobieda, which had been first seen in 1945. Production was slow to start (with just 75 cars built in the first year), but assembly gradually sped up; by 1956, the M20 had become an entirely Polish product. At that point in the proceedings, a new overhead-camshaft engine was fitted to replace the ageing side-valve unit. The new powerplant put out 70bhp (52kW), and that was enough to give the car a top speed of 105km/h (65mph).

An estate (station-wagon) version was produced in prototype form the following year. After that, a further face-lift was introduced, toning down the ornate grille. In 1960, the Ghia-designed saloon version was launched, but, from then until when it was phased out in March 1973, there were no other major changes made.

More than 250,000 examples were built, and they proved popular as taxis – thanks in no small part to their heavy construction and simple mechanics. The car's most famous owner was none other than Polish-born Pope John Paul II, before he became the Pontiff.

ENGINE: 2120cc (129cu in), four-cylinder
POWER: 70bhp (52kW)
0–60MPH (96KM/H): about 30 seconds
TOP SPEED: 105km/h (65mph)
PRODUCTION TOTAL: 254,470

AUSTIN A40 SOMERSET

In an era of massive technological leaps forward, it was good to see that, among other manufacturers, Austin was still able to afford only to produce poor updates of existing obsolete models. In the

The Austin Counties range of cars was curvaceously styled, distinctive on the road – and the Somerset was probably the nicest of all to drive.

light of such technical marvels as the Morris Minor and Saab 92, Austin's A40 Somerset was typical of this policy.

It may be a genuine classic today, but, by using the running gear of the A40 Dorset and Devon – which was already antiquated – and giving the car the same style as the A70 Hereford and the A30, the company was not able to offer a convincing case for itself at a time when it was important to tempt younger buyers with exciting products. Its B-series engine was still pegged at a mere 1200cc (73cu in) and, despite independent front suspension, the chassis was not able to conjure up inspiring handling.

Despite that, the portly little car soon won a place in the British public's collective hearts, and the prominent sweeping line down from the top of the front wing (fender) and the distinctive grille helped to stamp a strong identity on the car. As a result, sales were reasonably good and helped to pave the way for creation of the British Motor Corporation in 1952.

ENGINE: 1200cc (73cu in), four-cylinder
POWER: 40bhp (30kW)
0–60MPH (96KM/H): 31.6 seconds
TOP SPEED: 111km/h (69mph)
PRODUCTION TOTAL: 173,306

PACKARD CARIBBEAN

ENGINE: 5358cc (327cu in),
eight-cylinder
POWER: 210bhp (156kW)
0–60MPH (96KM/H): 12 seconds
TOP SPEED: 174km/h (108mph)
PRODUCTION TOTAL: 1150

During Packard's gentle decline during the post-war years, many of its traditional customers drifted away. This retreat saw the company lose ground to upmarket rivals such as Cadillac, and the resultant loss of prestige caused further losses – it was a vicious cycle of decline.

Only one 1950s Packard came close to stopping the rot, and that was the 1952 Caribbean. This was a stunning machine that looked like a real threat to Cadillac's equally imposing Eldorado convertible. Designed by Richard Teague, the softtop Packard had a huge chrome-laden frontage, a long wheelbase and continental-style rear wheel carrier. It certainly looked the part, even if, underneath, it still used an old side-valve straight-eight engine.

Production volumes were deliberately kept low to maintain the Caribbean's desirability, but the Packard brand could not compete with the Cadillac's glamour in the early 1950s. In a desperate bid to maintain its place in the elite, Packard bought ailing carmaker

The huge and impressively styled Packard Caribbean defined Detroit style for years to come – but the car drove less well than it looked.

Studebaker in 1954, but the debt-ridden company proved a fatal financial burden. Despite an exciting new range of cars launched in 1956, sales continued to slide; Packard closed in 1958.

SIATA 208S

The Siata 208S is based on perhaps the most collectable Fiat ever, the 8V, and for that reason is one of the more interesting sports cars of its era. Siata had been involved in the development of the 8V from the outset, as it had built the running prototype for Fiat. With a Vignale-styled bodyshell and featuring pop-up headlights, it was officially available as either a coupé (initially built by Stabilimenti Farina, then Carozzeria Balbo) or as a convertible – although there were numerous other special and one-off derivatives built. The car had all-round independent suspension mounted on a tubular chassis, to which was added a steel body.

When Fiat stopped production of the 8V, only 114 cars had been built, but 200 examples of the double-overhead camshaft 16-valve V8 engine had been produced; the balance was sold to Siata. With so few engines available, the 280's production was necessarily limited, but that did not stop Siata offering other variants, such as the long-wheelbase 208SC.

The engine was developed during the production run. An eight-port cylinder head to make it more efficient was introduced, but only about eight of these were built.

ENGINE: 1996cc (122cu in),
eight-cylinder
POWER: 128bhp (95kW)
0–60MPH (96KM/H): n/a
TOP SPEED: 205km/h (128mph)
PRODUCTION TOTAL: about 32

AUSTIN CHAMP

It was not only Rover that noticed the sheer all-round usability of the Willys Jeep during World War II. Austin's designers and engineers noted this, too, and, as a result, the company conceived plans to produce its own Jeep rival. It was not until 1952 that the vehicle appeared on the market – the Austin Champ. Bad timing was the order of the day, as the all-conquering Land Rover had already been on the market for four years by this time. Like the Land Rover, the Champ had four-wheel drive, and featured very basic bodywork.

Available in two versions – military and civilian – the Champ was not a success. The military version of the vehicle was powered by a special Rolls-Royce FB engine, with four cylinders and a capacity of 2.9 litres (177cu in), but the engine was considered far too sophisticated for army life. Partly because of this, the Champ ended up being an unreliable beast, and fell out of favour with the military, potentially its biggest customer. The civilian Champ used a detuned version of the A90 Atlantic four-cylinder unit, but, despite its positive points, the Champ failed in that market, too – thanks to the Land Rover.

Almost 13,000 were built, but just 1200 were civilian models, and most of those were exported.

ENGINE: 1971cc (120cu in), four-cylinder
POWER: 105bhp (78kW)
0–60MPH (96KM/H): 11.4 seconds
TOP SPEED: 168km/h (104mph)
PRODUCTION TOTAL: n/a

Conceived as Austin's response to the Jeep, the rugged and practical Champ certainly looked the part. However, it failed to stack up against the Land Rover.

BENTLEY R-TYPE

ENGINE: 4566cc (279 cu in), six-cylinder
POWER: 150bhp (112kW)
0-60MPH (96KM/H): 14.4. seconds
TOP SPEED: 172km/h (106mph)
PRODUCTION TOTAL: 2320

The Bentley R-Type, introduced in 1952, is generally regarded as one of the most beautiful saloon cars ever built. Perhaps its elegant styling was the direct consequence of the MK VI's bulky bodywork, but, whatever the reason, the R-Type's appearance put Bentley at the top of the prestige car tree once again. Power came from Rolls-Royce's acclaimed 4.5-litre (279cu in) six-cylinder engine, with inlet-over-exhaust valves. The car's spirited performance and smooth progress, married to excellent interior insulation, made it a quiet cruiser.

The new car again came with a standard body, but the chassis was longer and the bodywork more evenly proportioned, with a raked rear end, sweeping wheel guards and streamlined front wings (fenders). The bulky curves made access to the back seats a touch difficult, though, and the interior was cramped for such a large car.

Standard-bodied cars suffered from tinworm, despite well-built mechanicals. A variety of coachbuilt bodies was also on offer, perhaps the most famous of which was the H.J. Mulliner Continental R fastback, regarded as one of the most stunning car designs of all time. Most specials were aluminium and therefore did not rust.

It looks gorgeous, but the R-Type Bentley is equally smooth to drive thanks to Rolls-Royce power. Easily in contention for 'best car in the world'.

FIAT 8V

ITALY 1952–55

ENGINE: V8 1996cc (122cu in),
eight-cylinder
POWER: 105bhp (78kW)
0–60MPH (96KM/H): 12.6 seconds
TOP SPEED: over 193km/h (120mph)
PRODUCTION TOTAL: 114 (chassis)

When Fiat first decided to push upmarket and build a flagship V8, the industry was caught by surprise. That surprise turned to disappointment when the prototype ended up being slow and cumbersome; the project was ultimately cancelled as a result.

This left Fiat with a 2-litre (122cu in) V8 engine, but no car to put it in, and the solution was to use it in a sports car – and so the 8V, or Otto Vu, arrived at the Geneva Motor Show in 1952. The car looked fantastic, and Fiat design boss Dante Giacosa designed all the beautiful Pininfarina-inspired lines in-house. Siata was contracted to build the cars, and the bodies were built at Lingotto by Fiat's experimental workshop. Underneath that beautiful body was standard 1100 independent suspension that gave unusually crisp handling.

Even so, legendary companies such as Vignale, Bertone, Ghia and Pininfarina produced bodies for many of the 8V chassis. It is Fiat's effort, however, that remains the most memorable. It was aerodynamically efficient as a result of using Turin Polytechnic's wind tunnel, and this helped Fiat's chief test driver Carlo Salomano to record a top speed of more than 193km/h (120mph).

So far, the 8V remains the only V8-engined car that the Italian car manufacturer has ever made.

With supercar looks and a price tag to match, the Fiat 8V was a world away from the aspirations of most Fiat owners in the 1950s. A top speed of 193km/h (120mph) was exceptional.

ARNOLT MG

UNITED KINGDOM 1952–56

The American industrialist and importer Stanley 'Wacky' Arnolt created the Arnolt MGs during the early 1950s, after spotting a couple of Bertone-bodied MG TDs at the 1952 Turin Motor Show. Arnolt was so impressed by the efforts of the legendary coachbuilding company that he immediately ordered 100 roadsters and 100 cabriolets.

The order saved Bertone, as the coachbuilder had been going under at the time, and it used the last of its cash reserves to produce these specials as a way of attracting customers. As part of the deal, Arnolt himself became a director of Bertone, and the company went from strength to strength.

Although the Arnolt MGs looked fantastic, and were way ahead of the car they were based on in terms of styling, thanks to their all-enveloping bodywork, performance was a disappointment. The reason for this was simple – that pretty body was too heavy for the TD mechanicals.

Sales were correspondingly low as a result, and, with only 100 cars built, production of the Arnolt MG came to an end. The deal did not, however, and the equally attractive Arnolt Bristol and Arnolt Aston were built instead.

ENGINE: 1250cc (76cu in),
four-cylinder
POWER: 55bhp (41kW)
0–60MPH (96KM/H): n/a
TOP SPEED: 121km/h (75mph)
PRODUCTION TOTAL: 100

LOTUS MK VI

UNITED KINGDOM 1952–56

Often seen as the first true Lotus, the Lotus Mk VI had little in common with anything the company had produced up to that point. Lotus Engineering had moved quickly to arrive at this car. It had been conceived by Colin Chapman and his wife-to-be Hazel Williams in 1952, and Chapman had initially worked on a variety of Austin-based trials cars before moving on to sportscar production at his premises in Hornsey, North London, and later at Cheshunt, Hertfordshire.

Once established, the Mk VI impressed all those who drove it. Technically brilliant, it featured a tubular space frame steel chassis (which was light and strong), with stressed aluminium body panels forming the floor, scuttle and sides.

All were sold in kit form, using affordable parts taken mostly from the Ford Ten/Popular range, including these cars' rigid rear axle. Soft suspension combined with a rigid chassis endowed the Mk IV with great roadholding, making it a popular choice among club racers. Power came from Ford, too – using either the 1172cc (72cu in) side-valve unit or the larger Consul engine, reduced in capacity to qualify for the 1500cc (92cu in) competition category.

ENGINE: 1172–1500cc (72–92cu in),
four-cylinder
POWER: 40bhp (30kW)
0–60MPH (96KM/H): n/a
TOP SPEED: 120km/h (75mph)
PRODUCTION TOTAL: 110

With a lightweight aluminium body and spaceframe chassis, the Lotus Mk VI was a lot more advanced than its primitive looks would have you believe. Exceptional handling came as standard and was a Lotus defining feature.

WOLSELEY 4/44

UNITED KINGDOM 1952–56

ENGINE: 1250cc (76cu in),
 four-cylinder
POWER: 46bhp (34kW)
0–60MPH (96KM/H): 29.9 seconds
TOP SPEED: 117km/h (73mph)
PRODUCTION TOTAL: 29,845

Badge engineering was a fact of life in the Nuffield Group by the 1950s, and the Wolseley 4/44 was a prime example of this practice, being closely related to the MG Magnette ZA. Despite the relationship, both cars had separate personalities, with the Wolseley being the luxury option.

Those who bought the Wolseley appreciated how the car sat a little higher off the ground, behind the traditional Wolseley grille. A luxury feature included the option of wood veneers (from 1954) for the plain but well-equipped dash.

Suspension was a positive asset, having shared its DNA with the Morris Minor – and it received a coil and wishbone front suspension layout, making it much more modern than its predecessor (although there was still half-elliptic leaf spring suspension at the back). The steering was also updated with a rack-and-pinion unit – just like the Minor.

Despite that, the Wolseley 4/44 lasted only four years, when the 15/50 replaced it.

Although it was closely related to the MG Magnette ZA, and was a prime example of Nuffield Group badge engineering, the Wolseley 4/44 had a personality all of its own.

ARMSTRONG-SIDDELEY SAPPHIRE 346

Although it looked like an evolutionary effort, the replacement for the Armstrong-Siddeley Lancaster, the Sapphire 346, was an entirely new car from the ground up. Generally it was the other way round in the British car industry at the time, with new clothes hiding familiar components.

The Sapphire 346 featured an all-new chassis, with coil-sprung suspension at the front and leaf springs at the rear. Power came from a 3.4-litre (210cu in) six-cylinder engine that pushed the top speed to 154km/h (95mph). Star Sapphire versions appeared in 1958, fitted with a 4.0-litre (244cu in) six-cylinder unit, and could top 161km/h (100mph).

Two gearboxes were offered: a four-speed all-synchromesh manual or a Rolls-Royce-supplied Hydramatic automatic. Power steering was an option, a first for a UK market car. The Sapphire 234 and 236, introduced in 1955, were very different machines, despite their familiar names. These 2.3-litre (140cu in) six-cylinder cars had unhappy styling and were a sales disaster from the start; they were dropped after three years. That loss was bad enough to cause Armstrong-Siddeley to quit building cars completely in 1960.

ENGINE: 3435cc (210cu in), six-cylinder
POWER: 125bhp (93kW)
0–60MPH (96KM/H): 13.9 seconds
TOP SPEED: 154km/h (95mph)
PRODUCTION TOTAL: 8777

BMW 501

Having lost everything it had achieved by the end of World War II, BMW might have retained its excellent image built since the purchase of the Dixi car company in 1928, but it needed to start from scratch in a new factory in Munich. Despite this huge setback, it targeted the same middle- and upper-class customers that bought its cars before the war, in direct competition with Mercedes-Benz.

The car for this tough task was the 501, closely based on the pre-war 326. It featured overelaborate styling which resulted in the 501 being dubbed the 'baroque angel'. Under the bodywork, there was the old six-cylinder engine and all-new independent suspension. It was a good car, but Mercedes-Benz produced better cars and sold them for less money.

BMW improved the 501 during its life, first with the 501A, then the 501/3. The model eventually evolved into the V8-powered 502 – a much better machine. These cars did not save BMW, but they allowed it to stay in business during a time that saw off plenty of seemingly more stable car companies.

ENGINE: 1971cc (120cu in), six-cylinder
POWER: 65bhp (48kW)
0–60MPH (96KM/H): n/a
TOP SPEED: 135km/h (84mph)
PRODUCTION TOTAL: 6328

VANDEN PLAS PRINCESS 4-LITRE LIMOUSINE

The Vanden Plas 4-Litre Limousine was not really a new car at all, merely an evolution of the Austin A135 – a staple of the upper-class market in the United Kingdom which had enjoyed moderate success during its life. After a run of around 1250 examples, that car became the Vanden Plas in 1959 and would go on to live a remarkably long life. The A135 had been introduced in 1952, but, as the 4-litre (244cu in) was the largest car in the British Motor Corporation (BMC) family, the Vanden Plas badge seemed more fitting – which it received in 1959.

The Princess 4-Litre was offered in saloon or landaulette forms, and, although it was an expensive car, it was considerably cheaper than similar-sized rival limousines from the more prestigious marques. With seating for six in three rows of two (including a pair of forward-facing occasional seats in the middle), the Princess 4-Litre was clearly aimed at British captains of industry who expected to be chauffeured from one meeting to another.

Despite its size, the car could almost hit 161km/h (100mph), thanks to the game efforts of its 122bhp (91kW) 3993cc (244cu in) six-cylinder engine. A four-speed automatic transmission, servo-assisted brakes (drums all round) and power-assisted steering were standard fittings.

ENGINE: 3993cc (244cu in), six-cylinder
POWER: 122bhp (91kW)
0–50MPH (80KM/H): 11.5 seconds
TOP SPEED: 158km/h (98mph)
PRODUCTION TOTAL: about 3350

MERCURY MONTEREY

Big and expensive, the Mercury Monterey was a prime example of the marque's upper-middle market offerings. This pillarless two-door coupé version clearly showed that the company was adept at giving customers what they wanted.

The Mercury marque had been the creation of Edsel Ford in 1938, when he produced a car to plug the gap between the low-cost V8 range of Ford cars and the luxury Lincoln K-series of the 1930s. It was also there to provide competition for Oldsmobile and Buick – both well-established GM brands of their day.

By the late 1940s, Mercury was moving upwards into Lincoln's patch, and that eventually resulted in the launch of the stylish Monterey in 1952. A brave new world was ushered in, and the company's archaic flathead V8 finally ended, to be replaced by an all-new Y-block power unit that produced 161bhp (120kW).

The Monterey was available in convertible, pillarless coupé, four-door sedan, and estate (station-wagon) versions, and customers could choose from 35 different colour schemes. Despite its huge size and weight, the Monterey struggled along with drum brakes front and rear, and that did not help the driving experience a great deal.

Despite that, the car was an immediate success, promoted no doubt by its association with James Dean – it was the car famously driven over the edge of a cliff in the film *Rebel without a Cause*. Other Hollywood film stars were also drawn to the Monterey, and screen legend Gary Cooper was a proud owner of one.

ENGINE: 6502cc (397cu in), eight-cylinder
POWER: 161bhp (120kW)
0–60MPH (96KM/H): 14.0 seconds
TOP SPEED: 161km/h (100mph)
PRODUCTION TOTAL: 174,238

BRISTOL 404

UNITED KINGDOM 1953–55

ENGINE: 1971cc (120cu in), six-cylinder
POWER: 105bhp (78kW)
0–60MPH (96KM/H): 10.5 seconds
TOP SPEED: 170km/h (105mph)
PRODUCTION TOTAL: 52

The 404 was an evolution of the previous Bristol models, and it used a shortened version of the 403 chassis (which itself was almost the same as the 401 chassis, but with an anti-roll bar at the front, improved steering and finned brake drums). Powered by the famous six-cylinder engine, it boasted an all-new body with a distinctive gaping front grille, and one that most Bristol enthusiasts regard to be the best-looking car made by the company.

Its shortened chassis meant that driving the 404 was a much more sportscar-like experience than most Bristols. The more powerful engine, which increased output from 105bhp (78kW) to 125bhp (93kW), provided acceleration that was as keen as its handling.

An interesting long wheelbase version of the 404, named the 405, was also offered. It became the only Bristol ever to be built with four doors instead of two.

With the 404 came a few features that have since become Bristol hallmarks. The most obvious was the location of the spare wheel and the battery behind either front wheelarch, to provide extra luggage space elsewhere, and the shrouded instrument panel directly ahead of the steering wheel.

Bristol referred to the 404 as the 'Businessman's Express' – a term that has been used since.

Featuring a smooth six-cylinder engine, aerodynamic styling and excellent dynamics, many people consider the 404 to be one of the best and most sporting Bristols ever made.

FERRARI 250 EUROPA

ITALY 1953–55

Following Ferrari's early practice of numbering all of its production cars, the Ferrari 250 was launched at the Paris Motorshow in 1953, to effectively replace the 212. The car had a smaller 2963cc (181cu in) version of the Lampredi V12 that was exclusive to this model, producing 220bhp (164kW). Power was marshalled through a four-speed all-synchromesh gearbox.

Instead of being just an adapted racing car, the Europa was specifically designed as a road car and was a clear indicator of the direction Ferrari would take in the future. Even though it was the final version of the 166, the Europa was closely related to the America models, with similar coachwork, smaller engines and lower prices. The long wheelbase chassis came from the Type 375, to make it more comfortable and refined for road use. This also made the 250, along with the 375, the largest Ferrari for sale at the time.

Italian coachbuilders all offered their own interpretations of the Europa, while the 'standard' body style was similar to the America and mostly built by Pininfarina as an elegant 2+2. Europas were largely exported to the United States, though many Ferrari customers baulked at its civilized nature.

ENGINE: 2963cc (181cu in), 12-cylinder
POWER: 220bhp (164kW)
0–60MPH (96KM/H): 9 seconds
TOP SPEED: 217km/h (135mph)
PRODUCTION TOTAL: 21

SUNBEAM ALPINE

Although most readily associated with the successful 1960s Alpine, the original car was actually closely based on the Sunbeam Talbot 90 Mk II saloon. Effectively, it was a two-door, two-seater version of the more mundane family car, although the chassis was reinforced considerably.

The Alpine was really designed with the American market in mind, with both the engine and the suspension tuned for sportiness so that it felt less like a family car to drive. This meant stiffer springs up front, more positive steering and freer-breathing cylinder heads.

A high list price compared with rivals such as the Triumph TR2, meant that sales were slow, and success eluded the car. The Alpine retained the independent suspension set-up (coil springs at the front), and was powered by another Rootes family engine, the 2.3-litre (138cu in) four-cylinder engine from the Humber Hawk.

With just 80bhp (60kW) on offer and a portly body, the Alpine's performance was poor, and, despite rallying success – including an outright win of the 1955 Monte Carlo Rally at the hands of a privateer – sales of the car were slow, and, after two years, the Alpine was dropped.

ENGINE: 2267cc (138cu in), four-cylinder
POWER: 80bhp (60kW)
0–60MPH (96KM/H): 18.9 seconds
TOP SPEED: 152km/h (95mph)
PRODUCTION TOTAL: about 3000

TRIUMPH TR2

For ever synonymous with the TR range of sports cars, the Triumph marque was in a state of flux when the first of that famous line was introduced in 1953. From that point, it has never looked back. Yet, had it not been for the TR series – and most notably, the TR2 that started it all off – Triumph as a marque could well have died out long before it did. The success of these sporting roadsters also saw the marque become the dominant partner of the Standard-Triumph concern.

TRs became popular throughout the world, but it was in the United States that the cars really picked up a cult following, becoming – alongside the MG – among the most popular of the sporting European imports.

It was MG's success in the United States that spurred company boss Sir John Black to create the new sports car. The MG TD was doing great business and developing quite a reputation. If MG could become a success in export markets, reasoned Black, then so should Triumph.

The first car to wear the TR badge was the TRX, an abandoned replacement for the Roadster shown at the 1950 Paris Motor Show, but that car was never put into production. The TRX loosely set the template for what would become the new TR2, including its twin-SU carburettor four-cylinder Vanguard engine. The chassis was based on that of the Standard Flying Nine. Although it went out of production in 1939, it was chosen primarily because there were several hundred surplus Flying Nine frames lying around the factory, and that kept costs down.

Initially known as the 20TS, the new Triumph was unveiled at the 1952 London Motor Show. It had been developed quickly, and, when it came to testing, the flaws were very obvious. Ken Richardson, formerly involved with BRM Grand Prix, drove the 20TS and famously called it a 'death trap'. After that, he was invited to join Triumph and help to develop the car. Stiffening up the chassis improved the handling, and styling work was done to tidy up the rear end.

The old car (which became retrospectively known as the TR1) had been reworked into the TR2 by the end of 1952, and with its completely new chassis was unveiled – again – at the 1953 Geneva Motor Show. This time, it was clear that Triumph had made giant leaps, with the revised look and the new underpinnings, along with the power of the 90bhp 2-litre (121cu in) engine.

While the new car may have been better received than its predecessor, it did not prove itself until the summer of 1953, when a modified car was taken to Belgium for a high-speed run on the Jabbeke motorway. With Ken Richardson at the wheel, a speed of almost 201km/h (125mph) was achieved, a remarkable effort.

Conceived by Triumph to fight MG on the marketplace, the TR2 was quite slow to catch on, but it sowed the seeds for a long line of Triumph sportscars.

Other valuable racing laurels followed, including Le Mans, the Mille Miglia and an outright win in the 1954 RAC Rally.

Despite all that, the TR2 never sold in the quantities of its rival from Abingdon – perhaps because the early cars had teething problems. The company had faith in its product, however, and continued development, producing the TR3, introduced in late 1955. It never looked back.

ENGINE: 1991cc (121cu in), four-cylinder
POWER: 90bhp (67kW) at 4800rpm
0–60MPH (96KM/H): 12.2 seconds
TOP SPEED: 166km/h (103mph)
PRODUCTION TOTAL: 8628

ALLARD JR

Despite being based largely on the mechanical package of the Allard Palm Beach roadster launched a year earlier, the new JR series had been conceived clearly with competition use in mind – and that meant the use of austere-looking windscreens and a lack of bumpers. There were, however, improvements. Instead of the rigid rear axle used in the Palm Beach, the JR used the J2's de Dion set-up at the rear, to provide better handling and traction on the track.

A wide range of engines was available to fit the JR's chassis; the most popular with owners was the 5.4-litre (331cu in) Cadillac V8. That mighty engine pushed the car to a top speed of 224km/h (140mph) and gained Sydney Allard provisional pole position in the 1953 Le Mans 24-hour race. Allard's fortunes waned as more sophisticated competition from the likes of Jaguar's stunningly successful XK120 hit the market – and the company ceased production in 1962. The Allard name continued, however, being associated with aftermarket tuning.

After Sydney Allard's death in 1966, his son Allan became involved in the business, opening a factory in Daventry, before moving to Ross-on-Wye.

ENGINE: 5420cc (331cu in), eight-cylinder
POWER: 250bhp (186kW)
0–60MPH (96KM/H): n/a
TOP SPEED: 224km/h (140mph)
PRODUCTION TOTAL: 17

ALVIS TC21

The Alvis TC21 was not a new model at all, but merely an evolution of the existing TA21, which appeared in 1953. The TC21 also received further updates later that year, and the introduction of an additional higher performance model in the range called the TC21/100, or Grey Lady, as it was widely known.

The '100' in the TC21/100's designation was derived from its powerful 100bhp (75kW) output, as well as the fact that it was capable of topping the magic 'ton', or 161km/h (100mph).

Why the 'Grey Lady'? Because that was the colour of the 1953 Earls Court Motor Show display vehicle – and it made quite an impression. The extra performance of the new car came as a result of the higher compression ratio and rear axle ratios.

There were only small visual clues characterizing the 'new' Alvis. Twin cooling bonnet (hood) scoops were fitted, along with louvres on the side of the bonnet doors, while Dunlop wire wheels were an obvious improvement. As with the TA21, Mulliner built the saloon bodies and Tickford crafted the drophead coupés. Swiss coachbuilders Graber also built a number of stylish variations. The reliance on outside contractors was the reason for Alvis dropping car production – Mulliner agreed to work solely for Standard-Triumph, and Tickford was taken over by rivals Aston Martin.

ENGINE: 2993cc (183cu in), six-cylinder
POWER: 100bhp (75kW)
0–60MPH (96KM/H): 16.5 seconds
TOP SPEED: 163km/h (101mph)
PRODUCTION TOTAL: 805

Forever associated with the Grey Lady moniker (the first display model was grey), in '100' form the Alvis TC21 was a fast, imposing saloon.

ASTON MARTIN DB2/4

ENGINE: 2900cc (177cu in),
six-cylinder
POWER: 140bhp (104kW)
0–60MPH (96KM/H): 10.5 seconds
TOP SPEED: 192km/h (119mph)
PRODUCTION TOTAL: 764

Sometimes it takes a couple of tries to get the formula spot on, as was the case with the DB2. It may have been a great car, but it needed further refinement. That is why it was replaced after three years by the similarly named DB2/4.

The new model addressed most of the DB2's shortcomings – the split windscreen was replaced by a one-piece item, an opening boot (trunk) was added, and tiny rear seats were squeezed in to turn it into an effective 2+2. That extra practicality was at the expense of style, and the DB2/4 ended up with a more bulbous rear end. The visual assault was tamed by adding proper bumpers to effectively lengthen the car, though.

Predictably, the car's weight rose, so the DB2/4 was given the previous car's higher output Vantage tune engine as standard, thus ensuring a favourable power-to-weight ratio. Later the 2.6-litre (157cu in) unit was increased to 2.9 litres (177cu in), turning the DB2/4 into a genuinely quick car. The DB2/4 was offered in both

Unquestionably the car where everything came right for Aston Martin – the DB2/4 was quick off the mark in Vantage form and extremely sumptuous inside.

fixed-head and drophead forms. Both were considered a success, with 565 being produced in just two years. For 1955, Aston Martin improved the mix still further by introducing the DB2/4 Mk II.

DAIMLER CONQUEST

In the early 1950s, Daimler had been trying hard to move away from its traditionally staid image, and had been reasonably successful in the process. With the Consort, the company had established that there was a ready market for a compact model in the range, and the new Conquest was clear indication that Daimler was rapidly moving in that direction.

Announced in 1952 to coincide with Queen Elizabeth II's coronation, the new saloon may have been

It might have an upright and almost regal appearance, but in Century specification the Daimler Conquest was actually rather fun to drive.

styled like a traditional Daimler, but there was definite modernization going on. The headlights were now mounted on the wings (fenders), and the new integrated wing line was pleasingly modern.

The Conquest's new six-cylinder engine put out a healthy 75bhp (56kW), and the independent front suspension used laminated torsion bars, which ensured a fine ride and moderately interesting handling. Daimler also offered the Drophead Conquest, a two-door model with a partially powered hood.

The 100bhp (75kW) Conquest Century was a more sporting variation, which did well in saloon car racing. It was the Conquest Century roadster that was even more innovative, however, and it was the first genuine Daimler sports car since 1908.

This alloy-bodied sports car had cutaway doors and tail fins, and, although the whole package was not exactly good-looking, the coupé version would subsequently improve matters.

ENGINE: 6 cylinder 2433cc (148 cu in)
POWER: 75bhp (56kW)
0–60MPH (96KM/H): 24 seconds
TOP SPEED: 132km/h (82mph)
PRODUCTION TOTAL: 9749

RILEY PATHFINDER

For many Riley aficionados, the Pathfinder was the beginning of the end. To their horror, it shared its bodywork with the visually similar Wolseley 6/90 – and became another victim of the BMC policy of badge engineering.

The 2.5-litre (149cu in) straight-six was an RM range hangover, however, and was exclusive to the Pathfinder, delivering an impressive power output of 110bhp (82kW). Still, the car's dynamics were called into question, and, although the handsome car may have looked like a contemporary unitary design, there was still a separate chassis underneath. Couple that with front torsion bar suspension, and old-fashioned 'cam-and-roller' type steering, and the result was terminal understeer. Sadly, the car was nicknamed the 'Ditchfinder' by the British motoring press, and was a reason for its creator, Gerald Palmer, to lose his job at BMC.

It may have not handled well, but the luxurious interior and supple ride were positives, and the servo-assisted hydraulic brakes were powerful. The right-hand gearlever, fitted even on right-hand drive cars, took some getting used to, meaning the big Riley was an easier car to drive in two-pedal semi-automatic form, offered from 1955.

ENGINE: 2443cc (149cu in), six-cylinder
POWER: 110bhp (82kW)
0–60MPH (96KM/H): 16.7 secs
TOP SPEED: 165km/h (102mph)
PRODUCTION TOTAL: 5152

SALMSON 2300 SPORT

The best car to come out of Salmson's Billancourt factory was its last. The 2300 Sport certainly looked the part, with styling strongly redolent of cars from Pegaso, Facel Vega and Ferrari. It used a version of the company's double overhead-camshaft four-cylinder engine that had first seen the light of day in 1921 – in the first car produced by Salmson. When installed in the 2300 Sport, upping the engine capacity and boosting the power accordingly upgraded it further.

The car's all-steel coachbuilt body was seen as unnecessary and something that only added to production costs without being of any real benefit. More bizarrely, no fewer than seven bodystyles were tried before a definitive range was chosen in 1954.

France was still recovering from World War II when the 2300 hit the market in 1953, and few people could afford such an overtly sporting car – at such a high price. With no market, the Salmson factory was forced to close after three more years, with just 227 cars produced between 1953 and 1956.

ENGINE: 2312cc (141cu in), four-cylinder
POWER: 105bhp (78kW)
0–60MPH (96KM/H): n/a
TOP SPEED: 168km/h (105mph)
PRODUCTION TOTAL: 227

MG MAGNETTE ZA/ZB

With the Nuffield Group now part of the British Motor Corporation, the pre-war policy of badge engineering took on new heights. Bedfellows since before World War II, MGs and Wolseleys tended to be closely related, and this was a practice that only continued to gain momentum within the new company.

The Magnette ZA closed the gap even further, however, by using the bodywork from the Wolseley 4/44, even if it was attractive, thanks to its fluted MG grille and other accoutrements. The ZA was also the first MG to be powered by the venerable BMC B-Series – a significant moment because that engine would go on to power the MGA and MGB.

The ZA received an uprated platform, with rack-and-pinion steering and improved suspension, and 60bhp (45kW) meant that it accelerated as well as it handled. Despite being the sportier offering, there was still an agreeable amount of wood and leather used in the interior.

A more powerful ZB variant replaced the ZA in 1956, and it was offered with optional Varitone two-colour paintwork and a wraparound rear screen. A few cars also appeared with manumatic semi-automatic transmission – a novel although not hugely effective attempt at creating a clutchless manual set-up that was years ahead of its time.

ENGINE: 1489cc (91cu in), four-cylinder
POWER: 68bhp (51kW)
0–60MPH (96KM/H): 22.6 seconds
TOP SPEED: 129km/h (80mph)
PRODUCTION TOTAL: 36,600

Good to look at and better to drive, the MG Magnette ZA was the first car in the newly formed British Motor Corporation to be powered by what would become the B-Series engine.

OPEL KAPITAN

Just as the big Vauxhalls of the era had clear American influences, so the situation was similar for their German cousins at Opel. The company's flagship had obvious Detroit overtones, with vast metalwork, an ornate chrome grille with shining 'teeth', whitewall tyres and polished metal side flashes. Despite that, the Kapitan was a very well engineered car featuring a tough, solid body,

independent coil and wishbone suspension at the front and semi-elliptic leaf springs at the back. The 2.4-litre (151cu in) straight-six was smooth and lively, while the three-speed column change transmission and an engine so well endowed with torque meant that it was an effortless drive.

The Kapitan was given a face-lift in 1955, and the nasty grille was dropped in favour of something

much more European in feel. Other improvements such as an all-synchromesh gearbox and better trimmed interior were added.

When the Kapitan was replaced in 1958, it was by an even more transatlantic effort, which featured a wraparound windscreen that passengers could easily smack their knees on when trying to get in or out. A more powerful engine, which produced 90bhp (67kW),

four-speed gearbox and automatic transmission, was drafted in for the new model, which remained in production until 1964.

ENGINE: 2473cc (151cu in), six-cylinder
POWER: 75bhp (56kW)
0–60MPH (96KM/H): 21.4 seconds
TOP SPEED: 142km/h (88mph)
PRODUCTION TOTAL: 154,098

PONTIAC CHIEFTAN

ENGINE: 4638cc (283cu in), eight-cylinder
POWER: 122bhp (91kW)
0–60MPH (96KM/H): n/a
TOP SPEED: n/a
PRODUCTION TOTAL: 379,705

For many, the 1950s were a styling highpoint for the American car industry – it was a celebration of

the country's confidence and the growing wealth of its people. Pontiac was one of many carmakers which could translate those styling cues to any of its cars – even the more ordinary.

In 1953, an all-new design, the Chieftain, was rolled out, and it featured the by-then mandatory one-piece curved windscreen, stepped rear wings (fenders) and aerodynamic rear wheel covers. A

wide range of two-tone paint schemes, whitewall tyres and ornate chrome side flashes topped it off.

Inside, multicoloured fabrics, an ornate and colour-coded dashboard and a panoramic instrument panel that allowed all the car's occupants to view the gauges were a sight to behold.

Buyers could choose from two- or four-door saloons, a striking two-door 'Catalina' coupé (a big hit

with collectors in later years), an odd-looking four-door estate (station wagon), two- and four-door convertibles and a 'Custom Sedan', which came with a lower roofline and extra chrome trim.

One of Pontiac's classics – and with so much chrome on board, it's hard not to fall for the Chieftan's flashy charms.

PANHARD DYNA 54

FRANCE 1953–59

Underneath the amazing styling, the Panhard Dyna 54 did not disappoint. With a 50bhp flat-twin it could still top 148km/h (92mph) – a testament to its fine aerodynamic performance.

The 1946 Panhard Dyna was typical of the breed – modern with fully independent suspension, four gears and hydraulic brakes. It was the Dyna 54, however, that vaulted the company into the big-time as a maker of technically advanced but quirky cars.

Despite its tiny air-cooled twin-cylinder engine, the Dyna 54 was relatively quick – especially at the top end – and, thanks to clever packaging, it could accommodate six close friends.

The aerodynamic body was made from light alloy for maximum lightness, and it was superbly economical. The later Dyna 57 and Dyna 58 had more power and superior front coil springs instead of torsion bars.

ENGINE: 851cc (52cu in),
two-cylinder
POWER: 50bhp (37kW)
0–60MPH (96KM/H): 24.3 seconds
TOP SPEED: 148km/h (92mph)
PRODUCTION TOTAL: 155,000

The Panhard Dyna was proof-positive that the French car industry was at its best when producing innovative small cars. It was a dramatic change of policy following World War II that saw Panhard develop a new range of air-cooled twin-cylinder engines and target the mainstream car market. As a result, the company flourished on the back of its affordable range of cars for the masses because they offered more luxury or innovation than rival domestic products.

STANDARD EIGHT

UNITED KINGDOM 1953–59

ENGINE: 803cc (49cu in),
four-cylinder
POWER: 26bhp (19kW)
0–60MPH (96KM/H): n/a
TOP SPEED: 98km/h (61mph)
PRODUCTION TOTAL: 136,317

later, the range-topping Super Eight was introduced. A year later the Phase II version was launched, replacing the previous range.

Standard continued to develop the car, but sales never really took off. By 1959, it became clear that Triumph-badged cars were the way forward for the company. By the time the Eight disappeared in 1960, the Herald had become Standard-Triumph's new small car range.

The Standard Eight was a basic British saloon that didn't set the market alight. With very little charisma, it struggled against the likes of the Morris Minor and Austin A30.

The Standard Eight will always be remembered for offering motoring in its most basic form, and lacking anything in the way of charisma in doing so – something that is essential in minimalist cars. Launched in 1953 with an 803cc (49cu in) engine, the Eight did without a boot (trunk) lid and even its second windscreen wiper was an optional extra.

In May 1954, the Eight was upgraded to make it more saleable. An uprated 948cc (58cu in) engine was installed and it now featured wind-up windows and more trim inside. In doing so, it became known as the Standard Ten. The price rose, but times were changing and increasingly affluent buyers could afford the extra in return for these little luxuries.

The following year, the Family Eight replaced the most basic model and, a couple of months

NASH METROPOLITAN

ENGINE: 1489cc (91cu in),
four-cylinder
POWER: 47bhp (35kW)
0–60MPH (96KM/H): 24.6 seconds
TOP SPEED: 121km/h (75mph)
PRODUCTION TOTAL: 104,368

The Nash Metropolitan (also sold as a Hudson in the United States and an Austin in Europe) was one of the more curious Anglo-American motoring collaborations, which sadly proved ill fated, despite the car's many merits.

The result of a partnership between Nash and Austin, effected by Donald Healey, the Metropolitan had all the ingredients of a winner. Nash president George Mason wanted to build a small economical car that would appeal to the US market, and the new car promised to bring together American styling and British small-car know-how.

The Metropolitan suffered from corrosion, however, and the high-sided and stubby styling was ill at ease in both the American and European marketplaces. Handling was, at best, erratic and, at worst, dangerous, and it was not very practical either – despite its boxy styling, an opening boot (trunk) was not offered until 1960.

Despite these major deficiencies, the Metropolitan sold reasonably well, notably in the United States.

More than 100,000 Metropolitans found homes during its seven-year production life – and ended up being fitted with a variety of Austin-sourced engines, including long-lived A- and B-Series units.

This curious BMC-powered Anglo-American venture proved an unexpected hit in the USA – despite its poor handling and practicality.

FORD UK 100E

It looks utterly conventional now, but the Anglia/Prefect range was actually Ford's first attempt at a monocoque-bodied small car. It came in two forms: the entry-level Anglia (two-door only) and the higher specification Prefect model (with four doors). The engine was old school in design – a brand-new 1172cc (72cu in) side-valve engine, featuring adjustable tappets. The innovative MacPherson strut independent front suspension system first seen on the Consul/Zephyr ensured that handling was assured, turning the car into a very competitive racer when effectively tuned.

Both Anglia and Prefect were given a face-lift for 1957, gaining larger rear windows, redesigned taillights and new grilles. A semi-automatic transmission option was added. It was innovative and sophisticated, but unwanted on such a cheap small car; very few cars were specified with it.

The Popular and Prefect appealed to those looking for a basic and cheap car – and were very good at giving the customer exactly what they wanted. The cars sold very well and picked up quite a following. When the more radically styled Anglia 105E appeared in 1959, small Fords suddenly became desirable, as well as sensible. The 100E stayed on after the new car's introduction and was renamed the Popular in 1960.

ENGINE: 1172cc (72cu in),
four-cylinder
POWER: 36bhp (27kW)
0–60MPH (96KM/H): 29 seconds
TOP SPEED: 112km/h (70mph)
PRODUCTION TOTAL: 626,453

AC ACE

Until the 1953 London Motor Show, AC was well regarded as a maker of high-quality but ageing sports saloons – but all that changed overnight, with the appearance of the Ace. That car redefined AC – and the delightful little car overshadowed the saloons, becoming the darling of the public and press.

Specialist builder John Tojeiro, who had produced a number of highly successful racing cars using transverse leaf spring independent suspension front and rear, had inspired the Ace. His car impressed

With drop dead gorgeous styling, the AC Ace was another reason to believe that the British ruled the roost in the sportscar field.

the company's management, and AC struck a deal with Tojeiro to produce a new car. Following the positive reception given to the first Ace, he worked quickly to install the 2-litre (121cu in) saloon's six-cylinder engine into his chassis, and adapt the aluminium bodywork for production.

By 1954, the Ace was ready for sale and the car was already attracting plenty of positive press.

A remarkable – for AC – 60 cars were built in the first year, and it went on to sell well throughout the early 1960s.

Bristol's excellent 2-litre (121cu in) engine was offered as an option in 1956, and a Ford Zephyr 2.6-litre (156cu in) engine was added to the line-up in 1961. The AC company had reinvented itself as a sportscar manufacturer – and future greatness beckoned.

ENGINE: 2553cc (156cu in), six-cylinder
POWER: 170bhp (127kW)
0–60MPH (96KM/H): n/a
TOP SPEED: 210km/h (130mph)
PRODUCTION TOTAL: 723

LANCIA APPIA

ITALY 1953–63

ENGINE: 1090cc (67cu in), four-cylinder
POWER: 43.5bhp (32kW) at 4800rpm
0–60MPH (96KM/H): 23 seconds
TOP SPEED: 132km/h (82mph)
PRODUCTION TOTAL: 107,245

The Appia was Lancia's entry-level model during the 1950s and into the 1960s, and, although it was smaller and cheaper than the Aurelia, the Appia (named after a Roman road) shared a major family resemblance. It may have looked similar, but it was far more basic both mechanically and in terms of interior trim.

The Appia was blessed with a brand-new small-capacity V4 engine (with the V angle set at a

Despite being an entry-level model for Lancia, the Appia still had all the style of its bigger brothers. The V4 engine wasn't sparkling, but was fun.

very narrow 10 degrees), and, although it was not very powerful, performance was good. Favourable power-to-weight ratio helped – and clever detailing such as aluminium doors, boot (trunk), bonnet (hood)

and rear wings (fenders) showed that its designers were on the ball.

In 1956, a Series 2 model appeared, with a restyled rear end that resulted in a larger luggage compartment, as well as giving the

car a more contemporary look. Power output was given a useful uplift, which gave the car more performance. In 1959, power was raised again to 53bhp (39kW) for the Series 3 face-lift.

As well as van, ambulance and pick-up versions, coachbuilt models appeared from Vignale, Farina, Lombardi and others. Most notable of these special Appias was the rare Zagato GT coupé.

FIAT 1100 MK II

ITALY 1953–69

A brand-new monocoque bodyshell was the major department for the Fiat 1100-103, but the familiar 1089cc (66cu in) engine powered the new car, and its four-speed gearbox with column-mounted shift still drove the rear wheels.

Although the saloon was pretty standard fare, the 103 TV ('Turismo Veloce') was fun to drive, producing

50bhp (37kW). An estate (station-wagon) version, the Familiare, joined the range in 1954, and a distinctive 103 TV 'Trasformabile' roadster was introduced in 1955.

The second-generation models from 1956 boasted more power at 53bhp (39kW), and the 103D model, with a longer boot (trunk), revised grille and better brakes, was added to the range in 1957. A 103H

Lusso version with 50bhp (37kW) was offered at the same time.

The new 1100D came in 1963 and featured new, cleaner styling. The final 1100, the 1100R, was launched in 1968, and it saw the return of the 1089cc (66cu in) powerplant, along with the installation of front disc brakes. The innovative 128 soon replaced that in Europe, but the 1100 lived

on in India as the Premier Padmini, powered by 1100cc (66cu in) and 1400cc (85cu in) engines. That car remains in production today.

ENGINE: 1089cc (66 cu in), 4 cylinder
POWER: 40bhp (30kW)
0-60MPH (96KM/H): 30 secs
TOP SPEED: 124km/h (77mph)
PRODUCTION TOTAL: 1,019,378

VOLVO PV445

SWEDEN 1953–69

A fter Volvo realized that monocoque construction of its PV444 meant that producing one-off bodies for special customers was difficult, it introduced a version of the car with a separate chassis. Dubbed the PV445, the new car used the PV444's engine, electrics, transmission, brakes and front

suspension. Rear suspension was changed to a more conventional semi-elliptic leaf spring set-up, and double-acting hydraulic dampers were added. These were attached directly to the chassis, making bespoke bodies much less complicated to fit. New variants could be developed very quickly,

easily and cheaply. The first of these were commercial vehicles with a payload of about 500kg (1100lb). It was not long before independent coachbuilders were building ambulances, hearses and even convertibles. One of the most popular conversions was an estate (station wagon), encouraging

Volvo to develop its own version, which it launched in 1953.

ENGINE: 1414cc (86cu in), four-cylinder
POWER: 40bhp (30kW)
0–60MPH (96KM/H): 24.9 seconds
TOP SPEED: 118km/h (74mph)
PRODUCTION TOTAL: n/a

CADILLAC COUPE DE VILLE

UNITED STATES 1953–70

S ymbolizing Cadillac's golden years, the Coupe de Ville was certainly one of the most charismatic cars produced by this marque. The de Ville range was on its way by 1950 with the 62 Series – a V8 hardtop coupé with prominent chrome grille, long bonnet (hood) and pre-emergent rear fins.

By 1955, the de Ville's distinctive torpedo front bumpers gave the car aggressive and unforgettable looks. The 1959 6200 Series, however, was the classic Cadillac Coupe de Ville style. Outlandish fins were the order of the day, as were powerful V8s. It had both – fins to die for and a 6384cc (390cu in) V8 engine. Chromework was plentiful, and the interiors were lavish colour-keyed coded efforts with jukebox dashboards.

By 1960, the Coupe de Ville's wings had been clipped; in 1962, the model was downgraded to the status of subseries, as the 6300. A four-door pillarless saloon model appeared, and a convertible was added to the range. By 1967, the glory years were over.

ENGINE: 6384cc (390cu in), eight-cylinder
POWER: 345bhp (257kW)
0–60MPH (96KM/H): 12 seconds
TOP SPEED: 185km/h (115mph)
PRODUCTION TOTAL: 670,000

If any car epitomises the excesses of car design in 1950s USA, then it's the Cadillac Coupe De Ville. With prominent fins, acres of chrome, and battleship proportions, it is one of the most memorable cars produced in Detroit.

CADILLAC ELDORADO

The first Cadillac Eldorado was based on a 1952 concept car and featured a 'wraparound' windscreen – the first time a car had ever received such a feature. When it reached production the following year, its styling remained startling, and the details included a stylish dip in the cut-down doors and chromed wire wheels – all suitable touches for a car which has a name that means 'gilded one' in Spanish.

It was a vastly expensive car, but the range was expanded to include a hardtop version, known initially as the Seville, then, in 1956, the even more glamorous Eldorado Brougham. From 1961 to 1966, the hardtops were dropped, as these cars became available exclusively as convertibles.

The 1967 Cadillac Eldorado marked a new direction to front-wheel drive with a coupé bodyshell. Technically, it became the first car to combine front-wheel drive with variable ratio power steering and automatic level control. The new Eldorado was shorter and lower than any other Cadillac, but was still able to seat

six people in comfort. And because it was cleverly styled by Bill Mitchell, it bore no physical relation to the Oldsmobile or Buick Rivera on which it was based. The car sold like hot cakes until it was phased out in 1970.

ENGINE: 7021cc (429cu in), eight-cylinder
POWER: 340bhp (253kW)
0–60MPH (96KM/H): 9.2 seconds
TOP SPEED: 193km/h (120mph)
PRODUCTION TOTAL: 100,273

The Eldorado started out as a concept and evolved into a fitting flagship for the Cadillac range – and from those extravagant beginnings it grew into one of the largest coupés developed by the end of the 1960s.

CHEVROLET CORVETTE

Although the US car industry had produced a number of specialist sports cars, it had yet to produce something that could sell in large numbers and take on the British at their own game. With the Corvette, it finally looked as if the United States had found its national plaything.

General Motors unveiled an innovative sporting creation of its own that caused such a storm that, just six months after the debut of a stunning concept car at the GM Motorama, the first production version of it rolled off a makeshift assembly line in Flint, Michigan, on 30 June 1953 – its name was Corvette.

Originally only available as a two-seat convertible in Polo White with a red interior, the first cars were built by hand and had their pretty Harley Earl–designed body moulded from glassfibre. The Corvette sat on a shortened saloon car chassis, with a 259cm (102in) wheelbase, and was powered by a 3851cc (235cu in) six-cylinder Chevrolet engine producing 150bhp (112kW). A Powerglide

two-speed automatic gearbox was the only transmission available.

However, Zora Arkus-Duntov, a Corvette engineer, knew what was needed to give the car the success it deserved – a harder edge. For 1956, the car was restyled and the six-cylinder engine was replaced by a 4343cc (265cu in) V8. The following year, that 195bhp (145kW) engine was replaced by a four-barrel carburettor 4638cc (283cu in) V8, which produced 220bhp (164kW). The now-iconic

Corvette was on its way. It was when the second-generation Corvettes arrived in 1963, however, that things really picked up.

All loved the classic Sting Ray body – and a coupé version joined the convertible and featured a

The 1963 Corvette was curvaceous and sporting in a way that no other mass-produced American car was at the time. Corvettes made today still feature the same special DNA.

The Corvette was one of the world's fastest cars when it went on sale in 1963. Featuring the Sting Ray body, it could top 233km/h (145mph).

distinctive split rear-window design. The Z-06 version was unveiled – which was also created by Arkus-Duntoz – and this was a racer powered by a fuel-injected 5360cc (327cu in) V8.

An all-new Corvette appeared in 1968 – and the Mako Shark styling went down well. Under the bonnet (hood), the car gained the 5360cc (327cu in) V8 L79, rated at

350bhp (261kW), and the L89 aluminium head option for the L71. The following year, that car was officially listed as a 'Stingray'. At this point, the coupé became the most popular model.

In 1973, a new-generation Corvette appeared which featured a smooth body-coloured nose combined with the original 1968 cut off 'Kamm' tail. The engines

were required to meet stricter emissions regulations by this time, however, and that badly affected power outputs. By 1974, the Corvette was further compromised by the smooth new body-coloured rear, which incorporated the weighty compulsory Federal 8km/h (5mph) bumpers.

At this point, the Corvette was softer and far slower than its

illustrious forebears, and its hard-edged character seemed lost for ever. The top 5735cc (350cu in) V8 was now rated at a mere 205bhp (227kW). This was also the last year for the convertible, as falling sales and threatened safety legislation ended its production life.

As the Corvette celebrated its twenty-fifth anniversary in 1978, a new fastback roofline and special two-tone paint were incorporated. The four-speed manual gearbox returned as standard equipment and the higher-output 5735cc (350cu in) V8 engine made a welcome return to the price lists. The Corvette, it seemed, had survived the 1970s with its pride intact.

ENGINE: 5360cc (327cu in), eight-cylinder
POWER: 360bhp (268kW)
0–60MPH (96KM/H): 6 seconds
TOP SPEED: 233km/h (145mph)
PRODUCTION TOTAL: 684,652

KAISER-DARRIN
UNITED STATES 1954–55

The Kaiser-Darrin was reputedly created as the result of an argument between the ill-tempered boss of Kaiser and his chief creative designer Darrin. In a fit of pique, Darrin ended up spending vast amounts of his own money designing a sleek glassfibre-bodied two-seater sports car at his California studio. The result was

the Kaiser-Darrin, featuring a 'pursed-lipped' front end and unusual doors that slid into the wings (fenders). Safety was a factor, and the car became one of the first to feature seat belts.

It did not go as well as it looked, thanks to a weak 90bhp single-carburettor six-cylinder Willys engine, and sold poorly as a result.

A hardtop, giving the car a reasonable-looking profile, could be fitted to replace the folding Landau hood, but, despite its oddball styling and interesting character, the car was a flop and only 435 were made.

The final 100 or so cars were fitted with supercharged Cadillac V8s. These lifted the Kaiser-Darrin

into supercar territory, thanks to its 224km/h (140mph) top speed.

ENGINE: 2638cc (161cu in), six-cylinder
POWER: 90bhp (67kW)
0–60MPH (96KM/H): 15.1 seconds
TOP SPEED: 157km/h (98mph)
PRODUCTION TOTAL: 435

SWALLOW DORETTI
UNITED KINGDOM 1954–55

William Lyons had sold Swallow to Tube Investments when he moved into car production with Jaguar. When the sidecar market went into terminal decline in the mid-1950s, Tube Investments decided to go into the car market with its own car, the Doretti.

With a bodyshell built in-house by Swallow, the Doretti had mechanicals borrowed from the

Triumph TR2, and this meant reliable and well-proven engines and gearboxes. A hand-made sheet-steel skin clothed a tubular frame with aluminium panels hung off it, and the interior was leather-trimmed. Boot (trunk) space might have been limited, but the car was great to drive and had a top speed of near 160km/h (100mph), thanks to the TR2's 1991cc (121cu in)

four-cylinder engine developing a healthy 90bhp (67kW).

Production costs were high and some of the engineering a little basic, and, with the TR2 £250 less, buyers were quick to plump for the more familiar Triumph. It was clear the company could never make money from building bespoke sports cars in such small numbers, so production was halted in 1955.

It made no effort to build a replacement, unwilling to lose further money in a tough market.

ENGINE: 1991cc (121cu in), four-cylinder
POWER: 90bhp (67kW)
0–60MPH (96KM/H): 13.4 seconds
TOP SPEED: 156km/h (97mph)
PRODUCTION TOTAL: 276

AUSTIN-HEALEY 100
UNITED KINGDOM 1953–56

The year 1953 saw the introduction of the first of what would become a long line of 'big' Healeys. These were considered by many to be the archetypal British sports cars – uncomplicated and brutal, but effective and great fun to drive.

The Donald Healey Motor Company had been in business since 1946, producing low-volume sports cars. It all changed, however, when Donald Healey spotted a gap in the market between MG and Jaguar, and soon had a small team working on a prototype – known

as the Healey Hundred in 1952. Geoffrey Healey (Donald's son) designed the chassis in conjunction with Barry Bilbie, and a relative newcomer to the company, Gerry Coker, devised the body styling. Donald Healey had the final say over the look of the car, and many

of the defining features of what was to become the 100, such as the reclining windscreen, came about through offhand comments and instructions from Healey.

Tickford built the prototype in aluminium, and the engine was a 2.6-litre (162cu in) six-cylinder unit. Much of the running gear was borrowed from the Austin A90 (Healey had previously used running gear from Riley, Alvis and various other sources), and the seats were a straight copy of those in Coker's Austin Seven.

The prototype was shaken down in Belgium in October 1952, and then returned to the United Kingdom in time for the 1952 Earls Court Motor Show in London. Legend has it that the prototype appeared on preview day as the Healey Hundred, but an overnight meeting between Donald Healey and Leonard Lord of Austin resulted in a deal that saw the car rebadged as the Austin-Healey 100 for the rest of the show. It seems, however, that Lord and Healey had already discussed such a deal.

While Healey built the pre-production 100s, and Donald Healey toured the United States drumming up orders for the new car, Austin geared up its Longbridge plant for a planned output of 200 Austin-Healey 100s a month. There were problems between the Healey designers and those at Austin, who had been instructed not to interfere with the original plans for the car.

The first 100 left the Longbridge production line in May 1953. Although production was slow to build, once it was up to speed, the

motoring press loved the 100, and orders really started to flood in. Helped by the publicity gained by racing in the Mille Miglia, Le Mans and Carrera Panamericana, the Healey was soon a roaring success.

A factory upgrade kit inspired by the Le Mans-specification racers was introduced – and could be ordered with any new Austin-Healey 100, or be retrofitted. These so-called 100Ms are very valuable today and, by 1955, had

become a regular production model. The legendary 100S also joined the range. A true competition car, it had lightweight aluminium panels, no bonnet (hood) or bumpers, a high-output engine and disc brakes front and rear.

In the same year, the 100 was upgraded from BN1 to BN2 specification, which featured a new four-speed overdrive gearbox (replacing the old three-speed one), improved front drum brakes

and higher front wheelarch cut-outs. This model continued in production until mid-1956, by which time the Austin-Healey 100 had already become legendary.

ENGINE: 2660cc (162cu in), four-cylinder
POWER: 90bhp (67kW)
0–60MPH (96KM/H): 10.3 seconds
TOP SPEED: 166km/h (103mph)
PRODUCTION TOTAL: 14,634

The six-cylinder Austin-Healeys are considered to be some of the most charismatic sportscars ever, thanks to fantastic engine note and superb handling.

DAIMLER SPORTSMAN

UNITED KINGDOM 1954–57

Based on the Consort, the original Regency was conceived as an attempt by Daimler to build a new generation of limousines. The car's production never got into its stride, however, and major series production eluded it. The Regency II limousine was Daimler's second effort – again effectively just a scaled-up Consort. At the top of this new range was the Sportsman saloon.

Stylistically, the Sportsman was differentiated from the standard limousine by its four headlights, a wraparound rear window and prominent tail fins. Transmission was by manual plus overdrive, but a more fitting automatic transmission was added to the range for the first time in 1957. The traditional pre-selector gearbox and fluid flywheel remained as the standard transmission system,

though. Sitting on the standard 290cm (114in) wheelbase, it used the Regency limousine's front coil spring and rear semi-elliptic leaf springs, but power was by the larger 4.5-litre (282cu in) straight-six engine. Performance was much improved, and the hefty car was capable of reaching a top speed of 152km/h (95mph) – braking was suitably uprated, too, with its hydraulic assistance.

The Sportsman proved that big cars need not be stuffy, and it paved the way perfectly for the impressive Conquest.

ENGINE: 4617cc (282cu in), six-cylinder
POWER: 140bhp (104kW)
0–60MPH (96KM/H): n/a
TOP SPEED: 152km/h (95mph)
PRODUCTION TOTAL: 75

FAIRTHORPE ATOM

UNITED KINGDOM 1954–57

Founded by Air Vice Marshal Don 'Pathfinder' Bennett, Fairthorpe was initially involved with the aircraft industry, and later became a pioneer manufacturer of glassfibre bodies. The company's first car was called the Atom, and Fairthorpe described it as having 'a very low total weight for what is in effect a reasonably spacious car' in its sales brochures.

The styling was attractive and promised much more than the range of chain-driven motorcycle engines that were offered with the car. Anzani's 322cc (20cu in) unit and BSA's 250cc (15cu in) and 350cc (21cu in) motors were cornerstones of the engine range, enabling the aerodynamic lightweight to reach a surprisingly high top speed of 121km/h

(75mph). The main sticking point for many customers, however, was that the Atom was a strange mish-mash of ideas, and that it closely resembled the widespread bubblecars that were taking off in Europe at the time.

It could not be denied that its low running costs were a major bonus, and, with independent suspension, it handled fairly well.

The Atom was replaced in 1957 by the Atomota, a more conventional car also available in kit form.

ENGINE: 646cc (39cu in), two-cylinder
POWER: 35bhp (26kW)
0–60MPH (96KM/H): 25 seconds
TOP SPEED: 120km/h (75mph)
PRODUCTION TOTAL: 44

There's no other word for it – the Fairthorpe Atom is simply bizarre. With its wing mounted headlamps and soap bar styling, there's little to touch it for idiosyncrasy. Rear mounted BSA single- or twin-cylinder engines provided the motivation.

JAGUAR XK140

UNITED KINGDOM 1954–57

ENGINE: 3442cc (210cu in),
    six-cylinder
POWER: 190bhp (142kW)
0–60MPH (96KM/H): 8.4 seconds
TOP SPEED: 200km/h (125mph)
PRODUCTION TOTAL: 9051

For those who thought the XK120 was going to be tough to replace, the appearance of the XK140 in 1954 proved that William Lyons knew exactly what he was doing. Although there were very few cosmetic differences between the two cars, there were upgrades galore under the skin to make this a better car to drive than its predecessor. Powered by more powerful versions of the XK twin-camshaft engine, steered by rack-and-pinion, and with the option of manual plus overdrive, how could it not be? The radiator grille was slightly modified (it had a couple of extra chrome spokes) and there were bigger bumpers, and the

widened body released much-needed cabin space – especially on the fixed and drophead coupés.

Weight was up, and the increase in power to 190bhp (142kW) was necessary in order to stop the new car being slower than the car that it replaced. Sadly, the brakes were still inadequate, and the steering remained excessively heavy.

As before, a more powerful SE version was offered, which used the cylinder head from the C-type, developing 210bhp (156kW), but these are very rare. Three bodystyles were offered for the XK140 – a roadster, a coupé and a drophead coupé.

Following a legend is always difficult to do – and Jaguar's XK120 replacement didn't quite manage to retain the purity of line that the 1948 car had, but it was still a very fine motorcar.

AUSTIN A40/A50/A55 CAMBRIDGE

ENGINE: 1489cc (91cu in),
four-cylinder
POWER: 50bhp (37kW)
0–60MPH (96KM/H): 28.8 seconds
TOP SPEED: 119km/h (74mph)
PRODUCTION TOTAL: 299,500

As much as middle England seemed to appreciate them, Austin's offerings during the 1950s were rapidly falling off the pace technically. The company was failing to keep up with new technology, and continued to produce solid family cars based on a separate chassis, despite its rivals moving away from this construction method.

Austin's medium saloons, the Counties range, fell into this category – but the end was in sight. When they were replaced by the Cambridge and the similarly styled Westminster in 1954 they ushered in a not-so-brave new world of unitary construction. It was an important step forward for Austin.

The A40 Cambridge continued to use the 1200cc (73cu in) Somerset engine, but the A50 used a new version of the B-series engine, bored out to 1489cc (91cu in). The running gear was modernized, with independent front suspension, hydraulic brakes and a four-speed column-change gearbox.

The A40 and A50 were both replaced by the A55 in 1957, but the traditional styling would last only a couple of more years, until the much sharper Farina style made an appearance in 1958. In van and pick-up form, the A55 lasted until 1971.

Austin's staple saloons of the late-1950s might not have been the most exciting cars technically, but they were honest, solid and loved by buyers.

FACEL VEGA FV

For a short time during the 1950s and 1960s, France had a flagship car that could hold its head high among the cream of the opposition. Brainchild of Jean Daninos, the owner of Forges et Ateliers de Construction d'Eure et Loire – or Facel for short – the manufacturer of high-quality metal products, the Facel Vega was an impressive machine.

The company carved a reputation building complete car bodies for Panhard, Simca and Ford France, but Daninos wanted to build his own GT cars. He realized his dream when he introduced his first in-house car, the Facel Vega FV.

The Vega was underpinned by a tubular chassis frame and powered by a 4.5-litre (274cu in) DeSoto V8 engine producing 180bhp (134kW). Transmission was by two-speed automatic gearbox (although a four-speed manual was available), and suspension was by coils and double wishbone upfront and a live rear axle on semi-elliptic springs at the rear.

Accommodation was impressive for a GT car, seating four in relative comfort. Performance was pretty handy, too, with rapid acceleration.

Still, the finely crafted bodywork overshadowed what lay beneath – it was stunning to look at.

ENGINE: 5801cc (354cu in),
eight-cylinder
POWER: 325bhp (262kW)
0–60MPH (96KM/H): 8.5 seconds
TOP SPEED: 209km/h (130mph)
PRODUCTION TOTAL: 357

MORRIS ISIS

By the time the Morris Isis replaced the Six in 1954, BMC's model rationalization process was well under way. Effectively an upmarket version of the mid-range Oxford, it was fitted with Austin's new C-series 2639cc (161cu in) six-cylinder engine. Styling was pretty similar to the Oxford's, but the bonnet (hood) was necessarily stretched to accommodate the longer engine – and beefed-up suspension and brakes were fitted.

The Traveller version was an early version of a people carrier, as it offered a third row of seats, allowing eight people to be carried in relative comfort. The Traveller also featured wood panelling around the load area. Performance was reasonable, but handling lacked the finesse of its smaller cousins, and sales were slow as a result.

When the Oxford was restyled in 1956, the Isis was remodelled to match, and the wood-lined estate (station wagon) was dropped from the line-up. Power output was raised to 90bhp (67kW). Effectively the car was marking time until the introduction of the Farina-bodied replacement in 1958.

ENGINE: 2639cc (161cu in),
six-cylinder
POWER: 86bhp (64kW) at 4250rpm
0–60MPH (96KM/H): 17.8 seconds
TOP SPEED: 142km/h (88mph)
PRODUCTION TOTAL: 12,155

AUSTIN A90/A95/A105 WESTMINSTER

ENGINE: 2639cc (161cu in),
  six-cylinder
POWER: 92bhp (69kW)
0–60MPH (96KM/H): 19.8 seconds
TOP SPEED: 145km/h (90mph)
PRODUCTION TOTAL: 60,400

The formula that made up the Austin Westminster was simple and very effective. Take a straight-six engine and install it in a semi-upmarket saloon with plenty of resemblance to its smaller cousins, and you end up with a solid entry in the middle-class sector of the market. And it was a success.

Following on from where the A70 Hereford had left off, the A90 Westminster looked like the A40 and A50 Cambridge, but only the doors were actually interchangeable between the models. The A90 Westminster was significantly larger and its C-series six-cylinder unit was suitable for its role.

In 1956, the Westminster became the A95 and A105, and both were differentiated from their predecessor by their larger rear window, a squarer rear wing (fender) line and a new grille. The A95 gained a bit more power, but the A105 was the star of the range, featuring twin carburettors.

The Westminster range may have looked like a merely upscaled version of the Cambridge, but the smooth six-cylinder engine felt a lot more cultured.

The A105 also had lowered suspension, overdrive as standard and two-tone paint. A badge-engineered Vanden Plas version of the Westminster was also built.

MERCEDES-BENZ 220 PONTON

Called the Ponton (meaning 'pontoon' in German) because of its unitary construction (first used on its predecessor, the slightly smaller four-cylinder 180 of 1953), the 220 was a further step towards modernity for Mercedes-Benz.

The Ponton featured a full-width body, integrated headlights, a six-cylinder engine and longer 'alligator' bonnet (hood), as well as a wraparound windscreen. The brakes became servo-assisted a year after production started, and the 220S Ponton, introduced in 1956, gained twin carburettors and more power. In the same year, the shorter wheelbase 219 also appeared.

The 220 Ponton coupé and convertible bodystyles made their debut at the 1955 Frankfurt Motor Show and entered production with the more powerful twin-carburettor 'S' engine in 1956, and with the 'SE' fuel-injected engine in 1958. The 220 Series sold well and helped to establish Mercedes-Benz's reputation for thorough engineering and excellent build quality. The first-class dealer back-up and customer service were also strong points of the company highlighted by these cars – and export success followed.

The coupé and convertible versions remain the most sought after of the 220 Ponton range, and they fetch high prices from collectors today because of their rarity – only 7345 were built.

ENGINE: 2195cc (134cu in),
  six-cylinder
POWER: 85bhp (63kW)
0–60MPH (96KM/H): 15.2 seconds
TOP SPEED: 162km/h (101mph)
PRODUCTION TOTAL: 116,406

WOLSELEY 6/90

The Wolseley 6/90 was part of a badge-engineered pair of cars that included the Riley Pathfinder. Both cars shared the same styling, as well as the same basic chassis and suspension units. This meant torsion-bar independent front suspension with a rear axle located by coil spring and damper units, semi-trailing arms and a Panhard rod. When the 6/90 was launched it was powered by the new BMC straight-six 2639cc (161cu in) C-series engine, which in the Wolseley produced 95bhp (71kW).

Nice touches were the column-mounted four-speed gearbox, and twin carburettors. Solid build quality and performance resulted in the car becoming synonymous with British police forces, and regular film appearances in that role.

The Series II arrived in October 1955, updated with half-elliptic rear suspension and a floor-mounted gearchange. Eight months later, the Mk III appeared, and added servo-assisted brakes to the specification sheet.

ENGINE: 2639cc (161cu in), six-cylinder
POWER: 95bhp (71kW)
0–60MPH (96KM/H): 18.1 seconds
TOP SPEED: 150km/h (94mph)
PRODUCTION TOTAL: 11,852

MORRIS OXFORD/COWLEY

After disappearing during the 1930s, the Cowley name made a welcome return to Morris price lists in 1954. Effectively, it was an entry-level version of the Oxford, Morris's new mid-range saloon. Significantly, these were the first all-new models built since Morris and Austin merged in 1952 to form the British Motor Corporation (BMC).

The Oxford/Cowley was designed by Alec Issigonis and, as a result, was up to date in many aspects.

The bulbous styling hid unitary construction, and interior accommodation was good for its size. The Oxford was powered by the new B-series 1489cc (91cu in) engine, and the more basic Cowley had the smaller 1200cc (73cu in)

version under its bonnet (hood). Both received a face-lift for 1956, and the 1489cc (91cu in) engine was standardized across the range.

In 1957, there was another restyle, and the Cowley became the Traveller estate (station wagon). After the introduction of the Morris-badged Farina saloons in 1959, the Traveller remained in

production; however, when the Farina estate appeared in 1960, the Traveller was quietly dropped.

ENGINE: 1489cc (91cu in), four-cylinder
POWER: 40.5bhp (30kW) at 4200rpm
0–60MPH (96KM/H): 29 seconds
TOP SPEED: 122km/h (76mph)
PRODUCTION TOTAL: 167,494

BORGWARD ISABELLA

ENGINE: 1498cc (91cu in), four-cylinder
POWER: 75bhp (56kW)
0–60MPH (96KM/H): 17.4 seconds
TOP SPEED: 150km/h (93mph)
PRODUCTION TOTAL: 202,862

Fondly regarded today as an elegantly understated saloon that should have sold more, the Isabella was Borgward's staple product during the latter half of

the 1950s. More importantly, it sold moderately enough to keep the company afloat during those financially trying times.

In standard form, the Isabella was offered in saloon or estate (station-wagon) form, and was a technically conservative evolution of the earlier Hansa model. Its name came about because Borgward engineers wanted to put a badge on a pre-production model to disguise the car's origins and not run the risk of being identified

when testing on public roads. Carl Borgward suggested Isabella – his wife's name – and it stuck.

Despite being based on the Hansa, the Isabella was advanced for its time. It featured aluminium alloy construction and boasted fine build quality. Separate front and rear rubber-mounted subframes for improved noise insulation were a nice touch, too.

The saloon version was followed up by the launch of coupé and convertible models, which seemed

to suit perfectly the curvaceous, glamorous style of the marque. The 1498cc (91cu in) engines might not have endowed sparkling performance, but did little to dent the car's solid all-round appeal.

The Isabella was an advanced saloon that sadly died before its time. Thoroughly engineered and technically conservative, it was offered as a saloon, estate, convertible or coupe.

SIMCA VEDETTE

The Vedette may have started out life as a Ford, but French buyers would take the car to their hearts once it appeared under new management. Although the Ford Vedette had been around since 1949, it enjoyed little success, so, when Simca bought the French subsidiary in 1954, Simca's version soon followed. The Gallic Vedette shared little with its ancestor – just

the name and the flathead V8. The new car boasted monocoque construction, but remained conservative, thanks to leaf spring rear suspension and rear-wheel drive. Technically, it did not set the world alight, but the company's rivals certainly sat up and noticed.

When the cars first appeared in 1954, they were badged as Fords and came in three trim levels.

Trianon was the base model, followed by the Versailles and the top model, the Regence. There was also an estate (station wagon) called the Marly. Performance was not a strong point, thanks to a weedy 84bhp (63kW) from its 2353cc (144cu in) side-valve engine, but it was reliable and pleasant to drive. The three-speed gearbox was a bit of a disappointment.

French Vedette production ended in 1961, but the tooling was shipped to Brazil, where the car was made until the end of the 1960s.

ENGINE: 2353cc (144cu in), eight-cylinder
POWER: 84bhp (63kW)
0–60MPH (96KM/H): 18.4 seconds
TOP SPEED: 146km/h (91mph)
PRODUCTION TOTAL: 166,895

FERRARI 250GT

ENGINE: 2953cc (180cu in),
12-cylinder
POWER: 240bhp (179kW)
0–60MPH (96KM/H): 7 seconds
TOP SPEED: 202km/h (126mph)
PRODUCTION TOTAL: 1811

With the 250 range, Ferrari finally hit the big time. It was an important step for the company in several respects because it was the first Ferrari built in relatively large numbers, and it was the company's first road car with disc brakes. As well as that, the 250 was the first four-seat Ferrari and the first commercially available mid-engined Ferrari – and it was a proven race winner.

The 250 GT Europa had a 2953cc (180cu in) V12 engine developing 240bhp (179kW), and was followed in 1956 by the 250 GT Boano & Ellena (26 were built by Boano in Turin; the remaining 49 by Ellena the following year). Disc brakes later became standard equipment, and, in 1958, the introduction of the Pininfarina 250 GT coupé sent shockwaves through the industry – a total of 343 were built.

The Pininfarina-designed 2+2/ GTE arrived in 1960, and became

Ferrari's first production four-seater. The V12 engine was moved forwards, to create more space for passengers. It proved a big hit with customers, and 950 were built. The final 250 GT in 1962

was the Lusso, which had a shorter 240cm (94in) wheelbase, but more luxurious trim. Built by Scaglietti, the car had the familiar 2953cc (180cu in) unit, tuned to produce 250bhp (186kW).

The 250GT will be remembered as the car that immortalized Ferrari as a producer of the world's finest road going supercars. With a three-litre V12, it was fast and sounded great.

AC ACECA

Following on from the successful Ace model, AC produced the Aceca as a way of hopefully extending sales and encouraging new buyers to the marque. Initially, AC had experimented with

a glassfibre hardtop version of the Ace, but it was a technical failure, thanks to heat build-up and noise inside the car. In the end, the company persisted with the idea and embarked upon an extensive

re-engineering project, giving birth to the Aceca coupé.

The Ace's basic tubular chassis was retained for the new model, as was much of the bodywork, but the doors were enlarged and

strengthened with ash framing. A new fastback roof, fashioned out of aluminium and supported by an extra tubular framework, was added up top. To reduce noise, heat and fumes, the company's engineers developed a full-width bulkhead from glassfibre, to sit between the engine bay and the cockpit.

A novel feature was the rear hatchback, making the Aceca the second British sports car to boast this feature after the Aston Martin DB2/4. Refinement was helped by the carpeted wood-lined interior, excellent ventilation and demister systems, leather upholstery and wood trimmings, making the Aceca an effective grand tourer.

ENGINE: 1971cc (120cu in),
six-cylinder
POWER: 125bhp (93kW)
0–60MPH (96KM/H): 9.0 seconds
TOP SPEED: 189km/h (117mph)
PRODUCTION TOTAL: 328

AC's Aceca was a step upmarket for the long-lived specialist producer of sportscars. Underneath it was almost identical to the Ace, but the fastback roof and rear hatchback gave it real GT potential.

MERCEDES-BENZ 190SL

GERMANY 1954–63

Although the Mercedes-Benz looks simply like a smaller version of the considerably more glamorous 300SL, underneath that beautiful styling with its blistered wheelarches and purposeful grille, the two cars could not have been more different. The 190 was based on a shortened version of the saloon 180, and was a very conventional car.

Whereas the 300SL had a powerful six-cylinder engine, the 190 made do with a twin-carburettor version of the standard 1.9-litre (116cu in) overhead-camshaft unit, producing an ordinary 105bhp (78kW). Gone also was the column gearchange – a more conventional floor-mounted gearlever was fitted to the 190SL.

Aimed at the American market, the 190SL was expensive for what

it was and not particularly good to drive either, despite offering a firm ride from its all-round independent suspension. It was pretty, however, and it sold reasonably well for what it was – and, although it was no competition car, its prices remain high today.

The car received a slight face-lift in 1955, and was fitted with servo-assisted brakes a year later. A coupé version (without gullwing doors, sadly) was also offered, as well as a roadster with the option of a removable hardtop.

ENGINE: 1897cc (116cu in), four-cylinder
POWER: 105bhp (78kW)
0–60MPH (96KM/H): 13.3 seconds
TOP SPEED: 168km/h (105mph)
PRODUCTION TOTAL: 25,881

What appeared to be a smaller version of the 300SL, the Mercedes-Benz 190SL was in fact nowhere near as desirable. Its engine lacked power, the handling had little finesse, but it looked a million dollars.

MERCEDES-BENZ 300SL

GERMANY 1954–63

The Mercedes-Benz 300SL (Sport Leicht, 'leicht' meaning 'light') is arguably one of the most beautiful cars ever made – and the impact it had on the motor industry when it first appeared in 1954 was considerable.

Boasting breathtaking styling, sensational gullwing doors, and performance to match, the 300SL was considered by many to be the world's first modern supercar. The car's roots can be found in the sports racing prototype, the W194. This car appeared in 1952, and, powered by the 300S's impressive fuel-injected six-cylinder engine, and coupled with a complex multi-tube spaceframe chassis, it drove like a true thoroughbred.

Only 10 were made, but it still managed to take victory in the Carrera Panamericana and Le Mans 24-Hour. A road-car version code-named the W198 was conceived to capitalize on these successes and duly followed two years later.

The 300SL had true dream car qualities – the gullwing doors were created to maintain structural integrity, and the low, sweeping bonnet (hood) to maintain the car's aerodynamic qualities. The production version was unveiled in New York, and stunned customers loved its refined appearance, sensational proportions and Bosch fuel-injected 240bhp (179kW) powerplant. Much of the car's underpinnings were derived from the previous 300.

It was not cheap, costing similar money to the Jaguar XK140, and its dynamics left a lot to be desired, thanks to a tendency to oversteer, which was largely down to its lively swing-axle rear suspension. The 300SL needed a skilled driver to get the most from it, and the complex spaceframe construction meant that it was hugely expensive to repair.

After a production run of just 1400 cars, the 300SL Gullwing was replaced by a roadster version in 1957. Although it lost the sensational looks of its coupé predecessor, the 300SL roadster had improved low-pivot rear swing axle suspension, a modified spaceframe and a slightly more powerful fuel-injected engine –

and, in many ways, was the better car. Despite being a better car to live with, the convertible had lost much of the 300SL's original purity. Still, it was a sales success – 1858 cars found buyers before production finally ceased in 1962.

As with the gullwing it replaced, the bodyshell, doors, bonnet and boot (trunk) lid were made from lightweight alloy. Twenty-nine all-alloy bodied cars were also made, and these proved themselves in competition, including success in the 1955 Mille Miglia event, where a car finished fifth.

The same basic engine became the backbone for Mercedes' production car range until the end of the 1960s, when new 3.5-litre (214cu in) and 4.5-litre (275cu in)

V8 units replaced it. The use of gullwing doors, however, remained peculiar to the 300SL, although the De Lorean DMC12 later mimicked it.

The 300SL's potential top speed was a claimed 264km/h (165mph), but a more realistic estimate was 248km/h (155mph) – which still made it one of the world's fastest cars. When the roadster was discontinued in 1962, the 230SL Pagoda replaced it, and the SL legend was in good hands.

ENGINE: 2996cc (183cu in), six-cylinder
POWER: 240bhp (179kW)
0–60MPH (96KM/H): 8.8 seconds
TOP SPEED: 224km/h (140mph)
PRODUCTION TOTAL: 3258

Fast and expensive, the Mercedes-Benz 300SL is one of the most recognizable classics – especially when those gullwing doors are open.

ALFA ROMEO GIULIETTA

Rather unusually, when Alfa Romeo decided to launch its new range of family cars, it chose to unveil the coupé version first. The Giulietta appeared in 1954 and was the first in a line of cars that would eventually include a saloon, Spider and several bespoke derivatives. Each version may have looked very different, but they were all based on the same floorpan. The coupé was designed and built by Bertone, using a twin-camshaft 1290cc (79cu in) engine (later increased to 1570cc/96cu in on the Giulia Sprint version from 1962). A Sprint Veloce later appeared, which was powered by the same 1290cc (79cu in) engine tuned to produce an amazing 90bhp (67kW) – or 100bhp (75kW) in twin-carburettor Speciale form.

The Berlina arrived a year later and had plenty of interior room, but stll remained fun to drive. In 74bhp (55kW) TI guise, which appeared in 1957, the Giulietta was a genuine sports saloon. The legendary Spider, which featured attractive open-top bodywork by Pininfarina, then joined the range completing the Giulietta range.

The 1.6 Giulia Spider replaced the open-topped Giulietta in 1962, and offered a much more torquey engine, as well as a five-speed gearbox. Much faster Veloce versions of the Spider and Giulia were offered; these remain sought after and highly prized today.

ENGINE: 1290cc (79cu in), four-cylinder
POWER: 65bhp (48kW)
0–60MPH (96KM/H): 13 seconds
TOP SPEED: 154km/h (96mph)
PRODUCTION TOTAL: 258,672

CHRYSLER C300

Forever associated with the legendary 'Hemi' V8 engines; the Chrysler C300 remains potent and charismatic to this day. It was the first genuine muscle car produced by Chrysler – not surprising with 300bhp (224kW) on tap.

Generally regarded as the first American 'muscle car', the Chrysler C300 was powered by a grunty 5425cc (331cu in) Hemi V8. With two four-barrel carburettors (and, in full race specification, camshaft) with solid lifters, special manifolds and large-diameter dual exhausts, power was a very respectable 300bhp (224kW).

Combining this rather powerful engine with a modified PowerFlite automatic transmission was an inspired move by Chrysler and guaranteed that the C300 could be driven quickly and smoothly by anyone. Suspension was uprated to cope with the demands put on it, with a heavy-duty suspension set-up and Blue Streak racing tyres.

The C300 was an exclusive car available in just three colours: black, red and white. Inside, leather upholstery was standard, and the car was only ever available as a two-door hardtop. At the front of the vehicle was an imposing Imperial model-type grille.

Part of its muscle-car image was the lack of a door mirror – the driver of a 300 was supposedly never going to need to watch out for faster cars coming up from behind. The C300 was able to win both the NASCAR Grand National and AAA stock car racing championships. The legend of the Chrysler 'letter' cars and, indeed, the great American muscle car had been born – and would live on for many years to come.

ENGINE: 5425cc (331cu in), eight-cylinder
POWER: 300bhp (224kW)
0-60MPH (96KM/H): 9 seconds
TOP SPEED: 206km/h (128mph)
PRODUCTION TOTAL: 1725

HRG TWIN CAMSHAFT

In the mid-1950s, HRG, a producer of traditional sports cars, investigated the possibility of developing a contemporary sports car – the result was known as the Twin Camshaft. In terms of styling, it really was a step forward, with its modern-looking lightweight alloy racing body, which had been bolted to a twin-tube chassis. Independent suspension all-round, four-wheel disc brakes and novel magnesium alloy wheels meant that it drove as well as it looked.

Powered by a modified 1497cc (91cu in) HRG twin camshaft engine, based on a Singer SM block, the lightweight sports car could power to a very impressive 184km/h (115mph) – excellent for a car of its size. Although it seemed to have all the ingredients for success, demand for the HRG Twin Camshaft was extremely sadly lacking, and buyers were put off by what they saw as excessive cost and complexity. Subsequently, existing HRG enthusiasts seemed to be generally ignoring the car, despite its long list of merits.

Only four examples ever left the Surrey factory before the company finally gave up making cars altogether and, consequently, the blisteringly quick roadster is extremely sought after today.

ENGINE: 1497cc (91cu in), four-cylinder
POWER: 108bhp (80kW)
0–60MPH (96KM/H): n/a
TOP SPEED: 184km/h (115mph)
PRODUCTION TOTAL: 4

TRIUMPH TR3

The Triumph TR line was all about evolution and refining of the breed – so, although there was very little to distinguish the TR3 from the TR2, it was usefully improved. The new name gave more clues to the improvements than the styling, but behind the new egg-crate grille covering the radiator-cooling intake was a more powerful engine, developing 5bhp (3.5kW) more than its previous incarnation, thanks to its bigger SU carburettors. In addition to that, a Le Mans-type head was available, upping the power to a handy 100bhp (75kW).

The main development, however, came in 1956, when it became the first British car to be fitted with disc brakes, made by Girling, as standard. Further improvements were not long in coming. For 1957, the styling was updated to include a full-length grille and, finally, external door handles. This

model was known as the TR3A, and it remained in production until 1962.

Sales of the TR3 picked up as a result of the improvements, and the United States became an

important export market as it took notice. A short-lived US-market-only TR3B version appeared in 1962, powered by the 2138cc (130cu in) engine; it remained on sale after the launch of the TR4.

ENGINE: 1991cc (121cu in), four-cylinder
POWER: 100bhp (75kW) at 4800rpm
0–60MPH (96KM/H): 12.0 seconds
TOP SPEED: 169km/h (105mph)
PRODUCTION TOTAL: 74,944

The TR3 looked a lot like the TR2 that immediately preceded it, but under the skin there were many notable changes to make it a far more drivable car. The most significant development came in 1956 when Girling discs were fitted as standard.

DKW 3=6 MONZA COUPE

GERMANY 1956–59

The DKW 3=6 had picked up a string of victories in European touring car racing, when two of its drivers decided to turn it into a road car by developing a sports body for it. Günther Ahrens and AW Mantzel designed a record-breaking car based on the 3=6, clothed in a lightweight plastic

body specially manufactured by Dannenhauer & Stauss.

The 980cc (60cu in) engine was tuned to deliver more than 50bhp (37kW) for racing purposes, but some engines reached 100bhp (75kW). Several long-distance speed records were set at Monza, Italy, in December 1956.

A limited edition of about 230 of these models was made and called 'Monza'. Heidelberg DKW dealer Fritz Wenk had them built. These cars used a 55bhp (41kW) 980cc (60cu in) engine, which could deliver a top speed of 161km/h (100mph). Luckily, the car's handling was as impressive as its

speed, but only a handful of these cars were sold.

ENGINE: 980cc (60cu in), three-cylinder
POWER: 50bhp (37kW)
0–60MPH (96KM/H): 25 seconds
TOP SPEED: 135km/h (84mph)
PRODUCTION TOTAL: 230

PEGASO Z103

SPAIN 1955–58

Moving up a gear from the impressive Z102, Pegaso's new Z103 was claimed by its maker to be one of the most advanced performance cars ever made; however, the technology used in the car was a retrograde step compared to its predecessor.

The Z103 used the same steel bodywork construction methods as the Z102, but was lighter

because of intelligent weight reduction. That made it a faster but scarier car to drive, with a very unstable back end and severely limited grip.

The V8 engine put out masses of power (as much as 400bhp/298kW was rumoured in tuned cars), but it was a simple overhead-valve unit compared with the Z102's complex but fascinating

quad camshaft set-up. Despite the immense power output and Formula One–style production technology, these Pegasos never really enjoyed successful competition. By the late 1950s, Don Wilfredo Ricart began to concentrate on the firm's core output of trucks and buses.

In eight years, Pegaso had built just over 100 sports cars and

proved that Ricart could build a suitable alternative to Ferrari – but at what cost?

ENGINE: 3988cc (243cu in), eight-cylinder
POWER: 350bhp (261kW)
0–60MPH (96KM/H): 5.5 seconds
TOP SPEED: 274km/h (170mph)
PRODUCTION TOTAL: 112 (incl. Z102)

BMW 503

GERMANY 1955–59

ENGINE: 3168cc (193cu in),
  eight-cylinder
POWER: 140bhp (104kW)
0–60MPH (96KM/H): n/a
TOP SPEED: 190km/h (118mph)
PRODUCTION TOTAL: 412

BMW might have been struggling for survival in the 1950s, but the 503 remained one of the most effective upmarket sporting cars

money could buy. It topped the BMW range, which could not have been more unbalanced, with this range of luxury cars at one end of the spectrum, and the tiny Isetta microcar at the other – and nothing in between.

The glorious-looking 503 was designed by Count Albrecht Goertz, a man who years later was closely involved in the best–selling Datsun 240Z, among many others. The 503 was sold alongside the

curvaceous 501 and 502 saloon models, and used the same running gear as the 502 (including the V8 engine).

The long and angular-looking cabriolet featured protruding headlights and a tall, bulbous version of the BMW kidney grille; this was an exceptionally good-looking car. It was much lighter than the 501 and 502, so the V8 engine had been uprated to produce 140bhp (104kW), making

The BMW 503 may have looks to die for, and was very nice to drive, but it very nearly ended up killing the company that produced it.

it fast and enjoyable to drive.

The price tag matched the exclusive looks – and, as a result, the car found few buyers. Despite its contemporary styling, the BMW 503 proved an expensive disaster.

FERRARI 250 GT BERLINETTA 'TOUR DE FRANCE'

ITALY 1955–59

This car was so named because of the 250GT's victories in the road race of that name in 1957, 1958 and 1959. Ferrari celebrated the fact that it had achieved what it set out to with this version of the car – achieve competition success. The 250 GT Berlinetta 'Tour de France' was created specifically as a result of Ferrari's experiences with the 250 Mille Miglia and the 250 Europa.

Power came from the Colombo designed 3-litre (180cu in) V12, which progressively increased its power output over the years from 240bhp (179kW) to 260bhp

So-called because of Ferrari's successes in road racing, the 250GT 'Tour De France' was distinguished by its particularly effective fastback styling.

(194kW) at the height of the model's success on the track.

The first official car was originally a 250 GT Europa with an all-aluminium body built by Pininfarina in 1955 for competition, but was not released until a year later.

Pininfarina built three more 250 GTs during 1955 that were 250 MM lookalikes. In 1956, specialist builder Scaglietti unveiled its own prototype with distinctive 14-louvre panels at the bottom of the front wings (fenders), but production of these competition-orientated 250GTs was now the sole responsibility of Scaglietti in Modena.

However, Zagato also built special-bodied coupé versions of this car for their customers to use on the road.

ENGINE: 2953cc (180cu in), 12-cylinder
POWER: 260bhp (194kW)
0–60MPH (96KM/H): 7 seconds
TOP SPEED: 202km/h (126mph)
PRODUCTION TOTAL: 84

JAGUAR MK I

Although never officially known as the Jaguar Mk 1, these saloons became commonly known by this moniker as a result of the widespread success of the 1959 Mk 2. It might have lived in the shadow of the later car, but the 1955 Mk 1 was actually a tremendously important car, as it spearheaded Jaguar's entry into the lucrative small luxury car market. It was influential in shaping the company's future because it was compact and good to drive – and

quick, too, thanks to the lusty XK engine. Featuring unitary construction, early Mk 1s were heavy-looking and had rear wheel spats, deep side panels, smaller windows and wide wraparound chrome bumpers.

The short-stroke version of Jaguar's twin-camshaft six-cylinder engine came with manual with overdrive or a poor-quality standard automatic transmission. Suspension was by effective independent coils and springs.

The range expanded, and the 3.4-litre (207cu in) version appeared in 1957. This delivered 210bhp (156kW) and gave the Mk 1 a real turn of speed and a 192km/h (120mph) top speed. These later, more powerful cars were distinguished by a slightly wider grille, cutaway rear spats and wire wheels.

At the same time, all-round disc brakes were introduced on all models. Soon after, the 2.4-litre version also gained the wider grille.

ENGINE: 2483cc (152cu in), six-cylinder
POWER: 112bhp (83kW)
0–60MPH (96KM/H): 14.1 seconds
TOP SPEED: 162km/h (101mph)
PRODUCTION TOTAL: 37,397

The Mk I started the long and successful line of compact sporting saloons that revolutionized Jaguar's image.

SIATA AMICA

The Societa Italiana Applicazione Transformazione Automobilistiche (Siata) was a tuning company set up by amateur racing driver Giorgio Ambrosini in 1926, with a view to making Fiats go faster – and, because of the focus on Fiats until now, it was no surprise that, when the company branched into car production, it would use mainly Fiat parts. Until the Amica arrived, Siata had not

sold many cars. As it was a small independent company that made most of its money from tuning, this did not matter much. It was not trying to be a mass-producer, and its expertise lay in selling performance equipment.

Launched in 1950, the Amica was a two-seater available as either a coupé or a roadster, and was the company's first serious effort at a standalone car. Suspension was

courtesy of Fiat, but Siata developed the tubular chassis. At the front was independent suspension with a transverse leaf spring and lower wishbones, while at the back, there was a live axle suspended by quarter-elliptic springs.

Power was also provided by Fiat, its 500 engine being available in various states of tune, including a 26bhp (19kW) 750cc (46cu in) version. Sales were sluggish,

however, and, when the company branched into the United States with a Crossley-engined model, few buyers were interested.

ENGINE: 596cc (36cu in), four-cylinder
POWER: 22bhp (16kW)
0–60MPH (96KM/H): n/a
TOP SPEED: about 100km/h (62mph)
PRODUCTION TOTAL: n/a

DEUTSCH-BONNET HBR

Charles Deutsch and René Bonnet were enthusiasts who decided to make their own Citroën-based sports and racing cars, with their first cars unveiled at the 1952 Paris Motor Show. Their first cars were road-going coupés, but, in 1955, a wider selection of models was made available. The standard Deutsch-Bonnet was the fascinating HBR luxe. Available in two- or four-seat versions, and powered by either a basic 750cc (46cu in) two-cylinder engine or supercharged 1100cc (67cu in) or 1300cc (79cu in) units, these cars were custom built to order.

Based on the chassis of the Dyna-Panhard, and clothed with glassfibre bodyshells, the cars looked fresh and modern. Their downward-sloping noses were particularly contemporary.

By 1957, there were just two engine options, a base 750cc (46cu in) unit and an 850cc (52cu in) unit, both twin-cylinder motors. Despite their low power, these cars could reach a high top speed of 144km/h (90mph). This efficiency was down to excellent aerodynamics and a supremely small frontal area.

ENGINE: 851cc (52cu in), four-cylinder
POWER: 55bhp (41kW)
0–60MPH (96KM/H): 21 seconds
TOP SPEED: 144km/h (90mph)
PRODUCTION TOTAL: n/a

LLOYD 600

The West German Lloyd company was a subsidiary of Borgward, and existed as a separate company merely to allow its parent to claim a larger allowance of steel, as the distribution of this was being strictly rationed by the government and two companies would be entitled to more.

Despite that, and because of these shortages, Lloyds were made from fabric body panels stretched over a wooden frame. The prices were low, and the cars very economical to own.

They also featured twin-cylinder air-cooled engines. The bigger engined LP600 version, introduced in 1955, featured an all-new four-stroke overhead-camshaft two-cylinder engine. After 1957, it was renamed the Alexander and gained fully independent suspension and a four-speed gearbox, with the added option of Saxomat automatic transmission. Quicker off the mark than its main rival, the popular Volkswagen Beetle, due to its lightweight construction, it had a higher price, which saw its success wane as the 1950s progressed.

A van-like version called the LT600 was added to the range to give it more appeal, as well as a smart-looking convertible, but were not enough to save the company.

ENGINE: 596cc (36cu in), two-cylinder
POWER: 19bhp (14kW)
0–60MPH (96KM/H): n/a
TOP SPEED: 99km/h (62mph)
PRODUCTION TOTAL: 176,524

MGA

Few companies make quantum leaps in their history, with most generations of cars being a solid evolution of the last. When the stylish MGA first appeared, however, it was every bit as important to MG's development as a sportscar manufacturer as the DS was to Citroën's continued existence.

The MGA was a particularly pretty car and managed to usher in a new era of modernity for the Abingdon-based manufacturer. And it did so with clever use of a large number of mechanical components borrowed from other cars in the BMC range. A major leap forward was its independent front suspension and rack-and-pinion steering – the first appearance of these on an MG sports car. The body was heavy and meant that the MGA was difficult to steer and stop, especially with drum brakes all round. The earliest models also had the ubiquitous 1489cc (91cu in) B-Series engine, which provided steady performance. Luckily the car was entertaining to drive, while a range of tuning accessories made it quicker.

The 0–60mph (96km/h) was 15 seconds, which was reasonable, although its looks promised so much more. Undeniably the styling was the MG's most modern aspect. Derived from a special 1954 Le Mans car, based on the MG TD and

With its aerodynamic looks, the MGA was stylistically a quantum leap forward over the existing Midget range of cars.

built on a strengthened box-section chassis, the car was designed from the outset to have a slippery, aerodynamic appearance.

A fixed-head coupé model joined the line-up in 1956 and offered better aerodynamics, but the trade-off was a cramped and claustrophobic cabin, a problem helped significantly in 1960 by the introduction of proper sliding windows. Both cars drove similarly impressively and ensured MG's continued popularity. In 1959, both the coupé and roadster received the power they deserved when the

B-Series was upgraded from 1489cc (91cu in) to 1588cc (97cu in). Maximum power was now 80bhp (60kW), and it was the right time for front disc brakes to be fitted.

Harry Weslake developed a new twin-camshaft head for the B-Series engine, and it was offered as option for two years in the late 1950s. Only 2111 MGA Twin Cams were made, and, although they were impressively quick, with 108bhp (80kW) on tap and a top speed of 177km/h (110mph), they suffered from engine fragility. Piston damage was the major

problem and consequently few survive today. Lightweight wheels with centre-spinners, all-round disc brakes and a slightly modified bonnet (hood) distinguished the Twin Camshaft model.

A more modern Mk II was launched in 1961. Visual changes were minor, limited to different rear light clusters and a recessed radiator grille. The B-Series block was further bored out to 1622cc (99cu in), upping the power to 86bhp (64kW). All-round discs brakes were added as an option on the De Luxe models. The Mk II was

the better car to drive, thanks to more flexible engine response.

The final MGA rolled off the production line in 1962, to make way for Britain's most successful sports car ever, the MGB – although many people argue the earlier car is the more pretty.

ENGINE: 1489cc (91cu in), four-cylinder
POWER: 72bhp (54kW)
0–60MPH (96KM/H): 15 seconds
TOP SPEED: 138km/h (100mph)
PRODUCTION TOTAL: 101,081

FORD THUNDERBIRD

UNITED STATES 1955–63

Think of the Ford Thunderbird as Uncle Henry's answer to the Chevrolet Corvette and you will not be a million miles away. The new car was also introduced, however, to slow the tide of British sports cars into the United States, led by the Jaguar XK120.

Introduced in 1955, the car had style, refinement and V8 power – and that was enough to make it an irresistible proposition for most buyers. Available only in open-topped form, the Thunderbird also came with the option of distinctive removable hardtop with circular porthole windows. The new car was underpinned with conventional parts from the Mainline and Fairlane models.

In 1956, a larger V8 option with 5113cc (312cu in) and 225bhp (168kW) was offered, indicating that Ford took performance seriously. Next year was when the fun began, however, with the introduction of the Y-block V8-powered models – the E-code 312

V8 was rated at a cool 270bhp (201kW). The F-code 312 V8 added a supercharger to produce 300bhp (224kW), and 340bhp (253kW) with the optional NASCAR 'racing kit'. The following year saw what, for enthusiasts, will always be the classic Thunderbird introduced.

The new-generation Thunderbird that came next had four seats, and a hardtop coupé as well as the convertible bodystyle. It became known as the 'Squarebird'. Engine choices widened – all-new 5768cc (352cu in) V8 and 7046cc (430cu in) V8 options were introduced. All of these things helped sales. A special 'Golden Edition' hardtop was unveiled in 1960 and featured America's first post-war sliding steel sunroof.

Third-generation Thunderbirds arrived in 1961 and sported a brave new look, which earned the nickname 'Projectile Birds', thanks to the quad headlighted arrow-front and modest fins above huge round taillights. One innovation

was the 'Swing Away' steering wheel, which would pivot to the side when the car was parked – the idea never took off.

The two-seat Thunderbird made a return the following year. A Sports Roadster package, which featured a glassfibre tone cover, designed by Bud Kaufman, covered the rear seat and effectively transformed the four-seat Thunderbird into a roadster. The tone cover even featured twin headrests, which flowed back to the rear, but the convertible top could still operate even with the cover in place. The package also included a dash-mounted grab bar for the passenger, and wire wheels.

Ford catered to the enthusiasts by offering a special 'M-code' 6391cc (390cu in) FE V8 rated at 340bhp (253kW). It featured three Holley two-barrel carburettors and an aluminium manifold, which kept the carburettors level and at the same height. Only 145 Thunderbirds were built with the

The Thunderbird is one of Ford's most famous products, and was introduced as a direct response to the Chevrolet Corvette.

'M-code' option, including 120 Sports Roadsters.

The Thunderbird stayed in production for the 1963 model year, with the Sports Roadster and M-code 390 engine still available. A new option was a landau hardtop with simulated hood irons on its rear roof panels, which was featured on the Thunderbird range for many years after, as gradually the car became more conventional, less sporting and lost its iconic status. It would return in later years.

ENGINE: 5113cc (312cu in), eight-cylinder
POWER: 225bhp (168kW)
0–60MPH (96KM/H): 9 seconds
TOP SPEED: 182km/h (113mph)
PRODUCTION TOTAL: 447,660

JENSEN 541

UNITED KINGDOM 1955–63

The 541 was a major step forward for Jensen when it was launched in 1953. In one fell swoop, the evocative streamlined styling (by Eric Neale) and panoramic windscreen introduced more dynamic styling to the company. Although it was unveiled in 1953, it would not be until 1955 that the 541 went into production, by which time the company had chosen glassfibre instead of steel for construction of the body. Underneath, a new type of chassis featuring longeron tubing braced by box sections and flat floor platforms featured. Up front, Austin-type wishbone front suspension ensured keen handling. Austin also provided much of the drivetrain, with its 4.0-litre (244cu in) six-cylinder engine and gearbox.

The car may have looked exciting, but the performance was adequate in the early models – although an upgrade to 150bhp (112kW) in 1956 improved the situation markedly.

The 541 became one of the first British production cars to feature all-round disc brakes – and, to that, a 541R version was launched the following year. Powered by the same engine, along with rack-and-pinion steering and an opening boot (trunk) lid, the R was a major improvement. The 541S released in 1960 was even better, thanks to a wider body and a standard limited slip differential.

ENGINE: 3993cc (244cu in), six-cylinder
POWER: 130bhp (97kW)
0–60MPH (96KM/H): 12.4 seconds
TOP SPEED: 174km/h (109mph)
PRODUCTION TOTAL: 546

SUNBEAM RAPIER

UNITED KINGDOM 1955–67

The first of the Sunbeam Rapiers was launched in 1955, as a four-seater sports saloon, despite becoming more widely known as a tuned two-door Hillman Minx. The Rapier was a typically intelligent creation plucked from the Rootes Group parts bin, and sold in large numbers as a result.

The Rapier closely resembled the Minx, and featured its coil spring and wishbone front suspension and overhead-valve 1390cc (85cu in) engine, although the gearbox and standard overdrive were based on the unit seen in the Humber Hawk.

The Series II version received a more powerful 1494cc (91cu in) engine, a new floor-mounted gearchange and minor steering and suspension changes. The Series III arrived in 1959, featuring plenty of crossover between the Rapier and the then new Alpine sports car.

An alloy cylinder head, front disc brakes and closer ratio gears improved the car, but, in 1961, further tweaking resulted in the Series IIIa being unveiled. This was powered by a 1592cc (97cu in) engine, but had no other changes. These were reserved for the final version, the Series IV of 1963.

Changes included smaller wheels, a tweaked interior and an all-synchromesh gearbox.

ENGINE: 1494cc (91cu in), four-cylinder
POWER: 68bhp (51kW)
0–60MPH (96KM/H): 20.2 seconds
TOP SPEED: 144km/h (90mph)
PRODUCTION TOTAL: 68,809

MESSERSCHMITT KR200

GERMANY 1955–64

ENGINE: 191cc (12cu in), single-cylinder
POWER: 10bhp (7kW)
0–60MPH (96KM/H): n/a
TOP SPEED: 100km/h (62mph)
PRODUCTION TOTAL: 41,190

During the 1950s, there was a need for inexpensive and no-frills transport – and bubblecars were perfectly placed to meet the demand, even though they seem laughable today. Known as the 'Kabinroller', and the brainchild of German aircraft engineer Fritz Fend, the first bubblecar appeared out of the Messerschmitt aeroplane factory in 1953. The uprated KR200 appeared in 1955 and featured an aeroplane-like one-piece Perspex canopy through which the cabin was accessed. Just as in a plane's cockpit, passengers sat in tandem, while steering was via a pair of motorcycle-style handlebars.

Powered by a 191cc (12cu in) single-cylinder engine, developing 10bhp (7kW), it was surprisingly quick, thanks to the car's minimal weight, tubular spaceframe construction and impressive aerodynamics. A 100km/h (62mph) top speed was positively scary.

With cable-operated brakes and a rudimentary swing-beam suspension set-up, this was fast enough for most, while those requiring hood-down motoring could opt for a convertible version. It was the ultimate in low-cost wind-in-the-hair motoring.

Kabinrollers sold well and their simple construction and ease of maintenance meant that they had a high survival rate and are not too difficult to find.

The Mini was introduced as a direct response to these cars – and their popularity waned as a result.

Given its heritage, it's not surprising that the Messerschmitt KR200 owes much of its design to the aviation industry. Introduced as a form of basic transport for young drivers, the 'bubblecar' ended up being a surprise sales hit.

ROLLS-ROYCE SILVER CLOUD

UNITED KINGDOM 1955–65

Despite its traditional styling and separate chassis, the Rolls-Royce Silver Cloud was a wonderfully capable car, offering unparalleled luxury inside.

Although the Silver Cloud retained a separate chassis – to facilitate those customers who demanded special bodies – it was actually the first Rolls-Royce to have a standard body produced in-house. That was not the only reason it was considered a hugely important car for Rolls-Royce. For one, it was incredibly beautiful and ended up selling in serious numbers.

The adaptable separate chassis was readily turned over to other projects within Rolls-Royce – most famously, the incredibly stylish Bentley Continental S, which was launched in 1955. Apart from that, the Silver Cloud sired the Bentley S1 and S2 saloons.

Rolls-Royce had enjoyed plenty of success during the 1950s, and chief engineer Harry Grylls commissioned the Cloud as an entirely new vehicle, to take the esteemed marque forwards into the 1960s. When it appeared in April 1955, it lived up to the brief. Although the early cars were available only with the 4887cc (298cu in) inlet-over-exhaust valve six-cylinder, more impressive armoury would appear later in the car's life.

Outside the Silver Cloud was imposing, and inside it lived up to expectations of the marque, retaining the traditional gentlemen's club interior, with a beautifully veneered dash and deep leather chairs. Further luxury adornments included GM's Hydramatic automatic transmission as standard, as well as power steering and optional air conditioning.

The impressive bodywork was 5.4m (17.6ft) long, which meant that the Cloud was suitably imposing, inevitably taking its toll on the car's six-cylinder engine. In 1959, that situation was put right with the introduction of the Silver Cloud II, which used Rolls-Royce's brand-new aluminium V8, initially available in a 6.2-litre (380cu in) capacity. The new engine transformed the Cloud's character, and, although it remained serenely quiet and supremely refined, it was now quick enough to cruise at high speeds in well-damped silence. As ever, Rolls-Royce never revealed the unit's power output, but, at an estimated 200bhp (149kW), it was more than adequate compared to the previous six-cylinder, which produced somewhere in the region of 150bhp (112kW).

It also enjoyed better fuel economy, although a leap from 19L/100km (12mpg) to 17L/100km (15mpg) hardly made the Silver Cloud an inexpensive car to run. The Cloud was no sports car, however, and enthusiastic driving resulted in very ungentlemanly behaviour on the road.

The Silver Cloud III, launched in 1963, saw the car gain twin headlights similar to those on the Phantom VI, a lower grille, new power steering and a higher compression ratio, although the engine's true power output still remained a closely guarded secret.

As well as the standard saloon, buyers could choose a Park Ward–bodied limousine, with an extended wheelbase and even more sumptuous interior, a striking two-door coupé or an H.J. Mulliner–designed drophead convertible (from 1962), which offered incredibly stylish looks and an even more exotic price tag.

The Silver Cloud started to struggle into the 1960s, and, although it had been modern when it was launched, by the time that production ceased a decade or so later, cheaper rivals were offering unitary construction, disc brakes and fully independent suspension – none of which featured on the Rolls-Royce.

The Crewe company had it in hand, however, and, when the Cloud went out of production in 1965, the far more progressive unitary-bodied Silver Shadow replaced it – bringing the marque more up to date. The Silver Shadow went on to become the marque's best–selling car ever.

ENGINE: 6230cc (380cu in), eight-cylinder
POWER: n/a
0–60MPH (96KM/H): 11.5 seconds
TOP SPEED: 182km/h (113mph)
PRODUCTION TOTAL: 7374

BENTLEY S-SERIES

UNITED KINGDOM 1955–66

The Bentley S1 and S2 were closely related to the Rolls-Royce Silver Cloud. In fact, although it might be vulgar to use such a term on cars that cost so much money, they were little more than badge-engineered specials. Despite the fact that many Bentley aficionados denounced them as the beginning of the end for the marque's individuality, they were well built, refined and luxurious cruisers.

The S1, launched in 1955 alongside the Silver Cloud, used the same 4.9-litre (298cu in) six with inlet-over-exhaust valves, and was the standard car in the range from 1959 to 1962. Also launched at the same time was the S1 Continental, a two-door grand tourer available as a hardtop or drophead coupé.

Major developments occurred in 1959 with the appearance of the S2 powered by the all-new 6.2-litre (378cu in) V8 engine developed for the Rolls-Royce Silver Cloud. Power steering and automatic transmission came as standard in all V8-engined cars.

A Continental version of the S2 appeared with the same mechanical changes and a few front-end styling changes, while S3 versions of the saloon and Continental both appeared in 1962. The saloon had twin headlights and two-tone paintwork, while the Continental acquired unusual front-end styling and angled headlights.

ENGINE: 4887cc (298cu in), six-cylinder
POWER: 175bhp (130kW)
0–60MPH (96KM/H): 13.7 seconds
TOP SPEED: 170km/h (105mph)
PRODUCTION TOTAL: about 8000

Bentley's version of the Rolls-Royce Silver Cloud retained all the qualities of its sibling, but also came in a spectacular range of coachbuilt body options. When the 6.2-litre S2 came along, it was a genuine contender for 'best car in the world'.

PEUGEOT 403

FRANCE 1955–66

Although the 403 was originally developed as a replacement for the popular 203, in traditional Peugeot style the two cars ran alongside each other for the first five years' production of the new car. Although they looked pretty similar, the 403 featured larger Pininfarina-styled bodywork, and ended up being a much more spacious vehicle.

Available with the 203's 1290cc (79cu in) engine, as well as a bored-out 1468cc (90cu in) version, the 403 was adequately lively – although buyers in France and Spain could choose the slow and noisy but highly economical 1.8-litre (110cu in) diesel version.

An estate (stationwagon) model was offered from 1956 onwards, and could be specified with eight seats arranged in three rows, suggesting the 403 was significantly ahead of its time given the current popularity of people carriers. The 404, 504 and 505 all had the same option offered. A Décapotable cabriolet model was also offered between 1956 and 1963, but this accounted for only 2000 of the 403's seven-figure production run.

In other respects, the 403 was a very conventional machine, but rugged build and its solidity meant that it was successfully exported around the globe, became a huge hit for Peugeot and was a big money spinner for France.

ENGINE: 1290cc (79cu in), four-cylinder
POWER: 54bhp (40kW)
0–60MPH (96KM/H): 29.5 seconds
TOP SPEED: 121km/h (75mph)
PRODUCTION TOTAL: 1,119,460

Although it was a far more conventional–looking car than the earlier 402, the Peugeot 403 was a more modern car to drive – and enjoyed considerable success as a result. Available in diesel and eight-seat versions.

FIAT 600

ITALY 1955–69

With the Nuova 500, Fiat proved that it could build a genuinely fun small car that people wanted – and, when it came to producing a larger brother to it, Fiat used the same ingredients to achieve pretty much the same result.

The 600 had a monocoque body with two B pillar hinged 'suicide' doors, which opened backwards and seated four. It was powered by a 633cc (39cu in) 29bhp (22kW) water-cooled four-cylinder engine, which sat behind the rear wheels.

This layout was excellent for space efficiency if not ultimate handling, despite independent suspension.

A full-length canvas sunroof became an option a year into the production run, and, at the same time, the Multipla was launched.

Arguably, the Multipla was the first genuine people carrier (as opposed to eight-seater estate car/station wagon), as it could accommodate three rows of seats or six people in the same footprint as a standard car. Alternatively, the two rear pairs of seats could be folded into the floor, turning the Multipla into a cute small van. Revised in 1960, to become the 600D, the upgunned 767cc (47cu in) 29bhp (22kW) car gained front opening quarterlights and the boot (trunk) lid with new cooling vents. In 1964, the 600D received front-hinged doors.

ENGINE: 633cc (39cu in),
four-cylinder
POWER: 29bhp (22kW)
0–60MPH (96KM/H): 40 seconds
TOP SPEED: 106km/h (66mph)
PRODUCTION TOTAL: 2,695,197

The tiny Fiat 600 was a four-seater – although getting in via the forward hinged doors could be interesting. The Multipla variant even boosted the seat count to six!

GLAS GOGGOMOBIL

The Goggomobil was a clever two-cylinder four-seater that quickly established itself in Europe, mainly because it was economical and significantly undercut the Volkswagen Beetle. The Goggomobil was the brainchild of Hans Glas,

Despite being cheaper and cleverer than the more expensive Volkswagen Beetle, the Glas Goggomobil never really took off in the same way.

and was his first attempt at vehicle manufacture. The name came from Glas's grandson, who was nicknamed 'Goggo', and the marque currently has a cult following.

A two-cylinder two-stroke 250cc (15cu in) engine mounted in the rear powered the diminutive car, but its performance was unsurprisingly poor, especially when the car was fully loaded. The later, bigger engined T300 and T400 versions were to improve matters marginally.

The car underwent various minor changes during its production run, and, in 1964, the original suicide-type forward-opening doors were reversed. There was also a two-seater TS Coupé available from 1956, with a dummy grille and stylish wraparound rear window. Less practical than the saloon, it could still seat 2+2 in an overall length of just 305cm (10ft). There was even a TS300 Cabriolet built between 1957 and 1958, though only seven were built.

The Goggomobil is known mainly in the United Kingdom for being the car that the Rootes Group benchmarked during the early development phase of its Hillman Imp.

ENGINE: 247cc (15cu in),
two-cylinder
POWER: 14bhp (10kW)
0–60MPH (96KM/H): n/a
TOP SPEED: 75km/h (47mph)
PRODUCTION TOTAL: 280,709

VOLGA M21

The Volga M21 was launched in 1955, as a successor to the popular M20 Pobjeba model, and, in true Russian style, an all-new body design clothed familiar mechanicals. Also known as the GAZ M21 Volga, it was considered by many to be the first Soviet car to compare favourably with Western standards of technology and build quality.

Under the skin, many of the parts were carried over from the M20, the componentry of which had been proven to be extremely reliable in service. The first 1955 cars, which became known retrospectively as the Series 1, used the M20 side-valve engine enlarged to 2432cc (148cu in). By 1957, an all-new 2445cc (149cu in) overhead-valve powerplant had

been developed, and this was installed in the Series 2 M21 the following year. Despite being called the Series 2, changes were actually very minor, with cosmetic alterations to the grille and dashboard.

The major addition to the range came in 1962, when the estate (stationwagon) version was rolled out. Called the M22, it was treated as an entirely new model by Volga.

Further trim changes in 1962 resulted in the Series 3 mode; after that, the range was unchanged until being phased out in 1971.

ENGINE: 2445cc (149cu in), four-cylinder
POWER: 95bhp (71kW)
0–50MPH (80KM/H): 18 seconds
TOP SPEED: 137km/h (85mph)
PRODUCTION TOTAL: 638,875

VOLKSWAGEN KARMANN-GHIA

The legendary Karmann-Ghia came about following negotiations between Karmann and Volkswagen, which had been instigated in 1950. The idea was for Karmann to build a sporting car for Volkswagen using the floorpan and components of its best-selling Beetle. It was not until 1955, however, that the car first appeared, after design house Ghia had been approached by Karmann to design and build a prototype.

The pretty car was soon a roaring success, despite a high purchase price and less than outstanding performance. Calling it a sports car was ambitious; it may have looked like one, but It certainly did not go like one.

Happily, the Beetle's excellent reliability and low running costs made it through to the Karmann-Ghia, and that was more than enough to tempt many buyers. Initially, only a 1200cc (73cu in)

coupé was offered, but, from 1965, buyers were able to specify a 1300cc (79cu in) version – and, in 1970, a 1.6-litre (98cu in) model was introduced.

The most sought after are the cabriolets, launched in 1957 with 1200cc (73cu in) engines, later upgraded to 1300cc (79cu in), then 1600cc (98cu in). Today, these cars have a cult following largely in line with the rest of the air-cooled Volkswagen line-up.

ENGINE: 1192cc (73cu in), four-cylinder
POWER: 30bhp (22kW)
0–60MPH (96KM/H): n/a
TOP SPEED: 115km/h (72mph)
PRODUCTION TOTAL: n/a

Despite being saddled by a high list price and poor performance, the pretty Volkswagen Karmann-Ghia sold exceptionally well.

CITROËN DS

When the Citroën DS was launched at the 1955 Paris Motor Show, most people were left absolutely dumbstruck – it looked like nothing that had gone before it and introduced a generation of drivers to the joys of fully powered brakes and Hydropneumatic suspension. It was the star of the show, and 749 orders were taken

within 45 minutes of its unveiling Citroën was always going to replace the Traction Avant with something special, but few were prepared for what eventually appeared.

The idea of a new big Citroën had originally been proposed in 1938, but World War II got in the way. Italian stylist Flaminio Bertoni had designed the basic DS shape

by 1945, and gradually refined that into production reality as the engineers developed the vehicle's mechanicals.

Citroën had been working on Hydropneumatic suspension since 1939. But it was not until the 1950s that it started working satisfactorily, at which point it made an appearance in the Citroën

'Heavy 15', which was regarded more as a commercial testbed than a production model.

When the DS finally went into production, it was powered by the tried and tested Traction Avant 1911cc (117cu in) engine – and that let down the rest of the car. It could have been an air-cooled flat-six, however, had development work on the car not stalled and finances tightened.

The advanced Citroën was extraordinary for its era, and, in the years of post-war austerity, it was in contrast to what all other manufacturers were offering because the space-age DS looked out of this world. Technically, it was a marvel, too – and Hydropneumatic assistance for the clutch, power steering, brakes and self-levelling suspension, which resulted in a supremely cushioned ride of unparalleled smoothness, pointed to a bright future. As with the Traction Avant, the first DSs suffered from Hydraulic teething

troubles, which threatened to overshadow its successful launch.

A cheaper DS, called the ID (or *idée* – 'idea' – in French) was launched in 1956, and featured a pared-down interior, detuned engine and conventional brakes and steering. The Safari estate (station wagon) with a longer wheelbase and enormous carrying capacity appeared in 1958, and, for 1960, the magnificent Décapotable was launched. Effectively a DS with the roof cut off – and fashioned by France's last remaining traditional coachbuilder, Chapron – the chic convertible became a legend in its own lifetime.

The DS was continually developed throughout its life, with the Pallas version appearing in 1965, and all manner of other special-bodied versions, including presidential limousines, kept the coachbuilders busy into the 1970s.

Engines were enlarged to 2175cc (133cu in) for the DS21 and 2347cc (143cu in) in the DS23 in 1973. Faired-in headlights were added in 1968, giving the car a shark-like look, and the inner set of light units now swivelled in the direction of the front wheels – an industry first.

It is a testament to the rightness of the design that it still looked fresh when it was replaced by the

CX in 1974 and 1975. For many, no other car ever managed to make such a big impression at its show launch.

ENGINE: 2175cc (133cu in), four-cylinder
POWER: 109bhp (81kW) at 5500rpm
0–60MPH (96KM/H): 14.8 seconds
TOP SPEED: 171km/h (106mph)
PRODUCTION TOTAL: 1,455,746

The Citroën DS must have looked like a spaceship on earth when it was unveiled at the 1955 Paris Motor Show.

TATRA 603

The 1957 Tatra 603 was a pure product of its creator, and could clearly trace its heritage back to Ledwinka's first T77 with its trademark rear-mounted air-cooled V8 and room inside for six passengers. The 603 was an update of the concept, though – and used a hemi-head 2.5-litre (151cu in) V8. Air scoops were moulded into the rear wings (fenders) and did an effective job

of cooling the car, as well as adding considerable visual interest.

The four-speed gearbox was operated by a column-mounted gearshift, and early cars featured drum brakes all round, although discs were fitted later. Changes throughout production were gradual, the biggest ones being reserved for the 603-2 of 1967.

Although the engine was reasonably light, it certainly was

not powerful – in low compression ratio form (with a ratio of just 6.5:1), the power output was only 100bhp (75kW). This was not really enough to push a car that weighed nearly 1500kg (3300lb), resulting in a poor power-to-weight ratio. Acceleration might have been sluggish, but the Tatra's slippery shape meant that it could hit almost 161km/h (100mph) if you could find a long enough road.

The later 603-2 had headlights placed further apart in a new grille, and owners similarly upgraded many earlier cars in later years.

ENGINE: 2472cc (151cu in), eight-cylinder
POWER: 105bhp (78kW)
0–60MPH (96KM/H): 15.2 seconds
TOP SPEED: 158km/h (99mph)
PRODUCTION TOTAL: 20,422

HILLMAN MINX SERIES I

The Hillman Minx Series I is a perfect example of why the Rootes Group had picked up a small but enthusiastic following for its well-built range of cars

during the 1950s and 1960s. Launched in 1956, the new car may well have been little more than a four-door version of the Sunbeam Rapier, which had been

announced the previous year, but it had a style all of its own.

The new car was bigger than the previous Minx and was far roomier, but it was heavier, too – although

the extra weight was offset by an extra 9bhp (7kW), meaning that the top speed remained unchanged at 128km/h (80mph). Being the staple family car that it was, the Minx was offered in several trim options, including the Special, which had floor gearchange (and separate front seats, as opposed to the usual bench seat), and a De Luxe version with column change and bench seats. In 1957, the estate (stationwagon) version followed just prior to the arrival of the Series II.

Continual evolution saw the Series III in 1958, the Series IIIA in 1959, the IIIB in 1960 and the IIIC a year later – each one received minor improvements.

ENGINE: 1390cc (85cu in), 4-cylinder
POWER: 51bhp (38kW)
0-60MPH (96KM/H): 27.7 secs
TOP SPEED: 128km/h (80mph)
PRODUCTION TOTAL: 500,000

Featuring well sorted styling and excellent build quality, the Hillman Minx Series I was a major hit for the Rootes Group.

VOLVO P1900

ENGINE: 1414cc (86cu in), four-cylinder
POWER: 70bhp (52kW)
0–60MPH (96KM/H): n/a
TOP SPEED: n/a
PRODUCTION TOTAL: 67

After a trip to the United States in 1949 where he saw just how popular European sports cars had become there, Volvo boss Assar

Gabrielsson decided to build one of his own. He commissioned the California-based company Glasspar, to design, engineer and build the new car, figuring that it would be perfect for the American market.

A number of exciting designs were penned in which the car was powered by a 1.4-litre (86cu in) B14 engine from the PV444 and many other components from the model were used. A pair of SU

carburettors was added to the engine to boost power to a more suitable 70bhp (52kW), and this powerplant was mated to a standard Volvo three-speed gearbox. The body used glassfibre panels, which were still a new, largely untested construction material.

Debuting September 1954 – and still without a name – the new car was pencilled for production later that autumn, at the rate of a car a

day. The first cars were delivered in 1956, but only 44 were built that year. Just 23 cars were added the next year before Volvo pulled the plug on what had finally become known as the P1900.

The P1900 was Volvo's first sportscar, and it was a long way from being a success. Only 67 were built.

BERKELEY 322/328

Small and perfectly formed, the Berkeley 322/328 featured some very advanced styling touches for its day.

It is not often that caravan manufacturers get into the business of building cars, but that is exactly what happened in the mid-1950s with the Berkeley Coachwork Company. The company commissioned small-time vehicle manufacturer Laurie Bond to design a new car – naming it the Berkeley Sports 322.

Laurie Bond had already earned a reputation for innovative design, having produced the Bond Minicar (a Villiers-powered three-wheeler), and the Unicar for another manufacturer – both featured glassfibre for bodywork. Given that the Berkeley Company was expert in the use of glassfibre, it is no surprise that the new car would be built from the same material.

The Berkeley 322/328 was a small and perfectly formed sports car, powered by a 322cc (20cu in) Anzani two-cylinder two-stroke engine. That was later replaced by a 328cc (20cu in) Excelsior twin. Gearboxes started out with three speeds, but were upgraded to four for the later models – and all had chain drive to the front wheels.

Performance in all cars was surprisingly quick, a testament to their low weight construction.

ENGINE: 328cc (20cu in), two-cylinder
POWER: 18bhp (13kW)
0–60MPH (96KM/H): n/a
TOP SPEED: 105km/h (65mph)
PRODUCTION TOTAL: 1418

DUAL GHIA

Conceived purely to build a production version of Virgil Exner's Dodge Firebomb/Firearrow concept car from the early 1950s, Dual Motors was the creation of haulage contractor Eugene Casaroll in Detroit. It had been expected that Dual would be building the cars for Chrysler. When that never happened, Casaroll simply bought the Firebomb and made it himself.

A 5162cc (315cu in) engine from the Dodge D-500 was installed, and designer Paul Farago managed to squeeze some more passenger and luggage space, making it a little more practical.

Assembly was a nightmare, though, as the chassis were shipped to Turin, Italy, where the Ghia coachworks hand-produced the bodies. An exquisite interior was added, swathed in Connolly hide, and after that exterior detail was added using chrome-plated brass clips to hold trim in place. After work had been completed in Italy, the drivetrain and interior trim were fitted back in Detroit.

The price was a reasonable US$7646, which pitched it below rivals from Cadillac. The car was a hit with the Hollywood elite, but a loss was made on each one, and production was wrapped up after just 117 had been built.

ENGINE: 5162cc (315cu in), eight-cylinder
POWER: 230bhp (172kW)
0–60MPH (96KM/H): 9 seconds
TOP SPEED: 193km/h (120mph)
PRODUCTION TOTAL: 117

MOSKVICH 402

The Moskvich 402 appeared in 1956 looking like a reasonably up-to-date effort with unitary construction and crisp styling, but underneath was the same archaic platform used in the 400/Opel Kadett. With no investment money for new car development and no tooling to build it, Moskvich's attempts to modernize amounted to a new-looking car riding the same old beam axle suspension.

The suspension might have been old, but the 1930s Opel side-valve engine developing a mere 35bhp (26kW) was from another age. The three-speed gearbox, wayward steering and harsh ride belied the car's origins, and meant that the driving experience was unpleasant.

It was suited to Russia, however, as it was pretty indestructible, and, with buyers issued with cars, Moskvich sold every example it could make. Exports did not happen until 1958, when the government-developed and vastly improved 407 appeared. Its aluminium cylinder head and reasonable performance meant that the marque enjoyed moderate success in the budget car market.

ENGINE: 1288cc (79cu in), four-cylinder
POWER: 35bhp (26kW)
0–60MPH (96KM/H): n/a
TOP SPEED: about 96km/h (60mph)
PRODUCTION TOTAL: n/a

AUSTIN-HEALEY 100-SIX

The original four-cylinder Austin-Healey 100 was a fine sports car, but it had faults, and, by the mid-1950s, changes were needed. The US market, where it had been unexpectedly successful, wanted more power than Austin's big four-cylinder engine could deliver; the 100 received a major update to answer those criticisms.

A small number of prototypes, named 100-Six BN3s, was built using BMC's six-cylinder 2.6-litre (161cu in) C-Series engine, and the production versions duly appeared in 1956, called the 100-Six BN4.

The 100-Six received a 5cm (2in) wheelbase stretch, which meant that a pair of small seats could be accommodated in the back. The general specification was also improved. The new engine added weight and was only 12bhp (9kW) more powerful than the previous unit, making the new car slightly slower than its predecessor. This was rectified in 1957, when a more powerful version of the C-series engine was fitted. In 1958, the 100-Six BN6 arrived, returning to the old two-seater format. It became Healey's legendary rally weapon.

ENGINE: 2639cc (161cu in), six-cylinder
POWER: 102bhp (76kW)
0–60MPH (96KM/H): 12.9 seconds
TOP SPEED: 166km/h (103mph)
PRODUCTION TOTAL: 14,436

BMW 507

ENGINE: 3168cc (193cu in),
eight-cylinder
POWER: 150bhp (122kW)
0–60MPH (96KM/H): 9.5 seconds
TOP SPEED: 193km/h (120mph)
PRODUCTION TOTAL: 253

The 1955 Frankfurt Motor Show was a busy event for BMW, where it managed to unveil a family of three cars, all based upon the same platform. The first was a limousine, which never made it into production, while the other two were sports cars designed by Albrecht von Goertz. The 503 and the 507 were both impossibly pretty, and proved that BMW had ambitions to become a world-class car manufacturer.

Although the 503 appeared first, the 507 was the better of the two. A lithe, low two-seater, it had a detachable hardtop and a folding hood that tucked out of sight

behind the seats. The clean but muscular lines meant performance, which was amply provided by the running gear. That performance was impressive, with BMW's V8 engine propelling the 507 to a top

speed of 193km/h (120mph). Predictably, the 507 was extremely expensive and, in five years, just 253 examples were sold.

The car attracted celebrity owners, such as Elvis Presley (he

gave the car to actress Ursula Andress) and Frank Sinatra. Its styling and superstar associations have made the 507 one of the most legendary BMWs produced, along with the pre-war 328.

Another absolutely glorious failure produced before BMW got its act together in the 1960s. Sales were hard to come by, but it's revered by its owners today.

FERRARI 410 SUPERAMERICA

The Ferrari 410 Superamerica took over from where the 375 had left off, and, as its name intimated, it was aimed squarely at the American market. The car was

designed to be the fastest and the best of its kind. To achieve Enzo's goals, Ferrari installed the largest and most powerful engine it could design – a 4963cc (303cu in) V12

producing 340bhp (254kW). Although the power unit had previously been seen in a racing 375, where it had stormed to victory at Le Mans, this was the

Offered in a wide range of stylish coachbuilt bodies, the Ferrari Superamerica deserved its tag – because everything about it was indulgent.

first application of the V12 in a 'standard' road car. A brand-new chassis with coil spring independent front suspension was built, and it was also used on the 250 GT cars.

Series II models arrived in 1957, with a shorter 250 GT wheelbase (259cm/102in rather than 279cm/110in), and just eight examples were built, including a 380bhp (283kW) 'Superfast' version.

The Superamerica was then put on ice, before returning in 1959 in Series III form. Now powered by a 4963cc (303cu in) 400bhp (298kW) engine, just 14 of these supercars were built. Although the Superamerica was fabulously fast and poised, sales of the car were a disappointment – partially due to its astronomical price.

ENGINE: 4963cc (303cu in), 12-cylinder
POWER: 340bhp (253kW)
0–60MPH (96KM/H): 8 seconds
TOP SPEED: 257km/h (160mph)
PRODUCTION TOTAL: 38

FORD FAIRLANE SKYLINER

UNITED STATES 1956–59

Introduced in 1955 as the new top-of-the-line full-size Ford, the Fairlane was actually named after Henry Ford's Fair Lane mansion in Dearborn, Michigan. Originally offered in six different bodystyles, the Fairlane range included saloons, a plastic-topped Crown Victoria, a steel-roofed Victoria and the convertible. The most distinctive version of the lot was launched for 1957 – in the shape of the Ford Fairlane 500 Skyliner.

The Skyliner also had the world's first production retractable hardtop, which, although stunning, proved to be very complicated and troublesome in the extreme.

The Skyliner was also expensive at $400 more than the convertible Sunliner – and many buyers wondered whether it was worth the effort. Ford stylists designed its roof to be shorter than on other models, and the car's front section was hinged to fold for more

compact storage into the larger boot (trunk), but the Skyliner still ended up with a bulky rear end.

It also differed from other Fairlanes with its standard V8 engine and the relocated petrol tank, now found behind the back seat. Also, there was little luggage space when the top was down. It briefly became the Galaxie in 1958, but the troublesome car was a liability, and, after a three-year run, it was phased out.

Short-lived in American production terms, the Fairlane Skyliner was of interest for its retractable steel hardtop roof.

ENGINE: 4453cc (271cu in), eight-cylinder
POWER: 190bhp (142kW)
0–60MPH (96KM/H): 12 seconds
TOP SPEED: 177km/h (110mph)
PRODUCTION TOTAL: 48,394

VANDEN PLAS PRINCESS IV

UNITED KINGDOM 1956–59

The Vanden Plas Princess IV was a limited production grand tourer of the old school, developed from the Austin Sheerline and Princess saloons. It was built the traditional way, with the chassis by Austin and the bodyshell produced by Vanden Plas at the Kingsbury Works in North London. The arrangement worked well, as both parties were within BMC's bosom.

Automatic transmission and power-assisted steering were standard. When *Autocar* magazine reviewed the Princess IV in 1958, testers were very impressed with the level of refinement. Not only was the car extremely quiet, even at high speed, but also the lack of vibration and smoothness of the transmission were something to be savoured.

The Princess IV was an imposing car, with a length of 510cm (16.6ft) and a weight of more than 2200kg (4850lb). Its performance was sluggish, however, even with a full 150bhp (112kW) produced by its 4-litre engine.

Typical fuel consumption was alarming, with little more than 28.4L/100km (10mpg) expected in normal running. The car's vast

thirst was matched by an even greater price tag, and that resulted in limited sales.

ENGINE: 3993cc (244cu in), six-cylinder
POWER: 150bhp (112kW)
0–60MPH (96KM/H): 16.1 seconds
TOP SPEED: 161km/h (100mph)
PRODUCTION TOTAL: n/a

ARNOLT BRISTOL

After Stanley 'Wacky' Arnolt's first cars proved a little on the underpowered side, he decided it was time to move up a gear. The early Arnolt MGs were based on the MG TD and dressed in Bertone bodies. They proved sluggish on the road, thanks to heavy bodywork and an unspectacular amount of power from its four-cylinder engine.

Aa Arnolt was also an importer for Bristol in the United States, however, the answer was obvious. He persuaded Bristol to supply its impressive new 404 chassis and six-cylinder engine, which the company then clothed in pretty sports bodies built by Bertone. The resultant Arnolt Bristol not only looked and went well, but also

unbelievably cost less than half the price of the Bristol 404.

The Arnolt Bristol proved a success in the marketplace, and production only ended when Bristol stopped supplying chassis – perhaps upset about the massive price difference between its own cars and the Arnolts. As a footnote, an Arnolt Aston Martin, pre-dating

the Bristol, was also made, but just eight of those were built.

ENGINE: 1971cc (120cu in), six-cylinder
POWER: 132bhp (98kW)
0–60MPH (96KM/H): n/a
TOP SPEED: 181km/h (112mph)
PRODUCTION TOTAL: 142

Although based on the Bristol saloons, the Arnolt cars were a far different concept. Starkly appointed inside and wonderfully styled on the outside, these cars had a character all of their own – as well as being cheaper than the cars they were based on.

LOTUS ELEVEN

The Eleven featured a clever spaceframe chassis and wonderfully aerodynamic and imaginative bodywork. It was a definite fantasy car, but could be bought for realistic money – perhaps because it was really just a track car converted to everyday road use by the addition of headlights and a basic fabric roof.

The Perspex wraparound screen was so shallow that even drivers of a moderate height could look over it. The nose section was hinged at the front to expose the

With its complex spaceframe construction and lightweight body, the Eleven was typically Lotus in its execution. Effectively a racing car for the road.

entire engine, and the rear-hinged tail section provided space for the battery, spare wheel and room for a toothbrush.

Three versions of the Eleven were available: Le Mans (with a Coventry Climax engine and a de Dion rear end), Club (again with a Coventry Climax unit and live axle/coil springs) and Sport (with a Ford side-valve engine and live rear axle). Series 2 cars were launched in 1957, and featured advanced wishbone and coil spring independent front suspension and strengthened rear axles.

Effectively, the Eleven was a competition car and dominated the racing scene in the 1950s – with considerable success at Le Mans in 1956 and 1957.

ENGINE: 1098cc (67cu in), four-cylinder
POWER: 75bhp (56kW)
0–60MPH (96KM/H): 10 seconds
TOP SPEED: 200km/h (125mph)
PRODUCTION TOTAL: 426

DESOTO FIREFLITE

The Chrysler Corporation's 'Forward Look', as penned by stylist Virgil Exner, has become the look of 1950s America. When DeSoto incorporated the style into its 1955 range of cars, sales picked up strongly, as cars took the tail fin fashion to its conclusion – with many observers concluding that they were the most successfully styled of all the big tail fin machines of the 1950s.

In one fell swoop, DeSoto's image was transformed, and the Fireflite headed the range in suitable style. It was charismatic and was powered by a strong 255bhp (190kW) engine. Sales were further improved in 1957 when a face-lift saw its fins grow ever larger.

The 5588cc (341cu in) V8 produced 295bhp (220kW), thanks to four-barrel carburettors, and the range included a saloon, two-door coupé and estate (station wagon). A six-seater wagon was called the Shopper and the nine-seater version was labelled the Explorer.

The 1960 model was DeSoto's first monocoque design, but sales were already slowing at this point, and the marque's future looked bleak. The top-of-the-range Fireflite withered and, in November 1960, it was finally cancelled. Since then, though, the DeSoto and the

Fireflite in particular have emerged as icons of the 1950s, simply because *Happy Days* character Richie Cunningham drove one.

ENGINE: 6277cc (383cu in), eight-cylinder
POWER: 255bhp (190kW)
0–60MPH (96KM/H): 9 seconds
TOP SPEED: 193km/h (120mph)
PRODUCTION TOTAL: 95,000

FAIRTHORPE ELECTRON

ENGINE: 1098cc (67cu in), four-cylinder
POWER: 90bhp (67kW)
0–60MPH (96KM/H): 10 seconds
TOP SPEED: 177km/h (110mph)
PRODUCTION TOTAL: 30

In 1957, the Electron Minor was introduced, and was built to a price – which meant that it proved popular despite its ugliness. The Minor used the same the ladder chassis as the grown-up Electron and had Triumph front suspension and engine. Power units ranged from the 948cc (58cu in) 50bhp (37kW) unit to the 1969 1.3-litre (79cu in) version. It could even be specified with a supercharger.

Featuring far more palatable styling and more useable power than its predecessor, the Fairthorpe Atom, the Electron was a very useable and affordable sportscar.

Fairthorpe's first entry into the car market, the Atom, was a quirky car with plenty going for it. What did let it down was its questionable styling. After that, the company got it right with the attractive glassfibre-bodied Electron.

The formula remained simple, though – a Microplas Mistral-designed body, available at the time to specialist builders, was fitted on a Fairthorpe ladder frame. Upfront, a Coventry Climax FWA engine provided power. Performance was rapid, and the 90bhp (67kW) engine had little trouble propelling the 508kg (1120lb) Electron to high speeds in no time. Handling was balanced, too. Overall, the car was excellent value for money, but sales were slow in a market crowded with low volume specials, and it was dropped in 1965.

CHRYSLER IMPERIAL

Chrysler's prolific stylist Virgil Exner produced some stunning cars during the 1950s, and the company's re-created flagship model, the Imperial, was no exception. Introduced as an independent brand, the new Imperial was distinguished by its long bonnet (hood) and short boot (trunk), and the bold grille work and tall freestanding taillights were styling highlights – even if

Chrysler's claim that it was the Finest Car America Has Yet Produced' was questionable.

In 1957, the styling, again by Virgil Exner, was revised, and its majestic tail fins were considered outstanding compared with the Imperial's contemporary rivals. The excesses were toned down, and the car had chrome-free flanks – and its curved door glass was a real industry first. Body variations were the two-door hardtops, four-door hardtops, pillared saloons and convertible – all of which looked the business. Power was an impressive 325bhp (424kW) and was delivered through a TorqueFlite push-button automatic gearbox.

Each model year brought saw new styling to the Imperial, but the 1961 design was dominated by large tail fins. Chrysler claimed that wind tunnel tests proved that

these fins gave its cars high-speed stability, but that was merely a cover for what was undoubtedly a fashion accessory.

ENGINE: 6769cc (413cu in), eight-cylinder
POWER: 345bhp (257kW)
0–60MPH (96KM/H): 9.8 seconds
TOP SPEED: 201km/h (125mph)
PRODUCTION TOTAL: 171,000

Built while Chrysler was at the height of its powers in the 1950s, the Imperial was a fine example of large-scale Americana. Power and presence was never an issue with the Imperial – and neither were its growing tail fins.

HEINKEL

Professor Ernst Heinkel's rounded three- and four-wheeler was launched a year after BMW's Isetta in order to satisfy the bubblecar boom of the mid-1950s. Its individual styling meant that it became known as the bubblecar.

The Heinkel and BMW looked very similar, but it was the former car that was technically superior. Heinkel, an aircraft-manufacturing company, had developed a lighter car, with room for at least four people, and it was arguably better looking. The Heinkel's body featured unitary construction and boasted refinements such as hydraulic front brakes. The single front door was not a great idea, especially as it lacked the BMW's swing-away steering wheel. Bolstering the range, a number of narrow-track four-wheelers were produced to run alongside the conventional three-wheel configuration with a single wheel at the back and two at the front.

Production in Germany ceased in 1958. The design was subsequently sold to Dundalk Engineering in Ireland; from 1961, Trojan also built the car in England. Additionally, 2000 or so were built in Argentina.

ENGINE: 174cc (27cu in), single-cylinder
POWER: 9bhp (7kW)
0–60MPH (96KM/H): n/a
TOP SPEED: 83km/h (52mph)
PRODUCTION TOTAL: 29,000

Along with the Isetta, the Heinkel was considered almost the definitive bubblecar. Produced at a time when the continued stability of fuel supplies was called into question, these low powered high economy cars proved very popular.

WARTBURG 311 & 312

EAST GERMANY 1956–66

The Wartburg 311 and 312 are proof positive that it was possible to produce handsome and well-engineered cars from behind the Iron Curtain. First shown at the 1956 Leipzig Spring Fair, the 311 was a well-engineered if slightly old-fashioned car with a superbly designed body.

Similar in many respects to the Borgward saloons of the same era,

the 311 was sold in either a four-door saloon or two-door estate form (known as the Kombi) – although, later, pretty cabriolet and coupé versions were introduced.

Suspended by transverse leaf springs at both front and rear, there was no doubt that the car's underpinnings were long in the tooth, even for 1956. When the 312 replaced by the 311 in 1964,

a new chassis and gearbox were finally introduced to Wartburg.

However, as the bodyshell was unchanged, all the benefits of all-round independent coil sprung suspension were lost on the car's customers because of the familiar style. Service intervals were impressive – 48,200km (30,000 miles) between visits to the garage, good by 21st-century standards.

When the 353 replaced the 312 in 1967, the chassis was carried over and the bodyshell updated.

ENGINE: 900cc (55cu in), three-cylinder
POWER: 37bhp (28kW)
0–60MPH (96KM/H): n/a
TOP SPEED: 115km/h (72mph)
PRODUCTION TOTAL: n/a

SINGER GAZELLE

UNITED KINGDOM 1956–67

ENGINE: 1497cc (91cu in), four-cylinder
POWER: 49bhp (37kW)
0–60MPH (96KM/H): 23.6 seconds
TOP SPEED: 125km/h (78mph)
PRODUCTION TOTAL: 83,061

The Singer Gazelle was a prime example of Rootes Group badge engineering – producing identifiably different cars from the same basic

platform and giving them a character all of their own. When Singer became part of the Rootes Group in 1956, it was clear that new metal would be needed quickly.

When it appeared, the Gazelle was really a Minx with a new 1497cc (91cu in) overhead-valve engine, different front-end styling and a restyled dashboard. Like its Hillman cousin, the Minx was offered in a choice of two- or four-door saloons and a convertible –

all with a four-speed gearbox column-mounted gearchange. Also like the Minx, it was revised on an almost annual basis, but 1957's update to Mk II spec was significant because an estate (station wagon) was added to the range and overdrive became available.

From 1958 to 1961, the Mk IIA, Mk III, Mk IIIA and Mk IIIB appeared with detail changes. As the Mk IIIC, it gained the 1592cc (97cu in) powerplant. Next was the Mk V

(there was no Mk IV) in 1963. The new car had smaller wheels, better brakes and a slightly revised look. The final derivative, the 1965 Mk VI, had a 1725cc (105cu in) engine and a slightly restyled nose.

A more sporting and upmarket version of the Hillman Minx, the Singer Gazelle was a popular car with buyers. It was offered in a bewildering array of versions.

ZIL 111

USSR 1956–67

Firmly at the top of the Communist car tree, the ZIL was very much Russia's flagship car. Built between 1956 and 1967, the ZIL was so prestigious a limousine, it was reserved for top officials. Effectively, the 111 was unbridled Russian luxury in a very American-looking

package. It was powered by a 230bhp (171kW) 5980cc (365cu in) V8 engine, driven through a push-button automatic gearbox, similar to the US PowerFlite gearbox.

In 1962, the enormous car was restyled and gained sleeker front and rear panelling. The US school

of design still heavily influenced the styling, both inside and out.

It was the first ever Russian car to feature air conditioning as an option. For those who needed more, a super-stretch version (the 111A) or a convertible (the 111V) was available for the really flamboyant.

ENGINE: 5980cc (365cu in), eight-cylinder
POWER: 230bhp (171kW)
0–60MPH (96KM/H): n/a
TOP SPEED: 161km/h (100mph)
PRODUCTION TOTAL: 112

DKW MUNGA

The DKW Munga was created after the company successfully bid for the German Federal Army's contract for an all-purpose vehicle with an off-road capability. In doing so, it beat competition from both Porsche and Borgward, hitting the market in 1956.

Originally fitted with the familiar three-cylinder 896cc (55cu in) two-stroke engine, it was not powerful enough for the task in hand, with an output of 40bhp (30kW). From 1958, the situation was reversed with the fitment of a 980cc (60cu in) 55bhp (41kW) engine, which at least meant that the Munga could cope with tough conditions.

The Munga had utilitarian styling with flat ribbed panels and a flat upright front screen, and most were open with canvas hoods. Although given the model designation F91/4 from 1962, the car was officially described as a 'Multi-Purpose Universal Off-Road Vehicle with All-Wheel Drive', which the Germans contracted to the acronym Munga. The vehicle remained in production until 1968, when the German army contract finally expired.

ENGINE: 896cc (55cu in), three-cylinder
POWER: 40bhp (30 kW)
0–60MPH (96KM/H): n/a
TOP SPEED: 97km/h (60mph)
PRODUCTION TOTAL: n/a

RENAULT DAUPHINE

Despite its much larger passenger compartment and lengthened chassis, the Dauphine was effectively an uprated 4CV. Powered by an enlarged 845cc (52cu in) version of the original car's engine, the Dauphine shared the 4CV's gearbox and braking system. When the boxy Renault 4 replaced the 4CV, its spirit essentially lived on in the Dauphine, which first appeared in 1956.

The suspension set-up was all-new, with independent coil springs and wishbones at the front and the option of 'Aerostable' semi-pneumatic springing at the rear – a real innovation that tried to answer Citroën's softly sprung 2CV and variants.

The most interesting Dauphine variation was the Gordini, although it was was never especially fast in standard form, struggling to reach 130km/h (80mph). The tuning brigade took the car to their hearts, however, and turned it into an effective road racer. There was one factory version built to be a quicker car, though. The 1093 Rallye, which was offered only in France and Spain, boasted 55bhp (41kW), came with garish body stripes and could top 170km/h (105mph).

The clunky three-speed gearbox was replaced by a much-improved four-speeder version for the 1960s, and all-round disc brakes were an important innovation for the last four years of production.

ENGINE: 845cc (52cu in), four-cylinder
POWER: 49bhp (36kW)
0–60MPH (96KM/H): 28.2 seconds
TOP SPEED: 119km/h (74mph)
PRODUCTION TOTAL: 2,120,220

VOLVO 120 AMAZON

Volvo's long-running PV-series cars were in need of replacement by the 1950s, and, as they had carved themselves a reputation for longevity, creating a suitable successor could not be rushed. When it was launched after a long and thorough development programme, the Volvo 'Amason' was launched in 1956 to a warm reception – especially in its home market. The name would not stick, however, as the motorcycle manufacturer Kriedler also produced a product with this name and claimed the trademark was its. The two parties settled, and Volvo was allowed to use the Amason name in its home market, but exported cars would have to wear another badge. All export models were known as the 120, 130 and 220-series, with the original car being called the 121. Needless to say, the enthusiasts had the final vote, adopting the more familiar 'Amazon' tag for the car.

The first cars were equipped with a single-carburettor 1583cc (97cu in) version of the PV444 engine, which delivered just 60bhp (45kW) – not enough – and the performance was poor. A couple of years later, an 85bhp (63kW) version known as the 122S was launched – complete with an all-synchromesh four-speed gearbox –

and the Amazon was transformed. Front disc brakes were phased in during 1965, and a more affordable Amazon, known as the Favorit, was introduced. It looked cheaper, though, and lost much of the chrome trim and equipment. More sadly, it reverted to the older car's three-speed gearbox.

The Amazon was selling well across the world, and further cemented Volvo's reputation as a producer of solid and dependable cars – and, because of this, the car looked set for a long production run alongside the 140, which had initially been introduced in 1966 to replace it. A new sports Amazon

badged the 123GT (or the 120GT in some export markets), was introduced in 1966, and it proved appealing, marrying the 1.8-litre (110cu in) engine from the 1800S with the two-door bodyshell of the 122. With 115bhp (86kW) on tap and a four-speed manual with overdrive gearbox, it was practical

Volvo could never be accused of rapid model turnover – and the long life of the Amazon clearly shows that the company was all in favour of gradual evolution.

and sporting, as well as affordable when compared with the 1800S.

At the end of 1967, the four-door Amazon was taken out of production, as the Volvo 144 had become the more popular car. For the first half of the year, however, the 121 was still the best–selling car in Sweden. The two-door and estate (station-wagon) versions continued in production and, in autumn 1968, it was announced that the cars would upgunned by the addition of the B20 2-litre (122cu in) engine.

This bored-out version of the B18 powerplant was rated at either 90bhp (67kW) or 118bhp (88kW), depending on the level of tune. The extra power available was less important, however, than the greatly improved torque, which turned the Amazon into an appealing quick car.

In 1969, the Amazon estate was discontinued, superseded by the boxy 145 and leaving just the 122 – it was inevitable that the end was near, and, in the summer of 1969, the final Amazon rolled off the production line, after a long and distinguished career.

ENGINE: 1583cc (97cu in), four-cylinder
POWER: 66bhp (49kW)
0–60MPH (96KM/H): n/a
TOP SPEED: 144km/h (90mph)
PRODUCTION TOTAL: 667,323

LANCIA FLAMINIA
ITALY 1956–70

Lancia's aristocratic Flaminia was intended to replace the Aurelia, but the two cars ended up running side by side for a couple of years. Most importantly, the pretty new car ushered in a new design era at Lancia. Out went the slightly chubby looks of the Aurelia, and in came the more angular Pininfarina look that would be used to varying degrees on many other cars. Small tail fins were a bit of a culture shock, giving the Italian saloon something of an American look.

Lancia developed a new 2458cc (150cu in) V6 unit for the Flaminia, as well as new wishbone and coil spring front suspension. It remained like this until 1959, when a new Flaminia range appeared. A very elegant coupé (based on the Pininfarina Floride II show car) was joined by the more striking Flaminia GT coupé and convertible. Built on a substantially shortened wheelbase, and very effective use of quad headlights to give a purposeful front aspect, these cars were very desirable. Zagato also came up with pretty two-seater coupé versions, the Sport and Supersport.

From 1963, all Flaminias were uprated with a 2775cc (169cu in) V6 engine, although the coupés and convertibles were tuned to produce more power than the saloon.

ENGINE: 2458cc (150cu in), six-cylinder
POWER: 110bhp (82kW) at 5200rpm
0–60MPH (96KM/H): 14.5 seconds
TOP SPEED: 169km/h (105mph)
PRODUCTION TOTAL: 12,685

PLYMOUTH FURY
UNITED STATES 1956–74

Released in 1956, the two-door Plymouth Fury became one of the most famous American cars of its era, and ended up outliving its decade to become one of the most popular models in the country's long and sometimes glorious motoring history. With more than 200 derivatives of the Fury during its lifetime, the model range was all things to all men.

The Furys that most people will remember the clearest were produced in the late 1950s, and sported enormous tailfins, twin headlights and a wraparound radiator grille to distinguish them from the rest of the contemporary opposition. Four-door models were offered shortly after the car's announcement, but there was no appealing pillarless option on offer.

The Fury remained distinctively styled well into the 1960s, until it became part of Chrysler's characterless range of badge-engineered three-box saloons. From that point on, the Fury was robbed of its identity. For many, the final interesting Furys were built in 1974 – when Chrysler went all energy-conscious.

One of the most famous cars in the world was the 1958 Plymouth Grand Fury two-door coupé that achieved immortality – literally – in the Stephen King book and horror movie *Christine*, as a car possessed by the devil.

It's hard to imagine anyone mistaking a Plymouth Fury, thanks to its hooded headlamps, lashings of chrome and tail fins.

ENGINE: 5212cc (318cu in), eight-cylinder
POWER: 225bhp (168kW)
0–60MPH (96KM/H): 10.8 seconds
TOP SPEED: 169km/h (105mph)
PRODUCTION TOTAL: n/a

JAGUAR D-TYPE

Alongside the Mercedes-Benz 300SL Gullwing, the Jaguar D-type remains one of the 1950s most beautiful poster cars – and, like its German counterpart, it was also rather handy in competition. Announced in 1954, the D-type was the spiritual successor to the earlier C-type, and is still seen as one of the most evocative sports cars of its generation.

The styling was no accident of design, though. Its sleek lines and curious stabilizing fin running directly behind the driver were all in the name of aerodynamics. The low bonnet (hood) – and superb aerodynamic qualities – was down to Malcolm Sayer, who devised a way of reducing frontal area by dry sumping the engine and devising a separate radiator header tank.

Although it used the six-cylinder XK engine from the production cars of the time, the rest of the D bore little resemblance to its predecessor. It was smaller, lighter and far more modern in conception.

The all-new magnesium-alloy monocoque was a serious step forward from its predecessor, as the engine and suspension were held in a tubular frame. In its lifetime, alloy disc wheels replaced traditional wire wheels and a new Jaguar four-speed gearbox was specially developed for the car.

The D-type enjoyed many spectacular race successes, including outright wins at Le Mans in 1953, 1955, 1956 and 1957.

ENGINE: 3442cc (210cu in),
six-cylinder
POWER: 245bhp (183kW)
0–60MPH (96KM/H): n/a
TOP SPEED: 288km/h (180mph)
PRODUCTION TOTAL: 45

A proven race winner, the Jaguar D-type's enduring success was down to the attention to detail lavished on it by designer, Malcolm Sayer.

JAGUAR XKSS

Although the Jaguar XKSS was a development of the D-type, conspiracy theorists claim that the car was only produced because the company wanted to shift its stock of unsold D-types. The difference

There may have only been 16 built, and it might have been a development of the D-type, but the Jaguar XKSS was a sensational car.

between the cars was that the XKSS had been devised for the road, whereas the D-type was purely a limited-market racecar.

Either way, by cutting a door in the D-type's centre section, dropping the fin, adding a full-width screen and offering a primitive hood, Jaguar managed to create a road-going supercar. The XKSS ended up being a sensation and had a top speed of 240km/h (150mph), with handling to match.

While it was true that it was a two-seater with little in the way of creature comforts, that was not what the car was about.

Sadly, the model's future was dashed when Jaguar's Coventry factory suffered a major fire, in which several of the cars were destroyed along with the production line. The XKSS setback coincided with Jaguar shifting focus onto saloon car production – although fans insist the XKSS was reborn with

the E-type's launch in 1961. Only 16 examples of the XKSS were made, making it extremely rare; as with the C-type, the market is flooded with modern replicas.

ENGINE: 3442cc (210cu in),
six-cylinder
POWER: 250bhp (186kW)
0–60MPH (96KM/H): n/a
TOP SPEED: 238km/h (149mph)
PRODUCTION TOTAL: 16

ZUNDAPP JANUS

USSR 1957–58

The German microcar maker Dornier thought that it was on to something when it unveiled the Delta, its tiny new product in 1955. It was an angular-looking car that was interestingly symmetrical along its length and width. The car had two pairs of seats arranged back to back; passengers accessed these seats via a door on the front or an identical one on the back.

It was an odd concept, but that did not stop German motorcycle-maker Zundapp from buying the rights and producing it. The result was the aptly named Janus, which went on sale in 1957. It featured several detail changes from the original Delta's design.

The doors were no longer top-hinged, but instead conventionally hinged at the side. The styling was also toned down somewhat. The

One of the surprise hits of 1957, the Zundapp Janus is perhaps one of the weirdest cars produced in the post-war era.

centrally mounted engine remained. This was still a car that defied all convention when it came to design and construction.

The engine itself was less idiosyncratic, as it was similar to the powerplants installed in many microcars. In 1958, the car was dropped, and Zundapp returned to focusing on motorbike production.

ENGINE: 248cc (15cu in), single-cylinder
POWER: 14bhp (10kW)
0–60MPH (96KM/H): n/a
TOP SPEED: 80km/h (50mph)
PRODUCTION TOTAL: 6800

ASTON MARTIN DB MK III

UNITED KINGDOM 1957–59

ENGINE: 2922cc (178cu in),
  six-cylinder
POWER: 162bhp (121kW)
0–60MPH (96KM/H): 9.3 seconds
TOP SPEED: 192km/h (119mph)
PRODUCTION TOTAL: 551

In an ideal world, the next Aston Martin to follow the DB2 (or the DB2/4) should have been the DB3, but the company had already produced a DB3 – a racing car that was then updated to become the successful DB3S and the legendary DBR1. Instead, the company came up with the DB Mk III moniker for its newly improved version of the DB2/4. It was an elegant car and clearly defined Aston Martin as a successful British supercar manufacturer. Improvements were a general tidy-up of the exterior trim and the fitment of vertical rear lights to replace the ugly round lenses of the previous models. The grille design was improved, and its shape was echoed by the instrument binnacle inside the car.

The real innovations on the DB Mark III were the introduction of

front disc brakes and an updated version of the previous model's engine. The new version of the old 2.9-litre (178cu in) unit was much stronger and more efficient, with much-improved power outputs –

allegedly up to 214bhp (159kW). A legion of small improvements added up to a significantly better car.

The DB Mark III was chosen as the first James Bond Aston Martin, in the book *Goldfinger*.

An important step in Aston Martin history, the DB Mk III was a halfway point between the DB2 and the epic DB4. Upgrades included a more powerful engine and front disc brakes.

OPEL OLYMPIA P1

GERMANY 1957–63

Just as was the case with GM-owned sister company Vauxhall, Opel's products were increasingly being influenced by its American counterparts. By the time the Olympia P1 appeared, Opel freely admitted that US styling influence was strong – perhaps as an excuse to justify the P1's ungainly looks.

On a smaller car, details such as the wraparound screens, tail fins

and chrome adornments simply did not work as they should have. The P1 was a small two- or four-door saloon the same size as the Vauxhall Viva, and the effect was confused. The stubby bodywork looked at odds with the curved front and rear screens, while the huge radiator grille made the Olympia P1 look like a cheap caricature of some of the United States' more

impressive models. Despite that, the P1 was a massive sales success. During its six–year production run, over 1.5 million cars were sold.

An estate car (station wagon), the 'Caravan', was offered from 1958 – and it looked even stranger. The P1 range offered a choice of engines, including the earlier Olympia's 1488cc (91cu in) overhead-valve unit, as well as a

new 1205cc (74cu in) overhead-valve engine or a livelier 1680cc (98cu in) car, the Rekord P2.

ENGINE: 1488cc (91cu in),
  four-cylinder
POWER: 45bhp (34kW)
0–60MPH (96KM/H): 28 seconds
TOP SPEED: 116km/h (72mph)
PRODUCTION TOTAL: 1,611,445

RAMBLER REBEL

The 'full-size' Rambler marked a dramatic change in approach from parent company AMC. It boasted an all-new body and controversially angular styling. AMC had previously been respected for building well-engineered but dull cars under the Nash and Hudson names, and Rambler represented a brave new world. The new cars were not dull – and, indeed, their rakish front-end styling and huge fins were for extroverts only.

The Rebel was the flagship model in this range, and was powered by a suitably grunty 215bhp (160kW) V8 engine in place of standard cars' six-cylinder units.

A four-door 'Country Club' sedan, with an unusual pillarless profile and a glass area that cut deep into the car's waistline, and an even more challenging estate (stationwagon) version, with an odd luggage rack over the rear area of the roof, were offered to brave buyers. The two-car range was a charismatic addition to a sector of the market crowded with talent.

Rebels were distinctive for their torpedo-shaped badging, ornate hubcaps and excess chrome. Otherwise, they looked identical to lesser Ramblers. Optional extras included 'Flash-O-Matic' push-button overdrive, power steering, electric windows, a radio, record player and reversing floodlights, guaranteed to blind following motorists.

ENGINE: 4704cc (287cu in), eight-cylinder
POWER: 215bhp (160kW)
0–60MPH (96KM/H): n/a
TOP SPEED: 169km/h (105mph)
PRODUCTION TOTAL: n/a

RILEY 2.6

After the folly of the Pathfinder, its replacement certainly looked like a retrograde step – gone was the nicely detailed Gerald Palmer–styled bodywork, and in its place was a much older looking car. It even had separate wings (fenders) and running boards. But the car was produced on purely economic grounds. The old and much-lamented RM-Series engine was replaced by the recently launched BMC C-Series engine in 2.6-litre (159cu in) six-cylinder form. Shared with the Wolseley 6/90, it gave a boost in power that went some way to placating traditionally sporting-minded Riley drivers.

The use of semi-elliptic leaf springs at the back instead of the previous model's unsteady Panhard rod and coil spring arrangement was a notable advantage over the Pathfinder. However, this never fully countered the Pathfinder's understeer. The Riley 2.6 never achieved much in the way of popularity, and the car remains largely forgotten today.

ENGINE: 2639cc (161cu in), six-cylinder
POWER: 102bhp (76kW)
0–60MPH (96KM/H): 17.8 seconds
TOP SPEED: 153km/h (95mph)
PRODUCTION TOTAL: 2000

EDSEL

Asked to name great automotive disasters, most people will instantly think of the Edsel, even if they do not fully understand the story. However, there is no denying the numbers – the Edsel adventure lost Ford $300 million.

Born out of a need for Ford to have a mid-market car to which owners of more basic models could aspire, the Edsel brand was created and named after Henry Ford II's father, Edsel. The idea was to plug the small gap between the Lincoln and Mercury ranges, and the good-value Edsel Rangers and Pacers were slightly more expensive than Fords, while the Edsel Corsair and Citation were more costly than a Mercury.

The models looked identical, but the more expensive versions had larger V8 engines. Despite lots of hype, sales were slow and dealers who overordered went bankrupt. These were good cars, unfortunately launched at a time when buyers had started to 'downsize'. Also, the Edsel had a 'horse collar' grille that some customers likened to a toilet seat. The expensive models were dropped in 1959, and the Villager estate (station wagon) was introduced. The redesign in 1960 was too little, too late, and failed to save the marque.

ENGINE: 3655cc (224cu in), eight-cylinder
POWER: 147bhp (110kW)
0–60MPH (96KM/H): 12 seconds
TOP SPEED: 174km/h (108mph)
PRODUCTION TOTAL: 111,000

Synonymous with automotive failure, the Edsel name has now passed into motoring folklore. It was actually a perfectly adequate product, simply badly judged for the prevailing market conditions, proving you can have too many marques.

STANDARD PENNANT

The Standard Pennant was simply an upmarket version of the Standard Ten, which in itself was a development of the Standard

Developed from the Standard Ten and Eight, the Pennant was a short-lived model, and was indicative of the downfall of the Standard marque.

Eight, and is largely forgotten now. The Ten was launched in 1954 as a response to the sheer sparseness of the Eight, which was so basic that it was scaring off customers.

What was effectively a deluxe variant of the Eight, the Ten was marketed as a new car that could be sold alongside the original model. However it was dressed up, the Ten still was not enough to

encourage customers back into the Standard fold – hence the arrival of another model and a new name, the Pennant. The new car was powered by a more useful 37bhp (28kW) version of the 948cc (58cu in) engine, with two-tone paintwork, hooded headlights and longer front and rear wings (fenders).

A larger rear window and a more flamboyant three-bar grille were

also Pennant identifiers. It sold steadily during its production run, but never set the world on fire.

ENGINE: 948cc (58cu in), four-cylinder
POWER: 37bhp (28kW)
0–60MPH (96KM/H): 34.9 seconds
TOP SPEED: 106km/h (66mph)
PRODUCTION TOTAL: 42,910

WARTBURG SPORT

The Wartburg Sport was a pretty addition to the company's three-car range that borrowed a number of styling cues from the West German opposition. Listed as a separate model, the Sport actually shared almost all of its components with its more common 311-based Coupé and Cabriolet counterparts. The transverse leaf springs all round were range

carryovers, and the three-cylinder 900cc (55cu in) engine still drove the front wheels via a four-speed gearbox. The flowing lines and wraparound window glass front and rear of the 311 were also retained – these were cars which were genuinely good-looking.

First unveiled in 1957, the Sport's major selling point was that its power had been boosted to

50bhp (37kW), which was a fair upgrade from the standard car's 37bhp (28kW). Performance was significantly improved, and a top speed of 140km/h (87mph) was not to be sneezed at when compared with the 311's 115km/h (72mph) maximum.

From 1958, in common with the rest of the Wartburg range, the four-speed gearbox received

synchromesh on all the forward gears – and, yet, the Sport was dropped two years later.

ENGINE: 900cc (55cu in), three-cylinder
POWER: 50bhp (37kW)
0–60MPH (96KM/H): n/a
TOP SPEED: 140km/h (87mph)
PRODUCTION TOTAL: n/a

GOLIATH 1100

In 1957, the car manufacturer Goliath finally made the transition to the modern era, by advancing technically and moving away from the continued reliance on pre-war mechanicals on its cars. The 1100 spearheaded this move, and came with a number of company firsts.

The brand-new water-cooled four-stroke flat-four engine was one, and the column-change four-speed

gearbox ended up being replaced with a much nicer floor-mounted all-synchromesh unit. Coil suspension replaced the leaf-sprung front suspension, and improved ride and stability. One backward step was the return to standard carburettion, as the previous car's fuel injection system delivered shaky results. The 1100 was renamed Hansa in 1958; to mark

the occasion, delicate fins were added to the rear wings (fenders).

Available in four bodystyles, the range comprised of a saloon, estate (station wagon), coupé and a cute-looking convertible model. Although the coupé was little more than a lightly modified saloon with a slightly shorter roof, its role was to go head to head against the more expensive Volkswagen Karmann

Ghia. Over 40,000 examples of the 1100 in its various guises were sold during its four-year lifespan.

ENGINE: 1094cc (67cu in), four-cylinder
POWER: 40bhp (30kW)
0–60MPH (96KM/H): 19 seconds
TOP SPEED: 125km/h (78mph)
PRODUCTION TOTAL: 42,695

JAGUAR XK150

Compared with the sublimely beautiful XK120 and XK140, the replacement model, rather unimaginatively called the XK150, was something of a disappointment to look at. Heavier than its predecessors, and looking just a little overweight, the XK150 gained a less distinctive higher

The XK150 is seen as the final flowering of the X120 line before the E-type burst onto the scene.

waistline and a welcome one-piece wraparound front screen.

Despite the unconvincing styling, the car was far more refined, and had become more comfortable and more civilized to drive in the process. Dunlop disc brakes were fitted to all four wheels, and handling was more assured than that of the earlier XKs. The continuation of the rear bench seat from the XK140 and the Borg Warner automatic transmission underlined the fact that Jaguar was

pitching the XK150 in the GT, rather than sportscar, market.

The 210bhp (156kW) Blue Top engine continued alongside the 190bhp (142kW) unit, although top speed fell to 200km/h (125mph). In 1958, the balance was restored with the introduction of a new version. To counter accusations that the XK150 had become 'middle-aged', Jaguar launched the S version, with 250bhp (186kW) on tap. From 1959, all cars were fitted with the 3.8-litre (232cu in)

engine, increasing power to 220bhp (164kW), or 265bhp (197kW) on the S versions. The XK150, however, represented little more than the calm before the E-type shaped storm...

ENGINE: 3442cc (210cu in), six-cylinder
POWER: 190bhp (142kW)
0–60MPH (96KM/H): 8.4 seconds
TOP SPEED: 198km/h (125mph)
PRODUCTION TOTAL: 9398

SIMCA ARONDE OCÉANE

The Simca Aronde Océane proved once and for all that it was possible to launch a two-seater open-topped car that was not remotely sporting. Available as a convertible or coupé, the Océane was powered by a big-valve version of Simca's well-established 1290cc (79cu in) four-cylinder engine, rated

at 57bhp (42kW). A revised five-bearing engine appeared from 1961, upping the ante to 62bhp (46kW), but the car was still no ball of fire. The next year, further tuning produced another 8bhp (6kW).

When the Océane was first displayed, it had something of the Ford Thunderbird about it – at the

time, Simca had often looked to the United States for inspiration. In 1959, that changed. The Océane picked up an Aston Martin–style grille, a look that stayed with the car until it went out of production three years later.

Although it appears the Océane lasted five years, it was actually

double that, as it was an update of the Simca 9, first seen in 1951.

ENGINE: 1290cc (79cu in), four-cylinder
POWER: 57bhp (42kW)
0–60MPH (96KM/H): n/a
TOP SPEED: 139km/h (87mph)
PRODUCTION TOTAL: 11,560

VESPA 400

Although Vespa is most readily associated with Italian scooters, the cars that carry the legendary name were actually produced in France. The reason for this anomaly was that Fiat's control over the car industry was already widespread, and it had established an agreement that no motorcycle producer would challenge its

market domination. In effect, Vespa needed to produce cars elsewhere in order to bypass the agreement. As a result, the Vespa 400 was made in Nievre, France.

The Vespa 400 was undoubtedly one of the better built microcars of the time, as it had a monocoque construction. With independent suspension all round, a three-speed

gearbox and hydraulic brakes, this was no crudely engineered backyard special. It was a 2+2 coupé featuring the additional benefits of a roll-back cloth sunroof. The air-cooled vertical twin engine was mounted at the car's rear, leaving the front for carrying luggage.

Although it was not fast, the car could cruise quite happily all day

at 65km/h (40mph). Production of the Vespa 400 ended in 1961.

ENGINE: 393cc (24cu in), twin-cylinder
POWER: 15bhp (11kW)
0–60MPH (96KM/H): n/a
TOP SPEED: 80km/h (50mph)
PRODUCTION TOTAL: about 34,000

VAUXHALL CRESTA PA

ENGINE: 2262cc (138cu in),
 six-cylinder
POWER: 82bhp (61kW)
0–60MPH (96KM/H): 16.8 seconds
TOP SPEED: 145km/h (90mph)
PRODUCTION TOTAL: n/a

Vauxhall's cars of the 1950s were smaller facsimiles of what was being produced in the United States at the time. This was no surprise, given the fact that GM owned the company – and it was certainly apparent in the design of the Cresta PA. It sported relatively large fins, a wraparound windscreen and heavy chrome-laden bumpers front and rear – pure Americana.

The concept of a large, unstressed engine was very American, too – and, although in the Cresta it had six cylinders in place of the favoured American V8, it was large compared with the mainly four-cylinder opposition.

The 2262cc (138cu in) engine produced just 75bhp (56kW), but there was plenty of torque and no need to use the three-speed

column-mounted gearshift with any frequency. The ride was supreme, helped by the bodyshell's huge bulk, and the boot (trunk) was also very large – but space efficiency was no great shakes.

In 1960, a 2651cc (162cu in) engine with an extra 20bhp (15kW) was drafted in, and the car became even more enjoyable to use, especially if the optional Hydramatic automatic gearbox was specified.

The Cresta PA is a fine antidote for all those who say old Vauxhalls are boring. Featuring amazing styling, there's a lot to like about the car, despite its terrible corrosion reputation.

LOTUS ELITE

Alternatively known as the Lotus 14, the Elite was part of a two-pronged attack (along with the Eleven) by Lotus on the sports-car market. The two cars could not be more different, though, with the sublime Elite contrasting nicely with the stark track-biased Eleven.

The Elite was Chapman's first attempt at a true road car, and it was judged to perfection. Technically, it was a fantastic,

featuring the world's first glassfibre monocoque, made by Bristol Aircraft in England. The Elite was aerodynamic (0.26cd), attributable to its stylist, Peter Kirwan Taylor. The sleek little GT took the 1957 London Motor Show by storm.

Coventry Climax engines were used, and S2 cars had optional twin carburettors. The 1962 SE had 85bhp (63kW) on tap, while the Super 95, Super 100 and Super

105 Elites were named according to their power outputs.

Using independent wishbone/coils at the front and Chapman struts at the rear, the mechanical components were bolted through the glassfibre, with metal inserts at mounting points. The ride was firm, but fabulously well damped, handling was amazing, and disc brakes were fitted all round. It was also noisy and harsh, however,

with plenty of vibration from the poorly ventilated monocoque shell. A real sportscar advancement, but it lost Lotus much money.

ENGINE: 1216cc (74cu in),
 four-cylinder
POWER: 75bhp (56kW)
0–60MPH (96KM/H): 11.4 seconds
TOP SPEED: 183km/h (114mph)
PRODUCTION TOTAL: 1078

MASERATI 3500GT

When the Maserati 3500GT hit the market in 1957, Ferrari found itself fighting for honours in the supercar market with a fearsome foe that was based locally. The car signalled Maserati's move into Ferrari's patch – producing some of the world's most desirable sports cars.

The 3500GT was a successor to the A6G/2000, but represented the transformation of Maserati from racing car manufacturer to fully fledged road-car builder. The new, immensely stylish car ushered in higher levels of production, although only 2223 examples of the 3500GT coupé and convertible Spider version were built in seven years. In specialist car manufacturing terms, however, this was a serious number of cars in a short space of time.

Although much of the 3500GT was completely new, elements were carried over from Maserati's previous models. The tubular steel chassis was based on the A6G, with coil spring independent front suspension and a live rear axle on semi-elliptic springs. The straight-six engine, substantially more powerful than the A6G's, was distantly related to the one that powered the 250F Grand Prix cars, as well as the 300S and 350S sports racers.

The twin overhead camshaft was reworked by Chief engineer Guilio Alfieri to make it road car tractable, using three Weber carburettors and two spark plugs per cylinder. To the untrained eye, it looked like a straight 12-cylinder engine, due to 12 plugs fitted where there usually would be just

six. The results were impressive, and it produced 220bhp (164kW).

The bodies were pretty special, with the majority of the attractive coupé shells being produced by Touring using aluminium panels and Superleggera (extra light) principles, but Bertone, Allemano and Frua also produced their own striking styles, while Moretti and Boneschi built one-offs.

The company continuously developed the 3500GT during its life, and 1959 saw front disc brakes introduced – but the most noteworthy issue was the appearance of the Spider convertible. Responsible for the beautiful body design was Giovanni Michelotti, who worked for Vignale. While much of the engineering was the same as the fixed-head models, the Vignale-

built bodies were substantially different to the Touring coupés, and were made out of steel.

The year 1961 saw the next major changes to the 3500GT formula. In response to the Jaguar E-type – which worried the Italian supercar manufacturers – Maserati fitted Lucas fuel injection to create the 3500GTI, thus building the first Italian production car to feature an injection system. Ironically enough, it was the same system as used by many Jaguar racing cars. It proved troublesome, but, when working properly, power was lifted by 15bhp (11kW), and the car's top speed also went up significantly.

Other changes around this time included the introduction of a five-speed manual transmission, disc brakes all round, a rerouted exhaust system, deletion of the front fog lights and revised indicators and rear lights. The end of production in 1964 even saw automatic transmission introduced, reinforcing the car's GT status.

The 3500GT enhanced the company's reputation and gave it the confidence and financial ability to start building some real supercars with which to fight Ferrari.

ENGINE: 3485cc (213cu in),
 six-cylinder
POWER: 220bhp (164kW) at 5500rpm
0–60MPH (96KM/H): 8.1 seconds
TOP SPEED: 204km/h (127mph)
PRODUCTION TOTAL: 2223

A true supercar when it appeared, and unmistakably a Maserati, thanks to the bold trident emblem on the radiator grille, the 3500GT was fast, well equipped and expensive.

RILEY 1.5

UNITED KINGDOM 1957–65

ENGINE: 1489cc (91cu in),
 four-cylinder
POWER: 62bhp (46kW)
0–60MPH (96KM/H): 17.4 seconds
TOP SPEED: 135km/h (84mph)
PRODUCTION TOTAL: 39,568

Although the Riley 1.5 was a badge-engineered Wolseley, which in itself was based heavily on the Morris Minor, it actually went some way towards reviving the marque's sporting spirit. Whatever enthusiasts thought about Wolseley and Riley coming together as they did, the 1.5 emerged as a pleasingly driver-focused saloon car, although Riley traditionalists must have been disappointed by what lay underneath the pretty four-door bodywork. This was despite the fact that the Minor was regarded as one of the most entertaining small cars on Britain's roads at the time of the new model's launch.

It made do with an awkward, short-looking wheelbase because of the car's humble underpinnings, but a boost was provided by the ubiquitous BMC B-Series engine, in 1489cc (91cu in) twin-carburettor form. This meant the car offered almost as much performance as the flamboyant MGA and could be tuned further to offer 160km/h (100mph) performance if desired.

The only downsides were very average brakes and, like many cars of the era, terrible rust problems.

Despite being a badge-engineered Wolseley 1500, the Riley One-Point-Five was a genuinely sporting car to drive.

WOLSELEY 1500

ENGINE: 1489cc (91cu in),
four-cylinder
POWER: 43bhp (32kW)
0–60MPH (96KM/H): 24.4 seconds
TOP SPEED: 125km/h (78mph)
PRODUCTION TOTAL: 93,312

The formation of BMC in 1952 had seen two once-great marques, Wolseley and Riley, brought together in an alliance that fans of the respective marques were not that keen on. Effectively the same car as the Riley 1.5, the Wolseley 1500 was developed from an aborted project to replace the Morris Minor, which never saw the light of day thanks to the original car's considerable success. Originally planned to have a 1.2-litre (73cu in) engine (destined to become the B-Series engine), the final car, which became the Wolseley 1500, was equipped with a 1489cc (91cu in) version of the old BMC B-Series powerplant.

The Minor's suspension was carried over and, with compact dimensions (just 386cm/152in long with a 218cm/86in wheelbase),

the 1500 was sold as a small luxury car. But it was not quick, and made do with 43bhp (32kW).

In 1960, the Mk II arrived, with hidden bonnet (hood) and boot (trunk) hinges, along with some minor engine modifications. The Mk III version appeared in 1961, with a new grille, taillights and lower suspension, but it faded away in light of the front-wheel drive Wolseley 1100.

Originally developed from the abandoned plans to replace the much-loved Morris Minor, the Wolseley 1500 retains that car's excellent steering and handling. A genuinely nice car to drive.

WARTBURG COUPÉ AND CABRIOLET

During the 1950s, Wartburg was producing a range of attractive saloons and coupés – a far cry from the modern perception that the marque's output was painfully square, smelly and noisy. The two-stroke Wartburg 353 Knight is the reason for the 'smoker' reputation.

The first post-war Wartburgs had been built by the state-owned IFA Company in 1950 and were badged as the F9. When a replacement was devised, it was decided to revive the Wartburg name, which had been used for cars built at Eisenach in East Germany until production had ceased in 1904. Using the same DKW-inspired 900cc (55cu in) three-cylinder two-stroke engine used in the F9, power was boosted from 30bhp (22kW) to 37bhp (28kW).

Another hangover from the old car was the four-speed gearbox and innovative front-wheel drive layout. That meant that, although the Wartburg looked all new, it was almost unchanged under the skin. The Coupé and Cabriolet did not major on interior space, but they looked good.

ENGINE: 900cc (55cu in),
three-cylinder
POWER: 37bhp (28kW)
0–60MPH (96KM/H): n/a
TOP SPEED: 115km/h (72mph)
PRODUCTION TOTAL: n/a

Extremely pretty styling was a major feature of the Wartburg Coupé and Cabriolet range – and had there been more power available than the 900cc (55cu in) engine was prepared to give, it could have achieved so much more.

AUTOBIANCHI BIANCHINA

Created by Edoardo Bianchi in 1899, the company that bore his name had been around since the earliest days of the motor industry. Although Bianchi was a name seldom heard outside its home country of Italy, Autobianchi played a major part in the Italian car industry over the years.

Originally called simply Bianchi, the company started out building motorcycles, before moving into car manufacture, competing against the all-powerful Fiat in some of its favoured market sectors. However, car manufacture ceased after World War II, leading to severe financial problems. In 1955, Edoardo's son, Guiseppe (who has been in charge since 1946), approached Fiat and Pirelli with a proposal to create a new manufacturer – and all three parties subsequently reached an agreement to create Autobianchi.

The first car to come out of the new company was the Bianchina.

Launched in 1957, the good-looking coupé was a rebody of the Fiat 500 (called the Trasformabile), with its two-cylinder, air-cooled engine mounted in the rear.

Luigi Rapi, who was in charge of Fiat's special body unit and helped to set up production in Desio, had designed the completely new and stylish body. Marketed as a luxurious 'recreational vehicle', it mirrored the increasing affluence in Italian society. It remained the sole bodystyle until 1960, when a two-door cabriolet was introduced, followed by a three-door estate (stationwagon) version, which was called the Panoramica.

ENGINE: 479cc (29cu in), twin-cylinder
POWER: 13bhp (10kW)
0–60MPH (96KM/H): n/a
TOP SPEED: 100km/h (62mph)
PRODUCTION TOTAL: 273,800

ENZMANN 506

A cross between a boat and a small sportscar – the Enzmann 506 was based on the floorpan of the Volkswagen Beetle.

The Enzmann 506 was one of the earliest examples of a kit car based entirely on the running gear of the Volkswagen Beetle. Designed and marketed by Swiss company Garage Enzmann, the car was not sold as a self-assembly kit. Unusually, the company actually purchased brand-new Beetles from Volkswagen and removed what it needed, particularly the floorpan and engine. It then commissioned a boatyard called Staempfi to mount the glassfibre body on top of the rolling chassis.

The result was very attractive, if unorthodox, and more than a little boat-like. The car had no doors, and the rear-mounted engine meant a smooth and featureless front end, with a nautical 'bow' – a type of boat guardrail bumper.

A removable hardtop was made available that resembled a futuristic aircraft canopy, which cantilevered backwards onto the rear engine deck. The engine and gearbox were barely changed from standard 1192cc (73cu in) aircooled flat-four engine, but the light body ensured reasonable performance. An Okrasa tuning kit was available, resulting in more impressive performance. Production just topped 100 units.

ENGINE: 1192cc (73cu in), four-cylinder
POWER: 56bhp (42kW)
0–60MPH (96KM/H): 20 seconds
TOP SPEED: 121km/h (75mph)
PRODUCTION TOTAL: 100

STEYR-PUCH 500

Following its near destruction during World War II, Steyr decided to forgo car production. The hiatus from the car industry was temporary, however, and, in 1948, a deal was signed with the Italian car producer Fiat. The deal resulted in Fiats being produced in Austria and would eventually see Steyr versions of the Nuova 500 being made at the Puch factory in Graz. Using a Fiat bodyshell and powered by the 493cc (30cu in) two-cylinder Steyr powerplant, the Steyr-Puch 500 was bargain basement motoring typified.

A Steyr version of the Mini Cooper was introduced in 1964. The higher performance of the car, called the 650 TRII, was powered by a 660cc (40cu in) horizontally opposed twin-cylinder engine. With up to 40bhp (30kW), its top speed was impressive – 128km/h (80mph).

ENGINE: 493cc (30cu in), twin-cylinder
POWER: 16bhp (12kW)
0–60MPH (96KM/H): n/a
TOP SPEED: 100km/h (62mph)
PRODUCTION TOTAL: n/a

PONTIAC BONNEVILLE

Having appeared on a pair of bubble-topped GM Motorama concept cars, the Bonneville name was rather important to Pontiac. As a result, when it was ushered into production in 1957, the Bonneville was very much Pontiac's 'trophy' car. During the era of fins and chrome adornments, Semon 'Bunkie' Knudsen's design stood out as one of the principal proponents.

It featured huge rear fins and an ornate rear bumper that appeared to have downward-pointing overriders, and incorporated two horizontal taillights. With a two- or four-door saloon, a huge split-tailgate estate (station wagon), coupé or convertible, there was a Bonneville for all buyers.

Power came from the engine of the existing Pontiac Star Chief, but bored out to 6063cc (370cu in) and offering 255bhp (190kW); some fuel-injected versions could produce over 300bhp (224kW).

A huge car, the Bonneville weighed in at more than 2000kg (two tons) and was 583cm (17ft 8in) long, meaning it struggled for room even in the United States, and its sheer size meant that it was no driver's car. Power steering and automatic transmission were standard, while convertible models also came with electric windows and a power folding roof.

ENGINE: 6063cc (370cu in), eight-cylinder
POWER: 255bhp (190kW)
0–60MPH (96KM/H): 10.1 seconds
TOP SPEED: 161km/h (100mph)
PRODUCTION TOTAL: 180,531

Pontiac's full-sized coupé and convertible Bonneville range was never the success that its company hoped for it. Lavish proportions, huge fins and chrome were all features of the car, as were the larger than life V8 engines.

LOTUS SEVEN

UNITED KINGDOM 1957–73

In an era when the rest of the car industry was producing ever bigger and more complex cars, the Lotus Seven was a breath of fresh air. When it was launched in 1957, the Seven boasted a minimalist specification that was as much about what did not feature on the equipment tally. With its skinny tyres, minimal body and rock-hard ride, it still managed to become one of Britain's best-loved and most enduring sports cars, enjoying a production run of 16 years before going on to a rather lucrative afterlife as a Caterham.

The first Seven was a kit based on the Mk VI chassis, which was progressively strengthened as the Seven gained extra power and performance during its production run. The suspension system was simple, using wishbones and coil spring/damper units at the front, and a live rear axle.

There were no driver comforts, and early cars did not even have opening doors. The cockpit was narrow and cramped, and was useless for taller drivers. Those that did fit had to adopt the notorious 'elbows-out' driving position. Two cushions – one on the floor, the other on the back panel – were the only seating. Entry-level models were so stark, even the canvas hood and windscreen wipers were listed as options. There was not even a

fuel gauge as standard until the S3 arrived in 1968. As with traditional 1930s sports cars, the spare wheel was boot (trunk) mounted.

Various engines were used during the Seven's life. The first cars used the 40bhp (30kW) 1172cc (72cu in) Ford side-valve engine, but the Super Seven had a 75bhp (56kW) 1097cc (67cu in) Coventry Climax unit married to a four-speed BMC gearbox. This short-lived option was replaced by the 95bhp (71kW) Cosworth 109E engine in 1961.

With its flared glassfibre front wings (fenders), the 1960 S2 version was instantly recognizable, and most cars left the factory with Ford

engines and gearboxes. The S3 was the ultimate Seven, powered by either a 1.6-litre (98cu in) Holbay-tuned Ford engine or Lotus's own fiery Twin Camshaft unit as found in the Elan. Only 15 Twin Cam Sevens were produced.

The S4 was a restyle too far. Introduced in 1970, and fashioned in glassfibre by Alan Barrett, it was not a successful look. The chassis was new, too, with suspension from the Europa at the front and Watts linkage at the rear.

When the car moved over to Caterham in 1973 (following Lotus creator Colin Chapman's decision to stop selling kit cars), company owner Graham Nearn's first step

was to relaunch the S3, accepting that the S4 did not have the same timeless appeal with buyers.

Thanks to the Caterham efforts, the Seven lived on indefinitely, remaining in production well into the twenty-first century. When Lotus stopped producing the car, it was the end of an era, signalling the beginning of the company's ill-fated push upmarket.

ENGINE: 1599cc (98cu in),
four-cylinder
POWER: 115bhp (86kW)
0–60MPH (96KM/H): 7.7 seconds
TOP SPEED: 163km/h (102mph)
PRODUCTION TOTAL: 2477

For many, the Lotus offered the opportunity to experience enormous grip and roadholding for very reasonable money.

SEAT 600

Across Europe, the post-war years were an exciting time for car manufacture – each country's population was looking for an inexpensive and simple car with which to get motorized. In France, it was the Citroën 2CV; in Italy, it was the Fiat Nuova 500 – and, in Spain, the car that gave the people their mobility was the Seat 600.

First shown at the 1955 Geneva Motor Show, the new baby car was not only cheap to buy, but also cost pennies to run. Based closely on Dante Giacosa's design for Fiat, the 600 finally went on sale in May 1957 and was an instant sales success. As well as the Fiat-derived 600 two-door model, the company also offered commercial derivatives, a convertible and, later, a four-door version called the 800.

Powered by a rear-mounted 633cc (39cu in) engine, the first cars were imported from Italy (as part of a joint venture); however, within months, a new factory in Barcelona was mass-producing them in large quantities. During the vehicle's 16-year production run, more than 800,000 examples of the Seat 600 were built.

ENGINE: 633cc (39cu in), four-cylinder
POWER: 21.5bhp (16kW)
0–60MPH (96KM/H): n/a
TOP SPEED: 95km/h (59mph)
PRODUCTION TOTAL: about 800,000

FIAT NUOVA 500

The successor to the legendary pre-war Topolino, the Nuova 500 was Fiat's most famous people's car. Relatively quick and frugal, the car possessed efficient handling and boasted wonderfully direct steering – a recipe that won it millions of fans in car-loving Italy.

This 'Nuova 500' was technically similar to the 600 – a rear-mounted engine drove the rear wheels, and the car featured all-round independent suspension with rear-hinged 'suicide' doors. A first for Fiat was the air-cooled engine, which was a two-cylinder 479cc (29cu in) unit producing 13bhp (10kW) in basic form.

A four-speed gearbox with a floor-mounted gear lever was precise and fun to use.

Initial sales were slow, however, and that led Fiat to launch two new versions, the 15bhp (11kW) Economica and the Normale. Essentially, the Economica was the original car, but with a more powerful engine and lower price tag. The Normale also had the uprated engine, plus various other upgrades that made the car easier to live with.

In 1958, the Sport model was introduced as a result of a spate of track successes, such as a first, second, third and fourth in class at the Hockenheim 12-hour race. This model was fitted with an uprated version of the standard engine, enlarged to 499cc (30cu in), with a revised camshaft, valves, cylinder head and fuelling. As a result, it now produced a very creditable 21.5bhp (16kW). With a distinctive red stripe down each side, the Sport was difficult to miss. Another feature was its solid roof, compared to the canvas roll-back roof found on standard production cars. The Sport was offered with an open-air option from 1959.

A Giardiniera estate (station wagon) version was introduced for 1960, which rode on a stretched wheelbase and differed from the saloon by having a horizontally mounted engine. Later that year, the 500D arrived with a 499cc (30cu in) engine from the discontinued Sport, but a reduced power output of 18bhp (13kW).

The 500D was replaced by the 500F in 1965, where the most noticeable changes were the overdue adoption of front-hinged doors and a revised transmission. In 1968, the 500F was joined in production by the Lusso, which offered several touches of big-car luxury, including reclining seats and even carpet.

There were literally dozens of 500 spin-off models – as well as the famous sporting Abarth-tuned models, some of Italy's most famous coachbuilders transformed the 500. Vignale's Fiat Gamine was a smart little roadster, while the Ghia Jolly had the roof removed. Siata built a miniature open-topped classic car. The 500 was also a genuine world car, built by SEAT in Spain and Motor Holdings in New Zealand, while the NSU-Fiat Weinsburg 500 from Germany was a Teutonically styled version.

The final version emerged in 1972 as the 500R, which used a new 594cc (36cu in) engine from the 126, with a reduced output of 18bhp (13kW). The R also had the floorpan from its successor and adopted the new Fiat logo, with different wheels and a few other changes. The car's basic drum brakes were never updated, however, while the 'crash' non-synchromesh gearbox provided lots of noisy entertainment.

ENGINE: 499cc (30cu in), four-cylinder
POWER: 18bhp (13kW)
0–60MPH (96KM/H): 45 seconds
TOP SPEED: 98km/h (61mph)
PRODUCTION TOTAL: 3,678,000

Responsible for motorizing the masses in Italy, the Nuova 500 was a taste of motoring at its most basic, with a generous dose of charisma thrown in for good measure.

PEERLESS

Based on Triumph TR3 mechanicals and using the same 100bhp (75kW) 1991cc (121cu in) engine, the Peerless was an interesting special. Like so many low-volume sports cars, it was never developed thoroughly.

Built on a unique spaceframe chassis, the Peerless featured glassfibre bodywork, and it was considerably quicker than the Triumph it was based upon because of its relative lightness. The two-door coupé body looked good and was spacious. Passenger comfort was not bad considering the stiff suspension set-up, but bumpy roads upset the equilibrium. A de Dion rear end meant that handling was safe and predictable.

The Peerless Phase Two appeared in 1959 and featured recessed headlights and a one-piece body that was simpler to produce. The Peerless had so much going for it, such as pretty styling and a realistic price, but lack of development and poor sales let the car slip into obscurity when the company closed in 1960. It was briefly revived as the Warwick, but new styling and a Buick 3.5-litre (213cu in) V8 were not enough to save it.

ENGINE: 1991cc (121cu in), four-cylinder
POWER: 100bhp (75kW)
0–60MPH (96KM/H): 12.3 seconds
TOP SPEED: 189km/h (117mph)
PRODUCTION TOTAL: 290

FACEL VEGA HK500

The Facel Vega HK500 may have been an update of the previous FVS model, but it was a considerably quicker car, thanks to the massive 360bhp (268kW) 6.3-litre (384cu in) engine found under the bonnet (hood). Styling was also pleasingly tweaked, with stacked quad headlights, more angular bodywork and a lean-forward nose. The effect gave the car a completely livelier look. Undoubtedly, with the HK500, Facel Vega took a definite step forwards. It was a truly impressive machine, especially when options such as power steering and disc brakes became standard.

Although priced to compete with the cream of the Italian supercar crop, it had no trouble keeping up with any of them – sadly, the handling was not in the same league. Despite that, the HK established Facel Vega in the supercar league, and also set the template for countless burgeoning manufacturers of fast cars to emulate during the 1960s. In particular, both Bristol and Jensen in the United Kingdom began installing similar or identical-sized Chrysler V8 engines to power their own coupés. Facel Vega cars were always more expensive than their European rivals, but build quality and styling justified the premium.

ENGINE: 6286cc (384cu in), eight-cylinder
POWER: 360bhp (268kW)
0–60MPH (96KM/H): 8.5 seconds
TOP SPEED: 225km/h (140mph)
PRODUCTION TOTAL: 500

JAGUAR MK IX

As was the fashion with Jaguar in the 1950s, saloon development was all about evolution, rather than revolution. The Mk IX was typical of the breed. Cosmetically, it was very similar to the last of the Mk VIII versions, and most of the improvements took place under the four-door's imposing skin.

A welcome addition to the Mk IX's armoury was a bored-out twin carburettor version of Jaguar's 3.8-litre (232cu in) XK engine – and that was a detuned version of the unit that had already proved itself so effectively in the D-type racing car. As a result, the Mk IX turned out to be an excellent high-speed cruiser.

Power steering was fitted, and, predictably, all-round disc brakes also made an appearance – and, although most cars came fitted with automatic transmission as standard, the option of four-speed manual with overdrive has proved very popular with classic car buyers in later years.

A total of just over 10,000 cars were built at Jaguar's Browns Lane

plant in Coventry during its three-year production lifespan. Despite the rust problems inherent in big Jaguars of this era, survival rate of the Mk IX has been high, as enthusiasts appreciate the modern dynamics of this big saloon.

ENGINE: 3781cc (231cu in), six-cylinder
POWER: 223bhp (166kW)
0–60MPH (96KM/H): 11.6 seconds
TOP SPEED: 184km/h (115mph)
PRODUCTION TOTAL: 10,009

Despite its hefty looks, the Jaguar Mk IX was actually a very sweet car to drive quickly. It was the first production Jaguar to feature disc brakes and power steering as standard and had excellent twin-cam engines.

DAIMLER MAJESTIC

During the 1950s, Daimler had been dropping off the pace of its rivals, and the company's owner, BSA (Birmingham Small Arms), was not investing enough in its prestigious marque to allow it to catch up. New models were needed, and the company's engineers pursued a number of odd proposals before settling on the Majestic to herald in a more forward-looking era.

The new model may have featured styling modelled on the 104 limousine, but it was daring (for the company), and the Majestic's flush-sided bodywork and a gently sloping bonnet (hood) were pleasing to anyone who appreciated contemporary design.

For the new model in 1958, Daimler's existing six-cylinder engine was increased in size and given a higher compression aluminium head with revised porting, to help it push out an extra 10bhp (7.5kW). It was enough, and 147bhp (110kW) was competitive with its rivals. A top speed of 161km/h (100mph) and healthy acceleration impressed everyone. Disc brakes kept it all in order.

The Majestic was stretched by 15cm (6in) in 1960, and received a larger 4.5-litre (278cu in) V8 producing 220bhp (164kW). A new automatic gearbox and power steering complemented the chassis's competence. For many, the Majestic Major was the last real Daimler.

ENGINE: 4561cc (278cu in), eight-cylinder
POWER: 220bhp (164kW)
0–60MPH (96KM/H): 10 seconds
TOP SPEED: 193km/h (120mph)
PRODUCTION TOTAL: 2120

Despite having a reputation for producing stuffy cars, the Daimler Majestic Major was anything of the sort. It was capable of an un-limousine like 193km/h (120mph).

ALVIS TD21   UNITED KINGDOM 1958–63

Following the loss of the coachbuilders Mulliner and Tickford (which were now tied to other companies), Alvis turned to the Swiss coachbuilder Graber. The Swiss firm had a tradition of producing sleek, modern and very elegant saloon and drophead designs. To ease logistical problems, Willowbrook of Loughborough built the Graber-designed bodies in

the United Kingdom. There were issues with the quality of the Willowbrook bodyshells, and that led to work being transferred to Park Ward of London, an extremely experienced coachbuilder.

When the car received a face-lift to become the TD21, a number of improvements were incorporated, including a single-piece rear window, and more room in the

boot (trunk) and the back seat. An automatic gearbox was added, and power was boosted from 104bhp (77kW) to 115bhp (86kW). With the extra power came better braking, and front discs were added.

Introduced in 1962, the Series II TD21 had disc brakes on all four wheels, a five-speed gearbox and pretty recessed spotlights either side of the grille. The TD21

evolved into the TE21 and TF21. In 1967, the company's new owner, Rover, stopped Alvis car production.

ENGINE: 2993cc (183cu in), six-cylinder
POWER: 115bhp (86kW)
0–60MPH (96KM/H): 13.9 seconds
TOP SPEED: 171km/h (106mph)
PRODUCTION TOTAL: 1070

ASTON MARTIN DB4   UNITED KINGDOM 1958–63

With the introduction of the DB4, Aston Martin had joined the ranks of the world's most prestigious carmakers. With its light aluminium body, weight was kept down, and that maximized the car's performance potential.

The Aston Martin DB4 was a clean sheet design when it hit the market in 1958. Beneath the pretty styling lay a brand-new chassis and engine. Designed by Aston Martin engineer Tadek Marek, the new engine was over-engineered, leaving scope for expansion from its initial 3-litre (183cu in) capacity. The straight-six engine had twin overhead camshafts, and was built around a cast alloy cylinder block. Marek had originally wanted to use a cast-iron cylinder block, but the alloy design was chosen instead.

The previous square section chassis was replaced by a massive base unit structure made from sheet steel, with 15cm (6in) box section sills welded to either side. A steel plate cradle at the front supported the engine and suspension, and around this base unit, a lightweight aluminium body, supported by a network of steel tubes (a Superleggera construction), was devised. It was designed by Italian coachbuilder Touring.

The DB4 was a huge success both commercially and critically. Altogether more impressive to drive than previous Astons, it was more reliable as well.

Aston Martin's DB4 evolved gradually throughout its life – from the original 1958 Series 1 through to the 1962 Series 5, and with the addition of the high-specification Vantage version.

ENGINE: 3670cc (224cu in), six-cylinder
POWER: 240bhp (179kW)
0–60MPH (96KM/H): 8.5 seconds
TOP SPEED: 227km/h (141mph)
PRODUCTION TOTAL: 1213

DKW (AUTO UNION) 1000 S COUPÉ

At the end of 1957, a famous pre-war marque reappeared when the Auto Union 1000 Coupé de Luxe hit the market. Although it was styled similarly to the DKW 3=6, this was a more upmarket version of that car. And, although the DKW 3=6 had recently benefited from an increase in engine capacity from 900cc (55cu in) to 981cc (60cu in), with power rising to 44bhp (33kW), it was not enough. The car's styling was as unimpressive as the acceleration.

At least the 1000 S was a move in the right direction, and with a more powerful 50bhp (37cu in) engine and an eye-catching wraparound windscreen. The 1000 model fell behind the opposition, however, as it remained closely related to the pre-war F 9. The two-stroke engines had fallen off the pace, with a distinct lack of reliability, and the car possessed unimpressive fuel consumption.

The 1000 S is regarded by enthusiasts of the marque as the last of the 'true' DKW-based cars. Despite lacking the ability of its opposition, the car remained in production until 1961. When the F102 was introduced a couple of years later, it was to set the style of future Audis, despite remaining obstinately two-stroke-powered.

ENGINE: 981cc (60 cu in), three-cylinder
POWER: 44bhp (33kW)
0–60MPH (96KM/H): 25 seconds
TOP SPEED: 135km/h (84mph)
PRODUCTION TOTAL: 6640

FACEL VEGA EXCELLENCE

Facel Vega creator Jean Daninos was keen to extend the range while enhancing the appeal of his cars. With this in mind, the company displayed a prototype four-door car at the Paris Motor Shows of 1956 and 1957, and met a positive response. A production version was developed, and sales began in 1958.

Called the Excellence, the car was expected to appeal to heads of state and tycoons worldwide – and, with styling that predated the similar-looking Lincoln Continental, it was set fair to succeed.

Like the Lincoln Continental, the Excellence was pillarless, and the front doors hinged conventionally at the front, while the rear doors were hinged at the rear in a 'clap hands' arrangement. The car was suitably large, and with considerable reinforcement in the middle, it was exceptionally heavy, and therefore ponderous to drive. It got worse. When loaded, the Excellence would sag in the middle. The result of this was that the doors could not be opened or closed.

With 355bhp (264kW) on tap from the V8 engine, however, the Excellence had a surprising turn of speed. Still, this was not enough to convince the world's high rollers that this was the limousine in which to be seen. The final eight models off the production line were restyled and lost their fins and wraparound windscreen.

ENGINE: 5801cc (355cu in), eight-cylinder
POWER: 355bhp (264kW)
0–60MPH (96KM/H): 8.8 seconds
TOP SPEED: 209km/h (130mph)
PRODUCTION TOTAL: 230

GSM DELTA

GSM (Glass Sports Motor) was created by South Africans Bob van Niekirk and Vester de Witt, and the Delta was a low-cost sporting car. It featured a steel tube ladder chassis, and the underpinnings took the form of transverse leaf springs at the front and a Ford 100E rear axle with coil springs at the rear. A breathed-on Ford Anglia engine powered the Delta; for more ambitious drivers, there was the option of a more powerful Coventry Climax unit for racing purposes.

Two body options were available, either a roadster or coupé, the latter of which had a Ford Anglia-style reverse rake rear windscreen. Both cars shared the same sharp-finned rear wing (fender) tops, similar to the Daimler SP250 'Dart', a car Niekirk was also involved in developing. The Delta was a useful club racer throughout the 1960s. In the latter part of its production lifespan in South Africa, it was improved to become the Flamingo.

Production of this Ford-based two-seater sports car may have set out in Cape Town, South Africa, but it also ended up being built in the United Kingdom (in West Malling, Kent) for a single year – 1960. Production then moved back to South Africa, as the UK factory suffered mounting losses.

ENGINE: 997cc (61cu in), four-cylinder
POWER: 57bhp (42kW)
0–60MPH (96KM/H): n/a
TOP SPEED: 161km/h (100mph)
PRODUCTION TOTAL: 35 in UK

MESSERSCHMITT TG500

Rather like the Volkswagen Beetle, the Messerschmitt Tg500 never actually bore the name by which people knew it. The German truck manufacturer Krupp may have patented the name, but that did not stop the diminutive two-seater from becoming something of a microcar legend.

Unusually for a microcar, the Tg500 had four wheels, and that meant that it was considerably more stable than its three-wheel competition – including its three-wheeled brethren. The 493cc (30cu in) Sachs air-cooled two-cylinder engine was powerful enough to endow the Tg500 with a top speed of 121km/h (75mph) – and that was faster than many saloons of its era.

The Tiger stopped as well as it accelerated, thanks to hydraulic brakes. It also featured improved steering and suspension set-up over the KR200.

The individual tandem seating layout and handlebars remained, meaning that people new to the car needed to acclimatize before driving the car at speed.

A low-roof coupé version was also available, and became the most collectable variant. Despite the Tg500's cult-like status and enthusiastic following, few were made and sales were actually rather slow. It is estimated that fewer than 500 examples of the car left the factory.

ENGINE: 493cc (30cu in), two-cylinder
POWER: 20bhp (15kW)
0–60MPH (96KM/H): 18.7 seconds
TOP SPEED: 121km/h (75mph)
PRODUCTION TOTAL: about 450

With an amazing top speed of 121km/h (75mph), the Messerschmitt Tg500 was no ordinary bubblecar. The car's more than interesting handling was complemented by excellent fuel consumption, making it the pick of the breed.

ALFA ROMEO 2000/2600 SPIDER

ITALY 1958–65

ENGINE: 1975cc (120cu in),
four-cylinder
POWER: 115bhp (86kW)
0–60MPH (96KM/H): 14.2 seconds
TOP SPEED: 179km/h (112mph)
PRODUCTION TOTAL: 5698

When the 2000 Spider was launched, it continued Alfa Romeo's tradition of producing pretty roadsters available at a realistic price. Technically, it was nothing too radical – the Spider range used a reworked version of the old 1900 model's engine and chassis, but the elegant open-top bodies featured styling by the coachbuilder Touring of Milan.

The all-round drum brakes were a disappointment, but the car had a traditional floor-mounted gearshift and five gears. A detachable hardtop complementing the more usual fabric hood was a sound feature. Two additional passenger seats

were squeezed in at the back, and that turned the car into a 2+2 – a distinct advantage over its rivals.

The face-lift of 1962 saw new front-end styling, featuring a full-width bumper and single chrome strip along the side, and the air vents behind the front wheels were removed. The major change was the new twin-camshaft six-cylinder 2584cc (158cu in) engine developing 145bhp (108kW).

Despite all the extra power and the sporting looks, neither car was light, and the handling was ponderous. Of the 5698 cars built, 3443 examples possessed the 1975cc (120cu in) engine.

Alfa Romeo had carved itself an impressive reputation at making sports cars, and the 2600 was no exception. Styled by the coachbuilders, Touring of Milan, it looked good, and also offered excellent performance.

CHAIKA GAZ-13

USSR 1958–65

Large Russian cars built for the country's elite were an appealing mix of American excess and Russian solidity. Built by Zavod Imieni Molotova (Gorky Motor Works), the GAZ M-13 was a perfect example, despite being nicknamed the 'Seagull'.

The styling was typically chrome-laden, with brightwork and American-style tail fins. In fact, the GAZ M-13 was more than influenced by its American contemporaries; it was actually a very close copy of the 1955 Packard Patrician.

Although it was a step below the Zil in prestige terms, the GAZ M-13 was way beyond the means of all but Soviet society's most select members. Only state officials and important professionals were in a position to enjoy the luxuries that included electrically operated windows, push-button automatic transmission and a five-band radio. There were even two fully collapsible bucket seats for additional passengers.

Power for the vehicle was provided by a US-inspired 5.5-litre (336cu in) V8 engine. Although it was built as a four-door limousine, there was also a cabriolet version for the truly decadent.

Chaika production stopped in 1965, but the M-13 was to make a reappearance in 1977, with updated styling. The car was the favoured transport of former Soviet leader Leonid Brezhnev.

ENGINE: 5500cc (336cu in), eight-cylinder
POWER: 195bhp (145kW)
0–60MPH (96KM/H): 15 seconds
TOP SPEED: 161km/h (100mph)
PRODUCTION TOTAL: n/a

DKW (AUTO UNION) 1000 SP ROADSTER

GERMANY 1958–65

After the introduction of the 1000 S Coupé, it was inevitable that Auto Union would produce a roadster version. The surprise, however, was that the 1000 SP Roadster ended up being one of the most visually and dynamically accomplished European models of its era. With styling inspired by the designs coming out of the United States at the time – most notably, the Ford Thunderbird – the 1000 SP's prettiness was rooted in its proportions. It was a design correctly scaled to the car's size, and it fitted in perfectly with European motoring.

First presented as a coupé in 1957, the 1000 SP was bolstered by the appearance of a roadster in 1961. It was built in relatively small numbers – around 1640 were sold in the end. Sitting on a DKW 1000 chassis, the car also shared the DKW's all-independent suspension and front-wheel drive layout.

From 1963, the SP 1000 was improved by front disc brakes and the 980cc (60cu in) three-cylinder two-stroke engine, which was also used by Saab, was tuned to produce a useful 55bhp (41kW). The coachbuilder Baur, based in Stuttgart, manufactured the bodies, and a total of about 6640 coupés and roadsters was made.

ENGINE: 980cc (60cu in), three-cylinder
POWER: 55bhp (41kW)
0–60MPH (96KM/H): 25 seconds
TOP SPEED: 140km/h (87mph)
PRODUCTION TOTAL: 1640

ELVA COURIER

UNITED KINGDOM 1958–65

ENGINE: 1489cc (91cu in), four- cylinder
POWER: 66bhp (49kW)
0–60MPH (96KM/H): 9 seconds
TOP SPEED: 121–209km/h (75–130mph)
PRODUCTION TOTAL: 500

Another of those appealing sporting specials that were being produced in the United Kingdom in the 1950s, the Elva was an enthusiast's creation. Successful garage proprietor Frank Nichols was interested in motor racing and aimed to produce a low-cost racing car. This concept proved successful in the United Kingdom and also crossed the Atlantic, appealing in the United States to amateur drivers in the SCCA racing series.

The Mk I Courier had a tubular ladder frame, a 1.5-litre (92cu in) Riley engine and gearbox (later changed to MGA units), as well as a rigid rear axle with coils at the back. There was a choice of pretty roadster or coupé bodies. Initially the car was exported exclusively to the United States. In 1960, it was finally offered in the United Kingdom, but only in kit form.

In 1962, the Courier was taken over by Trojan, who created the Mark III and immediately ruined the handling. The Mark IV put things right, adding independent rear suspension, several bodystyles and even a Ford GT engine over and above the MGB unit now fitted. Production halted in 1965 due to lack of sales, but it was the first Courier road car to establish the company internationally.

A fine example of minimalist sports–car motoring concocted from a tried and tested list of ingredients.

VOLVO PV544

Introduced in 1958 to supersede the PV444, the PV544 looked rather familiar. It used almost the same bodyshell as its predecessor, but it was roomier and now had larger front and rear windscreens. Gone were the split screen and the flat glass of the PV444.

Offered in a wide choice of specifications in a bid to maximize popularity, the PV544 was offered with different trim levels, and a choice of standard or Sport engines. Most interesting was the Sport version, which was fitted with an 85bhp (63kW) 1.6-litre (96cu in) engine (which had been formerly reserved for US-market cars only) and which offered excellent performance. The price of the car went up, however, and Volvo needed to counter the costly

power unit with a raft of extra equipment, making the car better value for buyers.

In 1960, a 1.8-litre (110cu in) engine was offered which had up to 90bhp (67kW) available if twin carburettors were specified, and, at that point, a four-speed gearbox was offered alongside the standard three-speed. Although the Amazon was introduced to replace it, the

last PV544 was actually built in 1965, some 10 years after the introduction of the newer car.

ENGINE: 1580cc (96cu in), four-cylinder
POWER: 85bhp (63kW)
0–60MPH (96KM/H): n/a
TOP SPEED: 136km/h (85mph)
PRODUCTION TOTAL: 243,995

AUSTIN-HEALEY SPRITE

ENGINE: 948cc (58cu in), six-cylinder
POWER: 43bhp (32kW)
0–60MPH (96KM/H): 20.5 seconds
TOP SPEED: 139km/h (86mph)
PRODUCTION TOTAL: about 129,350

Many car manufacturers tried to grasp the nettle of producing a truly popular inexpensive sports car, but it was Donald Healey who correctly identified what was needed in order to give customers what they wanted. Although it was now working closely with Austin, Healey's team had little budget with which to create the new car.

Healey had the advantage of being able to dip into the BMC parts bin; a no-frills open-top sports car, the Sprite, emerged. It used the 948cc (58cu in) BMC A-series engine from the Austin A35. The gearbox, axle and front and rear suspension

of the Sprite were also lifted from the baby Austin. Cleverly, the steering and brakes came from the Morris Minor. Cute Gerry Coker styling and pod-mounted headlights saw the Sprite gain the UK nickname 'Frogeye', while in the United States it was the 'Bugeye'. The car had nimble and responsive handling. It was slow in a straight line, but competition success soon followed.

In 1961, the Sprite Mk II appeared alongside the near-identical MG

Created by imaginative use of the BMC parts bin, the Austin-Healey 'Frogeye' Sprite was a cheap and fun offering in the sports-car market.

Midget Mk I. Specification improved over the years, but, when the deal between Healey and Austin ended in 1970, the car became the Austin Sprite, before being dropped six months later.

AUSTIN A40 FARINA

Although it is often overlooked in BMC history, the Austin A40 is actually a very important car. It marked a turning point in the direction of BMC's design at the time – it was the first post-war Austin to be styled without input from Dick Burzi, the company's design director. More importantly, it predicted the fashion for using Italian design houses to style

family cars – in this case, Farina. Initially conceived to replace the ageing A35, the A40 emerged as a crisply styled two-box design that was so smart a premium could be charged for it, allowing the older car to remain in production.

Under the bodywork, the same A-series engine that powered the A35 and all but the earliest Morris Minors was used. The running gear

was utterly conventional, despite the daring styling. It used the A35 underpinnings, right down to the questionable hydro-mechanical brakes. When the A40 Farina Mk II was introduced in 1961, it gained all-hydraulic brakes, a slightly longer wheelbase and a new grille.

A year later, the car was fitted with a 1098cc (67cu in) version of the A-series engine, giving it a little

more power. A clever Countryman version previewed the hatchbacks that would dominate 15 years later.

ENGINE: 948cc (58cu in), four-cylinder
POWER: 37bhp (28kW)
0–60MPH (96KM/H): 27.1 seconds
TOP SPEED: 121km/h (75mph)
PRODUCTION TOTAL: 342,280

HUMBER SUPER SNIPE/IMPERIAL

ENGINE: 2651cc (162cu in),
six-cylinder
POWER: 112bhp (83kW)
0–60MPH (96KM/H): 19.0 seconds
TOP SPEED: 144km/h (90mph)
PRODUCTION TOTAL: 30,031

Humber's Super Snipe and Imperial were typically British upper-class saloons – solid and dependable, and very tasteful. When the 1957 version appeared, it modernized the marque's styling considerably, but under the skin was really nothing more than an upmarket monocoque Hawk (launched 18 months earlier) with a 2.6-litre (162cu in) six-cylinder engine. The power unit, developed in collaboration with Armstrong Siddeley, was interesting, and featured spherical combustion chambers, opposed valves and modern cross-flow breathing.

All that was different, visually, between the Super Snipe and the Hawk was a bonnet (hood) mascot, fluted chrome grilles surrounding the sidelights and the availability of classy two-tone colour schemes. A three-speed was fitted as standard, but optional overdrive, automatic transmission and power steering were available. The Series II in 1959 gained a 3.0-litre (183cu in)

engine and front disc brakes, while the Series III of 1960 had twin headlights arranged horizontally in each front wing (fender).

In 1963 the Series IV pushed out 133bhp (99kW) and gained more

chrome; the 1964 SV had the Hawk's new roofline, twin carburettors and power-assisted steering. The Imperial model was simply an SV with a black roof and automatic transmission fitted as standard.

Suitably dignified in appearance, the Humber Super Snipe and Imperial actually shared the Hawk's body shell, but with added cosmetic enhancements and a full-width chrome grille.

TVR GRANTURA

TVR Engineering had been around since 1947, but the company that Trevor Wilkinson set up in Blackpool did not actually start building production cars until

1958. The Grantura was the first of the line. Like most specials of the time, it used a variety of sources for its components. Volkswagen Beetle trailing arm rear suspension,

hard springing and a Coventry Climax overhead-camshaft four-cylinder were combined. The first Granturas were best remembered for their serious oversteer moments.

After a decade building small-scale specials, the Grantura became TVR's first full-scale production car. Handling was demanding and limited appeal.

THE ENCYCLOPEDIA OF CLASSIC CARS

Enthusiast buyers could specify the engine and tune, and, typically with 83bhp (62kW) and with only 660kg (1455lb), performance was sensational. Other popular engines were the 1.5-litre (92cu in) MGA unit, the side-valve Ford 100E engine or the new 105E 'Kent'.

In mid-1960, the Mk II was unveiled, and it was unchanged except for the single-engine option, the 1.5-litre (92cu in) MGA unit, and a few design details. The factory could not cope with demand, however, and the car was barely profitable at the price at

which it sold. The Mk III version arrived in 1962, with a new tubular chassis with independent suspension all round. From 1964, the MGB 1800cc (110cu in) engine was used, and the interior was improved and new taillights were fitted. This car became the Mk IV.

ENGINE: 1216cc (74cu in), four-cylinder
POWER: 83bhp (62kW)
0–60MPH (96KM/H): 10.8 seconds
TOP SPEED: 163km/h (101mph)
PRODUCTION TOTAL: about 800

AUSTIN GIPSY

UNITED KINGDOM 1958–68

The Gipsy was BMC's second attempt at producing a worthy rival for the Land Rover – and, after the failure of the Champ, it was

important to get it right. The new car was a massive improvement in many ways, although the styling, which was rather too similar to the

Land Rover, implied that it was merely a copy of its Solihull rival.

Although it was a sales failure, the Gipsy was actually a very

capable vehicle, and arguably better than the Land Rover in many ways. Its suspension used an all-independent Flexitor rubber set-up, as designed by Alex Moulton, and that meant it compared superbly with Land Rover's much less sophisticated leaf spring set-up.

The Land Rover's chief advantage over the Gipsy, however, was that it was alloy-bodied, while the Gipsy's body was made from steel and was susceptible to corrosion. After the problems with the Champ, the military unsurprisingly refused to buy the Gipsy, and that left the vehicle with no market.

When Rover (and hence Land Rover) joined British Leyland in 1968 (of which Austin was a part), the Gipsy was rendered irrelevant and dropped from the model line-up.

ENGINE: 2199cc (134cu in), four-cylinder
POWER: 62bhp (46kW)
0–60MPH (96KM/H): n/a
TOP SPEED: 102km/h (63mph)
PRODUCTION TOTAL: 21,208

Built as a direct response to Solihull's Land-Rover, the Austin Gipsy certainly looked the part of a rugged off-roader, but lacked the ability of its rival.

NSU SPORT PRINZ

GERMANY 1958–68

NSU's rear-engined small car the Prinz 4 was not universally admired for its styling, which had been criticized for being awkward. When the Sport Prinz appeared, however, it reversed the misdeed.

The pretty two-door coupé bodywork was the work of esteemed stylist Franco Scaglione, who at the time was working for the Italian styling house Bertone. The sleek little car was a delicate

thing, and yet it could be pushed along as quickly as some much larger and mature sports cars.

It was certainly not powerful – the standard Prinz's air-cooled twin put out just 30bhp (22kW) – but the car's light weight, quick steering and nimble chassis meant that it held the road brilliantly in the hands of an expert driver. Unfortunately, the car would snap into oversteer if driven too hard

through corners, especially in wet road conditions.

Although the cars were proudly German, all Sport Prinzes were actually built by Bertone in Italy for the first seven years, and only moved to Heilbronn in Germany for the final three years of the production run.

Despite remaining popular and still looking fresh, the Sport Prinz was killed off by NSU's parent

company in 1968, to allow it to concentrate on developing rotary engines – and the impressively forward-looking NSU Ro80.

ENGINE: 583cc (36cu in), two-cylinder
POWER: 30bhp (22kW)
0–60MPH (96KM/H): 31.7 seconds
TOP SPEED: 123km/h (76mph)
PRODUCTION TOTAL: 20,831

SUBARU 360

JAPAN 1958–71

Significant in motoring history for being the first car to be produced by Subaru, the 360 appeared in 1958 and enjoyed success in its homeland. Designed

with affordability and low running costs as its key selling points, it was a typical late 1950s economy car. Powered by an air-cooled twin-cylinder engine mounted at the

back of the car, driving the rear wheels, it followed the fashionable Fiat Nuova 500. An estate (station wagon) version of the 360, called the Custom, was also offered,

alongside a pick-up and a beach car, which drew its inspiration from Fiat's Jolly model.

At just 3m (9.8ft) long, it was a true mini car, and its 356cc (22cu in) two-stroke engine put out a mere 16bhp (12kW). The power output was later increased to 20bhp (15kW), before a 422cc (26cu in) engine, developing 22bhp (16kW), was introduced. Called the Maia, or K212, in Japan, the uprated car had a three-speed gearbox and independent suspension on all four wheels.

In 1969, a four-speed gearbox was fitted and superior torsion-bar independent suspension all round was added to the package.

ENGINE: 356cc (22cu in), twin-cylinder
POWER: 16bhp (12kW)
0–60MPH (96KM/H): n/a
TOP SPEED: 90km/h (56mph)
PRODUCTION TOTAL: 5000 approx

Subaru's baby 360 is a rare sight today despite selling strongly in its homeland when new – however, few remain in existence today, thanks to corrosion problems. It was a hoot to drive as long as you were small.

AUSTIN FX4

UNITED KINGDOM 1958–97

To most people, the name Austin FX4 will not actually mean a lot, but the new Austin introduced in 1958 is one of the most widely recognized vehicles in the world, and almost universally known as the London black cab. Since before World War II, Austin had done very well in the taxi market, and the FX4 was the latest in a successful line. Compared with its predecessor, the FX3, it had modern bodywork (for the period) and a series of minor luxuries that cab drivers really appreciated. An automatic-gearbox option made the biggest difference, but independent front suspension and hydraulic brakes were vital, too; cab designs had not been updated for years.

Gradually, the FX4 evolved with more powerful engines and a manual transmission option. Later, the Carbodies Company took over the FX4's manufacture. It became known as the Fairway before being replaced by the new generation TX1 model in 1997.

ENGINE: 2199cc (134cu in), four-cylinder
POWER: 56bhp (42kW)
0–60MPH (96KM/H): n/a
TOP SPEED: 121km/h (75mph)
PRODUCTION TOTAL: about 50,000

As much of a British institution as the red telephone box and St Paul's Cathedral, the Austin FX4 is one of the most identifiable cars ever produced.

BERKELEY T60

Although the agreeable combination of Laurie Bond's designs and the backing and manufacturing expertise of the Berkeley Coachwork Company (a caravan manufacturer) had produced a number of sweet little sports cars, as the years passed, the company's boss wanted to expand into new markets. The original four-wheeler baby sports cars, the

323 and 328, had become the 492, then the B95 and B105 (the numbers denote their respective top speeds), but Bond saw that the production of three-wheelers could affect the company's expansion.

It was perhaps inevitable that at least one of Berkeley's cars would be designed in this format. The car that emerged was the T60, a neat-looking sports car that tapered

into a semi-point at the rear end. Having just three wheels kept weight to an absolute minimum, and the 328cc (244cu in) Excelsior motorcycle engine that powered the T60 was capable of delivering excellent acceleration.

There is an inherent mistrust of three-wheelers in many buyers' minds, but the T60 was good to drive with excellent handling. A

handful of later T60s were built, but when the parent company collapsed, so did car production.

ENGINE: 328cc (244cu in), two-cylinder
POWER: 18bhp (13kW)
0–60MPH (96KM/H): n/a
TOP SPEED: 97km/h (60mph)
PRODUCTION TOTAL: 1830

BORGWARD P100

During the 1950s, Borgward had become a serious force in German car manufacturing, and, as well as successfully exporting its range of cars throughout the world, it also competed very effectively with the opposition from Opel and Mercedes-Benz in particular.

Borgward's mainstay at the time period was the P100, which was a big and impressive US-style saloon

powered by a 2.3-litre (137cu in) six-cylinder engine. It also offered the option of air suspension – which was not only innovative, but was also the first instance of a German car using pneumatics. Borgward had invested a lot of money in the car's development, but the P100 was let down by its engine. It was not powerful enough, and that resulted in lost sales.

Borgward's finances began to suffer as a consequence, and that forced the company to approach the Bremen Senate for cash assistance – after all, BMW had received similar help only a year before. No money was forthcoming, however, and Borgward fell into bankruptcy in 1961.

The P100 and Isabella's tooling was then sold to Mexico, where the

cars remained in production until 1970. Tragically, Carl Borgward died broken-hearted in 1963.

ENGINE: 2240cc (137cu in), six-cylinder
POWER: 100bhp (75kW)
0–60MPH (96KM/H): 14.6 seconds
TOP SPEED: 161km/h (100mph)
PRODUCTION TOTAL: 2587

WOLSELEY 6/99

Wolseley had been on the receiving end of Nuffield-sponsored badge engineering for at least 25 years, but the 1958 6/99 was a break with tradition. When it appeared, the Wolseley 6/99 had become part of the BMC game plan, and was actually a re-jigged Austin, the A99. With the exception of a few minor changes

to the styling, trim and equipment levels, the cars were identical, even though they were assembled at different factories.

The 6/99 was a massive leap forward from its predecessor, the 6/80. The body was a monocoque construction and was far roomier inside. Coil spring independent suspension at the front and a half-

elliptic spring set-up at the back – with anti-roll bars all round – ensured much tidier road manners.

Front disc brakes were fitted, but the camshaft-and-lever steering and three-speed all-synchromesh gearbox (with overdrive) were a bit passé. (A Borg-Warner automatic could be specified.) Power came from a 103bhp (77kW) 2912cc

(178cu in) version of BMC's C-Series overhead-valve six-cylinder engine.

ENGINE: 2912cc (178cu in), six-cylinder
POWER: 103bhp (77kW)
0–60MPH (96KM/H): 14.4 seconds
TOP SPEED: 157km/h (98mph)
PRODUCTION TOTAL: 13,108

AC GREYHOUND

Effectively a four-seater version of the Aceca, the AC Greyhound was meant to generate many more sales for the British sports–car producer. However, the engine's lack of ultimate power meant it was disadvantaged against rivals.

The Aceca had been an unexpected success for AC, and the company was keen to capitalize on its good fortune. It decided to build a more luxurious four-seater version of the car – called the Greyhound. It was not just a case of squeezing two back seats into the Aceca, though.

AC needed to lengthen the Aceca's wheelbase and replace the old transverse leaf suspension, which took up valuable space for the engine in the front and the rear passengers at the back. In its place, independent coil spring suspension was fitted. The chassis was comprehensively engineered

in order to cope with the car's extra weight and length. Despite this, the Greyhound did not handle nearly as well as the Ace and Aceca. The extra weight dulled performance, whatever the engine choice (AC, Bristol or Ford).

The programme proved a drain on company resources, but the

Cobra appeared on the scene, and the Greyhound was quietly dropped.

ENGINE: 1971cc (120cu in), six-cylinder
POWER: 105bhp (78kW)
0–60MPH (96KM/H): 11.4 seconds
TOP SPEED: 167km/h (104mph)
PRODUCTION TOTAL: 83

DKW JUNIOR

With its three-cylinder two-stroke engine and front-wheel drive, the Junior was a typical DKW. However, the torsion-bar front and rear suspension were new to the marque, and the body design now used obvious US stylistic elements. Vestigial tail fins and a 'shark' radiator grille were pure Americana,

and the fashionable wraparound rear window heightened the effect.

In 1961, a new Junior was introduced, powered by a larger 796cc (49cu in) engine, which produced the same 39bhp (29kW) as its predecessor. An automatic system injected the oil at the carburettor, which meant that

there was no longer any need to pre-mix the oil and petrol. The styling changed only slightly at this point, with the fitment of round sidelights at either end of the front grille.

This was the company's first big seller, so a new plant was set up in Ingolstadt to make the car. This

became Auto Union's headquarters in 1962; Audi is now based there.

ENGINE: 741cc (45cu in), three-cylinder
POWER: 34bhp (25kW)
0–60MPH (96KM/H): 27 seconds
TOP SPEED: 113km/h (70mph)
PRODUCTION TOTAL: 237,605

FACEL VEGA FACELLIA

ENGINE: 1647cc (101cu in), four-cylinder
POWER: 114bhp (85kW)
0–60MPH (96KM/H): 13.7 seconds
TOP SPEED: 183km/h (114mph)
PRODUCTION TOTAL: 1258

With the Facellia, Facel Vega made a concerted effort to reach a wider and more profitable

end of the market. By building a smaller four-cylinder convertible at a competitive price, Facel hoped to attract sportscar enthusiasts who usually bought British cars made by Austin-Healey, Triumph and MG.

The Facellia was based on the V8 Facel Vegas, but was much lower with a shorter wheelbase. Styling was very similar to the larger cars, with single round headlights above

the fog lamps in the same housing protected by a Mercedes-like cover. Allegedly this attention to aerodynamics boosted the top speed by 8km/h (5mph).

The convertible was launched first, followed by the optional hardtop, then the coupé in 1961. The Facellia did all it was asked to do, with perky performance, pretty styling and tidy handling, but the

A brave but vain attempt to revive the fortunes of the once great company, the Facel Vega Facelia still had glorious style.

Westlake-designed engine (built by Pont-a-Mousson in France) proved very unreliable. That killed sales, and eventually forced Facel into receivership in the mid-1960s.

FERRARI 250GT SWB

ITALY 1959–63

ENGINE: 2953cc (180cu in),
12-cylinder
POWER: 280bhp (209kW)
0–60MPH (96KM/H): 6 seconds
TOP SPEED: 241km/h (150mph)
PRODUCTION TOTAL: 250

Introduced at the 1959 Paris Motor Show, the 250 GT Berlinetta was named the SWB because a shorter 240cm (94in) wheelbase had been incorporated into the car's styling. It was significant for being the first Ferrari to feature disc brakes.

The reworked engine, with repositioned spark plugs and coil valve springs, helped to boost the power output to a cool 280bhp (209kW). The first 21 cars were competition models, which meant that the bodywork was all alloy rather than steel (resulting in a saving at least 91kg/200lb in weight). In competition, the SWB soon recorded strong performances, with fourth and fifth places in the 1960 Le Mans 24-hour race and Sebring 12-hour event. The shorter and stiffer chassis meant the handling was superbly balanced with tenacious roadholding.

Lusso-type road cars did not emerge until 1960 and, although the body was steel, lightweight alloy bonnets (hoods), boot (trunk) lids and doors were still used. Pininfarina styled the 250GT SWB,

Yet another variation of the 250, the Ferrari 250GT SWB was a shortened, sweeter handling version of the original. One of the ultimate roadgoing cars.

considered the designer's best work to this point. During 1959, a Spyder California with a Scaglietti body was made available – another very handsome interpretation of what is now a classic design.

RENAULT FLORIDE

FRANCE 1959–63

The Floride was a pretty rear-engined machine, styled by Frua. Effectively it was a standard-tune Dauphine Gordini engine, which meant that it came with the same 845cc (52cu in) engine and temperamental three-speed column-change gearbox, clothed in a beautiful body. A four-speed gearbox and 'Transfluide' semi-automatic were offered as options.

True to Renault's big-sellers of the time, the Floride was rear engined and powered by the familiar Gordini tuned four-cylinder engine.

With its stunning coupé or convertible styling, tactile controls and a high price tag, the Renault Floride was stopped from being a true sports car only by its lack of performance. Its styling worked best as a convertible, although the high ride height appeared at odds with the low-cut panel work. The Floride was typically Renault in that it was a fun car to drive. Light steering and a bumpy ride were memorable, as was the questionable grip when cornering quickly. The tiny engine always felt more powerful than it actually was.

Performance improved slightly in 1956 with the introduction of the S model, with its bored-out 956cc (58cu in) 51bhp (38kW) engine. All Florides were built externally by coachbuilders Brissoneau and Lotz, and suffered from the usual extensive rust problems.

ENGINE: 845cc (52cu in), four-cylinder
POWER: 38bhp (28kW)
0–60MPH (96KM/H): 28.7 seconds
TOP SPEED: 127km/h (79mph)
PRODUCTION TOTAL: 177,122

TRIUMPH ITALIA

UNITED KINGDOM 1959–63

British businessman Raymond Flower came up with the idea of introducing Triumph to the Italian stylist Giovanni Michelotti, to create an updated TR3. He came up with some alternative Triumph-based sports–car designs in 1957, and they seemed perfectly suited to the car, allowing it to become a competitive sports car again.

Suitably impressed, Triumph gave Michelotti a TR3 chassis to work with; within three months, he produced a flamboyant-looking machine in return, which had been built by Vignale of Turin. The car did not go into production, but Michelotti did very well out of the deal, being handed a contract to style future Triumph models.

One of the ideas he came up with was a pretty fixed-head coupé on a TR3A frame. When it appeared at the 1958 Turin Motor Show, with a streamlined front end, it was so well received that Vignale put it into limited manufacture as the Triumph Italia. The production version came with a conventional nose and chrome wire wheels, plus

the standard TR3A 1991cc (121cu in) 100bhp (75kW) engine. It was the start of something very big …

ENGINE: 1991cc (121cu in), four-cylinder
POWER: 100bhp (75kW) at 5000rpm
0–60MPH (96KM/H): 11.4 seconds
TOP SPEED: 174km/h (108mph)
PRODUCTION TOTAL: 329

CHEVROLET CORVAIR

UNITED STATES 1959–69

Famous because of the safety campaign it was responsible for launching, the Chevrolet Corvair was a disaster for General Motors. For ever known as the car that was killed by a book, the Corvair was General Motors' response to the increasing number of European economy cars imported into the United States.

Refreshingly different, the Corvair was like nothing else offered by the US industry at the time, with its rear-mounted, air-cooled, slat six-cylinder engine and independent suspension. It was clear that this was a genuinely new compact and not a scaled-down big car like those offered by Ford and Chrysler in the subcompact market. Buyers remained cautious and steered clear.

Although the saloons struggled, the Monza coupés and convertible were pretty and found a willing fan base in those who appreciated their unique style and decent performance. Unfortunately, Ralph Nader's book *Unsafe at any Speed*

highlighted handling problems and high-profile accidents on the early models. Even though the handling became unsafe only if tyre pressures were not properly maintained, the damage had been done.

Despite a new-generation Corvair available from 1964 with a pretty restyle and revised rear suspension, the innovative car never recovered. The later introduction of a turbocharged version that produced 180bhp (134kW) did not save it either.

ENGINE: 2377cc (145cu in), six-cylinder
POWER: 84bhp (63kW)
0–60MPH (96KM/H): 15 seconds
TOP SPEED: 144km/h (90mph)
PRODUCTION TOTAL: 1,695,765

Safety activist Ralph Nader made the Chevrolet Corvair the subject of his book *Unsafe at Any Speed*, with predictably detrimental effects on sales.

CITROËN BIJOU

FRANCE 1959–64

By the end of the 1950s, Citroën had become known as a maker of eccentric cars. Even by Citroën's own standards, however, the Bijou was a strange creature indeed. Built at the company's British factory in Slough, the Bijou was essentially a rebodied 2CV that was tailored especially for British buyers, who were turned off by the original car's quirky looks. Famous for penning the Lotus Elite, Peter Kirwin-Taylor designed the pretty Bijou. It was unfortunate that the glassfibre pseudo-French creation did not have the looks of the Lotus. In fact, most buyers found it hard to get on with.

The Bijou weighed more than the 2CV as well, so performance was extremely disappointing, and the top speed was only slightly more than 80km/h (50mph). Another setback was its high list price (it was more expensive than the Mini, launched the same year), although it did have the fact it did not rust and excellent fuel economy in its favour. Still, after five years and only 207 Bijous sold, the experiment was over, and the car was cancelled.

ENGINE: 425cc (26cu in), twin-cylinder
POWER: 12bhp (9kW) at 4000rpm
0–60MPH (96KM/H): n/a
TOP SPEED: 81km/h (51mph)
PRODUCTION TOTAL: 207

DAIMLER SP250 'DART'

UNITED KINGDOM 1959–64

When it first appeared, the Daimler SP250 sent shock waves through the British motor industry – and not just because of its looks. The SP250 was a departure from the limousines, saloons and special-bodied roadsters that Daimler had been producing to this point. With this model, Daimler was aiming directly at the sportscar market, and the new management, specifically ex-Triumph motor designer Edward Turner, was hoping to reinvent the company.

Originally called the Dart, until Dodge complained, the SP250 was so far removed from existing Daimlers that it was almost impossible to believe that it was a product of the same company. The Triumph TR3A heavily influenced the car's chassis and suspension, and the engine was all-new. The light alloy 2.5-litre (155cu in) V8 owed much to prevailing motorcycle engineering principles. Braking was by discs, and the SP250 was economical, powerful and competitively priced.

Not everyone, however, liked the ornate styling. The pronounced rear wings (fenders) and headlights took some getting used to, but what really set it apart was its use of glassfibre for the bodywork.

'B' models were introduced in 1961 and had a stiffer chassis and beefed-up bodywork. 'C' versions from 1963 incorporated better trim. As Jaguar had taken over the company, however, it did not want any competition for its own E-type, and production of the SP250 was phased out in 1964.

ENGINE: 2548cc (155 cu in), eight-cylinder
POWER: 140bhp (104kW)
0–60MPH (96KM/H): 10.2 seconds
TOP SPEED: 194km/h (121mph)
PRODUCTION TOTAL: 2650

Not a car that could be confused with any other, the Daimler SP 250 was a radical departure for its maker. With a glass fibre body and sublime V8 engine, it was a peach to drive.

FERRARI 400 SUPERAMERICA

ITALY 1959–64

Debuting at the Brussels Motor Show in 1960, the Ferrari 400 Superamerica replaced the 410 – it was a new car based on the shortened 250 GT chassis and was powered by a larger, 3967cc (242cu in) version of the Colombo-designed V12. Maximum power was an ample 340bhp (253kW).

Lighter than the V12 used in the 410, the newly developed power unit contributed to the lower overall weight of the 400 model. Employing cylinder heads also derived from the 250 GT, and triple Weber carburettors, the car was touted as being able to reach a top speed of 257km/h (160mph).

With that potential, the chassis had to be right. Luckily, the wishbone and coil spring front suspension, combined with the conventional live axle retained at the rear, was well honed and endowed the car with handling that matched the performance. A four-speed transmission with overdrive gearbox was used, and the braking was by discs all round.

Pininfarina built fewer than 50 examples, mostly with bodywork in various styles, including coupés and cabriolets. From 1962, about half the production run had a slightly lengthened wheelbase. Although it was a good car, the Superamerica proved to be another misjudgment of the US market. It was too expensive and did not offer many benefits over the 250GT.

ENGINE: 3967cc (242cu in), 12-cylinder
POWER: 340bhp (253kW)
0–60MPH (96KM/H): 8 seconds
TOP SPEED: 257km/h (160mph)
PRODUCTION TOTAL: 48

MASERATI 5000GT

ENGINE: 4941cc (302cu in),
eight-cylinder
POWER: 370bhp (276kW) at 6000rpm
0–60MPH (96KM/H): n/a
TOP SPEED: 282km/h (175mph)
PRODUCTION TOTAL: 32

After finishing its illustrious racing career in 1957, Maserati realized that real money could be made in the manufacture of road-going supercars. Although the legendary 450S had won plenty of races in the hands of Juan Manuel Fangio, the cost of running a Grand Prix team had proved crippling for the Italian company.

The 5000GT was a direct result of the withdrawal – Maserati was left with a number of 450S V8 quad-camshaft racing engines, of 4935cc (301cu in) capacity. Supposedly at the Shah of Iran's suggestion, the engines were fitted into the 3500GT chassis, resulting in the new and powerful 5000GT model.

Launched at the 1959 Turin Motor Show, it caused an immediate sensation. Not only did it look good, but it also featured disc brakes on the front brakes, a four-speed

gearbox and the same suspension as the 3500GT. Originally, the cars came with Weber carburettors, but, from 1961, Lucas fuel injection was fitted. All-round disc brakes and ZF five-speed transmission were later

upgrades. Of the 32 cars produced, 21 had bodies built by Allemano, with Touring responsible for another four. Pininfarina, Bertone, Frua, Michelotti, Vignale and Monterosa constructed the others.

Built because there was a stockpile of racing engines at Maserati's factory after it pulled out of Grand Prix racing, the Maserati 5000GT had a top speed of 282km/h (175mph).

SKODA FELICIA

ENGINE: 1221cc (75cu in),
four-cylinder
POWER: 53bhp (kW)
0–60MPH (96KM/H): 27.5 seconds
TOP SPEED: 135km/h (84mph)
PRODUCTION TOTAL: 15,864

No great shakes dynamically or in terms of performance, the Skoda Felicia was still a capable

car. In Communist Czechoslovakia, it attracted a waiting list that was years long. Based on the Octavia saloon, the Felicia was powered by a 53bhp (39kW) engine that did not demand its quirky swing axle suspension set-up. The separate chassis was a bit of a throwback and did not help handling. Despite that, drivers seemed to enjoy it.

British buyers were not so sure when the car appeared on UK price

lists in 1961. It was reliable and very well built, if not particularly highly specified, but sales struggled to take off. Perhaps potential customers were just unfamiliar with the Skoda name because the Felicia's 135km/h (84mph) top speed was no worse than that of UK-produced cars such as the Triumph Herald. Also, with low fuel consumption figures (30mpg, or 9.5L/100km) the car was cheap to run.

Equipment levels were not very impressive, with rubber mats in place of carpeting and plastic instead of leather seats, but they were acceptable, with a heater, a radiator blind and sun visors.

The Felicia predated Skoda's cheap and poor reputation: it was stylish, rugged and in the UK not inexpensive.

SUNBEAM ALPINE SERIES I–V

UNITED KINGDOM 1959–64

When the Sunbeam Alpine went on sale in July 1959, the Rootes Group had earned itself a reputation for building cars that put comfort, style and quality of finish above all else. What it was not readily associated with was the production of sports cars. The launch of the Alpine did much to reverse that image. Even though the cars made by MG, Triumph and Austin-Healey were seen as far more driver-focused, Sunbeam did not seem to mind at all.

Englishman Ken Howes styled the car, and it was clear that, after working with Studebaker and Ford in the United States, his thoughts were very much directed towards America with the Alpine.

When it was launched in 1959, the 78bhp (58kW) produced by its 1494cc (91cu in) four-cylinder powerplant was not really enough,

and, although it was more than the Husky put out, compared with its rivals, the Alpine's performance was a little limp-wristed. The top speed of just 163km/h (101mph) was not too much to complain about, but none of the subsequent Alpines beat it. The gearbox was shared with the Rapier, but with more closely stacked gear ratios and the option of a Laycock overdrive.

In October 1960, after 11,904 Series Is had been built, the Series II appeared. With a larger, 80bhp (60kW) 1592cc (97cu in) engine, the new update kept the fins and detachable aluminium hardtop of its predecessor, but the seating was made more comfortable. By the time it gave way to the Series III in March 1963, 19,956 had rolled off the production lines.

The third-generation Alpine brought a new option – the GT.

This car strangely had no folding hood, to keep weight and costs down, but the interior was much better with wood trim for the dash and a wood-rim steering wheel. Even more perversely, the GT is now the least sought after Alpine unless converted to have a folding roof – in which case it is one of the most desirable, thanks to its wooden trim and steering wheel.

The optional detachable hardtop on the Series III onwards was steel instead of aluminium (and was more angular), and twin fuel tanks replaced the single item fitted to earlier cars, which meant that the boot (trunk) space was increased. Just 5863 Series IIIs were made, making it the rarest Alpine (except for the Harrington fixed-roof Alpines), and one of the most desirable, too, as it is the most refined of the big-finned models.

In all, 12,406 Series IVs were built before production gave way to the Alpine's final version, the Series V, in September 1965.

With a five-bearing engine for the first time, the Series V sported a 1725cc (105cu in) engine and a pair of Stromberg carburettors producing 92bhp (69kW) – still only enough to push it to 161km/h (100mph). When Alpine production ceased in January 1968, a total of 19,122 Mk Vs had been built.

The Alpine's biggest moment was possibly its appearance in the James Bond film *Dr No.*

ENGINE: 1494cc (91cu in), four-cylinder
POWER: 78bhp (58kW)
0–60MPH (96KM/H): 13.6 seconds
TOP SPEED: 161km/h (100mph)
PRODUCTION TOTAL: 59,251

VANDEN PLAS 3-LITRE

UNITED KINGDOM 1959–64

Dismissed by many as a badge-engineered version of the Austin A99, the Vanden Plas 3-Litre did offer a level of luxury previously unseen in the big 'Farina' saloons. Sold alongside the Wolseley and Austin versions in BMC showrooms, the Vanden Plas 3-Litre was the most exclusive, featuring a special

radiator grille, extra soundproofing and more upmarket interior.

The car's roots were clear, but it sold well because of its high quality and the strength of the Vanden Plas name. When the Mk II version was launched in the autumn of 1961, the car was further improved. Now a genuine

161km/h (100mph) car, the Mk II featured a more highly tuned C-Series 2.9-litre (178cu in) straight-six engine, a longer wheelbase and changes to the suspension to make it more comfortable.

For those who chose to drive rather than be driven, power-assisted steering became optional

in 1962. In 1964, the car was discontinued in favour of the 4-Litre.

ENGINE: 2912cc (178cu in), six-cylinder
POWER: 103bhp (77kW)
0–60MPH (96KM/H): 17.9 seconds
TOP SPEED: 156km/h (97mph)
PRODUCTION TOTAL: 12,703

BMW 700

GERMANY 1959–65

The BMW 700's ultra-stylish Michelotti-penned body disguised basic underpinnings, which owed more to the Isetta bubblecar at the bottom of the range rather than the desirable saloons above – a handy seller, and worth more than the sum of its parts.

Billed as the car that saved BMW from ruin in the early 1960s, the 700 was actually just a stopgap model in the range that the BMW management was ashamed of. In a range that comprised of ultra-glamorous luxury saloons and high-performance sports cars, however, the 700 did look a little out on its own by the mid-1960s.

BMW produced the 700 because of the yawning gap in the range between its Isetta microcar and its big saloons and sports cars, which needed filling. As there was no budget available to produce a new mid-range car, BMW simply took the mechanicals from the Isetta and installed them into a pretty saloon body.

The 700 received its name from the newly expanded engine that powered the Isetta (now 697cc/ 43cu in) – and, in time, the range was expanded to include a 700 Sport model (which was later called the 700CS). Available as a coupé or a cabriolet, the Sport proved popular with younger buyers. A longer-wheelbase 700LS was then introduced, and that took the 700 even further away from its microcar roots.

The BMW 700 sold well for two reasons: its looks (the body had been penned by none other than Michelotti of Turin, and was unexpectedly good-looking) and because it was well equipped (for the market).

ENGINE: 697cc (43cu in), twin-cylinder
POWER: 30bhp (22kW)
0–60MPH (96KM/H): 33.7 seconds
TOP SPEED: 113km/h (70mph)
PRODUCTION TOTAL: 174,390

PANHARD PL17 FRANCE 1959–65

The Panhard PL17 continued in the spirit of the innovative cars previously produced by Panhard. Replacing the Dyna 54 would always be difficult, but, to keep costs to a minimum, the platform and central body panels of the earlier car were used. With the new car, however, the body was all steel, which had a tendency to rust quickly.

The PL17 Tigre introduced in 1961 was the most interesting variant because of its twin-choke 60bhp (45kW) engine and 145km/h (90mph) top speed. An all-synchromesh gearbox added in 1962 made the PL17 a much nicer machine to drive, and hydraulic brakes with supple suspension made it an effective touring car.

Also offered as a two-door convertible, with a roof that folded almost flat against the rear tonneau, the PL17 truly was the thinking man's choice. The drop-top was well designed, but it was expensive and sales were limited – convertibles were almost twice the price of saloons and rusted even more badly.

Still, a Panhard in any guise is never a boring car, especially if you value alternative designs. Challenging, futuristic styling, the norm for a Panhard, was married to class-leading aerodynamics and economy, and the same six-person seating capacity as its predecessor.

ENGINE: 851cc (52cu in), two-cylinder
POWER: 60bhp (45kW)
0–60MPH (96KM/H): 22.6 seconds
TOP SPEED: 145km/h (90mph)
PRODUCTION TOTAL: 130,000

The Panhard PL17 was a six-seater saloon with a 145km/h (90mph) top speed. A slow seller and an individual choice.

TURNER SPORTS UNITED KINGDOM 1959–66

The Turner Sports started life as a low-volume sporting special, The appearance of the extremely capable Austin-Healey Sprite, however, meant that the Turner Sports was unable to establish itself on the market. The problem was that the car cost a third more than an Austin-Healey Sprite when it was launched in 1959, yet it was more basic and not as well built. Using a glassfibre bodyshell on a tubular steel chassis, the Turner was very light, and, if the customer specified the 90bhp (67kW), 1220cc (74cu in) Coventry Climax engine option, it was very fast indeed. So powered it was in fact faster than the Sprite, but that extra speed came at a price.

Despite being costly, the Turner Sports did appeal to those who saw the cars being campaigned successfully by the Turner works racing team, which operated between 1960 and 1963. The Turner Sports Mk II arrived in 1960, and this model came with a better interior, an optional hardtop and Triumph Herald suspension in place of the A35 set-up that had previously been used.

Ford engines were then used, and, in 1963, the final Mk III version appeared. Changes to the car were slight, but the company folded after founder Jack Turner died in 1966.

Fewer than 400 cars were built during the Turner Sports's seven-year production run.

ENGINE: 948cc (58cu in), four-cylinder
POWER: 60bhp (45kW)
0–60MPH (96KM/H): 12 seconds
TOP SPEED: 152km/h (95mph)
PRODUCTION TOTAL: about 400

The UK market was awash with glassfibre-bodied two-seater low-volume sports cars in the 1960s, and the Turner Sports was another capable entry into the marketplace. However it never enjoyed lasting success thanks to the appearance of the cheaper Austin-Healey Sprite.

FORD UK ANGLIA

UNITED KINGDOM 1959–67

When Ford opened a research and development centre in the heart of the British motor industry in Birmingham in the mid-1950s, it meant that the company could produce cars specifically tailored for one of its most important markets. Despite the promise of a bright future, only one production model emerged from this creative 'hothouse', the 105E Anglia. The car was an interesting departure for Ford. Most obvious was the Americanized styling – hardly too surprising, as a visiting designer from Ford USA, Elwood Engel, was credited with many features and was responsible for the extensive wind-tunnel testing.

Main points of interest were the rear wings (fenders), reverse-rake windscreen and hooded headlights, which made the Anglia a bit of a landmark car for Ford.

One of the new Anglia's best features was the engine, which was an over-square, high-revving overhead-valve unit that was attached to Ford's first four-speed transmission. Combined with tidy and acceptable handling, it was a real step forward from the car it replaced, as well as one of 1959's brightest stars. A popular estate (station wagon) version was added to the range in 1962.

ENGINE: 997cc (61cu in), four-cylinder
POWER: 39bhp (29kW)
0–60MPH (96KM/H): 21 seconds
TOP SPEED: 128km/h (80mph)
PRODUCTION TOTAL: 1,083,960

GILBERN GT

UNITED KINGDOM 1959–67

For ever known as Wales' only car, the Gilbern GT originated in Pontypridd. Originally available as a kit, it was sold in component form in order to exploit a loophole which allowed potential owners to save money by avoiding paying purchase tax. The car provided an affordable entry into the sports–car market for many people. Underneath the glassfibre body was a tubular chassis and running gear taken from a combination of parts out of the BMC Parts bin.

Despite its diminutive engine size, the Gilbern's performance was reasonably impressive, thanks to the addition of an optional Shorrock supercharger to the standard Austin A-Series. That pushed power up from 42bhp (31kW) in the standard car to 68bhp (51kW). Successive cars were sold with either the 1098cc (67cu in) Coventry Climax unit, or the 1588cc (97cu in) or 1622cc (99cu in) engine from the MGA. After 1963, the company offered the 1798cc (110cu in) engine from the MGB to offer a suitably torquey experience.

Styling was unpretentious and neat, and the two wide-opening doors provided good access to a utilitarian bench seat in the back, enabling the GT claim that it could seat four in reasonable comfort.

ENGINE: 948cc (58cu in), four-cylinder
POWER: 42bhp (31kW)
0–60MPH (96KM/H): 17.4 seconds
TOP SPEED: 147km/h (91mph)
PRODUCTION TOTAL: 166

Take a BMC A-Series engine, and marry it up to a lightweight coupé body, and you've discovered Gilbern's sports–car recipe. Fun and frugal, the GT proved that you needn't be rich to have a good time on your favourite roads – although the optional supercharger added a certain something.

JAGUAR MK 2

UNITED KINGDOM 1959–67

ENGINE: 3781cc (231cu in),
 six-cylinder
POWER: 220bhp (164kW)
0–60MPH (96KM/H): 8.5 seconds
TOP SPEED: 200km/h (125mph)
PRODUCTION TOTAL: 83,980

Today revered as one of the greatest all-round classic cars, thanks to its fantastic styling, usable performance and impressive specialist back-up, the Jaguar Mk 2 made quite an impression when it was new, too. Introduced to replace what retrospectively became known as the Jaguar Mk 1, the new car featured a larger glass area (including a much bigger rear window), a better interior, a slightly wider rear track (to improve roadholding), a different grille and all-round disc brakes as standard.

The Mk 2 was also offered with a much wider range of engines, including the fabulous 3.8-litre (232cu in) twin-camshaft from the XK. Specified with option, the Mk 2 was one of the fastest production saloons of its era.

An all-synchromesh gearbox arrived in 1965 and, from 1966, there was a reduced specification,

which included Ambla plastic on the seats instead of leather, and no fog lamps. From 1967, there was optional power-assisted steering, which helped what was otherwise a heavy car to drive.

Loyal enthusiasts have ensured that the elegant Mk 2 remains as desirable today as it was when new. Its most famous TV appearance was on the long-running detective series *Inspector Morse*.

The Mk 2 immortalized Jaguar as a world-class producer of cars for the gentleman in a hurry. With perfectly judged styling, throttle adjustable handling and prodigious straight line pace.

AUSTIN A99 AND A110 WESTMINSTER

Applying the Pininfarina styling of the A55 and A60 Cambridge to the upscaled Westminster worked surprisingly well – in fact, it really suited the Westminster's more imposing look.

The previous pre-Farina Westminster had been a worthy car, and the new A99 took the best bits from that model and improved upon them. The C-series engine was enlarged to 3 litres (178cu in) and fitted with twin SU carburettors, while the three-speed gearbox was given a stronger synchromesh and the front brakes were upgraded to servo-assisted discs, a first for an Austin saloon.

In 1961, the Westminster was given a longer wheelbase to increase passenger room and give the car a more impressive road presence. The following year, Austin added power steering and air-conditioning options. Later, in 1964, the A110 Westminster Mk II appeared with a four-speed gearbox, the finishing touch for a surprisingly impressive machine.

ENGINE: 2912cc (178cu in), six-cylinder
POWER: 120bhp (89kW)
0–60MPH (96KM/H): 13.3 seconds
TOP SPEED: 165km/h (102mph)
PRODUCTION TOTAL: 41,250

AUSTIN-HEALEY 3000

ENGINE: 2912cc (178cu in), six-cylinder
POWER: 132bhp (98kW)
0–60MPH (96KM/H): 11.5 seconds
TOP SPEED: 180km/h (112mph)
PRODUCTION TOTAL: 42,926

The Austin-Healey 3000 was undoubtedly the most famous of all the 'Big Healeys' – and one which became a legend within its own lifetime. In production from 1959 to 1968, the 3000 began life as a simple upgrade to the previous 100-Six models. The 2.9-litre (178cu in) version of the BMC C-series six-cylinder engine was squeezed under the bonnet (hood), as well as new front discs brakes.

The 3000 came in two versions, the two-seater BN7 and the 2+2 BT7. The more practical latter version was by far the more popular choice with buyers. Given the useful boost in power compared with the previous 2.6-litre (161cu in) 100-Six models, performance was predictably impressive, with a top speed of 187km/h (116mph) and acceleration to match.

In 1961, the models were updated to the 3000 Mk II BN7 and BT7. The Mk II BJ7 followed hard on the heels of this car a year later. It featured a proper fold-down hood and wind-down windows. In 1963, the 3000 Mk III BJ8 Phase I was launched, featuring a restyled fascia using walnut and a new centre console; a year later, the BJ8 Phase II appeared. After the formation of British Leyland 1968, the marque was quietly dropped.

With that grinning mouth and bellowing straight-six engine how could you not fall for the open-topped charms of the 'big' Healey 3000?

FIAT 1800

A new range of four- and six-cylinder Fiat models was launched in 1959. The 1800 and 2100 were smart-looking cars, bringing the top of the Fiat range bang up to date. Powered by either a 1795cc (110cu in) unit with 75bhp (56kW) or a 2054cc (125cu in) with 82bhp (61kW), these cars were the first Fiats to use torsion bar suspension at the front. The 2100 was also the first post-war Fiat to use straight-six engines.

The pretty Pininfarina Berlina saloon and Familiare estate looked rather similar to the BMC 'Farina' saloons, as well as the Peugeot 404, which were also styled by the prolific Italian designer. From 1960, the 1800 could be ordered with many luxury car features including a sunroof, radio, electric radio aerial, whitewall tyres and a heated rear window. The 1800 did not sell well abroad, however, and few buyers fell for its charms – unconvinced by its average refinement and patchy build quality.

From 1962, the engine from the 1500 was added to the 1800 range, but it did not sell either – and started Fiat down a long road of slow-selling large cars.

ENGINE: 1795cc (110cu in), four-cylinder
POWER: 75bhp (56kW)
0–60MPH (96KM/H): 19 seconds
TOP SPEED: 145km/h (90mph)
PRODUCTION TOTAL: 30,000

MG MAGNETTE MK III/IV

UNITED KINGDOM 1959–68

The BMC 'Farina' saloon range was well established by the time the MG version was launched in 1959. The Magnette Mk III/IV was a member of the badge-engineered family that included cars produced by Austin, Morris, Wolseley, Riley, Vanden Plas and MG – and it was supposed to be the sporting option of the humble but worthy range of cars.

In order to live up this, the MG Magnette 'Farina' received an extra carburettor to give a minimal performance boost, a rudimentary anti-roll bar set-up on the front suspension and a well-equipped leather and wood interior. Magnette IIIs had a 1489cc (91cu in) engine, while later IVs had a 1622cc (99cu in) unit, plus optional automatic gearbox and two-tone paint.

Visual differences included a trademark if somewhat incongruous MG grille, plus different indicator light lenses. The car did not impress marque enthusiasts used to the more flamboyant pre-war cars, but it sold reasonably well anyway.

ENGINE: 1622cc (99 cu in), four-cylinder
POWER: 68bhp (51kW)
0–60MPH (96KM/H): 20.2 seconds
TOP SPEED: 142km/h (88mph)
PRODUCTION TOTAL: 30,996

ROCHDALE OLYMPIC

UNITED KINGDOM 1959–68

ENGINE: 948cc (58cu in), four-cylinder
POWER: 44bhp (33kW)
0–60MPH (96KM/H): 14.9 seconds
TOP SPEED: 134km/h (83mph)
PRODUCTION TOTAL: 400

The Rochdale Olympic may have been called after one of the least likely place names in history (it is a former mill town near Manchester, England), but what it lacked in glamour it made up for on the road. The small independent sportscar producer did well through the 1960s and survived longer than many of its contemporaries on the back of its interesting and pretty two-seater coupé.

The running gear came from a variety of BMC sources, with A-Series, B-Series or Triumph-based engines; some examples used Ford Cortina or even the aged side-valve Anglia units. The complex glassfibre monocoque construction body meant that body rigidity was surprisingly good. The earliest two-door versions even made do without a boot (trunk) opening. In 1963, the sporting car became a proper hatchback, and its appeal was widened considerably.

Later cars were the best, with significantly improved build quality and Triumph Spitfire front suspension. A Rochdale could take any engine that fitted – and the glass-reinforced-plastic body could handle it, too. Handling was neat, although it was twitchy at the rear end and suffered from a bumpy ride. It was a genuinely sporting car.

Powered by a range of humdrum engines, the Rochdale Olympic was quick and fun to drive – with tidy handling and excellent agility, but its interior was stark.

ROLLS-ROYCE PHANTOM V

UNITED KINGDOM 1959–68

In 1959, Rolls-Royce produced one of the largest cars ever to emerge from its Crewe factory, and used the occasion to launch its now-familiar 6.3-litre (380cu in) V8 engine. It was a suitably enormous car built for heads of state and the super-rich – tipping the scales at almost 3000kg (almost 3 tons). The Phantom V had a 3.6m (12ft) wheelbase, and the passenger space was suitably enormous – especially in the rear.

Under the bonnet (hood), the new pushrod V8 owed much to the engines built by Chrysler and GM in the United States – even down to the aluminium block and cylinder heads, which were fashionable there at the time. Power steering was standard – it needed to be – as was automatic transmission, while underneath the imposing bodywork was a lengthened version of the Silver Cloud's chassis. Coachwork options were offered, although most buyers went for the H.J. Mulliner six-light styling, usually painted black.

Performance was adequate, but fuel consumption was astronomical if the car was pushed. In 1968, it was replaced by the even more extravagant 6.7-litre (409cu in) Phantom VI, which remained available well into the 1990s.

ENGINE: 6230cc (380cu in), eight-cylinder
POWER: n/a
0–60MPH (96KM/H): 13.8 seconds
TOP SPEED: 163km/h (101mph)
PRODUCTION TOTAL: 793

The favoured transport for heads of state across the Commonwealth, the Rolls-Royce Phantom V was a monument to the art of the coachbuilders. The Rolls-Royce to be powered by the new V8 engine that remains in production in the 21st century.

AUSTIN A55 AND A60 CAMBRIDGE

UNITED KINGDOM 1959–69

ENGINE: 1622cc (99cu in),
  four-cylinder
POWER: 61bhp (45kW)
0–60MPH (96KM/H): 21.4 seconds
TOP SPEED: 131km/h (81mph)
PRODUCTION TOTAL: 425,500

After the success of the Austin A40, BMC's boss Len Lord commissioned Farina to work on styling other cars in the company's huge range. The bread-and-butter Cambridge and Westminster range were next in line for the Italian's attention, and, in 1959, the Austin and Morris versions of the new 'Farina' were introduced to an impressed public.

Gone were the downbeat lines of their predecessor, and, in return, the new models received a flamboyant European look. It was

A startling new Farina style ushered in the 1960s for BMC. A capable and worthy saloon that wasn't as exciting as it looked.

not perfect and, compared with the similarly styled Peugeot 404, looked a little fussy. Still, it was a breath of fresh air, and buyers warmed to the new look. The A55 was a simple remodelling of the previous 'pre-Farina' Cambridge, powered by the same 1489cc (91cu in) B-series engine. Apart from the addition of an SU carburettor, it was almost unchanged – but it was at least more powerful than the terrible diesel option that appeared with the Farina.

In 1961, the A60 appeared and benefited from an increased engine capacity to 1622cc (99cu in) – a worthwhile improvement. At the same time, the wheelbase was increased by 2.5cm (1in), and the front grille was redesigned, but the natty tail fins of the A55 were dropped. A Countryman version was also offered and proved popular.

RILEY 4/68 & 4/72 FARINA

UNITED KINGDOM 1959–69

ENGINE: 1622cc (99cu in), four-cylinder
POWER: 68bhp (51kW)
0–60MPH (96KM/H): 19.5 seconds
TOP SPEED: 147km/h (91mph)
PRODUCTION TOTAL: 25,011

By the time the rolling programme of 'Farina' introductions was well under way in 1959, BMC had well and truly abandoned the idea that more expensive Rileys and Wolseleys should be treated to the luxury of their own bodywork. Badge engineering seemed to work between the marques, so why not extend it to encompass an entire range of similarly sized cars?

And it was so. The Riley 4/68 – and latterly the 4/72 – was an adaption of the standard Morris Oxford. For its translation into Riley form, the Morris nose was removed and replaced by Riley's traditional 'grille and whiskers' style front-end. Two-tone paintwork was also added to give the car a visual lift.

The sporting Riley variant received a few performance enhancements, including front and rear anti-roll bars and a twin-carburettor engine – and was as quick as the MG Magnette version. Optional automatic transmission – a Riley first – was offered from 1962, along with a 1622cc (99 cu in) engine to replace the earlier car's 1489cc (91cu in) unit.

Based on the Morris Oxford 'Farina' saloon, the Riley 4/68 and 4/72 were affable mid-liners.

MORRIS OXFORD FARINA

UNITED KINGDOM 1959–71

The badge may have said Morris, but the engineering was BMC – and alongside the Cowley-built car were the mechanically similar Farina saloons, available in Austin, MG, Riley or Wolseley forms. The car took its name from the designer who penned the car, and it would be a look that would influence the design direction for BMC's mid-range cars for the following decade. Apart from its alternative grille arrangement, there was little to distinguish the Oxford from its Austin counterpart (called the Cambridge), but BMC sold plenty through its former Nuffield Group showrooms.

From 1959 to 1961, the Oxford had prominent rear fins and a 1489cc (91 cu in) B-Series engine. The practical Countryman estate (station wagon), available from 1960, complemented the four-door saloon and proved popular. In 1961, a slight restyle reduced the size of the fins, and engine capacity was increased by fitting to 1622cc (99cu in) B-Series unit – and it was in this form that the car remained largely unchanged until the Marina replaced it in 1971.

ENGINE: 1622cc (99cu in),
four-cylinder
POWER: 61bhp (45kW) at 4500rpm
0–60MPH (96KM/H): 21.4 seconds
TOP SPEED: 130km/h (81mph)
PRODUCTION TOTAL: 296,255

SKODA OCTAVIA

CZECHOSLOVAKIA 1959–71

Closely developed from the earlier 440, when it appeared in 1959, the Skoda Octavia actually looked a lot fresher than it really was. Still, it remained a worthy car, so named because it was the eighth in a line of small cars made by the Czechoslovakian manufacturer.

As well as the standard car, a Super version was offered. This, too, was based on an old car – the 445. A higher lift camshaft, new inlet and exhaust manifolds, twin carburettors, bigger valves and a higher compression ratio delivered extra performance.

Buyers could also specify the quicker and more focused Octavia TS (Touring Sport). Powered by a 50bhp (37kW) twin-carburettor Standard engine taken from the Felicia soft-top, it was fun to drive.

Although the trio of Octavias was essentially variations of the same car, the faster models always seemed worth their premium. At first, the engine was the familiar 1089cc (66cu in) unit; from 1961, this was uprated to a 1221cc (75cu in) powerplant, which also appeared in the Felicia, itself a variation of the Octavia.

ENGINE: 1089cc (66cu in),
four-cylinder
POWER: 40bhp (30kW)
0–60MPH (96KM/H): 36.6 seconds
TOP SPEED: 120km/h (75mph)
PRODUCTION TOTAL: 279,724

TRIUMPH HERALD

UNITED KINGDOM 1959–71

ENGINE: 1147cc (70cu in),
four-cylinder
POWER: 39bhp (29kW) at 4500rpm
0–60MPH (96KM/H): 28.6 seconds
TOP SPEED: 122km/h (76mph)
PRODUCTION TOTAL: Approx 544,210

In the pre-war years, the word 'standard' meant 'excellence'. Ten years later, that had all changed, with the word becoming associated with 'basic'. This was more than a little trouble for the Standard Motor Company, so, following its takeover of Triumph, it was only a matter of time before its range of cars began using the marque name from the company it took over.

As so it was – when the Standard Eight/Ten range was replaced in 1959, it was by a Triumph-badged car. The approach certainly worked because the Herald range became one of the most successful small British cars of the 1960s. Styling was by Michelotti, and engineering remained traditional. The Herald still used a separate chassis and drum brakes, and it was powered by modernized versions of the old

Standard engine. All-independent suspension was fitted, but the elementary rear set-up was poor.

The platform was adaptable, though, and it sired a number of variations – as well as the saloon, a convertible, a coupé, an estate (station wagon) and van were all offered. A bigger 1147cc (70cu in) engine was added in 1961, expanded to 1296cc (79cu in) in 1967. Production ended in 1971.

Conceived to replace the dull–but–worthy Standard Eight and Ten, the Michelotti–styled Triumph Herald had considerable panache. Offered in a wide range of options, it lived a long life.

BUICK ELECTRA

UNITED STATES 1959–72

The 1959 Electra brought extravagance to new heights when it was launched – with its enormous fins, stacked headlights and oodles of chrome fittings. The high performance Wildcat model defied belief and maintained the marque's success.

With the launch of the Electra, Buick returned to the large-car class with a more modern interpretation of the old Roadmaster range. The slightly sporting large car was huge – especially in 225 form, which as its name suggests, was 225in (572cm) long (in the stretched body version).

There was plenty of power, though. A 6571cc (401cu in) V8, producing 325bhp (242kW), delivered ample performance. Three years after launch, the standard car was dropped, and face-lifted models produced under the direction of Bill Mitchell, GM's chief designer, appeared in the range.

The bodies were simpler and less bulky, especially the 'convertible look' two-door coupés. For 1965, the Electra 225 received a major restyle and the same 325bhp (242kW) V8 as used in the high-performance Buick Wildcat model. This was further improved in 1966 with a Custom series featuring plush interior trim.

By 1967, the cars were getting bigger and bulkier again, but with more body contours and increased power output for the V8 engines – up to 360bhp (268kW). Two years later, the Electra 225 received another body rework. Although still a large car, it looked graceful.

ENGINE: 6571cc (401cu in), eight-cylinder
POWER: 325bhp (242kW)
0–60MPH (96KM/H): 9 seconds
TOP SPEED: 193km/h (120mph)
PRODUCTION TOTAL: 1,220,340

BUICK LE SABRE

ENGINE: 5965cc (300cu in), eight-cylinder
POWER: 250bhp (186kW)
0–60MPH (96KM/H): 9.2 seconds
TOP SPEED: 170km/h (106mph)
PRODUCTION TOTAL: 2,100,000

First seen in 1951 on a futuristic concept car built from cast magnesium and aluminium body panels and powered by a supercharged V8 engine, Buick's Le Sabre promised excitement. When the production car of the same name appeared in 1959, its initial promise was fulfilled – the Buick Le Sabre was a radically restyled range with prominent fins that ran from the front to the rear of the body. Available as a saloon, a two-door hardtop, a convertible and an estate car (station wagon), its power came from a 5965cc (364cu in) 250bhp (186kW) engine.

As the entry-level Buick, it was an immediate success – 165,577 were sold. In 1962, the looks were toned down when the car was completely restyled with clean square lines. Power was plentiful, and output climbed to 280bhp (209kW). In 1965, a new body with wider, softer lines kept Le Sabre as Buick's full-sized price leader.

A further rebody in 1967, as well as a Custom series, with enhanced levels of trim, saw the

Sitting below the Electra in the Buick range, the Le Sabre was equally flamboyant. Fins, chrome and a range of V8 engines were once again staple features.

car increase in size, although it was now available only in saloon and hardtop coupé guises. In 1969, a further restyle saw the arrival of the '400' option, which included a 280bhp (209kW) V8.

ROVER P5

For many, the Rover P5 summed up all that was good about the Rover company – it was solid, luxurious and built like a tank. The car was a step upmarket for Rover when it first appeared. Sales quickly took off within the United Kingdom's managerial classes – most notably, the British government, with examples being used by Prime

Although it didn't look like a technological leap forward, the Rover P5 sported unitary body construction.

Ministers well into the 1980s. The Queen also owned a couple.

The P5 was significant for Rover because it was the company's first monocoque construction vehicle, with a crisp and imposing style penned by David Bache. The interior was a traditional wood-and-leather affair. Initially, the P5 was powered by just one engine, a 2995cc (183cu in) straight-six developed from the earlier P3. In 1962, more power arrived. The new 'Weslake Head' (a modified cylinder head developed by performance expert Harry Weslake) version of the engine lifted power output from 115bhp (86kW) to 134bhp (100kW).

The introduction of the four-door low-roof coupé version in 1963 significantly increased the car's appeal, as did introduction of the newly acquired 3.5-litre (214cu in) V8 engine to create the P5B in 1967.

ENGINE: 2995cc (183 cu in), six-cylinder
POWER: 115bhp (86kW) at 4500rpm
0–60MPH (96KM/H): 16.2 seconds
TOP SPEED: 157km/h (98mph)
PRODUCTION TOTAL: 69,141

FORD GALAXIE

UNITED STATES 1959–74

ENGINE: 6386cc (390cu in), eight-cylinder
POWER: 300bhp (224kW)
0–60MPH (96KM/H): 9.5 seconds
TOP SPEED: 196km/h (122mph)
PRODUCTION TOTAL: 4,726,105

Detroit was in the throes of a major power war at the start of the 1960s, and Ford's contribution to the main event was the Galaxie. Although it outpowered the similar Chevrolet Impala, it never sold as well because of its dull styling, poor aerodynamics and sheer weight.

The Galaxie did, however, help to usher in the muscle-car era at the full-size end of the model spectrum. Despite slow sales, Ford continued with the Galaxie and fitted ever larger engines to it. The pinnacle surely had to be the most powerful engine Detroit ever made: the Cammer 427, which produced a whopping 657bhp (489kW).

Galaxies were revamped for 1965, with sharper styling and stacked headlights, and a redesigned front suspension. But buyers who wanted pure performance chose more compact models, so, from 1967, the company shifted the Galaxie's focus and turned it into a luxury car. The GT package separated

The Galaxie was Ford's flagship muscle car for much of the 1960s. The Cammer 427 engine was a 657bhp (489kW) beast.

performance Galaxies from the XL series, which no longer came with standard bucket seats and V8 power. By the end of its life in 1974, the Galaxie had completely lost its individual status within the range.

CHECKER MARATHON

UNITED STATES 1959–82

Just like the United Kingdom had the iconic Austin FX4, the United States boasted its own 'national' taxi – and one that could not be confused with any other. The Checker Marathon was a popular rugged car, built with the taxi trade in mind. It came with extra wide doors and lots of legroom.

Based on the Checker A-8, produced in 1956, the Marathon featured the now familiar quad headlights of the 1958 A-9. Checkers were also marketed to the private motorist. The first of these was the A-10 Superba, released in 1960, but its appeal was limited.

In 1962, Checker used the Marathon name for the first time on the A-12, which was available as a four-door saloon and an estate (station wagon). Essentially, the styling remained unchanged for the next 20 years, and the car became part of New York City's street furniture. Five thousand Checker cabs roamed the city as late as the mid-1970s, but numbers quickly declined by the end of the decade.

In the 1970s, oil prices doubled, which became a problem for the Marathon, as it averaged only 4km/L (11mpg). Cab drivers began buying smaller, more fuel-efficient vehicles. On 12 July 1982, Checker Motor Corporation of Kalamazoo, Michigan, made its last cab.

ENGINE: 3704cc (226cu in), six-cylinder
POWER: 122bhp (83.5kW)
0–60MPH (96KM/H): 15 seconds
TOP SPEED: 177km/h (110mph)
PRODUCTION TOTAL: 100,000

Its name might not be familiar, but the Checker Marathon is instantly recongnizable as the New York Taxi. Most often painted yellow and sporting chequered stripes along its side, the Marathon was tough in order to survive the punishment meted out by competitive cab drivers.

CHRYSLER 300F

UNITED STATES 1960

ENGINE: 6769cc (413cu in),
eight-cylinder
POWER: 375bhp (279kW)
0–60MPH (96KM/H): 7.1 seconds
TOP SPEED: 233km/h (145mph)
PRODUCTION TOTAL: 1212

The Chrysler 300 was legendary in the muscle-car scene even before the 1960 launch of the 'sixth in a famous line', the 300F. Built for outright performance, this latest in a long line of 'letter cars' was powered by a 6769cc (413cu in) engine delivering a spectacular 375bhp (279kW). Using a clever ram induction intake manifold system, 76cm (30in) induction tubes positioned over the carburettor fed each bank of cylinders out beyond the rocker cover of the opposing cylinder head. It was enough to add 5bhp (3.5kW), but a massive 61Nm (45lb ft) of extra torque at 800rpm lower in the rev range.

For drivers who wanted more outright power, an engine tuned to produce 400bhp (298kW) was fitted with a four-speed Pont-à-Mousson

manual transmission from France's big Facel-Vega models.

The monocoque body was structurally brand new, with a trapezoidal grille and fabulous sloping tail fins, as well as

boomerang-like taillights. The car's four bucket seats were divided by a console that ran from front to back, and the domed dashboard comprised a glass bubble in which the instruments seemed to float.

Chrysler was a prime mover in the muscle–car movement, and the 300F was one of the most feared of the bunch, developing upto 375bhp (279kW) straight out of the box.

GHIA L.6.4

The Ghia L.6.4 was closely based on the Dart, a show car built by the design house and coachbuilders in the late 1950s, and it proved to be an exclusive machine that found few homes. The company's most popular car was the Dual-Ghia Firebomb, which, like the L.6.4, was styled by the prolific designer, Virgil Exner, and proved to be less than faithful in service.

The fantastically styled coupé was built by Casaroll and Company, and lived up to its predecessor, thanks to its highly styled coachwork, panoramic windscreen, imposing frontal treatment, and liberal use of chrome trimmings. Unsurprisingly, the L.6.4 was targeted at affluent American buyers, and one such high profile owner was Frank Sinatra.

Powered by a lusty Chrysler V8 engine and featuring a body styled and built by Ghia in Turin, the L.6.4 had a top speed of 224km/h (140mph) with vivid acceleration to match. The Italo-American hybrid set the template for many exotic cars to come such as the Chrysler-powered and Italian-styled Iso, Jensen and Monteverdi.

A huge list price meant that only 26 examples were built during its

two-year production run, and few have survived today – when they come up for sale, the Ghia L.6.4 is enormously expensive.

ENGINE: 6279cc (383 cu in), eight-cylinder
POWER: 335bhp (250kW)
0–60MPH (96KM/H): 8 secs
TOP SPEED: 224km/h (140mph)
PRODUCTION TOTAL: 26

MORETTI 1000

Of all the strange and wonderful car companies to have ever existed, Moretti was one most curious. The marque was created in 1945 to build motorcycles of its own design, before switching to fascinating small cars. Although Morettis were expensive and no better than their mass-produced contemporaries, Italians valued the cars' individuality enough to ensure

the company remained independent (a big deal in the country dominated by Fiat) throughout its life.

The Moretti 1000 was one of the company's prettiest designs. Based on the underpinnings of the Fiat 1100 saloon, the angular range incorporated a two-door coupé, a saloon, a convertible and an estate (station wagon). Moretti went on to create a range of Fiat 500- and

126-based city cars, plus an oddball 127-based hatchback, in the 1970s.

Until 1957, Moretti designed and built its own overhead camshaft engines and fitted them to platforms also designed in-house. It then exclusively used Fiat chassis, and, while engines also came from the Turin manufacturer, these were significantly re-engineered. The company finally closed its doors in

the mid-1980s after widespread globalization destroyed hundreds of small vehicle manufacturers.

ENGINE: 980cc (60cu in), four-cylinder
POWER: 41bhp (31kW)
0–60MPH (96KM/H): n/a
TOP SPEED: 123km/h (76mph)
PRODUCTION TOTAL: about 1000

MARCOS GT

So called because Jem Marsh and Frank Costin had co-formed the company during the 1950s, Marcos built specials that were based on an unusual marine-ply wooden chassis. The first Marcos off the line was the odd-looking GT. It was innovative and looked very different to the opposition, thanks to its long nose and pod-like cabin. The gullwing coupé soon picked

up the nickname 'Wooden Wonder'. It featured a wooden monocoque construction and a glassfibre nosecone. The rest of the body was shaped exclusively from specially formed ply, and it was exceptionally aerodynamic.

Front suspension was borrowed from the Triumph Herald, and a Ford live axle, located by a Panhard rod, was at the back. Power came

from Ford's 105E engines, in a variety of forms.

While proving very successful on the track in the hands of drivers such as Jackie Stewart, the GT had challenging styling that resulted in slow sales. Indeed, in its four-year production run, and despite a makeover by Dennis Adams to improve its looks and increase the use of glassfibre instead of wood,

only 39 cars were ever sold. Still, the story of the GT ends well. Today, due to its rarity, existing examples draw very high prices.

ENGINE: 997cc (61cu in), four-cylinder
POWER: 41–64bhp (kW)
0–60MPH (96KM/H): 9.1 seconds
TOP SPEED: 152km/h (95mph)
PRODUCTION TOTAL: 39

INNOCENTI SPIDER

Innocenti originally set out making Lambretta scooters, but, by 1960, the company had broken into the world of car manufacturer. Its first product, a licence-built Austin A40, started a long British association, which before it had fully flowered resulted in the pretty Spider. The new car was essentially a rebodied Austin-Healey Sprite with bodywork designed by Tom

Tjaarda, an employee of the Ghia styling house in Turin. It was initially powered by a 948cc (58cu in) version of the A-Series engine and rode on Austin-Healey suspension, but modifications to the Spider were not long coming.

From late 1961, a removable hardtop was offered, and, in 1963, the Spider was fitted with the larger Austin 1098cc (67cu in)

engine producing 58bhp (43kW) at 5500rpm, along with front disc brakes as standard.

In 1966, the Spider went out of production when it was replaced by the new C (or Coupé) model, which was manufactured by Ghia's neighbour OSI. Production of this car, which used the same running gear as the Spider, lasted until 1968. Today, the Spider is rare and

valuable, and is a good example of the pretty, almost hand-built low-volume specials that Italy was producing at the time.

ENGINE: 948cc (58cu in), four-cylinder
POWER: 43bhp (32kW)
0–60MPH (96KM/H): 12 seconds
TOP SPEED: 136km/h (85mph)
PRODUCTION TOTAL: 6857

OSCA 1600

After selling their own company to the Orsi family in 1937 to avoid bankruptcy, the Maserati brothers ventured once again into small-scale performance car production at the start of the 1960s with OSCA (which stood for Officine Specializzate Costruzioni Automobili – Fratelli Maserati SpA).

OSCA's biggest commercial success was the 1600, which was

based on the floorpan of the Fiat 1600S. That gave the car superb handling and lively performance from its twin camshaft engine.

OSCA tuned the engine to deliver as much as 140bhp (104kW) – impressive for a 1.6-litre (96cu in) unit even today – but the units were fragile, and too many forays into the peak power zone of 7200rpm would usually result in a breakage.

Buyers could choose their own body styling, although most opted for the Zagato-designed two-door coupé, reminiscent of Pininfarina's Ferrari 275GTS. Other stylists included Fissore and Vignale, and a handful of convertible OSCAs were also made. These were hand-built cars of the highest quality and, despite the small engines, were a genuine alternative to a Ferrari or

Porsche. Production ceased in 1967 when the Maserati brothers went into retirement and sold the OSCA factory to MV Augusta.

ENGINE: 1568cc (96cu in), four-cylinder
POWER: 140bhp (104kW)
0–60MPH (96KM/H): 8.2 seconds
TOP SPEED: 210km/h (130mph)
PRODUCTION TOTAL: n/a

Consider the OSCA 1600 as a baby-Maserati and you'll not be far off the truth – based on the floorpan of the Fiat 1600S, the jewel-like sports car had superb handling and good performance, a sure sign of its exclusive DNA.

ZAZ 965

USSR 1960–63

Otherwise known as the Zaphorozhets, or Zaporogets, the ZAZ 965 was poorly engineered with decidedly ropey build quality. Described by many as the worst car ever conceived, this rear-engined car produced in the Soviet Union possesses origins which have been lost in the mists of time. The ZAZ 965 looked very similar to a Fiat 600 with a boot

(trunk), but it was powered by an air-cooled V4 engine.

The original powerplant was a 748cc (46cu in) unit developing just 23bhp (17kW). Within a year of its introduction, the 965 was upgunned with an extra 200cc (12cu in), increasing engine capacity to 887cc (54cu in) and 27bhp (20kW). The power boost coincided with a change in name to the 965A.

Throughout production, the suspension was independent at the front with longitudinal trailing arms and transverse torsion bars, while, at the back, there were semi-trailing arms with coil springs and lever arm dampers. Drum brakes were fitted all round, and the car was to remain unchanged until the launch of its replacement, the 966, in 1967.

The car's most famous screen appearance was in the James Bond movie *Goldeneye*.

ENGINE: 748cc (46cu in), four-cylinder
POWER: 23bhp (17kW)
0–60MPH (96KM/H): n/a
TOP SPEED: 80km/h (50mph)
PRODUCTION TOTAL: n/a

CHEVROLET IMPALA

UNITED STATES 1960–69

Credited by many as the first true muscle car, the Chevrolet Impala was originally created as the company's top-of-the-range model. The Impala soon became synonymous with performance, and was responsible for introducing Chevrolet's Super Sport SS performance brand. Available in saloon, estate (station wagon), convertible and two-door hardtop

versions, power was initially came from 5.4-litre V8s. Looking less outrageous than their be-finned predecessors, the SS models were launched in 1961, powered by an impressive 6702cc (409cu in) V8.

Redesigned for 1965, the Impala lost its box-like shape and had a much more streamlined look. The original and much-loved engine was phased out and replaced by

the Mark IV 6489cc (396cu in) V8, which went on to power Chevrolets for the rest of the 1960s.

By 1966, the Caprice became the new top-of-the-line Chevrolet, leaving the Impala somewhat overshadowed, especially as the SS was now a performance car in name only. At that time, it also lost its trademark six round taillights, an Impala feature since 1958. The

end of the 1960s had seriously watered down the Impala's image as a muscle car with edge.

ENGINE: 5359cc (327cu in), eight-cylinder
POWER: 250bhp (186kW)
0–60MPH (96KM/H): 10 seconds
TOP SPEED: 172km/h (107mph)
PRODUCTION TOTAL: 7,000,000

The Impala was responsible for ushering in the Chevrolet Super Sport SS performance brand – not surprising considering it was, for many, the USA's first true muscle car. Later versions featured toned down styling, but went faster.

ABARTH-FIAT 850/1000

ITALY 1960–70

In 1949, Carlo Abarth set up his own company and planned to develop a new version of the Cisitalia 1100 for racing. Abarth's credentials were impeccable – he was a self-taught engineer who had worked with many automotive greats, including Ferdinand Porsche. In time, however, the business evolved into a performance tuning parts company that specialized in modifying production cars. Abarth was well respected in the business, but the car that vaulted him into the big time was his version of the little Fiat 600.

The first of these came in 1956, followed by a 747cc (46cu in) version in 1959, but the best came when the Fiat engine was bored out to 847cc (52cu in). The car it created, the 850TC, was a true buzz-box, a fun combination of lightness, diminutive size, go-kart handling and a responsive engine.

The basic version came with 52bhp (39kW), but there was an 850S model with 55bhp (41kW) and an 850SS with 57bhp (42kW). Compare this to the standard 600, producing only about 20bhp (15kW), and you begin to understand the popularity of these cars. Other models followed, including the 1000, then twin-camshaft versions of both the 850 and 1000.

ENGINE: 982cc (60cu in), four-cylinder
POWER: 60bhp (45kW)*
0–60MPH (96KM/H): n/a
TOP SPEED: 201km/h (125mph)
PRODUCTION TOTAL: n/a

FORD FALCON

UNITED STATES 1960–70

A more usefully sized Ford for those on a budget that wouldn't stretch to a full-sized car. Offered in smooth six-cylinder form and as a higher-powered V8 Futura Sprint model, there was still plenty of appeal.

success of the Mustang, however, led to the Sprint being discontinued, as it was no longer required. In 1964, the Falcon gained extra weight and less appeal, while an even bulkier restyle in 1966 saw the convertible and two-door hardtop versions finally dropped.

By 1969, the range was badged as either Falcon or Torino, but the Falcon name was then dropped for the 1970s – a sad end for one of Ford's big successes.

Although it was almost 1m (3ft) shorter than the full-sized models, there was still plenty of room inside the Ford Falcon, in both the two- and four-door models. It was an important car – the Falcon marked Ford's entry into the 1960s compact car market, and it proved extremely successful. Styled simply yet handsomely, it was a car that had wide appeal, helped by its smooth six-cylinder engine.

In 1963, the range's appeal was widened considerably by the introduction of the convertible and two-door hardtop versions. The V8 engines that appeared at the same time also helped the car win friends.

The Ford Falcon Futura Sprint was an important part of Ford's Total Performance competition programme and was available with high-power V8s. The incredible

ENGINE: 4261cc (260cu in), eight-cylinder
POWER: 260bhp (194kW)
0–60MPH (96KM/H): 9 seconds
TOP SPEED: 197km/h (123mph)
PRODUCTION TOTAL: 2,700,697

MERCURY COMET

For the 1960s, Mercury set about widening its appeal, launching an offensive into the compact car market. Derived from the Ford Falcon, the new Mercury Comet originally borrowed its 2360cc (144cu in) six-cylinder engine, but, in 1961, the appealing car gained a more conventional V8 powerplant to win it extra customers.

Given the Mercury family look, the Comet's styling echoed the bigger cars, and was available in three bodystyles, the two- and four-door saloons and an estate (station wagon). The cars sold well, and the rather interesting sporting S-22 model from 1963 attracted buyers thanks to its 2785cc (170cu in) engine, 164bhp (122kW) power output and 11.5-second 0–60mph (96km/h) time. The sporting theme of the S-22 was echoed inside as well as under the bonnet (hood), with bucket seats being fitted.

On the road, the Comet stood aside from the Detroit norm, on account of its firm and responsive suspension, and its roll-free cornering – it was a very capable driver's car.

The car was renamed the Caliente (meaning 'hot' in Spanish) in 1964, by which time Mercury had fitted a 200bhp (149kW) V8 engine with optional power steering and power-assisted brakes.

ENGINE: 2785cc (170cu in), eight-cylinder
POWER: 164bhp (122kW)
0–60MPH (96KM/H): 11.5 seconds
TOP SPEED: 150km/h (94mph)
PRODUCTION TOTAL: n/a

The Comet became Mercury's first ever car to be offered with something other than a V8 cylinder option – and its more down-to-earth styling, positive handling and manageable proportions predicted Detroit's future direction.

VOLVO P1800

ENGINE: 1780cc (109cu in), four-cylinder
POWER: 100bhp (75kW)
0–60MPH (96KM/H): 13.2 seconds
TOP SPEED: 166km/h (104mph)
PRODUCTION TOTAL: 39,407

there were few other changes. It was not until 1968 that engine capacity increased to 2.0 litres (122cu in) and the excitement mounted, but the star turn was reserved for the 1800E in 1971 ('E' for Einspritz, or fuel injection), which offered more sparkling performance.

The P1800 became internationally famous, thanks to its appearances in the TV programme *The Saint*, starring Roger Moore.

Considering Volvo's reputation has been forged on the back of solid big saloons, the P1800 was a desirable diversion that was a commercial success and remains much in demand today.

The Volvo P1800 was an elegantly styled car that looked far more exciting than it actually was. In typical Volvo fashion, it was a totally conventionally engineered car – and just as solid as the rest of the range. However, that solidity was not due to fine build quality because the early cars were not exactly well made. Blame that on the fact that production of the P1800 was outsourced due to Volvo's lack of factory capacity.

An agreement had been reached for Jensen to put the cars together once the Pressed Steel Company had built the bodyshells at its Scottish Linwood factory. In 1963, production moved to Sweden, and the car was rebadged the 1800S – and matters improved considerably. The engine was uprated with higher compression and a better camshaft to increase power, but

LANCIA FLAVIA

ENGINE: 1.5-litre (92cu in),
four-cylinder
POWER: 78bhp (58kW) at 5200rpm
0–60MPH (96KM/H): 18.7 seconds
TOP SPEED: 154km/h (96mph)
PRODUCTION TOTAL: 106,476

When it appeared, the Flavia was a major step forward for Lancia. It may have been predictably named (after the Roman road), but the Flavia was the first front-wheel drive Lancia, and it was powered by an all-alloy flat-four 'boxer' engine. It did not stop there. The car had disc brakes on all wheels, with vacuum assistance and a dual hydraulic system for extra safety.

The styling was a bit of a letdown, and the overall look was angular and conventional, but the quad headlights did add a little flair. Pininfarina improved matters considerably with the coupé version in 1961, and Vignale built an attractive convertible from 1962. As usual, though, it was Zagato that built the most arresting – the uniquely styled and highly individual Flavia Sport of 1963.

The Flavia saloon remained in production for 14 years, during which time the engine size went up to 1.8 litres (110cu in), then 1991cc (121cu in). The saloon was also restyled, in 1967 and again in 1969, when the coupé was updated as well. Fiat took control of Lancia in 1969, and the coupé and convertible versions were dropped. In 1972, the car was renamed the Lancia 2000.

The Lancia Flavia was an advanced car when it appeared, benefiting from front wheel drive and many safety features, and consequently it remained in production for 14 years.

PEUGEOT 404

To British eyes, the Pininfarina-designed Peugeot 404 looks like a tidier version of the Austin Cambridge. Given both cars were penned by the same styling house, it is understandable, although Peugeot management must have wondered what they were paying for. Still, the 404 was an elegant and well-finished machine, and was comfortable thanks to its independent front suspension. Entry-level models came with the 403's 1.5-litre (90cu in) engine, although a new 1.6-litre (98cu in) model, based on the old unit, was also offered with a lively 85bhp (63kW) on tap. Some cars were fuel-injected, pushing the power output up to a class-leading 96bhp (72kW) and giving the 404 genuine 160km/h (100mph) cruising ability.

Like the 403, Peugeot offered estate (station wagon) versions of the 404, as well as an eight-seater Familiale model. The improved 53bhp (39kW) 2.0-litre (122cu in) diesel version also helped to satisfy the growth in popularity of this fuel in France. There were also coupé and cabriolet versions, but these were different enough to be considered as entirely new models.

They were also available only with the 1.6-litre (98cu in) engine, with or without fuel injection.

ENGINE: 1468cc (90cu in),
four-cylinder
POWER: 65bhp (48kW)
0–60MPH (96KM/H): 22 seconds
TOP SPEED: 135km/h (84mph)
PRODUCTION TOTAL: 2,769,361

DODGE DART

When it was introduced as Dodge's entry into the compact market, it was just little more than a Plymouth Valiant with edgier styling. The car established itself as a useful performance machine, however, available as three models, the Seneca, Pioneer and Phoenix, and that led to a range of engines being fitted. A 5211cc (318cu in) V8 with either a two- or four-barrel carburettor was first to go in, then a 5916cc (361cu in) V8 with 310bhp (231kW) was added to the range. All models were available with

Although it was a compact car by American standards, it was larger than the car it replaced, the Lancer. The Dart enjoyed great success during a long life.

Dodge's D500 performance option using the larger V8.

When relaunched in 1963, the Dart became a true compact, using a shorter wheelbase, but the bodywork was less well styled and the V8 option had been dropped from the hardtop or convertible. In

1964, the Dodge Dart GT received a performance boost with the addition of Chrysler's 4474cc (273cu in) V8 delivering 180bhp (134kW). In 1968, Dodge introduced a new GTS trim. The car was available with either a standard 5572cc (340cu in) V8 with 275bhp

(205kW) or an optional 6276cc (383cu in) V8 with 300bhp (224kW).

For 1971, an all-new Dodge Demon, based on the Plymouth Duster, was offered as a two-door fastback, but performance-minded buyers opted for the Demon 340, the Dart GTS's spiritual successor.

ENGINE: 5572cc (340cu in), eight-cylinder
POWER: 275bhp (205kW)
0–60MPH (96KM/H): 6.3 seconds
TOP SPEED: 196km/h (122mph)
PRODUCTION TOTAL: about 5,000,000

SAAB 96

SWEDEN 1960–80

It is difficult not to conclude that the way to produce a vehicle that stays in production for a very long time is to build an individual-looking and innovative car. That is precisely what Saab did with the 96.

When the 96 was launched in 1960, it had a 38bhp (28kW), 841cc (51cu in) two-stroke three-cylinder engine Saab engine, mated to a three-speed gearbox (with a

fourth speed as an option until 1966 when it became standard). An estate (station wagon) version, the 95, was also offered. Safety was very important from the outset – the car was not only very strong, but, from 1962, seatbelts were fitted. From 1964, the car featured dual-circuit brakes.

In 1962, the triple-carburettor Sport was introduced; in 1966, it

was renamed the Monte Carlo to celebrate Erik Carlsson's win in the famous rally. Meanwhile a face-lift in 1965 saw a new front end, which lost the characteristic bullnose front. Two years later, the two-stroke engine was replaced by a 65bhp (48kW) 1498cc (91cu in) V4. Front disc brakes were fitted as standard. After that, the only major updates were a new dashboard in 1971,

the fitment of impact-absorbing bumpers in 1975, and a quiet run to 1980 when it was phased out.

ENGINE: 1498cc (91cu in), four-cylinder
POWER: 65bhp (48kW)
0–60MPH (96KM/H): 17.1 seconds
TOP SPEED: 147km/h (92mph)
PRODUCTION TOTAL: 547,221

Originally powered by Saab's idiosyncratic two-stroke engine, the 96 also used Ford V4 power in later years. Highly aerodynamic and individual to look at and drive, the Saab 96 proved a huge success and benefited from a policy of gradual evolution, remaining in production until 1980.

MERCURY METEOR

UNITED STATES 1961–63

The Meteor was introduced to become the mid-sized car in the Mercury range, and was initially launched in two-door saloon form. Although it shared the same basic shell as the Ford Fairlane, it had a slightly longer wheelbase and bore a strong resemblance to the other cars in the Ford family with its clean and smooth styling.

The Meteor used Mercury's comfortable 'Cushion Link' suspension, with independent coils at the front and a rigid axle with a five-leaf semi-elliptic spring set-up at the rear. This quirky device allowed the front and rear wheels to move rearwards as well as up and down over bumpy roads – and proved rather effective at providing a smoother ride. The

build quality and panel fit were particularly good on the Mercury range of cars and set high standards – the Meteor was no exception in this respect.

Performance was only average for the mid-sized class, mostly because the Meteor shared the same engine as the smaller Ford Falcon and the Comet. Handling was slightly more balanced than these

cars because the engine was set back from the front of the car to provide better weight distribution.

ENGINE: 3645cc (222cu in), six-cylinder
POWER: 145bhp (108kW)
0–60MPH (96KM/H): 15.2 seconds
TOP SPEED: 152km/h (95mph)
PRODUCTION TOTAL: n/a

OGLE SX1000

ENGINE: 1275cc (78cu in),
four-cylinder
POWER: 76bhp (57kW)
0–60MPH (96KM/H): 11.0 seconds
TOP SPEED: 177km/h (110mph)
PRODUCTION TOTAL: 66

Although in production for only a couple of years, the Ogle SX1000 made a big impression because of its combination of good looks and impressive handling. Ogle Design became famous for creating the Reliant Scimitar, but it was the SX1000 that became the company's most popular and, ultimately, fateful machine.

Based on the platform of the front-wheel drive Mini van, it was marked out by its unusual bulb-shaped plastic bodywork. The car could be specified with any variant of the popular BMC A-Series engine, including the twin-carburettor 1275cc (78cu in) Cooper S version. So powered, it could reach a top speed of 177km/h (110mph). The SX1000 was luxuriously equipped and interiors could be tailor-made to customers' specifications. Ogle also offered to convert customers' Minis, but this was not cheap due to the high production costs.

The project collapsed when company owner David Ogle lost control of his SX1000 and was killed. Customers lost confidence, and the concept died in its infancy. Boat builder Norman Fletcher briefly revived the bodyshell, but just four of the renamed Fletcher GTs were ever completed before the SX1000 disappeared for ever.

Based on the underpinnings of the innovative BMC Mini, the Ogle SX1000 took many of that car's best qualities, such as keen roadholding, and improved them.

BONNET DJET

This sports car from France from an unassuming manufacturer was actually a major motoring milestone, although one can be forgiven for never having heard of it. The Bonnet Djet (pronounced D-jet) was the first ever mid-engined road-going sports car. Brainchild of Frenchman René Bonnet, who had previously made sports and racing cars with Charles Duetz under the banner of CD, the Djet relied heavily on the Renault parts bin.

The impressive package used Renault running gear, with a backbone chassis, independent suspension front and rear, and disc brakes all-round. Matra, a giant in the aerospace industry, made its glassfibre body – indeed, it would

To prove that René Bonnet's masterpiece was sensational, the Renault powered Djet beat the Lamborghini Miura to become the world's first mid-engined sports car.

move further into the car industry in later years.

With their Gordini-tuned 1108cc (68cu in) Renault engines, even the earliest Djets were fast. The later Djet Series II, 5 and 5S versions were even quicker.

By 1964, the company was in financial trouble, and owed Matra a significant sum of money. Matra took over Bonnet and kept the Djet alive. Soon Matra revamped the car with a larger 1255cc (77cu in) engine and named it the Jet,

before replacing it with the even more bizarre-looking M530.

From small beginnings, Matra became one of the most innovative niche car producers before being taken over by Pininfarina in 2003.

ENGINE: 1108cc (68cu in), four-cylinder
POWER: 65bhp (48kW)
0–60MPH (96KM/H): n/a
TOP SPEED: 165km/h (102mph)
PRODUCTION TOTAL: n/a

CISITALIA 750/850

Following the failure of the glorious Cisitalia 202, which saw its creator, Pero Dusio, relocate to Argentina, the Cisitalia story would revisit tragedy. Dusio then attempted to form a Grand Prix team, using the Porsche 360 to mount a campaign. The venture failed after a single race, however, and Dusio returned to Italy to start again. Dusio's ex-racing manager, Carlo Abarth, profited from the

situation by taking Cisitalia's advanced Porsche-designed Grand Prix car, as well as the team, and making it successful. That money was then used to launch the Abarth tuning company.

Meanwhile, Cisitalia took the sensible step of devising a special road car, which was based around the engine and running gear of the Fiat 1100. Dusio's son Carlo then built an unsuccessful version of

the Fiat 1900 before undertaking further experiments with the 1100. A break in production from 1958 to 1961 followed, before Cisitalia returned for one last try with the 750/850 Tourism Special.

Essentially, this was a rebodied Fiat 600 with the choice of 735cc (45cu in) or 847cc (52cu in) engines. It was undeniably pretty, reminiscent of Pininfarina's best. Production was erratic, however,

and too many models were offered. The cars were not tuned either, and that meant rival sports cars were much quicker.

ENGINE: 735cc (45cu in), four-cylinder
POWER: 29bhp (22kW)
0–60MPH (96KM/H): 18 seconds
TOP SPEED: 140km/h (87mph)
PRODUCTION TOTAL: n/a

FACEL VEGA FACEL II

ENGINE: 6286cc (384cu in), eight-cylinder
POWER: 390bhp (291kW) (manual)
350bhp (261kW) (automatic)
0–60MPH (96KM/H): 8.3 seconds
TOP SPEED: 240km/h (149mph)
PRODUCTION TOTAL: 184

A straight restyling exercise on the HK500 it might have been, but the Facel II was marketed as a completely new car. Visually, the

Facel II was similar to the old car, and the same two-door four-seat coupé-only layout was continued, with sharper, more contemporary styling. Really, the Facel II retained the original bodywork, but had a restyled cabin and doors, and the original swept-back 'dog-leg' front windscreen pillars were replaced. There was more glass area than before, with more angular pillars, a flatter roof and a considerably larger rear window. There was also

a smaller front end, with a narrower, squarer grille. Quad Marchal headlights were stacked vertically in oval housings, with amber lights between each pair.

Using the same 264cm (104in) wheelbase, power output from the Chrysler V8 rose to an almighty 390bhp (291kW), which put the Facel II in among the cream of the supercar opposition. Dunlop disc brakes, essential on such a powerful car, were standard.

Optional items included very attractive Borrani wire wheels. Most customers chose the automatic TorqueFlite gearbox, which no longer had distinctive push-button operation, and a reduced-power engine rated at 350bhp (261kW).

There's nothing like going out in style and Facel Vega's last car, the Facel II, had the strength as well to become an all-time great.

FORD UK CONSUL CLASSIC/CAPRI

Despite following on from the super-successful Anglia, the Ford Consul Classic/Capri didn't sell in the numbers Ford envisaged it would. Quad headlamps and bold styling meant it deserved a better fate – although the Capri name would live on in later years.

Following on from the attractive Anglia, the two- and four-door saloon Consul Classic and fastback Capri were designed and built in Dagenham, England, but had a strong American flavour. The Classic range had been created to plug the gap in the Ford range between the Anglia 105E and higher specification Consuls – and it was only partially successful.

It used the same gearbox and a reworked 1340cc (82cu in) engine version of the Kent engine used in the Anglia. The Classic was a good effort, especially when a 1500cc (91cu in) engine was fitted in 1962 to give better performance. Its production life was cut short by the all-conquering Cortina's arrival. For many, the biggest thing about the Classic was its boot (trunk),

with a massive 0.6 cubic metres (21cu ft) of space.

The pretty Capri was essentially a Classic with a sloping roof. Again, it had a large boot and subtle fins, and was suitably boosted by the arrival of the GT variant in 1963. Fitting twin-choke carburettors, four-branch exhaust, bigger exhaust valves and performance camshaft transformed the 1500cc (91cu in)

engine. Despite this, the Capri never took off, and production figures were poor by Ford standards.

ENGINE: 1340cc (82cu in),
four-cylinder
POWER: 57bhp (43kW)
0–60MPH (96KM/H): 13.7 seconds
TOP SPEED: 153km/h (95mph)
PRODUCTION TOTAL: 24,531/6868

LAGONDA RAPIDE

One of the prettiest saloons of its era, and redolent of the Facel Vega Excellence without the styling excesses, the Lagonda Rapide was like nothing that had gone before. But buyers baulked at the front end styling as penned by Touring, and sales were a fraction of what they could have been. The tiny cabin might have meant an impressive long bonnet (hood) and

boot (trunk), but the pay-off was a severe lack of room on what was actually a rather large car.

The Rapide's platform chassis was based on that of the Aston Martin DB4, but lengthened and featuring de Dion and torsion bar rear suspension instead of the donor car's coil-sprung set-up. The Rapide also had the new Tadek Marek 4.0-litre (244cu in) six-

cylinder engine, inherited by the DB5 three years later. Borg Warner's automatic transmission was fitted as standard, with a manual all-synchromesh gearbox offered as an option.

What promised to be a beautiful car, with its handcrafted aluminium body, wonderfully responsive engine and dual circuit servo-assisted all-round disc brakes,

proved a disappointment, but it did set a precedent for future amazingly styled Lagonda saloons.

ENGINE: 3995cc (244cu in),
six-cylinder
POWER: 236bhp (176kW)
0–60MPH (96KM/H): n/a
TOP SPEED: 224km/h (140mph)
PRODUCTION TOTAL: 54

VAUXHALL VICTOR FB

By the time the Victor FB was launched in 1961, the Vauxhall's F-series cars had become very successful indeed in the United Kingdom. The original 1957 car had dated very quickly, though, thanks to faddish US-inspired styling. When its replacement was being drawn up (with the help of Gerald Palmer), a much more timeless style was introduced to the range.

Vauxhall offered the FB in a variety of guises – a four-door saloon or five-door estate (station wagon), with a choice of either 55bhp (41kW) 1.5-litre (92cu in) or 59bhp (44kW) 1.6-litre (97cu in) engine. The new Victor was a notable success, and further established Vauxhall as a market leader. Comfort levels were also improved, with an increase in

interior space and large bench seats (which could be swapped for bucket seats instead).

The more generous exterior proportions helped greatly, and overall the car was much more refined. The standard three-speed gearbox was poor, so most customers specified the optional all-synchromesh four-speed unit. Again, the car lasted only a few

years in production, as Vauxhall persisted with its policy of continuous styling evolution.

ENGINE: 1508cc (92cu in),
four-cylinder
POWER: 55bhp (41kW)
0–60MPH (96KM/H): 22.6 seconds
TOP SPEED: 122km/h (76mph)
PRODUCTION TOTAL: 328,640

The Victor FB was a 100,000-cars per year hit for Vauxhall. A wide range of engines and trim options meant there was something for everyone. Sadly few survive today thanks to Vauxhall's inability to protect its cars from corrosion, which proved catastrophic for the company's image.

MERCEDES-BENZ 300 FINTAIL

GERMANY 1961–65

Designed by Karl Wilfert, the angular 'fintail' range produced by Mercedes-Benz came very close to defining the company's output for the next couple of decades or so. The first fintail, launched in 1959 as the 220, featured wraparound front and rear windscreens, along with the famous shark-fin pointed rear wing (fender) tips.

The 300SE, introduced in 1961, was the finest of the breed, and distinguished from the 220 by its extra chrome. Under the long bonnet (hood) a powerful 3-litre (464cu in) fuel-injected six-cylinder engine had been installed. The brakes were also uprated to discs all-round, and assisted. Following Borgward's lead, the car also featured air suspension, which was self-levelling at the rear.

The four-speed automatic gearbox was new to the car and featured pioneering technology that would be used later on various other models for years to come.

This was one of the most luxurious Mercedes-Benzes yet and also one of the most expensive, being almost double the price of the lesser 220. It was a more than suitable flagship, however, for the range, and won the company many admirers.

In 1963, the SEL version was introduced with a slightly longer wheelbase, providing its owners with an even more impressive 'magic carpet' ride.

ENGINE: 2996cc (464cu in), six-cylinder
POWER: 160bhp (119kW)
0–60MPH (96KM/H): 10.9 seconds
TOP SPEED: 171km/h (107mph)
PRODUCTION TOTAL: 6750

The Fintail Mercedes-Benz saloons showed that the German company was not averse to building stylish, dignified cars.

BMW 1500

GERMANY 1962–72

Following on from the successful and crisply styled 700 series, BMW launched a mid-sized range of cars that transformed its image and cemented its place in the upper echelons of the motor industry. The 1500, Neue Klasse (New Class), model proved quite a money spinner for BMW, and defined the role of the company's products for years to come: quality saloons with sporting appeal.

First shown in 1961, the 1500 immediately received a warm response from the motoring press. It looked right, with hints of the previous 700 in its styling, as well as an arrow-shaped nose that Albrecht von Goertz had added to the fantastic 507 sports car. Somehow the new car conveyed quality and prestige, without resorting to distasteful excesses of chrome or self-conscious design features. In fact, the 1500 had been designed mostly in-house at BMW, with some help from the Italian design house Michelotti.

The four-cylinder overhead-camshaft engine was all new, but also trouble-free, although the car's gearbox and axle were to prove not quite so successful initially. They suffered from failures, which almost destroyed BMW's reputation for quality.

Luckily, the 1500 survived these early problems and went on to flourish – with 1600, 1800 and 2000 versions later introduced.

ENGINE: 1499cc (91cu in),
four-cylinder
POWER: 80bhp (60kW)
0–60MPH (96KM/H): 14 seconds
TOP SPEED: 148km/h (92mph)
PRODUCTION TOTAL: 350,729

If the 700-Series was responsible for saving BMW in 1960s, the neu-klasse 1500 defined the breed for the next couple of decades.

JAGUAR MK X

At 193cm (6.3ft) wide, the Jaguar Mk X held the dubious distinction of being the widest British car ever made until the Jaguar XJ220's arrival in 1992. Despite being 5.2m (17ft long), the car had a low roofline and high sills, which meant that it was actually quite awkward to get into.

The Mk X was a successful styling effort, but there was little that could be done to disguise its sheer bulk. Its cigar-like shape helped to disguise this.

Typically for a Jaguar, the car's road manners were exemplary, although it rolled a fair bit in corners. Sharing the same all-round independent suspension as other cars in the Jaguar range did it no harm at all. Effectively, it used the Mk II front and the E-type rear.

Refinements included Kelsey Hayes power-assisted all-round disc brakes and power steering as standard. Originally fitted with the 3.8-litre (232cu in) engine from the XK150, the Mk X gained the company's new 4.2-litre (258cu in) unit with its superb mid-range torque from 1964. At the same time, an all-synchromesh gearbox was fitted. The car was renamed the 420G from 1966, and it evolved into the Daimler DS420 Limousine in 1968.

ENGINE: 3781cc (231cu in),
six-cylinder
POWER: 265bhp (197kW)
0–60MPH (96KM/H): 12.1 seconds
TOP SPEED: 192km/h (120mph)
PRODUCTION TOTAL: 25,212

RELIANT SABRE

The Reliant company's evolution into a producer of full-sized cars was sporadic, to say the least. Alongside the quirky three-wheeled microcars (including the iconic Regal) and delivery vans (from

which the microcars originally evolved), the company decided what it needed was a two-seater sports car. The Sabre, however, had come about because of an interesting Anglo-Israeli deal,

which meant that development of the Sabre had already been paid for.

Reliant had originally built a similar car, known as the Sabra, for limited sales in the Israeli market, and, in order to maximize

the venture, Reliant changed this car in detail only, and put it into production at its factory in Tamworth, England.

The car's complex construction included a strange leading-arm front suspension (which was never very effective), as well expensive glassfibre bodywork supplied by Ashley Engineering (which meant that the car was never particularly profitable). The Sabre's distinctive styling was also compromised, and did little in the way of attracting prospective buyers.

The standard Sabre used a 1703cc (104cu in) Ford Consul engine and was not very fast; however, the more expensive Sabre Six had the Ford Zephyr Six's 2.6-litre (159cu in) engine and more conventional Triumph TR4 suspension, and was something of a minor sensation.

Neither Sabre was a great success for the company, but they did pave the way for the Scimitar.

ENGINE: 1703cc (104cu in), four-cylinder
POWER: 73bhp (54kW)
0–60MPH (96KM/H): 14.1 seconds
TOP SPEED: 145km/h (90mph)
PRODUCTION TOTAL: 285

HILLMAN SUPER MINX

UNITED KINGDOM 1961–67

ENGINE: 1592cc (97cu in), four-cylinder
POWER: 58bhp (78kW)
0–60MPH (96KM/H): 22.5 seconds
TOP SPEED: 128km/h (80mph)
PRODUCTION TOTAL: 135,000

The Rootes Group had enjoyed good years leading into the 1960s. Reflecting that confidence, Hillman's Super Minx burst onto the scene sporting exciting new styling. Hooded headlights, chiselled tail fins and American-influenced wraparound front and rear screens meant that the good-looking car stood out from the crowd. Underneath, existing Minx running gear was used, with the addition of a central gear lever.

It was called the Super Minx because its wheelbase was 5in (10cm) longer than the existing car, and the two ranges were sold alongside each other. Bodystyles offered were the two- and four-door saloon, an estate (station wagon) version and a very attractive drop-top, although this ran only from 1962 to 1964.

The 1962 Series II had front discs, the option of a Borg Warner automatic gearbox and individual front seats. The Series III from 1964 had larger front and rear windscreens, sharper roofline and veneer-effect fascia. The Series IV from 1965 had the new 1725cc (105cu in) powerplant and optional overdrive. The Series IIIA proved the most popular, with its classic looks and performance. The range was replaced in 1967 by the Arrow.

Larger than the car it was intended to replace, hence the SuperMinx tag, the new Hillman was a typically well-engineered, likeable Rootes Group product.

SINGER VOGUE

UNITED KINGDOM 1961–66

The Rootes Group was not averse to badge engineering its cars, so, when it came to launching the Hillman Super Minx, it ensured that there would be a slightly more expensive Singer version offered, too. The Vogue was bigger and more expensive than the Gazelle. Initially it was intended to be a replacement for it, but the Gazelle and the Vogue ended up being sold alongside each other as bedfellows in the Singer range.

Sharing much with the Hillman Super Minx, the Vogue had four headlights and a more luxurious interior than the Gazelle. There was a choice of automatic or manual/overdrive transmissions, and the front drum brakes were uprated to disc brakes when the Mk II arrived in 1962.

The Mk III of 1964 featured styling changes, larger rear doors, an alloy cylinder head and an all-synchromesh gearbox, along with better interior trim. The final version, the Mk IV, came in 1965. Apart from the adoption of the 1725cc (105cu in) engine seen elsewhere in the Rootes Group's cars, there were no other changes.

ENGINE: 1592cc (97cu in), four-cylinder
POWER: 62bhp (kW)
0–60MPH (96KM/H): 20.9 seconds
TOP SPEED: 133km/h (83mph)
PRODUCTION TOTAL: 47,769

TRIUMPH TR4

UNITED KINGDOM 1961–67

Triumph agonized over how to replace the TR3 – and, together with Michelotti, it worked on a new, more suitable style for its 1960s incarnation of the classic roadster. The Triumph Italia had been such a proposal. As attractive as the car looked, management at Standard-Triumph felt that it was not quite right for what it wanted to achieve with the new TR.

Italian stylist Giovanni Michelotti was asked to keep working on ideas for the new TR, and he produced a number of exciting designs, including two that would eventually become the TR4. In 1958, the Zest prototype was completed on a TR3A chassis, and it showcased many of the design cues that would later characterize the TR4, especially around the front, with its hooded headlights and long grille.

The alternative Zoom project that followed it had a longer wheelbase, and frontal styling that would later go on to evolve into Triumph Spitfire. The Zoom did

A programme of continued improvement refined the TR line of sportscars, so by the time the TR4 appeared in 1961, it was a very well sorted car. Michelotti once again was responsible for the excellent styling.

The TR4 looked very modern compared with its predecessors, and, although based on the chassis of the old car, the styling was a step forwards. Much of the original TR3 remained underneath, but it was updated with accurate rack-and-pinion steering and servo brakes, as well as an all-synchromesh manual transmission.

The enlarged 2138cc (130cu in) 100bhp (75kW) engine featured, although the old 1991cc (120cu in) engine could be specified. Sales of the car were strong enough to put MG and Austin-Healey under pressure and make them up their game as a consequence.

Following the launch of the MGB in 1962, Triumph revised the TR4 with updated underpinnings. Sportscar standards had moved on since the chassis was first designed, and the TR4 gained a new frame onto which all-independent suspension based on the new Triumph 2000 saloon's was fitted.

US dealers, however, demanded that a version with the old live beam rear axle be made available, too, so that they could sell a cheaper TR variant in this price-sensitive market. Triumph complied, and modified the new frame to take the old TR4 axle.

Now called the TR4A, the new car was actually difficult to differentiate from its predecessor. Apart from altered badging, a subtly modified grille and sidelights moved to the wing (fenders) tops, there were few clues to the improvements made in the new car. The TR4A was a little heavier than its immediate predecessor, but the engine manifold was slightly revised to add more power as compensation, the four-cylinder unit now capable of producing 104bhp (77kW). Performance remained similar.

The TR4A stayed in production until 1967, by which time Triumph had something very special planned for the next TR model.

ENGINE: 2138cc (130cu in),
four-cylinder
POWER: 100bhp (75kW) at 4600rpm
0–60MPH (96KM/H): 10.9 seconds
TOP SPEED: 167km/h (104mph)
PRODUCTION TOTAL: 68,718

include an innovative two-piece hardtop, and that particular feature would later make the transition to appear on the TR4.

In 1960, Triumph asked Michelotti to combine the shape of the Zoom with the shorter

wheelbase, nose, bonnet (hood) and hardtop of the Zest, to create the definitive TR4 shape. Once the car's style was decided on, the production version appeared very quickly, and the TR4 was on the scene in September 1961.

AMPHICAR

It might have seemed like the answer to a question no one was asking, but the Amphicar (a car that was also a boat) was developed for a very real purpose. It was the

brainchild of Hans Trippel, who had developed amphibious vehicles for the German army during World War II, and he had hoped that a new version of the

car-boat would become an important recreational vehicle in an increasingly affluent society.

Powered by a Triumph Herald engine, mounted in the back, and

a VW Beetle-type four-speed transmission, the Amphicar could reach 113km/h (70mph) on the road. In the water, a special unit made by Hermes (the makers of Porsche transmissions) could be used to switch to the two-speed water transmission, powering twin propellers. These allowed the Amphicar to reach a giddy 11km/h (7mph) in the water.

The Hermes transmission could even allow both driving wheels and propellers to drive at the same time, to help entry and exit to and from the water. Once floating, the front wheels acted as ineffective rudders. Predictably, the Amphicar was not particularly good either on road or in water, but it still remains the only civilian amphibious vehicle to ever be mass-produced.

ENGINE: 1147cc (70cu in),
four-cylinder
POWER: 38bhp (28kW)
0–60MPH (96KM/H): 42.9 seconds
TOP SPEED: 113km/h (70mph)
PRODUCTION TOTAL: 3878

The Amphicar was a brave idea that didn't look too bad at all, but didn't succeed commercially because few people needed a car that was a boat.

GINETTA G4

Ginetta was created by brothers Bob, Trevor, Ivor and Douglas Walklett, and began building specialist sports cars from a small factory in Woodbridge, England. In 1958, the company moved to Witham in Essex, and from there it launched the exciting new G2 – its first production vehicle.

Success followed later with the launch of the G4 in 1961; like most Ginettas, it was also sold in kit form to allow prospective owners to build the car while avoiding paying purchase tax. Underneath a sporty-looking glassfibre body was a tubular space frame chassis, initially with coil springs at the front, a live rear axle and optional front disc brakes. Powered first by the effective Ford Anglia 105E 997cc (61cu in) engine, then by

the 1498cc (91cu in) Ford Cortina unit, the G4 had a reasonable power-to-weight ratio that allowed it to be highly competitive.

In 1963, a short-tail Series II appeared, and a BMC rear axle replaced the Ford item. The Series III was radically updated with an improved chassis, Triumph Herald front wishbones and pop-up headlights – quite a novelty at the time. After a break in production of over a decade, the G4 was relaunched in 1981, albeit in updated S4 form.

ENGINE: 997cc (61cu in), four-cylinder
POWER: 39bhp (29kW)
0–60MPH (96KM/H): n/a
TOP SPEED: 144km/h (90mph)
PRODUCTION TOTAL: 500

The G4 was Ginetta's first attempt at a 'volume' selling car and it did fairly well, earning its maker plenty of kudos on account of its club events success. It was relaunched in 1981 after a 12-year hiatus.

RILEY ELF

Nicknamed the 'shelf', the Riley Elf was essentially a Mini with luxury equipment, treated to a Dick Burzi-penned facelift, and the addition of a boot at the back. The full-depth grille made it easier to work on.

When creating a posh Mini to wear the Riley (and Wolseley) badge, BMC's director of design Dick Burzi was tasked with grafting a boot (trunk) onto the rear end of the car. The Mini's creator, Alec Issigonis, had been so

appalled by the idea that he refused to have anything to do with it.

In Riley form, the notchback Mini ended up sharing all the original car's prize assets, such as lively performance and clever packaging, but combined them

with a more mature feel and more luggage capacity. Developed alongside the Wolseley Hornet, the Riley Elf ended up being surprisingly attractive, sharing the Mini's wings (fenders), doors and windows, but with an entirely new

shell and a choice of traditional-looking Riley grille (which also aided engine accessibility).

The interior was befitting of the marque and featured a wood-veneer dashboard and deep-pile carpets, and the 1963 face-lifted models also benefited from an increase in engine capacity to 998cc (61cu in). In Mk III form, from 1966, it also received winding windows and hidden door hinges.

Despite protestations from Riley traditionalists, the Elf (or 'Shelf', as it was nicknamed) proved to be something of a sales success.

ENGINE: 998cc (61cu in), four-cylinder
POWER: 38bhp (28kW)
0–60MPH (96KM/H): 24.1 seconds
TOP SPEED: 124km/h (77mph)
PRODUCTION TOTAL: 30,912

VOLKSWAGEN KARMANN-GHIA TYPE 34

As its name suggests, Type 34 was designed by Ghia but built by Karmann, and sold by VW alongside its other cars, including the now-coveted razor-styled Karmann-Ghia 1200. The Karmann-Ghia 1500 and 1600 were an integral part of the Type 34 family, and were added to the expanding range of Volkswagen saloons, convertibles and estates (station

wagons) that had been introduced in an attempt to expand the range for the 1960s. Wider, longer and higher than the older Karmann-Ghia 1200, the stylish 1500 and 1600 were based on a wider floorpan, to accommodate luggage and passengers more convincingly.

The Type 34 was certainly an appealing car – it had comfort, reliability, chic styling and good

performance – but its high purchase price and poor fuel consumption meant that fewer buyers were attracted to it than anticipated.

The car made its debut in 1961, but did not arrive in the United Kingdom until 1963 and was not exported to the United States at all. By 1967, automatic transmission and fuel injection were available; by 1969, the car was obsolete and

dropped out of production. Today, it is one of the most desirable air-cooled Volkswagens available.

ENGINE: 1493cc (91cu in), four-cylinder
POWER: 45bhp (34kW)
0–60MPH (96KM/H): n/a
TOP SPEED: 144km/h (90mph)
PRODUCTION TOTAL: 42,563

WOLSELEY HORNET

UNITED KINGDOM 1961–69

The Wolseley Hornet name featured prominently in the history of the marque – although those cars of the 1930s were a long way removed from their similarly named descendants that appeared in 1961. The new car was little more than a badge-engineered Riley Elf, itself closely based on the 1959 Mini. The Wolseley Hornet and Riley Elf were considered different enough to satisfy their owners, but they were difficult to tell apart, and continued the process that was bringing the two marques closer to each other.

Sharing the Mini's rubber cone suspension, the Mk I Hornet remained a very responsive car to drive, with a pleasing level of luxury inside. It was powered by the same 848cc (52cu in) A-Series engine seen in the Mini.

In March 1963, the Mk II Hornet appeared, with a more powerful 998cc (61cu in) engine and the inventive Hydrolastic suspension system. The Mk III version arrived in 1966, and that saw the addition of winding windows (instead of sliding ones), better ventilation, concealed hinges and the option of automatic transmission from 1967. The car was dropped in 1969 and was not replaced.

ENGINE: 848cc (52cu in), four-cylinder
POWER: 34bhp (25kW)
0–60MPH (96KM/H): 32.3 seconds
TOP SPEED: 114km/h (71mph)
PRODUCTION TOTAL: 28,455

Like its twin, the Riley Elf, the Wolseley Hornet topped the Mini range and stood apart from humbler versions because of its larger boot.

HINO CONTESSA

JAPAN 1961–71

Having initially been set up to assemble Japanese market Renault 4CVs, Hino began making its own car in 1961. The Contessa was actually closely based on the mechanicals of the small French car with which the Japanese engineers had become so familiar.

The styling of the four-door saloon, with its boxy looks and small glass area, was what would later become known as the Oriental style of design. In fact, it was actually a nice design – and impressive for a first effort. The Michelotti-styled two-door coupé version, which was introduced in 1962, was even better, but was unfortunately shelved soon after production started. When the entire range was restyled in 1964, Michelotti was given the job. As well as looking better, the car went better, too, thanks to a newly expanded 1251cc (76cu in) engine.

Hino could have been a household name like Nissan, Honda and Toyota, but its car-making operation was bought by rival Toyota in 1966 and killed off completely four years later. Very few cars were ever made; even fewer exist today outside of Japan.

ENGINE: 893cc (54cu in), four-cylinder
POWER: 35bhp (26kW)
0–60MPH (96KM/H): n/a
TOP SPEED: 115km/h (72mph)
PRODUCTION TOTAL: n/a

MINI COOPER

UNITED KINGDOM 1961–71

It was obvious to anyone who drove the Mini at its 1959 launch that its fantastic roadholding was like nothing anyone had seen before at this price level. If anything, it was begging for more power – and, thanks to the efforts of racing driver and engineer, John Cooper, the Mini would get it.

When Cooper approached BMC in 1960 with the idea of creating a performance Mini, BMC was quick to agree – although the car's creator Alec Issigonis could not see what all the fuss was about. The first Mini Cooper to appear on the market in 1961 used a 997cc (61cu in) A-Series engine, and Cooper was able to obtain the extra power by increasing its bore and stroke. As a result, top speed was improved to almost 145km/h (90mph), with acceleration and handling to match.

The next development on the theme was the Cooper S, which appeared in 1963. Initially built with a choice of 970cc (59cu in)

There were quicker competition cars, but thanks to unmatched roadholding, the Mini-Cooper was a mighty weapon in rallying.

and 1071cc (65cu in) engines, the car had the now-familiar 1275cc (78cu in) unit added to the range available from 1964. With twin SU carburettors fitted, 76bhp (57kW) was extracted, and the Cooper's top speed increased to an impressive 154km/h (96mph).

By this time, BMC had already achieved some rally success with the Cooper, and the car was also a regular performer on club circuits across the country. It was still putting in strong appearances in the British Saloon Car Racing Championship in the hands of famous drivers such as Sir John Whitmore, John Rhodes and Barrie

Williams. But the British company's works motorsport division pulled off the ultimate coup in 1964, when the Cooper S stormed to a shock victory in the prestigious Monte Carlo Rally. Despite being underpowered compared to some more exotic competitors, the Cooper proved ideal for the rally, while the icy conditions suited the car's front-wheel traction. BMC went back the following year and did it again, and, in 1966, should have had an impressive first, second and fourth, but officials disqualified them over a lighting infringement. Instead, the French organizers awarded Monte Carlo

victory to Citroën ... Angered by the decision, BMC competed in the rally again in 1967 (this time with headlights inspected before the start) and won – again.

The Cooper S was also a fine road car, with the same famed racing handling and lively performance passed on to enthusiastic road users. By 1971, however, BMC had become British Leyland, and the new company had its own ideas about what a performance Mini should be. It severed its links with Cooper Garages to cut costs, and replaced the car with the (admittedly cheaper) 1275GT, with a less

powerful version of the 1275cc (78cu in) engine.

The Cooper name reappeared on a Mini in 1990, and, complete with 30.5cm (12in) Minilite alloys and bonnet (hood) stripes, made a dashing comeback. It enjoyed further success lasting until 2000, when the last Mini Cooper came off the Longbridge factory's line.

ENGINE: 1275cc (78cu in), four-cylinder
POWER: 76bhp (57kW)
0–60MPH (96KM/H): 10.1 seconds
TOP SPEED: 156km/h (96mph)
PRODUCTION TOTAL: 144,910

BUICK SKYLARK

The Skylark name had been dormant since the first Buick bearing that name in 1954 went out of production the following year. For 1961, the name was revived – this time attached to an all-new car. Originally launched as a coupé and fitted with a standard 3528cc (215 cu in) V8 with a four-barrel carburettor, which was rated at 185bhp (138kW), the cleanly

styled Coupé soon won plenty of new friends. The performance was impressive for the size, and the model's appeal was boosted when the convertible version joined the range in the year after.

As the years passed, the Skylark became bigger and more imposing. For 1964, it received a new body and a performance boost with the addition of a new 4916cc (300cu in)

V8 with a four barrel carburettor. A top-of-the-line 'High Performance' V8 engine rated at 210bhp (156kW) was also added to the range.

In 1965, the Gran Sport option was introduced, and eventually became a model in its own right. A four-door Sport Wagon was an interesting new estate (station wagon) model with a distinctive raised rear roof panel. At its peak,

the Skylark produced 285bhp (212kW), but the 1970s saw the model go into decline.

ENGINE: 6571cc (401cu in), eight-cylinder
POWER: 325bhp (242kW)
0–60MPH (96KM/H): 7.4 seconds
TOP SPEED: 194km/h (121mph)
PRODUCTION TOTAL: 1,462,316

The Skylark was one of the first American sports compacts, and thanks to the aluminium V8 engine which endowed the car with a fair turn of speed, it soon became a big success. The earliest models are now rare and collectable, especially the convertible version.

NSU PRINZ 4

Often referred to as the German Hillman Imp because of its similar styling and mechanical layout, the NSU Prinz was a popular car. Basic three-box styling, a rear-mounted engine and entertaining handling were hallmarks of both. The NSU actually beat the Hillman onto the market by a year, and its popularity was quick to come – especially in Germany.

The air-cooled twin-cylinder engine was not very advanced or powerful, but it was strong and reliable. Thanks to the car's low weight, performance never seemed lacking. The Prinz was actually a very pleasant car to drive, feeling light on its feet, and boasted a slick synchromesh gearbox and effective disc brakes on all but the earliest versions. It was surprisingly

well planned, too, and despite its minuscule external dimensions, had a spacious cabin and a useful boot (trunk) space at the front.

The car would not have a future, and neither did the company that produced it. NSU was absorbed into the VW-Audi group in 1969, and the Prinz range was left to decline. Sales continued until 1973, but the car was not actively marketed by

VW-Audi, which threw too much of its resources into the ill-fated rotary engine development programme.

ENGINE: 598cc (36cu in), two-cylinder
POWER: 30bhp (22kW)
0–60MPH (96KM/H): 32.2 seconds
TOP SPEED: 121km/h (75mph)
PRODUCTION TOTAL: 576,023

VOLKSWAGEN TYPE 3

ENGINE: 1493cc (91cu in),
four-cylinder
POWER: 45bhp (34kW)
0–60MPH (96KM/H): n/a
TOP SPEED: 130km/h (81mph)
NUMBER PRODUCED: 1,542,342

Despite the Beetle having been around a very long time, by the time the Volkswagen Type 3 appeared, it was only the second car to be launched by the company. When it appeared at the 1961 Frankfurt Motor Show, the 1500, as it was called, closely followed the basic principles defined by the Beetle. A rear-mounted air-cooled engine powered it – yet, despite the position of the flat-four, there was still a luggage compartment at the car's rear and another at the front.

Initially, a Karmann-built cabriolet was shown alongside the two-door saloon, but it never went into production. In 1962, an estate (station wagon) did, though, and the following year the 1500S was launched with twin carburettors.

By 1965, a 1584cc (97cu in) engine complemented the 1493cc (91cu in) unit, and was used in a version called the 1600TL. This heralded the launch of the TL-badged fastback saloon, a car that looked like a modern hatchback, but had a conventional boot (trunk) and just two doors.

By 1966, the 1500cc (91cu in) engine was dropped; all Type 3s used 1584cc (97cu in) units instead.

Bolstered by the huge success of the Beetle, Volkswagen embarked on a programme to introduce bigger and more appealing models. The Type 3 was simply bigger and pricier.

JAGUAR E-TYPE

Considered by many to be the most beautiful sports car of all time, the Jaguar was certainly groundbreaking when it burst onto the scene at the 1961 Geneva Motor Show. Its beautifully sleek profile was no accident, but more a lesson in aerodynamics, having been crafted by aerodynamicist Malcolm Sayer, after learning so much from earlier racing D-types.

The origins of the car can be traced back to a lightweight prototype raced at Le Mans in 1960, but, when the E-type was first unveiled, both open roadster and fastback coupé versions hit the market only four months after it made a big splash in Geneva.

The E-type was not such a landmark car because of its looks alone – it was incredibly quick, achieving an impressive 240km/h (150mph) in contemporary road tests (although few owners could replicate that top speed with their own cars). The reason for the turn of speed was simple: the E-type was powered by the legendary 3.8-litre (232cu in) XK twin-camshaft engine that had proved its worth at Le Mans during the previous decade. Roadholding was good enough to match the car's

performance and was helped by the impressive grip from its new wishbone and coil-sprung independent suspension set-up, which at the same time provided occupants with a relaxed and reasonably comfortable ride.

The really clever thing about the E-type, however, was its price – at less than half the cost of the Aston Martin DB4 GT, you got more performance and better dynamics.

The original 3.8-litre (232cu in) version that was built between 1961 and 1964 had cleaner lines and ultimately better performance than the later 4.2-litre (258cu in)

version. It was available as an open-top roadster or slightly more practical fixed-head coupé with hatchback rear door.

The Series 1, introduced in 1964, had a new 4.2-litre (258cu in) XK engine with more torque, and came with much a better gearbox and brakes, along with improved electrics and more opulent trim. For many, this was the best version of the car – technically advanced, while retaining much of the original's purity.

In 1966, a third model, the 2+2, arrived, with an extra 23cm (9in) in the wheelbase, a reshaped,

The unmistakable profile of a Jaguar E-type Series I: the long bonnet, cigar like styling, feline curves and potential top speed of 150mph (240km/h) took it to the top of the supercar class.

The handling of the Jaguar E-type did not disappoint, and for less than half the price of most of the opposition it created a new set of standards. Later models became less 'pure', but remained popular.

slightly higher roofline and 110kg (243lb) more weight. Two years later, US safety legislation resulted in the Series 2, with its uncowled headlights, bigger raised bumpers and bigger front and rear light clusters mounted below bumper level. The bonnet (hood) also lost its characteristic streamlined shape. At the same time a number of technical changes were made, including twin electric fans for improved cooling, improved brakes, power-assisted steering, an automatic option on the 2+2, and even the option of air conditioning.

In the final transformation of Jaguar's supercar, the Series 3, introduced in 1971, the company brought in its new alloy 272bhp (203kW) V12 engine with its massive torque and incredible acceleration. For many E-type enthusiasts, the Series 3 was a revision too far, as it was far more soft and lazy to drive than previous versions. As a GT car, it predicted the introduction of the 1975 XJ-S perfectly.

ENGINE: 4235cc (258cu in), six-cylinder
POWER: 265bhp (197kW)
0–60MPH (96KM/H): 7.1 seconds
TOP SPEED: 218km/h (136mph)
PRODUCTION TOTAL: 72,507

SIMCA 1000

FRANCE 1961–78

Although it is hard to believe now, at the time the 1000 was introduced, Simca was France's largest privately owned car manufacturer. Having produced conventional front-engine/rear-drive saloons for years, and picked up a great deal of success in doing so, the company surprisingly chose to launch a rear-engined, rear-wheel competitor for the Renault 8 1961.

But the Simca 1000 was a hit in France – even though it was not without faults. The rearward weight bias meant that handling was strange. With just 40bhp (30kW) from the 944cc (58cu in) cast-iron powerplant, performance was also pretty leisurely. The car featured all-round drum brakes and worm-and-roller steering, so was lacking in engineering innovation. Still, it was cheap to buy and run, which was what most French car buyers were looking for at the time.

In 1962, Abarth launched the 1136cc (69cu in) Simca-Abarth 1150 version, sporting between 55bhp (41kW) and 85bhp (63kW) depending on tuning. By 1965, major changes had been made to the interior so the 1000 could compete with Renault's R8. In 1969, brakes, steering and suspension were uprated, and the exterior design tidied up. Now part of the Chrysler Group, the Simca 1000 remained largely ignored and stayed in production until 1978.

ENGINE: 944cc (58cu in), four-cylinder
POWER: 35bhp (26kW)
0–60MPH (96KM/H): 27 seconds
TOP SPEED: 118km/h (74mph)
PRODUCTION TOTAL: 1,642,091

CITROËN AMI

FRANCE 1961–79

Considering the now iconic status of the Citroën 2CV, it may seem strange that, during the 1950s and the 1960s, it was actually a slow seller everywhere except France. To try to make the most of the capable platform, Citroën introduced a number of different 2CV-based cars to boost sales, all of which met with varying degrees of success.

The Ami 6 was created with good intentions, but ended up being one of the more eccentric attempts to extend the 2CV theme. More powerful than the 2CV, thanks to its flat–twin 602cc (37cu in) engine, the Ami had styling which featured an awkward reverse-rake rear window, and DS-style rear end.

Sales in France were typically strong, but the unconventional looks failed to convince customers elsewhere, so Citroën redesigned it in 1969 with a more conventional rear window line, and added a new grille and front disc brakes. In this more export-friendly form, it was renamed the Ami 8.

The conventional Ami was quick enough, but, in 1972, Citroën put in a four-cylinder 1015cc (62cu in) engine from the GS. The 61bhp (45kW) Ami Super possessed performance that was not only impressive, but scary as well. Not for the faint-hearted.

ENGINE: 602cc (37cu in), two-cylinder
POWER: 22bhp (16kW) at 4500rpm
0–60MPH (96KM/H): 44 seconds
TOP SPEED: 112km/h (70mph)
PRODUCTION TOTAL: 1,840,159

As prosperity in France increased during the 1950s, the popularity of Citroën's ultra-basic 2CV began to wane. The Ami was an attempt to repackage the car with more civilized styling.

MG MIDGET

UNITED KINGDOM 1961–79

Launched in 1961, the smallest MG was based entirely on the underpinnings of the Austin-Healey Sprite – proving that badge engineering could indeed work.

The Midget was one of the first fruits of the merger between Austin and Nuffield Motors, which owned the Morris and MG brands – and, although Austin-Healey and MG had been deadly rivals in the past, their cars were now sharing components. Although the cute Austin-Healey 'Frogeye' (or 'Bugeye', if you are American) Sprite was first on the market, it was the MG that would go on to enjoy truly remarkable international sales success.

By late 1961, the Frogeye was dead, and, while badge-engineered Austin-Healeys continued, they were identical to the Midget in all but name. Only the earliest Midgets were identical underneath to the Frogeye Sprite, with their quarter-elliptic leaf springs and an eager but breathless 948cc (58cu in) A-Series engine.

By mid-1962, the Midget had been improved, and gained a more powerful 56bhp (42kW) 1098cc (67cu in) engine and those all-important front disc brakes, while further improvements in 1964 saw installation of larger semi-elliptic springs aimed at aiding ride comfort and making the back end less twitchy in the wet. Added to these were a more rounded windscreen, wind-up windows in place of sliding ones and, for the first time, lockable doors.

A Mk III model appeared in 1966, which this time possessed the performance the Midget had always craved, with a 65bhp (48kW) 1275cc (78cu in) A-Series engine under the bonnet (hood) and the ability to almost reach 160km/h (100mph). The car's practicality was improved, too, with a proper folding hood instead of a removable hardtop.

When British Leyland took control of MG in 1968, the plan was to not interfere too much with the Midget, and so it continued largely unchanged until 1974. A matt black grille and sills, and slimmer bumpers, appeared in 1969. By 1972, the squared-off rear arches were swapped for round ones to make wheel changes easier. But any car from the 1966–74 era is enjoyable to drive.

There were, however, troubled times ahead – and it was down to the impending environmental and safety legislation that was just about to hit the United States. The lively A-Series engine was dropped, as it would have been too difficult for British Leyland to develop a version that would pass US emissions regulations. Instead, it was replaced by the 1493cc (91cu in) overhead valve unit from the Triumph Spitfire (once a deadly rival; now an uneasy bedfellow). The 65bhp (48kW) unit offered good performance; as it has since been retrofitted to earlier Midgets, it may well have been a popular engine option. But new laws also meant visual changes, which ruined the looks. Regulations on headlight height meant the ride had to be jacked up by nearly 8cm (3in), while black polyurethane impact bumpers were attached front and rear.

Although the Midget remained a fun car to drive, its ungainly new appearance, coupled with the introduction of new, exciting and more practical sports cars from other manufacturers, meant that, by 1979, sales had almost completely dried up and the car ceased production.

ENGINE: 948cc (58cu in),
   four-cylinder
POWER: 46bhp (34kW)
0–60MPH (96KM/H): 20 seconds
TOP SPEED: 140km/h (87mph)
PRODUCTION TOTAL: 226,526

Based on the Austin Healey Sprite, the Midget was an opportune – and welcome – piece of BMC badge engineering. The back-to-basics sports car was fun and cheap to run, and enjoyed remarkable global success.

OLDSMOBILE CUTLASS

UNITED STATES 1961–74

ENGINE: 4184cc (255cu in),
   six-cylinder
POWER: 155bhp (115kW)
0–60MPH (96KM/H): 10.9 seconds
TOP SPEED: 177km/h (110mph)
PRODUCTION TOTAL: n/a

As a result of the increasing affluence of American car buyers during the 1960s, vehicles produced in Detroit were becoming increasingly large and expensive to buy. The fin and chrome excesses of the 1950s may have subsided in the new decade, but cars were still getting bigger. By the end of the decade, it was impossible to buy a compact vehicle.

General Motors realized this and introduced the F-85 Cutlass to appeal to buyers on a budget. The car shared its platform and many body panels with models from Pontiac and Buick, but the Cutlass Supreme notchback coupé and Cutlass S fastback were individual to Oldsmobile. There was also a bewildering range of engine options. The base model's 4.0-litre (244cu in) Chevrolet-sourced straight-six was at the bottom of the range, while the enormous 390bhp (291kW) 7.4-litre (452cu in) V8 topped it. A five-speed manual gearbox was also made available as an option in the 1972 Hurst Oldsmobile, named after the gearbox maker.

Despite being marketed as an entry-level compact car, the Cutlass predictably grew with the wealth of its customer base. By 1964, it was as large as anything offered by the 'Big Three' US manufacturers.

More compact cars like the Ford Falcon were taking off in the American market, and General Motors introduced the stylish Cutlass to capitalize on this.

RENAULT R4

FRANCE 1961–92

Rarely seen outside France these days, the Renault 4 became one of the world's biggest selling cars during its lifetime – and, out of the all-time classics, its figure of eight million sales in three decades of production remains an impressive achievement to this day.

The massive success of the R4 was unexpected for Renault. The car had been launched as a more practical hatchback rival to the Citroën 2CV, which had already established itself as France's bestselling car, and would prove to be a tough nut to crack. Like the Citroën, the R4 had a bouncy ride, super-soft suspension, tenacious roadholding and a strange push-pull gearchange.

The R4's rather basic-looking bodywork looked even more like corrugated iron than the Citroën 2CV's, and many assumed that it would struggle against such well-established opposition. However, its simple mechanical layout and very low running costs meant that the R4 was an inexpensive and popular choice, and exports were strong – which was not the case at Citroën.

Early cars came with a 603cc (37cu in) straight-four, but capacity grew on numerous occasions throughout its life, borrowing units from the 4CV, Dauphine and Caravelle, and, later, the 1.1-litre (67cu in) motor from the Renault 5.

ENGINE: 1108cc (68cu in), four-cylinder
POWER: 34bhp (25kW)
0–60MPH (96KM/H): 25.7 seconds
TOP SPEED: 116km/h (72mph)
PRODUCTION TOTAL: 8,135,424

The charming Renault 4 lacked some of the idiosyncrasy of its rival from Citroën, but that helped it sell in far more serious volumes. This late-model in GTL form boasted an 1108cc (68 cu in) engine.

FERRARI 250GTO

ITALY 1962–64

Ferrari's reason for developing the GTO was obvious. The name, Gran Turismo Omologato, was supposed to mean that this model was the homologated racing version of the 250 GT SWB. What is truly surprising is that Ferrari managed to convince the racing authorities that the GTO was simply an evolution of the existing SWB, when in fact it seemed to be an all-new design.

Another surprise is that the GTO must have been technically illegal, as Ferrari never made the required 100 models to qualify for racing. So, although Ferrari kept the 250 GT's short wheelbase, it set about changing much of the tubular steel frame's bracing and mounting joints for extra rigidity. A live axle

was retained, but it was well located with parallel trailing arms and the addition of a Watts linkage. As a result, this set-up provided exceptional poise and balance on the racetrack.

Providing the power was the Colombo-designed V12 used in 250 TR, with just a few modifications, such as bigger valves and dry sump lubrication, so that it would fit under the lower bonnet (hood). The aim was to exceed a target of 100bhp (75kW) per litre, and it is said that any engine that failed to develop between 296 and 302bhp (221 and 225kW) when bench-tested had to be rebuilt.

Ferrari had realized that, although the SWB had been a fast car, its aerodynamics had let it down. So,

using the same short chassis, the bodywork was designed from scratch by Giotto Bizzarrini with the extensive use of a wind tunnel. Thus a distinctive shape emerged, rather than being deliberately styled. Step by step, the GTO's bodywork gradually and scientifically evolved into a slippery shape that is now renowned as one of the most beautiful automotive designs ever.

With its low nose and high tail, it was certainly eye-catching, and featured a body-integrated rear spoiler, which was the first time this innovation had ever been seen on a road car. However, Ferrari never really intended the 250 GTO to stray too far from the track, even though the entire model needed to be legal on the road and

therefore there was the installation of a speedometer.

The great V12 engine and superb aerodynamic body comprised to give the GTO a phenomenal top speed in excess of 274km/h (170mph). Soon, the GTO was racking up impressive results and overall victories. There were class wins in the Sebring 12-hour, Targa Florio, Spa 1000km and Le Mans, where it also came second overall in 1962 and 1963. Ferrari also won the GT World Championship in 1962, 1963 and 1964.

Just three 4-litre GTOs were built with 3967cc (242cu in) engines producing 390bhp (291kW) at 7500rpm. They needed a large and rather ugly bulge on the bonnet to accommodate the units. Another development occurred in 1964, when three 'second series' GTO/64 cars were built. Bizzarrini and Piero Drogo also made some lightweight racers based on 250 SWB components with distinctly odd though very aerodynamic van-type styling. However, the GTO's competitive racing days were over. Nevertheless, the car had assured its place in history, explaining why collectors pay huge sums for them.

ENGINE: 2953cc (180cu in), 12-cylinder
POWER: 300bhp (224kW)
0–60MPH (96KM/H): 6 seconds
TOP SPEED: 274km/h (170mph)
PRODUCTION TOTAL: 39

With pumped up bodywork and air intakes galore, there's no mistaking the GTO's legendary sporting credentials.

STUDEBAKER AVANTI

The Avanti was a commercial flop and yet its refreshing minimalist look and technical specifications had a large influence on the industry.

When it was launched in 1962, the Studebaker Avanti was so far away from what was fashionable in the American car industry at the time that it remains a surprise that the company had the bravery to produce it. In an era of fins, chrome and excess, the svelte-looking car was completely out of place.

When unveiled in 1962, it was one of the best cars on the market, but Studebaker's South Bend factory was such a distance from its component suppliers that productivity could never match that of its competitors. Innovative features included disc brakes at the front, which had never been specified on a US mass-produced car before. Styling was distinctive, too, penned by Raymond Loewy, also responsible for the famous Coca-Cola bottle. Power was supplied by a 4.7-litre (291cu in) V8 engine and fed through a four-speed manual gearbox. If this standard power output was not enough, tuning options were available which saw outputs rise to more than 300bhp (224kW) through the use of a supercharger.

Perhaps the main failings of the Avanti were that it was built at the wrong place and in the wrong time. Either way, the car failed so dismally that it lasted only a single year in production.

ENGINE: 4763cc (291cu in), eight-cylinder
POWER: 210bhp (156kW)
0–60MPH (96KM/H): n/a
TOP SPEED: 200km/h (125mph)
PRODUCTION TOTAL: 4643

VAUXHALL CRESTA PB

When the Cresta PB was launched, anyone could have been forgiven for confusing it with the visually similar Victor FB. Not only did it look the same, but also the underpinnings were all but identical. The PB was essentially a six-cylinder version of the smaller car. It had the same basic structure, and the doors were carried over, giving it the same basic look.

It was launched as a four-door saloon in 1962, and a five-door estate (station wagon), built by coachbuilder Martin Walter, arrived a year later. Using a saloon as its basis, but with the roof chopped off and replaced by a bespoke glassfibre shell, the estate was a luxurious carryall built at a time when estates were not seen as anything other than workhorses – it even found favour with British royalty. The only engine initially on offer was a 2651cc (162cu in) straight-six, with three transmission options. The standard car came with a three-speed manual gearbox, with overdrive as an option; an alternative was a Hydramatic self-shifting automatic transmission.

From 1965, this became the two-speed Powerglide, and the engine was also upgunned to a 3294cc (201cu in) straight six, with a useful increase in performance.

ENGINE: 2651cc (162cu in), six-cylinder
POWER: 95bhp (71kW)
0–60MPH (96KM/H): 19.5 seconds
TOP SPEED: 149km/h (93mph)
PRODUCTION TOTAL: 87,047

JENSEN CV8

The Jensen CV8 was another one of those British specialist cars that evolved visually, rather than technically. It effectively replaced the 541S and utilized the same PW chassis and glassfibre body combination that had been put to such good use previously.

The controversial styling was all new and featured slanting quad headlights and redesigned front and rear end. The platform was familiar, but a huge Chrysler V8 installed under the bonnet (hood) meant that the driving experience was something else entirely.

Coupled up to a TorqueFlite automatic transmission, the new V8 option meant that the CV8 could top 208km/h (130mph) with ease, and that figure rose to nearer 224km/h (140mph) when the 6.3-litre (383 cuin) V8 was installed in 1964. The Mk II, which appeared in 1963, had adjustable Selectaride shock absorbers, while the Mk III of 1965 had equal-sized front headlights, better brakes, reclining front seats, and a number of other refinements to the interior.

It was expensive at launch, so very few cars were sold, but many have survived thanks to being made from corrosion-proof glass fibre and powered by bulletproof American engines.

ENGINE: 5916cc (361cu in), eight-cylinder
POWER: 305bhp (kW)
0–60MPH (96KM/H): 8.4 seconds
TOP SPEED: 206km/h (129mph)
PRODUCTION TOTAL: 499

MASERATI SEBRING

First shown in 1962, and based upon the Maserati 3500GT, the Sebring was a graceful addition to the supercar ranks. Styled by Vignale and mounted on the short wheelbase 3500GTI convertible chassis, the Sebring certainly seemed to have it all.

Originally, the car was called the 3500GTI, but almost instantly it became the Sebring instead, the name reviving Maserati's past glories on the racetrack. It was publicized as a 2+2, but rear-seat accommodation was really unsuitable for anything other than hand luggage. Although most of the body was made out of steel, an alloy boot (trunk) lid and bonnet (hood) were fitted. Also, as the US market was so important to the car, the options list was long. Buyers could add air conditioning, radio, a limited slip differential and a three-speed automatic transmission to their Sebrings. Standard equipment was important where it mattered – disc brakes on all four wheels, fuel injection and a five-speed manual gearbox.

The Series II was introduced in 1965, powered by a larger 3694cc

(225cu in) or 4014cc (245cu in) engine. Externally, changes were less noticeable. The quad headlights received hoods, the rear lights were redesigned and the bonnet air intake was remodelled.

ENGINE: 3485cc (213cu in), six-cylinder
POWER: 235bhp (175kW) at 5500rpm
0–60MPH (96KM/H): 8.4 seconds
TOP SPEED: 222km/h (138mph)
PRODUCTION TOTAL: 444

With a pretty body by Vignale underpinning shortened 3500GT running gear and a five speed gear box, there was little wrong with the Maserati Sebring.

GHIA 1500GT

ITALY 1962–67

Following the excesses of previous ventures, Ghia went back to basics, deciding it needed to get into series production. In 1962, the company began production of a specially bodied Fiat-based car, the fastback Coggiola-styled Ghia 1500GT.

Built at a peak rate of four units a day in Ghia's body shop in the Via Agostino di Montefeltro, the stylish Ghia 1500GT used the powertrain of the Fiat 1500, with a sheet steel box-section and tubular frame, setting the engine further back than in the standard car. And the wheelbase was shorter too.

Performance though didn't match the looks, and with a top speed of just over 100mph (161km/h) there were many faster cars available for the same money.

And unlike many other sporting specials at this level in the market, the 1500GT didn't make up for this performance shortfall in the handling department, which was underwhelming.

Despite these shortcomings, the 1500GT was a likeable, surprisingly practical car and because its list price wasn't in the stratosphere, buyers were prepared to make these sacrifices. Almost non-existent rust protection meant that the few that have survived are very expensive.

ENGINE: 1481cc (90 cu in), four-cylinder
POWER: 84bhp (63kW)
0-60MPH (96KM/H): 12 secs
TOP SPEED: 168km/h (105mph)
PRODUCTION TOTAL: 925

AC COBRA 289

UNITED KINGDOM 1962–68

The AC Cobra is one of the most famous cars ever built, and the story of how it came into existence is one of motoring's legends. Texan chicken farmer (and racing driver) Carroll Shelby spotted the quintessentially English AC Ace roadster and, in order to give it more potential as a racing car, shoehorned a Ford small-block V8 engine into the engine bay, and created one of the most fearsome cars of the 1960s.

The AC Ace had always sold well in the United Kingdom, but its two-litre (122cu in) engine hardly delivered exciting performance. When Shelby discovered that the then-new small-block Ford fit straight in, the rest came easily. The first V8 to be installed in the Cobra was the 4.2-litre (260cu in) version. As it weighed only a little more than the existing engines used by AC, balance was not adversely affected. AC was so impressed with the V8 and Carroll Shelby that its contract with Ked Rudd, the existing supplier of the Ace's six-cylinder, was terminated. After a year the 4.2-litre (260cu in) engine was upgraded to a 4.7-litre (289cu in) version.

The Cobra 289 was to become the second best known AC of all time. The wheelarches remained unflared, and that meant the 289 was a pretty effective Q-car.

ENGINE: 4727cc (289cu in), eight-cylinder
POWER: 300bhp (224kW)
0–60MPH (96KM/H): 5.5 seconds
TOP SPEED: 250km/h (155mph)
PRODUCTION TOTAL: 673

It looked like an AC Ace on steroids, and went like a bat out of hell – a Ford V8 engine stuffed into a lightweight roadster.

ASA 1000GT

Often referred to as a 'Ferrarina' because it started out as a pet project of Enzo Ferrari, the ASA 1000GT was a delightful little sports car set perfectly in the Italian mould. Enzo had always wanted to create a small sports car, and so his team, headed by chassis engineer Giotto Bizzarini, went away and designed one. A baby Ferrari, with

a body styled by Bertone – it should have been a roaring success.

Although the Italian design house Bertone produced the body, the actual styling was attributed to Giorgetto Giugiaro (who worked there at the time), and was one of the first in a long line of his influential designs. The prototype was displayed at the 1961 Turin

Motor show and attracted plenty of attention, but Enzo Ferrari made it clear that the company would not be building it. Instead, the design was sold to the affluent De Nora family, who formed ASA to build it.

The production version was called the 1000GT, and was later joined by a glassfibre-bodied convertible. The cars were a joy

to drive and surprisingly fast, but they were also very expensive.

ENGINE: 1032cc (63cu in), four-cylinder
POWER: 84bhp (63kW)
0–60MPH (96KM/H): n/a
TOP SPEED: 185km/h (115mph)
PRODUCTION TOTAL: 101

RENAULT CARAVELLE

The Renault Caravelle was an uprated and face-lifted rear-engined Floride. Renault did the simple thing, and applied the name the Floride always went by in the United States. To distinguish new from old, the Floride included smaller chrome strips and lost its trim from around the air vents. A larger rear cooling grille, bigger bumpers, heater vents under the

front bumper and Caravelle badging across the front panel made it easily identifiable, as did larger wheels and revised wheel trims. The new car's roof was also raised in order to improve headroom – a criticism of the outgoing car.

The first Caravelles used the tried and tested 956cc (58cu in) engine from the Floride S. It was a power unit derived from that used

in the Renault 8 and was reliable. From 1963, engine capacity was increased to 1108cc (67cu in). The extra power certainly showed the coupé's performance potential to its best advantage. The downside was wayward handling, especially in the wet. Other modifications for 1963 included an all-synchromesh gearbox and larger petrol tank, while convertible models came with

a detachable hardtop as standard. This car was always a curiosity, but never a brilliant seller.

ENGINE: 1108cc (68cu in), four-cylinder
POWER: 54bhp (40kW)
0–60MPH (96KM/H): 17.6 seconds
TOP SPEED: 144km/h (89mph)
PRODUCTION TOTAL: n/a

DAIMLER V8 250

In a straight comparison between the Jaguar Mk 2 and the Daimler V8 250, it's usually the Daimler that takes the spoils.

powerplants, but the V8 250 had Daimler's small Edward Turner–designed V8 shoehorned under the bonnet (hood). Previously used to power the SP250 sports car, the fine engine perfectly suited the sporting Jaguar chassis.

Jaguar charged more for the V8 250 because the Daimler marque was considered more prestigious. Thus the Daimler came equipped with standard automatic transmission, more chrome trim and a distinctive fluted bonnet grille. The result was the best-selling post-war Daimler to date. Today, despite being such an appealing package, the V8 250 is worth less than Jaguar's Mk II.

ENGINE: 2548cc (155cu in), eight-cylinder
POWER: 140bhp (104kW)
0–60MPH (96KM/H): 13.8 seconds
TOP SPEED: 177km/h (110mph)
PRODUCTION TOTAL: 17,620

Once Jaguar had taken over Daimler, it was inevitable that there would be rationalization of the two ranges; badge engineering would be the way to do it. The company needed to develop a

hybrid model that would be both profitable and enhance the old marque's image. The result was the 2.5-litre (155cu in) Daimler saloon, rebadged in 1968 as the V8 250. Jaguar took the best elements from

each product line and combined them. Jaguar's Mark II was the basis for the new car, a curvaceous and compact-looking saloon. Jaguar cars were usually powered by its legendary XK twin-camshaft

DATSUN FAIRLADY

The Japanese motor industry was effectively still in its infancy in the 1960s, but that did not stop Nissan having a go at developing its own rival for the all-conquering MGA and TR3, and aiming it at the American market.

For a first attempt at building a sports car, it was pretty good – and, although similar in layout and style to the MGB, it appeared on the market two years before the British roadster. Under the pretty skin, however, it was a step

behind technically – unlike the MG, it had a separate chassis with front coil spring suspension and double wishbones. At the rear was a live axle, hung on semi-elliptic springs.

Initially powered by a 1499cc (91cu in) engine that produced

only 71bhp (53kW), it was not exactly quick. It took more than 15 seconds to get from 0–60mph (96km/h), and that was way behind contemporary UK cars. However, a programme of development saw that rise – to a more usable 85bhp (63kW) in 1963. In 1967, a 1596cc (97cu in) engine producing 96bhp (72kW) was introduced, along with synchromesh on first gear and front disc brakes.

The ultimate Fairlady appeared in 1967. This version featured a brand-new overhead-camshaft 1982cc (121cu in) engine that produced 135bhp (101kW).

ENGINE: 1982cc (121cu in), four-cylinder
POWER: 135bhp (101kW)
0–60MPH (96KM/H): 10.3 seconds
TOP SPEED: 173km/h (108mph)
PRODUCTION TOTAL: 40,000

Rare and desirable today, the Fairlady was Datsun's first real attempt at producing a car to fight in the MGB/TR4 market. It was a good try, too, although the early versions were slow.

ISO RIVOLTA

From little acorns – that is how the Iso story panned out. Initially, the company built fridges and motor scooters, but, by the 1950s, it had branched out into car production. Its first model was a bubblecar, later built by BMW under licence, but its next product was something entirely different.

The Rivolta was its first venture in the GT market, and the car was very impressive. A young Giugiaro designed the bodywork, and former Ferrari engineer Giotti Bizzarrini created the chassis. It was a recipe that worked, and in many ways was similar to what Gordon Keeble was doing in the United Kingdom. The elegant Bertone-built steel body clothed a similar box-section frame with de Dion rear suspension. The Rivolta had an American V8 under the bonnet (hood), giving it an impressive turn of speed. In fact, it was easily capable of more than 224km/h (140mph).

Being less than two-thirds of the cost of an entry-level Ferrari at the time, commercially the Rivolta picked up plenty of sales, being fast as well as practical, with its four-seat capacity. Only a few good examples of this exotic sports car exist today. Like much Italian exotica from the 1960s, the car succumbed to corrosion.

ENGINE: 5357cc (327cu in), eight-cylinder
POWER: 300bhp (224kW)
0–60MPH (96KM/H): 8.0 seconds
TOP SPEED: 224km/h (140mph)
PRODUCTION TOTAL: 797

Considering the Rivolta was Iso's first venture into the four-seat GT market, it was a very impressive effort indeed. With a finely honed chassis and prodigious performance thanks to the use of Detroit muscle, it gave Ferrari a run for its money.

TRIUMPH VITESSE

Standard-Triumph had done well with the Herald since its launch in 1959 – the small car had proved popular with the car-buying public, and it had been selling in large numbers. Its simple separate chassis meant that a number of different bodystyles could be spun off the same platform – a great way of increasing the range without major investment.

In 1962, Triumph launched the Vitesse, a clever extension of the Herald. It was a more powerful six-cylinder version of the car, with a strengthened chassis, disc brakes up front, a sportier gearbox and overdrive as an option.

A 2-litre (122cu in) six-cylinder engine and all-synchromesh gearbox came in 1966, but handling problems caused by the independent rear swing axle meant a hasty redesign which appeared in 1968, in the form of the Vitesse Mk II. As well as revised suspension, there was more power with this update.

The Vitesse was distinguished from its less powerful sister by its slanted quad-headlight front styling. It could be bought in both

saloon and convertible versions, with the latter being a competent budget sports car that was packed with character.

Like the Herald range on which it was based, the Vitesse was dropped in 1971.

ENGINE: 1998cc (122cu in), six-cylinder
POWER: 104bhp (77kW) at 5300rpm
0–60MPH (96KM/H): 11.9 seconds
TOP SPEED: 164km/h (102mph)
PRODUCTION TOTAL: 51,212

Essentially this was a Triumph Herald with more power – but because a smooth six-cylinder engine provided that, there was plenty of fun to be had. Wayward handling hamstrung original cars, but this was cured by 1968.

RENAULT 8

FRANCE 1962–72

Creating a car to succeed the mega-successful Dauphine was easy for Renault – the new car should be more of the same. As a result, the company stuck with the same formula, building a new car that used the same 956cc (58cu in) engine, again mounted at the rear. The Renault 8's styling, however, was a much more modern affair indeed. Out went the Dauphine's

curvaceous looks, scalloped sides and bulbous cabin, replaced by a boxy and much more angular design that seemed utterly contemporary. The look was improved further after the 1964 face-lift, when larger headlights were introduced.

All R8s were surprisingly quick and agile, and the tuned Gordini, unveiled in 1964, was a rare treat. It had a 103bhp (77kW) 1255cc

(77cu in) engine, with a hemi-style cylinder head and twin-choke carburettors, plus a five-speed manual gearbox. Top speed was over 160km/h (100mph). More than 12,000 Gordini versions were sold.

The R8 was more advanced under the skin, too, with fully independent suspension, all-round disc brakes and a four-speed synchromesh gearbox. An unusual

automatic gearbox was available as an option, operated by pushing buttons on the dashboard.

ENGINE: 1108cc (68cu in), four-cylinder
POWER: 57bhp (42kW)
0–60MPH (96KM/H): 16.5 seconds
TOP SPEED: 145km/h (90mph)
PRODUCTION TOTAL: 1,316,134

BUICK RIVIERA

UNITED STATES 1962–73

During the 1960s, the American car industry changed – cars remained as large as ever, but the previous styling excesses were exorcized to create a cleaner generation of cars. Riding on the crest of that wave was the Buick Riviera – one of the most successful attempts by Detroit at capturing European styling and performance tailored for the home market. The

Riviera was Buick's flagship coupé, and it was the company's best styling and performance package.

Known as model 4747, the Buick Riviera was a huge success straight out of the box, selling around 40,000 in its first year. The styling pioneered a new concept – frameless side windows. It looked good and went well. The standard engine was a 6571cc (401cu in) V8

with 325bhp (242kW), although a 6964cc (425cu in) V8 with 340bhp (253kW) was available for a small premium. In 1964, there was nothing to revise on the styling front, but the 6964cc (425cu in) engine could be ordered with a second four-barrel carburettor, upping the power by 20bhp (15kW).

In 1965, a minor restyle introduced retractable headlights

and expansive rear taillights, but, more importantly, the Riviera joined the muscle-car set in Gran Sport guise. This included the 6964cc (425cu in) engine now boasting 360bhp (268kW) and Posi-Traction rear end to keep it in check. The following year saw more styling tweaks and even more power – 340bhp (253kW) was now the standard package available.

In 1968, GM badge engineering reared its head, and the Riviera now shared bodywork with both the Cadillac Eldorado and the Oldsmobile Toronado. The grille was restyled again, with large parking lights housed in a new front bumper, although headlights still retracted above the grille. The Gran Sport option delivered real performance, with a 209km/h (130mph) top speed, despite its huge 1915kg (4222lb) kerb weight.

The year 1970, however, was not a good one for the Riviera. A dreadful redesign added rear

The Riviera rode on the wave that swept through the Detroit design houses, turning its back on monster chrome and tail fins.

wheel skirts and deleted the retractable headlights. A new standard engine was introduced, a 7459cc (455cu in) 370bhp (276kW) V8, but the extra weight blunted performance, and buyers deserted the model.

GM's styling boss Bill Mitchell revitalized the car in 1970. Dubbed 'the boat-tail', the car had a look that was supposed to draw upon stylish cars of the 1930s, but resulted in a truly remarkable look. The dramatic lines featured a more aggressive front end and curved hips as the bodywork rose over the rear wheels. The fastback roofline then narrowed down to a pointed boat-tail, which allowed for a sporty wraparound rear window, similar to that of the old Corvette Stingray. Power was down to 315bhp (235kW), and that affected sales – even in Gran Sport guise, the car was now rated at 330bhp (246kW).

Riveria sales actually picked up for the last year of the boat-tail look, but the model went into decline. For 1974, an all-new model looked clumsy and weighed more than ever at 2074kg (4572lb), and the 455 V8 produced just 210bhp (156kW). Not surprisingly, sales of the Riviera dived, and the model drifted into obscurity.

ENGINE: 7459cc (455cu in), eight-cylinder
POWER: 330bhp (246kW)
0–60MPH (96KM/H): 8.5 seconds
TOP SPEED: 200km/h (125mph)
PRODUCTION TOTAL: 441,501

LOTUS ELAN

Lotus had been building up to the Elan – the Elite proved it could build a beautiful car that handled, but the Elan went one step further by being powered by Lotus's own engine and marrying with the best bits produced by the company. For the first time, international sports–car manufacturers began to take notice of Lotus, and its brand-new world-class budget sports car.

The secret to the Elan's success was its superb handling. Based on a steel backboned chassis with forked sections front and rear, the Elan enjoyed rigidity that had been so lacking in the Elite. Independent wishbone and coil suspension at the front (derived from the Triumph Herald), with Chapman struts and lower wishbones at the back, made the car impressively agile and responsive. It also had good ride quality to complement the excellent roadholding – it was soft but sure-footed and predictable. The steering came courtesy of Triumph, and Girling provided the all-round disc braking system.

The engine used in the Elan was Lotus's own twin-camshaft unit, with the block and bottom end coming from a Ford Cortina, but with an aluminium twin-camshaft head designed by Harry Mundy fitted. This powerplant was then mated to a slick-shifting Ford four-speed gearbox.

Early Elans had 1498cc (91cu in) and 100bhp (75kW) to play with, but these were soon replaced by the high-revving and extremely flexible 1558cc (95cu in) version, rated at 105bhp (78kW). Being so light and compact, with a kerb weight of just 688kg (1473lb), the Elan possessed a fantastic power-to-weight ratio, and that endowed the car with rapid performance and cornering.

Although hardly luxurious, cabin space was good for two, with ample luggage space for a weekend's excursion. Lotus's own design and development engineer Ron Hickman designed the body, and it was made by Lotus. It was offered only as an open-top car at launch, and the hardtop version followed in 1963 – with the coupé appearing with the S3 Elan in 1965.

The S2 of 1964 featured better brakes and more impressive instrumentation, while the S3 of 1965, now available as a coupé, gained a higher final drive. A year later, the SE was also introduced, with an 115bhp (86kW) rated engine, servo-assisted brakes, centre-lock wheels and the luxury of fitted carpets. The 1968 S4 also received more powerful brakes, as well as flared wheelarches to accommodate lower profile tyres.

The final incarnation of the Elan came in 1971 with the introduction of the Sprint. Tuned by engine specialist Tony Rudd, giving it 25 per cent more power, the Sprint was almost supercar quick. These 'big-valve' Sprints used twin Weber carburettors and proved more reliable and less raucous than the older engines. The Sprints were distinguishable by their two-tone 'Gold Leaf' paintwork (echoing the Formula 1 team colours), slightly extended wheelarches and knock-off centre wheel nuts, and they remain the most sought-after model in the Elan range.

In 1973, the last Lotus Elan left the factory in Norfolk, England. Lotus wanted to lose its 'kit car' image, and it was determined to move upmarket, with the exciting wedge cars of the 1970s, the Elite, Eclat and the Esprit.

ENGINE: 1558cc (95cu in), four-cylinder
POWER: 106bhp (79kW)
0–60MPH (96KM/H): 8.7 seconds
TOP SPEED: 185km/h (115mph)
PRODUCTION TOTAL: 9150

The Elan will probably stand as one of Lotus' greatest cars – deliciously styled, it possessed dynamics far in excess of what the driver should expect.

MG 1100/1300

Based on the Austin/Morris 1100, the MG 1100 may well have been another example of BMC badge engineering, but it was an excellent car and sporting in the true MG tradition. Fine front-wheel drive handling, sharp steering and willing engines, even in the earliest 1098cc (67cu in) models, meant that the small MG saloons could be driven flat out almost all the time.

The final versions, built from 1968, were the best. They were powered by the 1275cc (78cu in) twin-carburettor version of the popular A-Series engine, and had a top speed of 145km/h (90mph) and a characterful exhaust note that was reminiscent of the Mini Cooper. Inside, the MG 1100/1300 was luxuriously appointed and boasted usefully more equipment than its more humble Austin and Morris siblings. Rust killed most of the cars during the 1970s, however, and the majority had gone to the crusher before classic status had been assured.

ENGINE: 1275cc (78cu in), four-cylinder
POWER: 70bhp (52kW)
0–60MPH (96KM/H): 15.6 seconds
TOP SPEED: 145km/h (90mph)
PRODUCTION TOTAL: 157,409

Following on from the groundbreaking Mini, the Morris 1100 was BMC's successful attempt to produce a family car true to the smaller car's principles. It worked, too – because as well as driving as responsively as a Mini, it was usefully sized and eminently practical.

MORRIS 1100/1300

UNITED KINGDOM 1962–73

Given BMC's need to sell its vitally important new family car, the 1100, through both its Austin and Nuffield dealer networks, the only solution was to offer a version that catered for every sales outlet. This meant that Austin and Morris both had ostensibly identical cars to sell. In the case of the BMC 1100, the Morris version appeared first, in August 1962. It was then followed by Austin, MG, Wolseley, Riley and Vanden Plas examples – all essentially the same car, differentiated by trim and badging.

Alec Issigonis designed the 1100 by extending the Mini. It shared the Mini's A-Series engine mounted transversely and driving the front wheels, and its all-independent suspension was a novel gas/fluid Hydrolastic system. The Mk II 1100 appeared in 1971, the same year as the 1300 version with its 1275cc (78cu in) unit. A sporty version, the Morris 1300GT, appeared in 1969. The Mk III version was available only as a Traveller estate (station wagon), from 1971 to 1973.

ENGINE: 1098cc (67cu in), four-cylinder
POWER: 48bhp (kW) at 5100rpm
0–60MPH (96KM/H): 22.2 seconds
TOP SPEED: 126km/h (79mph)
PRODUCTION TOTAL: 801,966

FORD TORINO

UNITED STATES 1962–76

The Ford Torino was a straightforward extension of the Fairlane range, which had been a Ford success during the 1960s. When the Fairlane range was repackaged and relaunched in 1962 as Ford's entry into the muscle-car market, its spin-off, the Torino, made an appearance.

Both cars soon established themselves as street and drag-strip legends. In 1968, a completely new Torino series was announced, featuring a GTS version that was powered by a standard 4949cc (302cu in) V8 engine. The emphasis was on sportiness, with

Enthusiasts will always know the Torino as the Starsky and Hutch car – but it appeared in the early 60s, long before the series was a twinkle in its producer's eyes.

bucket seats, centre dashboard console, decals, side stripes and distinctive trim and deluxe wheel covers all on the equipment list.

Muscle-car options included a 6391cc (390cu in) V8 and the 7022cc (428cu in) V8 390bhp (291kW) engine. Available as fastback, hardtop and convertible, entry-level Cobra models were added a year later with a 7022cc (428cu in) Cobra Jet V8, rated at 335bhp (250kW).

Also new for 1969 was the introduction of the Torino Talladega, which had been specifically aimed at NASCAR. Based on the two-door hardtop, it received an extended sloped nose, flush grille and revised rear bumper, adding 15cm (6in) to the length of the car. The Torino was to remain in production throughout the 1970s, but its importance in the Ford range waned.

ENGINE: 7022cc (428cu in), eight-cylinder
POWER: 335bhp (250kW)
0–60MPH (96KM/H): 8 seconds
TOP SPEED: 217km/h (135mph)
PRODUCTION TOTAL: 2,024,189

ALPINE A110

Alpine had been created in Dieppe, France, by rally driver and Renault dealer Jean Rédélé in 1954, to modify competition cars and overcome their shortcomings. His first production car, the A106, was aluminium-bodied and powered by a rear-mounted Renault 4CV engine. Rédélé rapidly followed up this success with the A108, then the A110 – the car considered by enthusiasts to be the definitive Alpine.

Introduced in 1961, the A110 made heavy use of Renault parts. Based on the R8, it was available only as a coupé – with a heavy slant on competition and featuring few creature comforts. The A110 had a steel backbone chassis with glassfibre bodywork; the design was influenced by the Lotus Elan and shared its stiff tubular backbone chassis, which featured on all subsequent Alpines.

The A110 was a very successful rally car. After winning several French rallies in the late 1960s with iron-cast R8 Gordini engines, the car was fitted with the aluminium-

block Renault 16 TS engine. With two dual chamber Weber 45 carburettors, the new engine could deliver 125bhp (93kW), and the production 1600S had a top speed of 210km/h (136mph). The company hit financial trouble, and was absorbed by Renault in 1974.

ENGINE: 1647cc (101cu in), four-cylinder
POWER: 138bhp (103kW)
0–60MPH (96KM/H): n/a
TOP SPEED: 214km/h (133mph)
PRODUCTION TOTAL: 8139

Conceived by a rally driver, it's no surprise to learn that the Alpine A110 was very successful in this sector of competition. With its Renault engine mounted in the back, the lightweight car takes time to master, but once there, it's magic.

MGB

Hailed throughout its life as the world's best–selling sports car, the MGB found a place for itself in the hearts of car fans right across the world. Today, that enthusiasm continues, and the MGB remains the world's most popular classic car – with devoted fans worldwide ensuring the car's continued survival. When it first appeared in 1962, the MGB Roadster looked like a straightforward replacement for the MGA. It was fairly sophisticated, however, and became the first MG sports car to boast a monocoque body. Other advancements over the MGA included wind-up windows, an easy-fold hood and a relatively spacious interior.

The car's chassis set-up was simple but effective – and it was rear-wheel drive, which meant that the MGB was enjoyable to drive. A further advantage over the MGA was the MGB's newly enlarged 1.8-litre B-Series engine, which delivered torquey performance from its 95bhp (71kW).

The appeal of the range was massively expanded with the coupé version, dubbed the MGB GT, which was launched in 1965. The rear hatchback and extra rear

Introduced in 1962, and remaining in production until 1980, the MGB was a big success for its makers and is legendary today. Quick and fun to drive, the 'B was a major step forward.

seats added extra versatility to the MGB. With its Pininfarina-styled roofline, it was certainly pretty.

In 1967, the MGB received the tougher five-bearing version of the B-Series, a full-synchromesh gearbox, an improved rear axle and different gear ratios, which allowed for reasonably relaxed high-speed cruising. Overdrive was also offered as an option across the MGB range.

As the 1970s drew nearer, it was clear that an MGB replacement would not be coming, so a programme of regular improvements continued to keep the model fresh. In 1970, a revised radiator grille, more sumptuous interior and

Rostyle polished steel wheels were introduced, all of which remained in place until 1974. At that time, the Rover V8-powered MGB GT V8 was introduced.

The ex-General Motors 3.5-litre (214cu in) alloy engine was used in low compression form, and developed 137bhp (102kW), but it still turned the MGB into a quick road car, with a top speed of almost 225km/h (140mph). The after-effects of the world energy crisis in 1973, however, meant that the car flopped, with only 2600 examples sold.

From 1974 onwards, American legislation changed the look of the MGB completely. The ride height

was increased to raise the headlight aim, while thicker rear bumpers and huge polyurethane bumpers became standard fittings. Handling was adversely affected, and ride quality did not improve. British Leyland, which by now owned MG, realized that the MGB needed to be a better car to drive. It was still a strong seller in export markets, so as a result the company extensively revised the car for 1976. A thick anti-roll bar addressed the handling issues and that interior was revised.

Ultimately, the changes were not enough. The Datsun 260Z took over as the United States' best–selling sports car, and

patriotic British buyers could only keep the flag flying until 1980, when the Abingdon plant closed. The last 1000 MGBs, which were badged LE, were all finished in silver and black, and they marked the end of an era in the British car industry.

MG would return – although it was not until 1995 and the MGF, when the MG octagon appeared on a brand-new sports car.

ENGINE: 1798cc (110cu in), four-cylinder
POWER: 95bhp (71kW)
0–60MPH (96KM/H): 12.2 seconds
TOP SPEED: 166km/h (103mph)
PRODUCTION TOTAL: 513,272

TRIUMPH SPITFIRE

UNITED KINGDOM 1962–80

The Triump Herald's separate chassis construction meant that producing new models based on it could not be easier. The Spitfire was a direct Herald-based offering and came at exactly the right time – competing with MG's Midget in the budget sports–car class.

Triumph had always planned a sporting offshoot of the Herald, but procrastinated until its management saw a sketch Michelotti had prepared for a pretty little roadster in 1960. Initially called Project Bomb, the Spitfire emerged as a remarkable, pretty open-topped roadster in 1962. Built on a shortened chassis,

Based on the flexible underpinnings of the Herald, the Spitfire was an appealing and pretty sports car introduced by Triumph to compete head on with the MG Midget.

and powered by the Herald's 1147cc (70cu in) engine fitted with twin carburettors to produce 63bhp (47kW), it was fun to drive. Front disc brakes were standard and, out of the box, the Spitfire was capable of 145km/h (90mph), although handling was 'exciting'.

In 1963, the Mk II version added more power, a new grille and a nicer interior. Another update in 1967 saw the Spitfire upgunned to 1296cc (79cu in) and given repositioned bumpers. Michelotti redesigned the front and rear for the Mk IV in 1970, and the final major update came in 1974, when the Spitfire received a 1493cc (91cu in) engine, which eventually was also fitted to the MG Midget.

ENGINE: 1296cc (79cu in), four-cylinder
POWER: 75bhp (56kW) at 6000rpm
0–60MPH (96KM/H): 13.6 seconds
TOP SPEED: 161km/h (100mph)
PRODUCTION TOTAL: 314,332

FORD UK CORTINA

UNITED KINGDOM 1962–82

If ever there was a case of launching the right product at the right time, then Ford did it with the Cortina. Although it was impeccably costed, lightweight and offered family men in the United Kingdom exactly what they wanted, the Cortina's implications on the UK car industry were far wider ranging than that.

What Ford managed to achieve with the Cortina was the creation of a new medium-sized family car that also defined how the perfect company car should look.

Launched to fill the gap between small and large cars, the Cortina was born out of rivalry between Ford UK and Germany. When the UK chairman Sir Patrick Hennessy discovered that a front-wheel drive model, code-named Cardinal, was

being developed in Germany with Ford US assistance, he initiated Project Archbishop.

Launched in 1962 with a name inspired by the venue of the 1960 Winter Olympics, the Cortina also carried Consul badging on the bonnet (hood) for the first two years. The crisp styling was the work of American Roy Brown, who had previously designed the ill-fated Edsel. When lined up against the opposition, principally the BMC 1100, the Cortina scored highly because it was roomier, cheaper and quicker. The BMC 1100 outsold the Cortina Mk 1 and Mk 2 for most of their lives, but the Cortina scored well with fleet buyers, who loved the car's simplicity and ease of service. Within a year, more than 250,000 examples had been sold –

a record at the time – and, though it was nicknamed the 'Dagenham Dustbin', the Cortina quickly became established as a national favourite in the United Kingdom.

In 1966, the Cortina Mk 2 appeared. In the process it received smart new styling (credited to Roy Haynes), and the engine range was shifted upwards, with a new base engine being set at 1.3 litres (79cu in). Part of the Cortina's appeal was the number of variants in which it was offered, and the Mk 2 was certainly no exception. It came in Base, De Luxe Super and GT forms, with the Lotus Cortina at the top of the range. In 1967, a new 1600cc (98cu in) and the 1600E (for Executive) were created.

When the Mk 3 was launched in 1970, the Cortina grew up. In

1973, it became the United Kingdom's best–selling car (a title it retained until 1981) and featured American styling, penned by Harley Copp. Nicknamed the 'Coke Bottle', the Cortina model range had become the perfect home for all company car owners – with Base, L, XL, GT and GXL models offered, and a range of engines that spanned 1.3 to 2 litres (122cu in). The last Cortina in 1976 was another clever redesign, this time by Uwe Bahnsen. After the Coke Bottle, the Mk 4 Cortina adopted a very square look (which was by now shared with the German Ford Taunus), but the glass area was increased, giving a feeling of space in the cabin.

An S replaced the GT model, and the engine options offered were

1300cc (79cu in), 1600cc (98cu in) and 2000cc (122cu in), although a 2.3-litre (140cu in) V6 was added in 1977. A minor face-lift in 1980 freshened up the style and meant even larger windows, but a new and more radical design was just around the corner.

ENGINE: 1198cc (73cu in), four-cylinder
POWER: 49bhp (37kW)
0–60MPH (96KM/H): 15 seconds
TOP SPEED: 153km/h (95mph)
PRODUCTION TOTAL: 4,299,669

Known as the 'Dagenham Dustbin', the original Cortina was actually a masterful piece of design and deserved the success it enjoyed over five generations.

SUNBEAM VENEZIA

UNITED KINGDOM 1963–65

The Sunbeam Venezia was one of those cars that looked a lot better than it drove. Built by Touring of Milan, the Venezia stuck to the Superleggera (superlight) principles of a tubular steel frame, over which aluminium panels were stretched – but, underneath the beautiful styling, it was nothing more than a prettier version of the Hillman Super Minx.

Apart from the standard overdrive and a slightly more powerful version of the engine that was usually fitted to the more mundane cars in the Rootes line-up, there were no mechanical differences between the Venezia and the more ordinary models in the range. Still, that did not stop Sunbeam from charging Jaguar prices for its new car, despite its 1592cc (97cu in) four-

cylinder engine. As a result, the company struggled to sell the Venezia in any numbers. Rootes Group management was keen to maximize the concept-mooted convertible and V8 versions, but they were never built.

After appearing in September 1963, the car lasted less than two seasons. Unexciting mechanicals and a high purchase price ensured

demand was low, and just 145 cars were built, seven of which were sold in the United Kingdom.

ENGINE: 1592cc (97cu in), four-cylinder
POWER: 88bhp (66kW)
0–60MPH (96KM/H): n/a
TOP SPEED: about 161km/h (100mph)
PRODUCTION TOTAL: 145

ABARTH-SIMCA 1150

ITALY 1963–65

Considering Carlo Abarth's well respected tuning firm had concentrated on uprating Fiat's smaller products, it came as a big surprise when he launched an uprated Simca in 1963. Based on the popular and boxy rear-engined 1000, the Simca-Abarth 1150 showed that there was plenty of potential in the French car – a factor which would become

obvious once Simca began launching ever more powerful Rallye versions in later years.

Although the original car didn't seem too promising, and suffered from a number of handling quirks, it didn't stop Abarth shoehorning in a more powerful version of its engine enlarged to 1137 (69 cu in). Cosmetically, its Abarth grille and wider wheels differentiated

the tuned car – it was a real Q-car.

However, the Simca-Abarth 1150 also paved the way for the Corsa, a pretty coupé built on the same floorpan, as well as other larger engined Abarth-Simca specials.

As the partnership bloomed, faster and more interesting cars were introduced. These included a 2-litre (122 cu in) version, which had a top speed of 150mph

(241km/h) – both frightening, and totally unexpected from something so mundane as a Simca.

ENGINE: 1137cc (69cu in), four-cylinder
POWER: 55bhp (41kW)
0–60MPH (96KM/H): 12 secs
TOP SPEED: 151km/h (94mph)
PRODUCTION TOTAL: n/a

ASTON MARTIN DB5

UNITED KINGDOM 1963–66

Often referred to as the most famous car in the world, thanks to its appearance in several James Bond films, when the Aston Martin DB5 was launched it did not make much of a splash at all. The reason for this indifference was because it seemed so similar to the older DB4 – in fact, there were even plans to call the new model the DB4 Series 6. However, the DB5 was soon recognized as a fine

Volante version of the DB5 combined wind-in-the-hair fun with the traditional elegance that comes as standard with a DB5.

model in its own right. It replaced the two factory DB4 models, the DB4 and DB4GT, by incorporating many of the features used on the GT, including Girling disc brakes front and rear, a 4-litre (243cu in) engine, triple SU carburettors and faired-in headlights.

The new model had gained weight and had become less demanding to drive, so the cabin was quieter and the ride more civilized. The triple Weber carburettor-equipped Vantage model added performance to the mix, and a five-speed ZF gearbox

made the DB5 one of the finest high-speed touring cars you could buy. A convertible version of the DB5 was also launched, called the Volante, Unusually, a 'Shooting Brake' version was also offered, as built by Radford. These cars looked surprisingly good.

ENGINE: 3995cc (243cu in), six-cylinder
POWER: 282bhp (210kW)
0–60MPH (96KM/H): 8.1 seconds
TOP SPEED: 227km/h (141mph)
PRODUCTION TOTAL: 1063

OPEL REKORD A/B

GERMANY 1963–65

After what seemed like years of building smaller versions of American cars, Opel had a change of heart with the Rekord A and B. When it appeared in 1963, the Rekord A had a much more European look to it, with squared-off, boxy lines. Upsides of this new look were the spacious passenger compartment and rectangular headlights. The new Opel looked

clean and modern, if a little dull. As well as the standard saloon, an interesting-looking coupé was launched in 1964, followed by the Rekord B the next year.

The Rekord B's engines were all new, replacing the original overhead-valve engines that could trace their roots to the pre-war Olympia. The modern overhead-camshaft engines were offered in

1.5-, 1.7- and 1.9-litre (92, 103, and 116cu in) forms. With a monocoque bodyshell and front disc brakes (from 1965), the Rekord had been brought up to date – especially compared to Opels of old. Rear suspension was still by live rear axle and leaf springs, though.

The Rekord was a big success for Opel, with over a million sold in a relatively short production life.

It was replaced by the similar-looking but much more modern Rekord C/Commodore in 1966.

ENGINE: 1680cc (103cu in), four-cylinder
POWER: 55bhp (41kW)
0–60MPH (96KM/H): 21.0 seconds
TOP SPEED: 147km/h (91mph)
PRODUCTION TOTAL: 1,152,824

PANHARD CD

FRANCE 1963–65

With a name fashioned after Panhard director Charles Deutsch's initials, the CD was created as a testbed for the company's air-cooled engine and highly developed aerodynamic

Named after Panhard's director, Charles Deutsch, the CD could just as well stand for Co-efficient of Drag – as it was slippery in the wind tunnel.

techniques. Deutsch commissioned a racing project that would take the small French manufacturer to Le Mans, and in doing so scored a considerable success.

The CD won the 'Index of Performance' class with ease in the 1962 24-hour, proving that the air-cooled engine was remarkably reliable when run at consistently high speeds. To celebrate, Panhard put the CD into limited production as a road car, although its price

was very much on the high side. The oddball glassfibre bodywork certainly looked individual, and, when mounted on a tubular steel backbone chassis, its stiffness and low weight meant that acceleration was exceptional for a two-cylinder engine of its size.

The CD was not built for comfort, with seating strictly for two (small) people. But it was a great car to drive, with accurate handling, a fantastic exhaust note and the

ability to outrun many more powerful cars in competition. Just 92 cars were built over three years, before Citroën bought Panhard in 1965.

ENGINE: 848cc (52cu in), two-cylinder
POWER: 60bhp (45kW)
0–60MPH (96KM/H): 10 seconds
TOP SPEED: 169km/h (105mph)
PRODUCTION TOTAL: 92

TVR GRIFFITH

The TVR Griffith was created (and named after) an American motor trader who first fitted the V8 engine in one of Trevor Wilkinson's cars in 1962. Jack Griffith had seen the works cars racing at the American Sebring race circuit and decided that fitting a Ford 4.7-litre (288cu in) V8 into a Grantura chassis – a car designed for an engine less than half the size – was a good idea.

Griffith negotiated a deal with TVR to sell the uprated Granturas with his own name on, and these first cars went under the name Griffith 200. The car was based on the Mk III Grantura and offered with the option of manual or automatic transmission. Suspect engine cooling and poor brakes meant that development work was required. That resulted in the 400, which was based on the Mk IV Grantura and introduced in 1964.

But there were insurmountable hurdles in developing this four-cylinder sportster into a V8-engined beast: weight distribution. In standard form, the Grantura had been fun; with that heavy motor upfront, things got a bit hairy.

ENGINE: 4727cc (288cu in), eight-cylinder
POWER: 271bhp (202kW)
0–60MPH (96KM/H): 5.7 seconds
TOP SPEED: 248km/h (155mph)
PRODUCTION TOTAL: about 300

TVR's legacy as a producer of monstrously quick V8 powered giant killers starts here. Inspired by the AC Cobra 289, an American motor trader had the bright idea of slotting in a Ford V8 into the diminutive chassis – hair-raising handling and dragster-like acceleration were the result.

FERRARI 330GT

ENGINE: 3967cc (242cu in), 12-cylinder
POWER: 300bhp (224kW)
0–60MPH (96KM/H): 7 seconds
TOP SPEED: 230km/h (143mph)
PRODUCTION TOTAL: 950

An all-new car, the 330GT was launched in January 1964 and, because of its additional interior space, lengthened wheelbase (which was 5cm/2in longer) and uprated disc brakes with two separate front and rear systems, it was a less 'extreme' way into the Ferrari camp. It had evolved from the 250 GTE 2+2, as, at the end of

Not the prettiest of Ferrari by a long chalk, the 330GT was a useful four-seater with the usual Ferrari qualities.

1963, Ferrari started to deliver these cars equipped with the new 330 engine. With 50 or so cars converted, they became known as the 330 America. The styling had been changed, too, and, although it was more modern, it was not nearly as beautiful as the 250's.

The quad headlight installation looked garish and clumsy; after just 18 months, one on each wing (fender) replaced them. The 330GT did show that Ferrari was willing to listen to its customers now. As well as restyling the front end, it added power steering and air conditioning to the options list. One thing it did not do was install an automatic transmission, but the US importer Luigi Chinetti certainly did. He acquired a General Motors Hydromatic transmission (used in the Chevrolet Corvette) and even had unofficial assistance from GM.

HUMBER SCEPTRE I/II

By the mid-1960s, Humber had long since become just another brand within the Rootes Group portfolio. Following the launch of the Super Snipe, no further models were designed specifically for Humber. The Sceptre was a case in point – it was really just a restyled Hillman Super Minx or Singer Vogue, with a slightly modified roofline and wraparound front screen.

The front-end styling was similar to the Sunbeam Rapier, but that was because it had actually been developed as a Rapier until a late stage in production. It was even powered by the Rapier's 80bhp (60kW) twin carburettor engine at the outset – which gave the superbly appointed saloon peppy performance. The interior was new, and the modern dashboard was very well stocked with instruments. Servo front disc brakes and self-cancelling dual overdrive made it the Super Minx family's most upmarket car at that time, and an interesting alternative to the Wolseley/Riley saloons offered by BMC.

The Mk II from 1965 was fitted with the Rootes Group five-bearing crankshaft 1725cc (105cu in) engine, with automatic transmission as an option. It, too, borrowed from the Hillman Super Minx by copying its frontal styling.

ENGINE: 1592cc (97cu in), four-cylinder
POWER: 80bhp (60kW)
0–60MPH (96KM/H): 17.1 seconds
TOP SPEED: 141km/h (88mph)
PRODUCTION TOTAL: 28,996

MORGAN PLUS 4 PLUS

ENGINE: 2138cc (130cu in), four-cylinder
POWER: 105bhp (78kW)
0–60MPH (96KM/H): 14.9 seconds
TOP SPEED: 177km/h (110mph)
PRODUCTION TOTAL: 26

Morgan's cars tended to evolve with all the zeal of a glacier, but the antiquated sports cars that emerged from the Malvern Link factory were exactly what the company's customers wanted. As proof, whenever Morgan attempted to modernize, it would meet failure.

The Plus 4 Plus was a brave attempt by Morgan to create a genuine contender in the grand tourer market – and, with an elegant closed body, a drooping MGA-style nose, a bubble-shaped hardtop and graceful rear-end styling, it should have succeeded. Technologically, it was radical – for Morgan – and featured a glassfibre body, gas-filled suspension dampers and wind-up windows.

Morgan fans rejected it, however, and sports–car fans chose to stick with what they knew, as the Plus 4 Plus suffered from a bumpy ride, flimsy construction and – still – an archaic chassis.

The outcome was predictable. Production ceased after just 26 cars, and the company suffered a financial setback because of it. The outcome was that Morgan went back to concentrating on its core products. In doing so, it ensured its future through the 1970s and 1980s, a difficult time for many other small sports–car producers.

The idea of a modern Morgan back in the 1960s must have seemed like a strange idea – so when the company launched its Plus 4 Plus, buyers stayed.

PANHARD 24-SERIES

One company that could never be accused of selling out to the lowest common denominator was Panhard – it prided itself on the advanced, forward-thinking cars it produced, and that it was still able to produce cars that were able to challenge conventional wisdom. Aerodynamically sculpted, the Panhards may have been styled for form, but there was also a quirky beauty that still stands up. The Panhard 24CT was a perfect example of form and function.

Loosely based on the PL17, the CT was a two-door coupé with an unusual but effective trapezoidal roofline, angular rear end, faired-in headlight lenses and a sharp aerodynamic snout. It looked years ahead of its time – and, again, managed to extract a high top speed from its low-powered engine. The engine was taken from the PL17, but, like the earlier car, the 24 always felt a lot quicker than its performance on paper suggests.

Despite being one of the most technologically advanced and strikingly styled cars on the market, the 24CT never sold in great numbers. This is not surprising, as, for, the same price as this flat-twin-powered coupé, buyers could invest in an equally unusual but much more practical Citroën DS22.

ENGINE: 848cc (52cu in), two-cylinder
POWER: 50bhp (37kW)
0–60MPH (96KM/H): n/a
TOP SPEED: 145km/h (90mph)
PRODUCTION TOTAL: 23,245

JAGUAR S-TYPE

ENGINE: 3781cc (231cu in), six-cylinder
POWER: 210bhp (156kW)
0–60MPH (96KM/H): 10.2 seconds
TOP SPEED: 195km/h (122mph)
PRODUCTION TOTAL: 25,171

Jaguars are emotional cars, and nowhere is this more evident than with the S-type. Although a newer and arguably more capable car than the Mk II, it is a much less desirable classic. When new, there was no comparison. though. It handled and braked better, thanks to independent rear suspension and extremely powerful in-board all-round disc brakes. Styling was a different matter. It was sleeker, having adopted the flatter rear end from the Mk X, but it somehow failed to look as pure.

There was no arguing about the power – of the two engines on offer, the 3.8-litre (232cu in) provided good acceleration and a top speed of over 192km/h (120mph). An all-synchromesh gearbox was made standard in 1965, as well as the popular Borg Warner automatic transmission. As with the Mk II, later versions had Ambla plastic trim instead of leather. The S-type never received the recognition it deserved and is overlooked by enthusiasts, so it is cheaper than the Mk II. Of the 25,171 cars made, 10,036 were fitted with the 3.4-litre (210cu in) engine and 15,135 with the 3.8-litre (232cu in) unit.

Based on the Mk 2, the Jaguar S-type never captured the imagination of its intended buyers as the older car.

BOND EQUIPE

Bond might have cut its teeth in the immediate post-war years building three-wheeled microcars echoing what Reliant was offering, but, in 1963, all that changed. Lawrie Bond's company then added the Equipe GT4 to the line-up.

Based closely on the Triumph Herald, and using its chassis, bulkhead and doors, the Equipe was a pleasantly styled coupé that was actually rather practical. Much of the bodywork was glassfibre, and in contemporary advertising it was described as 'the most beautiful car in the world'. That was a matter of opinion, but, overall, the GT4 was a good car that further improved in 1964 when the GT4S, with its twin headlights, opening boot (trunk) and more headroom than the GT4, was launched.

The totally restyled Equipe 2-litre (122cu in), based on the Triumph Vitesse, also put in an appearance. Along with the new six-cylinder engine, the car also inherited the Vitesse's unpredictable rear suspension, but the Mk II Equipe put that right and also introduced the convertible option.

These Bonds were cheap and sporty, and now enjoy quite a following, even if the chassis and bulkheads are even more rust-prone than those of the Herald and Vitesse.

ENGINE: 1998cc (122cu in), six-cylinder
POWER: 95bhp (71kW)
0–60MPH (96KM/H): 10.7 seconds
TOP SPEED: 165km/h (102mph)
PRODUCTION TOTAL: 4381

The Mk II Bond Equipe featured Bond's own styling and did away with the Herald doors that made the original car look too much like a facelifted Triumph. With such familiar underpinnings and glassfibre bodywork, the Bond Equipe should have been the best of both worlds, but sales never lived up to expectations, so when the company merged with Reliant, it was quietly dropped from the lineup.

DAIHATSU COMPAGNO

JAPAN 1963–70

Small and not quite perfectly formed, the rather unremarkable Daihatsu Compagno didn't make too many waves.

synchromesh four-speed gearbox. In 1965, it was upgraded to 958cc (58cu in), and power increased to 55bhp (41kW), giving the car a useful performance boost.

The range expanded to include a four-door saloon and estate car (station wagon) based on the saloon body. More interesting was a convertible with a more powerful engine, thanks to a twin barrel carburettor that boosted output to 65bhp (48kW) and produced a top speed of 145km/h (90mph).

Daihatsu became part of the Toyota empire in 1967, effectively becoming its small car division.

Few would have predicted it at the time, but the Daihatsu Compagno was the beginning of what turned into a tidal wave of Japanese cars imported into Europe during the 1970s. The car itself was a rather unremarkable two-door saloon that failed to set the world on fire, but it was the first four-wheeled Daihatsu to go into production, and the company made an effort to get it right first time. Styled by Vignale, the look was neat and stylish without much of the clutter and chrome that became associated with its Japanese decedents during the 1970s.

The Compagno was powered by a water-cooled 797cc (49cu in) four-cylinder engine driving the rear wheels, and featured an all-

ENGINE: 797cc (49cu in), four-cylinder
POWER: 55bhp (41kW)
0–60MPH (96KM/H): 35 seconds
TOP SPEED: 113km/h (70mph)
PRODUCTION TOTAL: 120,000

FORD UK CORSAIR

UNITED KINGDOM 1963–70

The Corsair was introduced by Ford as an attempt to plug yet another gap in its range – above the Cortina but below the Zephyr/Zodiac. Known internally as the 'Bucaneer', the Corsair was the product of intense market research, and the slightly ornate styling was a result of that.

Its distinctive arrow-shaped nose looked like a cross between that of the Taunus in Germany and the Thunderbird in the United States. It never really caught the imagination of buyers, and sales

Arrow–nosed styling and V4 engines dared to be different, but the new range-plugging Ford didn't spark massive interest.

were slower than anticipated – despite the printed circuit board inside the instrument panel, an industry first.

Replacing the existing 1498cc (91cu in) engines with the new V4s at 1663cc (101cu in) and 1996cc (122cu in) actually removed some of the appeal, and the car was slower and less economical with these new and less efficient engines. Also, a lot of the car's weight was positioned over the front wheels, which did not inspire confident handling. Ford released versions with reworked engines and high levels of standard trim to tempt buyers, but most customers still preferred the better value Cortina, and sales remained poor until the car's demise in 1970.

ENGINE: 1498cc (92cu in), four-cylinder
POWER: 60bhp (45kW)
0–60MPH (96KM/H): 14 seconds
TOP SPEED: 158km/h (98mph)
PRODUCTION TOTAL: 331,095

MASERATI MISTRAL

ITALY 1963–70

ENGINE: 3692cc (225cu in), six-cylinder
POWER: 245bhp (183kW) at 5500rpm
0–60MPH (96KM/H): 7.5 seconds
TOP SPEED: 233km/h (145mph)
PRODUCTION TOTAL: 948

With the Mistrale, Maserati continued with its programme of recycling the tried-and-tested chassis of the 3500GT to produce another supercar. Regarded as one of the better Maseratis, the Mistral appeared in prototype form at the 1963 Turin Motor Show.

It used the same engine as the Sebring, and the chassis had been shortened and strengthened with square section tubing to enhance handling. A year later, the convertible Spider appeared. The coupé had the 3694cc (225cu in) engine from new, while the Spider used the older 3485cc (213cu in) unit. The Sebring's 4014cc (245cu in) unit became available from 1967. All had Lucas fuel injection.

The design for both was by Frua, with the bodies built by Maggiora using aluminium for the panels, except the rear wings (fenders) of the Spider, which were made of steel. The coupé was notable for its large glass hatchback, while the Spider had a hardtop, included a sloping rear window and small buttresses. Mechanically, the Mistral had a similar suspension layout to the 3500GT, with disc brakes on all four wheels. Frua used nearly the same design for the British AC 428, even recycling some Maserati panels for it, thus compromising the Mistral's individuality.

Based on the familiar chassis of the 3500GT, the Maserati Mistral was a tried and tested package wrapped in stylish new clothes.

MASERATI QUATTROPORTE

ITALY 1963–70

When Maserati rolled out the Quattroporte of 1963, it reintroduced the saloon supercar concept to European buyers – something that had been missing since the golden era of the 1920s. The Quattroporte combined luxury with superb performance, and it was a theme that would be adopted by Lamborghini with its Espada, and Ferrari with the 365 GT4 2+2 – although neither had four doors. Introduced at the Turin Motor Show in 1963, the Quattroporte was the fastest four-door car in the world when launched, and it was not convincingly topped until the launch of the Jaguar XJ12 in 1972.

Frua designed the coachwork, but Vignale built it. It was powered by a 4.2-litre (252 cu in) quad camshaft V8 derived from the racing engines, and featured a new chassis with the engine mounted on a subframe to cut down on noise and vibration. The front suspension followed established double-wishbone practice, but at the rear was a de Dion axle which proved troublesome in operation. By 1966, a conventional live axle with semi-elliptic springs had replaced it. In 1969, the Type 107A Quattroporte was launched. this version had a 4.7-litre (287cu in) engine with an extra 30bhp (22kW).

ENGINE: 4136cc (252cu in), eight-cylinder
POWER: 260bhp (194kW) at 5200rpm
0–60MPH (96KM/H): 8.3 seconds
TOP SPEED: 222km/h (138mph)
PRODUCTION TOTAL: 759

PONTIAC GTO

For muscle-car fans, the Pontiac GTO is the Holy Grail – where it all began. It was a brave effort by General Motors and bucked many trends in the motor industry. At a time when the rest of the US industry was developing ever larger behemoths, Pontiac decided to combine big block power with the relatively compact body of the Tempest coupé.

Pontiac's chief engineer John De Lorean developed the Pontiac GTO. Fast cars were seen as politically incorrect within GM at the time, but his perseverance paid off. The car was launched, and was ecstatically greeted by young American buyers who craved performance. As well as the 6555cc (400cu in) engine, the GTO option gave buyers more responsive steering, firmer suspension, twin exhausts and wider tyres – all for a $300 premium over the standard Tempest.

With the GTO name lifted straight from the eponymous Ferrari, where GTO stood for 'Gran

Turismo Omologato' in reference to its racing exploits, it was obvious that comparisons would be made between the two cars. Although any collector would immediately choose the Ferrari, performance-wise the Pontiac actually ran the thinly disguised racing Ferrari pretty close, being able to accelerate from 0–60mph (96km/h) in under seven seconds. As the GTO was further developed, that figure continued to tumble, making the car a pretty special proposition. Owners joked that the GTO initials on the Pontiac stood for 'Gas, Tyres and Oil', as the overpowered car consumed all three at an alarming rate.

By 1965, GM's anti-performance policy had been reversed, and, to celebrate, John De Lorean decided the GTO should become a model in its own right. The 1966 GTO was similar to the earlier cars, but its profile was tweaked to give a more elegant, flowing appearance, with contoured 'Coke bottle'

styling along the flanks. In order to give it more power, the flagship GTO received a massive 7457cc (455cu in) engine, giving it 370bhp (276kW) and 209km/h (130mph) performance, plus the ability to sprint from 0–60mph (96km/h) in six seconds.

An all-new bodyshell was introduced for the 1968 model year, which brought the car up to date. One of the main new features was the 'Endura' front bumper, which satisfied new US safety legislation by being made of deformable polyurethane, yet at the same time was cleverly disguised not to look like a bumper, wrapping around the entire front of the car and housing the mesh radiator grille. De Lorean proved the new bumpers' efficacy by appearing on US television repeatedly bashing one with a sledgehammer, to absolutely no effect.

The ultimate version of these second-generation GTOs was the 'Judge', offered as an option pack.

The mother of all muscle cars is the GTO – and in Mk 2 form, as introduced in 1968, it proved incredibly quick and not far off the Ferrari it was named after.

Its power output was nearly 400bhp (298kW), thanks to a quad-carburettor 'Ram Air' set-up, and it also had large front and rear spoilers, bright paint schemes, a three-speed manual shift transmission and 'Judge' decals.

Sales of the GTO as a model in its own right died in 1971, after a massive drop in muscle-car popularity and an increasing trend towards less powerful, more luxurious cars in the United States.

ENGINE: 6555cc (400cu in), eight-cylinder
POWER: 345bhp (257kW)
0–60MPH (96KM/H): 6.8 seconds
TOP SPEED: 200km/h (124mph)
PRODUCTION TOTAL: 486,591

SINGER CHAMOIS

Rootes badge engineering was alive and well with the group's new Hillman Imp. The rear-engined baby car suited the sportier Singer treatment perfectly, and the smooth

engine and neat road behaviour were complemented by the higher quality interior trim, and higher equipment levels fitted as standard. The sportier looking car

was launched in 1963, and, by 1965, a Mk II version arrived. A year later, the Chamois Sport appeared, which was a more highly equipped version of the

Sunbeam Imp Sport, featuring the same mechanicals under the skin.

In 1967, the suspension on the standard car was fettled, and in the same year the Chamois Coupé went on sale. This was the same as the Hillman Imp Californian, but, again, had a better interior. In 1968, the Chamois's fascia was changed and twin headlights added. The cars were all dropped in 1970 when the Singer marque died.

ENGINE: 875cc (53cu in),
  four-cylinder
POWER: 51bhp (38kW)
0–60MPH (96KM/H): 16.3 seconds
TOP SPEED: 144km/h (90mph)
PRODUCTION TOTAL: 49,798

The upmarket and more powerful version of the Hillman Imp was an absolute delight to drive – a smooth, revvy engine and sweet steering made it a treat. Later Mk II and Coupé versions were even more desirable.

ABARTH-FIAT 595/695 ITALY 1963–71

One of the legendary names in the tuning industry, Carlo Abarth had cut his teeth tuning and improving the Fiat 500 – and producing his famous 595 and 695 models. These were based on Fiat's updated version of its tiny 500, named the 500D.

Abarth transformed the Fiat from a basic budget runaround to a pocket rocket that could challenge the performance of many larger and more expensive sports cars – including the Mini Cooper.

Handling options were offered, while the 695SS could be bought with front disc brakes and wider wheelarches. The cars became so sought after that they are still made by replica manufacturers, with Abarth stripes and the distinctive Abarth scorpion badge.

The two-cylinder engine was tuned and bored out to 593.7cc (36.2cu in), and power went up to 27bhp (20kW). The rise may not seem significant, but it was enough in such a tiny, lightweight machine. Little else was changed for this new model, named the 595.

Following that, a more powerful version, known as the 595SS, appeared which was boosted to 32bhp (24kW) by using a bigger carburettor. By enlarging the Fiat engine still further, Abarth managed to obtained 30bhp (22kW) from a 689.5cc (42cu in) unit (in the 695) and 38bhp (28kW) for the 695SS.

ENGINE: 689.5cc (42cu in),
  twin-cylinder
POWER: 38bhp 28(kW)
0–60MPH (96KM/H): n/a
TOP SPEED: 142km/h (88mph)
PRODUCTION TOTAL: n/a

MERCEDES-BENZ SL 'PAGODA' GERMANY 1963–71

ENGINE: 2778cc (170cu in),
  six-cylinder
POWER: 170bhp (127kW)
0–60MPH (96KM/H): 9.3 seconds
TOP SPEED: 192km/h (127mph)
PRODUCTION TOTAL: 48,902

So called because of the shape of its hardtop roof, which was concave in profile, the Mercedes-Benz SL proved a popular roadster in the 1960s and is an enduring classic to this day.

Based on the floorpan of the Mercedes-Benz 220, but with a necessarily shorter wheelbase, the chassis boasted double wishbone suspension at the front and swing axles at the rear. Styling was by

Beautifully styled, thanks to that individual looking hardtop roof and stacked headlamps, the Mercedes-Benz SL 'Pagoda' remains one of the defining cars produced by the company during the 1960s. Long-lived, and much missed when it was replaced.

sculptor and painter Paul Bracq, and the convertible was available with either a four-speed manual or with automatic transmission.

As Mercedes offered both a coupé and a convertible, cars were available with a hood only, a hardtop and hood, or a hardtop alone, which made room for back-seat passengers – one in the 230SL and two, on a bench seat, in the 250 and 280SL. The 230SL had front disc brakes, while the bigger engined 250 (introduced in 1966) featured all-round discs and the option of a five-speed gearbox. Both the 250 and the 280 that followed in 1968 had much-improved torque.

Being more of a tourer than a sports car, this machine set the tone for future Mercedes performance cars, single-handedly taking over from both the magnificent 300SL and the 190SL.

MERCURY CYCLONE

In order to give its upper-class Comet range a bit of a sporty edge, Mercury introduced the Cyclone. Available in convertible guise, then, four years after the launch of the original, as a fastback coupé. It was clear that the emphasis was on performance.

In addition to the sporting bodystyles, a notchback version with bucket seats and an optional glassfibre roof with simulated air scoops was launched – it certainly managed to grab the attention of onlookers. As well as these 'surprise and delight' features, the Cyclone had an odd aluminium visor in the screen designed to reduce radio interference from the ignition system.

As was the case with all the muscle cars in the 1960s, the engine capacity of the Cyclone increased as the years passed, and at its peak in 1976 it had reached 425bhp (317kW). A couple of years later the Cyclone CJ appeared, which was powered by the Ford 7030cc (428cu in) Cobra engine and was bedecked with all manner of aerodynamic spoilers – and bonnet (hood) scoop with Ram Air induction fitted.

Production of the Cyclone drew to a close at the start of the 1970s, after around 90,000 cars had left the Mercury production line.

ENGINE: 7030cc (428cu in), eight-cylinder
POWER: 425bhp (317kW)
0–60MPH (96KM/H): 8.8 seconds
TOP SPEED: 213km/h (133mph)
PRODUCTION TOTAL: 90,236

LANCIA FULVIA

Long-lived and ultimately very popular, the Lancia Fulvia was a forward-looking product from a company that was confidently looking towards a prosperous 1960s. While Lancia's Appia was certainly an advanced car, the Fulvia went one step further – it featured a completely new V4 engine, The new car continued to use the front-wheel drive layout that had started with the Flavia.

The Fulvia also shared the same suspension and disc brakes as its mid-sized sibling and similar box-like styling. Once the Fulvia saloon was up and running, Lancia began to roll out a number of variants.

First came the iconic Fulvia coupé in 1962. Built on a shortened floorpan, the compact coupé was an attractive design. Following a year later, the HF (High Fidelity) coupé version was introduced. Stripped for competition, with no bumpers, additional power, aluminium panels and Plexiglas windows, it was intended more for competition than for road use.

A Zagato version of the Fulvia appeared in 1967, and it managed to look radically different to the mainstream efforts, especially at the front, with its strange headlight layout. There were constant evolutions made to the Fulvia until 1973, when the Fiat-based Beta replaced it.

ENGINE: 1298cc (79cu in), four-cylinder
POWER: 87bhp (65kW) at 6000rpm
0–60MPH (96KM/H): 15.6 seconds
TOP SPEED: 164km/h (102mph)
PRODUCTION TOTAL: 339,653

Lancia Fulvia Coupés such as this one have a particularly aggressive stance, especially when riding on wide wheels.

NSU 100/110/1200

During the 1960s, NSU continued developing its rear-engined platform to accommodate a larger range of cars. Launched in 1963, the family-oriented version of the Prinz, the 1000, featured larger, more spacious bodywork and a bigger engine – a four-cylinder air-cooled design. Styling was partially successful, but the elongated wheelbase and plastic cooling fins gave the 1000 a strange appearance. An even longer version, named 110, joined the range in 1965. Powered by a larger 1.1-litre (67cu in) version of the 100's engine, it was then joined by a 1.2-litre (73cu in) variant, called the 1200, in 1967.

An innovative optional semi-automatic transmission was added in 1970, creating a full range of cars. Despite their relatively small dimensions and small engines, the 1000 Series cars were all well made and felt larger than they actually were.

The 1000 also spawned the sporting TT version, which shared the same bodywork as the standard 1000 saloon. With lively acceleration and a 161km/h (100mph) top speed, the TT was a popular car with boy racers looking for an alternative to the Mini Cooper. On the road, it could be a handful, though, with the rear engine, rear-wheel drive layout, and lightweight body leading to serious spins in the wrong hands.

ENGINE: 996cc (61cu in), four-cylinder
POWER: 40bhp (30kW)
0–60MPH (96KM/H): 20.5 seconds
TOP SPEED: 129km/h (80mph)
PRODUCTION TOTAL: 423,704

VAUXHALL VIVA

Introduced in 1963 and powered by a 44bhp (33kW) 1057cc (65cu in) engine, for Vauxhall the Viva was a much-needed entry into the small family car market, traditionally dominated by Ford and BMC. Immediately successful, the Viva soon sired a number of variations.

In 1965, the Viva SL was launched with 66bhp (49kW), but Vauxhall did not rest on its laurels,

giving the car a serious face-lift to create the HB model. With a larger, all-new body, more modern styling, improved suspension, uprated brakes and a 56bhp (42kW) 1159cc (71cu in) engine, it seemed like a natural rival to Ford's Cortina Mk 1.

It continued to grow, and, in 1970, the Viva HC was unveiled with a choice of two- or four-door saloons, a coupé or three-door

estate (station wagon) and engines ranging from 1159cc (71cu in) to 1599cc (98cu in). This truly was Vauxhall's attempt at beating Ford at its own game.

Although mechanically similar to its predecessors, the HC's new styling and various options gave it a more grown-up feel. In 1971, the Coupe Firenza made its debut with 1159cc (71cu in), 1599cc (98cu in)

or 1975cc (121cu in) engines, and was then supplemented by a luxury Viva, called the Magnum.

ENGINE: 1057cc (65cu in), four-cylinder
POWER: 44bhp (33kW)
0–60MPH (96KM/H): 22.1 seconds
TOP SPEED: 123km/h (77mph)
PRODUCTION TOTAL: 321,332

VANDEN PLAS PRINCESS 1100 & 1300

ENGINE: 1098cc (67cu in), four-cylinder
POWER: 55bhp (41kW)
0–60MPH (96KM/H): 21.1 seconds
TOP SPEED: 136km/h (85mph)
PRODUCTION TOTAL: 43,741

Keen to capitalize on the demand for luxury small cars, BMC wasted no time in producing a Vanden Plas version of its popular 1100. Its creation was down to Fred Connolly, of the famous leather company bearing the same name, who requested that an 1100 be given the full luxury treatment for his personal use.

When BMC management saw the result, they were so impressed that the company made its own version. Arriving in 1963, the production version was available with four doors only and proved an instant success, appealing to drivers who wanted a small car with luxury. Mechanically, the car was identical to all the other 1100s produced by the BMC empire.

In 1967, a 1275cc (78cu in) engine became available, as did an automatic gearbox and a Mk II version of the 1100, complete with cropped fins. The next year the 1100 was dropped, but the Mk II

1300, with a more powerful twin-carburettor engine, was made until 1974. Today, the Vanden Plas 1100, often referred to as the Princess, enjoys a cult following – as it did in Japan during the mid-1990s.

Despite wearing the imposing grille typical of the marque, the BMC 1100 based Vanden Plas 1100 manages to pull off this feat of badge engineering with great aplomb.

AUSTIN 1100 AND 1300

Although the Mini is the most famous of Alec Issigonis' front-wheel drive creations, it was the Austin 1100 (and its derivatives) that was the most optimal. Using the same principles that he pioneered in the Mini, Issigonis developed a larger car and made it work incredibly well.

The new medium-car design was technically brilliant in many respects: the 1100 was remarkably spacious inside, thanks to clever touches and the neat layout of its transversely mounted front-wheel drive A-series engine and integral transmission, mounted in the sump. It also looked right – and the

This Mk 3 1300GT was in many ways the best and the worst of the breed. It had the panache of other 1100s, but suffered from dismal build quality.

styling tweaks that Farina applied to the design during development certainly did the trick.

The suspension was by an interconnected Hydrolastic unit, which used fluid within rubber spheres as the springing medium.

The cooling system was sealed, which put an end to the need to constantly top up the system, and there were disc brakes at the front.

The 1100 was joined by the uprated 1300 version in 1967, as well as a bewildering variety of

badge-engineered variants. The range was Britain's bestselling car for most of the 1960s and into the 1970s. It was never really profitable, however, thanks to its advanced engineering and low purchase price.

ENGINE: 1275cc (78cu in), four-cylinder
POWER: 58bhp (43kW)
0–60MPH (96KM/H): 17.3 seconds
TOP SPEED: 142km/h (88mph)
PRODUCTION TOTAL: 1,119,800

HILLMAN IMP

The brave experiment by the Rootes Group – and it may have worked too, had it not been for the delayed launch and early build glitches. Roadholding was unencumbered by the rear-engine layout.

The Hillman Imp was supposed to be the next great thing from the Rootes Group. The brave new mini-sized car was well into development before the BMC Mini was launched, but a troubled process and problems over planning permission for its new factory at Linwood near Glasgow in Scotland meant that the Imp did not appear until 1963 – four years after the launch of its major rival from Austin.

Suffering from poor build quality, early Imps were plagued with problems that damaged its image – a shame because, in many ways, the Imp was a very accomplished little car. Following the European car maker's trend of positioning the engine in the rear, the Imp's alloy Coventry Climax engine weighed very little and was surprisingly lively. The Imp was also technically advanced, with

independent suspension all-round and a clever hinging rear window giving access to folding rear seats to simulate a hatchback.

The Super Imp from 1965 gained a few luxuries, while the trendy Californian from 1967 had a coupé roofline and no hatch. Particularly sought after are the other two coupé options, the Chamois (1967–70) and the Sunbeam Stiletto (1967–72), which boasted the fast 51bhp (38kW) sports engine, a tauter suspension, servo-assisted brakes and spectacular quad headlights.

ENGINE: 875cc (53cu in), four-cylinder
POWER: 37bhp (28kW)
0–0MPH (96KM/H): 25.4 seconds
TOP SPEED: 130km/h (81mph)
PRODUCTION TOTAL: 440,032

ROVER P6

ENGINE: 1978cc (121cu in), four-cylinder
POWER: 90bhp (67kW) at 5000rpm
0–60MPH (96KM/H): 15.3 seconds
TOP SPEED: 163km/h (101mph)
PRODUCTION TOTAL: 439,135

For many Rover enthusiasts, the P6 was the high-water mark for the company, which had built an enviable reputation for quality and

solidity. When it was launched, the P6 caused quite a sensation with its daring styling and interesting technical make-up.

The new Rover was a smart car, with modern square-cut styling and a capable new overhead-camshaft 2-litre (121cu in) four-cylinder engine. Servo-assisted disc brakes were fitted all round. The P6's method of construction was unusual, effectively a steel skeleton onto which the body panels and

mechanicals were attached. Initially available only as the 1978cc (121cu in) Rover 2000, the range was to expand – first, with the automatic option in 1966, then with more power in the twin-carburettor TC model and, finally, in 1968, as the powerful Rover 3500.

The new model was the making of the Rover P6, created by using the company's alloy V8 engine to make a superb cruiser. At first this was available only in automatic

form, but the manual 3500S version followed in 1971.

Credited with helping create the 2-litre executive class (alongside the Triumph 2000), it was replaced by the equally advanced SD1.

Encompassing design flair and traditional Rover dignity, the P6 was a towering achievement. With luxury and agility it became the UK's executive car of choice.

TRIUMPH 2000

UNITED KINGDOM 1963–77

The Triumph–Michelotti partnership really bloomed with the appearance of the 2000 in 1963, a rival for the Rover 2000.

Triumph was a successful company in the ascendancy in the 1960s. As well as producing sports cars to fight MG in the US market, it was going toe to toe with Rover in the executive saloon market. Although the Rover and Triumph 2000 were very close rivals and ended up cornering the market for several years, neither company's design team (officially) knew of the existence of its rival's offering.

Both cars had their individual strengths. The Rover was more solid, whereas the Triumph boasted a smooth six-cylinder engine lifted from the outgoing Standard Vanguard. The Michelotti-styled Triumph 2000 was as sharp as it was handsome. All-independent suspension ensured a fine ride and handling. The estate (station wagon) appeared in 1965; in 1969, the Innsbruck face-lift resulted in a far stronger-looking car, thanks to a longer restyled nose and tail.

In 1968, the 2.5PI was created, by fitting a fuel-injected TR5 engine. The Lucas injection system proved unreliable, though, so a twin-carburettor version was introduced alongside it in 1974. This power boost was enough to maintain the car's competitiveness against the Rover P6B. In the end, it was replaced by the Rover SD1.

ENGINE: 1998cc (122cu in), six-cylinder
POWER: 90bhp (67kW) at 5000rpm
0–60MPH (96KM/H): 13.5 seconds
TOP SPEED: 150km/h (93mph)
PRODUCTION TOTAL: 219,816

ALFA ROMEO GIULIA

ITALY 1963–78

ENGINE: 1290cc (79cu in), four-cylinder
POWER: 55bhp (41kW)
0–60MPH (96KM/H): 15.3 seconds
TOP SPEED: 138km/h (86mph)
PRODUCTION TOTAL: 486,801

The Giulia was not exactly the most exciting model ever produced by Alfa Romeo, but it managed to sell in significant numbers in its home market. Known as the 105 series, the Giulia's conservative but neat styling reflected its underpinnings, which were closely related to the 1950s Giulietta Berlina. Despite its plain Jane looks, it was a sporting saloon with plenty of character. Styled by Alfa's star designer Dr 'Satta' Puliga, it was created to be small on the outside, but with the spaciousness of a bigger car on the inside.

Initially, it was available with a 1600cc (98cu in) engine, a five-speed gearbox, column gearshift, front bench seats and a rigid rear axle. The range expanded to include a 1290cc (79cu in) version in 1964 – identified by its single headlights and four-speed gearbox. Throughout its long production lifespan, the car's specification was gradually improved; all-round disc brakes replaced drums, and all models received a five-speed gearbox. The 1974 Giulia Nova had a slightly revised body, but the shape otherwise remained much the same until 1978, when the wedge-shaped Giulietta replaced it.

The company made its first foray into diesel power with the oil-burning Giulia in 1976.

An Alfa Romeo mainstay for a decade and a half, the Giulia proved very popular in its homeland.

MARCOS 1800

UNITED KINGDOM 1964–65

When it appeared in 1964, the Marcos 1800 was a much more handsome-looking machine than its predecessor. With styling by Dennis Adams, and a Volvo engine, the new car retained the trusted laminated plywood chassis as used in the company's previous car, the Marcos GT. With its enclosed sloping headlights, hinging front nose section, wide doors and aggressive Ford GT40-influenced rear end, it created a trademark Marcos look that became a classic and lasted the lifetime of the company.

The engine was Volvo's P1800 unit. Triumph again provided the front wishbones, with a semi de Dion and coil-sprung set-up at the rear. Sold mostly in kit form, at a fairly high price, the car held the road well and gained a strong reputation among sports-car enthusiasts. The cabin was cramped, with its fixed semi-reclining seats; adjustment of the pedal assembly was the only way taller drivers could squeeze in. The shape still looks modern today. When Marcos was relaunched in the 1990s, it was with a car that retained the 1800's memorable shape.

ENGINE: 1780cc (108cu in), four-cylinder
POWER: 114bhp (85kW)
0–60MPH (96KM/H): 9.1 seconds
TOP SPEED: 184km/h (115mph)
PRODUCTION TOTAL: 99

With its highly aerodynamic Dennis Adams designed body mounted to a plywood chassis, and powered by a Volvo engine, there was no way one could accuse Marcos for not producing a highly individual car. The styling endured, too – and reappeared on the market in the 1990s.

FERRARI 275 GTB

ITALY 1964–66

When it came time to replace the 250 GT, Ferrari produced what many critics feel is one of the most beautiful cars of all time. The 275 GTB was a Ferrari road car with state-of-the-art racing-car underpinnings, featuring a chassis with independent rear suspension and a five-speed transaxle.

The chassis may have been new, but its tubular frame construction was a mainstay of Ferrari design. The V12 engine was a development of the existing unit, but with a larger cylinder bore and dry sump lubrication – and that helped it to deliver a considerably more mid-range torque.

Three twin-choke Weber carburettors pushed the output to

280bhp (209kW), although a six-carburettor 320bhp (238kW) version was an option. The transaxle gearbox arrangement had the effect of giving even weight distribution and allowing more interior space.

The beautiful Pininfarina styling seemed to encompass the best

elements of the previous GT and a GTO, such as the cut-off tail, and bring them up to date. The cowled headlights formed part of what was called the 'short nose' body and, from 1965, a 'long nose' style was also offered.

By 1966, a 275 GTB/4 had made an appearance, which had a twin

camshaft version of the 3.3-litre (201cu in) engine.

ENGINE: 3286cc (201cu in), 12-cylinder
POWER: 280bhp (209kW)
0–60MPH (96KM/H): 7 seconds
TOP SPEED: 246km/h (153mph)
PRODUCTION TOTAL: 735

With fine aerodynamics, and near perfect 50/50 weight balance, the 250GT had a few advantages over older Ferraris. Rare and extremely desirable in any form.

GORDON-KEEBLE GK1/IT

UNITED KINGDOM 1964–66

ENGINE: 5395cc (329cu in), eight-cylinder
POWER: 300bhp (224kW)
0–60MPH (96KM/H): 7.5 seconds
TOP SPEED: 217km/h (135mph)
PRODUCTION TOTAL: 99

A short-lived but well-respected classic that combined the best of Britain, Italy and the United States is an apt description of the Gordon-Keeble GK1. Nicknamed the 'Growler', it was the brainchild of John Gordon and Jim Keeble, and first appeared as a steel-

bodied prototype at the 1960 London Motor Show.

It was not until 1964, however, that the car went into production, renamed GK1, but also known as the 'International Tourer'. The car utilized inexpensive American V8 power and possessed blistering

Of the 99 Gordon-Keebles built, an exceptionally high proportion still exist today thanks to its glassfibre bodywork. The GK1 was called 'The Growler' thanks to its ample performance and melodic soundtrack.

performance. Handling was very good, too, thanks to de Dion rear suspension and a complex square section space-frame chassis.

The styling was the work of 21-year-old Giorgetto Giugiaro, then chief stylist at Bertone, who later moved to Ghia before setting up his own studio. 'The car that was built to aircraft standards' was how the company from Eastleigh, England, marketed its glassfibre-bodied four-seater coupé. After a year, the company had produced just 80 cars, and component supply problems and underinvestment meant that Gordon-Keeble never realized its true potential.

Another 19 cars were built in 1966 under new management, but the company ceased trading later that year. Made from glassfibre and therefore rustproof, about 90 of the original 99 are still on the road.

HONDA S800
JAPAN 1966–70

In an era where most affordable sports cars soldiered on with overhead valves and low rev limits, the Honda S800 must have come as something of a shock to anyone who was fortunate enough to drive it. Thanks to the use of motorcycle technology in its exciting new engine, Honda's first effort at an open-topped sports car was the S600. It featured chain drive and its maximum power was delivered at a giddy 8000rpm.

When introduced at the 1965 Tokyo Motor Show, its replacement, the S800, revealed itself as a delicate car – available in coupé or roadster form. It continued to use advanced technology, not least the 791cc (48cu in) four-cylinder engine, which produced 70bhp (52kW) at 8000rpm – nearly 100bhp/litre.

Early examples continued to use the chain drive, and independent suspension in the rear, but Honda switched to a conventional live axle rear end with four radius rods and a Panhard rod. Later, front discs were introduced.

In 1968, the S800M was launched, which featured flush door handles, dual-circuit brakes and safety glass. These changes were made for the American market, even though the car was never actually imported there.

ENGINE: 791cc (48cu in), four-cylinder
POWER: 70bhp (52kW)
0–60MPH (96KM/H): 13.4 seconds
TOP SPEED: 152km/h (95mph)
PRODUCTION TOTAL: 11,536

FERRARI 500 SUPERFAST
ITALY 1964–67

The Ferrari 500 Superfast was a replacement for the 400 Superamerica. Unveiled to massive acclaim at the 1964 Geneva Motor Show, the car was powered by a new 4962cc (303cu in) engine, which was an interesting development of both the Colombo and Lampredi V12s; it generated a phenomenal 400bhp (298kW).

The chassis was similar to the 330 GT, and, after the first 25 500 Superfast cars had been built using the four-speed gearbox from the 400 Superamerica, the five-speed gearbox was introduced. Indeed, some 12 second-series cars, built during 1966, and identifiable only by louvres on the front wings (fenders), had the five-speed gearbox.

As befitting the name 500 Superfast, the car was capable of more than 274km/h (170mph), and reportedly could exceed 161km/h (100mph) in second gear. The body was a development of the Pininfarina 'Coupé Aerodynamico' seen on the 400 Superamerica, but it was not one of the most successful or coherent designs.

Just 37 cars were built in all, which indicated that another Ferrari attempt to break into the United States had failed. Ferrari had offered lots of luxury options and features fit for wealthy, high-profile customers such as actor Peter Sellers, but there were not enough multimillionaires in the world to buy these cars.

ENGINE: 4962cc (303cu in), 12-cylinder
POWER: 400bhp (298kW)
0–60MPH (96KM/H): 6 seconds
TOP SPEED: 280km/h (174mph)
PRODUCTION TOTAL: 37

Although in replacing the 400 Superamerica the 500 Superfast had a lot to live up to, it was a much more discreet-looking car.

LAMBORGHINI 350GT
ITALY 1964–67

Celebrated as the supercar company that had been created as the result of a spat with Ferrari, Lamborghini has become a major member of the Italian establishment. Ferruccio Lamborghini made his living making air-conditioning equipment and air-cooled diesel tractors, but his lifelong obsession was with motor cars. A former competitor in the 1948 Mille Miglia, he was not a bad driver either. After receiving a dismissive response from the Maranello factory when his car broke down, Lamborghini began a personal feud that was to result in him starting up his own sports-car manufacturing company, poaching some of Ferrari's top engineers in the process.

The 350GT was the company's first production car. Ex-Ferrari man Giotto Bizzarini was responsible for the chassis and superb V12 engine, and Touring of Milan styled the lightweight aluminium body. Giampaolo Dallara then developed the car, introducing a number of technical improvements such as the Girling disc brakes, ZF steering box, five-speed transmission and Salisbury differential at the back.

Despite being very fast, flexible and exhibiting superb handling, the 350GT lacked finesse. That said, it was an impressive first effort and paved the way for a glorious line of bedroom-wall supercars in later years.

ENGINE: 3463cc (211cu in), 12-cylinder
POWER: 270bhp (201kW)
0–60MPH (96KM/H): 6.8 seconds
TOP SPEED: 243km/h (152mph)
PRODUCTION TOTAL: 120

NSU WANKEL SPIDER

Although Felix Wankel's engine design ultimately became one of the industry's white elephants, every car powered by a rotary seemed to have a delightful character. The first car to appear with a Wankel engine under its bonnet (hood) is one not too many people will have heard of – the NSU Wankel Spider. The cute little cabriolet may have been the first car powered this way, but it was not until 1967 and the introduction of the NSU Ro80 that rotary engines were produced in any real volume. Based on the pretty Sport Prinz coupé, the Spider lost that car's roof for an even more stylish design. It may have been desirable, but its price seriously hampered sales.

The Spider had many other positive points. It was capable of a top speed of 161km/h (100mph), and the engine's lightness meant that the Prinz's already impressive handling was significantly improved.

It should have been a success, but like all early rotaries, the Wankel Spider was hampered by reliability problems that put buyers off who had not been scared away by the price. Without doubt, the Spider was interesting and a missed opportunity, but it was merely a prelude to the next – much more impressive – rotary-powered NSU.

ENGINE: 497cc (30cu in),
rotary
POWER: 50bhp (37kW)
0–60MPH (96KM/H): 16.7 seconds
TOP SPEED: 148km/h (92mph)
PRODUCTION TOTAL: 2375

VAUXHALL VICTOR FC

Making it longer and wider – and heavier in the process – the Victor FC was more spacious than its predecessor, but had a higher fuel consumption too.

Continuing Vauxhall's policy of regular skin changes for its family cars, the Victor FC (also known as the Victor 101) appeared on the scene just three years after its predecessor. Although it looked significantly different from the FB, under the skin, little had changed.

Still powered by the familiar 1594cc (97cu in) unit seen before, it was still suspended by wishbones and coil springs at the front, along with a live axle and semi-elliptic springs at the rear. The new styling was much sleeker, though, with thinner pillars, more curvaceous panels and a slightly concave rear window – a trend which did not catch on (unless you count the Citroën CX and C6). The choice of transmission was a three- or four-speed manual, along with a two-speed Powerglide automatic gearbox, available from 1966. The bold new styling offered another significant upside – the Victor 101 had one of the largest boots (trunks) in its class, more interior space and class-leading ride quality.

There was a choice of six cars across saloon and estate (station-wagon) bodyshells, including the range-topping VX4/90, which had a four-speed all-synchromesh gearbox as standard. The sporting Victor boasted a power output of 85bhp (63kW), compared to the standard car's 76bhp (57kW).

ENGINE: 1594cc (97cu in),
four-cylinder
POWER: 60bhp (45kW)
0–60MPH (96KM/H): 17.1 seconds
TOP SPEED: 137km/h (85mph)
PRODUCTION TOTAL: 219,814

MATRA DJET

One of the more technically interesting cars of the 1960s, the Djet was the first car to wear the Matra badge. Up to that point, the French Matra company was better known for making missiles, but it decided to buy out the financially ailing Bonnet Company, based in Champigny-sur-Marne, rather than let it go to the wall, following a loss-making period.

Based on René Bonnet's existing Renault-engined car, the Matra-Bonnet Djet 5, to give its full name, featured an aerodynamic plastic body with a sleek nose (much like the later Opel GT), pencil-thin chrome inserts in the front and rear bumpers, large-diameter steel wheels and a typical GT-style rear end with a reasonable-sized boot (trunk) for luggage. The tuned Renault 8 powerplant produced 70bhp (52kW) and delivered suitable performance. A later 5S version gained the Gordini engine producing 95bhp (71kW), which was then uprated in 1966 to 1255cc (77cu in) and 103bhp (77kW), and delivered truly impressive acceleration. At this point, it was renamed the Jet 6.

Once the Matra company had learned the basics of making frames and bodywork, it produced a more ambitious plan to build a larger machine – the M530.

ENGINE: 1108cc (68cu in),
four-cylinder
POWER: 70–95bhp (52–71kW)
0–60MPH (96KM/H): 9.8 seconds
TOP SPEED: 174km/h (109mph)
PRODUCTION TOTAL: 1681

OPEL DIPLOMAT

Launched in 1964, the Admiral and Diplomat made it clear that Opel was harking back to its tradition of US-inspired styling. Still, these cars, which featured lines almost identical to GM's (US) Buick Special, were actually very handsome, doing much to bolster Opel's image. A genuine rival to the prestige products of Mercedes-Benz and BMW, but at a lower price, the Admiral was relatively cheap and a very spacious big saloon, powered by the Kapitan's 2.6-litre (159cu in) engine. The luxurious Diplomat, however, aroused more interest with enthusiasts.

Under the bonnet (hood) a 4.6-(283cu in) or 5.3-litre (323cu in) V8 engine was fitted, taken from the Chevrolet Chevelle, so the Diplomat was a quick and refined cruising machine – ideal for Germany's de-restricted autobahns. Good points included a cosseting ride and excellent standard equipment, but it was very prone to rust and used a lot of fuel. Also worthy of note is the ultra-rare Diplomat Coupé, built in 1967 by coachbuilders Karmann. Elegant but very expensive, just 304 were built.

ENGINE: 4638cc (283cu in),
eight-cylinder
POWER: 230bhp (171kW)
0–60MPH (96KM/H): 10.3 seconds
TOP SPEED: 210km/h (130mph)
PRODUCTION TOTAL: 89,277

SUNBEAM TIGER

After the success of the AC Cobra, it seemed as though the rest of the British sports-car industry wanted to get in on the act. Rootes' pretty Alpine Series IV roadster seemed like an unlikely choice to go supercar chasing, but that is what happened when the company installed a 4261cc (260cu in) Ford V8 in its engine bay to create the Tiger. The car's structure was barely altered, although rack-and-pinion steering was fitted and the rear suspension modified with the addition of a Panhard rod.

Launched in 1964, and more successful in the United States, the Tiger did not inspire British buyers because of its poor braking and undersized wheels and tyres. US buyers were also much happier with its soft ride – but trouble already lay ahead. In late 1964, Chrysler took a financial stake in the Rootes Group, and that meant using a Ford engine was no longer a politically expedient move.

A Mk II version of the car was marketed for a short period in 1967 (including just 12 right-hand drive cars), with a 4727cc (288cu in) Ford engine producing 220bhp (164kW), but the Tiger was doomed – Rootes experimented with a new Tiger, but could not get the Chrysler V8 to fit.

ENGINE: 4261cc (260cu in), eight-cylinder
POWER: 164bhp (122kW)
0–60MPH (96KM/H): 9.5 seconds
TOP SPEED: 188km/h (117mph)
PRODUCTION TOTAL: 7,066

Despite having never been built for speed, the Rootes Group thought it would be a jolly good idea to install an American Ford V8 engine in the Alpine roadster. Performance was boosted, handling was upset – and in the end, the car was discontinued when Chrysler took control of Rootes.

VANDEN PLAS 4-LITRE R

ENGINE: 3909cc (239cu in), six-cylinder
POWER: 175bhp (130kW)
0–60MPH (96KM/H): 12.7 seconds
TOP SPEED: 179km/h (112mph)
PRODUCTION TOTAL: 6555

During the early 1960s, BMC and Rolls-Royce entered into discussions about a number of future collaborations. The only road car to see the light of day, however, was a relatively affordable luxury saloon, known as the Vanden Plas 4-litre R. Based on the Farina-bodied Vanden Plas 3-litre, the new car used a 4-litre (239cu in) Rolls-Royce six-cylinder engine mated to a Borg-Warner automatic gearbox. The powerful 175bhp (130kW) all-alloy engine offered refinement and torque, but too many people were aware of its military heritage, and it also used a lot of petrol.

The styling was perfectly judged, though, and more steeply raked front and rear windscreens increased headroom inside. The interior was suitably upgraded with Connolly leather seats and walnut veneer on the dash and door cappings.

From the outset, the aim was to produce 100 cars a week, but buyers remained unconvinced by the 'affordable' luxury car. By 1968, production was halted after just 6555 cars had been built. A Bentley-badged version, the Java, was also planned, but Rolls-Royce saw trouble ahead and pulled out.

The most exotic of the Farina bodied BMC saloons the Vanden Plas 4-Litre R was powered by a Rolls-Royce FB60 engine. Styling was impeccable, but handling didn't match expectations.

SKODA 1000MB

A switch to rear engines and the introduction of a less traditional and rather ugly new style marked the beginning of a downhill slide in Skoda's fortunes, when the 1000MB made an appearance in 1964. After years of producing solidly dependable cars, Skoda turned to this saloon inspired by the Renault 8 in a move to modernize its products.

The rear-engined 1000MB was powered by an overhead-valve 988cc (60cu in) engine, using an aluminium cylinder block to help keep weight down, a necessity with the powerplant hanging over the rear axle. The low compression ratio of 8.3:1 helped the engine to run on poor-quality fuel, but did not do much for the power output, which was rated at 43bhp (32kW).

From the outset, only a four-door saloon was available, but, from 1966, a twin-carburettor two-door pillarless coupé was offered. Called the 1000MBX, very few were built, as the cars were too expensive to buy. It lasted only five seasons before being replaced by the face-lifted S100/110 and, after that, the 105/120 Estelle, which lasted until 1990. The car outlived its welcome by a considerable margin and became something of an international joke.

ENGINE: 988cc (60cu in),
  four-cylinder
POWER: 43bhp (32kW)
0–60MPH (96KM/H): 30.8 seconds
TOP SPEED: 120km/h (75mph)
PRODUCTION TOTAL: 419,540

RELIANT SCIMITAR GT

The Reliant Scimitar GT car originally started life as a styling exercise built on a Daimler SP250 'Dart' chassis as designed by Ogle. The Tamworth-based company liked the shape of the SX250 so much it bought the rights, and introduced it in 1964. Suitably remodelled for the Sabre-

Six platform and called the Scimitar GT SE4, the car had the honour of becoming the company's first genuine sports-car success.

It had the by-now Reliant-traditional glassfibre bodywork, and power was lifted directly from the Ford range – initially the 2.6-litre (159cu in) Zephyr Six unit,

and, later, the V6 Essex engine developed for the Capri.

Early cars were tricky to handle at speed, but the addition of trailing arm rear suspension in 1965 reversed this defect significantly, making the later versions genuine performance cars, with excellent handling,

potent acceleration and surprisingly good build quality.

Were it not for the amount of time required to hand-build the cars, Reliant could easily have sold more Scimitars, and it stacked up quite a waiting list. However, the company – and Ogle – were already working on a larger and more powerful successor which became a serious player in the sports-car market of the late 1960s and early 1970s – the innovative hatchbacked Scimitar GTE.

ENGINE: 2994cc (183cu in),
  six-cylinder
POWER: 136bhp (101kW)
0–60MPH (96KM/H): 8.9 seconds
TOP SPEED: 195km/h (121mph)
PRODUCTION TOTAL: 1005

The Scimitar GT was a gamble upmarket for Reliant. But with Ford power and the Ogle body, sales didn't take long to pick up.

FIAT 850

ENGINE: 843cc (51cu in),
  four-cylinder
POWER: 37bhp (28kW)
0–60MPH (96KM/H): 27 seconds
TOP SPEED: 125km/h (78mph)
PRODUCTION TOTAL: 2,670,913

The Fiat 850 was directly based upon the successful rear-engined 600. As a result, it retained many of that car's mechanical components. Apart from the new and more spacious bodywork, a fresh 843cc (51cu in) four-cylinder water-cooled engine powered the 850. Two versions of the saloon were produced, the 'Normale', with 34bhp (25kW), and the 'Super', with 37bhp (28kW).

Although based on the 600, the Fiat 850 boasted sweet handling and a bigger body. The Coupé model was deliciously styled.

A Familiare model was also offered, replacing the old 600 Multipla, again using three rows of seats. This variant was in production until 1976, using a 903cc (55cu in) engine from 1970 onwards.

The 850's appeal was improved considerably with the launch of the pretty Coupé and Spider versions in 1965. Designed by Centro Stile Fiat and built by Fiat, the Coupé was an impressive in-house effort, while the Spider was designed and built by coachbuilders Bertone. The Coupé's tuned engine produced 47bhp (35kW) (49bhp/37kW for the Spider), so the addition of disc brakes was welcome. In 1966, a semi-automatic transmission was made available. An 850 Special went on sale in 1968, and was a saloon with the coupé's engine and disc brakes. The Fiat 127's arrival rendered the 850 obsolete.

TOYOTA CORONA

JAPAN 1967–72

A mainstay of the Toyota range since 1957, the Corona was typically Japanese in the way that it constantly evolved to meet the demands of its customers. During the following three decades, well into the 1980s, there was always a Corona model in Toyota's line-up.

Always intended to be a staid family saloon, by the mid-1960s it was Toyota's most successful car, earning it valuable income to develop other models. When the third-generation Corona went on sale in 1964, it represented a big leap forwards in engineering terms, with monocoque construction and a new 92bhp (69kW) 1591cc (97cu in) four-cylinder engine.

A big seller in its home market and considerably more export-friendly than the company's previous efforts, the Corona made many friends in the United States, where it was voted Imported Car of the Year in 1969 – and, in 1971,

the next-generation version was given the Car of the Year accolade.

The fourth-generation car had been launched in 1970, with a new 1707cc (104cu in) engine rated at 95bhp (71kW) or 105bhp (78kW) depending on compression ratio. To maximize sales, a whole range of bodystyles was offered, from a saloon and a coupé, to a hatchback and an estate (station wagon).

ENGINE: 1591cc (97cu in), four-cylinder
POWER: 92bhp (69kW)
0–60MPH (96KM/H): 17.2 seconds
TOP SPEED: 150km/h (94mph)
PRODUCTION TOTAL: 1,788,000

Although conventional in its engineering, the Corona proved a massive success in its home market because it delivered all that was expected with no fuss.

RELIANT REBEL

UNITED KINGDOM 1964–73

R eliant came up with the neat idea of building a Mini rival by converting its small Regal three-wheeler into four-wheel spec. There was another good reason for producing the car, too – drivers who liked the Reliant Regal, but had earned a full driving licence, now had a car they could buy without leaving the fold. The Rebel

used the same engines, gearbox and rear-end set-up as the three-wheeler version, and was a relatively easy car for Reliant to develop.

The glassfibre bodywork was not pretty, but the car was surprisingly useful, especially in estate (station-wagon) form. The Rebel never really posed a threat to more conventional compact cars

such as the Ford Anglia, Mini or Hillman Imp, however, because of its relatively high price.

Handling was entertaining, although the trade-off was a bumpy ride and large amounts of interior noise from the Austin Seven-based aluminium engine. It was very slow, even with the largest capacity 748cc (46cu in)

unit installed, but non-metal bodywork meant it did not rust and was surprisingly tough.

ENGINE: 700cc (43cu in), four-cylinder
POWER: 31bhp (23kW)
0–60MPH (96KM/H): 35.9 seconds
TOP SPEED: 110km/h (68mph)
PRODUCTION TOTAL: 700

PLYMOUTH BARRACUDA

UNITED STATES 1964–74

T he Ford Mustang might have been a massively important 'pony car', but GM had recognized the significance of Ford's upcoming new sports car and introduced its similarly conceived Barracuda in the same year. Although it was pretty, the 'Cuda simply could not match Ford's combination of performance, value and versatility.

Based on the Valiant saloon and sharing its frontal styling, the Barracuda could still seat six people on two bench seats. The distinctive styling was certainly pretty, featuring a huge curved screen, which wrapped round into the D-pillars. Considering its sporting styling, the Barracuda was practical – its clever folding

rear seat allowed for plenty of room for carrying loads.

A 'Formula S' performance option was introduced in 1965 with about 10 per cent more power; however, the 'Cuda still could not compete with the fastest Mustangs or Pontiacs. The S-pack also helped the car's handling by needing firmer suspension bushes and anti-roll bars, which helped to improve the standard model's handling at speed.

In 1967, an all-new Barracuda was launched and was a much more competitive proposition in the pony-car market, thanks to a longer wheelbase and bigger engine range, lead by a 6.3-litre (384cu in) V8, plus potent smaller units (although the base 5.0-litre

(305cu in) model still delivered only a very modest 145bhp (108kW). The wraparound rear screen had gone and three different bodystyles were now offered – a fastback coupé, a notchback coupé, ande a two-door six-seat convertible.

Again, a Formula S pack was offered and came with suspension modifications, fatter tyres and a rev counter, plus special Formula S decals. Power steering and a 330bhp (246kW) engine introduced in 1969 helped to boost the car's appeal, but it was not until 1970 that Plymouth got really serious about performance.

The Barracuda for the new decade was introduced in late 1970. Body panels, engines and

transmission were shared with the equally muscular Dodge Challenger, and, at last, Chrysler had created a brace of muscle cars that could compete with Ford and GM. The styling was similar to the Chevy Camaro, with barrel sides, a four-headlight snout and pillarless coupé panels on hardtop models, but the V8s were more potent than ever, especially when equipped with the tuned 7.2-litre (440cu in) Hemi engine lifted from the Plymouth Superbird. This gave the Barracuda a sensational 0–60mph (96km/h) time of 5.2 seconds and a top speed of 233km/h (145mph).

Hemi-engined cars also came with a large bonnet (hood) scoop, and, unlike most American cars with this feature, it was actually essential to the engine's induction efficiency; the additional air intake was routed directly to the carburettor housing. Between 1970 and 1972, the Barracuda achieved considerable success both in the showroom and in competition, although it still remained a slow seller compared to the mighty Ford Mustang.

The introduction of environmental legislation in 1972 saw the Hemi engines dropped and the most powerful 'Cuda putting out 240bhp (179kW). That, combined with the 1970s energy crisis, marked the end of the Barracuda. It slipped away quietly in 1974.

ENGINE: 4490cc (696cu in), eight-cylinder
POWER: 235bhp (175kW)
0–60MPH (96KM/H): 8.8 seconds
TOP SPEED: 181km/h (112mph)
PRODUCTION TOTAL: 391,887

Fans of the Rootes Group in the UK might find the original Plymouth Barracuda rather familiar-looking because the later Sunbeam Rapier looked like a scaled-down version. However, the later car pictured here made no bones about its thundering performance.

AUSTIN 1800 AND 2200
UNITED KINGDOM 1964–75

By the mid-1960s, BMC had transformed itself into a forward-thinking producer of innovative cars. The Mini and 1100 had popularized front-wheel drive, but what was needed next was a larger car to replace the stuffy Farina range of saloons.

Clever though it was, the bigger 1800 range struggled on the market, despite its resemblance to the bestselling 1100. It won Car of the Year when it was launched, an accolade previously enjoyed by the Rover 2000. The first version, the 1800, used a detuned MGB engine mounted transversely and linked to a new front-wheel drive transmission. The suspension was, like the 1100, Hydrolastic.

Following the 1100 range, BMC introduced its front wheel drive 1800. Ungainly styling and odd proportions led to its nickname 'Landcrab'.

It should have been a success. The 1800 was strong and very spacious, but let down by heavy steering, a poor driving position and terrible gearchange. Power assistance came in 1967, but the spartan interior (another Issigonis feature) turned buyers off.

In 1972, the 2200 arrived. To improve performance and refinement, a six-cylinder engine, also mounted transversely, was fitted. The engine was actually based on the four-cylinder Maxi E-series overhead-camshaft unit and very refined. Still, this upward extension of the range failed in the face of in-house competition from the Rover and Triumph 2000s.

ENGINE: 1798cc (110cu in), four-cylinder
POWER: 80bhp (60kW)
0–60MPH (96KM/H): 17.1 seconds
TOP SPEED: 145km/h (90mph)
PRODUCTION TOTAL: 221,000

FORD MUSTANG
UNITED STATES 1964–78

The Mustang was a surprise hit for Ford – one that caught the imagination of an entire generation. It was originally designed as a European-style two-seater, but Mustang creator, Lee Iacocca, knew that volume sales were crucial for the breed's future success. Sharing the platform and as many parts as possible with the compact Falcon to keep production costs down, the Mustang was powered by a either a six-cylinder or V8 engine.

In mid-1964, Ford introduced the sporting 2+2 fastback bodystyle to go along with the hardtop coupé and convertible. Enthusiasts loved the new 271bhp (202kW) V8 that finally delivered the performance to match the sensational looks. For those who wanted more, Carroll Shelby and Ford collaborated on the Shelby GT-350, a Ford Mustang fastback. The 4736cc (289cu in) V8 produced 306bhp (228kW) in standard tune and 360bhp (268kW) in GT-350R race tune.

Development continued apace, and, in 1967, a considerable revision saw the styling become more aggressive, with a new grille, a concave tail panel and a full fastback roofline for the coupé. There was now more room for a big block 6391cc (390cu in) unit to replace the 4727cc (288cu in) engine. Shelby-tuned Mustangs became more outrageous, as the new GT500 was powered by a reworked 7014cc (428cu in) V8; these were the last Shelby Mustangs actually built by Shelby-American.

The Mustang was completely restyled for the 1969 model year, and the character began to change –

it was growing. A new Mach 1 was powered by a 5752cc (351cu in) V8, but also available with the 7014cc (428cu in) Cobra Jet unit.

The 'Boss' series Mustangs were named after stylist Larry Shinoda's nickname for Ford president Semon Knudsen. Boss Mustangs were built to qualify for the NASCAR series and came with a race-ready 7030cc (429cu in) V8 with ram air induction, header-type exhaust manifolds running through a four-speed manual gearbox and a 3.91:1 Traction-Lok axle.

The original 'Pony Car' was an astute creation. European in thinking, great looking but affordable, it became the fastest-selling car of its era.

The year 1971 was a watershed one for the Mustang, as it grew again – but just as damaging to the Mustang image was the disappearance of the Shelby and some of the Boss models. Engines were detuned for emissions, and the 351 V8 had dropped to just 156bhp (116kW).

The restyled Mustang of 1974 abandoned any pretence of offering performance. In the post-energy crisis years, and at a time when safety regulations were coming thick and fast, Ford responded in the only way it knew how – by downsizing. The top speed from the six-cylinder 2.8-litre (171cu in) version was now a paltry 164km/h (102mph), and, worse than that, 60mph (96km/h) came up in over

13 seconds. Although the Mustang has been neutered compared with its predecessors from only a decade previously, these European-sized cars kept the name alive, even if enthusiasts did not like what had happened to the once-great car. Sales remained strong, though. By 1978, over 1 million Mustang IIs had found new homes. A sad decline for a once-great name ...

ENGINE: 4727cc (288cu in), eight-cylinder
POWER: 271bhp (202kW)
0–60MPH (96KM/H): 8.3 seconds
TOP SPEED: 193km/h (120mph)
PRODUCTION TOTAL: 2,385,039

EXCALIBUR

Back in the 1960s before the classic movement had taken off, there was no such thing as the nostalgia car – assuming you discount the Morgan, which had been in continuous production since the 1930s. So when Brooks Stevens, a leading industrial designer, came up with the Excalibur, he arguably created the market for this new breed of faux-historic cars.

Although content to build racing cars based on Kaiser Chassis and using a variety of engines from Willys to Jaguar, in 1964 Stevens conceived a road car which he called the Studebaker SS. Essentially a high-quality contemporary replica of a Mercedes SSK, it was based on a Lark Daytona convertible chassis with a glassfibre body.

Studebaker withdrew its endorsement of the project, but so stunning was the reaction to the car at the 1964 New York Auto Show that Stevens built it anyway. The Excalibur was powered by the Chevrolet Corvette's V8 engine, and a four-door body was offered. By 1970, production was in the hands of Stevens's sons, David and William, and the Excalibur II now had a purpose-built chassis and a bigger 350 Chevrolet V8 engine.

They restricted production to no more than five cars a week to maintain demand. The Excalibur Series III from 1975 was the last car to be directly descended from the original SS and had a big block 454 V8 powerplant.

ENGINE: 4738cc (289cu in), eight-cylinder
POWER: 289bhp (215kW)
0–60MPH (96KM/H): 7 seconds
TOP SPEED: 201km/h (125mph)
PRODUCTION TOTAL: 1848

Designed to look like a pre-war Mercedes-Benz SSK but with simple homegrown mechanicals, the Excalibur was a long-lived nostalgia car. Although lacking taste it undeniably stood out in a Las Vegas car park.

RENAULT 16

Not an obvious candidate for stardom, the Renault 16 was actually one of the 1960s most important cars. The monocoque body housed Renault's first front-wheel drive arrangement on a large car, although, unlike the BMC equivalents, the engine was mounted longitudinally. The unit was thoroughly modern, however, with an aluminium cylinder head and block and wet liners. It would go on to power millions of Renault vehicles well into the 1990s.

The long-travel fully independent suspension, which employed all-round torsion bars, guaranteed a soft ride, and soft and supportive seats and a well-trimmed cabin merely enhanced the feeling of luxury. The column-change gearbox was popular on the Continent, but British buyers could not get on with it, although this was not a problem for most owners, as it was light and smooth to operate.

The R16's claim to fame was its hatchback rear end. Other cars had been built with an opening rear hatch before, including the Renault 4, but it was the 16 that introduced such practicality to large mainstream family cars, and it would not be rivalled until Austin's Maxi debuted in 1969. The 16TX and TXE were the top models, with luxury cabins.

ENGINE: 1647cc (101cu in), four-cylinder
POWER: 93bhp (69kW)
0–60MPH (96KM/H): 12.9 seconds
TOP SPEED: 152km/h (94mph)
PRODUCTION TOTAL: 1,846,000

CHEVROLET CHEVELLE

The Chevelle Supersport SS was Chevrolet's entry into the mid-size muscle-car market battle against the Pontiac GTO, and was suitably quick.

The ultimate Chevelle SS soon had the most powerful rated engine in muscle-car history, pushing out a magnificent 450bhp (336kW), in the LS6 454 in 1970. The last year for the SS before the whole range was redesigned and the engines detuned was 1973. The new Colonnade hardtop styling meant that inner and outer shells and heavy roof pillars were used.

Designed to fit between the compact Chevy II and the company's full-sized cars, the all-new Chevelle of 1964 was labelled as a 'senior compact'. Eleven models were available in two basic lines, called the Chevelle 300 and the Malibu, although a convertible was added to the range. The Chevelle Supersport SS started out life with a 5359cc (327cu in) V8, and was later fitted with a more powerful 6489cc (396cu in) V8. In 1968, the Chevelle received a thorough face-lift, and an estate (station wagon) variation was launched. The front end looked rakish, the bonnet (hood) was stretched out and the boot (trunk) line shortened, while the two-door got a new fastback look.

ENGINE: 6489cc (396cu in), eight-cylinder
POWER: 375bhp (279kW)
0–60MPH (96KM/H): 7 seconds
TOP SPEED: 193km/h (120mph)
PRODUCTION TOTAL: 3,282,066

TRABANT 601

Before the Iron Curtain came down in 1989, the Trabant 601 provided cheap and no-frills transport for millions of families in the Eastern Bloc. After that event, it became an unwanted object of mirth.

The Trabant 601 emerged, blinking, into the limelight with Germany's reunification In 1989. When the borders between East and West were opened, lines of Trabbies pressed into Western Europe. Seen everywhere, they became obsolete (and almost worthless) overnight, yet were seen as the ultimate in ironic chic. Based on the 600, the 601 entered production in 1964 with almost no development. Various 601 bodystyles were on offer, the most popular being the saloon, known as the Limousine. There was also the option of a military version, an estate (station wagon) (Universal) or a cabriolet, built by Osnabruck-based coachbuilder Osterman.

During 26 years of production, there remained little development.

From 1965, an automatic gearbox was offered as an option, and, in 1969, an extra 3bhp (2kW) was added to the engine. Twelve-volt electrics arrived in 1983 and, from May, 1990 a 1.1-litre (67cu in) VW Polo engine was used. With the new power unit, acceleration in this lightweight saloon was almost indecently quick. But the Trabant's strongest point was its reliability, based on its simplicity – important when its customers had little money to fix it when it went wrong.

ENGINE: 594cc (36cu in), two-stroke four-cylinder
POWER: 26bhp (19kW)
0–60MPH (96KM/H): n/a
TOP SPEED: 100km/h (62mph)
PRODUCTION TOTAL: about 3,000,000

MINI

ENGINE: 848cc (52cu in), four-cylinder
POWER: 33bhp (25kW)
0–60MPH (96KM/H): 27.1 seconds
TOP SPEED: 116km/h (72mph)
PRODUCTION TOTAL: 5,505,874

Without doubt, the Mini did more to popularize the front-wheel drive layout than any other car. There were many front-driven cars before it, but what the baby saloon, designed by Alec Issigonis, did was to combine a clever engine/gearbox arrangement with an amazingly packaged car – and make it fun to drive. In many ways, the following generations of superminis all owed their existence to the small car from BMC that had been conceived to drive the bubblecars off the roads.

When it was launched in 1959, it was incredibly well priced – just £496 – almost £50 cheaper than the Ford Anglia. Mechanical space-savers included a sump-mounted four-speed gearbox, plus an unusual rubber cone suspension system developed by Dr Alex Moulton, who would also create the unusual fluid and gas-filled Hydrolastic and Hydragas systems fitted to later BMC products.

It was not just the clever layout and low pricing that made the Mini a big hit. The car was also had cute looks, a sporty exhaust note and a hard and bumpy ride giving it immense character. Driven hard, it could be cornered at incredible speeds and was much quicker than the performance figures suggested. As well as the excellent handling, the steering was incredibly communicative. In an era of podgy family saloons, the Mini's range of abilities was absolutely amazing.

When it was announced, it was badged either the Austin Seven or Morris Mini Minor, but most people just called it 'Mini' – the title it officially received in 1968. In 1967, the Mini received its first face-lift, and received a new radiator grille, larger door handles, a bigger rear window and all-synchromesh gearchange, and the adoption (briefly) of Hydrolastic suspension. The floor-mounted ignition (which caused problems in the wet) had been dropped by this time.

A 1.0-litre (61cu in) A-Series engine joined the range on top-specification cars, providing 42bhp (31kW) and a 137km/h (85mph) top speed. British Leyland, as Britain's biggest car maker was now known, introduced the Mini Clubman in 1969 by adding a Roy

Haynes–styled squared-off snout and flat bonnet (hood). Buyers preferred the original, and the Clubman never met its sales targets. In 1980, it was dropped when the Metro was introduced, leaving the original car to soldier on through the 1980s.

Basic City and luxury Mayfair specifications were offered in the 1980s, plus a host of special editions using both 1.0- (61cu in) and 1.3-litre (79cu in) A-Series engines. Sales dwindled, but demand remained strong enough to make Mini production worthwhile, especially in Japan.

BMW took over the Rover Group (which replaced BL) in 1994, and allowed company to press on with plans for a replacement. After 5.5 million cars had been sold, a record for a British car, the last Mini rolled off the production line at Longbridge, Birmingham, England, in October 2000. It was the end of an era.

The Mini was an incredibly compact design, and the driver's proximity to the road seemed to amplify the perceived speed – in reality, standard minis had a top speed of just 116km/h (72mph).

MINI MOKE

UNITED KINGDOM 1964–94

Both the Gipsy and the Champ, BMC's previous attempts to produce cars for the military, had failed. When Mini designer, Alec Issigonis, penned the Moke, the new car followed its predecessors' into obscurity, but for its cult following.

A lot of money was invested in creating a basic, low-maintenance Mini variant to use for ferrying army personnel, but the armed forces dismissed it because of its lack of ground clearance.

BMC tried to sell the Moke to the public, but sales were never strong. The problem was simple: it was very open, and the British climate was wet. In 1966, production shifted to Australia, where the Moke enjoyed more success as a basic carry-all. A factory opened in Portugal in 1980 to build Mokes under licence.

ENGINE: 848cc (52cu in), four-cylinder
POWER: 34bhp (25kW)
0–60MPH (96KM/H): 27.9 seconds
TOP SPEED: 135km/h (84mph)
PRODUCTION TOTAL: 14,518
(UK production)

PORSCHE 911

GERMANY 1964–PRESENT

Along with the MGB and the Datsun 240Z, the Porsche 911 is one of the most iconic sports cars ever produced. Unlike its classic counterparts, the 911 remains very much in production today and still at the cutting edge of supercar technology.

The original 911 was launched in 1964 as a replacement for the 356, although this time it had an extra bank of cylinders and was targeted at a more sporting, and wealthy, sector of the market. Ferdinand Porsche's sons, Ferry and Butzi, designed the 911 to iron out the 356's unpredictable on-limit handling characteristics, and it had a more forgiving all-new rear suspension. Even so, the car

still had a strong tendency to oversteer and needed expert handling at high speeds.

From launch, all 911s came with a five-speed gearbox, with a dog-leg first gear and all-round disc brakes, while quick steering and a clever torsion bar suspension set up at the rear made the 911 a particularly agile and encouraging car for a competent driver to drive quickly. The first cars used a 1991cc (121cu in) flat-six, which developed a sporting 130bhp (97kW) and gave a top speed of 210km/h (130mph). By 1967, three power outputs were available, with the quickest cars boasting 170 bhp (127kW), while engine capacity increased to

2.2 litres (134cu in) for 1969, with a more even spread of torque and flexible in-gear performance.

The power continued to rise, and in 1971, the 2.4-litre (146cu in) unit was introduced – and, the following year, the Carrera name made a return with the legendary 2.7 RS (165cu in). Built for just one year, the Carrera RS could easily top 250km/h (155mph). For 1973, the 2.7-litre (165cu in) engine was standardized, and power outputs rose to between 150 and 210bhp (112 and 156kW). A two-pedal semi-auto Sportomatic transmission was also offered as an option on all examples – it never took off.

A legend was unveiled at the 1974 Paris Motor Show. As a direct

consequence of the competition cars, a turbocharged model was announced. Although expensive, the production version (which appeared the following year) could storm from 0–60mph (96km/h) in just 5.6 seconds and hit 257km/h (160mph). Power delivery was not smooth, mostly because of turbo lag. The 911 continued strongly into the 1980s; as the economic boom in Europe and the United States saw demand for sports cars rise, Porsche capitalized. In 1983, the Carrera name was to return, and the engine range was expanded to 3.2 litres (195cu in).

All-new Carrera 2 and Carrera 4 models appeared in 1989, which were heavily revised versions of the original car, but, when the 993 appeared in 1993, the air-cooled engines were finally dropped. An all new bodyshell appeared in 1998 with the Porsche 996, which was then subtly revised in 2004 to become the type 997. Although the 911 has evolved, it retains the same basic look and rear-engined layout of the original 1964 car.

ENGINE: 2993cc (183cu in), six-cylinder
POWER: 230bhp (171kW)
0–60MPH (96KM/H): 5.5 seconds
TOP SPEED: 250km/h (155mph)
PRODUCTION TOTAL: n/a

Introduced in 1964 and available in a similar form today, the Porsche 911 is proof positive of sticking with a winning formula.

CHAPTER FOUR

A TRULY GLOBAL INDUSTRY

1965–1980

The late Sixties saw the excesses of the previous decade rapidly toned down – but not without a fight!

For a period of almost ten years, America was gripped by the muscle car phenomenon, with the likes of the Pontiac GTO, Chevrolet Chevelle SS, Plymouth Barracuda and Dodge Charger cleverly combining the affordability and practicality of a family sedan with the performance of a sports car.

Fascinating as muscle cars were, however, they were killed by environmental legislation and fuel shortages, which saw more and more compact cars coming onto the market.

America brought in sports cars from Europe, as they were more economical than homegrown models, while in Japan a fledgling car industry was readying itself to make a huge impact. Japan's first sports car, the Datsun 240Z, made its debut in 1969

and left both American and British manufacturers reeling in shock – nobody was prepared for the 240Z's impact, which gave the Japanese a real foothold in both the American and European markets and proved they were able to compete with the best domestic manufacturers.

Over the next decade, the Japanese industry became as large as those in the US and Europe, while elsewhere across the globe major manufacturers emerged from Australia, Korea and South Africa, importing and exporting cars the world over. The automotive industry truly had become a global stage.

By the 1980s, the motor industry had become huge, and a car was a commodity owned by most people. Luxury, performance and comfort had reached new levels, and there was a car to suit all tastes and pockets, from a humble city runaround to a fully-fledged supercar.

As the motor industry grew more and more global, car makers looked for opportunities to export to other markets where they saw potential for their cars. The Sonnet was Swedish maker Saab's attempt to grow its sales in America, although the car was never a huge success.

DE TOMASO VALLELUNGA

ITALY 1965–67

The first-ever De Tomaso model might have been seriously flawed, but it was a great example of one man's vision being turned into a reality, despite having the odds stacked against him. Argentinian Alejandro de Tomaso fled his home country because of

With its rounded nose and faired-in headlamps, the Vallelunga looked almost like a Ferrari from the front.

the fraught political climate there, and ended up in Italy, where he indulged his passion for racing cars, working closely with the Maserati brothers.

De Tomaso's dream was to build his own car, and so he did. In his own time, Alejandro assembled a bespoke spaceframe chassis and fitted it with the engine from a humble Ford Cortina, simply because the four-cylinder unit did not take up much space and was relatively straightforward to tune.

He approached others in the motor industry with his idea, and won the backing of top stylist Giorgetto Guigiaro, who designed the two-seater bodywork that surrounded it. The result was the astonishingly pretty Vallelunga – a car that looked great, but suffered from dramatic chassis flex and some startling handling characteristics.

Despite the faults, the seed had been sown, and de Tomaso went on to build a whole range of individually styled Ford-engined

cars with bespoke chassis and great styling, against the odds and with incredibly tight finances. The Vallelunga became the opening chapter in one of the most defiant stories in motoring history.

ENGINE: 1498cc (91cu in), four-cylinder
POWER: 100bhp (75kW)
0–60MPH (96KM/H): 10 seconds
TOP SPEED: 176km/h (110mph)
PRODUCTION TOTAL: 50

GLAS 2600 V8

GERMANY 1965–67

German engineer Hans Glas had achieved a surprising amount of success with his off the-wall Goggomobil microcar, so his next project was a somewhat surprising choice. Aimed at buyers who would usually have chosen a Porsche, or possibly one of the less sporting Aston Martins, the Glas 2600 V8 was an interesting venture into the

unknown. Nicknamed the 'Glaserati', thanks to its pin-sharp styling, carried out by Frua of Italy, the 2600 V8 had a semi-fastback appearance and unusual frontal styling. The interior was adorned with wood and leather, and power came from a 2.6-litre (159cu in) V8 engine of Glas's own design – effectively two 1300cc units welded together.

In concept, the 2600 V8 was a great car, and it won praise for its build quality, neat handling and styling. Despite the best efforts of BMW, which invested in the project and attempted to sell the car as its own for the last two years, the Glas did not have the market presence or reliability to deliver what German executive car buyers wanted. After

just three years, this brave effort was consigned to the history books.

ENGINE: 2.6-litre (159cu in), eight-cylinder
POWER: 140bhp (104kW)
0–60MPH (96KM/H): 8.7 secs
TOP SPEED: 193km/h (120mph)
PRODUCTION TOTAL: 300

AC COBRA 427

UNITED KINGDOM 1965–68

There are legends of motoring, then there are the cars that go on to attain hero status, adorning the bedroom walls of teenage boys

throughout the world, regardless of when they were built.

These are cars such as the AC Cobra 427, a car so desirable that

it has managed to transcend time and, despite being an ancient design, is even today still in some kind of production, albeit as the

toned-down AC Superblower. The 427 first appeared in 1965, on the back of the already rapid Cobra 289. It was built primarily for

motorsport homologation purposes, after former chicken farmer and Ford's racing supreme Carroll Shelby decreed that the 289 simply was not fast enough to be guaranteed success on the racetrack.

At the time, Ferrari was starting to make a comeback, and the Cobra 289's dominance on the world's circuits was coming to an end. Rumours were rife of a 7-litre (427cu in) Chevrolet Corvette in the offing, and the Ford-backed AC enterprise looked as if it was about to lose its footing. But not if Shelby could help it.

Even then, the 427 came about by accident. In December 1963, Shelby and his workforce were busy preparing some Ford Galaxies for a NASCAR race, when one of his mechanics suggested that the

big sedan's 7-litre (427cu in) powerplant could be just the thing to make the Cobra go faster. After all, in those days there really was no substitute for cubic inches. The idea sounded ridiculous, not least because the Cobra's bodyshell was based on the compact AC Ace and was originally designed to house a four-cylinder engine. Yet Shelby's team managed to shoehorn the big-block V8 under the bonnet (hood) and fit a larger radiator and bigger wheels and tyres.

On its first trial, it became immediately apparent that the 427 was utterly terrifying. The 289's leaf-spring chassis could not cope with the 427's power, making it impossible to accelerate in a straight line. Luckily, by this point, Ford had regained interest in the

project, and the company paid for the rear suspension to be completely overhauled, with coil springs and a wider rear track helping the Cobra to deliver more grip and unbelievably quick acceleration. The concept was then handed over to AC to finish, and, rather than create a whole new body for the car, AC instead gave the 427 huge flared rear wheelarches and beefy side exit exhaust pipes.

The 427 was amazingly well received, and was of course a huge success on the racetracks. Yet, despite this, few were ever sold to members of the public, who were put off by the 427's impracticality and reputation for being thoroughly frightening to drive, especially in the wet. Nonetheless, the car remains one

It was the fastest car of its day, and also a real brute. Cobra 427s required very careful handling! A huge success on the racetracks, but the general public were put off by its frightening reputation.

of motoring's all-time legends, and spawned hundreds of copies from kit-car manufacturers, as well as a raft of similar models from AC itself, which continues to trade off the 427's reputation.

ENGINE: 6984cc (427cu in), eight-cylinder
POWER: 425bhp (317kW)
0–60MPH (96KM/H): 4.2 seconds
TOP SPEED: 266km/h (165mph)
PRODUCTION TOTAL: 306

GHIA 450SS

The concept behind the Ghia 450SS was an interesting one – to create a European car for the American market. The brainchild of US businessman Bert Sugarman, the car was styled on the look of Fiat's 2300S, which Sugarman had seen on the cover of an Italian car magazine and had instantly fallen in love with. He approached the Ghia styling studio in Turin and

asked them to create a car for him, based on the chassis of a stock Plymouth Barracuda and sharing the American car's 4.5-litre (274cu in) Chrysler Commander V8 engine.

In profile, the 450SS looked stunning, its squared-off rear and flat waistline giving it an appearance to match contemporary Ferraris. It was not so successful at the front, where critics drew attention to its

twin headlight and excessive use of chrome – styling traits that Sugarman saw as essential to make the car appeal to the US market, but which, in the eyes of some enthusiasts, detracted from the Ghia's appeal to those who put style before status. All 450SSs were handmade, and it is unclear how many were built in total; the outright figure is believed to be

somewhere in the hundreds, of which only a handful still survive. They are coveted by collectors and rarely come onto the open market.

ENGINE: 4490cc (274cu in), eight-cylinder
POWER: 235bhp (175kW)
0–60MPH (96KM/H): 8.9 seconds
TOP SPEED: 200km/h (125mph)
PRODUCTION TOTAL: n/a

BIZZARINI GT STRADA 5300

ITALY 1965–69

The GT Strada 5300 is the work of the man behind one of the most famous car designs of all time. Giotto Bizzarini was one of Ferrari's top designers and was responsible for the look of the famous 250

Although based on the ISO Grifo, the aerodynamic nose of the Strada meant it looked completely different.

GTO. But behind the scenes at Ferrari, Bizzarini was one of many engineers and designers who failed to see eye to eye with boss Enzo Ferrar. Eventually he walked out of the Maranello factory in order to set up his own car company.

Initially working as a consultant for Lamborghini and ISO, designing the ISO Grifo, Bizzarini continued working for Ferrari on motorsport projects, but it was his work with

ISO that would eventually see his life's dream become a reality. He competed behind the wheel of an ISO Grifo at the 1964 Le Mans 24-Hour and won the GT class, which helped him to negotiate a deal with ISO boss Renzo Rivolta to create his own race-bred version of the Grifo for road and track use.

The car became the GT Strada 5300. Like the Grifo, it was powered by a 5.3-litre (326cu in) Chevrolet

small-block V8, mounted on a low-slung chassis and clothed in a more aerodynamic version of the Grifo's body, cast from aluminium. Only a handful was ever made.

ENGINE: 5343cc (326cu in), eight-cylinder
POWER: 365bhp (272kW)
0–60MPH (96KM/H): n/a
TOP SPEED: 258km/h (160mph)
PRODUCTION TOTAL: 149

PORSCHE 912

GERMANY 1965–69

The Porsche 911 might have been a legend, but it was the 912 that was closest to Porsche's roots. Launched in 1965 to plug the gap left in the range by the decision to withdraw the 356C, the 912 shared the 911's pretty coupé bodywork and chassis set-up, but had only four cylinders instead of six.

The 1582cc (97cu in) unit was the same as used in the 356 and offered a modest 90bhp (67kW) power output, while the standard transmission was a four-speed

Aside from the more basic trim, it was difficult to tell the Porsche 912 apart from the legendary 911. Most differences were mechanical.

manual instead of the 911's five-speed shift (although the 911 gearbox was offered as an option in later cars).

To keep costs low, the 912 also had a much more basic cabin than the 911, with plastic seats, fewer

dials and a generally lower level of standard equipment.

While not earning itself the legendary status of the 911, the 912 does have its followers, who appreciate the car's lighter weight. It is easier to drive than an early

911, with less tendency towards oversteer, while even some of the 911's biggest fans will tell you that the smoother clutch and lighter steering make the 912 a more entertaining car to drive away from a high-speed environment.

ENGINE: 1582cc (97cu in), four-cylinder
POWER: 90bhp (67kW)
0–60MPH (96KM/H): 11.8 seconds
TOP SPEED: 177km/h (110mph)
PRODUCTION TOTAL: 30,300

RILEY KESTREL

The British Motor Corporation created the concept of 'badge engineering', where one particular design of car is sold with various different brand names in order to broaden its appeal to buyers of other brands. The BMC 1100/1300 series of cars, introduced in 1963, was the most varied selection of

badge-engineered models yet, with the Austin, Morris, MG, Riley, Wolseley and Vanden Plas names all appearing at some stage during the model's career.

The Riley Kestrel debuted in 1965 and used the MG version's sportier engine, coupled to the luxury interior features that buyers

expected from a Wolseley. The latest Kestrels were really quite lively, fitted with a 1275cc (67cu in) version of Austin's venerable A-Series and twin carburettors. As long as you kept on top of the bodyshell's keenness to rust, the Kestrel was a pleasant and entertaining car to own. While it

may not be especially collectable, it remains an interesting curiosity.

ENGINE: 1098cc (67cu in), four-cylinder
POWER: 55bhp (41kW)
0–60MPH (96KM/H): 17.3 seconds
TOP SPEED: 144km/h (89mph)
PRODUCTION TOTAL: 21,529

ASTON MARTIN DB6

You could be forgiven for thinking that the DB6 was merely an update of the existing DB5, but to do so would be wrong. Visually, the car was unmistakably a member of the DB family, and from a distance it is almost impossible to tell it and the earlier car apart. But look closely and you will see that every single panel is different, most notably at the rear where the roof is extended out to the boot (trunk) to give the car a more streamlined profile.

The engineering was significantly different, too. Instead of stretching the aluminium panels out over a lightweight separate chassis, as with previous cars, Aston Martin used folded metal panels to add extra lateral strength and make the car much easier to produce. Under the skin, revised suspension, steering and dampers made it a

much more compliant car to drive, while the 4.0-litre (243cu in) straight-six engine was both smooth and lively. A Mk 2 version appeared in 1969, and along with it came a convertible model called the Volante. A soft-top had been offered previously, but, although it looked like a DB6 it was actually based on a DB5 chassis and was nowhere near as good to drive.

Earlier cars are known as 'short-chassis' Volantes, to distinguish them from the much better later cars, but their rarity means that they have greater collector interest.

ENGINE: 3995cc (243cu in),
 six-cylinder
POWER: 325bhp (242kW)
0–60MPH (96KM/H): 6.5 seconds
TOP SPEED: 239km/h (148mph)
PRODUCTION TOTAL: 1755

Longer, wider and lower than the DB5 it replaced, the DB6 was still unmistakably an Aston Martin. Under the skin, revised suspension, steering and dampers made it a much more compliant car to drive.

TOYOTA SPORTS 800

Had the Japanese car industry been the global superpower it is today, then, in 1965, Toyota could have had a real winner on its hands. Interestingly styled, great to drive and amazingly cheap to run, the Sports 800 was Toyota's first toe in the sports-car water.

The car may have had offbeat styling, but there was no denying that the Sports 800 was a true

delight to drive. Derived from the very ordinary Publica saloon (sold as the Corolla in Europe), the Sports 800 was powered by an air-cooled flat-twin engine of just 790cc (48cu in), which delivered only 49bhp (37kW). Yet despite the modest power output, the car was incredible fun. It was light in weight, which meant that it was able to reach 154km/h (96mph)

flat out and had surprisingly peppy acceleration, coupled to a lively, rasping exhaust note. The steering was superbly weighted, and, although the live rear axle could make the car a little tricky to handle in the wet, on dry roads the grip and handling were great.

The car had a four-speed all-syncromesh gearbox and effective brakes; top models came with

removable roof panels for wind-in-the-hair thrills. Had the Sports 800 been exported, its final production figures could have been far higher.

ENGINE: 790cc (48cu in), twin-cylinder
POWER: 49bhp (37kW)
0–60MPH (96KM/H): n/a
TOP SPEED: 154km/h (96mph)
PRODUCTION TOTAL: 3131

TRIUMPH 1300 FWD

ENGINE: 1296cc (79cu in), four-cylinder
POWER: 61bhp (45kW) at 5000rpm
0–60MPH (96KM/H): 19 seconds
TOP SPEED: 138km/h (86mph)
PRODUCTION TOTAL: 148,350

When Triumph came to replace its ageing Herald model, which had been built as simply as possible to keep costs to a minimum, the British manufacturer tried to create a car that would shun conventional thinking in

every respect. The result was the front-wheel drive 1300, which used an unusual combination of longitudinally mounted engine and driven front wheels in a pressed steel monocoque body, with independent suspension all

round – very unlike the rear-drive Herald with its separate chassis and spring axles.

Triumph also marketed the car as more upmarket than its contemporary rivals. Even the most basic 1300s came with Ambla leather-style upholstery, a wooden dash and deep-pile carpets.

But Triumph's 'Junior 2000' was not to be a success. Traditional buyers preferred the Herald, while those in the market for a family car often shopped for cheaper models such as the BMC 1300 and Ford Escort. In a dramatic rethink, Triumph dropped the 1300 FWD before the Herald had even ceased production, replacing it with a 1500 version in a revised bodyshell. The 1500 was an equally slow seller, and was superseded by the Dolomite, which looked almost identical, but came with a more conventional rear-drive layout.

Michelotti's styling was angular and modern, under the skin was a longitudinally mounted engine and inside the Triumph 1300 FWD was a classy package.

VIGNALE-FIAT 850

ENGINE: 843cc (51cu in), four-cylinder
POWER: 35bhp (26kW)
0–60MPH (96KM/H): n/a
TOP SPEED: about 136km/h (85mph)
PRODUCTION TOTAL: n/a

Few cars were as easy to tune or as fun to drive as Fiat's little 850 saloon, so it is hardly a surprise that, soon after its 1964 launch, several Italian styling houses were commissioned to create their own interpretations of the diminutive model.

One model, designed by Bertone, was snapped up by the Italian giant and went into production as a Fiat, but Vignale had three of its own designs, and was not going to

It wasn't great to drive, but Vignale's adaptation of the Fiat 850 was undeniably pretty. All of the Vignale's carried over the Fiat's body parts apart from the shell. Prone to corrosion, few survive today.

be put off building them as its own individual projects.

The Vignale-Fiat 850 debuted in 1965 and was a seamlessly pretty interpretation of the original Fiat 850 design, available as a coupé, a 2+2 (called the Special Saloon) and a 2+2 Special Spider, which was an especially good-looking two-door convertible. All of them carried over all of the Fiat parts apart from the bodyshell, which meant that they were easy to maintain and equally as fun to drive as Fiat's baby.

Inside, the cabin came with extra luxuries, including fake leather trim, chrome detailing around the controls and the option of metallic paint on the bodywork. While not a great performer, the Vignale-Fiat 850 was sweet to drive and developed quite a cult following. It was prone to corrosion, however, so there are few survivors today.

INTERMECCANICA ITALIA

ITALY 1965–71

You have to admire the Intermeccanica Italia's reason for being. Conceived by British sports-car maker TVR as a larger version of the Griffith, called Griffith Omega, the project was canned as it neared completion. It was so far down the line that it seemed foolish to throw the plans away, so US-based Hungarian businessman Frank Reisner bought the rights to the design and resurrected it. It was designed by Franco Scaglione, a former Bertone stylist, and 150 bodies and chassis units had already been built in Italy before TVR withdrew from the project. Reisner set about finishing them and seeing them through to final production.

As the Intermeccanica was now targeted at the American rather than European market, the original four-cylinder engine was replaced by a 5.0-litre (302cu in) V8 from the Ford Mustang. There was even an automatic transmission option – a feature that definitely was not there at the project's conception.

A convertible model, dubbed Torino, appeared in 1967 to further broaden the range, but sales were never especially good and build quality was, at best, suspect. Despite this, about 1000 cars were built overall.

ENGINE: 4949cc (302cu in), eight-cylinder
POWER: 200bhp (149kW)
0–60MPH (96KM/H): 8.8 seconds
TOP SPEED: 200km/h (125mph)
PRODUCTION TOTAL: about 1000

AUDI 60

GERMANY 1965–72

Today, the Audi name is synonymous with fine handling luxury cars with a premium image, but things were not always that way. Back in the 1930s, the Audi name had been lost in part of the Auto-Union empire, when it joined forces with fellow German makers Horsch, Wanderer and DKW.

But with falling sales, Auto-Union revived the Audi name for its new luxury saloon, aimed at models such as the BMW 2000 and Opel Rekord. It was initially called the D-B Heron, but the not-so snappy title (given because the engines used 'Heron'-type long combustion chambers) was dropped in favour of 'Audi 75'; this was soon joined by the less powerful (and far more popular) Audi 60. Unlike most of its contemporary rivals, the Audi was front-wheel drive, so it enjoyed greater cabin space and a bigger luggage compartment – traits that proved popular in its home market.

Although it was never especially exciting to drive, with an underpowered 1.5-litre (91cu in) engine, the 60 was a pleasant car to drive, with excellent ride comfort, competent handling and good fuel economy. It was also very solidly built, with some neat design features that included a sliding sunroof with its own pop-up wind deflector.

Not a brilliant car by any means, the Audi 60 was nevertheless a good enough package to attract the might of Volkswagen, which bought the rights to Audi and developed the brand to the premium level where it sits today.

ENGINE: 1496cc (91cu in), four-cylinder
POWER: 55bhp (41kW)
0–60MPH (96KM/H): 18 secs
TOP SPEED: 138km/h (86mph)
PRODUCTION TOTAL: 416,852

MASERATI MEXICO

ITALY 1965–72

The Maserati Mexico had a difficult birth. It was based on two very different designs, one by Vignale and another by Michelotti, and the end result was a compromise between the two, albeit quite a successful one in terms of the car's appearance.

Built as a replacement for the ageing Maserati 3500 GT, the Mexico was built on a shortened version of the Quattroporte chassis to save costs, but with a live rear axle and ventilated disc brakes to give it more sporty driving characteristics. The car's all-steel body was welded onto an oval tube frame. This labour-intensive and not especially effective method of construction allowed all the panels to be beaten into shape by hand, but later led to horrific corrosion issues that saw the end of many a car at a fairly youthful age.

Two engine variants were offered – a 4.1-litre (252cu in) quad cam V8 at launch, and an uprated 4.7-litre (287cu in) variant from 1969 onwards, while inside the Mexico was a true four-seater, with supple leather trim and opulent wood and chrome trimmings.

Yet, despite being quite an attractive package, the Mexico could never quite manage to fire enthusiasts' passions in the same way as its 3500 GT predecessor, and, when production ceased after only seven years, just 250 cars had been completed.

ENGINE: 4136cc (252cu in), eight-cylinder
POWER: 260bhp (194kW) at 5200rpm
0–60MPH (96KM/H): 7.5 seconds
TOP SPEED: 230km/h (143mph)
PRODUCTION TOTAL: 250

Despite being a compromise between two different designs by Vignale and Michelotti, the Mexico is an imposing looking car. This is probably its best angle.

MERCEDES BENZ W108/109 S-CLASS

GERMANY 1965–72

A familiar sight all over the globe, the Mercedes W108 was tough, durable, technically advanced and simple to maintain.

Karl Benz may have been the inventor of the automobile, but it was always Rolls-Royce that took credit for building the best cars in the world. The 1965 S-Class was Mercedes-Benz's attempt to capture that title as well, by introducing what it called the most luxurious and most advanced car ever made.

The W108 and long-wheelbase W109 were certainly impressive, with long, sleek bodywork and an imposing stacked headlight arrangement either side of Mercedes' trademark 'horseshoe' radiator grille, while inside the cars were beautifully appointed, with hand-stitched leather trim, deep pile carpets, ornate chrome details and acres of rear legroom.

But it was the technology that was the S-Class's biggest trump card. Under the skin, the car had all-independent suspension and

disc brakes on all-four wheels, while top models (called SE in short-wheelbase form or SEL for long-wheelbase models) had even more technical developments in the form of gas-filled air suspension and power-assisted disc brakes. Build quality was exquisite, despite the S-Class being much cheaper than the equivalent Rolls-Royce Silver Shadow.

Power came from a choice of engines, including 2.5- (153cu in), 2.8- (170cu in) and 3.0-litre (183cu in) straight-sixes, and a 3.5-litre

(214cu in) V8, all of which were smooth and reliable. The range topper was the 300SEL 6.3, with its huge 6.3-litre (383cu in) V8 and startlingly quick performance. Was it the best car in the world? For a while, probably, yes.

ENGINE: 2778cc (170cu in), six-cylinder
POWER: 128–250bhp (95–186kW)
0–60MPH (96KM/H): 9.8 seconds
TOP SPEED: 206km/h (129mph)
PRODUCTION TOTAL: 56,092

AC 428

UNITED KINGDOM 1965–73

ENGINE: 7014cc (427cu in), eight-cylinder
POWER: 345bhp (257kW)
0–60MPH (96KM/H): 5.45 seconds
TOP SPEED: 234km/h (145mph)
PRODUCTION TOTAL: 81

Despite the enormous success of the Cobra on the world's racetracks, like most manufacturers, AC could not survive with only one model in its product line-up. The problem was, apart from the money poured into Cobra development by Ford, AC itself did not have huge cash reserves, and what new

Largely forgotten, the 428 is one of the best-kept performance secrets of the classic car world and underrated by collectors.

additions it could make to its range could be carried out only at minimum cost. That meant using the Carroll Shelby–developed Cobra 427 chassis, a long-wheelbase version of which had already been commissioned by Ford for a Ghia show car, and interpreting it in its own way. AC appointed Frua of Italy to build a smart 2+2 body that would go straight onto the lengthened chassis, incorporating the 7.0-litre (427cu in) Ford Galaxie powerplant used in the Cobra 427.

In the end, two versions of the AC 428 appeared, a 2+2 coupé and a pretty convertible. Despite their pretty grand tourer looks, both versions were very much Cobras at heart, meaning that they had phenomenal performance and a chassis that was great in a straight line, but needed concentration if driven round corners at any speed.

OPEL KADETT B

As part of GM Europe's versatile product development, the Opel Kadett B, which replaced the 1962 Kadett A, was designed from its conception to include several variants to broaden its appeal in the competitive small-saloon sector of the European car market.

Based on the same fairly competent chassis as the Kadett A, the Kadett B looked much prettier and came with a wider choice of engine variants, ranging from 1.0 litres (61cu in) to a high compression 1.5-litre (92cu in) twin carburettor unit, which gave it 100mph (160km/h) performance.

As well as four-door and two-door saloons, the Kadett B was offered as a convertible and a very attractive two-door coupé model, which served as the basis for the 1967 Kadett Rallye. The Rallye had the look of a scaled-down American muscle car, with pressed-steel sports wheels, twin coachlines and a matt black anti-glare bonnet (hood). Fun to drive, it also had the liveliness to match and is today one of motoring history's most underrated performance cars. The Kadett was sold in Britain as well as Western Europe, despite GM's presence with the Vauxhall brand, and it enjoyed reasonable success.

ENGINE: 1492cc (91cu in), four-cylinder
POWER: 90bhp (67kW)
0–60MPH (96KM/H): 12.6 seconds
TOP SPEED: 165km/h (102mph)
PRODUCTION TOTAL: 2,649,501

WOLSELEY 1100 AND 1300

In much the same way that the Riley Kestrel took BMC's method of badge engineering to a surprisingly successful extreme, the Wolseley 1100 (or 1300 from 1967) managed to retain most of the traits of the historic Wolseley marque, despite the use of a BMC 1100/1300 bodyshell. As with all previous Wolseley models, the ornate chrome radiator grille featured a badge that illuminated with the headlights, while inside the wood-capped door trims, leather seats and beautifully detailed wood-veneer dashboard added to the upmarket appeal. Also, the Hydrolastic gas-filled air suspension gave the Wolseley a far better ride than most small cars of the era.

The best versions were built from 1968 until 1973, and came with a twin-carburettor version of Austin's 1275cc (78cu in) A-Series engine, delivering surprisingly lively performance and good motorway refinement for such a small car. Although not especially sought after, the Wolseley 1100/1300 range today enjoys a cult following.

ENGINE: 1098cc (67cu in), four-cylinder (1100)
POWER: 55bhp (41kW)
0–60MPH (96KM/H): 18.4 seconds
TOP SPEED: 137km/h (85mph)
PRODUCTION TOTAL:
17,397 (1100);
27,470 (1300)

ISO GRIFO

Based on the chassis of the Rivolta, named after ISO's founder Renzo Rivolta, the Grifo was heavily influenced by former Ferrari engineer Giotto Bizzarini. Bizzarini sharpened up the Rivolta's chassis and enlisted the help of Bertone to style a two-door coupé, touted as a 'Corvette for Europe'. The result was truly one of the most beautiful European sports cars ever, with hunched front and rear wings (fenders), bulbous wheelarches and a pretty twin-headlight front end. The style was matched inside by soft Italian leather seats, chrome-ringed dials and a matt black dashboard, lending the car a sporting aura.

Power came from the same General Motors V8 engine that powered the Corvette, lending even more credence to ISO's marketing strategy. The Grifo even enjoyed some motorsport success, winning its class in the 1964 Le Mans 24-Hour race. A choice of manual or automatic transmissions was offered. In 1968, the engine size was upped from 5.4 litres (327cu in) to 7.0 litres (427cu in) to provide credible opposition to newcomers such as the Ferrari 365 GTB Daytona and Maserati Ghibli.

The last Grifos, introduced in 1970, were given a moderate face-lift, with pop-up headlight covers and a more rounded rear end. These made them look spookily like a Corvette Sting Ray, but it is the original that is by far the best remembered and most cherished.

**'A Corvette for Europe':
Enormous rear tyres helped the Grifo transfer its prodigious power output to the road.**

ENGINE: 5359cc (327cu in), eight-cylinder
POWER: 300bhp (224kW)
0–60MPH (96KM/H): 7.4 secs
TOP SPEED: 241km/h (150mph)
PRODUCTION TOTAL: 504

INNOCENTI MINI

ITALY 1965–76

The success of the original Mini in the United Kingdom was phenomenal, and, in Italy, where small cars had ruled for years, it made sense to take on the locally built Fiat 500 at its own game, in a more space-efficient package. But tough Italian import rules made it difficult for British-built Minis to sell there, so instead the British Motor Corporation signed a deal with Italian coachbuilder Innocenti to build Minis under licence, to meet local demand.

Innocenti Minis were more upmarket than British ones, appealing to the kind of buyer who wanted the compactness of a Fiat 500, but with a bit more in the way of creature comforts. They came with opening front quarterlights, hinged back windows, proper door-pull levers and more upmarket trim materials, while on the outside the Innocenti cars featured a different grille, numberplate housing and unique 25cm (10in) sports wheels. As in

the United Kingdom, sporty Cooper variants were produced, and later cars came with an elaborate five-dial dashboard, never to be seen in Birmingham-built Minis.

With British Leyland rationalizing its model range in the early 1970s, Innocenti saw a new opportunity open up and, for a short while, exported its own Minis to the car's home market in Britain, where instead of the austere and basic Mini 850 or Mini 1000, you could choose a plush Innocenti model

with better seats and extra instruments. The Leyland/Innocenti tie-up broke down in 1976 with the British company facing financial turmoil, but not before almost half a million Innocenti Minis were built.

ENGINE: 1275cc (78cu in), four-cylinder
POWER: 76bhp (57kW)
0–60MPH (96KM/H): 10.9 secs
TOP SPEED: 152km/h (95mph)
PRODUCTION TOTAL: 450,000

BENTLEY T-SERIES

UNITED KINGDOM 1965–80

Launched at the same time as the Rolls-Royce Silver Shadow, and very much the same car in all but badging and trim, the T-Series was the first Bentley to have a full unitary construction bodyshell. Like the Silver Shadow, it had self-

A Rolls-Royce in all but name? It was certainly difficult to tell the T-Series Bentley apart from the Rolls-Royce Silver Shadow.

levelling suspension developed with the help of Citroën, plus all-round disc brakes – but, being a Bentley, it was set up to have a firmer, more sporting ride quality, to suit traditional buyers of the marque.

Visually, the differences between the two included a different radiator grille, with no mascot on the Bentley, and different wheel trims, while the Bentley was also offered in only one wheelbase, instead of the long and short

versions offered on the Rolls-Royce. From 1969 onwards, all Bentleys had air conditioning as standard, while, in 1970, the original car's 6230cc (380cu in) V8 engine was increased to 6750cc (412cu in), although, as with all Rolls-Royces, the power output was a closely guarded secret, described only as 'sufficient' in the sale brochures.

A face-lift came in 1977 and brought with it new bumpers with black inserts, and entirely new

fascia and large side repeater lights. There was now also rack-and-pinion steering and a sportier suspension set-up, to give the car more driver appeal.

ENGINE: 6750cc (412cu in), eight-cylinder
POWER: n/a
0–60MPH (96KM/H): 10.1 seconds
TOP SPEED: 194km/h (120mph)
PRODUCTION TOTAL: 2280

ROLLS-ROYCE SILVER SHADOW

UNITED KINGDOM 1965–80

Given that all its previous models were built along traditional separate chassis principles, the Silver Shadow represented a sea change for Rolls-Royce and its design direction. Launched in 1965 as a replacement for the beautiful

but old-fashioned Silver Cloud, the Shadow was something entirely new. It used a unitary construction monocoque, onto which all of the major components were attached. This reduced the build time necessary for each car and, at the

same time, vastly improved the driving characteristics.

Known in-house as the Tibet project, the Silver Shadow was signed off in 1958 by Rolls-Royce's chief engineer Harry Grylls, a whole seven years before the start

of production and fairly early into the life cycle of the Silver Cloud.

A huge amount of development work went into making sure the Silver Shadow was technically perfect – Rolls-Royce had to live up to its reputation for building the

Series 1 Silver Shadows, such as this one, had slimmer bumpers and more chrome trim than their later counterparts.

best cars in the world, so the company could not afford for Project Tibet to fail.

Citroën was drafted in to help develop a self-levelling suspension system for the car, based on the expertise it had gleaned from working on the DS, while supplies from Connolly Leather and Wilton

Carpets were brought in at an early stage, to ensure that the trim they built for the Silver Shadow was of the requisite exquisite quality and fitted perfectly.

By October 1965, the Silver Shadow was ready to hit the showrooms, and the initial response was brilliant. Wonderful to drive and even better to travel in as a passenger, the Shadow was smooth, powerful and whisper quiet, while the conventional three-box styling was subtly sharpened up by the addition of

a traditional-style Rolls-Royce radiator grille, complete with Spirit of Ecstasy winged mascot, and neat chrome bumper bars. Weight was kept down by the use of aluminium for the bonnet (hood) and boot (trunk) lid – a technique pioneered by Rover in the 1963 2000 saloon – while both short- and long-wheelbase versions were offered for buyers who preferred to drive, or be driven.

Initially, the car used the Silver Cloud's 6230cc (380cu in) V8 engine, but, in 1970, this was

upped to 6750cc (412cu in) in response to customers demanding more power from the engine – although, in true Rolls-Royce fashion, the power output for either unit was never disclosed.

Despite financial pressures faced by Rolls-Royce in the early 1970s, when it had to sell its military vehicle and aircraft engine divisions to survive, the Shadow's continual good sales meant that the model went from success to success. Tough US safety and emissions legislation saw a major face-lift occur in 1977. Called the Silver Shadow II, the newcomer looked almost the same as the Shadow I, save for its large impact bumpers, polyurethane front spoiler and big side repeater lights.

There were changes under the skin, too, with revised suspension and, for the first time, rack-and-pinion steering, which sharpened up the driving experience even further. Unusually, the original car's four-speed automatic gearbox was swapped for a three-speeder, although the engine's torque and flexibility meant that this cost-cutting measure made little difference to the way the car drove, and the Silver Shadow continued to be a great success for Rolls-Royce until it was replaced by the Silver Spirit in late 1980.

ENGINE: 6750cc (412cu in), eight-cylinder
POWER: n/a
0–60MPH (96KM/H): 9.4 seconds
TOP SPEED: 192km/h (119mph)
PRODUCTION TOTAL: 27,915

MARCOS MINI-MARCOS   UNITED KINGDOM 1965–81

The original Mini's handling characteristics made it drive like a sports car, but even so BMC had never seen fit to introduce a Mini-based sports car. Spotting this obvious gap in the market, Marcos owner Jem Marsh decided to launch his own car based on the idea. Originally shown as a prototype called the Dart, the Mini-Marcos went into production in 1965 and used a bespoke glassfibre body,

onto which were mounted the front and rear subframes and drivetrain of a standard Mini, powered by any choice of A-Series engine.

Sold in kit form or built to order, the Mini-Marcos was a rudimentary device utterly devoid of creature comforts, and its oddball styling did little to lend it appeal in the sales charts. But sharp handling and lively performance did make it a hit with competition drivers,

especially when the low purchase cost was taken into account. The Mini-Marcos even raced in the legendary Le Mans 24-Hour, finishing an impressive fifteenth overall in 1966 and being the only British-built car to complete the day-long event in 1971.

Marcos went bankrupt shortly after, but the design stayed in production as a private venture until 1981, as the Midas Bronze kit car.

It has since resurfaced several times, most recently in the late 1990s as a Mini-Marcos Mk V, so even now it may not be gone for good.

ENGINE: 1275cc (78cu in), four-cylinder
POWER: 76bhp (57kW)
0–60MPH (96KM/H): n/a
TOP SPEED: 168km/h (105mph)
PRODUCTION TOTAL: 1200

ALFA ROMEO DUETTO   ITALY 1966–67

Some cars are so perfectly styled that they transcend time, and the Alfa Romeo Duetto is one of them. It may have enjoyed only one full year in production, but the diminutive two-seater went on to spawn the Alfa Spider – a car that enjoyed more than 25 years and achieved legendary status.

Quite rightly, it is the Duetto that is most sought after by collectors.

Designed by Pininfarina, the little Alfa was based on the platform of the Giulia 105 model, introduced in 1963. The streamlined body had a pretty 'boat-tail' rear end, which tapered in towards the back and offered a long luggage hold, proving that styling and practicality do sometimes go well together. Power came from a twin-cam 1570cc (96cu in) engine producing

a lively 109bhp (81kW). The Duetto had great handling, lovely steering and a very sweet gearbox, along with a rasping exhaust note and ample performance, making it a great sports car – although the fragility of its rust-addled bodywork was always an issue.

Bizarrely, the name 'Duetto' was chosen as a result of a competition run by Alfa Romeo, which offered

a free car as the prize for someone who could come up with a name for its new sporty two-seater.

ENGINE: 1570cc (96cu in), four-cylinder
POWER: 109bhp (81kW)
0–60MPH (96KM/H): n/a
TOP SPEED: 187km/h (116mph)
PRODUCTION TOTAL: 6325

Best remembered for its appearance as Mrs Robinson's car in the cult movie *The Graduate*, the Alfa Romeo Duetto is one of the most attractive sports cars of the 1960s and yet only enjoyed one full year of production.

LAMBORGHINI 400GT

ITALY 1966–67

Although it looked outwardly identical to the 350GT that preceded it, the Lamborghini 400GT had no two body panels the same. Styled by Touring of Milan to replace the two-seater

Touring of Milan did a bold job of styling Lamborghini's grand tourers. The 400GT was a large, powerful car.

350GT, the 400GT had an extra pair of seats in the back to turn it into a 2+2, but those in the back turned out to be very cramped, with almost no leg or headroom.

Unlike the expensive-to-build all-alloy 350GT, the 400GT had a steel bodyshell and doors, although the boot (trunk) lid and bonnet (hood) were still cast from aluminium to keep weight down. The extra pounds added by the steel body

and extra seats would have taken its toll on performance, though, so to counter the power shortfall Lamborghini ousted the 350GT's 3.5-litre (211cu in) V12 engine and replaced it with a revised 3.9-litre (240cu in) unit developing 320bhp (238kW). This gave the 400GT more torque and a higher top speed than the 350GT, but it was the earlier car that was still quicker off the mark.

Not an especially successful car, with just 273 examples sold, the 400GT still represented an important chapter in Lamborghini's history.

ENGINE: 3929cc (240cu in), 12-cylinder
POWER: 320bhp (238kW)
0–60MPH (96KM/H): 7.5 seconds
TOP SPEED: 248km/h (155mph)
PRODUCTION TOTAL: 273

JAGUAR 420

Not to be confused with the gargantuan 420G, which succeeded the Jaguar Mk X, the 420 was actually a derivative of the much smaller and lighter S-type. Launched in 1966, three years after the S-type itself, the 420 was

Based on the S-Type, the Jaguar 420 had simplified trim, a luxurious interior and slimmer chrome bumpers.

the flagship Jaguar model (there was also a Daimler Sovereign, based on the same body) in the S-type model line-up.

The car came about to placate buyers who wanted a performance Jaguar and mourned the passing of the famous 3.8-Litre Mk II, after the range was rationalized for the 1967 model year. From the windscreen back, the 420 was pure S-type, with the same dropping rear and wheel spats, but

upfront the S-type's Mk II–style grille and single headlights were replaced by twin lamps and a larger horseshoe-style grille, as featured on the barge-like 420G.

Power came from the top-of-the-range 4.2-litre (256cu in) version of the XK engine, although it was detuned slightly from the unit that appeared in the 420G and E-type to offer 245bhp (183kW). That gave it enough power to reach 200km/h (125mph), while buyers

could choose from a four-speed manual or three-speed Borg Warner automatic transmission. Disc brakes were fitted all-round, and the cabin was dripping in luxury.

ENGINE: 4235cc (258cu in), six-cylinder
POWER: 245bhp (183kW)
0–60MPH (96KM/H): 9.9 secs
TOP SPEED: 200km/h (125mph)
PRODUCTION TOTAL: 9801

AMC RAMBLER

One of the most confusing model ranges of all time, the AMC Rambler line-up was a collection of different vehicles left over from the formation of the American Motors Corporation, through the merger of Nash and Hudson. Originally sold as the Nash Rambler in 1958, the name became a generic term for any number of models in the AMC range, including a compact car

called the Rambler American and Rambler Rogue Coupé, the bigger Rambler Classic and the top-of-the-line Rambler Ambassador. There was also the Rambler Marlin Coupé, which was a pretty but unsuccessful attempt to take on the all-conquering Ford Mustang.

All were strictly conventional in their layout, with straight-six or V8 engines, live rear axles, leaf springs and rear-wheel drive. The range

was gradually rationalized to make more sense, with the Ambassador becoming an AMC model in its own right from 1967. By 1969, the larger models had been dropped, and the Rambler American had its name changed simply to Rambler, as a last effort to boost sales of the long-established but not ultimately successful model.

Despite the massively confusing model range, more than four

million Ramblers were sold, but AMC failed to make much profit on them. The car marked the beginning of the end for the corporation.

ENGINE: 4752cc (290cu in), eight-cylinder
POWER: 200bhp (149kW)
0–60MPH (96KM/H): 9.9 seconds
TOP SPEED: 171km/h (106mph)
PRODUCTION TOTAL: n/a

DAIMLER SOVEREIGN

Until the Sovereign appeared in 1966, all Daimlers had managed to maintain an identity of their own, despite the company being taken over by Jaguar. Even

the Daimler V8 250, which looked outwardly identical to the Jaguar Mk II, maintained its own identity by virtue of its excellent Edward Turner–developed V8 engine.

The Sovereign, however, was to mark a turning point for Daimler. Replacing the outdated Majestic, the newcomer was nothing more than a Jaguar 420, with a few

visual tweaks to mark it out as a Daimler. Like the 420, the Sovereign used the entire rear section of the Jaguar S-type, but with a front end modelled on the look of the larger Jaguar 420G. Daimler's trademark fluted radiator grille remained, along with the 'Flying D' bonnet mascot, and the fluted pattern of the grille was repeated on the car's boot (trunk) lid handle. Unique hubcaps and a

more plush level of interior trim, with darker wood cappings and richer leather, provided the car with some upmarket appeal.

While some cynics rejected the Sovereign as a half-baked attempt by Jaguar to replicate the Daimler

marque, the car was nonetheless a very good one, and it achieved impressive sales success. The Sovereign name went on to appear on a succession of Daimler models from thereon in, right through to the late 1990s.

ENGINE: 4235cc (258cu in), six-cylinder
POWER: 245bhp (182kW)
0–60MPH (96KM/H): 9.9 seconds
TOP SPEED: 197km/h (123mph)
PRODUCTION TOTAL: 5700

FORD UK GT40

UNITED KINGDOM 1966–69

One of the biggest corporate fall-outs in motoring history inadvertently led to the creation of one of the world's greatest ever cars – the Ford GT40. The story began back in 1963, when Ford approached Ferrari with a view to buying out the Italian sports-car maker to give it a foothold in the lucrative sports-car market.

Ford spent a great deal of money researching the deal and got as far as writing up contracts, with the cooperation of the Italian firm's management, when at the eleventh hour Ferrari founder Enzo Ferrari decided that there was no way he was going to sell his company. Ford's management was so angry at the amount of time and money it had wasted trying to seal the Ferrari deal that it decided to form its own racing team and beat Ferrari at its own game by winning Le Mans 24-Hour race.

The United Kingdom was chosen as Ford's centre of excellence for

motorsport, given the country's reputation for building some of the world's greatest racing cars, and the finest designers and engineers from all over the world were brought in to create Ford's racer.

The style of the car came from Detroit, but the Lola-based V8 engine was the creation of British engineer Eric Broadley, while the fibreglass body and spaceframe chassis were assembled by Ford's Advanced Vehicle Operations centre in Slough, Berkshire.

The racer became known as the GT40 because of its height – 40in (102cm) in total. The suspension used independent coil springs and double wishbones all-round – an expensive arrangement, but the GT40 was built to win races, not to be a sales charts bargain. Although never officially tested, the car's top speed was estimated to be about 320km/h (200mph). The first prototypes were raced in 1964, and proved fast but fragile,

giving Ford hope for beating Ferrari. The pivotal moment came in 1966 when the first production GT40s arrived (a car had to exist as a road car before it could be raced at Le Mans), and Ford entered the famous French 24-Hour race head to head with Ferrari for the first time proper. Enzo Ferrari appeared unthreatened by the GT40's appearance, writing it off as a poor publicity stunt, but he was left eating his words when, at the end of the race, the three works-backed GT40s crossed the finish line one after the other to take all three podium places. Ford had conquered Ferrari, and went on to do so again in 1967.

Motorsport was an expensive business, though, and with its point proven Ford withdrew from endurance racing while at the top. The GT40's career carried on a bit longer thanks to Grady Davis, the vice president of Gulf Oil. Hearing of Ford's withdrawal, he secured

This is a Ford UK GT 40 Mk 2, which was longer and more comfortable than the original, although the comfort part was purely relative.

backing from his company to run the race team for a further two years, and Ford won Le Mans again in 1968 and 1969.

The GT40 was a true legend, and Ford marked the car's fortieth anniversary by introducing a special-edition Ford GT for the twenty-first century. It looked almost identical to the original, but had modern Mustang running gear.

ENGINE: 4737cc (289cu in), eight-cylinder
POWER: 335bhp (250kW)
0–60MPH (96KM/H): 6 seconds
TOP SPEED: 274km/h (170mph)
PRODUCTION TOTAL: 133

GILBERN GENIE

For those who wanted a car that had all the class of a grand tourer, but could be run and maintained on a shoestring budget, Welsh

The red dragon in the Gilbern's radiator grille is an indication of its origins – the car was built in Wales.

manufacturer Gilbern's pretty but unpretentious model range was well worth a look.

The Genie was a larger, more angular version of the maker's original GT, with a more luxurious passenger compartment that could seat four people in relative comfort, and even had a useful load bay in the rear. Power came from Ford V6

engines in 2.5-litre (152cu in) or 3.0-litre (183cu in) form, which gave the car lively acceleration and impressive cruising ability. It was not a car to be pushed, though, as the body tended to flex when pushed hard and the rear end could prove twitchy on wet roads.

Only 174 Genies were built, but a surprisingly high number survive,

thanks to their easy maintenance and a rot-proof fibreglass body.

ENGINE: 2495cc (152cu in), six-cylinder
POWER: 112bhp (83kW)
0–96KM/H (60MPH): 10.7 seconds
TOP SPEED: 176km/h (110mph)
PRODUCTION TOTAL: 174

OLDSMOBILE TORONADO

Oldsmobile completely bucked the muscle-car trend with its Toronado. The enormous coupé was front-wheel-drive, with pop-up headlamps and speed-sensitive power steering.

In a bid to fight off its staid image, Oldsmobile sought to defy convention when it introduced the Toronado. Rather than following the mainstream ideals of creating a muscle car by simply dropping a huge V8 engine into an existing bodyshell, GM's most traditional brand turned the rulebook on its head. The weird looks were one thing, but the off-the-wall engineering was something else.

The engine was longitudinally mounted, but, instead of a conventional rear-drive live-axle arrangement, it powered the front wheels via automatic transmission and huge torque converters to stop the immense power from destroying the driveshafts.

The car also got pop-up headlights, enormous wheels and speed-sensitive power steering, proving beyond doubt that boring old Oldsmobile was taking its image change seriously.

Never a huge commercial success, the Toronado was still a critical model for GM, both as a technology showcase and as a hint at future front-wheel drive models, including the Cadillac Eldorado. It even had all the ingredients of a true muscle car, including an enormous 7.4-litre (454cu in) big-block V8 engine and startlingly quick performance. One of the more interesting US cars of the era, even if not a true great, its influence on future vehicle design cannot be shrugged off lightly.

ENGINE: 7446cc (454cu in), eight-cylinder
POWER: 385bhp (287kW)
0–60MPH (96KM/H): 8.7 seconds
TOP SPEED: 210km/h (130mph)
PRODUCTION TOTAL: 143,134

SAAB SONETT II

SWEDEN 1966–70

Sweden's first attempt at a sports car was pretty unsuccessful, but still quite interesting. The Sonnet II (Sonett I had been a low-volume prototype) made its debut at the 1966 Geneva Motor Show and

A rare sight in both the USA and Europe, Saab's Sonnett was not the success that the Swedish company had hoped for.

drew plenty of attention, largely due to its unconventional looks.

The Sonett was not cheap either, although it did come with a high-tech fibreglass bodyshell wrapped around a steel frame. The first cars came with a two-stroke three-cylinder engine, which gave it a characterful exhaust note and surprisingly lively performance given its modest 60bhp (45kW) power output. For 1967, after only

258 two-stroke cars had been built, the larger V4 engine from the Saab 96 was squeezed into the compact body, resulting in some essential styling modifications, including an ugly bulge in the car's bonnet (hood). The 1498cc (91cu in) engine did at least give the car a power boost and make it more competitive with other European sports cars.

The car was not a huge success, and Saab went back to the drawing board to create a new Sonett, which appeared in 1970 as a different car entirely. Sonett IIs are now very rare and have a certain curiosity value.

ENGINE: 1498cc (91cu in), four-cylinder
POWER: 73bhp (54kW)
0–60MPH (96KM/H): 12.5 seconds
TOP SPEED: 165km/h (102mph)
PRODUCTION TOTAL: 258 (two-stroke), 1609 (V4)

UNIPOWER GT

UNITED KINGDOM 1966–70

A sports car may not seem like the most obvious vehicle to emerge from a forklift truck factory, but that is exactly what happened with the Unipower GT. The brainchild of Ford engineer Ernie Unger, who sketched a design for a sports car based on the Mini 850 in his own time, the project finally received investment courtesy of Universal Power Drives, a company better known for

building electric forklift trucks for the warehouse industry.

Universal believed that being associated with a sports car would improve its image, so it financed Unger's vehicle from the drawing board through to production car, which made its debut at the 1966 Racing Car Show in London. The mid-engined Unipower had a mid-mounted 998cc (61cu in) A-Series engine coupled to a four-speed

gearbox, with a gear lever to the right of the driver.

Such was the car's initial impact that Unger was inundated with orders; by 1967, the Unipower GT had its own one-make racing series. In 1968, Universal Power Drives lost interest, but the car was kept alive by Unger's own company, UWF. A revised model was unveiled, using a 1275cc (78cu in) engine, but the new car's

development proved too costly without a buyer. Unger wound up the company after only 15 second-generation cars had been built.

ENGINE: 998cc (61cu in), four-cylinder
POWER: 55bhp (41kW)
0–60MPH (96KM/H): 12.6 seconds
TOP SPEED: 153km/h (96mph)
PRODUCTION TOTAL: 75

The sports car that came out of a forklift truck factory: budgetary constraints meant the Unipower had to use as many Mini parts as possible. The headlight layout worked quite well, but the doors looked awkward.

VIGNALE-FIAT EVELINE

ITALY 1966–70

After enjoying some success with the Vignale-Fiat 850, the Italian styling house Vignale turned its hand to other models in the Fiat range so that it could offer its own bespoke conversions.

The French-sounding Eveline debuted in 1966 and was based on the standard 124 saloon, a car renowned for being a lively machine to drive, if lacking in styling flair. With only 1197cc (73cu in) under the bonnet (hood), the Eveline was never going to be a fire-breather, but it benefited from the 124 saloon's sweet-handling chassis and could be tuned to deliver enough power to at least feel lively off the mark; the Vignale-styled coupé bodywork gave it the look of a scaled-down Aston Martin DBS.

Vignale had also listened to criticism of its Fiat-based cars' build quality, and concentrated on making the Eveline feel much better screwed together. As a result, it resisted corrosion far better than its contemporaries and was one of the best-made Italian cars of its era.

It was also reasonably well equipped, with imitation leather seats, a five-dial dashboard and bespoke carpets and door trims, giving it the feel of a much larger car. Probably Vignale's best Fiat conversion, the Eveline never really achieved the recognition it deserved.

ENGINE: 1197cc (73cu in), four-cylinder
POWER: 60bhp (45kW)
0–60MPH (96KM/H): n/a
TOP SPEED: about 144km/h (90mph)
PRODUCTION TOTAL: about 200

Another stunningly pretty Vignale, the Eveline was a coupé version of the boxy Fiat 124 saloon car. It was probably the best Vignale-Fiat conversion, but has been under-appreciated.

VIGNALE-FIAT SAMANTHA

ITALY 1966–70

Following its tradition of giving its Fiat-based cars girls' names, Vignale's biggest model was known as the Samantha – an odd choice for a car that was aimed at testosterone-fuelled young male buyers. It was one of Vignale's prettiest Fiat designs, but, unlike the well thought out Eveline, the Samantha was not brilliantly executed. Build quality was terrible,

rust-resistance was almost nonexistent and it depended too much on the Fiat 125's construction, meaning that any modifications Vignale carried out were very much a compromise. The bodywork was too tall, so Vignale countered this by painting the sills black to make it look narrower, while, to drop the front end, the nose was made more slanted and round headlights were

faired in, rotating upwards when switched on. Vignale also used the 125's bulkhead, dashboard, rear lights and inner wings (fenders).

With the extra weight added by its own bodywork modifications, the Samantha was, embarrassingly, slower than standard 125 saloon models. A slower seller than Vignale anticipated, and far too costly, it eventually contributed to

Vignale winding up all of its Fiat projects in 1970. The car is a rarity today, but not especially valuable.

ENGINE: 1608cc (98cu in), four-cylinder
POWER: 90bhp (67kW)
0–60MPH (96KM/H): 12.6 seconds
TOP SPEED: 165km/h (103mph)
PRODUCTION TOTAL: n/a

DE TOMASO MANGUSTA

ITALY 1966–72

Italian for 'mongoose', the Mangusta was originally conceived as a sports racing car, commissioned by none other than legendary racer and engineer Carroll Shelby. But the project foundered, leaving Alejandro de Tomaso with a

Essentially a racing car tamed for the road, the Mangusta (mongoose) was a handful to drive, but fabulous looking.

complete chassis design and no bodywork to put on top of it. He approached designer Giorgetto Giugiaro, who had recently finished a project for ISO, but the rival firm had rejected his design.

De Tomaso put both abandoned projects together, creating the Mangusta, built by coachbuilders Ghia (of which de Tomaso was owner) using part steel, part aluminium construction. Effectively a racing car tamed for the road,

the Mangusta was brutally fast and difficult to drive at speed, especially as most of the weight was towards the rear, which housed the 4.7-litre (288cu in) US Ford V8 engine.

The Mangusta's stunning looks initially charmed more than 400 buyers, but some of them ended up cancelling their orders after discovering how challenging the car was to drive, leaving de Tomaso with some complete cars that he could not sell. It was a

lesson hard-learned by de Tomaso, who focused on a slightly less brash and more affordable car for his next project, which would become the legendary Pantera.

ENGINE: 4727cc (288cu in), eight-cylinder
POWER: 305bhp (227kW)
0–60MPH (96KM/H): 7 seconds
TOP SPEED: 249km/h (155mph)
PRODUCTION TOTAL: 400

LAMBORGHINI MIURA

ITALY 1966–72

The 350GT and 400GT models were a moderate success for Ferruccio Lamborghini, but it was not until 1966 that his sports-car firm really came to prominence. Beautiful in its simplicity, the Miura was a car that came to market driven by passion and enthusiasm. Lamborghini's engineers Giampaolo Dallara and Paolo Stanzani were huge motorsport fans and, impressed with the successes of the Ford GT40 and Ferrari 250LM, they put forward plans for a road car based on racecar engineering, which Lamborghini instantly approved on

the premise that it must also be stunning to look at.

The Miura, named after a fighting bull because Ferruccio Lamborghini was born under the star sign of Taurus, was born, and, to ensure that his desire for the car to look fantastic was met, Lamborghini appointed Bertone to style the body out of aluminium.

The Miura's seductive profile was the work of a young up-and-coming designer named Marcello Gandini, who tried to keep the panels as slender as possible, despite the need to house a wide V12 engine and a bespoke

spaceframe chassis. To do this, he designed a rear section that tilted backwards away from the car to give access to the engine compartment, using one of the car's few natural straight lines as the hinge point.

Gandini was also responsible for the trademark 'eyebrows' on the Miura, after Lamborghini deemed the original design (with the revolving headlights faired into a flat bonnet/hood) to be too stark in appearance. A simple fix, the black plastic strakes surrounding each light were to become an instant Miura trademark, and they

were beautifully effective despite their simplicity.

The car was first shown at the 1965 Turin Motor Show and went into production the following year, and it received almost universal praise for its seductive looks.

But the Miura was not perfect. The cabin was tiny, and the position of the engine as close to the centre of the car as possible to provide even weight distribution led to the cockpit getting uncomfortably hot – a situation not helped by the steeply raked front windscreen, which magnified the sun's heat in hot weather.

One of the most famous shapes in motoring, the Lamborghini Miura is remembered as one of the most stylish cars of all time. Even today, its looks are seductive.

The driving experience was not great either, with an incredibly heavy gearshift and weighty steering. Acceleration was, as you might expect, incredible, but the

Miura had an aerodynamic problem that led to air literally lifting the front end of the car up at high speed, with dramatic consequences. Later cars were better – they had been subjected to a reengineering program at the hands of New Zealand racing mechanic Bob Wallace, who made significant changes to the car's handling, ride and braking to make it more compliant, as well as ordering extra strengthening to

the centre section of the chassis, which had a tendency to flex if cornered too hard. To further improve matters, Lamborghini offered air conditioning from 1969 onwards, making the car much more comfortable.

While those expecting perfection might have been disappointed by the Miura when it made its debut, most of the problems had been sorted by the time the last SV models appeared in 1971. With

their fat wheelarches and larger wheels, however, they lacked the styling purity of the original model, which, like all true greats, was fundamentally flawed.

ENGINE: 3929cc (240cu in), twelve-cylinder
POWER: 350bhp (261kW)
0–60MPH (96KM/H): 6.7 seconds
TOP SPEED: 272km/h (170mph)
PRODUCTION TOTAL: 775

MAZDA LUCE

JAPAN 1966–72

Japan's assault on the European car market began in the early 1960s, with every manufacturer from the Land of the Rising Sun told to design cars that would bring them export success. It is no coincidence, therefore, that the Mazda Luce ended up looking like a cross between a Triumph 1300 and an Audi 60 – although the design originated in Italy from

styling house Bertone, which had the plans rejected by Alfa Romeo.

Mazda was quick to snap up the redundant blueprints, and the Luce was developed in record time, from conception to showroom in just one year. Power came from a 1490cc (91cu in) overhead-camshaft engine that was surprisingly refined and lively, while the front-wheel drive chassis was perfectly

acceptable, if not exactly thrilling in terms of handling characteristics.

While not a huge export success, the Luce did give Mazda a foothold in the European market, which it developed with quite some success. Mention must also go to the short-lived Luce R130 coupé, which appeared in 1969 and used a derivative of the twin rotary Wankel engine found in the Cosmo

sports car – an interesting technological diversion and pretty to look at, but ultimately a failure.

ENGINE: 1490cc (91cu in), four-cylinder or 655cc (40cu in) twin-rotor Wankel
POWER: 92bhp (69kW)
0–60MPH (96KM/H): 19.3 seconds
TOP SPEED: 161km/h (100mph)
PRODUCTION TOTAL: 160,845

VAUXHALL PC VISCOUNT

UNITED KINGDOM 1966–72

Despite pressures from within General Motors to make Vauxhall and Opel models more alike, the British arm of the company insisted on ploughing its own furrow throughout the 1960s, with its own design, engineering and development centres in Luton, Bedfordshire. The PC Viscount was the Vauxhall range's flagship model, and was based on the PC

Cresta – Vauxhall's rival to the Ford Zephyr and Zodiac ranges.

Power came from a 3294cc (201cu in) straight-six engine, fed to the rear wheels through GM's Hydromatic two-speed automatic transmission, with a four-speed manual available as an option. The powerplant was not the most refined and was fairly noisy at high speed, but it provided decent

acceleration and was supremely reliable. Standard equipment included a vinyl-covered roof, electric windows, power steering and luxurious wooden door cappings. For 1970, the range was enhanced with a new three-speed auto gearbox, along with a few minor tweaks to the exterior styling.

Behind the wheel, the Viscount was not especially sharp to drive,

but it was incredibly comfortable, making it ideal for families or high-mileage business users.

ENGINE: 3294cc (201cu in), six-cylinder
POWER: 120bhp (89kW)
0–96KM/H (60MPH): 15.5 seconds
TOP SPEED: 157km/h (98mph)
PRODUCTION TOTAL: 7025

FIAT DINO

A fruity V6 engine and alluring styling gave the Fiat Dino the perfect ingredients to become a classic Italian sports car.

suitable for road use, but it still delivered an impressive 119kW (160bhp), which fed its power to the rear wheels through a five-speed manual gearbox and limited slip differential. The Ferrari tie-up was deliberate, as the racing car maker needed to homologate a new engine to allow it to compete in Formula Two racing, and it did not sell enough of its own cars to meet the necessary target of 500.

A coupé version of the Dino followed in 1967 and was arguably even prettier than the soft-top, while its stiffer bodyshell meant that it was also a much sharper handling machine. A new engine came in 1969, with a less expensive cast-iron block to replace the original all-alloy unit. Power was upped to 180bhp (134kW) to compensate for the engine's extra weight, and this had no detriment on the car's performance.

ENGINE: 2418cc (148cu in), six-cylinder
POWER: 180bhp (134kW)
0–60MPH (96KM/H): 8 seconds
TOP SPEED: 208km/h (130mph)
PRODUCTION TOTAL: 7577

Despite its mainstream badge, Fiat has always been a manufacturer to pull a surprise out of the hat – and, at the 1966 Turin Motor Show, it did just that. The Dino Spyder caused onlookers to gasp in awe at its incredible Pininfarina-penned styling, and Fiat got enthusiasts even hotter under the collar when it announced that the car would go into production with a quad-cam V6 Ferrari engine under the bonnet (hood).

The reworked competition unit was detuned to make it more

JENSEN INTERCEPTOR

ENGINE: 7212cc (440cu in), V8-cylinder
POWER: 385bhp (287kW)
0–60MPH (96KM/H): 6.9 seconds
TOP SPEED: 240km/h (150mph)
PRODUCTION TOTAL: 6727

A combination of Italian styling coupled to an American V8 engine promised great things for the Jensen Interceptor. While the British-built grand tourer was not perfect by any means, it was still a seriously classy and desirable car in its day.

Problems manifested themselves right at the start, when the Jensen factory in West Bromwich, near Birmingham, was not ready in time to meet early production deadlines.

In photographs, it's difficult to imagine the Interceptor's overall size. American V8 engines ensured that there was enough grunt to haul the big body along. It developed a cult following.

This meant that the very first cars were assembled in Italy by styling house Touring, which was responsible for the car's external appearance, and build quality was not up to the standard that buyers expected for the price. Undeterred, Jensen continued development.

An innovative model called the FF (for Ferguson Formula) appeared in 1966 and was the world's first mass-produced four-wheel drive car, as well as being the first to feature an anti-lock braking system as standard, developed from the Dunlop-designed system used by aeroplane manufacturers. Available as a coupé, an odd-looking notchback or a very rare convertible, the Interceptor gained a cult following. The later Mk III models were especially extravagant, with cast-alloy wheels and a huge 7.2-litre (440cu in) engine.

MASERATI GHIBLI

ITALY 1966–73

Every car maker has an iconic model in its history books, and for Maserati that vehicle is the Ghibli. Built to compete with the Ferraris 365GTB Daytona and Lamborghini Miura, it faced stiff rivalry and had to be excellent to stand a chance in the sales charts. Luckily for Maserati, it was, outselling both its rivals and earning itself a rightful entry into the supercar hall of fame.

Named in traditional Maserati style after an African wind, the Ghibli featured a newly styled aerodynamic bodyshell stretched over a truncated version of the existing Mexico chassis. The V8 engine was bigger than the Mexico's, at 4719cc (288cu in), and developed an awesome 340bhp (253kW).

Perhaps Maserati's most famous model, the Ghibli was one of Giorgetto Giugiaro's most accomplished works of styling. It was an instant success.

The powerplant was entirely Maserati's own design and was cast entirely from alloy. It delivered quite incredible performance, although the downside was the car's incredible thirst for fuel, which made it even more expensive to run than the V12 Lamborghini Miura.

The Ghibli was not anything special under the skin either, relying on a simple arrangement of a live rear axle and leaf springs, rather than the more sophisticated independent suspension systems of rivals. This meant that, while it handled well most of the time, the Ghibli's rear end could get very twitchy in wet weather or under hard acceleration.

These flaws did not seem to matter much, though, as Giorgetto Giugiaro's beautiful styling managed to negate any bad feeling towards the car's rather basic underpinnings. By insisting on the engine having a dry sump, Giugiaro was able to lower the profile of the bonnet (hood), giving the Ghibli its distinctive wedge-like front end – a style that would go on to be used, with varying degrees of success, by a myriad of manufacturers throughout the late 1960s and into the 1970s.

A year after the coupé debuted, Maserati introduced a soft-top Ghibli intended to appeal to the American market, although it lost some of the coupé's styling harmony and only a handful was ever sold. Unlike most soft-tops, however, it benefited from the coupé's rigid chassis, which meant that no extra body strengthening was needed and it rarely suffered from flexing, except under extreme circumstances.

The most powerful Ghibli was the SS model, launched in 1970. It looked identical to the standard car, but had a more powerful 4930cc (301cu in) V8 engine, developing 385bhp (287kW). The more powerful unit really showed up the shortfalls of the Ghibli's chassis, though, and critics said that the original car was a much nicer machine to drive.

A major success for Maserati, the Ghibli nonetheless had a relatively short lifespan, and was withdrawn in 1971. It became a victim to the advancing march of technology in the sports-car market, and its traditional engine and chassis configuration was considered old hat. Maserati had already started production of the mid-engined Bora in 1971, and focused its attentions on the technically superior car for the mid-1970s, leaving the Ghibli to rest on its laurels as, quite deservedly, the company's true historical icon.

ENGINE: 4719cc (288cu in), eight-cylinder
POWER: 340bhp (253kW) at 5500rpm
0–60MPH (96KM/H): 9.5 seconds
TOP SPEED: 248km/h (154mph)
PRODUCTION TOTAL: 1372

MERCURY COUGAR

ENGINE: 4736cc (289cu in), eight-cylinder
POWER: 210bhp (156kW)
0–60MPH (96KM/H): 10.2 seconds
TOP SPEED: 168km/h (105mph)
PRODUCTION TOTAL: 90,236

Sharing its mechanical layout with the Ford Mustang, the Mercury Cougar had a pretty good start in life. Aimed slightly more upmarket than the original pony car, the 1966 Cougar first appeared as a two-door hardtop, with neat flaps that folded down over the headlights when not in use, giving the car a stealth-like appearance.

A wide range of engines was offered, from modest-powered V8 units to an astonishing 7030cc (429cu in) powerplant that developed in excess of 350bhp (261kW). Three-speed manual gearboxes were standard on all models; a four-speed Borg Warner automatic was listed as an option.

A convertible Cougar came along in 1967 to add more diversity to the range, while Mercury also concentrated on building a number of specials.

Most intriguing of these were the luxury-oriented XR-7, the GT-E (with sports suspension and handling upgrades), and the sinisterly badged Eliminator, which was aimed at taking on the might of the US muscle-car market.

Sections of the Cougar's front grille retracted at night to reveal twin circular headlamps.

TRIUMPH GT6

Often dubbed 'The poor man's E-Type', the GT6 was based on the simple chassis of a Triumph Herald, the Triumph Vitesse's six-cylinder engine and the Spitfire's styling.

ENGINE: 1998cc (122cu in), six-cylinder
POWER: 95bhp (71kW) at 5000rpm
0–60MPH (96KM/H): 12 seconds
TOP SPEED: 174km/h (108mph)
PRODUCTION TOTAL: 40,926

Billed as the 'poor man's E-type' due to its striking similarity to Jaguar's sporting flagship, the Triumph GT6 was a clever amalgam of the Triumph Vitesse's six-cylinder engine and the Spitfire's sports-car styling. Only ever sold as a coupé, to give it more lateral strength than the soft-top Spitfire, the GT6 was an arch competitor to the four-cylinder MGB GT. It stole a march on its rival, thanks to the 2.0-litre (122cu in) six-cylinder engine, which delivered more power and torque than the MG and was much more refined at speed.

The fastback styling was first seen on Triumph's Le Mans racing

Spitfire and was carried over to the GT6 almost unchanged, the individually moulded rear bodyshell mounted directly onto the steel chassis of a Triumph Herald, on which the Spitfire was also based.

The car's ancestry meant that the GT6 suffered from the same alarming handling tendencies as the rest of the Herald family, but this was vastly improved from 1968, thanks to a thoroughly

reworked rear suspension. A major face-lift occurred in 1970 with the GT6 Mk 3, which was tweaked by Italian stylist Michelotti to give it a more modern and arguably more attractive look as it entered a new

decade. Although the visually similar Spitfire soldiered on until 1981, the GT6 was dropped in 1973, as the worlwide fuel crisis saw demand dwindle because of its thirsty six-cylinder engine.

HONDA N600

JAPAN 1966–74

The concept of a microcar might seem like a modern idea, built to satisfy the demands of environmental legislation and traffic congestion, but it has been around in Japan for years. The N600 replaced the even tinier N360 in 1966, and featured packaging that made even the original Mini look badly designed. Its tiny body housed four adult-sized seats and

a reasonably generous luggage area, while power came from a tiny 599cc (37cu in) all-alloy engine that revved freely all the way to the 10,000rpm red line, making the little Honda incredible fun to drive.

It handled well, too, with a firm yet compliant ride, sharp steering and good brakes, while power was fed to the front wheels. The N600 started to show its weaknesses

outside city limits. The air-cooled engine might have been lively, but on the open road its incredible noise became intrusive. Also, the lightweight construction meant that high-speed stability was never a strong point, despite an impressive top speed of 136km/h (85mph).

To judge the N600 on its failings would be wrong. It was designed primarily as a commuting tool for

urban dwellers – a brief it fitted perfectly and, given today's car pool, one well before its time.

ENGINE: 599cc (37cu in),
two-cylinder
POWER: 42bhp (31kW)
0–60MPH (96KM/H): 29.3 seconds
TOP SPEED: 136km/h (85mph)
PRODUCTION TOTAL: n/a

MASERATI INDY

ITALY 1966–74

After the success of the Ghibli, Maserati wanted to transfer the angular looks of its top model to less performance-oriented models in its range. The Indy was conceived as a smaller alternative

Essentially a scaled-down Ghibli, the Indy was nowhere near as harmoniously styled and never shared its sister car's success.

to the Mistral, with the practicality of four seats and a rear fastback.

Instead of commissioning Giugiaro to design the Indy, Maserati asked Vignale to carry out the styling. The result was slightly awkward. Maserati wanted to continue the Ghibli's look, but Vignale did not want to copy Giugiaro, so the car was higher and wider, despite retaining the Ghibli's low nose and pop-up headlights.

Underneath came the chassis from the Quattroporte, but Maserati chose to seam-weld the body to the frame in an unusual method of semi-unitary construction. Its lack of experience in this department came home to roost several years later, when the Indy developed an unfortunate reputation for corrosion, due to water and dirt getting trapped inside the car's sill structure and rotting outwards.

Power came from a choice of engines – initially the Quattroporte's 4136cc (252cu in) V8, but later models used the 4930cc (301cu in) unit from the Ghibli SS.

ENGINE: 4719cc (288cu in), V8-cylinder
POWER: 290bhp (216kW) at 5500rpm
0–60MPH (96KM/H): 7.5 seconds
TOP SPEED: 253km/h (157mph)
PRODUCTION TOTAL: 1136

LOTUS EUROPA

UNITED KINGDOM 1966–75

Lotus has revived the Europa name for use in the twenty-first century, despite the fact that the first car to bear the name was not a huge success for the British sports-car maker. Built as a car for Europe, the Europa used the engine and gearbox from the Renault 16 hatchback to reduce Lotus's development costs. The Renault engine was not really the issue,

however, as it was fairly lively and quite reliable. It was the Europa's distinctive high-sided styling (designed by John Frayling) that was at best considered controversial, if not downright ugly.

It was also cramped inside and had extremely poor visibility, especially towards the rear, while the fixed-pane windows on early models meant that it was almost

impossible to get any ventilation into the cabin, making the car insufferable on hot days. All of which was a crying shame because, under the skin, the Europa was brilliantly designed. In the right environment it was thrilling to drive.

Series 2 cars, from 1968, were much improved, with electrically operated front windows and more leg and elbow room in the cabin,

while from 1971 a new twin-cam engine finally gave the car the performance it deserved.

ENGINE: 1470cc (90cu in),
four-cylinder
POWER: 78bhp (58kW)
0–60MPH (96KM/H): 10.7 seconds
TOP SPEED: 179km/h (112mph)
PRODUCTION TOTAL: 9230

It may have looked slightly odd, but the Lotus Europa was designed to have perfect 50:50 weight distribution front to rear. They also saved development costs by using the engine and gearbox from the Renault 16 hatchback.

MORRIS 1800/2200

UNITED KINGDOM 1966–75

For some reason, BMC waited almost two years to introduce the Morris version of its 1800/2200 'Landcrab' series of models, despite the car being identical to the existing Austin version in all but the minor details. The thinking at the time was to establish Austin as the 'innovator' of the BMC brands, while Morris was aimed more at traditional buyers who favoured proven technology rather than newfangled design. If that was the case, then fans of traditional big Morrises would have been rather fazed by the 1800/2200's oddball looks, front-wheel drive and bouncy Hydrolastic suspension, although they would at least have been impressed by the car's vast interior space and comfortable seats.

The four-cylinder 1800 went out of production in 1972 to make way for the Marina, while at the same time not stealing sales from the avant-garde Austin Maxi. Six-cylinder 2200 models soldiered on until 1975 and the arrival of the Princess 'Wedge'.

ENGINE: 1798cc (110cu in), four-cylinder
POWER: 80bhp (60kW) at 5000rpm
0–60MPH (96KM/H): 17.4 seconds
TOP SPEED: 148km/h (92mph)
PRODUCTION TOTAL: about 105,271

PONTIAC TEMPEST LE MANS

UNITED STATES 1966–75

If you couldn't afford a GTO, you could at least buy a car that looked like it! The Tempest Le Mans was Pontiac's less muscular offering. It received the same GTO-style pressed-steel sports wheels, sports front bucket seats and air intakes on the bonnet (hood).

The Le Mans was Pontiac's 'baby' GTO. Based on the body of a standard Tempest, much like the GTO itself, the Le Mans was available as a saloon, a two-door coupé or a convertible, although it was the latter two bodystyles that accounted for the lion's share of sales. Its popularity mainly came from its visual similarities to the iconic but expensive GTO, for it received the same GTO-style pressed-steel sports wheels, air intakes on the bonnet (hood) and rear wings (fenders), sports front bucket seats, electric windows and a 10 per cent boost in power over standard Tempest models.

On the outside, the car was identified by its unsubtle badging and a vinyl-covered roof, or electric folding top on convertible models. Pontiac also offered a Le Mans Station Wagon, but this was utterly unsporting and even featured fake wood self-adhesive panels down each side, replacing the other models' smart side flashes.

In line with the rest of the range, the Le Mans had a face-lift in 1969, ushering in a new era of bad taste. Chrome rings around the radiator grille and unconvincing fake wood panels splashed around the interior did little for the car's styling, and the Le Mans' reputation as a GTO wannabe was lost at the same time. Pontiac continued to offer 'sporty' Le Mans versions of its ordinary models until the late 1990s.

ENGINE: 4638cc (283cu in), eight-cylinder
POWER: 195bhp (145kW)
0–60MPH (96KM/H): n/a
TOP SPEED: n/a
PRODUCTION TOTAL: 831,331

SUNBEAM IMP SPORT

UNITED KINGDOM 1966–76

The Hillman Imp had plenty of tuning potential, but, for the Rootes Group, the marque simply did not have what was required to sell to a younger, more performance-oriented market. When the decision was taken to build a more lively Imp, with a revised engine, twin carburettors and wider tyres, the car was sold under the more dynamic Sunbeam name. To cope with the power increase (up to 51bhp/39kW from 39bhp/29kW), extra cooling was needed, especially as the Imp already had a reputation for overheating, so Rootes redesigned the engine cover to include slats that forced air over the powerplant.

The car was especially popular with budget-conscious rally drivers, as its rear-engined layout made it especially effective on gravel stages. In 1970, when Rootes rationalized the range, the Imp Sport became known as simply the Sport, and received a few minor styling and trim changes.

ENGINE: 875cc (53cu in), four-cylinder
POWER: 51bhp (39kW)
0–60MPH (96KM/H): 16.3 seconds
TOP SPEED: 144km/h (90mph)
PRODUCTION TOTAL: about 10,000

Visual differences between the Sunbeam and Hillman versions of the Imp included twin front headlights, wider tyres and a revised radiator grille. Very popular with budget-conscious rally drivers.

BMW '02-SERIES

GERMANY 1966–77

It might have gone about its business subtly, but the BMW '02 range was the car that saved the ailing BMW company and built it back up to its current position as one of the leading luxury car makers in the world. Neatly styled and beautifully built, the '02 was aimed at a slightly less affluent market than previous BMWs, and was initially available only with a 1600cc (98cu in) slant-four engine.

Reviewers raved about the new car, which had great steering and handling, was exceptionally well put together and was both practical and affordable. Initially, BMW could not cope with demand, which delayed the introduction of further models. They did arrive, though, in the form of the ground-breaking hatchback-cum-estate (station wagon) Touring model in 1968 and, a year later, the famous 2002. Using a 1990cc (121cu in) engine, the 2002 gave the baby BMW enough power to sell well in the United States, while the twin carb Ti model was even more lively.

A fuel-injected version, called Tii, debuted a year later, while the ultimate version of the '02, the 2002 Turbo, became the first production car to be offered with a turbocharger as standard, and was very potent indeed. The '02 is today regarded as a mould-shattering design classic, with good reason.

ENGINE: 1990cc (121cu in), four-cylinder
POWER: 130bhp (97kW)
0–60MPH (96KM/H): 8.3 seconds
TOP SPEED: 187km/h (116mph)
PRODUCTION TOTAL: 698,943

The top version of the '02 was the Ti; one of the first commercially available cars with fuel injection as standard.

HILLMAN MINX/HUNTER

Believe it or not, the Hillman Minx and Hunter were regarded as forward-thinking designs when they first appeared. Known internally as the 'Arrow' range, the newcomers marked a significant leap forward for the ultra-conservative Hillman brand, which took a long time to finally give up styling cars with curves, fins and chrome, and concentrate instead on moving forwards with the times.

Some of the best engineers in the automotive industry were called upon for their input, including Aston Martin engineer William Towns. At launch, the car was seen as a bold and almost dynamic new look. Looking back, there was nothing especially unique about the Minx/Hunter models (which were also sold as Singer Vogues, Singer Gazelles and, dripping with chrome, as the

Humber Sceptre). Regardless, they were good sellers for Hillman, and the simplicity of their engineering, which consisted of a proven range of overhead-valve engines, live rear axles and worm-and-roller steering, meant that they were perfect for home maintenance. The 1725cc (105cu in) versions were surprisingly lively, especially the 93bhp (63kW) Hunter GLS of 1972. When the Hunter was withdrawn in

1977, the design was shipped off to Iran, where it reappeared for almost 30 years as the country's national car, the Paykan.

ENGINE: 1496cc (91cu in), four-cylinder
POWER: 60bhp (45kW)
0–60MPH (96KM/H): 17.8 seconds
TOP SPEED: 138km/h (86mph)
PRODUCTION TOTAL: 470,000

TRIDENT CLIPPER

It may have sounded like a boat, but there was nothing aquatic about the Trident Clipper. First shown at the 1966 Racing Car Show in London, the Clipper began life as a TVR prototype, but ended

For a car that cost more than an E-Type, the Trident Clipper wasn't exactly a looker. It was tricky to drive, too.

up being disposed of as part of the demise of TVR's partner, the Grantura Engineering company. Initially based on the TVR Grantura chassis, no longer available as Grantura had stopped trading, the first production Clippers used a 390bhp (291kW) Ford V8 engine, mounted on an Austin-Healey 3000 chassis. But no sooner had the Clipper entered production than the Austin-Healey went out of

production, leaving Trident with the task of reengineering the car to sit on a Triumph TR6 frame.

In the end, the Clipper cost more to buy than a Jaguar E-type and almost as much as an Aston Martin DB5. Unsurprisingly, this led to the company facing bankruptcy in 1972. The Clipper project was briefly revived in the mid-1970s, using a 6-litre (366cu in) Chrysler V8 engine, which turned the original

Clipper's already precarious handling into something truly terrifying. It was a brave effort, but ultimately a complete disaster of a car.

ENGINE: 4727cc (287cu in), V8-cylinder
POWER: 390bhp (291kW)
0–60MPH (96KM/H): n/a
TOP SPEED: 219km/h (137mph)
PRODUCTION TOTAL: 225 (including Venturer and Tycoon)

FIAT 124 SPIDER

Fiat's 124 saloon was an unlikely basis for a sports car, yet, despite its mundane family car origins, the 124 Spider was an unprecedented success, becoming Italy's most successful sports car ever in terms of sales and lasting for almost 20 years, even doing well to infiltrate the US market. Much of its success was, of course, down to its charming looks. Styled and built by Pininfarina on a

shortened 124 saloon chassis, the Spider looked dropdead gorgeous.

But it was not only the car's appearance that made it attractive, for under the bonnet (hood) was a superb twin overhead-camshaft engine, initially in 1438cc (88cu in) 90bhp (67kW) form with a five-speed manual gearbox. Revised models, from 1969, received a more powerful 1608cc (98cu in) engine with twin Weber carburettors,

developing 82kW (110bhp), and these cars are recognizable by their twin bonnet humps, which house the larger carbs.

The fastest and most collectable Spider was the Abarth, with 95KW (128bhp), revised suspension, a limited slip diff and glassfibre bonnet and boot (trunk) to keep weight to a minimum.

Later models were detuned to comply with American emissions

legislation, and are identifiable by their black plastic bumpers, which also make them less stylish and much less collectable.

ENGINE: 1438cc (88cu in), four-cylinder
POWER: 90bhp (67kW)
0–60MPH (96KM/H): 12 seconds
TOP SPEED: 170km/h (106mph)
PRODUCTION TOTAL: 198,000

Production of the Fiat 124 Spider, Italy's highest-selling sports car of its day, officially stopped in 1979, but Pininfarina assembled several cars itself to keep the car going well into the 1980s.

WARTBURG 353/KNIGHT

EAST GERMANY 1966–88

One of the more successful Eastern European cars, if a long way from being perfect, the Wartburg 353 (or Knight, in some markets) was based on the chassis of the outgoing Wartburg 312

Smoke from the rear end was a trademark of Wartburg's two-stroke engineering. Today's environmentalists would hate it.

models, with various modifications to make it safer and more modern.

Built for ease of maintenance, it retained Wartburg's trademark three-cylinder two-stroke engine, which was incredibly economical, but had an alarming habit of belching out thick clouds of oily smoke, especially in cold weather. The engine was simple to repair, though, and all of the body panels were bolted on so that they could

be simply and easily replaced. An unusual estate (station wagon) model, the Tourist, debuted in 1967 and was unusual to look at; its development costs were kept down by moulding the rear end out of fibreglass.

Wartburgs sold with some success in Western Europe, where they were much cheaper to buy than mainstream models, but disappeared in the mid-1970s as

new emissions laws made them impossible to sell. In less stringent Eastern European markets, they sold well up until the late 1980s.

ENGINE: 991cc (60cu in), three-cylinder two-stroke
POWER: 45bhp (34kW)
0–60MPH (96KM/H): 22.8 seconds
TOP SPEED: 118km/h (74mph)
PRODUCTION TOTAL: n/a

FORD OSI 20M

Italy's OSI always turned up at international motor shows with cars of its own design, usually based on those of Fiat or Alfa Romeo. But, in 1966, the company built an intriguing concept car based on the popular and reliable German Ford Taunus 20M. Reaction from showgoers was so positive that Ford's European headquarters in Cologne commissioned OSI to build a limited run of the cars to add more glamour to the marque outside of its home market, where sales were generally slow.

Based entirely on the Taunus, the OSI used both its 2.0-litre (122cu in) and 2.3-litre (140cu in) V6 engines, along with the same axles, suspension configuration, gearboxes and brakes. Although utterly conventional underneath, the OSI handled well and enjoyed quite lively performance, but the high price meant that it only ever sold in limited numbers.

OSI was acquired by rival coachbuilder Ghia in 1968, and the 20M Coupé project was cancelled, but not before OSI had made a big enough name for itself for Ford to consult with new owners Ghia over various future projects, before eventually taking over the company itself and using Ghia as a model name for its more upmarket cars.

ENGINE: 1998cc (122cu in), four-cylinder
POWER: 90bhp (67kW)
0–60MPH (96KM/H): 10 seconds
TOP SPEED: 172km/h (107mph)
PRODUCTION TOTAL: n/a

TRIUMPH TR5/250

If one criticism could be levelled at the pretty TR4, it was the car's lack of power, which led Triumph to upgrade to a six-cylinder engine for the last three years of the car's production. The new model, dubbed TR5, appeared in late 1967 and

Although outwardly similar to the TR4, the TR5 was completely different under the skin, with a new six-cylinder engine.

used a 2498cc (152cu in) engine based on the smaller 2.0-litre (121cu in) unit fitted to the Triumph 2000 saloon. The engine size was increased by lengthening the stroke of the engine, while Triumph pulled off a further coup by becoming the first British manufacturer to use fuel injection as standard on a car, courtesy of the TR5's Lucas-developed system.

The body looked almost identical to the TR4, but there were changes under the skin. Larger brakes were fitted, the rear suspension was revised and modifications were made to the interior to make it look more modern, with safer padded fascia surfaces.

Unfortunately for Triumph, the innovative fuel injection system failed to meet tough US emissions legislation, so cars sold in the United States had the injectors replaced by a pair of Zenith carburettors, significantly reducing the power output from 150bhp (112kW) to 105bhp (78kW). Nowhere near as good as their European contemporaries, these cars were called TR250s.

ENGINE: 2498cc (152cu in), six-cylinder
POWER: 150bhp (112kW) at 5500rpm
0–60MPH (96KM/H): 8.8 seconds
TOP SPEED: 195km/h (121mph)
PRODUCTION TOTAL: 11,431

ALFA ROMEO 33 STRADALE

In Europe's style capital of Italy, even racing cars had to be stunningly beautiful – and the Alfa Romeo 33 certainly did not disappoint. Styled by ex-Bertone designer Franco Scaglione, the two-door coupé bodywork was reminiscent of the classic Ferrari Dino and was considered so stunning that Alfa Romeo decided to build a road-car variant, on a 10cm (4in) longer chassis to improve ride comfort. Known as the Stradale, the road car had handmade light alloy bodywork and was built on Alfa Romeo's behalf at Scaglione's workshop in Turin.

It was powered by a detuned version of the racing 33's twin overhead-camshaft V8 engine, although it was still a very potent machine. The 1995cc (122cu in) delivered 230bhp (171kW) – enough to propel the Stradale to a top speed of 259km/h (162mph).

Only 18 cars were completed, including three special motor show models – the Bertone-bodied and wedge-shaped Carabo, Guigiaro's 33 Iguana coupé, and a two-seater convertible by Pininfarina, called the P33 Roadster.

ENGINE: 1995cc (122cu in), eight-cylinder
POWER: 230bhp (171kW)
0–60MPH (96KM/H): n/a
TOP SPEED: 259km/h (162mph)
PRODUCTION TOTAL: 18

BIZZARINI 1900 EUROPA

ITALY 1967–69

Having already created his own supercar in the form of the huge V8-powered Strada 5300, ex-Ferrari engineer Giotto Bizzarini decided that he had more chance of appealing to the mass market, and making a profit in the process, by creating a smaller, more affordable sports car that borrowed heavily from the Strada's styling cues. Instead of running a

Chevrolet V8 engine under the bonnet (hood), Bizzarini approached German manufacturer Opel, which provided its 1897cc (116cu in) engine from the A-Series Manta, as its compact dimensions were perfect for squeezing into the low-slung Europa's bodyshell.

Styling-wise, the Europe looked very similar to the Strada. It was much smaller, obviously, but most

of the original dimensions were simply scaled down to fit onto Bizzarini's newly designed compact chassis. There were a few changes, including a more pointy front end, curved glass tops to the doors to make the interior appear more airy, and repositioned air vents.

The Europa was fairly quick and drove impressively well, but it was not much cheaper than the V8

Strada. Its high development costs forced Bizzarini to close down after only 15 cars had left the factory.

ENGINE: 1897cc (116cu in),
four-cylinder
POWER: 135bhp (101kW)
0–60MPH (96KM/H): n/a
TOP SPEED: 206km/h (128mph)
PRODUCTION TOTAL: 15

DODGE CHARGER

UNITED STATES 1967–69

General Motors may have invented the muscle car, but there was a time when Chrysler-Dodge was considered America's keenest exponent of the iconic macho saloons. The Dodge Charger

One of the muscle-car icons of the 1960s, the Dodge Charger has now become massively collectable.

and its sisters – the Dodge Challenger, Plymouth Roadrunner and Plymouth Barracuda – were the best-selling cars on the muscle-car scene. The Charger was Dodge's flagship muscle machine, powered by its famous 440 Magnum or 428 Hemi engines, both of which were blisteringly quick. The top model, called the R/T, came with a neat rear boot (trunk) spoiler, to echo the look of Dodge's NASCAR racers.

In 1970 came the most extreme Charger of the lot – the Daytona. Built in a limited run of just 500 for motorsport homologation purposes, the Daytona had a huge rear wing (fender) and pointed polyurethane nose to improve its aerodynamics, giving it an incredible top speed of 322km/h (200mph).

Successful on the racetrack, the Charger also had an impressive television and film career, as the

'General Lee' in *The Dukes of Hazzard* and as the sinister black car that pursued Steve McQueen's green Mustang in the movie *Bullit*.

ENGINE: 7211cc (440cu in),
eight-cylinder
POWER: 375bhp (279kW)
0–60MPH (96KM/H): 7.2 seconds
TOP SPEED: 217km/h (135mph)
PRODUCTION TOTAL: 201,088

JAGUAR 240/340

UNITED KINGDOM 1967–69

In a bid to cut costs and rationalize its range, Jaguar made a raft of changes to its popular and successful Mk II model to make it appeal to less affluent buyers. Purists were horrified by what Jaguar did to the car. Even today, the car is snubbed by aficionados of the marque in favour of its almost identical predecessor, despite the

fact that the 2.4-litre (152cu in) 240 and 3.4-litre (210cu in) 340 were actually good-quality cars that proved popular with a new breed of Jaguar customer. Some even argue that the 240 and 340 are better looking than the Mk II, as the original's overly elaborate chrome bumpers were replaced by less intrusive, slimmer items.

Other cutbacks included imitation leather Ambla upholstery in place of premium hide, thinner carpets, dummy grilles where the Mk II's fog lamps would have been and a simpler dashboard. To drive, the 240 and 340 were little different from the Mk II, but the lack of power-assisted steering made them hard work to park. Sadly, there

was no 3.8-litre (231cu in) option, despite the larger engine's success in the previous generation of cars.

ENGINE: 2483cc (152cu in), six-cylinder
POWER: 133bhp (99kW)
0–60MPH (96KM/H): 12.5 seconds
TOP SPEED: 170km/h (106mph)
PRODUCTION TOTAL: 856,428

Purists may have been horrifed by the low budget version of the legendary Mk 2, but the 240/340 series of Jaguars were still incredibly beautiful and desirable beasts, whose handling was much the same as the more luxurious Mk 2.

MG MGC

On paper, the MGC should have been a great car. It was built to compete with larger sports cars such as the Triumph TR4, when BMC decided to redesign the front end of the popular MGB to house the straight-six engine from the ill-

The only external difference between an MGC and an MGB is the squared-off bonnet hump, to accommodate the larger engine.

fated Austin 3-Litre saloon. The theory was that the MGB's pretty body, coupled to the more potent six-cylinder engine, would make the car a worthy successor to the aged Austin-Healey 3000.

But it was not to be. Despite some moderate racing success at Daytona, Sebring and Le Mans, the MGC did not translate especially well into a road car. The big six-cylinder engine was simply too heavy to put in the MGB's nose,

which meant that the steering felt impossibly heavy at low speeds, and the back end was twitchy and prone to losing grip, especially in the wet. MG tried to counter this by firming up the suspension, but this only served to ruin the MGB's compliant ride. Its case was not helped by independent MG specialists fitting Rover V8 engines instead, a move that MG later pursued itself when British Leyland Corporation took over Rover.

Externally, the MGC looked little different from an MGB, apart from a pronounced hump in the bonnet (hood) and different wheel discs. It was offered as a roadster and a GT.

ENGINE: 2912cc (178cu in), six-cylinder
POWER: 145bhp (108kW)
0–60MPH (96KM/H): 10 seconds
TOP SPEED: 202km/h (125mph)
PRODUCTION TOTAL: 8999

AMC REBEL

Starting life as one of the myriad of confusing models in the AMC Rambler range, the Rebel became a car in its own right in 1967, marketed between the upmarket Ambassador and smaller American.

Rebels were not especially attractive, and were available as two-door sedans, fastbacks and convertibles, plus an awkward-looking estate (station wagon)

variant. A range of options was offered, including both six-cylinder and V8 engines.

A subtle restyle occurred in 1968, which made the front end styling much more attractive, while the range was cut back to just two trim levels – base and SST. The SST, which stood for Super Sport Touring, was marketed as a junior muscle car to try to cash in

on America's latest performance craze, but the AMC name did not have the kudos associated with bigger muscle cars such as the Pontiac GTO and Dodge Charger.

Undeterred, AMC tried to cash in on the muscle-car market proper in 1970, with the extremely styled and very quick Rebel Machine. It came with a 5.6-litre V8 (343cu in) engine, producing a remarkable

340bhp (253kW), making it AMC's most powerful model ever. Despite this, it was not a huge success.

ENGINE: 5619cc (343cu in), eight-cylinder
POWER: 280bhp (209kW)
0–60MPH (96KM/H): 9 seconds
TOP SPEED: 177km/h (110mph)
PRODUCTION TOTAL: 284,326

OPEL OLYMPIA

Historically, the Olympia name was always used on Opel's flagship models, but, in 1967, the German maker applied it to a different class of car. Aimed at buyers who knew the company's history, but wanted a smaller, more modern car than Olympias traditionally had been, the badge was applied to upmarket versions of Kadetts. In essence, they were very pleasant cars. The standard

Kadett on which they were based was a well-made and pleasant car to drive, while the choice of two- or four-door saloon or two-door coupé bodystyles were all modern and smart looking.

Extra trim included neat chrome wheel trims, whitewall tyres and a vinyl-covered roof, plus a unique radiator grille that curved round to meet the front wings (fenders). The cabin was well trimmed, with

wood-effect details and extra dials. All came with twin carb engines for a little more performance than standard Kadetts, while the basic car's chassis delivered obedient handling and a comfortable ride.

Despite being a likeable machine, the Olympia was not overly successful simply because of its price. Buyers could have moved up to a car a class larger for the same price as an Olympia, even if those

cars were not anywhere near as luxurious. Most people valued extra space and practicality over the Olympia's creature comforts.

ENGINE: 1078cc (66cu in), four-cylinder
POWER: 60bhp (45kW)
0–60MPH (96KM/H): 19.3 seconds
TOP SPEED: 145km/h (90mph)
PRODUCTION TOTAL: 80,637

TOYOTA 2000GT

Toyota tried everything to make the world take its first proper sports car seriously, including a special arrangement to feature a one-off convertible version in the James Bond movie *You Only Live Twice*. Toyota was desperate to infiltrate the US market, and built the 2000GT by using knowledge gleaned from taking apart and inspecting some of the world's

finest sports cars, including the Lotus Elan and MGB. The car was based on a steel backbone chassis and came with the Toyota Crown's twin-cam six-cylinder 2.0-litre (121cu in) engine. The engine was lively, and the Lotus-style chassis meant decent roadholding as well.

The huge cost of development meant that Toyota could not afford to offer the 2000GT at as low a

price as it hoped. The company's lacklustre image, coupled to the GT's rather odd styling, meant that the car flopped at launch; Toyota canned the project after just 337 examples had been built.

It was not until the Datsun 240Z appeared two years later that the Western world woke up to the threat of the Japanese car market, and, while Toyota's first attempt at

conquering the United States was a failure, it now sells more cars there than any other manufacturer.

ENGINE: 1998cc (122cu in), six-cylinder
POWER: 150bhp (112kW)
0–60MPH (96KM/H): 8.4 seconds
TOP SPEED: 219km/h (137mph)
PRODUCTION TOTAL: 337

VIGNALE-FIAT GAMINE

ENGINE: 500cc (30cu in), twin-cylinder
POWER: 34bhp (25kW)
0–60MPH (96KM/H): n/a
TOP SPEED: 120km/h (75mph) approx.
PRODUCTION TOTAL: 2000 approx.

It might look like the kind of car Noddy might drive, but the Vignale Gamine was a serious attempt at appealing to Italy's vintage and veteran car enthusiasts. Built on the chassis of the Nuova 500, the Gamine recalled the look of earlier cars such as the Topolino of the 1930s and the pre-war Balilla roadster. Vignale got the radiator grille spot on, but sadly failed with the rest of the bodywork, which ended up looking rather

Most Vignale-Fiats were beautiful cars, but the Gamine wasn't the company's finest hour.

silly. The 500's chassis was shorter and wider than the original vintage Fiats', giving the Gamine a squat, cartoonish appearance, while the addition of several bright and lurid colour schemes did little to make

enthusiasts take the car seriously. The Gamine was dreadful to drive, too, with a noisy 500cc (30cu in) engine and no soundproofing whatsoever, plus a complete lack of weather protection.

Taking all of these things into account makes it even more unusual to learn that almost half of the 2000 or so Gamines built were sold in the relatively cold and wet United Kingdom, where they

were imported by Greek business tycoon Frixos Demetriou. Demetriou had spotted one in Italy, and fell in love with it enough to set up a retail network in London, which was surprisingly successful.

ZAZ 966

USSR 1967–68

The ZAZ 966, also known as the Zaporozhets outside of the former Soviet Union, was a rather unusual little car. Following on from the truly awful ZAZ 965, the 'Zappo' was unusually pretty, styled to look similar to the German NSU Prinz. It had a rear-mounted air-cooled engine and

huge air intakes in each side, although a fundamental design flaw was that the air intakes were too large, and sucked large pieces of debris up from the road to go smashing into the engine block.

Like its predecessor, the 966 was precarious to drive, with ineffective brakes and dubious

handling, although it was modified for sale in Europe (as the Yalta 1000) to use an engine and braking system borrowed from Renault, with reasonable results.

One of the Zappo's more curious attributes was a lift-out panel in the floor of the passenger compartment, designed to allow

its occupants to take the car fishing on frozen lakes!

ENGINE: 1196cc (73cu in), four-cylinder
POWER: 45bhp (34kW)
0–60MPH (96KM/H): n/a
TOP SPEED: 120km/h (75mph)
PRODUCTION TOTAL: about 2,000,000

AUSTIN 3-LITRE

UNITED KINGDOM 1967–71

There was some confusion surrounding the debut of the Austin 3-Litre, as by the time it debuted its parent company already

This was a parts-bin special: the doors were from the 1800, the engine from an Austin-Healey and the suspension from a van.

owned Rover and Triumph, and pundits questioned the need for a luxury car wearing the downmarket Austin badge. The car's case was not helped by its styling. Budget cuts at BMC meant that the designers had to use the doors and centre body section from the Austin 1800/2200 models, which were much smaller. The result was

a car that looked as if it had been pinched in the middle.

Self-levelling rear suspension and power steering were standard, while BMC faced a huge challenge re-engineering the front-wheel drive 1800/2200's midriff to accept the rear-drive layout of the 3-Litre. Power came from the same straight-six engine as the MGC.

The 3-Litre's odd looks and lack of prestige contributed to this fairly decent car being a very poor seller.

ENGINE: 2912cc (178cu in), six-cylinder
POWER: 124bhp (92kW)
0–96KM/H (60MPH): 15.7 seconds
TOP SPEED: 161km/h (100mph)
PRODUCTION TOTAL: 9992

FERRARI 365 GT 2+2

ITALY 1967–71

Ferrari's largest and most luxurious model ever, the 365 GT 2+2 was the replacement for the 330 2+2. It retained the platform of the 330, with its

264cm (104in) wheelbase, but the overall length was significantly increased, with long overhangs and the front and rear of the car. This helped to make the 365 a

genuine four-seater, with generous passenger and luggage space, and a greater level of practicality than any Ferrari before or since. Standard equipment included air

conditioning, electric windows and power-assisted steering, although this latter development met with disapproval from some enthusiasts, who specified the car without.

At 1588kg (3500lb), the 365 GT was heavy. Thanks to a 4.4-litre (268cu in) V12 engine, however, the performance was undiminished, and the car was able to sprint to 60mph (96km/h) in just seven seconds and on to a top speed of 152mph (245km/h). To save interior space, the gearbox was mounted at the front with the engine, rather than at the rear over the axle, as in other Ferrari models.

A great grand tourer and a convincing sports car to boot, the 365 GT was an unusual offering from the Ferrari stable, but at the same time a very welcome one.

ENGINE: 4390cc (268cu in),
V12-cylinder
POWER: 320bhp (238kW)
0–60MPH (96KM/H): 7 seconds
TOP SPEED: 245km/h (152mph)
PRODUCTION TOTAL: 801

A Ferrari for all the family? Well, maybe not quite, but the GT 2+2 was Ferrari's largest car ever, with back seats and some useful luggage space.

OLDSMOBILE 4-4-2

Oldsmobile had tried to redefine the muscle car with the Toronado, but its avant-garde approach had met with resistance from technophobic US buyers. But Oldsmobile did not want to miss

There were both Fastback and Convertible versions of the 4-4-2. The former was a better drive, the latter is more collectable.

out on the muscle-car revolution, and as a result the 4-4-2 was born.

Looking unashamedly like its arch rival, the Plymouth Barracuda, the 4-4-2 was a pretty two-door fastback or convertible, with a choice of V8 engines, including the incredible 7.4-litre (455cu in) unit taken straight from the innovative Toronado. Underneath, the chassis was from the Oldsmobile Cutlass Sedan and as simple as they came,

with drum brakes and leaf springs giving the 4-4-2 the same hairy handling characteristics as the rest of the muscle-car clan. Incidentally, the 4-4-2 name stood for 400 cubic inches, a four-barrel carburettor and two exhausts, meaning Oldsmobile was not shy about the car's performance aspirations.

Like all cars of its type, the 4-4-2 was killed off in its prime, not by a lack of customer demand, but by

the combination of tough new emissions legislations that led to vastly reduced power outputs, and the oil crisis of the early 1970s.

ENGINE: 6551cc (400cu in),
eight-cylinder
POWER: 290bhp (216kW)
0–60MPH (96KM/H): 10.3 seconds
TOP SPEED: 194km/h (120mph)
PRODUCTION TOTAL: 86,883

TVR TUSCAN

UNITED KINGDOM 1967–71

With the Tuscan, TVR finally built the car that its Griffith should have been. Dramatically better made than its predecessor, the Tuscan boasted a timeless bodystyle that would grace TVR's models for the best part of two

The first in a series of similar-looking TVR sports cars, the Tuscan is one of the company's all-time icons.

decades, along with a better chassis, blistering performance and seat-of-the-pants roadholding. It was not for the faint-hearted by any means, but, on the right road, the Tuscan could be a real hoot to drive. TVR thought carefully about the car's weight distribution, and ousted the Griffith's big V8 engine in favour of a Ford-sourced V6, which made the front end lighter and the car better balanced overall. The four-speed gearbox also came

from Ford and had a light, precise action, giving the Tuscan the feel of a true lightweight sports car.

Later on in the model's life, in a bid to attract people away from kit cars into fully built sports cars, TVR offered a variant with a four-cylinder Ford engine, which also proved impressively popular, especially when emissions legislation in the United States dramatically slashed sales of big-engined performance models.

Although not many Tuscans were sold, the car evolved into the M-Series, which proved to be the Blackpool-based company's most successful model ever.

ENGINE: 2994cc (183cu in), V6-cylinder
POWER: 128bhp (95kW)
0–60MPH (96KM/H): 8.3seconds
TOP SPEED: 201km/h (125mph)
PRODUCTION TOTAL: 156

MAZDA COSMO

JAPAN 1967–72

Although most people credit NSU for bringing the twin rotary Wankel engine to market with the Ro80, it was actually Mazda that introduced this innovation in the low-volume, rather odd-looking Cosmo sports car. Introduced in 1967, the Cosmo was powered by a twin-rotor engine of just 982cc (60cu in) and produced about 110bhp (67kW). The rotary engine worked

by means of a pair of triangular-shaped rotors, which spun quickly to compress the air inside the combustion chambers, allowing much smoother acceleration than a standard petrol engine and the ability to rev much more freely.

Despite the technical advances under the bonnet (hood), the Cosmo was fairly ordinary under the skin, with a live rear axle, front coil springs and disc brakes at the

front, drums at the rear. A Series II variant was introduced in July 1968 and had a more-powerful 128bhp (95kW) engine, plus five-speed manual transmission in place of the original car's four-speed unit.

Visual changes included a larger grille under the front bumper with two additional air vents. Each Cosmo was fully put together by hand and took over a day to build, with just 1519 cars finished in

total before Mazda withdrew the model and focused on making its rotary engines fit into more mainstream cars.

ENGINE: 491cc (30cu in), twin-rotor Wankel
POWER: 110bhp (82kW)
0–60MPH (96KM/H): 10.2 seconds
TOP SPEED: 185km/h (115mph)
PRODUCTION TOTAL: 1176

SUNBEAM STILETTO

UNITED KINGDOM 1967–72

The most desirable and sought-after version of the Hillman Imp is the Sunbeam Stiletto. Based on the same coupé bodywork as the Singer Chamois and Imp Californian, the Stiletto came with four round headlights and a different front grille. It also had

a black vinyl-topped roof and smart black fake leather interior trim. The dashboard had wooden inserts and extra dials to further mark out the car as an upmarket model.

The engine was the same as that fitted to the Imp Sport. While its 875cc (53cu in) displacement was

identical to a standard Imp, its improved gas flow cylinder head, larger inlet valves and high-lift cam gave it far more lively performance. Sunbeam owners, Rootes Group, fitted stronger pistons and a self-adjusting clutch mechanism to complement the extra power.

ENGINE: 875cc (53cu in), four-cylinder
POWER: 51bhp (38kW)
0–60MPH (96KM/H): 17.6 seconds
TOP SPEED: 139km/h (87mph)
PRODUCTION TOTAL: about 10,000

VAUXHALL VICTOR FD

UNITED KINGDOM 1967–72

ENGINE: 1975cc (121cu in),
four-cylinder
POWER: 104bhp (77kW)
0–60MPH (96KM/H): 14 seconds
TOP SPEED: 153km/h (95mph)
PRODUCTION TOTAL: 198,085

Vauxhall was used to its cars being criticized for being bland, but that was certainly not a charge that could be levelled at the stylish Victor FD, with its smart four-headlight front end and side panels that were pinched in the middle like a Coke bottle.

The FD also came with a decent engine range, kicking off with a 1599cc (98cu in) unit that offered modest performance and good reliability. A 1975cc (121cu in) mid-range unit was the most popular, with its good compromise of performance and economy. The flagship models, dubbed 'Ventora', came with a 3294cc (201cu in) straight-six and optional automatic transmission, giving them the feel of a small luxury car.

All FD's were good to drive, with sharp handling and a comfortable ride, plus accurate rack-and-pinion steering. A fairly attractive estate (station wagon) model joined the line-up in 1968, giving the Victor FD greater appeal to fleet customers. Sadly, this very good car is remembered more for its bad corrosion than its many positive attributes. The FD was replaced by the squared-off FE in 1972.

With its swooping centre-line and vast bonnet, the FD Victor was heavily influenced by General Motors stylists in Detroit.

ASTON MARTIN DBS

UNITED KINGDOM 1967–73

The DBS came as quite a shock for fans of Aston Martin's more traditional models. The delicate curves and understated elegance of the iconic DB models may have proven a successful formula for almost two decades, but, to ready itself for the 1970s, Aston took a completely new tack. The new car, styled by William Towns, was much bolder and brasher than Astons of old. At a full 1.8m (5ft 11in) wide, the DBS's squat nose with twin headlights gave it the appearance of an American muscle car, and clearly indicated in which part of the world Aston wanted to increase its market share.

Some people loved the looks; others found it offensive. Still, the DBS did have a number of good points. Although based on the basic architecture of the DB6, the revised rear end used a de Dion rear axle arrangement, pioneered in the Rover P6, which made a significant difference to the way the car went round corners. Given the DBS's colossal weight, it was still inadvisable to attack bends with too much enthusiasm.

The first DBSs used the DB6's 4.0-litre (244cu in) straight-six engine, but Aston Martin made clear from the start that the car had been designed for further power choices, and, in 1970, the DBS V8 appeared. Its 5.3-litre (326cu in) engine developed 375bhp (279kW) and was designed entirely in-house by Aston Martin, surviving in the company's models well into the 1990s.

Early models suffered reliability problems courtesy of the Bosch fuel injection system, but these were ironed out fairly quickly.

ENGINE: 5340cc (326cu in),
eight-cylinder
POWER: 375bhp (279kW)
0–60MPH (96KM/H): 6 seconds
TOP SPEED: 256km/h (159mph)
PRODUCTION TOTAL: 962

The angular styling of the Aston Martin DBS marked a sharp change of direction for the company, although purists missed the curviness of earlier models.

GINETTA G15

Kit cars were commonplace throughout the 1960s, but only a handful ever made a big enough name for themselves to end up going into proper production. Ginetta, based in Witham, Essex, in the United Kingdom, created cars stylish enough to win the hearts and minds of sports-car enthusiasts, and priced them keenly enough to secure a steady flow of orders over the years. The G15 was the company's best-selling model, and

it is not difficult to see why. Looking almost like a Lotus Elan, but with the engine tucked away in the rear, the G15 was offered as a coupé or a convertible, both of which were beautifully stylish.

The car used the all-alloy engine from the Hillman Imp to keep weight to a minimum, coupled to an Imp gearbox and rear suspension, plus front suspension from a Triumph Spitfire. These units were mounted on a handmade tubular

steel frame, cloaked in a gorgeous glassfibre body, while a few models were fitted with a 998cc (61cu in) BMC A-Series engine in place of the Imp unit.

The G15 performed well and was extremely economical on fuel because of its minimal weight, as well as being rewarding to drive. Sadly, changes to British tax laws in 1973 made kit-derived cars such as those offered by Ginetta less viable, and the company

suffered as a consequence, although, despite production officially ending in 1973, kit-based G15's have continued to appear over the years since.

ENGINE: 875cc (53cu in), four-cylinder
POWER: 55bhp (41kW)
0–60MPH (96KM/H): 12.9 seconds
TOP SPEED: 152km/h (95mph)
PRODUCTION TOTAL: 796

MATRA 530

If the original Matra Djet could be considered one of the prettiest cars of its era, then the Matra 530 that succeeded it must have raised a few eyebrows. Intended as a longer, wider and more practical alternative to the Djet, the 530

The 530 had weird revolving headlights, plastic bodywork and a mid-mounted V4 engine. It was never going to be conventional.

was the first car to come out of Matra's new, bigger factory at Romarantin, western France. Its curved front end sat uncomfortably with the trapezoid-shaped roof line, while the flat rear end did little for the harmony of its looks.

But the 530 was an intriguing machine even so. Power came from a German Ford V4 engine, mounted right in the middle of the pressed-steel monocoque inner structure, while plastic outer panels

kept everything well protected. Two especially odd features of the 530 were its pop-up headlights, which were operated by the driver using a pedal in the footwell, and the gearchange, which was back-to-front. The engine was designed for front-wheel drive cars in Germany and so was effectively mounted the wrong way round in the rear-drive Matra. First gear was top right and fourth was bottom left, which took some getting used to!

Noisy and not especially rapid, the 530 was nevertheless an exciting car to drive, with incredible roadholding, thanks to its near-perfect weight distribution.

ENGINE: 1699cc (104cu in), four-cylinder
POWER: 75bhp (56kW)
0–60MPH (96KM/H): 15.6 seconds
TOP SPEED: 161km/h (100mph)
PRODUCTION TOTAL: 9609

TVR VIXEN

The TVR Vixen was closely related to the earlier Grantura, but came with a larger rear window, a bonnet (hood) scoop and different rear end treatment,

with new light clusters borrowed from the Mk 2 Ford Cortina.

It also came with a new engine – a Ford-sourced 1599cc (98cu in) crossflow unit developing 88bhp

(66kW), coupled to a smooth shifting four-speed manual gearbox. Although the power output sounds modest, especially compared to TVR models of recent years, the

little four-cylinder powerplant made the Vixen a pleasant and lively car to drive. The lightweight glassfibre body panels obviously helped, as did the car's delicate tubular chassis. Changes occurred after a year of production, with a longer wheelbase chassis and some minor tweaks to the car's rear bodywork to give it a smoother ride, while the addition of a servo to assist the brakes made it much easier to exploit the car's performance. Called the S2, the visual differences between it and the first Vixen were limited to a distinctive bonnet bulge and two small air intakes at the front, while for ease of maintenance the body panels were bolted, rather than bonded to the chassis, making them far less complex to replace.

The last Vixens, known as S3s, were introduced in 1970 and had a more powerful engine, borrowed from the Ford Capri.

ENGINE: 1599cc (98cu in), four-cylinder
POWER: 88bhp (66kW)
0–60MPH (96KM/H): 11 seconds
TOP SPEED: 170km/h (106mph)
PRODUCTION TOTAL: 746

A smaller, more tame version of the Tuscan, the Vixen was cheaper and less challenging to drive, with a Ford-sourced engine which although not as powerful as more recent TVRs, was very pleasant to drive.

AMC JAVELIN

UNITED STATES 1967–74

AMC always tried its best, but sometimes its cars just did not quite hit the mark – and the Javelin is a case in point. With the Ford Mustang completely dominating the market for stylish, performance-oriented coupés in the United States, AMC decided that it, too,

Yet another 'nearly' car from AMC – the Javelin was a good car in concept, let down by penny-pinching and poor design.

wanted in. With a 6392cc (390cu in) V8 under its bonnet (hood), the Javelin had all the right mechanical ingredients to appeal to fans of the higher powered Mustangs and other junior muscle cars. But in true AMC fashion the car failed to spark the emotions in the way that similar Ford, GM or Chrysler cars did. The slightly bulbous frontal styling and truncated rear end made the Javelin appear at odds with itself, while committee-led costcutting within AMC led to

shoddy build quality and the use of very cheap materials inside the cabin. This would have been fine if the Javelin had undercut its rivals in the price lists, but it did not.

The Javelin was given some minor styling tweaks from year to year up until the end of production, but the most significant changes came in 1971, with the addition of bulging curves in the top of each wing (fender), giving the car an even more unconventional look that was definitely not a huge hit

with customers. This, coupled to increasing legislation governing engine emissions and the car's greater-than-average weight led to AMC dropping the model altogether in 1974.

ENGINE: 6392cc (390cu in), eight-cylinder
POWER: 315bhp (235kW)
0–60MPH (96KM/H): 7 seconds
TOP SPEED: 174km/h (108mph)
PRODUCTION TOTAL: 235,497

FERRARI DINO

Acombination of Enzo Ferrari being too stubborn to build a V6-engined Ferrari and his desire to build a car in tribute to his late son Alfredino led to the smallest ever Ferrari model simply being called the 'Dino' until the mid-1970s. Launched in 1967 as the Dino 206GT, the car had a 1997cc (121cu in) V6 engine that was built for Ferrari by Fiat, and, despite its compact dimensions, it developed an impressive 180bhp (134kW).

Styling house Pininfarina was responsible for the car's gorgeous lines, which Enzo Ferrari was allegedly upset about because a number of pundits described the Dino as the most beautiful Ferrari ever, despite its initial lack of Ferrari badges.

To save space at the main Ferrari factory, the Dinos' bodies were made by coachbuilder Scaglietti, then transported to the Ferrari factory at Maranello for final assembly.

In 1969, the 246GT version arrived, with a larger 2418cc (148cu in) engine, now producing 195bhp (145kW), although the extra weight of the engine meant that there was negligible difference in performance between it and the 206GT. A further change came in 1972, with the addition to the range of the 246GTS, which had a removable targa roof panel, which saw the rear windows removed from all models and replaced by three vent slats.

The last Dinos were the best because, by the time Enzo Ferrari finally allowed them to wear a Ferrari badge, they received extra body stiffening and strengthening to sharpen up the handling.

ENGINE: 2418cc (148cu in), six-cylinder
POWER: 195bhp (145kW)
0–60MPH (96KM/H): 8 seconds
TOP SPEED: 227km/h (141mph)
PRODUCTION TOTAL: 4064

The earliest Dinos weren't known as Ferraris, hence the small 'Dino' nose badge. But its success meant that it was soon accepted as a Ferrari.

ISO FIDIA

The beautiful Rivolta had been a fairly successful car for ISO, given the fact that the Italian manufacturer was only a very small operation. In order to try to broaden its appeal and reach out to more practical-minded buyers, ISO wanted a four-door rival to the established Maserati Quattroporte. That car was the Fidia, styled by Ghia and based on a stretched Chevrolet chassis, complete with a GM small-block V8 engine and a choice of three-speed manual or two-speed automatic transmission.

Sadly for ISO, where the Rivolta was harmonious-looking and pretty, the Fidia turned out to be an oversized slab of a car, with far too much width and bulky flat body panels that did little to give it the impression of agility. The fact that ISO priced the car at the same level as a Rolls-Royce Silver Shadow did not help matters, nor did the patchy build quality and lack of rust resistance.

Fewer than 200 Fidias were built before the ISO company went bankrupt during the oil crisis of 1974, although a handful of cars appeared right through until 1979 under the name 'Ennezeta'.

ENGINE: 5359cc (327cu in), eight-cylinder
POWER: 300bhp (224kW)
0–60MPH (96KM/H): 8.1 seconds
TOP SPEED: 205km/h (128mph)
PRODUCTION TOTAL: 192

LOTUS ELAN+2

ENGINE: 1558cc (95cu in), four-cylinder
POWER: 118bhp (88kW)
0–60MPH (96KM/H): 8.2 seconds
TOP SPEED: 185km/h (115mph)
PRODUCTION TOTAL: 3300

In a bid to expand the appeal of its model range, which had so far allowed only up to two passengers, Lotus decided to develop a four-seater car based on the popular Elan. With assistance from Italian

Bearing in mind how pretty the Elan convertible was, the +2 was a disappointment in styling terms.

styling house Frua, which penned the car's not especially inspiring looks, Lotus lengthened the Elan's steel backbone chassis to allow longer, taller bodywork, and fitted wider doors to provide greater

passenger access to the rear. That said, the back seats were tiny and suitable for small children only – an adult, even of the slightest build, would struggle to get comfortable in the narrow bucket seats.

The Elan+2 was slightly more upmarket than the standard Elan, with a more luxurious cabin and more instruments, plus improved cabin ventilation. The car's added weight meant that it was never as

quick as the roadster models, but the car was more aerodynamic and had better levels of grip, which meant that it could still be hustled along quite quickly. The car was a reasonable success for Lotus.

TOYOTA CROWN

JAPAN 1967–74

Toyota's first attempt to conquer the US sedan market came in the form of the third-generation Crown – a car previously sold only in its home market and certain European countries. That meant it featured an all-new chassis designed

The first Crown's slab-sided style was proof that Japan's fledgling automotive industry was heavily influenced by that of America.

to meet tough US safety legislation, making it significantly heavier and softer to drive than its predecessors.

In order to appeal to the United States, Toyota also took a braver approach with the car's styling, although its success in this department was somewhat limited. The car's excessive chrome at the front and weird, angular bodywork were certainly unique, but failed to win huge praise from the media. The Crown did have its good

points, though, not least in terms of passenger comfort, which was perfect for the luxury demands of the American market, while the build quality was also impressive compared to most US and European offerings of the period.

Two six-cylinder engines were offered, with ample if not exhilarating power, while later models came with anti-skid brakes and an electronically managed automatic gearbox. Although

never a huge seller in the United States, the Crown was a moderate success, and one that helped Toyota to grow into the automotive superpower it is today.

ENGINE: 1988cc (121cu in), six-cylinder
POWER: 125bhp (93kW)
0–60MPH (96KM/H): 12.7 seconds
TOP SPEED: 163km/h (102mph)
PRODUCTION TOTAL: n/a

VOLVO 140

SWEDEN 1967–74

Safety was always a Volvo byword, so, when it came to replacing the much-loved and highly successful 120 Amazon models, the Swedish maker had to ensure that the company's next model reinforced this image.

The new car featured bulky monocoque bodywork, and the slab-sided and squared-off 140 was designed to perform well in

an accident. Crumple zones front and rear were designed to absorb the forces of an accident, while the car also had anti-burst door locks to prevent the doors flying open in the same situation, as well as a collapsible steering column and rear seat-belt anchorages.

Some of the mechanical features of the 120 were carried over to the 140, including modified versions

of the front and rear suspension and two of the engine choices.

The 140 was also offered as an enormous estate (station wagon), with acres of luggage capacity. It was famous for being the first of a whole generation of 'boxy' Volvos. Withdrawn in 1974, the 140 Series was replaced by the even more safety-oriented 240 models, which used the same rear bodywork and

mechanical set-up as seen in the 140, and remained in production as late as 1994.

ENGINE: 1778cc (109cu in), four-cylinder
POWER: 85bhp (63kW)
0–60MPH (96KM/H): 12.5 seconds
TOP SPEED: 163km/h (102mph)
PRODUCTION TOTAL: n/a

A Volvo 140 in weather that it could simply shrug off. Arctic conditions and harsh winters were nothing for the sturdily constructed Swede. Replacing the 120, the 140 had many more advanced safety features and was the first of Volvo's 'boxy' cars.

DAF 33

THE NETHERLANDS 1967–75

Britain had its Mini, France had its Citroën 2CV and Germany had its VW Beetle, but, in the Netherlands, the small car of choice was the DAF 33 – an unusual device, but, to the Dutch, a car just as emblematic and well loved as those other European icons.

To complement its range of trucks and commercial vehicles, DAF first ventured into car

manufacturing with the DAF 600 of 1963. It was the 1967 DAF 33, however, that was the company's big success. Powered by a two-cylinder, air-cooled Boxer engine of just 746cc (46cu in), the 33 produced just 32bhp (24kW). But, as it weighed only 660kg (1455lb), the DAF was surprisingly lively.

The car's by far most interesting technological element was its

transmission. Only available as an automatic, called Variomatic, the transmission did not actually feature any gears, but used a centrifugal clutch attached to a series of conical metal wheels, driven by rubber bands. This gave the DAF incredibly sharp acceleration from a standstill, and also meant that it could be driven as quickly in reverse as it could forwards.

The 33 had several face-lifts in its life, later becoming the DAF 44 and DAF 55. There was also an odd-looking coupé called the Daffodil.

ENGINE: 746cc (46cu in), two-cylinder
POWER: 32bhp (24kW)
0–60MPH (96KM/H): 43 seconds
TOP SPEED: 113km/h (70mph)
PRODUCTION TOTAL: 312,367

HUMBER SCEPTRE

UNITED KINGDOM 1967–76

Humber's last-ever model marked a sad demise for one of Britain's most famous and established luxury brands. Following Chrysler's takeover of the Rootes Group in 1964, the company's model lines were gradually rationalized. In 1965, a decision was taken to introduce a new range of cars that would wear all of the former Rootes brand names.

The 'Arrow' range of cars started life as the Hillman Minx and Hunter in 1966, but later evolved into the Singer Vogue and Humber Sceptre. The Sceptre was not a bad car, with a well-appointed, luxury cabin, good performance, but it was the cynicism with which Chrysler treated the Humber name that rankled enthusiasts. Previously, the

Sceptre had always been a uniquely styled junior executive car with its own distinct identity. Despite the vinyl roof, side trims and wood trim of the latest model, however, it was impossible to tell it apart from a Hillman Hunter at 10 paces. The final ignominy came in 1970, when Chrysler introduced an estate (station wagon) to appeal to sales reps. The Humber brand was

finally put out to pasture in 1976, when the Arrow cars were replaced by the Chrysler Alpine.

ENGINE: 1725cc (105cu in), four-cylinder
POWER: 82bhp (61kW)
0–60MPH (96KM/H): 13.1 seconds
TOP SPEED: 161km/h (100mph)
PRODUCTION TOTAL: 43,951

A Hillman Hunter in all but name, which rankled enthusiasts, the last of the line Sceptres were pleasantly trimmed and comfortable, but marked an ignominious end for the once proud Humber name.

SUNBEAM RAPIER AND ALPINE

UNITED KINGDOM 1967–76

In contrast to the Sceptre, which was based on the Arrow saloon, the Sunbeam Rapier and Alpine variants were actually quite interesting cars, and far more loyal

Attractive and well made, the Rapier and Alpine were the most interesting cars from the Rootes Group in the late 1960s.

to the brand's heritage. Using a new two-door coupé bodystyle, with a wraparound rear screen that made it look like a miniature Plymouth Barracuda, the Sunbeam Coupé was both pretty and well proportioned.

Power came from Rootes Group's established 1725cc (105cu in) engine, developing 76bhp (57kW) in Alpine models and 88bhp (66kW) in the more upmarket and

more powerful Rapier. There was also a hot performance version, the Holbay-engined Rapier H120, with its modified cylinder head, two twin-choke Weber carburettors and styling changes to include Rostyle wheels, a small boot (trunk) lid spoiler, sill finishers and a range of exclusive, brighter colour schemes.

Sunbeam built almost 50,000 Alpine and Rapiers in a seven-year

production run, and the coupé is by far the most sought after of the Arrow cars today.

ENGINE: 1725cc (105cu in), four-cylinder
POWER: 76bhp (57kW)
0–60MPH (96KM/H): 12.8 seconds
TOP SPEED: 165km/h (103mph)
PRODUCTION TOTAL: 46,204

ALFA ROMEO 1750 BERLINA

ITALY 1967–77

Telling the difference between the Alfa Romeo Giulia and the car that replaced it was difficult. The 1750/2000 Berlina models appeared in 1967 and had the same boxy, upright shape. But the new car was bigger, with a longer boot (trunk) lid and bigger bonnet (hood). The sides were also more rounded to increase the passenger space. This gave the car a more rounded, bloated look lacking the sharpness of Pininfarina's original. The car was also 70kg (154lb) heavier than its predecessor, which did little to improve its handling.

It did have one big saving grace, in the form of its engine. The twin-cam 1779cc (109cu in) unit gave impressive performance, while disc brakes all round made the car feel safe and secure on the open road.

In response to bigger engined German competitors, Alfa increased the Berlina's engine size to a 2.0-litre (122cu in) unit in 1970, with 132bhp (98kW) and a top speed of 189km/h (118mph), giving the Berlina a new lease of life. The car enjoyed just over 10 years of production, during which time almost 200,000 cars were sold.

ENGINE: 1779cc (109cu in), four-cylinder
POWER: 113bhp (84kW)
0–60MPH (96KM/H): 10.8 seconds
TOP SPEED: 179km/h (112mph)
PRODUCTION TOTAL: 191,720

MONTEVERDI 375

SWITZERLAND 1967–77

Swiss car dealer Peter Monteverdi had always harboured a desire to run his own car company. When the multimillionaire found himself disillusioned with the usual crop of Italian sports GTs and supercars, he decided to take matters into his own hands and create a machine to suit his personal tastes.

The first car that was to bear the Monteverdi name was the little-known but spectacularly beautiful 375 Coupé. Its chiselled lines were created by Frua, to sit on a heavy tubular steel chassis of Monteverdi's own design.

Power came courtesy of a huge big-block Chrysler V8 engine of 7.2 litres (440cu in) in capacity, although a smaller 6.9-litre (421cu in) unit was available in the earliest examples. Initially, two different bodystyles were available – a two-seater coupé and a slightly larger 2+2 – although later variants of the car included a convertible and the 375/4, which used a stretched chassis and had four doors to give limousine-like internal accommodation.

Never a sports car, thanks to its soft suspension and mighty weight, the 375 was nonetheless a fine grand tourer. Monteverdi, though, wanted to build himself a supercar, which led to the birth of the oddly named Hai three years later.

ENGINE: 7206cc (440cu in), V8-cylinder
POWER: 375bhp (279kW)
0–60MPH (96KM/H): 6.9 seconds
TOP SPEED: 250km/h (155mph)
PRODUCTION TOTAL: n/a

Peter Monteverdi's eccentric cars were nothing if not interesting – this is the enormous 375/4, the largest model in the range.

NSU RO80

GERMANY 1967–77

ENGINE: 2 x 497cc (30cu in), rotary
POWER: 115bhp (86kW)
0–60MPH (96KM/H): 13.1 seconds
TOP SPEED: 181km/h (112mph)
PRODUCTION TOTAL: 37,398

Although ultimately so badly flawed that it wiped the NSU name out of the market, the Ro80 was considered so brilliant to drive and technologically advanced at its birth that it was immediately crowned European Car of the Year.

Powered by a twin rotary Wankel engine, the Ro80 was supremely smooth to drive. Its innovative semi-automatic clutchless transmission

The world wasn't ready for the NSU Ro80, nor the NSU Ro80 ready for the world – it was blighted by reliability problems.

and beautifully set up chassis gave it wonderful road manners. The modern styling was also highly praised for its aerodynamic efficiency, as well as its smart and curvaceous yet angular looks.

So what went wrong? In one simple word: breakdowns. Despite the amount of money ploughed into developing the rotary engine, the first Ro80s were spectacularly unreliable; within months, the

manufacturer faced a barrage of warranty claims caused by failed rotor tips causing the engines to break into pieces. The Ro80 also suffered from dreadful fuel consumption and dubious quality

control, which was a crying shame, as time has shown rotary engines can be efficient and reliable. NSU's brave attempt at bringing them to the mainstream could well have turned out so differently.

ALFA ROMEO SPIDER

ITALY 1967–93

Criticisms of the beautiful Duetto's lack of practicality forced Alfa Romeo to redesign its iconic sports car less than two years after it went on sale, and the result was the Spider. It was still an attractive car, but the Italian

Not as pretty as the original Duetto but the Alfa Romeo Spider was nonetheless an attractive car, and a big success.

maker had redesigned the rear end to make it longer, offering greater luggage space, and upsetting the harmony of the Duetto's original lines. Two engines were offered, a lively 1750 (109cu in) and a 1300 (79cu in) unit. The latter powered the Spider Junior, distinguishable from its bigger brother by its lack of faired-in headlight covers.

In 1970, the boat-tail rear end was modified further and made completely flat, in a design known

as the Kamm tail. This balanced up the styling quite nicely, as well as making the luggage area even more practical. The following year, the 1750 was replaced by the 2000, with a 2.0-litre (122cu in) twin-cam engine and power outputs as high as 133bhp (99kW).

After 1975, the Spider got ugly plastic impact bumpers to satisfy US safety legislation, but the car continued to sell well. After 22 years in production, the Spider received

a final face-lift in 1989, courtesy of Pininfarina, with more modern-looking bumpers and a significantly revised cabin, which allowed the car to continue selling until 1993.

ENGINE: 1779cc (100cu in), four-cylinder
POWER: 113bhp (84kW)
0–60MPH (96KM/H): 9.2 seconds
TOP SPEED: 189km/h (117mph)
PRODUCTION TOTAL: 104,958

CHEVROLET CAMARO

UNITED STATES 1967–81

ENGINE: 5733cc (350cu in), eight-cylinder
POWER: 224kW (300bhp)
0–60MPH (96KM/H): 8 seconds
TOP SPEED: 209km/h (130mph)
PRODUCTION TOTAL: 2,636,007

In response to Ford's success with the Mustang, in 1964 General Motors began designing its own rival to the 'pony car'. By 1966, the car had a name, Camaro, an archaic French slang term for 'friend'. Production began in 1967 with a hardtop coupé and a convertible offered with both V6 and V8 engines. The Camaro could be ordered with nearly 80 factory options and 40 dealer accessories arranged into three different packages. The RS package included cosmetic changes, such

as a blacked-out grille with hidden headlights and revised light clusters. Better, though, was the SS package that included as standard a modified 5733cc (350cu in) V8 engine. A 6489cc (396cu in) big-block version producing 325bhp (242kW) and a 375bhp (279kW) unit raised the stakes even further, complete with extra air intakes on the bonnet (hood), bumble-bee striping, and a blacked out grille.

Even more exciting was the Z-28, specifically designed to compete in the Club of America Trans Am racing series. This had competition suspension, and the engine could produce a mighty 400bhp (298kW). With a 225km/h (140mph) top speed, it dominated track racing for quite a few years.

The diversity of GM's tuning programme also meant that dealers could make high-performance

models specifically for each customer, but these were nothing compared to the factory-built Camaro ZL-1, which was designed to compete in the NHRA Super Stock drag racing classes. At the heart of this model was an all-alloy engine producing 498bhp (373kW), making it the most powerful engine Chevrolet ever offered to the public. The unit weighed just 227kg (500lb), the same as Chevy's 5359cc (327cu in) small-block engine, and came with a remarkable five-year/80,000km (50,000-mile) warranty. Despite this, the high price made them very difficult to sell, and new ZL1s were still on offer in the early 1970s.

An all-new Camaro arrived for 1970 with a great-looking restyle, influenced by GM Europe. This car formed the basis of every Camaro for the next decade. The new car

was 5cm (2in) longer, had 12.5cm (5in) longer doors and was more refined, thanks to better noise insulation. For 1971, there were major changes under the bonnet. GM decreed that all of its cars had to run on unleaded petrol, meaning lower compression ratios and power. The high-output Z-28 saw its 5733cc (350cu in) engine drop from a compression of 11:1 to 9:1, and horsepower fell from 360bhp (268kW) to 330bhp (246kW).

This was the shape of things to come, as the 1970s were unkind to performance cars in general. A 174-day strike in 1972 at GM's Ohio plant did not help matters. Even worse, 1100 unfinished Camaros had to be scrapped, as they did not meet 1972 US Federal bumper safety standards. There were even rumours that the Camaro name was to be dropped.

In 1973, the legendary SS option was discontinued. The only true performance Camaro was now the Z-28. Another indicator that the Camaro's character, and, indeed, its buyer profile, was changing was that air conditioning was available on the Z-28 for the first time. This also explained the new Type LT, effectively a luxury package, including a weak V8 and several trim items. Ironically, the neutering of such sports cars broadened their appeal and boosted sales. In 1979, the Camaro had its best-ever year, with 282,571 finding owners. By then, more than two and a half million Camaros had been sold.

In its original form, the Camaro was quite subtle and unostentatious, although it grew more bold and brash as the 1970s progressed.

PONTIAC FIREBIRD

Similar in more than just concept to the Camaro, the Pontiac Firebird was more or less the same car beneath the skin and, in the process, gave General Motors the opportunity to mount a double-pronged attack on the all-conquering Ford Mustang. Many components were shared between the Firebird and the less expensive Camaro, including chassis and body panels, with GM correctly hoping that brand loyalty would see both the Pontiac and the Chevrolet account for sales that between them matched those of Ford's phenomenal Mustang.

The Firebird appeared half a year later than the Camaro, giving Pontiac time to further develop its car, adding Ram Air power, extra chrome, a new twin-headlight nose and distinctive cooling fins in the rear quarter panel to feed a stream of air to the rear brake drums.

Top models also got the 7.5-litre (455cu in) V8 from the Pontiac GTO – an option never offered in the Chevrolet, which had a 6.5-litre (397cu in) engine in its most powerful model.

The Firebird was also better equipped than the Camaro, with a choice of four-speed manual or three-speed automatic gearboxes over the standard three-speed heavy-duty unit, plus free-flow exhausts, a performance rear axle and the option of front disc brakes.

The trade-off was a higher asking price, with Firebirds costing between $200 and $600 more than the equivalent Chevrolet. The

Famous for its role in the *Smokey and the Bandit* movies, the Trans Am was the ultimate model of the Pontiac Firebird.

Camaro outsold the Pontiac by a ratio of more than two to one over the next decade and a half, but loyalty, plus perceived better quality, meant that the Firebird was still a strong seller. In 1969, Pontiac introduced the first Trans Am models, sold initially as a special edition in white with blue racing stripes. Fewer than 700 were built, but the name would go on to be an iconic one for the Firebird.

The first major change came in 1970, when the Firebird got a new bodyshell and revised interior, again like the Chevy, but some customers preferred the simple lines of the original. The biggest changes also happened in 1970, when, in line with the Camaro, a completely new body was offered. A new quad-headlight nose made from 'Endura' plastic appeared, attached to longer, wider panels. The convertible option was dropped, although a T-top roof could be ordered as an option. At this time, the Trans Am became a standard addition to the range and could be ordered in either blue with white stripes, or vice versa. Two heavy-duty gearboxes were introduced to cope with the Trans Am's extra power, either a four-speed manual Hurst unit or a three-speed 'Turbo-Hydramatic' automatic.

Power outputs were reduced drastically the following year to comply with new US emissions legislation, and sales plummeted as a result. The Firebird nearly ceased production altogether in 1972 when the Pontiac factory went on a six-month strike, and serious questions about the model's future were asked at GM's Detroit headquarters.

Luckily, the car's future was secured by the introduction of a new high-performance 7.5-litre (455cu in) engine, marking the return of a genuine performance offering in the Trans Am. A face-lift carried out in 1974 was not a success, however, although buyers welcomed the introduction of a larger rear screen to aid visibility.

Any performance aspirations were killed altogether the following year, as power outputs were again cut to cope with the introduction of mandatory catalytic converters, although sales remained strong enough to keep the Firebird in production.

The last cars built on the Camaro platform were completed in 1981, more than a year after the Camaro went out of production, although the Firebird went on to appear on later models. More than 1.3 million were made in total.

ENGINE: 7457cc (455cu in), eight-cylinder
POWER: 345bhp (257kW)
0–60MPH (96KM/H): 5.5 seconds
TOP SPEED: 210km/h (130mph)
PRODUCTION TOTAL: 1,339,100

SIMCA 1100

FRANCE 1967–82

Not an especially exciting car, the Simca 1100 was actually a ground-breaking model for the French company. With independent suspension, front-wheel drive and a full rear hatchback, it brought new levels of comfort and practicality to buyers of the company's small cars, who previously had endured noisy rear-engined machines with cramped interior space.

As well as the added practicality, which gave the 1100 the appeal of a miniature Renault 16, the car was surprisingly lively to drive, with peppy performance courtesy of its 1118cc (68cu in) engine and precise rack-and-pinion steering.

As well as a hatchback, the 1100 was offered as an estate (station wagon) and a panel van, and formed the basis for the Matra Rancho of 1978. It can also claim to be the first-ever hot hatchback, in the form of the Ti model, with its fuel injection and revised suspension and steering that appealed to the performance market. It may be largely forgotten today, but the Simca 1000 (also sold as a Talbot and a Chrysler) made a significant contribution to motoring history.

ENGINE: 1118cc (68cu in), four-cylinder
POWER: 50bhp (37kW)
0–60MPH (96KM/H): 19.6 seconds
TOP SPEED: 134km/h (84mph)
PRODUCTION TOTAL: n/a

Sometimes, simple is best. The Simca 1100 was a straightforward little hatchback, yet at the same time was both fun to drive and versatile.

CITROËN DYANE

FRANCE 1967–85

ENGINE: 602cc (37cu in), two-cylinder
POWER: 31bhp (23kW) at 7000rpm
0–60MPH (96KM/H): 31.7 seconds
TOP SPEED: 126km/h (78mph)
PRODUCTION TOTAL: 1,443,583

In much the same way as British Leyland tried to replace the Mini with the Mini Clubman, Citroën decided to replace its 2CV with something a little more modern.

With the 2CV fast approaching its twentieth birthday, Citroën unveiled the Dyane, a car that used the standard 2CV chassis as its basis, but had a newer looking and more practical body on top. Gone were the 2CV's vulnerable separate headlights and impractical boot (trunk), to be replaced by a proper lift-up hatchback and faired-in lights. The interior space was also increased to give passengers in the back more legroom.

Two models were offered: the Dyane 4, with a 425cc (26cu in) engine, and the much more useful and livelier Dyane 6, with a 602cc (37cu in) unit and a top speed of 126km/h (78mph). But the Dyane failed to oust the original 2CV, which was still going strong when Citroën stopped making Dyanes in 1985.

Originally intended as a facelift to replace the near on 20-year-old 2CV, France's love of the original 'Tin Snail' meant that the Dyane actually died six years before the car it was supposed to have replaced.

PUMA GT

There are not many classic sports coupés to have emerged from the Brazilian motor industry, but the Puma was just that. Launched in 1967, the glassfibre two-door was the brainchild of Italian engineer Genaro Malzoni, who left his home country to live in South America in the late 1950s.

Although tiny, the GT resembled a Lamborghini Miura, with similar slatted B-pillars and large oval headlights. Underneath, however, it was much more ordinary. Power came from a variety of Volkswagen air-cooled engines, which were built for the South American market in a factory close to Malzoni's São Paulo factory. It was not just the engines that came from VW either, as the GT was constructed on a Karmann Ghia platform and was even sold through some smaller VW dealerships in Brazil, which also provided the car with the requisite service back-up. Later cars were built on standard Beetle platforms after the Karmann Ghia ceased production, and were shorter and less elegant as a result.

Other cars built by Puma included a Fissore-designed two-door coupé and the GTB, which, while it looked similar to the GT, was a larger car altogether, using a locally built Chevrolet platform and front-mounted engine. As well as the 30,000 or so Pumas built in Brazil, a further 357 cars were built by Bromer in South Africa as CKD kits.

ENGINE: 1493cc (91cu in), four-cylinder
POWER: 72bhp (54kW)
0–60MPH (96KM/H): 11.7 seconds
TOP SPEED: 161km/h (100mph)
PRODUCTION TOTAL: about 30,000

SAAB 99

After years of producing the successful 92 to 96 series, Saab needed a dramatic change of approach. For a manufacturer known more for evolution than revolution, this could prove tricky – but the result was a remarkable success.

First seen at the end of 1967, the Saab 99 used a slant-four engine developed in partnership with British manufacturer Triumph, but Saab's engine differed in that it was mounted the opposite way round to make the car front-wheel drive. It also was not afflicted by the same reliability issues that confronted Triumph owners.

Initially available as a two-door saloon only, the 99 range soon diversified to include four-door saloons, as well as three and five-door hatchbacks that were known as Combis. The most significant development was the 99 Turbo of 1978. Although BMW had been the first maker to offer a turbocharged saloon car, the Saab model had greater poise and performance. It enjoyed a long, successful career in circuit racing and rallying, much to the delight of Saab's Scandinavian fans, for whom rallying was considered a national sport.

ENGINE: 1709cc (104cu in), four-cylinder
POWER: 80bhp (60kW)
0–60MPH (96KM/H): 15.2 seconds
TOP SPEED: 150km/h (94mph)
PRODUCTION TOTAL: 588,643

ZIL 114

In Soviet Russia, luxury cars were very much the preserve of government officials and the moneyed classes. And with a kerb weight of 3048kg (6720lb) the ZIL 114 really needed its 300bhp

Bold, imposing and quite scary, someone in a ZIL in Soviet Russia was probably capable of having you thrown into jail.

(224kW) power output. The engine was made out of aluminium (ironically, to help keep weight down), and it struggled to deliver fuel consumption any better than 18.9L/100km (15mpg).

Like its predecessor, the 111, the 114 borrowed heavily from US designs, and looked surprisingly modern when it was launched in 1967. Equipment levels had grown steadily since the first post-war limousines had rolled out of the ZIL factory. By the time the 114 reached production, the cars featured servo-assisted ventilated disc brakes all round, while those being chauffeured had electrically adjustable seats, vacuum-operated locks, tinted glass and a stereo radio to play with.

On the flip side, the ZIL was not especially brilliant, nor was it comfortable to drive. But then again, the driver was very rarely in a position to afford a ZIL, and was merely an employee of the far more important person in the back!

ENGINE: 6962cc (425cu in), eight-cylinder
POWER: 300bhp (224kW)
0–60MPH (96KM/H): n/a
TOP SPEED: 188km/h (118mph)
PRODUCTION TOTAL: n/a

LAMBORGHINI ISLERO

ITALY 1968–70

ENGINE: 3929cc (240cu in),
12-cylinder
POWER: 325bhp (242kW)
0–60MPH (96KM/H): 6.3 seconds
TOP SPEED: 260km/h (162mph)
PRODUCTION TOTAL: 225

The Islero took over where the 400GT left off, and was so popular with company boss Ferruccio Lamborghini that he had one as his personal car. He also played a part in its rather subdued styling, making it look more like an upmarket GT car than an out-and-out performance car. More of a 2+2 than a four-seater, the Islero did have a rear bench as a token gesture. It continued Lamborghini's tradition for naming its cars after fighting bulls – Islero killed a famous matador in the late 1940s.

The car was based on an adapted version of the square-tube chassis used on the earlier 350GT and 400, but was wider and slightly shorter. Styling was by Marazzi and featured retractable headlights and extremely narrow chrome bumpers to give it a clean, understated look. Underneath the shallow bonnet (hood) line was the company's famed V12 powerplant, which, although it offered great performance, provided dreadfully bad access for mechanics.

The S version was announced to answer criticism that the Islero was just a bit too subtle. The addition of wider wheels and flared arches, fog lamps, air vents behind the front wheels and, most importantly, a power increase up to 350bhp (261kW) made a significant difference to the car.

Not one of the best remembered Lamborghinis, the Islero was effectively a modernized version of the old 400 GT.

PLYMOUTH ROAD RUNNER

UNITED STATES 1968–71

Knowing that popular culture sold cars, Plymouth paid $50,000 to Warner Brothers for permission to use its Road Runner cartoon bird on its entry-level full-sized V8 muscle car. The car also came with the cartoon character's

It was no coincidence that the Road Runner looked like the Dodge Challenger – the two cars were very similar under the skin.

trademark 'meep-meep' horn, tuned by Warner Bros' engineers to match the tone of its star character.

Alloy wheels were an option, with patterned steel road wheels as standard, and the car had various styling tweaks over the standard Valiant sedan on which it was based. Some of the modifications were purely for show, including the huge air ducts cut into the bonnet (hood), which did not feed any extra air to the combustion chambers, but did look extremely aggressive. Offered as either a coupé or convertible, the Road Runner had standard four-speed manual transmission or an optional three-speed self-shifter.

A new three-speed manual transmission appeared for 1970, when the engine acquired increased torque and Plymouth deemed the extra ratio an unnecessary expense. New emissions legislation killed the car's awesome performance in 1970; the last Road Runners saw power output drop by as much as 75bhp (56kW), making them less desirable among street racers. Rare today, a neat original Road Runner is highly prized by collectors.

ENGINE: 6276cc (383cu in), eight-cylinder
POWER: 335bhp (250kW)
0–60MPH (96KM/H): 7.1 seconds
TOP SPEED: 182km/h (113mph)
PRODUCTION TOTAL: 125,904

PLYMOUTH SUPERBIRD

Although they were both part of the huge Chrysler Corporation, Plymouth and Dodge were keen rivals on the United States' NASCAR oval racing circuits. After Dodge won the 1969 NASCAR championship with its Daytona,

A Road Runner built for NASCAR racing, the Superbird sported a love-it or hate-it aerodynamic body kit and huge rear wing.

Plymouth's response was to design and develop the stunning Superbird, based on the Road Runner.

NASCAR regulations meant that, in order to compete, at least one car had to have been sold by each of the manufacturer's dealers. For homologation purposes, Plymouth built 1920 Superbirds, each with a huge rear aerofoil and sculpted shark-style nose, moulded out of soft polyurethane. The aerodynamic nose added 48cm (19in) to the

Road Runner's overall length and made the car difficult to park, as the first few feet of bodywork was invisible from the driver's seat.

Inside, it was standard Road Runner (although bucket seats and harnesses could be fitted as an option), while extra dials included oil-pressure and oil-temperature gauges. Outside, unsubtle decals marked the rear wings (fenders). Colour schemes were generally lurid yellows, greens or oranges. With

incredible performance off the track, and a myriad of race victories, the Superbird quickly became America's most revered muscle car and one of the most successful NASCAR racing machines ever.

ENGINE: 6974cc (426cu in), eight-cylinder
POWER: 425bhp (317kW)
0–60MPH (96KM/H): 5.1 seconds
TOP SPEED: 234km/h (145mph)
PRODUCTION TOTAL: 1920

AMC AMX

Despite the Javelin being of only limited success, AMC persisted with building its own muscle cars to take on the big boys. AMC's smallest and sportiest offering was the AMX. The name stood for 'American Motors Experimental',

AMC claims of the AMX being a latter day Thunderbird was lost on the buying public, and not without good reason...

the experimental part referring to the fact that this was the first two-seat-only, steel-bodied US sports car to go into mass production since the original 1955 Ford Thunderbird.

To look at, the AMX was much like the larger Javelin, but towards the rear end the styling looked more than a little odd, with the metalwork steeply cut off to give the car a blunt, slightly awkward appearance. Underneath was a shortened version of the Javelin

chassis, while mechanically the two cars shared the same six-cylinder or V8 engine options.

The AMX was actually sharper handling and more rewarding to drive than the Javelin, but the US public was not convinced. It was not as exotic as other two-seaters around, and looked a bit weird. On top of that, AMC had the temerity to charge more for the AMX than it did the larger Javelin, and some buyers felt they were being fleeced.

The AMX was unceremoniously dropped in 1971. The name remained for use on range-topping versions of the Javelin and the exceptionally odd-looking Gremlin.

ENGINE: 6392cc (390cu in), eight-cylinder
POWER: 319bhp (238kW)
0–60MPH (96KM/H): 7.2 seconds
TOP SPEED: 177km/h (110mph)
PRODUCTION TOTAL: 19,134

MARCOS 3-LITRE

Marcos's distinctive styling first appeared in 1968, but was still seen on production cars well into the 21st century.

If there was one major criticism of the original Marcos 1800, it was that the Volvo-engined coupé lacked power, an issue that Marcos addressed with the launch of the 3-Litre. In 1968, Marcos boss Jem Marsh decided to fit the powerful Ford 3.0-litre (183cu in) V6 'Essex' unit, coupled to a four-speed overdrive gearbox as fitted to the Zephyr saloon, but with revised, closer ratios. Despite concerns from contemporary road testers about the effect on the Marcos's weight distribution, 3.0-Litre cars were actually better to drive. The extra weight reduced the tendency of the nose to suffer from aerodynamic lift, and, as a result the top speed increased to around 200km/h (125mph).

A year after production started, a coil-sprung live axle took the place of the de Dion unit originally fitted at the rear, but this affected the handling quite badly and was widely criticized. After 100 cars were built, a switch was made from the original wooden chassis to a much more modern steel crosstube construction, sorting out the handling, but enthusiasts were a little baffled when, in 1970, Volvo's 3.0-litre (183cu in) powerplant from the dowdy 164 saloon replaced the Ford engine.

Fans were slightly appeased when the 2.5-litre (153cu in) unit taken from the Triumph TR6 was offered as an alternative, along with Ford's rough and ready 2.0-litre (122cu in) V4 unit from the Corsair. Marcos went bust in 1971 and the 3-Litre died, only to reappear 13 years later as the Mantula and 3000GT, the latter of which was reunited with the V6 Ford engine that had made the original car great.

ENGINE: 2978cc (182cu in), six-cylinder
POWER: 140bhp (105kW)
0–60MPH (96KM/H): 7.8 seconds
TOP SPEED: 200km/h (125mph)
PRODUCTION TOTAL: 350

VOLKSWAGEN 411

Volkswagen's first real foray into the large family car market was the 411, also known as the Type 4. For the first time, the company created a car with more than two doors. In other respects, it followed Volkswagen traditions to the letter, with a rear-mounted air-cooled engine and a derivative of the Beetle's chassis. The underpinnings were significantly altered, though. As well as being much longer, the 411 featured transverse links and MacPherson struts in place of the original Beetle's trailing link front axle and torsion bars.

Despite lots of investment, the 411 was not a huge success. It was considered too similar to the Beetle and Type 3, both of which were rapidly being thought of as old-fashioned. The car was also expensive and, with its cramped front luggage bay, was less practical than many of its contemporary rivals. On the plus side, it was comfortable and pleasant to drive, and the build quality was superb. VW had originally envisaged building at least a million Type 4s, but in the end achieved only a third of its original target.

ENGINE: 1679cc (102cu in), four-cylinder
POWER: 68bhp (51kW)
0–60MPH (96KM/H): 13.8 seconds
TOP SPEED: 155km/h (97mph)
PRODUCTION TOTAL: 355,300 (incl. 412)

OPEL GT

ENGINE: 1897cc (116cu in), four-cylinder
POWER: 90bhp (67kW)
0–60MPH (96KM/H): 12 seconds
TOP SPEED: 185km/h (115mph)
PRODUCTION TOTAL: 103,373

With the Corvette proving to be an extraordinary phenomenon in the United States, Opel decided to take the best of GM's global design knowledge and bring it to Europe. It's own 'Mini-Corvette', the GT, was the first truly sporting Opel and shared much of its underpinnings with the Kadett. First shown as a styling exercise at the 1965 Frankfurt Motor Show, it proved so popular that GM gave it the green light for production.

While the Corvette-like styling was done in-house at Opel, the car's manufacture was outsourced to French coachbuilders Brissoneau and Lotz. Unusual features included headlights that rotated out of the

Built as a baby Corvette for Europe, the Opel GT was actually assembled in France as Opel's own factory near Frankfurt didn't have the space to dedicate to a low volume sports car. The GT's lightweight body made it quick and surprisingly agile.

bonnet (hood) through a linkage operated by a lever alongside the gear stick, and there was a useful amount of rear luggage space. The GT's lightweight body made it quick and surprisingly agile, its

compact 1897cc (116cu in) engine delivering a modest but adequate 90bhp (67kW). The steering and chassis composure were excellent.

Despite the car being designed primarily for Europe, more than 80

per cent of GTs ended up being exported to the United States, where buyers loved the car's compact Corvette looks. Built in left-hand drive only, the GT was still sold in some right-hand drive markets,

such was the demand for its lithe looks. But it suffered badly from corrosion, and many American cars from dry states have been reimported to Europe by enthusiasts undertaking restoration projects.

FERRARI 365 DAYTONA

ITALY 1968–74

Bucking the industry-wide trend for launching supercars with mid-mounted engines, Ferrari stuck with its tried-and-tested front-engined formula for the 365 GTB/4, even going so far as to offer a pair of rear seats to demonstrate the 'practicality advantages' of keeping such a layout.

The GTB/4 received the Daytona name in honour of Ferrari's incredible 1-2-3 line-abreast finish in the Daytona 24-hour race in 1967, although the name was never an official one and did not appear in any brochures. But Daytona was how it was always known. It was a heavy car, weighing more than 1600kg (3527lb), but it had more than enough power to cope. The 4.4-litre (268cu in) overhead-camshaft V12 was a derivative of the company's original V12, which was renowned for its performance, smoothness and reliability – things that Ferrari saw no point in superseding.

But the engineers at Maranello managed to increase the bore and stroke of the engine, enlarging it from 3.3 litres (210cu in), as used in the 275 GTB/4, to 4.4 litres (268cu in) in the process. With an output of 352bhp (262kW) and producing about 429Nm (318lb ft) of torque, it certainly was not lacking anything in performance or flexibility, but it did drink fuel.

Arguably the greatest front-engined GT of all time, the 365's beautiful, aerodynamic body was styled by young designer Leonardo Fioravanti at Pininfarina. His achievement was to design a car with a massive engine in the nose that still looked sleek and well proportioned, rather than nose-heavy and bulky. He did this by making the bonnet (hood) as long as he could, and mounting the engine as close to the bulkhead as was feasible, not only adding harmony to the lines, but also evening out the car's weight

distribution, which was further helped by mounting the gearbox in the rear axle rather than on the back of the engine. To offset the extra length at the front, Fioravanti restricted the rear overhang to the bare minimum.

Initially, and only for the European market, the headlights were hidden behind glazed panels, but cars sold in the United States and other territories had pop-up headlights instead.

Underneath, the Daytona was an extended version of the 275 GTB/4's chassis, with revised independent front and rear suspension, having firmer damper rates over the earlier car. The decision to use a rear 'transaxle' gearbox meant that the Daytona's gearshift was sometimes heavy and unpleasant to use, but this did nothing to stunt performance.

The Daytona was capable of sprinting from 0–60mph (96km/h) in just 5.4 seconds, and had a top

speed in excess of 280km/h (174mph). This, crucially, made it faster than its greatest rival, the Lamborghini Miura.

In 1969, Ferrari added an open-top Spyder model to the line-up, although only 122 were ever built and were badged 365 GTS/4. The specification was the same as for the coupé, but the majority came with wire spoke wheels in place of the coupé version's cast five-spoke alloys. Collectors are wary of these, though, as a number of coupés were modified during the classic-car price boom of the late 1980s, with the result that there are many fakes around.

So why is the Daytona such a classic? All the design and engineering elements came together to make a car that offered pin-sharp handling. At the same time, however, the car was comfortable, enjoyable to drive and had a good ride quality. On top of that, it was also stunningly beautiful. In most cases with a car such as this, you either trade dynamic ability in favour of good looks, or go for the looks and put up with compromised dynamics. The Daytona, unlike any car before or arguably since, managed to successfully combine the two and is quite rightly revered as one of the greatest cars of all time.

ENGINE: 4390cc (268cu in), 12-cylinder
POWER: 352bhp (262kW)
0–60MPH (96KM/H): 5.4 seconds
TOP SPEED: 278km/h (174mph)
PRODUCTION TOTAL: 1423

A true Ferrari icon, the Daytona was nowhere near as good to drive as it was to look at – but it didn't matter.

VOLVO 164

SWEDEN 1968–75

Effectively a 144 with a six-cylinder engine, the 164 was Volvo's attempt to cash in on the growing luxury saloon car market and go head to head with the likes of the Ford Zodiac and Citroën DS.

The car was also charged with offering traditional Volvo buyers a car with a little more class and luxury, as the existing 144 and run-out Amazon models were fairly

basic in trim levels, and the Swedish firm had identified a demand for a more premium model.

From the A-pillars backwards, the 164 was identical to its four-cylinder cousin, with the exception of some extra chrome trim around the sills and wheelarches, and standard mud flaps at the rear. But the front end was significantly modified, with a longer wheelbase

to accommodate the larger engine and a more ostentatious front end.

Rather than stick with the flat nose of the 144, Volvo fitted an incongruous Rolls-Royce–style radiator grille to the 164, and fitted Jaguar-style headlights into the rounded front wings (fenders). Auxiliary driving lights in the front panel were standard. The engine was a 2979cc (182cu in) straight-six,

which was effectively one and a half 144 engines welded together. Although smooth and refined, it was not especially lively.

ENGINE: 2979cc (182cu in), six-cylinder
POWER: 130bhp (97kW)
0–60MPH (96KM/H): 11.3 seconds
TOP SPEED: 170km/h (106mph)
PRODUCTION TOTAL: 155,068

AUDI 80

With its clean, modern lines and durable interior, the Audi 80 was the first of the cars that earned the company the reputation it enjoys today. The 80's basic platform became the basis for the later Quattro.

Audi's designs were well made and neatly designed, but when Audi was taken over by Volkswagen in 1967, from that date onwards there was an internal directive that all Audi and VW models should share a certain number of common parts – a tradition that continues to this day. The Audi 80 was the first fruit of this collaboration, and would go on to share many of its panels and mechanical components with the Volkswagen Passat.

From the outside, the 80 looked almost identical to the larger 100, but was powered by a new Audi-designed overhead-camshaft engine. The suspension was different, too, with MacPherson struts all round, while the geometry of the front struts were set deliberately for extra stability and safety, even in the event of a tyre blow-out.

Several engines were used, ranging from an entry level 1.3-litre (75cu in) unit up to a range-topping 2.0-litre (121cu in). Later versions were fitted with Audi's unusual 2.2-litre (132cu in) five-cylinder engine. The 80's basic platform also went on to provide the basis for the all-conquering Quattro, which became the rally car legend of the 1980s.

ENGINE: 1296cc (79cu in),
four-cylinder
POWER: 55bhp (41kW)
0–96KM/H (60MPH): 16.9 secs
TOP SPEED: 145km/h (90mph)
PRODUCTION TOTAL: 939,931

MERCEDES-BENZ W114/115

Sharply styled, elegant and durable, the W114/115 Series was one of Mercedes' best-selling models of all time, proving popular with anyone ranging from the landed gentry to taxi drivers. Launched as a smaller, entry-level Mercedes, the cars had a shape that was all new, distinguished by unusual vertical headlight units in the wings (fenders) which incorporated the sidelights and indicators. The unitary construction body, semi-trailing link suspension and ubiquitous upright Mercedes grille were pretty much the same as fitted to larger Mercedes models.

A confusing range of engines included the entry-level 2.0-litre (122cu in) unit and a new twin-camshaft straight-six petrol. Innovation came in the form of the diesels. Sold as 220D and 240D, the 2.2-litre (134cu in) and 2.4-litre (147cu in) derv-fuelled units were not especially quick, but they were incredibly reliable and economical. The first diesel engine to be a sales success in a passenger car was derived from Mercedes' success in the commercial vehicle market,

This is a CE version of the W114 series and was bought by a different kind of customer from the more workaday saloon.

and it was not unusual for either powerplant to exceed a million kilometres (620,000 miles) in its lifetime. Automatic transmission and power-assisted steering was an option on all cars, including the diesels, although with a self-shifting gearbox they were especially slow.

Other interesting variants were an extra-long-wheelbase limousine version and a very pretty two-door pillarless coupé. This was slightly shorter and lower than the saloon, as well as being significantly more expensive. Badged CE to distinguish them from the saloons, they are the only W114/115 models that have any real collector value.

ENGINE: 2778cc (170cu in),
six-cylinder
POWER: 185bhp (138kW)
0–60MPH (96KM/H):
13.7–24.2 seconds
TOP SPEED: 198km/h (124mph)
PRODUCTION TOTAL: 1,326,099

LAMBORGHINI ESPADA

Concept cars very rarely reach production unchanged, but Marcello Gandini's four-seater Lamborghini Marzal, previewed at the 1967 Geneva Motor Show, was an exception, The car went on to become the incredible Espada, with very few styling tweaks. With further styling work completed by Bertone, the V12-engined 'Lamborghini for the family' went into production on a steel platform chassis with integral bodywork.

The Espada continued the bull theme common to the Lamborghini range, its name meaning 'matador's sword'. It was a wide and bulky car, but the clever design made it look sleek from any angle, with its low bonnet (hood) and gently

The Espada's styling polarised opinion – but it was certainly distinctive from whichever angle you viewed it.

raked rear end assisting in the optical illusion that made the car appear much smaller than it was. Wide-opening conventional doors replaced the Marzal's odd roof-hinged items, while its glass door panels were replaced by aluminium door skins, as the design was thought a little too extreme to

reach production. Extra glass was fitted into the car's rear end, though, making the Espada much easier to reverse-park than was the case with most supercars.

Inside, the Espada provided its occupants with every luxury, including leather seats and walnut trim, while legroom in the rear was

more generous than you would expect from a 2+2. A major irritation with the car was its poor driving position, and it seemed that little thought had been given to the location of instruments and other controls. Some drivers even reported that they could not reach the handbrake with their seat belt

on, while the car's gearshift was renowned for being awful.

ENGINE: 3929cc (240cu in), twelve-cylinder
POWER: 350bhp (261kW)
0–60MPH (96KM/H): 6.9 seconds
TOP SPEED: 248km/h (155mph)
PRODUCTION TOTAL: 1217

FORD UK ESCORT

Ford's Escort became one of the most successful rally cars of all time, seen here competing in the 1970 Mexico rally.

The oddball Anglia had been an incredibly successful car for Ford, but the speed at which automotive technology advanced throughout the 1960s soon rendered it out of date. Determined to ensure the Anglia's replacement would be cutting edge, Ford invested in a pan-European development programme for its eventual replacement – the Escort.

The car was styled in the United Kingdom, as Britain was considered the best country in Europe for car styling, and much of the Escort's engineering, including designing its superb all-synchromesh gearbox, was carried out in Germany at the Blue Oval's new technical development centre near Cologne.

Designated production plants were Halewood, England, and Saarlouis, Germany. There were minor visual differences between cars produced at the two locations, with German-built cars getting

different wheels and bumpers.

A spacious, good-value and reliable newcomer, the Escort was initially available only as a two-door model. An unusual double wishbone front suspension set-up was replaced in less than a year by the proven (and far cheaper) MacPherson strut system, while the Escort became the first Ford to have rack-and-pinion steering. The engines were reworked versions of the existing Anglia and Cortina units, but now with five bearing cranks and crossflow cylinder heads. A new 1098cc (67ci) engine provided entry-level power in the Basic, De Luxe and Super models. The 1298cc (79cu in) engine powered the Super, but the GT had a new cylinder head, high-lift camshaft, revised manifold and a dual-choke Weber carburettor producing 72bhp (54kW). This was the first 'performance' Escort – a trend that would very soon establish itself as one of the small Ford's

most significant developments.

In 1969 came the Twin Cam, which had the running gear of the Lotus Cortina, but in a shell that was 136kg (300lb) lighter. Modified suspension and a quicker steering rack were developed by Ford's Special Vehicle Operations (SVO), and these were squeezed into a modified shell, with bubble-shaped wheelarches and extra lateral strengthening.

The more ordinary Escorts, though, were the ones that were critical to Ford of Europe's success, and the range finally received two much-needed additions in 1969 in the form of a four-door saloon and an estate (station wagon). A panel van was also introduced and became especially popular as a rival to the older Vauxhall Viva-based Bedford Beagle.

The sporting Escorts were still massively important, though, and, following the success of the Twin Cam, Ford set up an Advanced Vehicles Operation (AVO) in Aveley, near Windsor, in the United Kingdom, to hand-build its specials. Its first project was the RS1600 with a new 16-valve twin-camshaft Cosworth engine. Inspired by the RS1600's impressive victory in the 1970 World Cup Rally, the company launched the Mexico, which had a larger 1558cc (95cu in) engine for reliability, while the later RS2000 had the 2-litre (122cu in) Pinto engine from the Cortina Mk 3 and unsubtle body graphics.

The Mk 1 Escort was eventually replaced by a Mk 2 model in 1975, and this version was known internally as Project Brenda during its development – the name apparently taken from the name of the secretary in the company's styling studio offices. Styled by

Uwe Bahnsen, who was appointed to give all European Fords a uniform appearance, it was much squarer and neater than the Mk 1, with immediate similarities to the Mk 4 Cortina and Mk 2 Granada.

The model range was just as vast as before, and under the skin the Mk 2 varied little from the Mk 1. Like its predecessor, the Mk 2 also spawned a whole family of performance models.

The RS1800 with a double overhead-camshaft BDA engine was a homologation special for rallying. In fully modified form, it had a 2-litre (122cu in) engine, uprated suspension, ZF close ratio gearbox, disc brakes all round and a bigger axle. This was the car that went on to win the World Rally Championship in 1979.

Less motorsport-oriented, but inevitably resting on the RS1800's laurels in order to sell to paying customers, were the Mark 2 Mexicos and RS2000s. The Mexico had a 1.6-litre (95cu in) engine which produced 95bhp (71kW), but was not a brilliant seller. The RS2000, meanwhile, had a distinctive moulded polyurethane nose, with four headlights and a prominent spoiler.

It was the standard Escorts, however, that were to prove the most important. The three-door estate was always a popular choice, and Ford reintroduced the Popular name for its base, no-frills model, which was later joined by the marginally more plush Popular Plus. The Mk 2 continued until 1981, when Ford replaced it with the much more modern but less involving to drive Mk 3, which had modern hatchback styling and front-wheel drive.

ENGINE: 1993cc (122cu in), four-cylinder
POWER: 110bhp (82kW)
0–60MPH (96KM/H): 8.6 seconds
TOP SPEED: 175km/h (109mph)
PRODUCTION TOTAL: 2,906,144

ISUZU 117 COUPÉ

Japanese maker Isuzu made most of its money building commercial vehicles and farming equipment, plus the odd four-wheel drive off-

roader, but the company also had the occasional moment where it diversified into the fringes of the car market. One of its more

intriguing offerings was the 117 coupé, launched in 1967.

With the assistance of top Italian stylist Giugiaro (then working at

Ghia of Turin), Isuzu launched what turned out to be a very attractive little coupé that looked almost like a scale replica of the Fiat 124 Dino with its rakish lines, four-headlight grille and delicate chrome bumpers.

The 117 shared its running gear with the Florian saloon, sold only in Japan. It was utterly conventional in every respect, thanks to its 1.6-litre (97cu in) engine, rear-wheel drive and live rear axle. Inside, high-back sports seats and extra dials made the 117 Coupé feel fairly sporty, while the driving position was excellent. Later models were the most exciting, with 1.8-litre (111cu in) twin-cam engines from 1970 onwards; the range-topping XE model came with fuel injection, pushing power up to a respectable 140bhp (104kW). The 117 Coupé developed a cult following, meaning it stayed in production until the early 1980s almost unchanged.

ENGINE: 1584cc (97 cu in), four-cylinder
POWER: 90bhp (67kW)
0–60MPH (96KM/H): 8 seconds
TOP SPEED: 161km/h (100mph)
PRODUCTION TOTAL: n/a

PEUGEOT 504

FRANCE 1968–82

The sedan version of the Peugeot 504 was universally praised – not only was it comfortable and good to drive, but it was also rugged, reliable and easy to maintain.

Mechanical simplicity made the 504 highly adaptable. For a while in the 1980s and 1990s pick-up trucks were built in Kenya and even imported into Europe.

Thanks to its durable design and solid engineering, the Peugeot 504 is one of motoring's stalwarts. European production ended in the early 1980s (except for the pick-up truck, which lasted until the mid-1990s), but the 504 remains in production in some African countries, where its good ground clearance, mechanical simplicity and spaciousness mean that it still has huge appeal.

The best version was (and still is) the estate (station wagon), which appeared in 1971 and was truly massive. The usual eight-seat Familiale option and fold-flat rear bench made these vehicles immensely useful as taxis, as well as family cars. There was also a truly beautiful Pininfarina-styled coupé, introduced in 1970; this had little in common with the standard 504 except for its running gear.

Petrol engines were 1.8-litre (110cu in) or 2.0-litre (121cu in) four-cylinder units, both with ample performance and a fuel injection system offered as an option from launch. But it was the diesels that were key to the 504's appeal. Initially a 2.0-litre (121cu in) unit borrowed from the 403 was fitted, until a much-improved 2.1-litre (128cu in) and more powerful 2.3-litre (140cu in) engine appeared from 1977 onwards. By the time European sales ceased in 1982, well over two million had been sold, making the 504 France's most popular saloon car ever.

ENGINE: 1971cc (120cu in), four-cylinder
POWER: 97bhp (72kW)
0–60MPH (96KM/H): 12.4 seconds
TOP SPEED: 166km/h (103mph)
PRODUCTION TOTAL: 2,836,837

VOLGA M24

USSR 1968–82

Volga's most successful model was heavily influenced by Detroit – it almost looked like a scaled-down Chevrolet Impala, with its solid three-box styling and imposing chrome radiator grille. Longer and lower than the M21 it replaced, the M24 was an attempt to offer better packaging and a more up-to-date design. It had the same 2445cc (149cu in) engine as the M21, but the car's overall top speed increased as a result of better aerodynamics and a raised compression ratio of 8.2:1, which increased the power output while still allowing it to run on the relatively poor-quality fuel then common in Eastern Europe.

First shown in 1968, the M24 saloon did not go into production until 1970, with a bespoke taxi version following soon after. This featured an engine with a lower compression ratio, so that it could run on even lower quality fuel and return better fuel economy.

All M24s were fairly good to drive, with servo-assisted brakes and a floor-mounted gearshift. Volga's build quality was still not up to Western standards, but the M24 required far less maintenance than its predecessor and was supremely reliable. Production of the M24 continued until 1982, when a face-lifted M21 appeared.

ENGINE: 2445cc (149cu in), four-cylinder
POWER: 112bhp (83kW)
0–60MPH (96KM/H): n/a
TOP SPEED: 144km/h (90mph)
PRODUCTION TOTAL: n/a

CITROËN MEHARI

FRANCE 1968–86

Proving that the 2CV was all things to all people, the Mehari brought an all-new fun dimension to Deux Chevaux ownership. Built on a standard 2CV chassis, the Mehari's simple body tub was made out of reinforced plastic that would absorb small impacts without malformation, although, as some owners found out to their peril, it was not so good at resisting fire... An incredibly simple concept, the Mehari was designed for light off-road use and took advantage of the 2CV's excellent ground clearance and skinny tyres to go places you would not necessarily expect a front-wheel drive car to go. It had clip-on canvas sides and a roof as token gestures towards weather protection, but unless you were a true martyr it was very much a summer-only vehicle.

Citroën briefly experimented with a 4x4 Mehari, which came with a separate engine for each axle, but it was of little success. There was also a van variant, which was a bit more popular, but still no great seller. All Meharis came with the 602cc (37cu in) engine from the standard 2CV, but were faster because of their lighter weight.

ENGINE: 602cc (37cu in), two-cylinder
POWER: 31bhp (23kW) at 7000rpm
0–60MPH (96KM/H): 40 seconds
TOP SPEED: 108km/h (67mph)
PRODUCTION TOTAL: 143,747

Certainly a car that defied convention, the Mehari was based on a 2CV chassis but its unusual off-road looks, canvas roof and one-piece plastic bodyshell made it best suited to warm climates.

RELIANT SCIMITAR GT/E

UNITED KINGDOM 1968–86

ENGINE: 2996cc (183cu in),
   six-cylinder
POWER: 138bhp (103kW)
0–60MPH (96KM/H): 10.7mph
TOP SPEED: 189km/h (117mph)
PRODUCTION TOTAL: 10,425

If it was good enough for Britain's royal family, then it was good enough for Reliant – which may explain why the Scimitar remained in production for almost 20 years. The car was a favourite of Princess Anne, who owned at least 10 Scimitars over the years and went as far as endorsing the car as the perfect combination between sports car and shooting brake.

The GT/E was certainly an interesting concept. Part estate (station wagon), part GT, it was built along Lotus principles, with a smart glassfibre body stretched over a steel backbone chassis.

SE6 versions of the Scimitar were slightly longer and wider than the earlier SE5 versions, but looked almost identical.

The first cars, called SE5s, were the prettiest, and came powered by a 3.0-litre (183cu in) Ford V6 engine. The SE6 was introduced in 1973, with a slightly taller and notably wider body, although the shape remained the same. From 1980, the cars had 2.8-litre (171ci) fuel-injected engines from the Ford Capri Injection Special, giving them huge driver appeal. A convertible model was also briefly offered, but by 1986 Reliant was in financial difficulties and the Scimitar was no more. It was briefly revived in 1988 by a small company called Middlebridge, which built 86 examples before it, too, folded.

JAGUAR XJ6/XJ12

UNITED KINGDOM 1968–91

A make-or-break car for Jaguar, the XJ saloon range proved to be far more than just the company's saviour. Brilliantly conceived and

brought to production in record time, the XJ was charged with reinventing the brand to appeal to a newer, younger audience.

The traditional Jaguar mantra of space, grace and pace was still very much in evidence, and the car drove with an incredible agility

that completely defied its size, but much more than that it was a car bristling with technical innovation. In-board rear disc brakes, power

Series 3 XJ6s went out of production in 1986 to make way for the XJ40, which proves that this 1989 car (on a UK G-registration) is an XJ12. The V12 models remained on sale until 1991.

steering and new automatic transmissions benefited the car greatly, while the neat monocoque construction vastly reduced Jaguar's build costs. Initially available with two six-cylinder engines, the XJ inherited the fabulous 5.3-litre (326cu in) unit from the E-type in 1971, along with the option of a long wheelbase chassis to turn it into a credible Rolls-Royce rival at a fraction of the price.

A Series 2 model came in 1973, with higher bumpers to meet US safety requirements, and, while it was quite pretty, it was a victim of the cost-cutting that was rife within British Leyland at the time.

Build quality suffered, equipment levels were down, and it took until 1979 and a mild Pininfarina restyle before the XJ was a great car again.

Of special interest during the Series 2 years was the gorgeous XJC – a six-cylinder or V12 version of the XJ in a unique two-door pillarless coupé bodystyle. This was definitely a hidden gem from the British Leyland years.

ENGINE: 5343cc (326cu in), twelve-cylinder
POWER: 285bhp (212kW)
0–60MPH (96KM/H): 8.8 seconds
TOP SPEED: 237km/h (148mph)
PRODUCTION TOTAL: 328,800

DAIMLER DS420

UNITED KINGDOM 1968–92

By taking over Daimler, Jaguar found itself in a situation where it could possibly mount a direct challenge to Rolls-Royce, and the DS420 was its rival to the much pricier Rolls-Royce Phantom V.

It had very similar dimensions to the Rolls and, in profile, even looked similar. Under the bonnet (hood) was Jaguar's proven (and

thoroughly excellent) 4.2-litre (258cu in) XK engine, mated to standard automatic transmission.

In the rear, there were two rows of seats – a standard bench at the far rear with a foldout centre armrest, plus two occasional foldout seats in the middle, which could be stowed away against the central divider panel.

The chauffeur's compartment was separated from the main cabin by a glass shield and featured an intercom system. Daimler did not intend production of the DS420 to last as long as it did, but a steady stream of orders, mostly from funeral parlours, meant that it was in production until 1992, by which time production had moved from

Daimler's premises to Vanden Plas Coachworks in Hendon, London.

ENGINE: 4235cc (258cu in), six-cylinder
POWER: 245bhp (183kW)
0–60MPH (96KM/H): 15 seconds
TOP SPEED: 169km/h (105mph)
PRODUCTION TOTAL: 3717 limousines and 802 chassis

MORGAN PLUS 8

UNITED KINGDOM 1968–PRESENT

ENGINE: 3528cc (215cu in), eight-cylinder
POWER: 190bhp (142kW)
0–60MPH (96KM/H): 5.6 seconds
TOP SPEED: 202km/h (125mph)
PRODUCTION TOTAL: about 5000

After criticism that the 4/4 simply was not quick enough, Morgan ordered a batch of Rover 3.5-litre (214cu in) V8 engines to fit into the 4/4's body. The Plus 8 was born. While it might have looked slightly twee with its vintage-car styling and ornate wooden dashboard, it was a real brute. Some road testers compared it to the AC Cobra, such was its propensity to slide its tail around under even moderate acceleration, while its wet weather handling was utterly terrifying.

Like the 4/4, the car was built on a wooden frame with steel panels stretched across it; aluminium

panels were offered from 1977, making the car even lighter and even more of a handful. Despite the car being difficult to drive and even trickier to stop, Morgan kept increasing the power, first in 1990

with a 3.9-litre (238cu in) Range Rover, then in 1994 with 4.0-litre (244cu in) and 4.6-litre (281cu in) versions. Amazingly, the Plus 8 is still in production, with a waiting list of over five years to own one.

The much-prized Morgan Plus 8 is not a car for the faint-hearted. Morgan even vetted each Plus 8 customer to check that they knew they were buying a car suitable only for experienced drivers.

WOLSELEY 18/85

UNITED KINGDOM 1969–72

As with the 1100/1300 Series of cars, BMC decided to offer various different badges on the 1800/2200 'Landcrab' series of family saloons. The most upmarket of these was the Wolseley 18/85, designed to appeal to traditional luxury-car buyers. Available with an automatic gearbox, unlike

Austin and Morris variants of the same car, the 18/85 also came with standard power steering, a wood-finished dashboard and leather trim; in traditional Wolseley fashion, the name badge of the radiator grille illuminated with the headlights. In 1969, the 18/85 was joined by the Wolseley Six,

which used the 2.2-litre (136cu in) engine from the Austin/Morris 2200 and was both quicker and more refined than the standard 1.8-litre (110cu in) model.

The same year also saw the launch of a Mk 2 version, with much-improved seats, a different dashboard and the option of twin

carbs on the 18/85 model for a much-needed performance boost.

ENGINE: 1798cc (110cu in), four-cylinder
POWER: 85bhp (63kW)
0–60MPH (96KM/H): 18 seconds
TOP SPEED: 145km/h (90mph)
PRODUCTION TOTAL: 35,597

DATSUN 240Z

For years, the Japanese had threatened to infiltrate the US and European car markets, and, for years the threat had been shrugged off by complacent industry bosses as a feeble attempt from a country that knew little about car manufacturing to scare them into investing into its industry.

The Datsun 240Z, then, came as something as a shock. When car industry bosses in Detroit heard that Datsun was planning to build a sports car to rival the Ford Mustang and Chevy Camaro, they laughed it off, saying that the Land of the Rising Sun could never produce a serious rival to the established American giants.

Similarly, bosses at MG and Triumph in the United Kingdom were blind to both the ambition and the quality of the Japanese company, so none of the main sports car players was quite ready when the 240Z snuck onto the market almost overnight and beat the Mustang at its own game, becoming America's best-selling sports car more or less as soon as it went on sale.

So what was the 240Z secret formula? First, it was very, very pretty. Styled by a Japanese team under the influence of Count Albrecht Goertz, who was responsible for the stunning BMW 507 in the 1950s, the Z-Car sported an incredibly long bonnet (hood) and neat, chopped-off tail.

The straight-six engine was created cheaply by adding two more cylinders to the overhead-camshaft engine from the Datsun

1600 saloon, which itself had been a copy of the early 1960s Mercedes 220 six-cylinder engine, with two cylinders removed and suitably stroked and bored. The result was a smooth and punchy unit that delivered a useful 151bhp (112kW) from 2393cc (146cu in).

Power was fed via a five-speed gearbox to a well-designed strut and wishbone rear suspension set-up. With struts at the front end and precise rack-and-pinion steering, the handling was a revelation, while the gutsy straight-six both sounded and performed like a grown-up sports car.

So successful was the 240Z at launch that Datsun had to restrict sales to the United States only for the first 18 months of production,

simply to meet customer demand, while even Japanese buyers were denied the opportunity to purchase one until mid-1969. A launch price in the United States of $3526 made it look incredibly cheap – at least $750 cheaper than a similar-performance Mustang – but, as waiting lists were so long at first, owners could actually sell their cars on for over $4000 to those who wanted to beat the waiting lists.

For the Japanese market only, where tax was based on engine size, the 240Z was known as the Fairlady Z and had a 2-litre (122cu in) 130bhp (97kW) engine.

But it was in Europe and the United States that the car made its biggest impact, and even today remains iconic. The 240Z was

This 240Z was restored in 2003 by Nissan GB, stripping it to bare metal and fitting new panels all round.

superseded in 1974 by the similar-looking and just as popular 260Z, which had a larger engine and a 2+2 option. It would be 1979 before the furore surrounding the car died down, when Datsun replaced it with the massively inferior 280ZX.

ENGINE: 2392cc (146cu in), six-cylinder
POWER: 151bhp (112kW)
0–60MPH (96KM/H): 9 seconds
TOP SPEED: 201km/h (125mph)
PRODUCTION TOTAL: 150,076

GILBERN INVADER

Gilbern eventually replaced the moderately successful Genie with the Invader – a more modern interpretation of what was effectively the same type of design.

The new car's chassis was stiffer, the suspension was firmer and the steering was sharper, making it more of a driver's car, while it was also more refined in many ways. The fit and finish were better, and ride comfort was much smoother, despite the firmer chassis set-up.

Power came from the Ford 3.0-litre (183cu in) V6 'Essex' engine offered in later versions of the Genie, with overdrive on third and fourth gears as standard, as well as the option of automatic transmission. Performance was

Gilbern's beefiest model, the Invader, used a Ford V6 powerplant and had proper sports car acceleration.

lively, with good acceleration and a top speed of 192km/h (120mph).

The Mk II had a few detail changes, including new door handles and a black radiator grille, while the Mk III was heavily modified with a lower overall ride height, flared wheelarches, revised rear end and wider front end. It also gained Ford Cortina front suspension and a Ford Taunus live rear axle, which improved ride quality and handling.

The most intriguing model was the Invader Estate (a station wagon), aimed at the Reliant Scimitar. It came out in 1971, but was dropped after a year, by which time only 105 cars had been built. Although a good

The Invader could trace its roots to the original Gilbern Genie, the Welsh manufacturer's first car, which had similar styling.

car, the Invader was not strong enough to help Gilbern survive; the Welsh manufacturer closed its factory in 1974 after 15 years.

ENGINE: 2994cc (183cu in),
  six-cylinder
POWER: 144bhp (107kW)
0–60MPH (96KM/H): 10.7 seconds
TOP SPEED: 192km/h (120mph)
PRODUCTION TOTAL: 561

ISO LELE ITALY 1969–74

Built to replace the Rivolta saloon, the Lele was a more modern and more angular machine built to suit the tastes and styles of the 1970s. It used the same Corvette-based chassis as all the other Iso cars, with the styling

carried out by Marcello Gandini of Bertone. The new bodywork was not innovative, but it was fairly smart-looking and offered the practicality of being able to seat four adults in reasonable comfort in its two-door coupé shell.

Under the bonnet (hood), true to form, was a Chevrolet small-block V8, providing it with a better power output than the Rivolta – although, like the Fidia, the Lele switched to a Ford 5.8-litre (351cu in) 325bhp (242kW) powerplant in its final

year of production. Iso also took the unusual step of offering an automatic gearbox as an option alongside the standard four-speed manual transmission, despite the car's sporting pretensions.

But sales of big supercars were falling rapidly as trouble in the Middle East threatened to cut off oil supplies, and Iso felt the pinch heavily, being left with stacks of unsold cars and mounting debts. The company went under in 1974, and the Lele went with it after only 317 cars had been built, which adds to the car's rarity value today.

ENGINE: 5359cc (327cu in),
  eight-cylinder
POWER: 300bhp (224kW)
0–60MPH (96KM/H): 7.3 seconds
TOP SPEED: 224km/h (140mph)
PRODUCTION TOTAL: 317

Unusually styled, the Iso Lele was a bizarre mix of sports car and family saloon. Well regarded, it couldn't save the company.

LMX 2300 HCS ITALY 1969–74

There were literally hundreds of design studies coming out of Italian styling houses in their 1960s heyday, but without the backing of a big manufacturer very few actually made it into series production. The LMX 2300 HCS was one of the rare exceptions. It was unusually based on Ford running gear, including the platform of the Taunus 20M and its 2.3-litre (140cu in) V6

engine, along with the suspension and all-round disc brake set up of the ageing Zodiac Mk IV.

Two bodystyles were offered: an odd-looking coupé or attractive two-door convertible. For those seeking a little more performance, LMX also offered a supercharged 210bhp (156kW) version, which had phenomenal acceleration and could crack 200km/h (124mph).

The glassfibre body was designed by a company called Eurostyle, based in Turin, and featured slightly strange rectangular headlights, a US-style power bulge in the bonnet (hood), flared arches and an aggressive-looking rear end. Despite this, the overall result was a car with clean lines, and one that looked good among its more exotic Italian sports-car rivals.

Only a handful of the 43 2300s made are still in existence and are very keenly coveted by collectors.

ENGINE: 2293cc (140cu in),
  V6-cylinder
POWER: 108bhp (80kW)
0–60MPH (96KM/H): n/a
TOP SPEED: 197km/h (123mph)
PRODUCTION TOTAL: 43

THURNER RS CZECHOSLOVAKIA 1969–74

A little-known but exceptionally pretty car, the tiny Thurner RS looked very much like a scaled-down Porsche, with curvy bodywork

and a neatly rounded front end. Indeed, the car even used some Porsche parts, including the windscreen from the 904 GTS.

The brainchild of German engineer Rudolf Thurner, the RS was to be a car that offered all the appeal of a Le Mans racer, but for

the masses. He aimed to bring the car to market for a bargain price, and to ensure that the car would be inexpensive for owners to run.

Most of the running gear, as well as the lively 1177cc (72cu in) engine, came from the rear-engined NSU 1200TT, and the car was built onto a shortened version of the 1200TT's chassis.

With a kerb weight of only 570kg (1250lb), the Thurner was a nippy little beast despite what could have been the constraints of its tiny engine, which could be tuned to provide an impressive 125bhp (93kW). The sleek lines, including Mercedes 300SL-style gullwing doors, gave the car efficient aerodynamics and incredible grip.

This was a truly stunning little sports car, and one that easily would have sold in much greater numbers than the 121 examples Thurner created were it not for the fact that each one was hand-built and, to Rudolf Thurner at least, a labour of love.

ENGINE: 1177cc (72cu in), four-cylinder
POWER: 65bhp (48kW)
0–60MPH (96KM/H): 7.1 seconds
TOP SPEED: 180km/h (112mph)
PRODUCTION TOTAL: 121

ALFA ROMEO JUNIOR ZAGATO

ITALY 1969–75

With no new models to announce and draw the crowds to its stand at the 1969 Turin Motor Show, Alfa Romeo instead turned to styling house Zagato to produce a limited-edition special, based on the chassis of the Spider and the engine and five-speed transmission from the Giulietta

The car was the Junior Zagato, and, despite Alfa's best attention, it looked clumsy at best, and downright awkward at worst. The drooping bonnet (hood) and sheared-off rear end gave the car unbalanced proportions, while the expanded glass area added to the Junior's somewhat unusual look.

It was a practical design, though, with room inside for four people and a well laid out cabin, and its clever aerodynamics and stiff bodyshell at least made it drive superbly, with great performance and tremendous agility. Another good idea was to hide the headlights behind a transparent panel made from thick impact-absorbent plastic, protecting them from stones flying up from the road or from falling victim to a bit of traditional Italian-style parking!

Initially a 1.3-litre (79cu in) engine was offered, but later a more potent 1.6-litre (96cu in) powerplant was provided, giving ample performance for its light weight. Although it was never intended for mainstream production, the Junior Zagato remained on sale for six years.

ENGINE: 1290cc (79cu in), four-cylinder
POWER: 87bhp (65kW)
0–60MPH (96KM/H): n/a
TOP SPEED: 168km/h (105mph)
PRODUCTION TOTAL: 1510

PORSCHE 914

GERMANY 1969–75

Originally planned to be developed by Porsche on behalf of Volkswagen, and sold purely with VW badges, the 914 ended up being a collaboration between the two manufacturers. Its development costs were too

Sold as both a Porsche and a VW, the 914 was a surprising sales success. There was also a 914/6, with the Porsche 911 engine.

high for Volkswagen to continue the funding, but by the time this was realized the project was so far down the line that to can it completely would have been a huge waste. Instead, VW secured some financial investment from Porsche to bring the car to market, and the car was sold as a VW-Porsche.

Called the 914, and powered by an air-cooled mid-mounted version of the engine from the 411 saloon, the car had oddball styling, but was pleasant and incredibly agile to drive. A pop-off Targa roof panel also gave it wind-in-the-hair appeal, while the use of VW components meant that the car was the cheapest Porsche by a long stretch.

The car received a frosty reception from Porsche fans, who hated the fact that it was not purely a Porsche design. Still, it was a sales success, with well over 100,000 cars leaving showrooms in a six-year career. In a bid to appease the purists, Porsche fitted the 911's flat-six engine to the flagship version, called the 914/6. It did not take off, and only 3500 were made before that model was withdrawn.

ENGINE: 1971cc (120cu in), four-cylinder
POWER: 100bhp (75kW)
0–60MPH (96KM/H): 8.2 seconds
TOP SPEED: 192km/h (119mph)
PRODUCTION TOTAL: 115,646

BRISTOL 411

UNITED KINGDOM 1969–76

Although thoroughly British in its eccentricity and in its unique breed of 'gentleman's club' style luxury, the Bristol 411 was actually powered by a thundering American heart. Power came from a 6.3-litre (383cu in) Chrysler V8 engine, coupled to Chrysler's 'Torqueflite' automatic transmission. Nonetheless, the character of the low-revving V8 suited this great British barge perfectly.

Based on the body of the existing 410, with its rounded front wings (fenders) and chrome grille, not to mention headlights taken from the humble Austin 1100, the 411 was a little more sporty than previous Bristols, It also featured slimmer bumpers front and rear, and a Bristol nameplate mounted on the grille and boot (trunk) lid. Nevertheless,

the vast weight of its separate chassis and sumptuous interior furnishings rendered the two-door four-seater saloon much more of a grand tourer than a sports car.

For the 1970s, the 411 received a new, squared-off nose and huge

slab-sided body panels that gave it a rather incongruous if individual look that was, if nothing else, more aggressive and sporty than its previous incarnations. The car also received a new engine with a lower compression ratio.

ENGINE: 6277cc (383 cu in), V8-cylinder
POWER: 335bhp (250kW)
0–60MPH (96KM/H): 7 seconds
TOP SPEED: 222km/h (138mph)
PRODUCTION TOTAL: 600

TRIUMPH TR6

UNITED KINGDOM 1969–76

With the United States being its biggest market for sports cars, Triumph could not afford to see its sales tumble. With the detuned TR250, however, the company was struggling. If it were going to claw its way back up the sales charts, a more powerful, meaner-looking sports car was needed. Enter the TR6, the first Triumph sports car to come out of the merger with British Leyland that took place in 1968.

Instead of using Michelotti, which had styled all previous generations of TR sports car, Triumph chose to approach German design house Karmann to try to give the TR6 a completely different appearance to its sports cars of old. Using the TR5/250 platform as a base, Karmann was given a tough task by the budget-squeezed Triumph.

Using the existing TR5/250 as a base, it had to transform the appearance of the car without altering its basic structure. The dictate from on high within British Leyland said that Karmann had to retain the wheel arches, floorpan, scuttle, windscreen, doors and even the inner panels from the original. To complicate matters further, the styling had to receive approval from all the various BL committees, and Karmann was expected to manufacture the new tooling as well. And it all had to be done within a mere 14 months.

British versions of the TR6, like this one, were much more powerful than their American counterparts.

To its credit, the German company managed to complete the task, and not without some success, for the TR6 filled the brief of looking meatier than its predecessor without being too costly to restyle. The new body hid the car's basic age well – but, as with the TR5 and 250, the US-market cars still had to make do with twin carburettors rather than the fuel-injection set-up enjoyed by European owners.

This time, though, US cars did have the same TR6 designation as their European counterparts, albeit with the 'Carb' suffix tacked on to create the TR6 Carb model. The TR6 proved the longest-lived of all the TR sports cars, and, although it did not sell as well as previous models in Europe, it turned around Triumph's fortunes in the United States and did a comprehensively good job of the task with which it was originally charged.

Very few changes occurred during the TR6's lifetime – with a stronger gearbox (from the Stag) fitted in 1971 and modifications to the car's interior the same year. In 1974, following on from ever more

stringent US emissions and safety laws, the TR6 was detuned and had big rubber overriders fitted to the bumpers, although cars in Europe were exempt from these ungainly modifications.

The TR6's sharp styling attracted a younger breed of buyers to the brand, despite the fact that the car felt very similar to drive to the earlier TR5. Regardless, its successful formula was not repeated for the next generation

of TR sports car – a model that was touted as truly avant-garde, but which turned out to be a damp squib in comparison to Triumph's heroic past offerings.

ENGINE: 2498cc (152cu in), six-cylinder
POWER: 142bhp (106kW) at 5700rpm
0–60MPH (96KM/H): 8.2 seconds
TOP SPEED: 195km/h (121mph)
PRODUCTION TOTAL: 94,619

FIAT 130

ITALY 1969–77

Replacing the dull but dutiful 2300 saloon, Fiat decided to go for a rakish new look with its 130 range. Launched in 1969 as a four-door sedan, the all-new 130 was powered by a 2866cc (175cu in) V6 engine developing 140bhp (104kW). The powerplant was based on the Ferrari Dino unit, but with only twin cams instead of four, while it used utterly conventional rear-wheel-drive running gear and a standard three-speed automatic gearbox.

The elegant good looks were the work of Pininfarina and looked very modern compared to rivals, while

Coupé versions of the Fiat 130 have become quite collectable. The appeal is in the rakish looks and Ferrari-sourced engine.

a mild face-lift in 1970 saw the original four-headlight grille swapped for a new front end with twin rectangular lights. A 3235cc (197cu in) engine debuted in 1971, upping power output to 165bhp (123kW), but, despite the 130's not inconsiderable charm, Fiat struggled to steal sales away from rivals such as Mercedes and Jaguar.

The most interesting version of the 130 was the Coupé, launched in 1971. Tabled by Pininfarina when it presented the original design, the good-looking two-door model was initially rejected by Fiat as surplus to requirements. Later launched to draw more attention to the 130 range, it was universally praised for its handsome styling. Pininfarina built the car for Fiat, using the same mechanical layout and floorpan as the saloon, which led to a number of quality problems.

ENGINE: 3235cc (197cu in), six-cylinder
POWER: 165bhp (123kW)
0–60MPH (96KM/H): 10 seconds
TOP SPEED: 189km/h (118mph)
PRODUCTION TOTAL: 19,385

OPEL KAPITAN/ADMIRAL/DIPLOMAT
GERMANY 1969–77

The Kapitan name, first used in the 1930s but most commonly known on Opel's large saloons of the 1950s, made a comeback for 1969 to mark out the most luxurious versions of the Admiral and Diplomat executive cars.

The Kapitan was powered by a 2.8-litre (170cu in) straight-six, producing an admirable 129bhp (96kW) – enough to give the car lively performance and a sweet-sounding exhaust note. The real brute of the range was the Kapitan Diplomat, which used a US-derived 5.4-litre (330cu in) V8 Chevrolet engine and had GM's Hydramatic automatic transmission as standard.

At the front end, stacked headlights gave the Kapitan models an appearance not dissimilar to the large Mercedes saloons of the era, or indeed GM America's Pontiac GTO. From the windscreen pillars back, however, the car had a vast slab-sided appearance that could not be described as pretty, but did have a certain, almost elegant presence. The rear end in particular was interesting, with an almost coupé-like look, thanks to its thick rear pillars.

ENGINE: 2784cc (170cu in), six-cylinder
POWER: 129bhp (96kW)
0–60MPH (96KM/H): 10.9 seconds
TOP SPEED: 176km/h (109mph)
PRODUCTION TOTAL: 61,019

SKODA S100
CZECHOSLOVAKIA 1969–77

Once known for building luxury cars, Skoda was firmly rooted in the budget-car market by the Skoda S100. It would remain in this position for the next 30 years. Designed as no-nonsense transport for Eastern European families, the

With the engine behind the rear axle and very little weight at the front, the Skoda S100 required careful handling through bends.

spacious, low-maintenance S100 was exported to other European markets, where it was one of the cheapest cars of its type.

It was not an especially great car to drive, with Triumph Herald–style swing axles at the back and a rear-mounted engine, which made the car particularly difficult to control if cornered too enthusiastically or driven in very wet conditions. It did have disc brakes all-round, which was good for the price, while the modern-looking body and black vinyl interior certainly looked no worse than contemporary Skoda rivals. Initially it was available with a 988cc (60cu in) air-cooled engine, but the powerplant was enlarged to 1107cc (67cu in) in 1968 – enough to give the car more respectable acceleration and answer one of the biggest criticisms it faced at its launch. As well as the most common saloon variant, there was a coupé version, the S110R, which was a rarity when new and is more or less extinct today.

The S100 was an honest, cheap car, one that enjoyed a surprising amount of rallying success.

ENGINE: 988cc (60cu in), four-cylinder
POWER: 43bhp (32kW)
0–60MPH (96KM/H): 30.8 seconds
TOP SPEED: 120km/h (75mph)
PRODUCTION TOTAL: n/a

TRIDENT VENTURER AND TYCOON
UNITED KINGDOM 1969–78

Trident updated its Clipper by introducing a pair of new cars which used a Triumph TR6 chassis and a choice of more economical six-cylinder engines in place of the original car's big V8. Called the Venturer and Tycoon, the cars looked very similar to the Clipper.

The faster version, the Venturer, used the same 138bhp (103kW) 2994cc (183cu in) V6 'Essex' engine seen in the range-topping Ford Capri 3000GT, while the Tycoon had the 150bhp (112kW) 2498cc (152cu in) fuel-injected straight-six usually seen in a TR6.

The Tycoon was by far the cheaper of the two cars, as no engineering work was required to mate the Triumph engine to the chassis. Despite this, Trident placed most of its emphasis on the more profitable Venturer, and only around seven Tycoons were ever completed. The Venturer, though, was more expensive than a Jaguar E-type, and the public was not prepared to have the wool pulled over its eyes, especially not after a road test in *Motor* magazine declared the car to be dangerous, with 'poor handling'.

An attempt to increase interest by entering the 1970 London to Mexico Rally came to nothing when the car retired near the start with terminal suspension, and, by 1972, Trident had gone bankrupt and the car ceased production.

Bizarrely, it was pulled back from the brink by a secret financier in 1976, and the Venturer was relaunched, this time with a live rear axle instead of the TR6 independent suspension. Again, nobody was interested, and, by the end of the year, the company had disappeared for good.

ENGINE: 2994cc (183cu in), six-cylinder
POWER: 138bhp (103kW)
0–60MPH (96KM/H): n/a
TOP SPEED: 192km/h (120mph)
PRODUCTION TOTAL: 225 (incl. Clipper)

VOLKSWAGEN 181

GERMANY 1969–78

Better known as the Kurierwagen, or even as the 'Thing' in the United States, the Volkswagen Type 181 was a road-going version of the old WW2 Kubelwagen troop carrier, revived in a period of peace, love and leisure narcotics to be seen as an icon of the hippy movement.

Using the Type 14 Karmann Ghia platform, the 181 had no fixed roof or doors, and the windscreen could be folded flat out of the way for maximum exposure to the elements, although quite why that was the case is anyone's guess.

There were no seats inside – just hard metal benches with pads on them, and, like the Kubelwagen, the 181 had absolutely nothing in the way of soundproofing or creature comforts. You could, quite literally, hose the car out after each use without fear of causing damage. The 181 was fairly light as a result, and, with a choice of Beetle 1500 or 1600 powerplants mounted in the rear, it was also frighteningly quick, especially given its incredibly hard ride and tendency to suffer chassis damage if driven on rough surfaces.

In 1975, production moved to Mexico – a country with a climate that was more suited to the 181's rudimentary design – and the final models were made in 1979.

ENGINE: 1493cc (91cu in), flat-four
POWER: 44bhp (33kW)
0–60MPH (96KM/H): n/a
TOP SPEED: 115km/h (72mph)
PRODUCTION TOTAL: 70,395

MINI 1275GT

UNITED KINGDOM 1969–80

Replacing the Mini Cooper was no mean feat, but with John Cooper Garages and British Leyland parting company after BL put the stoppers on the company's motorsport activity, the famous Monte Carlo Rally winner was destined for retirement. To succeed it, BL decided to place the emphasis on its new flat-fronted Mini, the Clubman. At the time, the plan was that the Clubman would replace the standard Mini, so it made sense to use the newer bodyshell and give it an image boost.

With its miniature Rostyle wheels and runflat tyres, sporty badging and black vinyl interior, the 1275GT was certainly a talking point, but at its debut it was missing one essential ingredient – power. The single carburettor 1275cc (78cu in) engine produced just 59bhp (44kW). While the car was easy to tune, enthusiasts could not understand why the 1275GT did not have the guts it needed from the start, and a range of special tuning kits was hastily produced to make the 1275GTs go faster.

In every other respect, it was a great car, with the legendary Mini handling and a more luxurious interior than previous Coopers.

ENGINE: 1275cc (78cu in), four-cylinder
POWER: 59bhp (44kW)
0–60MPH (96KM/H): 13.3 seconds
TOP SPEED: 145km/h (90mph)
PRODUCTION TOTAL: 117,949

The 1275GT benefited from the standard Mini's wonderful handling, but it was no match for the original Cooper S.

PEUGEOT 304

FRANCE 1969–80

Based largely on the outgoing 204, the 304 came with a dynamic new look for the 1970s that borrowed heavily from the look of the larger 504 saloon.

Available in a number of bodystyles, including two and four-door saloons, a smart two-door hatchback-cum-estate (station wagon) and a gorgeously pretty two-door convertible, the 304 was a versatile and well-designed car. It used the 204's range of excellent overhead-camshaft engines (which had been introduced in 1965 and powered some Peugeot cars right up until the twenty-first century), front-wheel drive, independent suspension and servo brakes, while an all-new floor-mounted four-speed gearbox was offered and was also heavily praised by the motoring media. The sportiest version was the 304S, which had a 1.3-litre (79cu in) petrol unit and anti-roll bars, plus a 160km/h (100mph) top speed.

All 304s were well equipped and had entertaining handling, making them far more appealing car than some of their mass-market rivals such as the Austin/Morris 1300 and Hillman Avenger. The 304 was incredibly tough mechanically, but the bodywork was a little fragile. Rust was a big problem, making survival rate low. Its replacement, in 1980, was the 305 – a much duller machine, but better made.

ENGINE: 1127cc (69cu in), four-cylinder
POWER: 45bhp (34kW)
0–60MPH (96KM/H): 14.7 seconds
TOP SPEED: 158km/h (98mph)
PRODUCTION TOTAL: 1,292,770

By far the most desirable of the 304 variants was this – the Pininfarina-styled convertible. It's a car cherished by enthusiasts today, unlike most other 304s.

AUSTIN MAXI

UNITED KINGDOM 1969–81

Great in concept, but definitely not in its execution, the Austin Maxi must be one of the most misunderstood models in motoring history. As a design, it was almost faultless. A huge hatchback bodyshell with front-wheel drive and a transverse engine meant that all of the space behind the front bulkhead could be given over to passengers and their luggage, so in essence it could become one

Later Maxis had black bumpers and full-size plastic wheeltrims to try to modernize them, but by then the car was badly outdated.

of the most versatile cars on the market. British Leyland went to town, creating a folding seat arrangement that could be turned into a double bed, boasting of rear legroom greater than that of a Jaguar and telling the world that not only was its Maxi a brilliant design, but that it also had the benefit of modern technology in the form of overhead-camshaft engines and a five-speed gearbox.

Sadly, it was the Maxi's mechanical components that were its nemesis. The engines were noisy, slow and prone to snapping their timing chains, with disastrous consequences, while the five-speed transmission used a series of cables to select the gears. The gearbox was dreadfully designed, though, which made gear selection, at best, tricky and, at worst, impossible, and completely destroying the driving experience.

It was a crying shame, as the later cars, which used BL's superbly supple Hydragas suspension and had revised gearboxes, were quite decent to drive. But the damage had been done, and the Maxi's reputation was tainted for ever.

ENGINE: 1748cc (107cu in), four-cylinder
POWER: 84bhp (63kW)
0–60MPH (96KM/H): 15.8 seconds
TOP SPEED: 144km/h (89mph)
PRODUCTION TOTAL: 472,098

FORD CAPRI

UNITED STATES 1968–87

ENGINE: 1297cc (79 cu in), six-cylinder
POWER: 57bhp (42kW)
0–60MPH (96KM/H): 7 seconds
TOP SPEED: 204km/h (127mph)
PRODUCTION TOTAL: 1,497,445

Billed as 'The car you always promised yourself', the Ford Capri was an engineering and marketing masterstroke. Following the success of the Mustang in the United States, Ford of Europe decided to build a car that would use all of the Mustangs key sales features, but targeted towards the European market. That meant that the car had to look fantastic, be good to drive and be affordable to all buyers, with a vast range of engine and trim options.

The first Capris appeared in showrooms in 1969, designed in the United Kingdom at Ford's engineering centre in Dunton, Essex. Available as a four-seater two-door coupé only, the Capri came with a range of different engines, kicking off with a 1.3-litre (79cu in) unit that was barely adequate, through to 1.6-litre (98cu in) and 2.0-litre (122cu in) four-cylinder options. The range-topper, though, was something else. Powered by a 3.0-litre (183cu in) V6, the fastest Capri was a real brute and could prove tricky to drive in the wet, as the power was fed through a live rear axle.

A large range of equipment packages and trim levels set each car apart in X, XL, XLR, or E formats, while an X-Pack styling kit was also available on all models – allegedly, there were more than 900 different ways you could specify a Capri, and this led to its appeal, as it was always difficult to find two cars exactly the same – ideal if you wanted a car that was personalized to your tastes.

The 3000GT in 1969 put a modified Zodiac V6 under the bonnet (hood), which needed a bulge to accommodate it. There were even limited-production high-speed RS versions – the RS2600 (sold only in Germany) and the

RS3100. Not surprisingly, the Capri excelled at motorsport and twice won the European Touring Car Championships.

A face-lift occurred in 1972 and gave the Capri new headlights and revised suspension, while an all-new model appeared in 1974. Using the same basic chassis as the original, the Mk 2 gained the addition of a hatchback. Unlike the Mustang, however, which had been severely watered down by the time it reached a second generation, the Capri continued to be just as desirable as ever.

Although the United Kingdom was the Capri's biggest market, all production was transferred to Cologne, Germany, for 1976, and these cars are arguably better built.

A final restyle in 1978 made the Capri look more aggressive than ever, with a smart four-light front end, a reprofiled bonnet, larger taillights, black wraparound bumpers and a revised cabin. The flagship model was the 3.0S, which came with four-spoke alloy wheels and smart side graphics, plus a smaller steering wheel and optional Recaro sports seats.

The 3.0-litre engine was replaced in 1981 by a fuel-injected 2.8-litre (170cu in) unit developing 160bhp (119kW). It was fitted to a new flagship, called the 2.8 Injection Special, complete with a sunroof, 'pepperpot'-style alloy wheels and standard Recaro seats.

There were two luxury versions: the Aston-Martin tweaked Tickford, which was offered in 1983 and 1984 only, and came only in white, with an odd-looking body kit; and the run-out Capri 280 Brooklands of 1986, which had leather trim, metallic green paint and masses of extra equipment to make it one of the best Capri variants ever.

Three generations of Capri were made, although some would argue there were actually four. This is the Mk 1 facelift, which got Mk 2-style rectangular headlights, a new grille and Ford's steel sports wheels.

LADA 2100 SERIES

Throughout the 1960s and 1970s, Fiat had a reputation for selling off its old models, along with its engineering expertise, to emerging car markets. In the case of the Fiat 124, it would go to Russia when it reached the end of its natural life. The first car to be built by VAZ of Togliattigrad was the VAZ 2101, made of Russian Glasnozt steel and using a 1.2-litre (73cu in) overhead-camshaft engine of VAZ's own design.

In Europe, VAZ was known as Lada, and, in 1971, the company began exporting cars to Western Europe, where they were sold at amazingly low prices. Also available as 1300, 1500 and 1600 models to suit different markets, the Lada was a cheap and cheerful offering, using flimsy plastic interior trim and a rugged but unpleasant-to-use gearbox. The Russian firm also modified the Fiat 124's suspension to cope with rough Russian roads; while this made the car more durable, it did nothing for its frightening roadholding.

In 1984, the 2101 was given a more modern-looking front and rear, and its name was changed to Lada Riva, but it was still an unpleasant machine. Regardless, VAZ has sold over 14 million 2101s. While exports have largely dried up, it still sells well in Russia.

ENGINE: 1198cc (73cu in), four-cylinder
POWER: 62bhp (46kW)
0–60MPH (96KM/H): 16.6 seconds
TOP SPEED: 139km/h (87mph)
PRODUCTION TOTAL: n/a

DE TOMASO PANTERA

The Pantera is known for its lack of reliability as much as its performance and good looks. Legend has it that Elvis Presley actually shot his Pantera in a fit of rage – and many owners have experienced a similar deflated feeling over the years. Yet, despite that, de Tomaso's most popular model has wormed its way into supercar fans' affections over the years, not least because of its brilliant simplicity.

Introduced at the 1970 New York Motor Show, the Pantera (Italian for 'panther') was a smaller version of the Mangusta, and de Tomaso's engineers had worked hard to iron out the criticisms of the larger car, which was berated for its tricky handling and poor weight distribution. The Pantera was still heavier at the rear than at the front, but motorsport engineering supremo Giampaola

Late Panteras like this one lacked the styling purity of the original – they succumbed to 1980s excesses, with over-the-top wings and body styling kits.

Dallara (of Dallara Formula One fame) considerably reworked the chassis, to deliver better grip and more predictable oversteer. It was still 'entertaining' in the wet, but the improvement was immense and made the Pantera appeal to a much broader spectrum of buyers than the earlier car ever could have wished.

The Pantera was also a more comfortable car to drive. Both the driver and the passenger had more elbow room, and there was even some space for their luggage. Most important of all, air conditioning was standard in the stuffy cabin. The car was offered in three states of tune – 280, 310 or 330bhp (209, 231 or 246kW), all powered by US Ford V8 engines.

The car's lithe styling was carried out by Tom Tjaarda, a stylist at the Ford-owned Ghia styling house, and the result was stunning, with a rakish profile and unusual angular rear end. Yet, under the skin, the car was as conventional as a supercar could be. A conventional monocoque body was used, with no complex spaceframe, while the big V8 fed power to the rear wheels through a live rear axle and five-speed manual gearbox.

Ford's involvement with the project from the outset meant that de Tomaso also secured a distribution network through some US Ford dealers, which saw his car smash all of his company's standing production records. While previous

de Tomasos were sold almost by the handful, over 9000 Panteras were sold over a 20-year career.

Things started well for this historic link-up between a small Italian supercar maker and one of the world's largest automotive corporations. In 1972, 2506 Panteras were built and sold, although this dropped to 1604 the following year. Clearly, there were some problems. One of them was the looming oil crisis, which meant that expensive and thirsty V8 supercars were losing their appeal.

Far more of an issue, however, was the Pantera's dreadful build. Owners complained about rust, overheating, noise and bits and pieces of trim falling off, and, tired of all the owners' frustrations,

Ford pulled its support out from underneath de Tomaso.

The bullish Italian entrepreneur would not let such a major vote of no confidence deter him, though. From 1978 through to 1990, de Tomaso continued to build cars at a rate of at least 50 a year, to satisfy the demand from sports-car enthusiasts, who were slightly more understanding of the fragility of a supercar than Ford dealers might have been.

ENGINE: 5769cc (352cu in), eight-cylinder
POWER: 330bhp (246kW)
0–60MPH (96KM/H): 5.5 seconds
TOP SPEED: 256km/h (159mph)
PRODUCTION TOTAL: 9500

MARCOS MANTIS

One of the rarest and ugliest cars of the 1970s, the Marcos Mantis shares its three-abreast seating layout with the rather more successful and attractive McLaren F1.

You certainly could not criticize Marcos for a lack of bravery when it announced the Mantis in 1970, but sadly there were plenty of other reasons to berate the car. First, and most obvious, was its ungainly looks. Marketed by Marcos as 'refreshingly different', the car was described by one car magazine as resembling a platypus, thanks to its turned-up nose and pod-mounted headlights.

Built from glass-reinforced plastic mounted on a steel tubular spaceframe, the wedge-shaped Mantis was a three-seater, with the seats mounted three abreast and the driver in the middle. The engine and suspension came from the Triumph TR6, while inside the

car was an incongruous mix-'n'-match of parts plucked from various British makers.

Launched to a furious backlash from fans of the marque, who valued the lithe, curvaceous styling of its earlier models, the Mantis received such bad press that Marcos withdrew it after it had been on sale for only a year. Only 32 were completed, making it, thankfully, a rare sight today.

ENGINE: 2498cc (152cu in), six-cylinder
POWER: 150bhp (112kW)
0–60MPH (96KM/H): n/a
TOP SPEED: 200km/h (125mph)
PRODUCTION TOTAL: 32

BOND BUG

ENGINE: 748cc (46cu in), four-cylinder
POWER: 32bhp (24kW)
0–60MPH (96KM/H): n/a
TOP SPEED: 126km/h (78mph)
PRODUCTION TOTAL: 2270

Both the Marcos Mantis and this creation turned 1970 into the year for bizarre wedge-shaped cars made from reinforced plastic. Unlike the Marcos, the Bond Bug was a surprising success. Built to offer more sporting styling to those who would usually buy a Reliant Robin, the oddball 'Bug' looked like a small wedge of cheese on wheels. Available only in orange (or for a short while lime green), the Bug's

You could have any colour as long as it was orange, or if you were lucky, lime green. The Bond Bug typified the 1970s.

emphasis was entirely on fun. Power came from a 748cc (46cu in) engine provided by Reliant, while the unique styling was the work of designer Tom Karen, who worked for British firm Ogle Design.

The car was accessed by hinging the whole windscreen and roof mechanism forwards. Other neat features included unique 22.5cm (9in) alloy wheels, pod-mounted headlights and muscle-car–style

black side graphics around the rear end. Its tripod layout meant that stability was not the Bug's strong point, but it was an entertaining machine, feeling remarkably responsive for its power output

and being an absolute hoot to drive round town. Initially it was planned to go on sale for only a year, but customer demand was so strong that Bond built the Bug until 1974, eventually selling over 2000 cars.

DODGE CHALLENGER

Both the Dodge Charger and Plymouth Road Runner were leading lights in the large muscle-car arena, but Chrysler Corporation took a while before it offered a true rival to compete in the burgeoning

pony-car market, spawned by the incredible success of the Ford Mustang. Its best effort came, eventually, in 1970, in the form of the Dodge Challenger and its sister car the Plymouth Barracuda.

An interpretation of the Mustang concept, almost to the point of duplication, the Challenger was a good-looking car. It could be bought as either a coupé or a convertible. Available in standard or R/T (Road

and Track) specification, the Challenger offered something for the enthusiast as well as the ordinary car buyer who just wanted some style. Over its four-year life, there was a confusing mixture of engine options, from a 5.2-litre (317cu in) 150bhp (112kW) unit up to the legendary 7.0-litre (427cu in) 425bhp (317kW) 'Hemi' power pack.

Despite its early promise, and some legendary one-off models, the Challenger was never the success that Chrysler Corp had hoped for. Its appeal was stunted partly by its late arrival, but more so by the constant need to reduce power outputs in light of US emissions laws and the fuel crises of the 1970s.

ENGINE: 7202cc (439cu in), eight-cylinder
POWER: 375bhp (279kW)
0–60MPH (96KM/H): 6 seconds
TOP SPEED: 209km/h (130mph)
PRODUCTION TOTAL: 188,606

Chrysler Group's answer to the Ford Mustang and Chevy Camaro, the Dodge Challenger was a good-looking car that was rewarding to drive, but never as successful as Chrysler hoped.

HONDA Z600

Based on the popular N600 K-Car, the Z600 started life as the 345cc (21cu in) Z Coupé, designed to suit Japan's stringent tax on engines over this capacity.

For the rest of the world, which did not get the car until 1972, the car came with a 599cc (37cu in) unit developing 42bhp (31kW).

This gave it just enough power to appear lively to drive in town, if not on the open road.

The Z600 was an interesting concept, designed as a sports GT for city dwellers. It had an exceptionally high level of trim for a car of its size, including aircraft-style overhead lockers and a six-

dial dashboard. All were finished in lurid bright orange.

For the Japanese market only, there was a special edition 'Hard Top' model (from 1972) which had stylish pillarless doors, but most other markets had only the four-seater two-door coupé model – although the four-seat designation

was at best a loose promise, as the rear bench was tiny.

ENGINE: 599cc (37cu in), two-cylinder
POWER: 32bhp (24kW)
0–60MPH (96KM/H): 32.6 seconds
TOP SPEED: 120km/h (75mph)
PRODUCTION TOTAL: n/a

SAAB SONETT III

Saab's determination to build a sports car continued with the Sonett III, which took the unsuccessful Sonett II concept a little further. In answer to criticisms of the earlier car's gawky styling, Saab enlisted the help of Italian styling house Coggiola to make the new Sonett more in tune with the demands of customers in the United States. Longer than the

outgoing car, the Sonett III had sleek, angular bodywork and a neatly chopped rear end, but its tall wheels and unusual windows, plus the need to incorporate a Saab 99 windscreen, meant that there were still areas of the car that looked a little incongruous.

First seen at the 1970 New York Auto Show, the car was deemed much more attractive than its

predecessor, and Saab's decision to replace the earlier car's 1.5-litre (92cu in) engine with a 1.7-litre (104cu in) V4 unit was well received.

Sadly, by the time the car was ready to go on sale in the United States, where Saab hoped most Sonetts would be sold, new safety laws meant that it acquired hideous black impact bumpers and side reflectors, making it ugly again.

It sold far better than the Sonett II, but, by 1974, Saab decided to stop making sports cars altogether.

ENGINE: 1699cc (104cu in), four-cylinder
POWER: 73bhp (54kW)
0–60MPH (96KM/H): 12 seconds
TOP SPEED: 171km/h (106mph)
PRODUCTION TOTAL: 8368

Better looking than the original, but still a little awkward, the Sonnet III enjoyed only limited success before Saab gave up on sports cars and reverted to its more profitable saloon car business.

VOLKSWAGEN K70

GERMANY 1970–74

Originally destined to be an NSU design, the K70 became a Volkswagen as part of the company's buyout of NSU in 1969. By then, the car was too advanced, and too much money had been spent, not to put it into production. With NSU's focus being the hi-tech rotary-engined Ro80, a conventional (and rather dull) saloon car would have had little synergy with the brand.

Instead, the car was introduced to the world as a Volkswagen, with a hasty restyle to make it fit in more with the VW family look.

Although not an especially bad car, the K70 nonetheless met with resistance from VW fans, as the engine was in the front and was water-cooled, unlike the company's other vehicles. It did set the scene for future VW cars, though, as the

company's next family models, the Scirocco and Golf, would feature the same layout.

Although a slow seller, the K70 was a decent enough car to drive and had fairly lively performance, as well as being fairly well made. It was difficult for VW to build, however, as no parts were interchangeable with other Volkswagens, meaning that the

K70 was taken out of production after a relatively short life to make way for VW's own new designs.

ENGINE: 1605cc (98cu in), four-cylinder
POWER: 75bhp (56kW)
0–60MPH (96KM/H): 10.5 seconds
TOP SPEED: 147km/h (92mph)
PRODUCTION TOTAL: 211,100

CITROËN SM

FRANCE 1970–75

ENGINE: 2670cc (163cu in), six-cylinder
POWER: 180bhp (134kW) at 6250rpm
0–60MPH (96KM/H): 9.3 seconds
TOP SPEED: 217km/h (135mph)
PRODUCTION TOTAL: 12,920

Trust Citroën to come up with the idea of combining the DS with a supercar. The French maker was renowned for its off-the-wall ideas, and, after buying the struggling Italian sports-car maker Maserati in 1968, it decided to combine its expertise of ride and handling, thanks to hydraulic suspension, with Maserati's incredible quad-cam V6 engine.

Styled by Citroën's in-house designer Robert Opron, the SM was a spectacular car to look at, with a brooding, angular profile,

Although not especially well made or reliable, the Citroën SM had stunning looks, which meant that loyal buyers loved it.

pretty chrome-shrouded rear end and innovative front that saw both the headlights and the number plate hidden behind a transparent plastic cover to protect them from stone chips or parking knocks.

In true Citroën style, the car was front-wheel drive, which meant that the Maserati engine had to be turned round to provide its power. The chassis, hydraulics and super-sharp self-centring steering were

taken directly from the DS, proving just how competent the original car was. When Peugeot took control of Citroën in 1975, the SM was instantly and unceremoniously dropped, infuriating the car's fans.

OPEL ASCONA

Launched at the 1970 Turin Motor Show, the Ascona was an utterly conventional design, but it was also a very important car for Opel. As a replacement for the smaller Olympia, it had much more interior space and a larger boot (trunk), making it a serious rival to cars such as Ford's Taunus and the Fiat 125, as well as new models such as the Audi 80. The car used a monocoque bodyshell, which was by now the industry-accepted standard, with either a 1.6-litre (98cu in) or 1.9-litre (116cu in) overhead-camshaft engine in a choice of two-door, four-door and estate (station-wagon) bodystyles. A strong four-speed manual gearbox was standard, along with the option of a three-speed automatic.

The Ascona's engines were its strongest point, offering good performance, excellent refinement and good fuel economy, which made them especially popular with drivers in the fuel-starved years of the mid-1970s. Light steering, coil springs all-round and front disc brakes also made the ride and handling competent.

While it never excelled at one particular thing, the Ascona was overall a very competent motor car and just what Opel needed at the time to grow its sales across Europe. It also provided the basis for the sporting Manta, which proved that, beneath the skin, the Ascona was very well thought out.

ENGINE: 1897cc (116cu in),
four-cylinder
POWER: 90bhp (67kW)
0–60MPH (96KM/H): 12.5 seconds
TOP SPEED: 158km/h (98mph)
PRODUCTION TOTAL: 641,438

OPEL MANTA A-SERIES

It was not just Ford that was looking to bring America's pony-car concept to the United Kingdom, and the proof was Opel's Manta. Like the Ford Capri, the Manta used transatlantic styling influences from its parent company to bring the concept of a 'personal coupé' to the masses – in the case of the Manta, a car that looked like a scaled-down 1968 Chevrolet Camaro. Also like its arch rival the Capri, the Manta came with a confusing engine range, from a tiny 1.2-litre (73cu in) four-cylinder engine to a 1.9-litre (116cu in) 105bhp (78kW) slant four, although the Manta never had a Capri-rivalling V6 option.

The Manta was neatly styled, using Ascona panels as far as the windscreen pillars to keep costs down. The fastest and most desirable variant was the 1973 Manta GT/E, which acquired Bosch fuel injection, Rostyle wheels, auxiliary driving light and a matt black bonnet (hood) to prevent glare from the sun blinding the driver. Like the Ascona, it was pleasant to drive, but lacking in driver involvement, although the supple ride and slick gearbox made it a comfortable cruising car. The Manta nevertheless won the hearts of enthusiasts who did not like the Capri, and its image was always considered slightly more upmarket than that of Ford's offering, as, indeed, was its price.

ENGINE: 1897cc (116cu in),
four-cylinder
POWER: 105bhp (78kW)
0–60MPH (96KM/H): 9.8 seconds
TOP SPEED: 189km/h (117mph)
PRODUCTION TOTAL: 498,553

ALFA ROMEO MONTREAL

First shown as a prototype at the 1967 Montreal Expo, Alfa's stunning two-door coupé was considered good enough to go into series production. Built on the existing Giulia GTV platform, the newcomer was designed to offer

From the show stand to the showroom almost without change, the Alfa Montreal was a concept car for the road which proved to be a steady seller.

less expensive competition to the likes of Maserati and de Tomaso.

By the time the concept reached production, some of the original prototype's sleek looks had been compromised by the need to fit extra safety equipment and also to house the 2.6-litre (158cu in) twin-cam V8 engine, which was effectively a detuned version of the unit found in the 33 racing cars. Despite this, the Montreal still looked well balanced and alluring, while the car's exquisitely detailed cabin was almost true to the original show car, save for some more conventional dials on the dashboard.

The V8 engine came with fuel injection, which made it less powerful than if it had been fitted with a carburettor, but, despite this the Montreal did not want for performance, with a 218km/h (136mph) top speed and impressive acceleration. Perhaps its most beguiling feature was its headlights, which were hidden beneath pop-up mesh covers to give it a mean and menacing look.

Sales were always steady rather than manic, but the Montreal was a good flagship for Alfa Romeo for nearly a decade.

ENGINE: 2593cc (158cu in),
eight-cylinder
POWER: 200bhp (149kW)
0–60MPH (96KM/H): 7.6 seconds
TOP SPEED: 218km/h (136mph)
PRODUCTION TOTAL: 3925

LIGIER JS2

Renowned for making racing cars, Guy Ligier made his first attempt at creating a road car in the form of the JS2 coupé, which was launched in 1970. The JS part of the name was in memoriam of Ligier's good friend Jo Schlesser, who was killed while competing in

Named after late racing driver Jo Schlesser, the JS2 was a pretty two-seater that should have been more of a success.

a race in 1968, and the car was targeted at wealthy buyers who, like Ligier himself, enjoyed supercars and a lavish lifestyle.

It was built on a pressed-steel platform chassis, around which was wrapped a stylish two-door glassfibre body, with the engine mounted in the middle.

The car was certainly distinctive to look at, with Le Mans-style Perspex-covered headlights, a large, steeply raked windscreen, alloy wheels and an air intake on

the back of the rear wing (fender) that forced air directly into the engine compartment. Power for the JS2 came from the same quad-cam 2.7-litre (181cu in) V6 engine that powered the Citroën SM, producing a healthy 192bhp (142kW) and giving the car phenomenal acceleration.

Only 150 JS2s were built in a seven-year career, largely due to the car's expensive price, and soon after Ligier withdrew from car production to concentrate on

Formula One. He later ventured back into the mainstream market with the Ligier Ambra microcar, a venture which was far removed from the company's previous road legal offerings.

ENGINE: 2965cc (181cu in), V6-cylinder
POWER: 190bhp (142kW)
0–60MPH (96KM/H): n/a seconds
TOP SPEED: 245km/h (153mph)
PRODUCTION TOTAL: 150

MAZDA RX4

Spurred on by the success of the Luce, Mazda decided to further its presence in the family car market with the RX4, which was aimed as a direct rival to the likes of the Ford Cortina and Peugeot 304. Available with a 1.8-litre (110cu in) petrol engine as a four-door saloon, an estate (station wagon) or a stylish two-door

coupé (which resembled a scaled-down Ford Mustang), the RX4 was a competent if uninspiring car.

It was utterly conventional to drive, with predictable handling, rear-wheel drive and steady performance. Mazda wanted to do something a little different to its rivals, however, so as well as the conventional 1.8-litre it offered an

RX4 with a rotary engine. Using a derivative of the twin rotary Wankel unit from the oddball Cosmo, the 573cc (35ci) motor produced an impressive 120bhp (89kW), but the extra power showed up the weaknesses of the standard RX4 chassis. On top of that, the early rotary engines were not especially reliable. Although

unique in its class, the RX4 Rotary was never a brilliant seller.

ENGINE: 17960cc (110cu in), four-cylinder or 573cc (35cu in) twin-rotor Wankel
POWER: 120bhp (89kW)
0–60MPH (96KM/H): n/a seconds
TOP SPEED: 189km/h (118mph)
PRODUCTION TOTAL: 213,988

MONTEVERDI HAI

Having seen his 375 GT turn into quite a success, Swiss business magnate Peter Monteverdi turned his attentions to his second dream car – a machine that would take on the cars of the ilk of the Ferrari 275 and Lamborghini Miura.

Unlike the 375, which was styled by Frua, the Hai was penned

This is one of only two Monteverdi Hais to have been 'officially' built – the other one was finished in silver. Are there any others?

entirely by Monteverdi's own hand, and it was every inch the car that he dreamed of producing, with stunning two-door coupé bodywork and a bespoke chassis.

His attention to detail in the plans made the Hai incredibly easy to produce, and, in less than 12 months, his own version of this

fabulous car was ready for him to use. The car was exceptionally well equipped, with leather trim, air conditioning and a beautiful dashboard, yet it was also a competent supercar. Its 7.0-litre (426cu in) Chrysler V8 engine fed power to the rear wheels through a five-speed manual gearbox.

Monteverdi made absolutely no secret of the fact that the Hai was built simply for his own use, and, while he was happy to sell cars to customers, they were hugely expensive. Officially, only two examples of the Hai were produced, although it is believed that a handful more of these

beautiful supercars were sold to customers on an unofficial basis.

ENGINE: 6974cc (426cu in), eight-cylinder
POWER: 450bhp (335kW)
0–60MPH (96KM/H): 5.4 seconds
TOP SPEED: 290km/h (180mph)
PRODUCTION TOTAL: 2

TOYOTA CELICA

JAPAN 1970–77

Having witnessed the success of the Datsun 240Z, especially in the United States, Toyota decided that it, too, would get in on the sports GT act. The Celica was based on the floorpan of the Carina saloon and was hastily

rushed into production in time for the 1970 Tokyo Motor Show, to capitalize on the booming sports-car market. Despite being brought to production in record time, it was a thoroughly developed and appealing machine.

Initially, only one bodystyle was on offer – a two-door notchback coupé – although a hatchback version, called 'Liftback', made its debut two years after launch and brought new elements of practicality to GT customers.

Power came from a choice of 1.6-litre (97cu in) or 2.0-litre (122cu in) engines, with a choice of single or twin camshafts, badged ST or GT accordingly. The power went to the rear wheels through a newly developed five-speed gearbox, while the handling was safe and predictable, thanks to the use of a conventional Macpherson strut system for the front suspension, and a live rear axle suspended by coil springs. Although not a mould-breaker in the vein of the Datsun 240Z, the Celica was still a great sales success.

ENGINE: 1588cc (97cu in), four-cylinder
POWER: 73bhp (54kW)
0–60MPH (96KM/H): n/a
TOP SPEED: 170km/h (106mph)
PRODUCTION TOTAL: 1,210,951

Japan's Mustang? The Celica was the first true personal coupé and a great sales success from the Land of the Rising Sun.

TRIUMPH STAG

UNITED KINGDOM 1970–77

The Triumph Stag could have been an incredible success were it not for the penny-pinching of British Leyland, a lack of development and the stubbornness of Triumph's own engineers to continue developing a new V8 engine that was surplus to the company's requirements.

Based on the platform of the upmarket Triumph 2000 saloon, the Stag was an incredibly good-looking four-seater cabriolet, with a soft top or detachable hardtop, meaning that it could be used all year round and serve as a grand tourer during the winter. Its existence was made all the more remarkable by the fact that it had been styled by accident.

Triumph's established designer, Giovanni Michelotti, got hold of an old styling prototype for the 2000 saloon and decided to amuse himself by chopping it around to create an open-top version. His intention was to build a motor show concept car. He remodelled

the shell of the 2000, turned it into a two-door car and cut the roof off to turn it into a soft-top convertible. One of the most notable features was the headlight arrangement. Michelotti put in a full-length grille, behind which twin headlights were concealed on each side – a look considered so neat that it was applied to the 2000 itself as a mid-life face-lift in 1970.

Triumph did not see the vehicle until 1966, when chief engineer Harry Webster visited Michelotti and 'discovered' the concept car. Webster immediately made arrangements to have the car taken back to Britain for appraisal, and the Triumph management originally intended it to become the new TR6.

That plan changed when the company realized that there would be a market for the car in its own right. Estimates put worldwide sales at around 12,000 a year, and the Stag (which was both its code name and final production name)

was scheduled for introduction in 1968. In reality, it took a couple of years longer to reach showrooms, largely due to arguments within British Leyland's various committees about which engine it should use.

One camp insisted that the car should have been fitted with the Rover-Buick V8 from the Rover P5B, but those involved with the project from the start had already begun to develop a 3.0-litre (183cu in) V8 that was effectively two Triumph 1500 engines welded together, with an alloy cylinder head atop the cast iron block.

In the end, it was the 3.0-litre unit that was given the go-ahead, as it would be lighter than the Rover engine. Despite being smooth, more economical than the Rover engine and pleasingly lively, however, the engine would prove to be the Stag's downfall.

Poor design within the cylinder head led to engines overheating and warping the softer alloy part of the engine, meaning that the

entire unit needed to be rebuilt. The glut of warranty claims affected triumph so badly that, in 1973, it withdrew the car from the US market, and the car's reputation for poor reliability was so bad that, even after the initial problems were ironed out, sales never picked up. When production ceased in 1977, fewer than a third of Triumph's original sales target had been met.

This was a great shame as, in every other respect, the Triumph Stag was a brilliantly conceived and well-executed car. Sadly, it will be remembered as yet another example of how British Leyland's committee-led thinking was capable of stifling potential.

ENGINE: 2997cc (183cu in), eight-cylinder
POWER: 145bhp (108kW) at 5500rpm
0–60MPH (96KM/H): 10.1 seconds
TOP SPEED: 188km/h (117mph)
PRODUCTION TOTAL: 25,939

AMC GREMLIN

USA 1970–78

Launching a car on April Fool's Day is not a great idea at the best of times, but when it is a car as dreadful as the Gremlin it is even more of an unusual decision.

Introduced on 1 April 1970, AMC's attempt at cashing in on the burgeoning compact-car market

Launched on April Fool's Day, the AMC Gremlin was an all round disaster: it looked ridiculous, fell apart and was awful to drive.

was not a good one. With little money to develop new cars, the company had to rely on its existing product base to take on America's 'Big Three', GM, Ford and Chrysler Corporation. It decided to enter the small-car market by taking a stock AMC Hornet and using all of its front panels as far back as the doors, before grafting on a new hatchback rear end to create a smaller car. The result was confounding.

AMC had reduced the length of the car by a third, but had simply

chopped off the rear and added an unusual back in the style of an estate (station wagon) directly behind the rear seats, leaving little room for luggage and giving the car the appearance of being overlong at the front.

AMC also missed the point of a compact car by insisting on using the Hornet's engines, including a 5.0-litre (304cu in) V8 – buyers would not even buy the car for its fuel economy. This was partly addressed in 1976, when AMC put

a 2.0-litre (122cu in) four-cylinder engine into the vast engine bay, courtesy of German maker Audi. But by then it was too late. By 1978, the Gremlin had shuffled out of production, largely unlamented.

ENGINE: 3802cc (232cu in), six-cylinder
POWER: 145bhp (108kW) at 4300rpm
0–60MPH (96KM/H): 12.5 seconds
TOP SPEED: 153km/h (95mph)
PRODUCTION TOTAL: about 650,000

LAMBORGHINI JARAMA

ITALY 1970–78

Introduced as a smaller alternative to the Espada, in keeping with tradition the Jarama also took its name from bullfighting, named after a town in Spain where the

sport was especially popular. Like the Espada, the Jarama was a 2+2, although the space in the rear was particularly cramped and suitable only for children or luggage.

Styled by Marcelo Gandini, the Jarama had a rakish, wedge-shaped profile and unusual headlights, which were partly hidden under hoods that lifted up when the

Although smaller than the Espada, the Jarama actually looked less sporty thanks to its higher roof and more wedge-like styling.

dipped beam switch was activated. Under the skin, the car had a cut-down Espada chassis, with a shorter wheelbase. The steel body, made by Bertone, was fairly heavy, which had some effect on performance, even if the car was still a fairly rapid machine with a top speed in excess of 260km/h (150mph).

A sportier model, called the Jarama S, was unveiled at the 1972 Geneva Motor Show and came with an even more powerful version of the 3.9-litre (240cu in) V12 engine, developing an impressive 365bhp (272kW). The Jarama was never an especially good seller. Lamborghini produced just a quarter as many Jaramas as it did Espadas, and this was despite the Jarama being the more affordable model.

ENGINE: 3929cc (240cu in), 12-cylinder
POWER: 350bhp (261kW)
0–60MPH (96KM/H): 6 seconds
TOP SPEED: 260km/h (162mph)
PRODUCTION TOTAL: 327

LAMBORGHINI URRACO

ITALY 1970–79

With its existing product range right at the top end of the market, Lamborghini wanted a car that would appeal more at the entry level to the supercar market. That car would be the Urraco (meaning 'young bull'), which made its public debut at the 1970 Turin Motor Show.

Although larger than Lamborghini originally planned, the Urraco was a well-packaged performance car, using the same mid-engined layout as the Miura, but with a smaller 2463cc (150cu in) V8 engine behind the cabin and a very simple yet effective chassis layout.

The car was styled by Bertone and looked sharp, with a low nose, pop-up headlights and a striking fastback rear, while the well laid out cabin was more spacious than people expected from a mid-engined performance car. There was also a reasonable amount of luggage space behind the engine. One of the Uracco's less than brilliant design cues was the fuel filler's position, inside the luggage bay – you had to lift the entire engine cover up to fill up with petrol.

An improved Uracco was released in 1974, with a larger V8, a more comfortable interior and improvements to the suspension and steering.

ENGINE: 2463cc (150cu in), eight-cylinder
POWER: 220bhp (164kW)
0–60MPH (96KM/H): 7.2 seconds
TOP SPEED: 232km/h (145mph)
PRODUCTION TOTAL: 776

CHRYSLER 180

UNITED KINGDOM/FRANCE 1970–80

Chrysler Europe's ill-judged attempt to find its footing in the large saloon-car market, the 180 was built to a design inherited when the global giant took over the British Rootes Group in 1970. Initially planned as an all-new Humber, it looked like an engorged Hillman Avenger, with a US-style front end and curved C-pillars leading into a drooping rear end.

Chrysler decided that the car would be built in France, and sold as both a Simca and a Talbot, as well as a Chrysler. In 1974, the 180 name was dropped, along with the 1.8-litre (111cu in) engine, and the car was renamed the 2-Litre, with a 2.0-litre (121cu in) engine and optional automatic transmission. The ungainly car was still no better than when it was launched, with dull driving dynamics, poor build quality and a total lack of character.

ENGINE: 1812cc (111cu in), four-cylinder
POWER: 97bhp (72kW)
0–60MPH (96KM/H): 13.6 seconds
TOP SPEED: 159km/h (99mph)
PRODUCTION TOTAL: 60,000

HILLMAN AVENGER

UNITED KINGDOM 1970–81

Hillman's key model in the fleet market, where it went head to head with the Ford Cortina and Vauxhall Viva, the Avenger was an utterly conventional car in almost every respect. The styling was fairly interesting, though, with unusual 'hockey stick'–shaped rear light lenses and a coupé-style rear end. MacPherson strut front suspension and a beam axle at the rear meant that the Avenger was light and easy to drive, although it was not as surefooted as some front-wheel drive rivals and had a tendency to slide if driven too quickly in the wet.

The sportiest model at launch was the GT, which had twin round headlights, Rostyle wheels, twin carburettors and sports seats. An even sportier version, the GLS, appeared in 1972, and added even more power and a vinyl roof. The original 1200 and 1500 engines were replaced by 1300 and 1600 units in 1973, with extra power.

The hottest ever model, the Avenger Tiger, came the same year. With 160km/h (100mph) performance, alloy wheels and bright yellow paint, the Tiger was not a car for shrinking violets.

The Avenger's name changed from Hillman to Chrysler in 1976 (when the car had an inadvisable face-lift), then to Talbot from 1979 as part of Chrysler's weird marketing strategy. Across the globe it was also sold as a Dodge, a Plymouth and even a Volkswagen!

ENGINE: 1248cc (76cu in), four-cylinder
POWER: 53bhp (39kW)
0–60MPH (96KM/H): 19.8 seconds
TOP SPEED: 134km/h (84mph)
PRODUCTION TOTAL: 826,353

CITROËN GS

FRANCE 1970–85

The brilliant little GS was Citroën's attempt to bring new levels of refinement to the small-car market, and in true Citroën style the car defied convention. As well as the mandatory hydraulic suspension, which gave superb ride and handling qualities for a car of its size, the GS was the most aerodynamic car in its class, with a sleek, rounded body penned by the SM's designer, Robert Opron.

More to be different than for any other reason, the first GSs came

One of Citroën's best ever cars, the GS made conventional rivals such as the Ford Escort and Morris Marina look ancient.

with a 1015cc (62cu in) air-cooled flat-four engine that was effectively two 2CV units welded together, but larger water-cooled units were available later. An exceptionally practical estate (station wagon) model was added in 1972. From 1979 onwards, the bodyshell was altered to incorporate a hatchback, and the range redesignated GSA.

One of the most intriguing models in the GS line-up was the Birotor, introduced in 1974. It was powered by a twin rotary Wankel engine, but, like other exponents of rotary technology, Citroën had difficulty in getting the engines to work properly; the project was canned after only 847 had been made. Most of these cars were bought back from customers by Citroën and scrapped, as the company did not want to maintain a parts supply network for them.

ENGINE: 1220cc (74cu in), four-cylinder
POWER: 60bhp (45kW) at 6500rpm
0–60MPH (96KM/H): 14.9 seconds
TOP SPEED: 154km/h (96mph)
PRODUCTION TOTAL: 2,473,997

RANGE ROVER

UNITED KINGDOM 1970–PRESENT

This is a prototype Range Rover, built while the name was still a top secret. The 'Velar' badge on the bonnet was fitted to try and stop rival companies from knowing whose car it was.

Originally intended as a dual-purpose vehicle that would take the role of a Land Rover as well as providing transport as a family car for farmers, the Range Rover evolved into a status symbol.

Before its introduction in 1970, if you wanted to go cross-country, you had to accept austerity and lack of comfort as part of the experience. But the Range Rover changed all that. Powered by the 3.5-litre (215cu in) V8 engine used in the Rover P5B and P6, the newcomer was both powerful and versatile, with an all-purpose coil-sprung separate chassis underneath and incredible axle articulation, meaning that it was a superb off-roader.

Like the Land Rover before it, the Range Rover was planned to be a short-term project, designed to help the company through a financial slump caused by a drop in orders from the military. The original intention was to build it for only a handful of years – little did Land Rover know at the time that it was about to kick off a global phenomenon across the entire motor industry, and that its new model would go on to enjoy a 25-year (and counting) life cycle.

The Range Rover's box-like two-door body was the result of a collaboration between engineers Spen King, Gordon Bashford and Phil Jackson. It was made of aluminium, and was designed with a large interior and a split rear-hatch opening for versatility. The vehicle's chassis featured permanent four-wheel drive, and there was to be a choice of manual or automatic gearboxes.

The first prototype was up and running by the end of 1967, and was then modified by Rover's design chief David Bache. Prototypes were tested in an assortment of climates, from the cold of Norway to the Sahara desert, before the car's launch in 1970.

Almost immediately, Land Rover was inundated with orders, and the Range Rover smashed the company's sales expectations by quite some margin. A four-door version was eventually launched in 1981, after 11 years of waiting, while a five-speed gearbox was finally offered in 1983.

A much-needed diesel model appeared in 1986, using a 2.4-litre (146cu in) four-cylinder unit that was provided by Italian maker V.M. Motori. In 1990, Land Rover finally offered the Range Rover with its own diesel engine, called the 200Tdi and developed for the new Discovery.

Long-wheelbase LSE models were also offered later in the Range Rover's life, while the V8 engine was increased from 3.5-litre to 3.9 in 1988. The most desirable Range Rover is probably the limited-edition two-door CSK, introduced as a top-luxury model to mark the car's twentieth anniversary. The CSK name stood for Charles Spencer King, a tribute to the original designer, who was better known as 'Spen'.

A new Range Rover came out in 1994, with more rounded styling and a thoroughly revised chassis, although it shared most of its architecture with the original car. It would do, however, until a newer, bigger and much more expensive model succeeded it in 2001.

ENGINE: 3528cc (215cu in), eight-cylinder
POWER: 130bhp (97kW) at 5000rpm
0–60MPH (96KM/H): 14.3 seconds
TOP SPEED: 161km/h (100mph)
PRODUCTION TOTAL: n/a

VOLVO 1800ES

SWEDEN 1971–73

With the P1800 advancing in years, Volvo decided to introduce something new for the 1970s in the form of the 1800ES. Identical to the P1800 from the windscreen forward, the new model had a rear like an estate (station wagon), much in the same way as the Reliant Scimitar against which it was benchmarked. With greater rear legroom than the coupé and a large load bay, the 1800ES was a practical car, but it did suffer from something of an identity crisis.

Despite having overdrive and all-round disc brakes, the Volvo was not an especially sporting drive, with heavy handling and performance that could best be described as modest – something that the P1800 coupé got away with because of its alluring GT looks, but which was to do the 1800ES few favours.

Nevertheless, the model was a steady seller throughout its short production life, which was curtailed in 1973 when its biggest market, the United States, demanded the use of energy-absorbent bumpers, which Volvo quite rightly claimed would ruin the car's looks. Rather than spend money reengineering it, it withdrew the car from sale and focused instead on developing its saloon and estate models.

ENGINE: 1986cc (121cu in), four-cylinder
POWER: 112bhp (83kW)
0–60MPH (96KM/H): 9.7 seconds
TOP SPEED: 181km/h (112mph)
PRODUCTION TOTAL: 8077

CLAN CRUSADER

The odd-looking Crusader was the work of ex-Lotus engineer Paul Haussauer, who was determined to create his own sports car. The two-door coupé, which was entirely his own design, was made out of glassfibre and mounted on a steel spaceframe chassis. All of the running gear came from the Hillman Imp Sport.

That meant that the Crusader came with a free-revving 875cc (53cu in) all-alloy engine and four-speed gearbox, producing a modest 51bhp (38kW), but weighing little enough for its requirements. Imp suspension was also used to keep costs to a minimum, while there were also several Rootes Group parts inside the cramped cockpit.

Despite its lack of outright power, the Crusader was a featherweight sports car, and that meant that it felt quite lively to drive. Haussauer's experience at Lotus also meant that the chassis was brilliantly designed, giving the car rewarding roadholding and great steering feel. The car's only downside was its cost, as by the time purchase

tax was added it was almost as expensive as a genuine Lotus.

ENGINE: 875cc (53cu in), four-cylinder
POWER: 51bhp (38kW)
0–60MPH (96KM/H): 12.5 seconds
TOP SPEED: 161km/h (100mph)
PRODUCTION TOTAL: 315

FERRARI 365 GTC/4

The 365 GTC/4 was a clever attempt by Ferrari to introduce an all-new model using parts that were already in existence. The car was a more spacious alternative to the Daytona, complete with four seats, and only the bodywork was

Based on the Daytona but nowhere near as attractive, the 365 GTC/4 enjoyed only limited success before Ferrari canned it.

entirely new and was styled by Pininfarina.

It soon accounted for half of Ferrari's front-engined production. Based on a Daytona chassis together with independent suspension from the 365 GTC 2+2, the car had a 4390cc (268cu in) V12 engine and a front-mounted gearbox. The power unit, revised from that in the outgoing 365 GTC 2+2, had a power output of 340bhp (253kW), which made it one of the most

powerful cars of its day. It also used the Daytona's ventilated disc brakes, plus air conditioning, power steering and self-levelling suspension from its predecessor.

The Pininfarina design was a two-door coupé with 2+2 seating which shared some styling elements with the Daytona, but had a lower, more angular nose and pop-up headlights, along with gorgeous Cromodora five-spoke alloy wheels. Ferrari completed

500 365 GTC/4s before the entire Ferrari range was given a shake-up in the mid-1970s, which would see big 2+2 models consigned to the history books.

ENGINE: 4390cc (268cu in), 12-cylinder
POWER: 340bhp (253kW)
0–60MPH (96KM/H): 7 seconds
TOP SPEED: 241km/h (150mph)
PRODUCTION TOTAL: 500

BMW 3.0CS

Big coupés had been part of BMW's line-up since the unusual-looking 2000CS of the 1960s, so, when BMW introduced its new large saloon models in 1968, a coupé variant was expected.

The 3.0CS appeared in 1971 and was incredibly elegant, with BMW's trademark shark nose at the front and unusual real light lenses mounted on a smart cigar-shaped

body. Power came from a 3.0-litre (182cu in) straight-six engine, which offered more than ample performance and was also extremely refined at cruising speeds, making the CS a superb high-speed grand tourer. Fuel injection came in 1973, boosting performance yet further and giving the car the ability to accelerate as quickly as a Porsche 911.

The most desirable CS also came in 1973, and it was originally intended as a homologation special for motorsport. Called CSL, the new car used lightweight alloy panels to keep its weight to a minimum and was nicknamed the 'Batmobile', thanks to its enormous wings (fenders), a huge boot (trunk) spoiler and wind deflectors mounted on the bonnet (hood).

The car had truly awesome performance and is today regarded as one of BMW's all-time classics.

ENGINE: 2985cc (182 cu in), six-cylinder
POWER: 200bhp (149kW)
0–60MPH (96KM/H): 7.5 seconds
TOP SPEED: 224km/h (139mph)
PRODUCTION TOTAL: 20,301

Beautifully balanced styling gave the 3.0CS masses of appeal, and elevated BMW's status as a manufacturer of luxury cars. It was also a fabulous car to drive. Today it's regarded as one of BMW's all-time classics.

INTERMECCANICA INDRA

ITALY 1971–75

Intermeccanica's second entry into the GT market came in the form of the Indra, developed by owner Frank Reisner in conjunction with former Opel engineer Erich Bitter (who would later go on to form his own sports-car company). As a result, there were a lot of Opel components in Intermeccanica's new model, which was based on a shortened Opel Diplomat platform and used the German car's 2.8-litre (170cu in) straight-six or 5.4-litre (327cu in) V8 engines.

The bodywork was styled by Italian designer Franco Scaglione, who had also penned the Intermeccanica Italia, and the car was available as either an attractive two-door coupé or an even more striking convertible. Unlike the Italia, though, the new car was made out of steel, so was heavier and less agile than its predecessor.

Reisner completed 127 Indras between 1971 and 1975, when he decided to withdraw from car making altogether and concentrate on other business interests. The plans for the Indra were borrowed by Erich Bitter, who used the car as the basis for his own SC models.

ENGINE: 2784cc (170cu in), six-cylinder
POWER: 190bhp (142kW)
0–60MPH (96KM/H): 8.2 seconds
TOP SPEED: 203km/h (127mph)
PRODUCTION TOTAL: n/a

GINETTA G21

UNITED KINGDOM 1971–78

Although it shared many styling cues with other Ginetta models, the G21 was the company's most daring model. With its scooped-out headlights and coupé-style rear, the G21 looked like a Triumph GT6, which was hardly a coincidence when you consider that the six-cylinder coupé was one of its most significant rivals.

The G21 used an all-new steel backbone chassis, cloaked in a well-constructed glassfibre shell that proved to be both rigid and lightweight. Ginetta opted for a Ford V6 engine to power what was to become its flagship model, preferring the 3.0-litre (183cu in) 'Essex' unit found in the Ford Capri, but soon after launch a cheaper four-cylinder version was introduced, with a 1725cc (105cu in) Rootes Group unit, found in the Sunbeam Rapier and tuned up by racing engineers Holbay.

Although Ginetta was primarily a kit-car maker, most of the 170 G21s that were built were supplied ready-made, to avoid swingeing tax rises, which came into effect in Britain in 1973 and made kit cars uneconomical to buy.

ENGINE: 1725cc (105 cu in), four-cylinder
POWER: 79bhp (59kW)
0–60MPH (96KM/H): 10.8 secs
TOP SPEED: 180km/h (112mph)
PRODUCTION TOTAL: 170

MASERATI BORA

ITALY 1971–76

Now under the ownership of Citroën, which took control of Maserati in 1968, the Bora was the Italian maker's first mid-engined model and was aimed as a rival to the likes of the Lamborghini Miura and de Tomaso Pantera. The car was unveiled at the 1971 Geneva Motor Show to universal acclaim, its stunning Giugiaro-penned bodywork making it an ideal companion for the beautiful Ghibli, which was also styled by the leading Italian.

Power came from a 4719cc (288cu in) all-alloy V8 engine that developed 310bhp (231kW) and was mounted on its own subframe within the car's steel body. Independent suspension came via double wishbones all round, giving the car excellent handling abilities, while Citroën's influence was evident inside the cabin, where the seats and pedal could be moved hydraulically to adjust the driving position. Citroën was also responsible for the Bora's brakes, which were sharp and progressive.

The Bora was also incredibly aerodynamic. Although Maserati did not use a wind tunnel at any point during the car's production, the sleekness of the car's profile gave it a drag coefficient of just 0.30, considerably lower than most sports cars of the era.

ENGINE: 4719cc (288cu in), eight-cylinder
POWER: 310bhp (231kW) at 6000rpm
0–60MPH (96KM/H): 6.5 seconds
TOP SPEED: 261km/h (162mph)
PRODUCTION TOTAL: 571

Under Citroën's stewardship, Maserati finally launched a worthwhile companion for the Ghibli and a rival to the Lamborghini Miura. The Bora went on to become Maserati's most successful model ever.

SUBARU LEONE

JAPAN 1971–79

Not a classic car in terms of its styling or desirability, the Subaru Leone is nonetheless notable for its contribution to automotive technology. Apart from the low-volume and expensive Jensen Interceptor FF, the Leone was the first passenger car to be offered with four-wheel drive as standard on all models. Subaru's plan was to sell more than a million worldwide (a figure it easily surpassed).

In the first year of production, only a four-door saloon was available, and sales were slow. The introduction of an estate (station wagon) model the following year saw sales boom dramatically, with the added practicality of the load bay making the car especially popular with farmers, who wanted a vehicle that drove like a car but had go-anywhere ability for far less financial outlay than a Range Rover. Picking up on this trend, Subaru developed a pick-up truck version, which farmers loved even more. Launched in 1977, the pick-up proved exceptionally popular and is still on sale in some markets today, although production of Leone cars drew to a close in 1979.

ENGINE: 1595cc (97cu in),
 four-cylinder
POWER: 65bhp (48kW)
0–60MPH (96KM/H): 16.7 seconds
TOP SPEED: 139km/h (87mph)
PRODUCTION TOTAL: 1,269,000

FORD PINTO

UNITED STATES 1971–80

ENGINE: 1599cc (98cu in),
 four-cylinder
POWER: 75bhp (56kW)
0–60MPH (96KM/H): 18 seconds
TOP SPEED: 131km/h (82mph)
PRODUCTION TOTAL: 3,150,943

With US buyers becoming ever more conscious of fuel economy, Ford developed the Pinto as a new subcompact model. Available as a two-door sedan, or an odd-looking hatchback model called the Runabout, the Pinto was powered by two Ford of Europe engines – a British-built 1.6-litre (98cu in) unit or a German-made 2.0-litre (122cu in) engine, which

Pintos hit controversy following a safety scare about its propensity to catch fire if involved in an accident.

was offered in conjunction with three-speed Cruise-O-Matic automatic transmission.

The Pinto was initially very popular, with more than 350,000 cars made in the first year alone, but it was subject to a huge safety scare when researchers from a US TV station learned that the Pinto could burst into flames if crashed into from behind. Ford received even more bad press when it was discovered that redesigning the fuel-filler neck to prevent the fires happening would have cost less than a dollar per car. As a result, sales dwindled quite dramatically. Later, revised Pintos sold better, and, with the fuel crisis out of the way, engine sizes rose to 2.3 litres (140cu in) and 2.8 litres (171cu in), again developed in Europe. There was even a performance version, called the 'Stallion'.

MORRIS MARINA

UNITED KINGDOM 1971–80

British Leyland's replacement for the Morris Minor was designed to take on the Ford Cortina in the fast-growing fleet market, but the company's haste to bring the car to production led to some serious engineering problems.

British Leyland's main competitor in the fleet market, the Marina, was available as a saloon or an oddly attractive two-door coupé.

Powered by a choice of 1.3-litre (78cu in) A-Series or 1.8-litre (110cu in) B-series engines, the Marina was underdeveloped, with crude front suspension and poor brakes, both of which combined to give the earliest models some alarming handling characteristics. These were addressed in 1973, and cars built from this year onwards were far better to drive.

Three bodystyles were offered – a four-door saloon, an estate (station wagon) and a curiously attractive two-door coupé, which managed to look more modern than the other variants.

In 1978, the Marina 2 appeared and had revised bumpers and a plastic front spoiler. The 1.8-litre engine was replaced by a new overhead-camshaft 1.7-litre (103cu in) unit, called the O-Series. It was both less powerful and less refined than the old 1.8, and was heavily criticized. Marina sales stopped in 1980, when the car was replaced by the Giugiaro-restyled Ital, built on the same basic structure. Saloon and estate models were offered, but there was never an Ital coupé.

ENGINE: 1798cc (110cu in), four-cylinder
POWER: 95bhp (71kW) at 5500rpm
0–60MPH (96KM/H): 12.3 seconds
TOP SPEED: 161km/h (100mph)
PRODUCTION TOTAL: 953,576

FIAT 127

ITALY 1971–83

ENGINE: 903cc (55cu in), four-cylinder
POWER: 47bhp (35kW)
0–60MPH (96KM/H): 17 seconds
TOP SPEED: 137km/h (85mph)
PRODUCTION TOTAL: 3,779,086

An impressive design, the 127 ushered in a new era of small-car excellence for Fiat. The 127 was so well packaged that it was voted Car of the Year 1971, and is also credited as being the first true 'supermini'. Built on a shortened 128 platform, the 127 featured front-wheel drive and a choice of lively overhead-cam engines in a choice of two-door saloon or three-door hatchback bodystyles.

As well as class-leading passenger space, the 127 had impressive handling and a good ride quality, while the brakes were

Simple, but effective, the Fiat 127 was fun to drive, cheap to buy, easy to tune and surprisingly spacious given its dimensions. It's no wonder that Fiat shifted almost four million in a 12-year production run.

also excellent. The car's dynamic ability led to the creation of a 'Sport' model in 1977, when the rest of the range was also given a face-lift to get a redesigned front and plastic bumpers.

The Sport had a 1049cc (64cu in) engine and developed 70bhp (52kW), which gave the car a good turn of speed and allowed drivers to exploit the impressive chassis. Further developments came in

1980, with a new five-door model added to the range, as well as an odd-looking estate (station wagon), called the Panorama. A diesel engine was also offered for the first time, the 1301cc (78cu in)

unit delivering especially thrifty running costs.

By the time production ceased in 1983, almost four million 427s had been sold, outselling even the hugely successful Nuova 500.

BENTLEY CORNICHE

Although only built by the handful, the Bentley Corniche was sold for 13 years alongside the Rolls-Royce that shared its name. Like the Rolls, the Bentley Corniche was a two-door version

of the Bentley T-series/Rolls-Royce Silver Shadow, available in coupé or convertible form, and the car based on a special body that was built by Mulliner Park Ward from 1967 onwards.

Production of 'official' cars began in 1971, and Bentley versions differed visually from the Rolls-Royce cars by featuring a different radiator grille, Bentley-branded wheel trims and a flaying

'B' mascot in place of the Rolls-Royce's Silver Lady. To drive, the Bentley was slightly firmer than the Rolls and had a more sporting feel to the brakes and steering, but mechanically the two cars were identical, sharing the same 6750cc (412cu in) V8 engine.

Series 2 models, from 1977, came with thicker bumpers and a front spoiler, and these were to remain in production until 1984 – although the Rolls-Royce Corniche continued to sell right through until the mid-1990s.

ENGINE: 6750cc (412cu in), eight-cylinder
POWER: n/a
0–60MPH (96KM/H): 9.9 seconds
TOP SPEED: 194km/h (120mph)
PRODUCTION TOTAL: 149

It was officially on sale for 13 years, but fewer than 150 Bentley Corniches were ever built – an average of fewer than 12 cars a year. In all but detail, it was identical to the more popular Rolls-Royce Corniche.

ALPINE A310

ENGINE: 2664cc (163cu in), six-cylinder
POWER: 150bhp (112kW)
0–60MPH (96KM/H): n/a
TOP SPEED: 221km/h (137mph)
PRODUCTION TOTAL: 11,616

You certainly could not fault Renault for a lack of ambition when it announced it was going to build a car to take on the Porsche 911. The Alpine A310 never quite achieved the same reputation as the cult German legend, but it did develop quite a following over its 14-year production life.

Using the same layout as the existing Alpine A110, which had proven a successful race and rally car, the A310 had a rear-mounted engine. The initial four-cylinder

unit from the Renault 17TS was soon superseded by a more potent 1.6-litre (163cu in) V6. In standard form, this developed 150bhp (112kW), but was easily tuned to give a greater power output.

From 1978 onwards, the A310 also received a five-speed gearbox, while the pretty two-door bodystyle was always clean and sharp-looking. Production of the A310 ceased in 1985, but the car morphed into the

Renault GTA, which was more or less the same car hidden beneath a body kit. The turbocharged GTA was much more powerful and, if anything, an even more credible rival to the Porsche 911.

Wedge-shaped and angular, the A310 was a comprehensive update of the pretty Alpine A110, 1970s style.

DE TOMASO DEAUVILLE

ITALY 1971–88

Squint, and you could almost believe that the de Tomaso Deauville was a Jaguar XJ6, so close was the car's styling to the British executive car. The XJ6 had raised the bar in the luxury-car market, bringing in new levels of agility, performance and clever packaging. Alejandro de Tomaso liked what he saw so much that he decided to copy the design. Although shorter than the XJ6, and slightly wider, the Deauville had the same sloping boot (trunk) lid and curved profile, while the four-lamp front end had a more rakish shape to it.

The Deauville was also more simple than the complicated British car, using the same Ford-sourced V8 engine as the Pantera, which fed its power to the rear wheels via a four-speed manual or three-speed automatic gearbox, while the suspension was by way of double wishbones front and rear.

This actually made the Deauville less impressive to drive than the Jaguar it aped, so very few people saw the point of paying more for one. Production numbers were tiny, but it stayed on de Tomaso's order books for 17 years.

ENGINE: 5763cc (351cu in), eight-cylinder
POWER: 330bhp (246kW)
0–60MPH (96KM/H): 8.6 seconds
TOP SPEED: 241km/h (150mph)
PRODUCTION TOTAL: 355

ROLLS-ROYCE CORNICHE

UNITED KINGDOM 1971–94

As soon as the Rolls-Royce Silver Shadow made its debut in 1965, coachbuilders were modifying examples to give them a unique look. One of the more popular conversions was a two-door coupé by Mulliner Park Ward. Rolls-Royce liked the look of it so much that it decided to incorporate the car into its standard model range from 1971.

Called the Corniche, the new car was offered as both a coupé and an incredibly elegant two-door convertible. Beneath the pretty body, the car was standard Silver Shadow, with a 6750cc (412cu in) V8 engine, self-levelling suspension and a four-speed automatic gearbox. Inside, the level of trim was exquisite. Hand-stitched leather seats, deep-pile carpets and polished burr walnut dashboard and door cappings gave the Corniche a sense of occasion. Cruise control and a radio-cassette were offered as standard equipment.

The Corniche II was introduced in 1977, featuring the same styling modifications as the Silver Shadow II, with rubber bumpers and a front spoiler. Silver Shadow production stopped in 1980, but the Corniche carried on for another 14 years, as there was no coupé or convertible version of the Silver Spirit.

ENGINE: 6750cc (412cu in), eight-cylinder
POWER: n/a
0–60MPH (96KM/H): 9.6 seconds
TOP SPEED: 194km/h (120mph)
PRODUCTION TOTAL: 6350

PLYMOUTH VALIANT

UNITED STATES 1972–74

Plymouth's first 'compact car', launched in response to the energy crisis of the early 1970s, was not very compact at all. But compared to the big V8-engined cars of the late 1960s, its 2.8-litre (2170cu in) slant-six engine made it look fairly economical in a climate of rising US oil prices.

Surprisingly pleasant to drive and capable of over 10L/100km (25mpg) if driven gently, the Valiant made for sensible yet stylish family transport. Sedan, coupé or estate (station wagon) versions were offered, the latter having a clever tailgate that split open in two parts for added practicality.

The slant-six engine could trace its roots back to the original Valiant of 1960, and as well as the economy 2.8-litre (170cu in) version, 3.2-litre (195cu in) and 3.7-litre (226cu in) versions of the six-cylinder were offered.

It was also one of only a handful of US cars to be exported to Europe. Plymouth even made a right-hand drive model for sale in the United Kingdom, although it was only ever sold in very small numbers.

Once the energy crisis had settled down, Plymouth upped the engine sizes and power outputs. The last cars came with big V8s, just as in the past.

ENGINE: 2789cc (170cu in), six-cylinder
POWER: 140bhp (104kW)
0–60MPH (96KM/H): n/a
TOP SPEED: 161km/h (100mph)
PRODUCTION TOTAL: about 900,000

JENSEN HEALEY

UNITED KINGDOM 1972–76

Ill-fated from the start, the Jensen-Healey had a difficult birth and never really recovered. In concept it was great, but the execution didn't match the original proposals and it never reached its sales targets.

With American businessman Kjell Qvale in charge of Jensen, the company decided to change its focus and aim itself at more of a mainstream sports-car market, rather than the most expensive luxury market where it had sat for the previous decade.

Qvale appointed Donald and Geoffrey Healey to help develop the new car, following their successes with the Austin-Healey range of sports cars. They not only styled the car, but also sourced most of the components.

The 2.0-litre (122cu in) four-cylinder engine came from Lotus, while the suspension and steering components were from Vauxhall and were the same as those fitted to the Viva. Initially, the power was fed to the rear wheels via a Hillman Avenger gearbox; this was uprated to a better Getrag unit after 1974.

By the time the Jensen Healey reached production, though, it was a long way away from Qvale's original vision. It was heavy, not especially agile to drive and had all sorts of reliability problems. It never reached the sales targets for which Jensen had originally hoped.

ENGINE: 1973cc (120cu in), four-cylinder
POWER: 140bhp (104kW)
0–60MPH (96KM/H): 8.8 seconds
TOP SPEED: 200km/h (125mph)
PRODUCTION TOTAL: 10.926

OPEL COMMODORE

GERMANY 1972–77

Opel's new large saloon, the second-generation Commodore (known as Commodore B) was based on the Rekord D and launched in 1972, two years after the base model. It had a new chassis, developed by GM Europe for use on Vauxhall models as well, and it came in two different bodystyles. The four-door saloon variant was conventional in every respect, but the two-door hardtop coupé version was neatly styled and resembled a scaled-down American muscle car.

Four models were offered: 2500 S, 2500 GS, 2800 GS and 2800 GS/E. Power ranged from 115 to 160bhp (84.5 to 118kW), making it more powerful across the range than the British Vauxhall Victor that shared its platform, but not its German-built engines. In the early to late 1970s, the Rekord and Commodore were also assembled as CKD kits in Switzerland. These cars carried the name 'Ranger' and had different grilles and trim. They were exported to various countries, including many outside Europe.

The best Commodores were those introduced before 1974, after which new German laws on exhaust emissions meant that they were detuned. Later cars were nowhere near as powerful.

ENGINE: 2784cc (170cu in), six-cylinder
POWER: 160bhp (119kW)
0–60MPH (96KM/H): 8.9 seconds
TOP SPEED: 194km/h (120mph)
PRODUCTION TOTAL: 140,827

TVR M-SERIES

UNITED KINGDOM 1972–79

The M-Series encompassed a myriad of different cars built over an eight-year period. All were based on the same steel backbone chassis and had styling that looked almost identical to the Griffith and

Bigger and beefier than even the Tuscan, thanks to its styling the M-Series was still instantly recognizable as a TVR.

Vixen models of the 1960s. The pretty glassfibre bodywork was TVR founder Trevor Wilkinson's design and had a timeless elegance, although the design was such that the body had a tendency to trap water between it and the chassis, causing difficult-to-repair corrosion.

Three engines were available at launch. The 1600M came with a 1.6-litre (98cu in) Ford 'Kent' engine, the 2500M got a 2.5-litre (170cu in) Triumph straight-six from the TR6 and the 3000M came with the 3.0-litre (183cu in) Ford 'Essex' V6 from the range-topping Capri. The ultimate incarnation of the M-Series was the 3000M Turbo, which used the Capri engine with a turbocharger fitted to deliver mind-blowing performance. Its tricky handling meant that was not a car for the weak-willed. The M-Series gave rise to the later Taimar, which was bigger, and also its replacement, the 3000S. Both had the traditional styling elements that made earlier TVRs famous.

ENGINE: 2498cc (153cu in), six-cylinder (2500M)
POWER: 106bhp (79kW)
0–60MPH (96KM/H): 9.3 seconds
TOP SPEED: 174km/h (109mph)
PRODUCTION TOTAL: 1749 (all types)

MERCEDES W116 S-CLASS

Mercedes' first S-Class was one of its most significant models. Not only did it raise the brand's profile among wealthy buyers, even appearing in TV series *Dallas* as the car of choice for oil baron J.R. Ewing, but it also introduced a raft of innovations in car safety.

With the exception of the Jensen Interceptor FF, always a very low volume model, the W116 was the first production car to come with standard anti-lock brakes. Other safety features included integrated crumple zones, which channelled energy away from the passenger cabin in the event of an accident.

Further technology came in the form of the 300SD, one of the world's first turbo diesel cars, but the star of the range certainly was not economy-minded. The 450 SEL had a 6.9-litre (420cu in) V8 engine which delivered incredible performance and refinement.

After a seven-year production run, the W116 was replaced by the new W126, which was even more technologically advanced, although some argued that it lacked the menacing styling and character of the original.

ENGINE: 2746cc (168cu in),
six-cylinder
POWER: 155bhp (115kW)
0–60MPH (96KM/H): 9.2 seconds
TOP SPEED: 189km/h (118mph)
PRODUCTION TOTAL: 437,240

TRIUMPH DOLOMITE

Following the vastly confusing range of front-wheel drive 1300 and 1500 models, plus the smaller rear-wheel drive 1300cc (78cu in) Toledo, Triumph decided to

It was a nice car in normal form, but in Sprint guise the Triumph Dolomite was a great machine. It was one of the first true sports saloons.

rationalize its small-saloon range completely in 1972 with the introduction of the Dolomite.

The new car used an identical bodyshell to that of the 1500FWD, confusing buyers further still. While 1300 and 1500 models were offered, the big news was the introduction of a new 1850cc (112cu in) slant-four engine, which Triumph had codeveloped with Swedish maker Saab. The unit was

lively, responsive and smooth, but the first buyers fell victim to reliability problems caused by leaking cylinder head gaskets.

Regardless of this, the Dolomite was a well-appointed, stylish and very popular upmarket saloon, made even more alluring by the introduction of the 16-valve Sprint model in 1973. The Sprint was the first mainstream production car to have a 16-valve head and also the

first to be offered with alloy wheels as standard. An exciting machine to drive, and successful in saloon car racing, it has a cult following.

ENGINE: 1854cc (113cu in),
four-cylinder
POWER: 91bhp (68kW) at 5200rpm
0–60MPH (96KM/H): 11.6 seconds
TOP SPEED: 166km/h (103mph)
PRODUCTION TOTAL: 177,237

VAUXHALL VICTOR FE-SERIES

Launched in 1972, the FE was last car to bear the famous Victor name, which had served Vauxhall well since 1957.

It signified a significant move towards platform sharing within

GM Europe because it was the first Vauxhall model to share most of its underpinnings with an Opel. Yet, although much of its running gear was the same as in the Opel Commodore, the FE looked notably

different to its German-built sister car, and the car was styled at Vauxhall's UK headquarters in Luton, Bedfordshire.

Two four-cylinder engines were featured in the FE – an entry-level

1.8-litre (110cu in) unit and a more potent 2.3-litre (134cu in) slant-four, which came with twin carburettors on the range-topping VX4/90. The 4/90 also had a closer ratio gearbox, and, while it looked fairly ordinary, it was quite an exciting car to drive.

The Ventora name, used on six-cylinder versions of the previous FD models, also made a brief appearance on the FE, although the 3.3-litre (195cu in) model was only ever sold in fairly limited numbers. When the FE was withdrawn in 1978, Vauxhall's new models were entirely based on their Opel cousins, and the FE's replacement, the Carlton, was identical to the Opel Rekord.

ENGINE: 3294cc (201cu in), six-cylinder
POWER: 124bhp (92kW)
0–60MPH (96KM/H): 12.6 seconds
TOP SPEED: 166km/h (104mph)
PRODUCTION TOTAL: 7984

Squarer and more angular than the FD it replaced, the FE Series was effectively the same car under the skin. It wasn't as well-built, however, and due to corporate cost-cutting nor was it as well equipped.

PANTHER J72

UNITED KINGDOM 1972–81

Businessman Bob Jankel certainly did not believe in fading into the background, and his wacky J72 was proof in point. Built to resemble the original Jaguar SS100, but in a uniquely 1970s way, the J72 looked

It could be considered kitsch, but the J72 was an expensive car in its day, costing the same as an Aston Martin DBS!

as if it should have been a kit car. In reality, it was not – it was hand-built to special order and was incredibly expensive, attracting a raft of wealthy customers, including the actress Elizabeth Taylor.

The J72 could be had with a choice of engines, both Jaguar units. The XJ6's straight-six was the standard offering, but most buyers plumped for Series 3 E-type's V12 unit, which gave the J72 startling

performance. But a combination of dreadful aerodynamics and a very basic chassis and suspension set-up made the J72 tricky to drive, the rigid front and rear axles offering little absorption against bumps and the overheavy steering providing little in the way of precision. On a wet road, feeding 266bhp (198kW) of power through the rear wheels was practically impossible without wheel spin.

The appeal of the J72 was in its exclusivity. It cost as much as an Aston Martin DBS, but without any of its classiness.

ENGINE: 5343cc (326cu in), 12-cylinder
POWER: 266bhp (198kW)
0–60MPH (96KM/H): 6.4 seconds
TOP SPEED: 219km/h (136mph)
PRODUCTION TOTAL: 300

MASERATI MERAK

ITALY 1972–83

With the Bora doing battle with the Lamborghini Miura, Maserati focused its interest on creating a smaller mid-engined car that would, it hoped, steal sales from the Ferrari Dino. Developed in record time, and at a surprisingly

The Merak and the Bora shared most of their body panels, but the Merak was lighter and less powerful.

low cost, the Merak was effectively a lightweight version of the Bora, fitted with a smaller V6 engine and with slightly fewer adornments.

Physically, it was hard to tell the two cars apart. The Merak did not get the Bora's distinctive polished alloy wheels, had only one door mirror and had slimmer bumpers, with fewer pieces of brightwork, but the panels and dimensions were identical. Otherwise, the only distinguishing factors were leaving

the car's rear buttresses unglazed and simplifying the frontal styling.

The V6 engine was the same unit as fitted to the Citroën SM, as Citroën owned Maserati at the time. Other influences from the elegant French coupé included the same instruments and steering wheel, excellent pneumatic brakes and hydraulic clutch. A basic 2.0-litre (122cu in) variant, the 2000, was added to the range for the Italian market only, but very few were sold.

The other rarity in the Merak range is the SS. Unlike the 2000, the SS is highly desirable, with 15 per cent more power and revised steering and suspension.

ENGINE: 2965cc (181cu in), V6-cylinder
POWER: 182bhp (135kW) at 6000rpm
0–60MPH (96KM/H): 9.5 seconds
TOP SPEED: 214km/h (133mph)
PRODUCTION TOTAL: 1140

ALFA ROMEO ALFASUD

ITALY 1972–84

One of motoring's greatest might-have-beens, the Alfasud was a brilliantly designed and beautifully agile car, upon which much praise was heaped at its launch. Using a lively flat-four engine mounted in a chassis that completely redefined the way a family car should handle, and topped off with pretty styling courtesy of Giugiaro, the 'Sud really should have been the car that made Alfa Romeo a household name.

The reality was far harsher. The car was called the 'Sud because it was built in a new government-funded factory in Naples, in the southern part of Italy, where unemployment and poverty were

Great to look at and fantastic to drive, if only the Alfasud were better made it would have been a world beater. Its recycled steel rusted very quickly.

rife. Labour relations were dreadful, however, after employees at the factory found out they were being paid far less than Alfa Romeo's workers at the company's other plant in Milan, and this led to some terrible build quality issues. On top of that, Alfa Romeo insisted on building the car out of cheap recycled steel, which was of such low quality that many cars went terminally rusty within just a couple of years, in turn giving the car a very poor reputation.

This was a crying shame, as, especially in sporty Ti guise, the Alfasud was a brilliant car to drive, and, on later models, quality was much improved. Several bodystyles were offered, including two and four-door saloons, three and five-door hatches, an estate (station wagon) and a gorgeous two-door coupé called the Alfasud Sprint.

ENGINE: 1186cc (72cu in), four-cylinder
POWER: 63bhp (47kW)
0–60MPH (96KM/H): 14.1 seconds
TOP SPEED: 149km/h (93mph)
PRODUCTION TOTAL: 567,093

ALFA ROMEO ALFETTA

ITALY 1972–84

Even Alfa Romeo's most conventional models had to be good to drive, so, when the Italian maker decided to enter the fleet car market with the Alfetta, it revived a great name from the past – Alfetta. The car shared little in common with its forebear, though. It had been a single-seat Grand Prix car, and the newcomer was a very ordinary-looking four-door family saloon. The styling was done in-house by Alfa Romeo's own designers and looked fairly boxy and plain, but the car was not without its charms. The ornate chrome radiator grille and prominently displayed Alfa Romeo shield indicated that some pride had gone into the project, and there were certainly no complaints about the way the car drove.

It used the same lively twin-cam engines that powered the Giulia saloons, which even in their most basic form were potent, while the handling was very carefully thought out. The gearbox, for example, was located on the back axle to balance weight distribution, while de Dion rear suspension made the car feel very stable and agile through bends.

At first, the car was offered only in 1800cc (109cu in) guise, but 1600cc (98cu in) and 2000cc (122cu in) models were introduced in 1976. After a fairly lukewarm reception, the Alfetta found a dedicated following and remained in Alfa's range for over 12 years.

ENGINE: 1570cc (96cu in), four-cylinder
POWER: 108bhp (80kW)
0–60MPH (96KM/H): 11.5 seconds
TOP SPEED: 174km/h (108mph)
PRODUCTION TOTAL: 450,000

RENAULT 5

FRANCE 1972–97

Renault invented the hatchback with the 16 in 1965, and followed up its innovation with the 5 in 1972 – a model that brought new levels of practicality to the small-car market. With its full-length tailgate and folding rear seat, the 5 had far more practicality than other cars of its size. Other benefits included superb ride comfort, good handling and cute styling that remained almost unchanged for a quarter of a century.

The first cars had a very odd engine and gearbox set-up, with the transmission mounted on the front of the engine, and the block mounted longitudinally despite an industry-wide preference for transverse engines in front-wheel drive cars. The angle at which the driveshafts came out of the engine meant that the 5 had a longer wheelbase on one side than the other, but this had little effect on the car's roadholding, which was always both reassuring and entertaining. A huge success for Renault, the 5 was even sold in the United States as 'Le Car'. There was a performance model in European markets called the Gordini which was an absolute hoot.

A five-door model expanded the range in 1981, while an all-new 5 appeared in 1984, not that you would have noticed. Completely reengineered to use a transverse engine and more modern engines, the new 5 – or 'Supercinq', as it was known in France – looked almost identical to its predecessor. The looks were so popular that the 5 kept in production, alongside the Clio that was supposed to replace it, for six years.

ENGINE: 1397cc (85cu in), four-cylinder
POWER: 63bhp (47kW)
0–60MPH (96KM/H): 12.2 seconds
TOP SPEED: 155km/h (96mph)
PRODUCTION TOTAL: 5,471,709

A brilliant design that would enjoy a 25-year production run and over five million sales, the Renault 5 became part of France's social culture.

FORD UK GRANADA

UNITED KINGDOM 1972–85

Replacing the much-loved Zephyr was a difficult task for Ford, as it needed to create a car that would not only appeal to existing Zephyr owners, but would also make its large models appeal to a newer, more youthful market. The first Granada appeared in 1972 and was codeveloped with Ford of Germany to have pan-European appeal. The car looked superb and satisfied the original design brief perfectly, with a spacious cabin, good levels of luxury and impressive ride and handling capabilities.

Entry-level cars were badged Consuls, as in the past; however, the Zephyr and Zodiac names disappeared for good in favour of the all-new moniker. All of the original engines were V-shaped, with a 2.0-litre (122cu in) V4 in basic models and a choice of

2.5-litre (152cu in) or 3.0-litre (183cu in) units further up the range. Automatic transmission was standard on all but a handful of the 3.0-litres. At launch, four-door saloon and estate (station wagon) models were offered, while a stylish coupé was added to the range in 1974, but was far more successful in Western Europe than in the United Kingdom.

In 1977, a revised Granada appeared. The new model was reskinned by Ford's design chief Uwe Bahnsen and looked much more angular and modern than the original, while it was given a mild face-lift again in 1981, when the 3.0-litre engine was replaced by the 2.8-litre (170cu in) fuel-injected unit from the Capri Mk 3.

ENGINE: 2495cc (152cu in), six-cylinder
POWER: 82bhp (61kW)
0–60MPH (96KM/H): 9 seconds
TOP SPEED: 193km/h (120mph)
PRODUCTION TOTAL: 1,486,049

LANCIA BETA

ITALY 1972–85

With Fiat in charge and desperately trying to cut costs, Lancia's reputation as a maker of fine automobiles started to crumble. Quite literally, in fact, into a pile of rust-coloured dust. Much like the

Several body styles were available for the Beta, of which the Coupé was the prettiest and the most corrosion-resistant.

similarly afflicted Alfasud, the Beta was a well-designed, characterful car ruined by dreadful build quality and a propensity to rust more quickly than a tin can exposed to the elements.

The situation was not helped by an exposé in the British newspaper the *Daily Mirror*, which found that some cars had started to corrode excessively in storage before they were even delivered to customers.

For Lancia, this was a tragedy, as the Beta was otherwise an impressive car. Available as a four-door saloon or, later, a hatch, it also spawned a coupé, a convertible and an oddball coupé-like estate (station wagon), called the HPE. Supercharged 'Volumex' models of the coupé and HPE were particularly appealing. All were fine handling and swift cars, with bulletproof twin-cam engines and beautiful interior styling, but poor customer confidence extended across Europe. The Beta was never the hoped-for sales success Lancia had wanted.

ENGINE: 1756cc (107cu in), four-cylinder
POWER: 110bhp (82kW) at 6000rpm
0–60MPH (96KM/H): 10.7 seconds
TOP SPEED: 175km/h (109mph)
PRODUCTION TOTAL: 387,365

FIAT 126

ITALY 1972–87

ENGINE: 594cc (36cu in), four-cylinder
POWER: 23bhp (17kW)
0–60MPH (96KM/H): 62 seconds
TOP SPEED: 104km/h (65mph)
PRODUCTION TOTAL: 1,970,000

Replacing the Nuova 500, which had worked its way into the hearts and minds of the Italian public for over 20 years, was no mean feat – so Fiat had to carefully manage the 126's introduction.

The little air-cooled city car was shown for the first time at the 1972 Turin Motor Show and was given a relatively low-key entrance to the world, as Fiat intended to sell it alongside the 500 until demand for the 126's predecessor finally tailed off.

It would be 1975 before the 500 was finally pensioned off, leaving the 126 alone in the city-car

A tiny engine in the back and a cramped cabin made the 126 the spiritual successor to the much-loved Nuova 500, although it never made it into the hearts and minds of the Italian public quite so well. In 1987 production was moved to Poland.

market. Although not as cute as its predecessor, the rather boxy-looking 126 did have much to recommend it. First, it was absolutely tiny and so ideal for Italy's traditionally manic urban streets. Furthermore, the tiny 594cc (36cu in) air-cooled engine sipped fuel, making the car one of the cheapest means of transport going.

It was sold almost unchanged for 15 years, with only minor details such as larger bumpers (in 1976) and a very slight power increase (in 1977). Big changes came in 1987, however, with the axe hanging over the 126's future, Fiat instead decided to fit the car with a new 704cc (43cu in) water-cooled flat-twin engine, giving it a new lease of life, and transferred production from Italy to Poland. Now called 126 Bis, the car soldiered on until September 2000.

FIAT X1/9 ITALY 1972–89

Built for Fiat by Bertone, the angular X1/9 was based on the 1970 Runabout Barchetta concept car.

Bertone tried to get Fiat to develop a mid-engine sports car based on 128 running gear for years, but the Italian company kept resisting, saying that there would not be a market for such a car. To prove Fiat wrong, a prototype called the Bertone Runabout Barchetta was shown at the 1970 Turin Motor Show and, so positive was the response, Fiat commissioned Bertone to build a similar car on its behalf.

That car was to be the X1/9, which came with alluring wedge-shaped bodywork, a targa roof and a finely honed chassis, which was helped by the car's almost perfect weight distribution.

The first cars appeared in 1972 and came with a 1.3-litre (79cu in) engine, although the power unit was enlarged to 1.5 litres (91cu in) in 1978. These later cars are by far the better to drive, as the increase in power makes them far more convincing as sports cars.

The original car's clean lines were blighted slightly in 1978, when American safety legislation forced Fiat to replace the X1/9's original slim chrome bumpers with impact-resistant rubber ones. On the X1/9, however, they were much less intrusive than those seen on some sports cars.

Fiat stopped building X1/9s in 1983, but Bertone continued to make them to satisfy what had become an unyielding demand. By the time production ceased in 1988, almost 200,000 had been built.

ENGINE: 1498cc (91cu in),
four-cylinder
POWER: 85bhp (63kW)
0–60MPH (96KM/H): 10 seconds
TOP SPEED: 180km/h (112mph)
PRODUCTION TOTAL: 180,000

ASTON MARTIN AM V8 UNITED KINGDOM 1972–90

Criticized for making the DBS look a little too soft, Aston Martin decided to put a bit of aggression back into its range with the AM V8. Launched in 1972 and based on the DBS chassis, the newcomer saw the return of the traditionally shaped Aston Martin radiator grille that had disappeared along with the DB6 in 1970. A large bonnet (hood) scoop, front spoiler and single round headlights completed the styling changes, with a rear end almost unaltered from the DBS that the AM V8 replaced – although Aston Martin did manage to increase the car's price by more than 25 per cent in the process.

Initially, the car was fitted with the DBS's fuel-injected 5340cc (326cu in) V8 engine, but this caused reliability problems, so in 1974 Aston went back to using four Weber carburettors instead and increased the size of the car's bonnet scoop to house them.

Further changes came in 1978 with the introduction of a face-lifted car, with thicker bumpers, a front spoiler and a new bonnet, which did away with the bonnet scoop and replaced it with a more subtle power bulge. A new fuel injection system then came in, developed by Weber and far more reliable than the old Bosch system, meaning that the last cars again had flat bonnets.

As well as the most common coupé variant, Aston Martin also offered a Volante cabriolet and, for a very short time, a four-door Lagonda variant, which was replaced by William Towns's rather wacky 'Lagonda Wedge' in 1977.

ENGINE: 5340cc (326cu in),
eight-cylinder
POWER: 340bhp (253kW)
0–60MPH (96KM/H): 6 seconds
TOP SPEED: 261km/h (162mph)
PRODUCTION TOTAL: 1600

More rounded and even more imposing than the DBS, the AM V8 became the face of Aston Martin for most of the 1970s and all of the 1980s. It was heavy to drive, but exceptionally luxurious.

DE TOMASO LONGCHAMP

ITALY 1972–90

Much in the same way as the de Tomaso Deauville had caused controversy the year previously for being a shameless facsimile of the Jaguar XJ6, the Longchamp was another blatant rip-off of a European luxury car. This time, Alejandro de Tomaso's target was the Mercedes 450SLC coupé – a long-wheelbase, elegant coupé version of the SL.

Like the Deauville was to the Jaguar, it was more or less identical proportionally to the Mercedes it aped, but with a quad-light de Tomaso grille and a typically Italian ornately finished interior.

The car was utterly conventional under the skin, however, with a thumping 5763cc (351cu in) US V8, borrowed from Ford, and a live

rear axle. This made the handling rather tricky and the car far more of a brute than its doppelgänger.

The Longchamp was very much a car that de Tomaso produced for the love of it, as only 400 were sold in an 18-year production run. He was such a fan of the car that, when he bought out the ailing Maserati company from Citroën in

1976, he commissioned a reworked version of it called the Kyalami, fitted with a Maserati V8 engine.

ENGINE: 5763cc (352cu in), eight-cylinder
POWER: 330bhp (224kW)
0–60MPH (96KM/H): 6.7 seconds
TOP SPEED: 241km/h (150mph)
PRODUCTION TOTAL: 410

DAIMLER DOUBLE SIX

UNITED KINGDOM 1972–92

ENGINE: 5343cc (326cu in),
12-cylinder
POWER: 253bhp (188kW)
0–60MPH (96KM/H): 8 seconds
TOP SPEED: 222km/h (138mph)
PRODUCTION TOTAL: 14,500

Some cynics did not like the way that Jaguar insisted on using the Daimler badge on its most upmarket models, rather than building unique

Long and short wheelbase versions of the XJ12 were available, the latter for those who enjoyed driving, and the former for those who were lucky enough to be able to afford a chauffeur.

Daimler models. But even they would have been hard pressed to find much to dislike about the original Daimler Double Six. The car developed such a following over the years that, when Jaguar tried to take it out of production in 1986, enough orders flooded in to keep it going for another six years.

In essence, the Double Six was a Jaguar XJ12 with even plusher furnishings, a fluted Daimler radiator grille and more discreet styling. The model developed such kudos in the United States, where it was also sold as the Daimler Vanden Plas, that it grew better equipped and more ostentatious with each passing year. Available in both long- and short-wheelbase versions (LWB only from 1986), the Double Six enjoyed the fabulous handling and cosseting ride of the Jaguar XJ, but even the earliest models had split-level air conditioning, hand-stitched leather trim, Wilton carpets and hand-polished burr walnut dashboards as standard. Initially, the Double Six was also terrific value for money, especially compared to a Rolls-Royce Silver Shadow or Mercedes 450SEL 6.9. By the time it was withdrawn in the early 1990s, it was one of the most expensive cars on the market.

LEYLAND P76

AUSTRALIA 1973–74

Leyland of Australia's first and only domestically produced and developed car was the P76 of 1973 – a car that the company had incredibly high hopes for, but which in reality ended up being a costly white elephant.

Designed exclusively for the Australian market to take on the might of US manufacturers, who were cashing in on the local desire for large V8-engined saloons, the P76 was expected to win the patriotic share of the market.

What Leyland had not banked on was the difficulty it would have getting the P76 to market. The ungainly styling did it few favours for starters, while build quality on the first batch of cars was so bad that most of them were practically rebuilt before going out to customers. Delays getting the car to market did little to improve buyer confidence, and the P76 ended up getting a dreadful press.

Despite Leyland's best attempts, including a prototype coupé version called the Force 7, which looked far better than the saloon, the P76 project was doomed from the start and was canned after only two years, by which time just 22,000 cars had been built. Only a handful was exported outside of Australia, and only a few survive.

ENGINE: 2622cc (160cu in), six-cylinder
POWER: 130bhp (97kW)
0–60MPH (96KM/H): n/a
TOP SPEED: 168km/h (105mph)
PRODUCTION TOTAL: 22,000

LANCIA STRATOS

ITALY 1973–75

Lancia's bid to win the World Rally Championship and at the same time boost its ailing image was carried out in a somewhat unique style. Rather than modify one of its existing models to competition standard, the Italian maker instead decided to put an

A Stratos driven in anger – this legend of rallying won three successive titles, despite being a real handful to control.

entirely new car into production, charged with winning the championship much more so than achieving showroom sales.

That vehicle was the Stratos, and, to make sure that the car turned heads, Lancia used a 1970 Bertone-styled prototype as the basis for the car, fitted with a mid-mounted Ferrari Dino V6 engine – fruit of Fiat taking over command of both companies in 1970. The Stratos used a centre fuselage, with the engine housed in the middle, around which was wrapped a stiff steel monocoque, wrapped in glassfibre panels.

Of course, for homologation purposes, the Stratos had to be sold as a road car as well as for rallying, so around 500 cars were sold to lucky customers, who soon found out from its cramped and excessively hot cockpit, appalling driving position and lack of ride comfort that they were fairly low down in Lancia's priorities. At the top, of course, was competition success, and the Stratos achieved what was expected of it with ease, trouncing its rivals and winning the World Rally Championship for three years on the trot, at a time when Lancia needed the publicity most.

ENGINE: 2481cc (151cu in), V6-cylinder
POWER: 190bhp (142kW) at 7000rpm
0–60MPH (96KM/H): 7 seconds
TOP SPEED: 225km/h (140mph)
PRODUCTION TOTAL: 492

VAUXHALL DROOP SNOOT FIRENZA

UNITED KINGDOM 1973–75

In essence a very simple concept, the Droop Snoot nonetheless changed Vauxhall's image among younger buyers, ushering in a new, much more dynamic era of styling to the British manufacturer and at the same time creating a cult of its own. Based on the standard Firenza coupé, itself little more than a coupé-bodied two-door Viva, the Droop Snoot added a breathed-on version of the Vauxhall Magnum's 2.3-litre (139cu in) slant-four engine developing 131bhp (98kW), coupled to a beefed-up gearbox.

A huge glassfibre nosecone was fitted to give the car a wind-cheating aerodynamic appearance that was not just for show – it cut the car's drag coefficient by 30 per cent.

The original plan was to build 1000 cars a year. Despite plenty of publicity (including a caravan towing race with some of the biggest names in motorsport), only 204 examples were built in two years, largely due to the high price.

As a result, Vauxhall found itself with a stack of nosecones in stock and no cars to fit them to, which resulted in the creation of the original Sportshatch. Based on a Viva estate (station wagon), the Sportshatch used a standard tune Magnum engine. Although it was never officially listed, almost 200 were built and sold to enthusiasts.

ENGINE: 2279cc (139cu in), four-cylinder
POWER: 131bhp (98kW)
0–60MPH (96KM/H): 9.4 seconds
TOP SPEED: 193km/h (120mph)
PRODUCTION TOTAL: 204

BITTER CD

GERMANY 1973–79

German businessman Erich Bitter started his car building business in 1971, after his relationship with the American-Italian firm Intermeccanica turned sour. Working out of his farmland in his hometown of Schwelm,

The Bitter CD was large, elegant and very expensive. Those with the cash often preferred a more exclusive and established name.

Germany, Bitter designed and developed the car in his barn, basing it on a shortened version of the Opel Diplomat chassis.

He did not have enough money to invest in his own production facilities for the car, nor the time or space, so he approached coachbuilders Baur to complete the cars for him. Baur was known for building prototypes and limited editions for various German makers, and the quality of the company's work was impressive. The Bitter CD, powered by a 5.4-litre (327cu in) Chevrolet V8 engine, was introduced at the end of 1973 after a very successful unveiling at the Frankfurt Motor Show that September. A euphoric Erich Bitter took 176 orders for his stylish new car at the show, but many of these were cancelled shortly after as the oil crisis loomed – people were put off by the car's prodigious thirst. Undeterred, Bitter kept the CD in production until 1979, by which time almost 400 cars had been built.

Its replacement, the SC, was more economical, and was based on the Opel Monza coupé.

ENGINE: 5354cc (327cu in), eight-cylinder
POWER: 230bhp (171kW)
0–96KM/H (60MPH): 9.4 seconds
TOP SPEED: 208km/h (129mph)
PRODUCTION TOTAL: 395

OPEL KADETT

GERMANY 1973–79

A truly global design, the Kadett C appeared in 1973, and was Opel's version of GM's T-Car – a small car that was designed to be sold, with various modifications, in markets all over the world.

It also formed the basis of the British Vauxhall Chevette, which had a more aerodynamic front end and used a 1256cc (76cu in) overhead-valve Vauxhall engine rather than the 1196cc (72cu in) Opel unit. The most popular Kadett was the two-door saloon; there was also a notable hatchback version, the Kadett City based on the Chevette and identical from the windscreen pillars backward.

Kadett C production ended in 1979, but the Chevette was produced until 1983 and was imported into Germany for a while after production ceased, as some traditional buyers hated the new front-drive Kadett D and wanted a rear-wheel drive car.

The most desirable versions of the Kadett C are the Rallye and GT/E Coupé models, which had pretty bodywork and impressive performance. These came with a Bosch fuel-injected 1897cc (116cu in) engine, bored out to 1998cc (121cu in). There was also a very unusual Kadett Aero, which had a pop-out Targa roof panel to turn it into a convertible.

The Kadett C was massively popular. It was also built in Japan as the Isuzu Gemini, Canada as the Pontiac Acadian, South Korea as the Daewoo Maepsy, the United States as the Chevrolet Chevette and Uruguay as the Grumett Color.

ENGINE: 993cc (61cu in), four-cylinder
POWER: 40bhp (30kW)
0–60MPH (96KM/H): 23.9 seconds
TOP SPEED: 123km/h (76mph)
PRODUCTION TOTAL: 1,701,075

FERRARI 308 GT4

Controversial as it was, the 308 GT4 was a groundbreaking model for Ferrari. It was Ferrari's first production car to come with a mid-mounted V8 engine – a layout that would become commonplace

Built to replace the Dino, but less good looking, the GT4 was styled by Bertone after Enzo Ferrari fell out with Pininfarina.

in the company's cars from there onwards. Far more shocking was the fact that the GT4 was the first production Ferrari to feature bodywork styled by Bertone, rather than Pininfarina. This upset Pininfarina a great deal, as well as Ferrari purists, who hated the new wedge-shaped looks.

Introduced at the Paris Motor Show in 1973, the car had angular lines entirely different from its

curvaceous two-seater predecessor, the Dino. Ferrari lovers were even more upset when, two years later, Ferrari announced a low-output version for Europe. The 208 GT4 used the smallest ever production V8 engine, which was effectively a de-bored version of the 308 unit.

Power output was 168bhp (126kW), giving a reasonable turn of speed, but the car's skinny tyres, simplified bodywork and lack of

equipment made it feel very stark. It was never a great success, and the GT4 series as a whole was not considered Maranello's finest hour.

ENGINE: 2927cc (179cu in), eight-cylinder
POWER: 250bhp (186kW)
0–60MPH (96KM/H): 6.4 seconds
TOP SPEED: 241km/h (150mph)
PRODUCTION TOTAL: 2826

MATRA-SIMCA BAGHEERA

ENGINE: 1294cc (79cu in), four-cylinder
POWER: 84bhp (63kW)
0–60MPH (96KM/H): 9.2 seconds
TOP SPEED: 163km/h (102mph)
PRODUCTION TOTAL: 47,802

Built by Matra in conjunction with Simca, the Bagheera was named after the panther from Rudyard Kipling's *The Jungle Book*. It used a plastic body mounted on a steel backbone chassis, and came with a practical opening rear hatch – an unusual feature on a mid-engined sports car. Even more

Three-abreast seating and a strange all glass tailgate proved that Matra would still challenge conventions.

bizarre was the seating layout – there was only one row of seats. The Bagheera was a three-seater with the driver positioned in the middle, so that there was no need to alter the car for right-hand drive or left-hand drive markets, and the driver's central position balanced out the car's weight distribution.

The car had two face-lifts. In 1976, the original 'hidden' door handles were replaced by cheaper, conventional items; in 1978, some more significant panelwork changes were made and the original 1.3-litre (78cu in) engine was replaced by a 1.5-litre (90cu in) unit. Matra also showed a prototype using the world's first and only U-shaped engine. The 2.6-litre (155cu in) U8 featured two 1.3-litre four-cylinder units, each with a separate crankshaft. It never went beyond prototype stage.

RENAULT RODEO

Citroën had the Mehari, so Renault decided to respond with the Rodeo. Effectively a broken-apart Renault 4, rebuilt in the same fashion as a Mehari to be a fun, summer vehicle, the Rodeo was an odd-looking but strangely alluring machine.

Like its arch rival, the Rodeo had reinforced plastic bodywork mounted atop a standard Renault 4 platform, with the same 845cc (52cu in) pushrod engine and push-pull gearchange.

With no real doors and no roof, the Rodeo was strictly a fair-weather vehicle, although it could be ordered with an optional canvas canopy that provided rudimentary protection from the elements. The car was two-wheel drive only, but conversion specialists Sinpar did offer a 4x4 option if you saw the point, which very few people did.

A larger Rodeo came in 1974 and was based on the Renault 6, with square headlights in place of round ones, larger bodywork and a larger 1108cc (68cu in) engine, which gave it the ability to reach a rather frightening top speed of 130km/h (80mph). In the right environment, though, the Rodeo was fun to own and drive. Many ended up operating as holiday hire cars in Mediterranean beach resorts.

ENGINE: 845cc (52cu in), four-cylinder
POWER: 34bhp (25kW)
0–60MPH (96KM/H): n/a
TOP SPEED: 100km/h (62mph)
PRODUCTION TOTAL: n/a

AUSTIN ALLEGRO

Lambasted by the press as soon as it hit the road, the Austin Allegro was born into a world of industrial turmoil, three-day weeks and dire labour relations. They did little for the build quality of the car that was charged with not only reinventing British Leyland, but also to a lesser degree reinventing the wheel. One of the Allegro's more eccentric traits, in more ways than one, was its square steering wheel – a design gimmick that ended up being a cruel joke, especially given that the car did not have the best start in life.

Built to replace the popular 1100/1300 Series, the Allegro was supposedly a thoroughly modern design, with fluid-based Hydragas suspension and a choice of overhead-valve A-Series engines, as seen on all Austins since 1948, or the new E-Series overhead-cam units from the Maxi. The height of the OHC units played havoc with designer Harris Mann's original rather streamlined shape, however, and what was supposed to be a sleek and elegant saloon ended up looking like an upturned bathtub.

There was worse. The five-speed gearboxes were truly horrible, reliability was questionable and it was impossible to get in and out of the back doors without twisting your ankle, as the gap between the seat and door pillar was too narrow.

Many of the Allegro's problems were addressed with the Series 2 model (complete with conventional round steering wheel), launched in 1976, and the Series 3 (from 1979) was actually quite a good car, with smart black bumpers and a plastic front spoiler. The damage had been done, however, and the car's reputation never recovered.

ENGINE: 1275cc (78cu in), four-cylinder
POWER: 59bhp (44kW)
0–60MPH (96KM/H): 18.4 seconds
TOP SPEED: 132km/h (82mph)
PRODUCTION TOTAL: 642,350

Its bathtub curves and roly-poly handling didn't do the Allegro a lot of favours, while shocking build quality caused a poor reputation. But it has its lovers.

LAMBORGHINI COUNTACH

Based on a concept car first seen three years previously at the Geneva Motor Show, the Countach was an avant-garde and strikingly different replacement for the legendary Miura. Legend has it that the car inherited its name when an engineer working at Lamborghini's Saint'Agata factory near Bologna, Italy, saw the car for the first time. He is said to have exclaimed 'Countach!' (an old Italian expression meaning something similar to 'Wow!') – a word he apparently used every time he saw a beautiful woman.

The project's chief engineer was Paolo Stanzani, who had worked with Giampaolo Dallara on the Miura, and he enlisted the talented race engineer Massimo Parenti to help him. Early prototypes had a semi-monocoque chassis, but this was soon replaced by a complex tubular spaceframe construction, over which was placed the unstressed aluminium bodywork.

Bertone stylist Marcello Gandini was the man responsible for the Countach's outlandish looks, which shared much in common with the racing cars of the late 1960s. Rather than being beautiful, like the Miura, the car was more brutal in appearance. Features included a short, stubby nose, pop-up headlights, a steeply raked rectangular screen and quirky scissor-hinged doors that opened upwards. Later cars also had a huge rear spoiler, although this contributed much more to cosmetics than it did aerodynamic downforce.

The mid-engined layout of the Miura was maintained, although rather than being transversely mounted the Countach's 4.2-litre (240cu in) V12 powerplant was fitted longitudinally to allow the body to taper upwards. Indeed, the model designation LP400, used on the first cars, was a result of this layout, the '400' standing for 4.0-litre and the 'LP' an abbreviation

The Countach assaults the eyes. Not conventionally attractive, the car's angular lines are nonetheless alluring.

for Longitudinale Posteriore (or 'lengthways and behind'). Most of the other running gear on the Countach, such as the suspension, steering, wheels and brakes, was carried over from the Miura.

Needless to say, the Countach's handling and performance were phenomenal – at launch it was the fastest car in the world, and not just in a straight line. The car's race-engineered chassis and carefully engineered weight distribution also meant that it had a limpet-like grip and was amazingly fast on twisty circuits, as well as in a straight line.

The cabin of the earliest cars mirrored the futuristic exterior, with a single-spoke steering wheel

and a variety of warning lights in front of the driver. As production went on, however, the car grew more conventional, with much use of black plastic and a huge central tunnel. Indeed, the car became more and more conventional as its life went on, with Lamborghini trying its best to make the Countach appeal to buyers in the United States, who struggled to understand its initial quirkiness.

Production had reached a total of just 23 cars by the time the LP400S arrived in 1978, the main difference being an improvement to the chassis and suspension, as wider Pirelli P7 tyres being fitted. The bigger wheels meant that wheelarch extensions were added.

In the mid-1980s, a larger 4754cc (290cu in) V12 appeared, and the car was renamed the LP500S. Later the same decade, engine capacity was increased again, this time to 5167cc (315cu in). Production ceased in 1990 with a 25th-anniversary car, which appeared two years after the Countach's official silver jubilee year – a fact conveniently overlooked by Lamborghini.

ENGINE: 3929cc (240cu in), 12-cylinder
POWER: 385bhp (287kW)
0–60MPH (96KM/H): 5.2 seconds
TOP SPEED: 288km/h (180mph)
PRODUCTION TOTAL: n/a

MASERATI KHAMSIN

ITALY 1973–82

Launched to replace the strong-selling Indy, the Khamsin was a slightly larger 2+2 coupé, styled by Bertone designer Marcello Gandini, the man behind the stunning Countach and various other Lamborghini projects. His brief was to create a 2+2 that would look, to the naked eye, as low and as mean as a mid-engined supercar – a tricky task, as economy dictated that the car would have to use

Maserati did well to create a 2+2 that lost little in the styling department, despite the demand to provide space inside.

Maserati's existing 4930cc (301cu in) quad-cam V8 engine.

The engine was redesigned to be fitted with a smaller, dry sump, to get the front as low as possible, while the use of independent double-wishbone suspension front and rear meant that the car could sit much lower on its haunches

than a more conventional layout. Indeed, there was less than 7.5cm (3in) from the top of the front tyres to the top of the front wings (fenders). But the Khamsin was not all about styling. It had to be practical, too. While the rear seats were not suitable for large adults, they were at least big enough to

fit a couple of children. It was also rewarding to drive. The suspension modifications necessary to keep the car so low benefited the handling as well, and the Khamsin was one of the best front-engined sports cars of its era for driving quickly. The car enjoyed a nine-year production run, although

sales were never as buoyant as they were with the outgoing Indy.

ENGINE: 4930cc (301cu in), eight-cylinder
POWER: 320bhp (238kW) at 5500rpm
0–60MPH (96KM/H): 6.5 seconds
TOP SPEED: 257km/h (160mph)
PRODUCTION TOTAL: 421

CATERHAM SUPER SEVEN

UNITED KINGDOM 1973–PRESENT

With Lotus abandoning its roots to move upmarket, one of its longest serving dealers decided to buy the rights to the classic Lotus Seven and keep it in production.

Caterham Cars of Surrey, Southeast England, dropped the ugly Series 4 model that Lotus had introduced in 1971, and instead

Caterham picked up where Lotus left off, and is still building its Seven replicas today with no signs of them ever going out of production.

focused on cars that were true to the basic spirit of the original.

Indeed, the car's tubular steel chassis, covered in aluminium panels with a plastic nose cone and wings (fenders) could not have been simpler. Mechanically, too, the 7 was made from readily available parts, with either Ford or Morris rear axles to start with, soon followed by a de Dion set-up designed by Caterham itself.

Initially, the Seven used Lotus's own 1558cc (95cu in) twin-cam engine, but, when supplies dried up, Caterham experimented with

various Ford-sourced units. Over the years, there was a vast myriad of engine options available. The hard-and-fast rule is: if its comes from a rear-wheel drive Ford and has no more than four cylinders, there is every chance it will fit.

Even with a tiny 1.3-litre (78cu in) unit fitted, performance was always outstanding due to a high power-to-weight ratio; the tiny Caterham always embarrassed more expensive machinery. The car appealed to drivers who liked their motoring to be a thrilling experience, while, in kit form, it provided buyers with a

real sense of satisfaction from building their own car.

Indeed, so successful was the Caterham formula that the cars remain in production today, with the most extreme versions using motorcycle engines to deliver frightening performance.

ENGINE: 1598cc (98cu in), eight-cylinder
POWER: 110bhp (82kW)
0–60MPH (96KM/H): 6 seconds
TOP SPEED: 177km/h (110mph)
PRODUCTION TOTAL: 11,000

BRICKLIN SV-1

CANADA 1974–75

ENGINE: 5896cc (360cu in), eight-cylinder
POWER: 220bhp (164kW)
0–60MPH (96KM/H): n/a
TOP SPEED: 197km/h (122mph)
PRODUCTION TOTAL: 2,854

The brainchild of eccentric Canadian billionaire Malcolm Bricklin, the SV-1 was supposed to be a sports car that was also the safest in the world. An honourable reason for building it, perhaps, but in reality the SV-1 was a bit of a disaster. Bricklin was so confident

that his sports car would be a huge hit that he convinced the Canadian government to invest 23 million dollars in the project, as well as providing a state-of-the-art manufacturing facility. With so much of the country's money at stake, the Bricklin had to succeed.

The styling was slightly odd, although its Camaro-like profile looked fairly neat, but the front end was very weird-looking, with a spring-loaded front bumper that was designed to withstand low-speed accidents and also reduce pedestrian injuries if a person was

The Bricklin's front bumper was spring-loaded to withstand impacts of up to 5mph (8 km/h) with no damage to the car's bodywork. The body itself was built from glassfibre and acrylic.

hit by the car. The body was built from a strange gel-like substance, made by mixing acrylic with glassfibre, and it even had gullwing doors. Power came from a 5.9-litre (360cu in) AMC V8 engine, not renowned for its reliability, and within the first few months the Bricklin project started to founder.

The sports-car market was shrinking (buyers wanted smaller, more economical cars), breakdowns were rife, and build quality was awful, with broken gullwing doors trapping some drivers in their cars. Within a year, Bricklin was bust, and the government had a lot of grovelling to do to its taxpayers.

MONICA GT

FRANCE 1974–75

An unusual Anglo-French project, the Monica GT was the dream of French railway tycoon Jean Tastevin. When he could not find a GT car to suit his needs, Tastevin decided to create his own, and have a go at selling it to other people in the process.

Rather than base his car on an existing chassis, which would have been the most obvious solution, Tastevin commissioned British engineer Chris Lawrence to design and build a bespoke spaceframe on which to build his car.

Meanwhile, Tastevin took care of the styling, using two of his favourite cars as influences. Those two vehicles were Jaguar's XJ6 and the Lotus Elan +2. While this may have seemed a rather incongruous pairing, when morphed together, the result looked much better than you could possibly expect.

Power for the car was provided by an extensively modified Chrysler V8 engine that developed 305bhp (227kW), while de Dion rear suspension and all-round disc brakes gave the Monica assured roadholding and stopping power.

After building and rejecting 25 development cars, perfectionist Tastevin finally decided that the car was ready for production, but he sold only 10 in total.

ENGINE: 5560cc (339cu in), eight-cylinder
POWER: 305bhp (227kW)
0–60MPH (96KM/H): n/a
TOP SPEED: 234km/h (145mph)
PRODUCTION TOTAL: 35

PANTHER FF

UNITED KINGDOM 1974–75

Commissioned by eccentric Swiss coachbuilder Willy Felber, the Panther FF was an interesting concept, but it is hardly surprising that only 12 were built. The car was a full-scale replica of the Ferrari 125 racer. Felber wanted it to be so authentic that he insisted Panther design it to house a Ferrari engine only. As the Italian company refused to supply its engines to anyone else, that meant that a Ferrari had to be broken up in order to provide its power unit. Few people were prepared to buy a new Ferrari, then tear it to pieces, so 11 of the 12 cars that did appear had engines from accident-damaged 330 GTCs. As a result, buyers found themselves paying an exorbitant amount of money for a car with a second-hand engine.

That said, Felber himself drove one and bought a new Ferrari 365 GTB Daytona, which he broke up for the parts. His unique car was sprayed bright metallic purple so that people would not accidentally mistake it for a Ferrari.

ENGINE: 3967cc (242cu in), 12-cylinder
POWER: 300bhp (223kW)
0–60MPH (96KM/H): n/a
TOP SPEED: 258km/h (160mph)
PRODUCTION TOTAL: 12

DATSUN 260Z

JAPAN 1974–79

ENGINE: 2565cc (157cu in), six-cylinder
POWER: 139bhp (104kW)
0–60MPH (96KM/H): 9.9 seconds
TOP SPEED: 193km/h (120mph)
PRODUCTION TOTAL: 472,573

Replacing the 240Z was a very sensitive job – Datsun had not only established itself in both the US and European markets with the iconic sports car, but it had also been a phenomenal success. Strict new emissions laws meant that the 240Z's days were numbered, however, and Datsun had to act quickly to maintain its strong position in the sales charts.

Its solution was brilliantly simple. By retaining the external panels of the 240Z, but refining the steering and suspension to make it feel more modern, Datsun could create a car that had all the iconic appeal of its predecessor. It was also the perfect opportunity to redesign the back of the car to allow a 2+2 variant to be produced, but this was never as pretty as the two-seater.

The engineering changes also gave Datsun time to develop a

Almost identical to the 240Z to look at, the 260Z had a larger engine, but was no more powerful thanks to emissions restrictions. Only in later models did they rectify this.

new engine for the car, in the form of a 2565cc (157cu in) straight-six. The engine was not allowed to be in as high a state of tune as its predecessor, though, as it would have breached the emissions laws.

As a result, although bigger, the unit was less lively, producing 139bhp (104kW), compared to the 151bhp (112kW) of the smaller engined 240Z. The law continued to cause Datsun problems.

Ungainly safety bumpers were added to the car in 1975, although, by fitting fuel injection and a five-speed gearbox, Datsun at least managed to get the power back up in its later models.

LOTUS ELITE

Not to be confused with the dainty 1960s sports car that shared its name, the Lotus Elite of the 1970s was an altogether different beast. Intended as an upmarket GT, complete with four seats, the new Elite was certainly distinctive, although its rakish

wedge-shaped profile was not the most harmonious shape of its era.

In traditional Lotus style, the car was constructed from glassfibre mounted on a steel backbone chassis, while the steering and suspension were designed in-house and had to be perfect before Lotus

boss Colin Chapman would sign them off. Coupled to a 1973cc (120cu in) all-alloy 16-valve engine of Lotus's own design, this meant that the Elite was terrific to drive, despite its gawky appearance. The engine was not renowned for its reliability, often suffering cooling

trouble, but it was one of the most potent 2.0-litre units in existence, developing 160bhp (119kW).

Three basic models of Elite were on offer: the 501, which was the basic specification variant; the 502, which had standard air conditioning; and the 503, which added power steering. There was also a 504 model, added later, which had Borg Warner automatic transmission as standard, although it was understandably quite rare.

From 1980 onwards, all Elites had a new 2.2-litre version of the alloy engine. The power output remained identical, but it had more torque and was coupled to a new close-ratio five-speed gearbox.

ENGINE: 1973cc (120cu in), four-cylinder
POWER: 155bhp (115kW)
0–60MPH (96KM/H): 7.8 seconds
TOP SPEED: 200km/h (124mph)
PRODUCTION TOTAL: 2535

Estate car or sports car? You decide... The Elite was certainly one of Lotus's more unusual product offerings.

MERCEDES-BENZ W107SL

One of Mercedes' most loved cars of all time, the W107 series enjoyed an impressive 18-year production run. Even more of a surprise is that much of its basic architecture came from the earlier

A timeless shape and a classless appeal – the W107 SL is one of Mercedes's most enduring and desirable models ever.

Pagoda, and could trace its origins back to the early 1960s.

Initially, two models were offered, both with V8 engines of 3.5 litres (214cu in) or 4.5 litres (276cu in). These were joined in 1974 by the entry-level 280SL, which had a fuel-injected straight-six twin-cam engine from the 280SE S-Class. The 1974 models also received an improved suspension system, with trailing arms at the rear and

standard power steering, although most owners had specified this much-needed option from the beginning of W107 production.

Further revisions came in 1980, when the old V8s were dropped in favour of a new 3.8-litre (230cu in) six to replace the 3.5, and a 5.0-litre (320cu in) V8 replacing the 4.5.

The most extravagant model was the 560SL, introduced in 1986. It had a 5.6-litre (342cu in) 227bhp

(169kW) V8 unit. Thanks to the wealthy profile of the average W107 buyer, this fast became the bestselling model in the range.

ENGINE: 4520cc (276cu in), eight-cylinder
POWER: 225bhp (168kW)
0–60MPH (96KM/H): 8.8 seconds
TOP SPEED: 214km/h (134mph)
PRODUCTION TOTAL: 107,038

VANDEN PLAS 1500

As If the Austin Allegro did not have enough problems, British Leyland decided to make even more of a joke out of it in 1974 when it introduced the Vanden Plas 1500, which took the car to an even sillier level. Built to appeal to older buyers who wanted a car with

the luxuries of a Jaguar or Daimler, but in a compact easy-to-drive package, the 1500 had a hideously incongruous Rolls-Royce–style radiator grille bolted to its snout. Inside, it featured full leather trim, a polished burr walnut dashboard and Wilton overmats, along with a

pair of neat folding picnic tables stowed away in the front seat backs. From the inside, the 1500 was quite pleasant, but in concept it was truly ridiculous. Still, it was quite a successful seller. The last models had bigger engines and were badged Vanden Plas 1750s.

ENGINE: 1485cc (91cu in), four-cylinder
POWER: 69bhp (51kW)
0–60MPH (96KM/H): 16.7 seconds
TOP SPEED: 144km/h (90mph)
PRODUCTION TOTAL: 11,842

MERCEDES-BENZ SLC

Launched soon after the SL, the SLC was a slightly larger, more mature offering than the smaller W107, but under the skin it was largely the same. Mechanically, it was little different from the W107 convertible, but the SLC was built on a longer wheelbase and was, by virtue of this, a much grander looking car, albeit not quite as pretty. The extra bodywork housed

a pair of fairly commodious rear seats, which gave the SLC quite generous interior accommodation and a much greater degree of practicality than its SL sister car.

It also had a unique styling feature of its own. All four windows could be wound down into the side panels to give the car a completely pillarless profile, making it look especially stylish in the summer.

The bigger bodywork did, of course, affect the car's weight, and it lacked the agility of the smaller SL, although the bulkier frame did little to affect the performance. The original V8 engines produced such high torque levels that power was never wanting, while even the six-cylinder 280SLC, introduced alongside the 280SL in 1974, was lively enough. The SLC never had

the SL's following, however, and was withdrawn a full eight years before the car on which it was based.

ENGINE: 4520cc (276cu in), eight-cylinder
POWER: 225bhp (168kW)
0–60MPH (96KM/H): 7.4 seconds
TOP SPEED: 214km/h (134mph)
PRODUCTION TOTAL: 56,330

The rigidity of the SLC's coupé body made it stronger than the SL, to the extent that Mercedes took it safari rallying. Not the most obvious place for a luxury grand tourer, but the car enjoyed surprising success.

VOLKSWAGEN SCIROCCO

GERMANY 1974–91

Contrary to popular belief, Volkswagen's first water-cooled car of its own design (excepting the VW K70, conceived by NSU) was not the Golf. Preceding the massively popular hatchback by almost six months, the two-door coupé Scirocco was originally proposed by Giorgetto Giugiaro alongside the Golf. VW initially turned down the idea, saying that it was not in keeping with its brand, so Giugiaro instead approached German styling house Karmann to see if it was interested.

Between them, Karmann and Giugiaro presented the idea again to VW, but this time the German maker said it could not afford to develop the project further. Determined to get the car into showrooms, Karmann carried out all the development work itself, and VW eventually yielded, saying that it would build the car after all.

Indeed, the Scirocco was ready before the Golf had reached final sign-off and appeared in showrooms first, thus giving the concept of a water-cooled VW a less shocking introduction. Although initially badly underpowered, a situation rectified much later, the Scirocco enjoyed an impressive 17-year production run, with only a couple of minor face-lifts.

ENGINE: 1588cc (97cu in), four-cylinder
POWER: 110bhp (82kW)
0–60MPH (96KM/H): 9 seconds
TOP SPEED: 185km/h (115mph)
PRODUCTION TOTAL: 504,200

It often played second fiddle to the Golf in terms of popularity, but the Scirocco was the car that spearheaded VW's water-cooled revolution.

It's hard to imagine the angular Scirocco on sale alongside the Beetle – with Giugiaro appointed to style its new look, VW also managed to completely review its image.

INNOCENTI MINI 90/120

ITALY 1974–82

Well ahead of its time in several ways, the Innocenti Mini 90/120 was the Italian firm's vision for how the original Mini should be replaced. Using a standard Mini platform, the Innocenti had some of its development financed by British Leyland, which could not afford to undertake such a big engineering study itself. Its design was refreshingly simple. The car's body was styled by Bertone in the form of a practical three-door hatchback, which made even greater use of the original Mini's brilliant interior layout by freeing up more cabin space and offering a much more useful boot (trunk).

The running gear came directly from the Mini, complete with bouncy rubber cone suspension and a 998cc (61cu in) A-Series engine or, in sportier versions, a detuned 1275cc (78cu in) Mini Cooper unit.

Although British Leyland was not brave enough to sell the car in its home market, where the Mini had become a much-loved part of British folklore, the Innocenti was a success, selling 220,000 over an eight-year period. The last of these were built by de Tomaso, which bought the remnants of Innocenti in 1976 when British Leyland went bankrupt again, and were fitted with Japanese Daihatsu engines.

ENGINE: 1275cc (78cu in), four-cylinder
POWER: 76bhp (57kW)
0–60MPH (96KM/H): 10.9 seconds
TOP SPEED: 152km/h (95mph)
PRODUCTION TOTAL: 450,000

VOLKSWAGEN GOLF MK 1

GERMANY 1974–83

ENGINE: 1272cc (78cu in), four-cylinder
POWER: 60bhp (45kW)
0–60MPH (96KM/H): 13.2 seconds
TOP SPEED: 147km/h (92mph)
PRODUCTION TOTAL: about 6,000,000

Volkswagen was initially resistant to the idea of making its core model water-cooled, but it need not have worried too much. The Mk 1 Golf got everything right from the start, but, then, VW did not exactly rush it into production.

The styling, from Giugiaro, was signed off in 1971, three years before the car made its debut, and, by the time it hit showrooms, any initial build-quality problems had been ironed out. The Golf was a superb design – economical, spacious, comfortable and well engineered. Very little fault could be found with it, other than perhaps being a little conservative. A diesel model came out in 1975 and was the world's first commercially successful oil-burning passenger car.

VW silenced its 'conservative' critics for good in 1976 with the GTI's launch. The hot hatchback defined an entirely new generation of performance cars and proved that, just like the Beetle before it, the Golf could be all things to all owners. When the Mk 2 Golf arrived in 1983, the range included a four-door model, called Jetta, and a very pretty cabriolet, which outlived the hatch and was built until 1993.

A legend in its own lap time – the VW Golf GTi was the original hot hatchback, and arguably the best.

PANTHER DE VILLE

UNITED KINGDOM 1974–85

The De Ville really wasn't a looker. Yes, Panther's rip-off of the Bugatti Royale really did use Austin Maxi doors and the windscreen from a Mini.

Not content with its J72 being a blatant rip-off of the Jaguar SS100, Panther decided to go down the road of ripping off another all-time classic with the 1974 De Ville.

Designed to look like the regal Bugatti Royale – a vehicle renowned for being the most lavish car ever built – the De Ville did a reasonable job of echoing its profile, although the build quality was not quite as exquisite. We doubt, for example, that the Royale would ever have used the doors from an Austin Maxi or the switchgear from a Vauxhall Chevette. That said, the Panther was well equipped and was also very expensive, largely because all the cars were hand-built.

A two-door version of the De Ville was also offered and was slightly less extravagant. By using the doors from an MGB instead of a Maxi, it was actually a far nicer looking car than the original.

ENGINE: 5343cc (326cu in), 12-cylinder
POWER: 266bhp (168kW)
0–60MPH (96KM/H): 8.8 seconds
TOP SPEED: 221km/h (137mph)
PRODUCTION TOTAL: 60

ALFA ROMEO GT/GTV

ITALY 1974–87

ENGINE: 1962cc (120cu in),
  four-cylinder
POWER: 130bhp (97kW)
0–60MPH (96KM/H): 8.7 seconds
TOP SPEED: 192km/h (120mph)
PRODUCTION TOTAL: 120,000

Initially conceived as the Alfetta GT by Giorgetto Giugiaro, the GTV was deliberated over for three years by Alfa Romeo management before the decision was taken to put it into production. Despite the initial resistance, the car was a huge success. Its stunning bodywork gave it plenty of appeal, regardless of the fact that the car was considerably pricier than similar coupés such as the Ford Capri and Opel Manta. The idea of a convertible version, to be called the Alfetta Spider, was also toyed with several times (a prototype was even shown), but it would never come to fruition.

The car was based on a shortened Alfetta floorpan and used the

Alfetta's 1.8-litre (110cu in) engine until 1976, when it was rebadged GT 2000 and given the 2.0-litre (122cu in) unit from the range-topping Alfetta. The best, however, was yet to come.

In 1981 Alfa fitted a 2.5-litre (152cu in) all-alloy V6 engine, developing 150bhp (112kW) and giving the car impressively rapid performance. The GTV6, as it was known, soon became the most

desirable GT of the lot, although it did lack the unusual interior design of the original, which had featured all of the dials except the rev counter in a pod towards the middle of the dashboard.

By far the best variant was the GTV6, a car with wonderful performance, a seductive engine note and very fluent handling.

CITROËN CX

FRANCE 1974–91

When Citroën's replacement for the DS finally arrived after 21 years, it was true to form – a car like no other on the road and an instant design classic in its own right. While the Citroën CX might not have made quite the same impact as its predecessor, that did

not stop the car from being weird and a technological tour de force at the same time – in other words, a proper large Citroën.

The suspension was, as you might expect, a self-levelling hydropneumatic system, while the Vari-Power self-centring power

steering was carried over from the SM. The car also had an unusual concave back window, which needed no rear wiper as air flow over the car kept it naturally clean.

Two engines were on offer initially, a 1985cc (121cu in) unit and a 2175 (133cu in) unit, both

carried over from the DS. These were followed by a turbocharged 2500cc (151cu in) powerplant in the 1977 GTI, and a range of diesels. Two estate (station-wagon) versions of the car were also on offer – the five-seat Safari and the seven-seat Familiale.

Citroën also manufactured a long-wheelbase model, called the Prestige, which had stunning leather seats and thick carpets, making it the car of choice for French government ministers.

In terms of build quality, Series 2 cars were the best due to better rustproofing, although they did lose some of the interior design ingenuity of the first cars.

ENGINE: 2473cc (151cu in),
  four-cylinder turbo
POWER: 168bhp (125kW) at 5000rpm
0–60MPH (96KM/H): 8.6 seconds
TOP SPEED: 206km/h (128mph)
PRODUCTION TOTAL: 1,042,300

Despite being a saloon car and not a sports model, the CX was the most aerodynamic car of its day, with a drag co-efficient of 0.29. A Ferrari Daytona's was 0.35. A fitting design classic successor to the DS.

ZAGATO ZELE

Famed for styling beautiful Aston Martins and Lancias, Zagato faced a new challenge as it went into the 1970s. Faced with bankruptcy, the Italian maker came up with an unusual antidote to the global oil crisis.

The wedge-shaped Zele was an all-electric city car designed for commuters, and was both cheap to buy and inexpensive to run. At only 196cm (77in) long, it was an interesting precursor to vehicles such as the Smart Car of today

Despite managing moderate sales, the Zele was perhaps a little ahead of its time. Moulded from plastic, the car was fairly light and had better performance than most electric cars, but its four 24-volt batteries gave it a range of only 69km (43 miles) before it needed plugging in and recharging, severely limiting its practicality.

Most of the 3000 or so Zeles were sold in the United States under the name Elcar, although a handful was also imported into Britain by Bristol.

ENGINE: 1000-watt motor
POWER: n/a
0–60MPH (96KM/H): n/a
TOP SPEED: 40km/h (25mph)
PRODUCTION TOTAL: about 3000

TATRA 613

Tatra's replacement for the iconic 603 was certainly as distinctive as its predecessor, but in a much more angular way. Styled by Vignale, the new car's angular bodywork featured a long bonnet (hood) and flying buttresses

Its slightly ungainly appearance disguised the fact that the Tatra 613 was a luxury car with an air-cooled V8 engine.

at the rear, while Tatra's trademark four-headlight grille remained.

Also carried over was the unusual concept of a rear-mounted air-cooled V8 engine, which presented Tatra with a huge engineering challenge. With all the weight over the rear end, the 613 had to have a number of chassis tweaks to keep it on the straight and narrow. While Tatra did not quite achieve the impossible (the 613 was tricky to drive in the wet), it did at least go some way towards making the car feel stable and secure, providing you did not provoke it too much.

A luxury car in its home market, the 613 was incredibly well appointed, with luxury seats, smart chrome trim inside and out, and acres of rear legroom. Heat taken directly from the engine kept the rear-seat occupants (who were usually the owners) nice and snug during cold Eastern European winters. Performance was admirable, too, and the car benefited from superb ride comfort. The 613 remained in production, albeit at a slow pace, for 23 years, changing its name to the T700 in 1996.

ENGINE: 3495cc (213cu in), V8-cylinder
POWER: 165bhp (123kW)
0–60MPH (96KM/H): 12 secs
TOP SPEED: 184km/h (115mph)
PRODUCTION TOTAL: n/a

WOLSELEY SIX

The luxury version of the BL Princess was also the last car to wear the Wolseley name, and to traditional fans of the marque it was a travesty. While the car was comfortable and well equipped, its Wolseley grille (complete with trademark illuminated grille badge), unique wheel trims and ornate rear reading lights did not make the car a true Wolseley. Buyers stayed away in their droves, despite the promise of a torquey 2.2-litre (136cu in) straight-six engine.

Only a few had been built when, less than a year after production started, British Leyland began a huge rationalization programme which saw the Wolseley name disappear from the British market altogether. The striking wedge-shaped car known variously as the Austin 18-22, Morris 1800 and Wolseley Six was rebranded under one banner as 'Princess'. It was an ignominious end for what was once one of Britain's most prestigious marques and a clear sign of the hard times Britain's motor industry faced.

ENGINE: 2227cc (136cu in), six-cylinder
POWER: 110bhp (82kW)
0–96KM/H (60MPH): 13.5 seconds
TOP SPEED: 166km/h (104mph)
PRODUCTION TOTAL: about 3800

JENSEN GT

With sales of the Jensen-Healey not reaching the heights that owner Kjell Qvale had anticipated, a new model was introduced in an attempt to inject some life into the model. Called simply Jensen GT, as by this stage the Healey family had

A desperate attempt to breathe new life into the Jensen-Healey project, the GT was an expensive and unsuccessful diversion.

withdrawn its interest from the company, the GT was a sports car-cum-estate (station wagon) in the same mould as vehicles such as the Volvo 1800ES and Reliant Scimitar.

The front part of the bodywork was identical to the Jensen-Healey's, right down to the awkward-looking safety bumpers, but from the windscreen pillars back it was all new, with taller windows, a higher roof and a tailgate rear end that, ironically, made the car look more

attractive than the convertible model on which it was based.

The same Lotus-derived engines were used as in the Jensen-Healey, complete with the same cooling problems, but all models had five-speed Getrag gearboxes as standard. At the rear, the new bodywork added some practicality in the form of a tailgate and decent-sized load area, but the 2+2 interior layout still came with unnecessarily cramped rear seats,

and access to the rear was difficult because of the doors' shape.

GTs were more luxurious than Jensen-Healeys, with wooden door cappings and dashboard trim.

ENGINE: 1973cc (120cu in), four-cylinder
POWER: 140bhp (104kW)
0–60MPH (96KM/H): 9 seconds
TOP SPEED: 192km/h (120mph)
PRODUCTION TOTAL: 473

PANTHER RIO

With sales of the playboys' playthings that made up most of its range starting to dwindle, Panther needed a new tack with which to approach the post–fuel crisis, recession-hit years of the mid-1970s. Its solution was a 'poor man's Rolls-Royce' in the form of the Panther Rio – a car that offered

the same level of luxury as the world's finest automobiles, but in a smaller, more affordable package.

In concept, it was not a bad idea. There was also no problem with Panther's choice of vehicle on which to base its unusual derivative. Under the skin, the car was a Triumph Dolomite Sprint, which meant that

it was good to drive, had lively performance and handled well.

The Rio had a Rolls-Royce–style radiator grille, flanked by the Ford Granada's rectangular headlights and attached to the nose of a smart, squared-off saloon body. It could have been a good car, but sold only by the handful, as it cost the same

to buy as three Dolomite Sprints, and was not especially economical.

ENGINE: 1998cc (122cu in), four-cylinder
POWER: 129bhp (96kW)
0–60MPH (96KM/H): 9.9 seconds
TOP SPEED: 185km/h (115mph)
PRODUCTION TOTAL: 34

AMC PACER

Criticized as the 'Edsel of the 1970s', the AMC Pacer was one of the most derided American cars of all time. Launched to an expectant public in 1975, the Pacer was designed to be a compact economy model, ready to do battle with the flood of Japanese and European imports that dominated this sector of the US market.

While there was no problem with the Pacer's concept, the execution

was not what buyers wanted. For a start, it was not compact, being bigger than most European luxury cars, and even the smallest, most fuel efficient engine on offer was a 3.8-litre (232cu in) straight-six – more than three times the size of the VW Beetle's engine and hardly what you would expect to find in an 'economy' model. Also, to make the car look compact, AMC made it incredibly wide to balance out the

looks. While this meant a spacious interior, it did little for the car's already goldfish-bowl-like looks.

One of the Pacer's more unusual marketing gimmicks was the fact that its passenger door was longer than the one on the driver's side, with the purpose of improving access to the rear seats for children and encouraging them to enter the vehicle from the kerbside rather than the road. The point of this

was lost when, in an effort to increase sales, AMC started selling the car in right-hand drive markets without altering the doors.

ENGINE: 4229cc (258cu in), six-cylinder
POWER: 100bhp (75kW)
0–60MPH (96KM/H): 15.8 seconds
TOP SPEED: 142km/h (88mph)
PRODUCTION TOTAL: about 280,000

More like a goldfish bowl on wheels than a compact car, the AMC Pacer was actually far larger than it looked. Like other AMC models, it failed to live up to its promise.

LOTUS ECLAT

UNITED KINGDOM 1975–82

ENGINE: 1973cc (120cu in),
four-cylinder
POWER: 160bhp (119kW)
0–60MPH (96KM/H): 7.9 seconds
TOP SPEED: 208km/h (129mph)
PRODUCTION TOTAL: 1519

Concerned that some people had criticized the Elite's looks as being too upright and not sporty enough, Lotus went back to the drawing board and came out with the Eclat. Built to complement rather than replace the Elite, the Eclat was more of a traditional sports model, although it still retained the Elite's four-seat layout. It also shared that car's excellent steel backbone chassis, while the lighter weight meant that it was faster.

Five models were offered. The entry-level Eclat was the 520, with

four-speed transmission, while the 521 differed only in that it had a five-speed box, wider wheels and a radio. The 522 came with air conditioning and electric windows, while the luxury 523 got wood trim

and power steering on top. The 524 was a real rarity, sold with an automatic gearbox on top of the 523 spec, and accounted for only a tiny minority of sales. As with the Elite, the Eclat received a 2.2-litre

(134cu in) engine in 1976 to replace the original 1973cc (120cu in) unit. There was also a special-edition model called the Riviera, with a lift-out glass roof panel and chintzy alloy wheels.

Based on the Elite but far more stylish, the Eclat outlived its sister car and evolved into the Excel.

AUSTIN 18-22 SERIES

UNITED KINGDOM 1975

More commonly known as the Princess, by which name it was known from 1976 onwards, the Austin 18-22 replaced the much-loved 1800/2200 'Landcrab' range. The controversial wedge-shaped machine was designed by British Leyland's in-house stylist Harris Mann and was as far removed from the rounded, dumpling-shaped Allegro as you could possibly

imagine. Its trapezoid looks, steeply raked bonnet (hood) and high back end soon earned it the nickname of 'Wedge'.

You either loved or loathed the looks, but with incredibly well damped 'Hydragas' suspension and an incredibly spacious cabin, helped by its transverse-engine front-wheel drive design, the Wedge was one of the most comfortable cars in its

class. It is alleged that Harris Mann originally designed the car to be a hatchback, hence the tapered rear end, but British Leyland's senior management insisted that this be changed to a traditional boot (trunk) so as not to steal sales from the already struggling Maxi. When the Ambassador replaced the Wedge in 1981 (and the Maxi was dead and buried), it finally got

the hatchback it so badly needed. But the new car looked even more unusual, and was never a success.

ENGINE: 1798cc (110cu in),
four-cylinder
POWER: 82bhp (61kW)
0–60MPH (96KM/H): 14.9 seconds
TOP SPEED: 155km/h (96mph)
PRODUCTION TOTAL: 43,427

FERRARI 308 GTB/S

Following the outcry caused by Ferrari asking Bertone to style its 308 GT4, the Italian supercar maker decided to play it safe with its latest model in 1975 and return to long-established stylist Pininfarina. And what a return it was. The 308 GTB (and later the convertible GTS) was an absolutely stunning machine, designed to replace the equally attractive 246 Dino. The talk of the 1975 Paris Motor Show, the car went on sale almost immediately afterwards.

Based on a shortened GT4 chassis, but with glassfibre bodywork except for an aluminium bonnet (hood), the 308 GTB had the same mid-mounted V8 engine as the GT4, albeit with a dry sump so that it could be mounted lower on the car's chassis.

Comparisons were inevitably made with the Dino, and not without good reason. Certainly, the dimensions and the market at which it was aimed were more or less identical to those of the Dino. Both cars had extremely low

waistlines, slim noses, a sleek overall shape and a large and steeply raked windscreen. Also, the flat engine cover and flying buttresses only served to emphasize the mid-engined layout. The 308's pop-up headlights helped to produce a more aerodynamic front end, beefed up with bonnet grilles and side air ducts. Its side windows were large and gave the cabin a light and airy environment.

Best of all, the 308 GTB was not just good to look at – it delivered a pure driving experience as well. Its transverse V8 had more than enough power and torque, and the car had a wonderfully smooth and direct gear change. The maximum European power output of 255bhp (190kW) was enough to push the car on to a top speed of 248km/h (154mph), while it could sprint from 0–100km/h (62mph) in just over six seconds. This was a great achievement from a normally aspirated and very compact V8 engine, with a displacement of only 2926cc (179cu in), no doubt

aided by the car's light weight and agile chassis.

In 1976, after 712 cars had been built, the bodywork was changed to all-steel construction to bring costs down (although this added some weight and stunted performance), and, in the following year, the GTS was added to the range. Unveiled at the Frankfurt Motor Show in 1977, this model, with a removable roof, had some additional strengthening to compensate. The roof panel could be stored behind the seats, while the rear windows of the GTB were replaced by louvred vent panels. The last few cars also lost some power due to more stringent emissions controls.

For 1980, the engines in both the GTB and GTS received a Bosch K-Jetronic fuel injection system and a Marelli Digiplex electronic ignition, and the models became known as the GTBi and GTSi, to compensate for the loss of power over the original. In Europe, the injected models developed 214bhp

One of Ferrari's most enduring shapes, the 308 GTB was a welcome return to form after the tepid reception given to the GT4.

(159kW), but in the United States this was lowered to 208bhp (155kW), thanks to the necessary addition of a catalytic converter in the exhaust system.

For the tax-sensitive Italian market only, there was also a 2-litre (122cu in) version producing 170bhp (127kW). A major boost came in 1982, with the launch of a turbocharged fuel-injected variant, offering 220bhp (164kW). This would become the mainstay of the GTB/S range until its eventual demise in 1986.

ENGINE: 2926cc (179cu in), eight-cylinder
POWER: 255bhp (190kW)
0–60MPH (96KM/H): 6 seconds
TOP SPEED: 248km/h (154mph)
PRODUCTION TOTAL: 5140

MORRIS 1800/2200 PRINCESS

The last big car to wear the Morris badge, the 1800/2200 series came with a choice of 1.8-litre (110cu in) four-cylinder or 2.2-litre (136cu in) six-cylinder transverse engines.

It was based on the platform of the existing 'Landcrab' models, but shared the bodywork of the Austin

and Wolseley 18-22 models, which would later become known simply as Princess. The dramatic Harris Mann–styled bodywork had a distinctive wedge shape, which was perhaps a little too controversial for the traditionally conservative Morris buyers, but the car's layout and Hydragas fluid suspension did

at least ensure that the 1800/2200 was exceptionally comfortable and had an excellent ride quality.

Despite this, with British Leyland becoming Leyland Cars in 1976, the Morris identity was dropped after less than a year, and the range became simply known as Princess, making the Morris variant

one of the rarest examples of this unusual avant-garde luxury car.

ENGINE: 2227cc (136cu in), six-cylinder
POWER: 110bhp (82kW) at 5250rpm
0–60MPH (96KM/H): 13.5 seconds
TOP SPEED: 169km/h (105mph)
PRODUCTION TOTAL: 225,842

TRIUMPH TR7

UNITED KINGDOM 1975–81

Harris Mann's designs were nothing if not individual, and the last-of-the-line of TR sports cars was yet another example of his forward-thinking design causing controversy.

Like the Princess, the TR7 was distinctively wedge-shaped, with its drooping nose, kicked-up rear and pop-up headlights, while it was also the first TR sports car to be offered only as a hardtop – a move that led to much derision from fans of the TR line and even led to Triumph introducing a soft-top TR7 later on.

Based on a prototype called the Bullet, the TR7 made its public debut in the summer of 1976, and, although the styling gave the impression of it being a mid-engined

Flawed, but admired by a devout band of followers, the Harris Mann-styled TR7 is certainly unique. Convertible models were only on sale for two years.

model, the TR7's engine was squeezed under the car's low nose.

This created some problems of its own, as the car was originally proposed to use the 2.0-litre (122cu in) 16-valve slant-four engine from the Dolomite Sprint. It soon became apparent during the design stage that the Dolomite's large cylinder head was too tall for the car's nose, and, short of adding an ugly ridge to the bonnet (hood) line and ruining the aerodynamics, there was no way that the engine could be used. Instead, Triumph used the Sprint's 2.0-litre block and fitted the smaller eight-valve head from the Dolomite 1850, meaning that the TR7 came with only 105bhp (75kW) of power in place of the intended 130bhp (96kW).

The interior was not the most sporting either. Rather than the basic sports-oriented cabin of previous TR cars, the TR7 was more of a luxury GT, with a full-width black plastic dashboard and

unusual tartan-trimmed half-vinyl sports seats.

After a slow start, TR7 sales started to pick up, although the new breed of buyer was o't the type traditionally associated with TR sports cars, and the car's good value pricing made it popular with those who wanted a comfortable, sporty-looking model, but did not need four seats.

Quality control was dire, however, and labour relations at the car's factory in Speke, Liverpool, were poor, which led to masses of warranty claims. Triumph closed the Liverpool plant in 1978 and moved production of the TR7 to Coventry, where it would be built alongside its other models and tighter quality control would be adhered to, resulting in later cars being significantly better than the earlier ones.

In 1979, the TR7 got a much needed five-speed gearbox, while a convertible model was also introduced, looking much sharper

than the coupé and answering many of the criticisms levelled at the original car. A meatier version, called the TR8 and equipped with the Rover V8 engine, also appeared the same year, but is covered in a separate entry.

Despite this added variety in the range, the TR7 had a fairly short life and was taken out of production in 1981 as part of Leyland's rationalization programme, which saw it significantly reduce the number of cars in its ranges. Even so, in only six short years, more than 100,000 TR7s had been built, proving that, despite the initial resistance and the early quality control issues, it was still the most successful TR derivative ever.

ENGINE: 1998cc (122cu in), four-cylinder
POWER: 105bhp (78kW) at 5500rpm
0–60MPH (96KM/H): 9.1 seconds
TOP SPEED: 177km/h (110mph)
PRODUCTION TOTAL: 112,368

VAUXHALL CAVALIER

UNITED KINGDOM 1975–81

The British version of GM's global J-Car, the Cavalier was a critically important car for Vauxhall. With the Viva range ageing rapidly and the Victor too large and thirsty to appeal to 1970s cost-conscious motorists, the Luton-based firm had seen its sales take a significant downturn in the highly competitive fleet market – and desperately needed a convincing answer to Ford's Cortina. The Cavalier was it. Neatly styled with Vauxhall's

trademark aerodynamic nose to distinguish it from the near-identical Opel Ascona, the new car was good-looking, well packaged and came with a broad enough model line-up to satisfy all tastes.

Three engines were offered – a 1.3-litre (79cu in), a 1.6-litre (98cu in) and a 2.0-litre (122cu in) – all of which were fairly lively and gelled well with the Cavalier's excellent rear-drive chassis to provide a rewarding driving experience.

Vauxhall had also listened to criticisms of its previous models, which had a poor reputation for corrosion, and treated the Cavalier to an 11-stage anti-corrosion treatment, including zinc coating of the panels and wax-injected sills to keep the dreaded rust at bay.

Most of the Cavaliers sold were either two- or four-door saloons, but the more intriguing variants included a stunning two-door coupé, which made for a very

affordable sports car, and the unusual three-door Sports Hatch – a 2+2 coupé with a practical rear tailgate, which was fairly popular because of its practicality.

ENGINE: 1584cc (97cu in), four-cylinder
POWER: 69bhp (51kW)
0–60MPH (96KM/H): 14.8 seconds
TOP SPEED: 157km/h (98mph)
PRODUCTION TOTAL: 238,980

Most Cavaliers were sold as four-door saloons, but Vauxhall also made a two-door coupé model, seen here, and a three-door model called the Sporthatch. A broad model line-up satisfied many tastes and the Cavalier became a highly successful competitor to Ford's Cortina.

BRISTOL 412

UNITED KINGDOM 1975–82

Bristol's first 'breeze-block' was the 412 – a very odd-looking car with slab-sided styling, a flat nose and a truly enormous chassis. Styled by Zagato – a company better known for its pretty European sports cars – the newcomer was certainly very different from anything the Italian company had ever produced before.

Whether or not you like its looks, the 412 was definitely imposing, although the Ford Granada headlights and Fiat-derived door handles might not be what you would expect to find on a car that, when new, cost three times the annual British salary.

The car was the first Bristol to be offered in convertible form directly from the factory, and the soft-top model accounted for about half of all orders, despite earning a reputation for being damp and leaky inside. In order to alleviate this, cars built from 1976 onwards had an external rollover bar and a lift-out Targa roof section that was far more watertight than the original canvas top.

Under the skin, the 412 offered little new. Mechanically, it was the same as the outgoing Bristol 411, complete with a 6556cc (400cu in) Chrysler V8 engine and standard automatic box.

The 412 was heavy and not especially dynamic to drive, although it was fairly quick and handling was never a major concern of Bristol's traditional buyers, who bought the car to make a statement much more than they did to make rapid progress.

ENGINE: 6556cc (400cu in), eight-cylinder
POWER: n/a
0–60MPH (96KM/H): 7.4 seconds
TOP SPEED: 226km/h (140mph)
PRODUCTION TOTAL: n/a

A typically British scene. Square, sturdy and old-fashioned, the Bristol matches the mews houses behind it! The soft-top model accounted for half of all orders, despite being leaky.

LANCIA BETA MONTECARLO

After it came home in first place in the 1975 Monte Carlo rally, Lancia decided to launch a special-edition car to celebrate its historic victory, and at the same time give the Beta range a much-needed boost. To do this, Lancia used an abandoned Fiat design, which was

The pretty styling did a good job of disguising the Beta Monte Carlo's many flaws, but a poor reputation meant Lancia pulled the car out of the US market.

effectively a larger version of the X1/9 sports car with neat Pininfarina-styled coupé bodywork.

The design was perfect for Lancia, as it featured the same mid-engined layout as the rally-winning Stratos, but had been engineered to house any existing Fiat group engine, including those from the Beta.

The car went on sale in the summer of 1975, powered by the 2.0-litre (122cu in) engine from the Beta, and it initially won praise for its pretty styling. It soon became

readily apparent, however, that the Montecarlo was not all that it was cracked up to be.

A lack of development threw up some serious handling and braking problems, while the 'Scorpion' model, which was introduced for the American market in eco-friendly detuned form, was so slow with its lowly 80bhp (60kW) power output that it could hardly be labelled a sports car.

The Montecarlo was withdrawn as early as 1978, as it was considered to be doing more

damage to Lancia's reputation – something it was supposed to rectify, not add to further. A revised model, with a heavily reworked platform, was introduced in 1980, but this was never sold in the United States.

ENGINE: 1995cc (122cu in),
 four-cylinder
POWER: 120bhp (89kW) at 6000rpm
0–60MPH (96KM/H): 9.8 seconds
TOP SPEED: 193km/h (120mph)
PRODUCTION TOTAL: 7595

VAUXHALL CHEVETTE

Although it was based on GM's global T-Car platform, sold as the Opel Kadett, Isuzu Gemini and Chevrolet Chevette, among others, the Vauxhall Chevette managed to maintain some autonomy in the form of its styling and powertrain.

It appears that GM relaxed its global rules and regulations for the UK market a little, as Vauxhall had its own design and engineering departments in Luton, and at the time the British market was still staunchly patriotic. This meant that the car had to be perceived as a 'British' product if it were going to offer serious competition to the Ford Escort and

Saloon, hatch and estate versions of the Chevette were made, and all came with an unusual grille-free front end for improved aerodynamics.

myriad of British Leyland small cars. As a result, the Chevette had a unique aerodynamic nose, which echoed the look of the 'Droop Snoot' Firenza. It also inherited the engine and transmission from the 1300cc (77cu in) Viva, rather than use the smaller overhead-camshaft engines that were popular in mainland Europe.

You certainly could not criticize the Chevette for having a limited range, as it was offered as both a three-door hatch and four-door saloon, while later on an estate (station wagon) and even a panel van, called the Chevanne, were introduced. The most exciting variant was the 2300HS, which was built to compete with Ford

on the international rally scene. Using a modified Vauxhall Magnum 2.3-litre (139cu in) engine, the Chevette was relatively successful, and had the added advantage of looking meaty.

A revised Chevette appeared in 1981 with a more modern interior, plus black plastic detailing to distinguish it from earlier cars, but

production ceased in 1984 to make way for the front-wheel drive Nova.

ENGINE: 1256cc (77cu in), four-cylinder
POWER: 59bhp (44kW)
0–60MPH (96KM/H): 16.7 seconds
TOP SPEED: 141km/h (88mph)
PRODUCTION TOTAL: 415,608

ROLLS-ROYCE CAMARGUE

An unusual attempt by Rolls-Royce to create a car that offered more modern, streamlined looks than its more traditional offerings, the Camargue was also Britain's most expensive car when it went on sale, costing the same as

four Jaguar XJCs. The controversial looks were styled by Pininfarina and polarized opinion among Rolls-Royce fans. Some loved the way the traditional Rolls-Royce style had embraced the modern age, while others found it a tad vulgar.

Under the bonnet (hood), the Camargue got a more powerful version of the 6750cc (412cu in) V8 engine fitted to the Silver Shadow, although, true to Rolls-Royce tradition the exact power output was never disclosed and

described merely as 'more than adequate'. Most commentators at the time estimated that the car's true output was around 220bhp (164kW), which, in truth, was quite modest for an engine of such a large cylinder capacity.

Camargue sales were never brilliant, despite a 10-year production run. This was partly because, under the skin, the Camargue had a normal Silver Shadow floorpan and was little different to drive than the car on which it was based, while the arguably prettier two-door Corniche was less expensive to buy, almost as fast and had a much more upmarket presence.

ENGINE: 6750cc (412cu in), eight-cylinder
POWER: n/a
0–60MPH (96KM/H): 10 seconds
TOP SPEED: 190km/h (118mph)
PRODUCTION TOTAL: 531

Loved by some, reviled by others, the Camargue is the car that broke the Rolls-Royce mode. It was slightly vulgar, but had some charm. Despite a 10-year run, sales were never brilliant.

CHRYSLER ALPINE

A one-time European Car of the Year winner, the Chrysler Alpine might appear incredibly conventional today, but in its heyday was an interesting car.

The Alpine's long hatchback body was unusual in itself, as most rivals were still offering four-door saloons in this sector of the market, while it was also the first car to come with electric windows and power steering as standard across the range – part of Chrysler's intention to offer incomparable value in the family car market and

Neatly styled, practical, comfortable and good to drive, the Alpine certainly had its followers, but build quality was never better than shaky, and they did like to rust...

win over buyers who simply were not able to find the same level of specification elsewhere.

The car was first introduced in 1975 and was built in Poissy, France, where it was sold as the Simca 1308, but from 1976 onwards the car was built in Coventry, England, and was sold as a Chrysler initially, then as a Talbot from 1978.

The Alpine was a practical and comfortable car that acquired a steady following over the years, but it was never an enormous success for Chrysler, who lost interest in 1978 and sold out to Peugeot (hence the name change to Talbot). Peugeot's first job was to make the range slightly more diverse, so a four-door variant called the Talbot Solara appeared in 1980. Even so, sales were never anywhere near the level of the Ford Cortina or Vauxhall Cavalier, which comprehensively outsold it despite being no better.

ENGINE: 1294cc (79cu in), four-cylinder
POWER: 65bhp (48.5kW)
0–60MPH (96KM/H): 16.9 seconds
TOP SPEED: 90mph/144km/h
PRODUCTION TOTAL: 108,405 plus 77,422 Talbots

OPEL MANTA B-SERIES
GERMANY 1975–88

Based on the platform of the Opel Ascona and Vauxhall Cavalier, the replacement for the A-Series Manta was a larger and more powerful car. Again going head to head with Ford's Capri, the Manta B-series came with a huge range of engine and trim options,

The B-Series Manta remained on sale for 13 years, as both a GT/E Berlinetta (two-door) and a three-door Coupé.

from 1.2 litres (73cu in) up to 2.0 litres (122cu in), and basic and luxury trims. It was initially only available as a two-door coupé, but a hatchback variant, based on the Vauxhall Cavalier Sports hatch, joined the range in 1978.

The Cavalier disappeared in 1981, to be replaced by a new front-wheel drive model, but the Manta soldiered on with a major face-lift, which saw it gain an all-new dashboard and more plush interior, plus two new engines. The larger

of the two, a 2.0-litre unit, was fuel-injected, and this model became known as the GT/E, the E standing for 'Einspritz', which is the German word for 'injection'.

The GT/E was by far the best mainstream Manta, although its desirability is surpassed by that of the rare Manta 400, which was built as an homologation special for Group B rallying in the early 1980s. It came with a 2.4-litre (146cu in) Cosworth-developed engine and sported lightweight

alloy body panels, wide arches and huge air scoops. The new-look B-series was in production until 1988, when it was replaced by the Opel/Vauxhall Calibra – a new kind of coupé for the 1990s.

ENGINE: 1979cc (121cu in), four-cylinder
POWER: 110bhp (82kW)
0–60MPH (96KM/H): 8.5 seconds
TOP SPEED: 194km/h (120mph)
PRODUCTION TOTAL: 603,000

JAGUAR XJS
UNITED KINGDOM 1975–93

Replacing the E-type was no mean feat, and it is fair to say that the car's eventual replacement did not have the same instant design harmony as its predecessor.

Based on the floorpan of the short-wheelbase XJ12 and sharing its 5.3-litre (326cu in) V12 engine, the XJS was initially offered as a coupé only, and its unusual flying

rear buttresses, wide-mouthed grille and squared-off wheelarches were to meet with some resistance from those fans who had loved the original E-type. On the plus side, though, the XJS was a good car to drive, with effortless performance, great handling and a typically well-trimmed cabin, making it an excellent grand tourer.

It continued almost unchanged until 1984, when Jaguar decided to give it a face-lift and introduce some more variants to provide the car with broader appeal. One of the most desirable additions was a cabriolet, which lost some of the coupé's awkward rear end styling, while there was also a new 3.6-litre (219cu in) 24-valve engine

called the AJ6, which Jaguar was developing for its forthcoming XJ40 saloon. The new engine was terrific, and with a manual gearbox fitted was even quicker than the V12, as well as being considerably more economical. The V12 was retained, though, as for some buyers the big engine was an essential choice.

It was never the E-Type successor originally intended, but the Jaguar XJ-S nevertheless carved out a niche for itself and became a popular car in its own right. It was a good car to drive, with excellent handling.

A second face-lift for the XJS came in 1991, when the car's rear lights were swapped for smoked dark plastic items and the engine sizes were increased to cope with the power that was sapped by new catalytic converters. The 3.6-litre engine was upped to 4.0 litres (244cu in), and the V12 was made into a 6.0-litre (366cu in).

By this time, the aged XJS had become an incredibly expensive car, but it still retained a loyal and traditional following.

ENGINE: 5343cc (326cu in), 12-cylinder
POWER: 285bhp (212kW)
0–60MPH (96KM/H): 5.5 seconds
TOP SPEED: 245km/h (153mph)
PRODUCTION TOTAL: 145,490

LAMBORGHINI SILHOUETTE

ITALY 1976–77

Following the dramatic success of its angular Countach, Lamborghini decided to try to replicate the car's angular features in a face-lift of the smaller Uracco.

The new car, called Silhouette, sported the same squared-off wheelarches as the Countach, as well as similar drilled alloy wheels, side air scoops and wedge-shaped front end, all of which were added by Bertone, which had styled the company's flagship. To add further appeal, Lamborghini removed the Uracco's roof and turned the car into a Targa-top, making it its first mid-engine open-top car.

Inside, the Uracco's 2+2 cabin was revised and turned into a two-seater, while extra soundproofing and a stiffened bodyshell made the car more refined to drive.

Despite this, the Silhouette was not a success. Lamborghini fans saw the car as cynical, trying to rest on the laurels of the Countach rather than be desirable through its own merit, while few people saw the point of buying it when it was considerably more expensive than the Uracco, which itself was still available.

Even Lamborghini's own efforts were half-hearted, It made no attempt to sell the Silhouette in the United States, where such a car might have proven popular. Instead, production was cancelled after only one year, and only 52 cars were ever built.

ENGINE: 2996cc (182cu in), eight-cylinder
POWER: 265bhp (197kW)
0–60MPH (96KM/H): 5.6 seconds
TOP SPEED: 250km/h (156mph)
PRODUCTION TOTAL: 52

TVR TAIMAR

UNITED KINGDOM 1976–79

Based on the M-Series, but larger and with a more practical hatchback, the Taimar marked two milestones for TVR. It was TVR's first car to feature any kind of practical luggage space, broadening its appeal instantly. Also, in optional soft-top form, it was the first officially available TVR convertible – a move that added significantly to the marque's popularity during the

Same styling, same engines, different name. The Taimar was the first TVR to be available as either a coupé or a convertible and the first TVR to feature any kind of practical luggage space.

late 1970s and 1980s. Underneath the glassfibre bodywork, the car used the same strengthened steel backbone chassis as the M-Series, and any extra length was simply in the bodywork, with the wheelbase remaining unchanged.

The interior, save for the luggage area, was also identical and used switches and dials from a number of British manufacturers' parts bins. Under the bonnet (hood) was the ubiquitous Ford 'Essex' 3.0-litre (183cu in) V6 engine, as featured in the upper-range Capri models.

The drop-top, available from launch, came with new bodywork from the windscreen pillars back and used the same Ford-sourced engine. It was a fairly easy car for TVR to engineer, as the glassfibre body/steel chassis layout meant that the convertible model needed no extra strengthening, but remained just as agile and exciting to drive as the coupé.

ENGINE: 2994cc (183cu in), six-cylinder
POWER: 142bhp (106kW)
0–60MPH (96KM/H): 7.7 seconds
TOP SPEED: 193km/h (121mph)
PRODUCTION TOTAL: 395 (plus 30 turbos)

LOTUS ESPRIT

The first James Bond car not to wear Aston Martin badges, the Lotus Esprit became one of the company's most successful models ever, enjoying a production run of more than 25 years in various guises. The striking wedge-shaped profile was the work of Giugiaro,

Wedge-shaped, distinctive and with wonderful handling, the Esprit was one of the highlights of the 1970s sports car scene.

who designed the car to wrap around the classic backbone chassis that had made the Elite and Eclat such exciting cars to drive.

This time, the engine would be mounted in the middle, so that the car could be designed to have an all-over trapezoid appearance, causing some detractors to suggest that you could not tell if it was coming or going. Power came from the same 2.2-litre (134cu in) engine as found in the Elite and Eclat, but in a higher state of tune,

while, from 1980 onwards, there was also a turbocharged version, which used a Garret G3 turbo and was blisteringly fast.

To cope with extra power, Lotus stiffened the chassis, making the already sharp handling even more edgy. From 1981 onwards, the Esprit S3 appeared and had a slightly softer appearance, as if someone had taken some sandpaper and rounded off the Esprit's sharpest edges. These cars were the most user-friendly, if

lacking the styling purity of the original. All that would change again in 1987, when instead of replacing the Esprit, Lotus had in-house designer Peter Stevens give it an all-new look.

ENGINE: 1973cc (120cu in), four-cylinder
POWER: 160bhp (119kW)
0–60MPH (96KM/H): 8.4 seconds
TOP SPEED: 200km/h (124mph)
PRODUCTION TOTAL: 2062

BRISTOL 603

Another oddball Bristol, the 603 was nonetheless the company's most popular model throughout the 1970s. The controversial restyle was not to everyone's tastes, described by those who were already concerned about Bristol's design direction as vulgar, but the car was still true to Bristol's traditional principles, with a ladder

frame steel chassis, the same suspension set-up as cars from the 1960s and a choice of Chrysler V8 engines that had already served Bristol well for over a decade.

The body panels were all alloy, and came with access panels in the wings (fenders) to get to the battery and the spare wheel – another curious Bristol tradition.

Two engines were on offer – the 5.2-litre (317cu in) 603E and the 5.9-litre (360cu in) 603S. The smaller of the two was supposed to be an economy model, but Bristol's definition of economy differed somewhat from those of the majority in the power-starved and recession-hit 1970s. Despite this, the 603 sold steadily and

became one of Bristol's most successful models of all time.

ENGINE: 5900cc (360cu in), eight-cylinder
POWER: n/a
0–60MPH (96KM/H): 8.6 seconds
TOP SPEED: 213km/h (132mph)
PRODUCTION TOTAL: n/a

PANTHER LIMA

The ill-fated Rio saloon had failed to tempt a new breed of buyer to Panther's cars, but this did not deter the company's irrepressible owner, Bob Jankel, from trying again. His second attempt at taking Panther towards the mainstream came in the form of the Lima, a retro-styled sports car made vaguely in the style of a Morgan, but based on modern running gear.

The main body tub was taken from the MG Midget, but, with no powerful Midget engines available, Jankel instead used the 2.3-litre (139cu in) Vauxhall Magnum slant-four – a unit renowned for being easy to tune and incredibly reliable.

It also used Vauxhall suspension and steering components, and was both agile and easy to drive as a result. Reasonable pricing ensured

that the Lima was a lot more accessible than earlier Panthers, especially when a deal was sealed with some Vauxhall dealers to sell the car through their showrooms.

Panther was taken over by a consortium of Korean businessmen in 1981, ending Jankel's association with the company he set up, and the car was developed further to become the Kallista, which looked

very similar to the Lima, but had a unique tubular steel chassis and Ford Cortina running gear.

ENGINE: 2279cc (139cu in), four-cylinder
POWER: 178bhp (133kW)
0–60MPH (96KM/H): 8.9 seconds
TOP SPEED: 202km/h (125mph)
PRODUCTION TOTAL: 918

FORD UK FIESTA

An unprecedented success for Ford and real milestone for the company's European arm, the original Fiesta was also an engineering milestone. It was the first front-wheel drive car that Ford had produced and came with a

Ford's first supermini quickly became a bestseller – almost two million first generation Fiestas were built, making it Ford's fastest-selling European model.

choice of transversely mounted small-capacity engines. The neat three-door body was the work of Ghia designer Tom Tjaarda – a man better known for penning sports cars than compact budget models.

Its introduction could not have been more timely, as it appeared in the middle of a global oil crisis, where the market for small and economical cars was booming. In traditional Ford style, the range was vast, with trim levels starting with the incredibly basic Popular,

which only had one sun visor, through Popular Plus, L, GL and the range-topping Ghia, which featured velour trim and wood door cappings. Sporty S models were also offered, but they differed from less youthful variants only in their styling, with bold side graphics and alloy wheels.

Fans had to wait until 1982 for a truly sporting Fiesta, which was called the XR2. Powered by Ford's 1598cc (98cu in) engine from the front-wheel drive Escort range, the

XR2 had revised suspension, fat tyres and Recaro sports seats. It lacked outright performance, but was easy to tune and became a popular choice in the burgeoning hot hatchback market.

ENGINE: 957cc (58cu in), 4-cylinder
POWER: 47bhp (35kW)
0–60MPH (96KM/H): 19 seconds
TOP SPEED: 127km/h (79mph)
PRODUCTION TOTAL: 1,750,000

LANCIA GAMMA

Originally planned as a joint project with Citroën, the Lancia Gamma was conceived as a large car for all of Europe. But the car suffered its first of many problems in 1972, four years before its launch, when French president Charles de Gaulle insisted that the collaboration be wound up as he felt that Citroën was sharing too much of its engineering knowledge with the Italians. This left Lancia to complete the project on its own.

The car was reengineered to feature a range of large flat-four engines of 2.0 litres (122cu in) and 2.5 litres (152cu in) in capacity, both of which would power the car's front wheels.

Two bodystyles were offered – a curvaceous but slightly awkward-looking saloon and a stunningly beautiful two-door coupé, both the work of Pininfarina. An estate (station wagon) and even a people-carrier, called the MegaGamma,

both went as far as the working prototype stage, but neither reached production.

Sadly for Lancia, the Gamma was blighted by build quality problems. To save space in the engine bay, the power steering pump was run by the same drivebelt as the camshaft, and, if the car was revved hard with the steering on full lock, the belt could slip off its teeth – with calamitous consequences. The Gamma's

engines were also prone to overheating problems. Neither of these issues was the tonic Lancia needed to mend its already badly bruised reputation.

ENGINE: 2484cc (152cu in), four-cylinder
POWER: 140bhp (104kW) at 5400rpm
0–60MPH (96KM/H): 9.7 seconds
TOP SPEED: 195km/h (121mph)
PRODUCTION TOTAL: 22,085

The lean and angular coupé was by far the most desirable incarnation of the Lancia Gamma line-up, although its spurious reliability put some buyers off: to save costs the power steering pump was run by the same drivebelt as the camshaft.

FERRARI 400 GT

ITALY 1976–85

Not one of the most memorable Ferraris, the 400 GT was developed for a market in which the manufacturer did not usually target its cars. Initially available only with automatic transmission, much to the horror of Ferrari traditionalists, it was essentially a revised 365 GTB Daytona – which angered Ferrari fans further by taking one of the company's most famous designs and giving it a new, less attractive look.

About the same size as a Jaguar XJS, the newcomer had hooded pop-up headlights to replace the Daytona's original lenses, while at the rear the separate light clusters were replaced by incongruous rectangular units. Power came from Ferrari's 4823cc (294cu in) V12 engine, which was an enlarged version of that in the 365 GTC/4 and required the Daytona bonnet (hood) to be lengthened, disturbing the styling harmony further.

The biggest shock, however, was the car's transmission – it was not even a Ferrari unit. The transmission was a very basic three-speed General Motors Hydramatic unit, found in mainstream Chevrolets and Buicks, and it did little to attract Ferrari buyers. Strangely, there was never an attempt to sell the car in the United States, where it might have proved popular, restricting the 400 GT's opportunities further.

After its first year, Ferrari offered a conventional manual version of the 400 GT, which enjoyed limited success, but at least rescued the model from near extinction.

ENGINE: 4823cc (294cu in), V12-cylinder
POWER: 340bhp (253kW)
0–60MPH (96KM/H): 7 seconds
TOP SPEED: 241km/h 150mph)
PRODUCTION TOTAL: 502

FERRARI 512BB

ITALY 1976–85

ENGINE: 4942cc (302cu in), 12-cylinder
POWER: 340bhp (253kW)
0–60MPH (96KM/H): 7 seconds
TOP SPEED: 282km/h (175mph)
PRODUCTION TOTAL: 1936

In a bid to match the success of rivals such as the Lamborghini Countach and Maserati Bora, Ferrari desperately needed a more dynamic mid-engined car in its

Easily identifiable by its huge orange lamp covers, the 512BB was Ferrari's first V12 engined model in years, and was mainly designed for motorsport.

line-up to match the success of its rivals' bigger models.

The new car would be called the BB, or Berlinetta Boxer, in which Boxer represented the horizontally opposed engine layout as found in the company's race cars. But the 365 GTB's engine was not good enough, as the environmental restrictions faced by the company meant that its power was vastly reduced from the glory days when it appeared in the likes of the Daytona and 365 GTC/4.

To rectify the situation, Ferrari increased the engine size to 5.0 litres (302cu in), actually losing 20bhp (12kW) in the process, but at the same time bestowing the car with much more mid-range torque, giving it a livelier performance under hard acceleration.

The new car was called the 512BB (the '5' stood for the engine's 5.0 litres and the '12' related to the number of cylinders). It was one of the prettiest Ferraris of the era, with prominent air ducts, low-slung bodywork (thanks to the engine's dry sump layout) and unusual amber driving lights incorporated flat against the car's nose for aerodynamic efficiency. The 521BB's engine was also a great technical advance for Ferrari, and went on to power the infamous Testarossa.

PORSCHE 924 GERMANY 1976–89

Porsche had already raised a few eyebrows by collaborating with VW to build the 914, so, when the 924 appeared in 1976, it caused even greater controversy. Not only was the new car another abandoned VW design, but it was also powered by a water-cooled VW engine, mounted in the front rather than aft of the rear axle, where Porsche traditionalists liked it.

Further ignominy came when customers learned that the VW engine in the 924 was not even from a car, but was a tuned-up version of the 2.0-litre (122cu in) straight-four unit fitted to the LT Transporter van.

Assembled for Porsche by Audi, the 924's overall build quality, affordable price and premium badge meant that, despite initial resistance, it earned itself a decent following over its life. It was good to drive, comfortable, sporty and practical. For many buyers, the opportunity to own a Porsche without any sense of compromise was appealing enough.

In 1978, Porsche proved the 924 had the company's true DNA by building a turbo version, with awesome performance and handling, while a pared-down lightweight Carrera GT was also briefly offered. The best standard models, though, came in 1985 and used a detuned 2.5-litre (153cu in) engine taken from the new 944. These cars offered excellent performance and great handling, and were great value for money.

ENGINE: 1984cc (121cu in), four-cylinder
POWER: 125bhp (93kW)
0–60MPH (96KM/H): 9.5 seconds
TOP SPEED: 203km/h (126mph)
PRODUCTION TOTAL: 138,586

It looked fairly smart, but Porsche fans were wary of the 924 as its engine was sourced from a Volkswagen van! Still, it had a decent following.

ROVER SD1 UNITED KINGDOM 1976–86

ENGINE: 3528cc (215cu in), V8-cylinder
POWER: 155bhp (115kW) at 5200rpm
0–60MPH (96KM/H): 8.4 seconds
TOP SPEED: 203km/h (126mph)
PRODUCTION TOTAL: 171,946

Rover's chief stylist David Bache openly admitted that the style of the SD1 was influenced by the Ferrari Daytona, which goes a long way towards explaining how the company's top-of-the-range hatchback came to have its rounded nose and wraparound indicator lenses. Styled to be as avant-garde as the P6 had been 13 years previously, the SD1 was charged

Rover stylist David Bache admitted that the SD1's sharp front end styling was influenced by the Ferrari Daytona.

with proving that Rover was still as innovative as it had been a decade earlier, despite being under the dubiously fragile wing of British Leyland.

The styling was futuristic, and the cabin's layout was also forward-thinking, with a clever instrument binnacle that could be moved from one side of the dash to the other, to reduce build costs for left- and right-hand drive markets.

In order to establish the SD1 as a premium model, Rover launched only one model to start with. That was the flagship 3500, using the 3.5-litre (215cu in) V8 engine from the P6 3500S; the four-cylinder P6s stayed in production for a short overlap period. In 1977, two straight-sixes joined the line-up. By the time production ceased in 1986, a 2.0-litre (122cu in) four-pot engine had appeared, along with a 2.4-litre (153cu in) turbo diesel.

Build quality problems blighted the earliest SD1s, but the car managed to pull its reputation back from the brink, and, towards the end, it was highly desirable. A face-lift in 1981 brought in front spoilers and softer front end styling, while in 1982 came the flagship 'Vitesse' performance models, which are highly prized by collectors today.

ASTON MARTIN LAGONDA

UNITED KINGDOM 1976–87

Penned by controversial designer William Towns, the shamelessly wedge-shaped Aston Martin Lagonda was far removed from the more traditional coupé models in the company's line-up.

Sick of being criticized for its old-fashioned styling, Aston Martin decided that the replacement for its Aston Martin V8–based Lagonda saloon would be the most modern car ever. On paper, it sounded sensational. A huge saloon car with distinctive wedge-shaped styling courtesy of William Towns, the Aston Martin Lagonda would come with all sorts of technology, including a fully digital dashboard, electric everything and automatic door locks should you forget to use the key.

The looks polarized opinion, but this was intentional. Aston Martin wanted the car to make a statement, and that it almost certainly did, drawing crowds from all over the world to its stand at the 1976 London Motor Show.

Making the car a technical tour de force was dangerous thinking, however, from a company that perpetually teetered on the brink of financial disaster, and, as Aston Martin did not have the money to invest in the most thorough of development programmes, the Lagonda stumbled into life without being thoroughly tested – and this led to a myriad of problems.

The LCD dashboards were a good idea, but the majority of them packed it in completely after just a few months, leaving most owners moderately disgruntled. Those who then found that their car had not so much automatically locked itself as become hermetically sealed, never to be accessed again, grew even more annoyed. The unfortunate few who, on top of this, went on to suffer the indignities of recumbent pop-up headlights and non-functioning electric windows were apoplectic with rage. This was a great shame because the Lagonda could have been one of the world's most amazing cars. Instead, it is remembered as a brave effort, but an ultimate failure.

ENGINE: 5340cc (326cu in), V8-cylinder
POWER: 280bhp (209kW)
0–60MPH (96KM/H): 8.8 seconds
TOP SPEED: 231km/h (143mph)
PRODUCTION TOTAL: 645

ALFA ROMEO ALFASUD SPRINT

ITALY 1976–90

Gorgeously pretty and brilliant to drive, the Alfasud Sprint was one of the best Italian cars of the 1970s, even if it did suffer from the same corrosion and electrical problems as the Alfasud with which it shared its floorpan. Styled by Giugiaro at the same time as the original 'Sud, the design languished for four years before being introduced to give the car a much-needed midlife popularity boost.

Engines and suspension were exactly the same as in the Alfasud, with the exception of the entry-level 1.2-litre (72cu in), which was

An even prettier version of the Alfasud, the Sprint was sadly blighted by the same rust-resilience issues.

not considered necessary in the sportier Sprint. A hatchback-style tailgate added practicality, and the car's quad-headlight front end made it look like a scaled-down GTV.

With fabulous handling, great steering and a seductive flat-four engine note, the Sprint was a driver's delight, for here was a car with all the usability of a family hatch in a beautiful compact bodyshell, complete with sportscar-like road manners – in other words, every inch an Alfa Romeo.

A face-lift in 1983 had a mixed reception, as the new plastic bumpers and front spoiler arguably spoilt the looks, but the new style did coincide with the introduction of the Sprint Veloce, which came with a 95bhp (71kW) version of the standard car's 1.5-litre (91cu in) engine, making it the pick of the range from a driver's perspective.

ENGINE: 1286cc (78cu in), four-cylinder
POWER: 76bhp (57kW)
0–96KM/H (60MPH): 13.1 seconds
TOP SPEED: 158km/h (99mph)
PRODUCTION TOTAL: 96,450

CHRYSLER LE BARON

UNITED STATES 1977–80

ENGINE: 3687cc (225cu in), eight-cylinder
POWER: 130bhp (97kW)
0–60MPH (96KM/H): 12 seconds
TOP SPEED: 185km/h (115mph)
PRODUCTION TOTAL: 360,000

The top model, the rather tacky-sounding Medallion, was aimed at Mercedes buyers and had deep-pile velour seats, a digital clock, fake wood dashboard inserts and electrically operated windows, air conditioning, electric mirrors and electrically adjustable seats. An estate (station wagon), the Town and Country, appeared in 1978. It added to the garishness with fake ash timber panels on the sides.

The most luxurious version, the 5th Avenue of 1980, had pintuck leather upholstery and a premium sound system. Despite Chrysler's best efforts, the Le Baron never challenged its true luxury rivals.

Not an especially upmarket brand, Chrysler decided it was still worthy of a share of the luxury-car market dominated by the likes of Cadillac and Mercedes-Benz. Its offering, the Le Baron, was based on the company's M-Car platform and was essentially the same as a Plymouth Volare under the skin, with a choice of six-cylinder or V8 engines, and a straightforward rear-drive, live rear axle layout, usually with automatic transmission.

Town and Country versions of the Le Baron were not aided by the addition of tacky, self-adhesive fake wood side panels.

CHRYSLER SUNBEAM

UNITED KINGDOM/FRANCE 1977–81

ENGINE: 928cc (57cu in), four-cylinder
POWER: 42bhp (31kW)
0–60MPH (96KM/H): 25 seconds
TOP SPEED: 123km/h (77mph)
PRODUCTION TOTAL: 104,547 plus 116,000 Talbots

Chrysler's response to the Ford Fiesta was developed in less than two years as a desperate attempt to play catch-up and become part of what had become a very lucrative market.

Badged Sunbeam, bringing back a name from the past, the car was neatly styled with smart, angular panel work that looked very similar to the Fiesta's, making it clear where Chrysler was headed with the project. Despite the modern looks, the Sunbeam relied very much on proven technology, with a shortened Avenger floorpan, rear

In the face of more modern rivals, the Chrysler Sunbeam was little more than a clever reskin of the Hillman Avenger.

leaf springs, a live rear axle and a range of old, underdeveloped engines including three overhead-valve units lifted directly from the Avenger. The entry level 928cc (57cu in) used an all-alloy engine derived from that in the Hillman Imp and was actually more popular with enthusiasts because of its free-revving nature. A Ti model appeared and was quite a decent performance hatchback, injecting much-needed life into the range, but the best version was yet to come.

Launched in 1979, the Sunbeam-Lotus used the 2.2-litre (134cu in) engine from the Lotus Esprit and was codeveloped with the sportscar maker for rally homologation purposes. A real beast, it was thrilling to drive, if a little tricky in the wet. In line with the rest of the former Chrysler range, the Sunbeam was rebadged Talbot in 1980.

MASERATI KYALAMI

ITALY 1977–83

After years of growing sales and bringing exciting cars to market, Maserati faced a bitter blow in 1975. Its owner, Citroën, had been taken over by Peugeot, and Maserati did not fit in with the newly formed PSA Peugeot-Citroën group's plans, so was immediately put into liquidation.

The marque's unlikely saviour came in the form of sports-car enthusiast and stalwart entrepreneur Alejandro de Tomaso, the boss of de Tomaso sports cars, whose passion for Italian sporting cars went way beyond his desire to make money. De Tomaso's vision was to make Maserati a little more mainstream, and a new model was introduced immediately.

The Kyalami looked familiar, largely because it was a de Tomaso Longchamp (itself a parody of the Mercedes-Benz SLC), with its front end restyled to incorporate quad headlights and Maserati's trademark trident grille badge. Other changes included a more ornate dashboard, greater interior luxury and a Maserati 4136cc (252cu in) V8 engine in place of the Longchamp's Ford-sourced powerplant. The Kyalami offered a new start for Maserati, but it was not a huge success. Only 150 cars were sold before production ceased in 1983.

ENGINE: 4136cc (252cu in), V8-cylinder
POWER: 270bhp (201kW) at 6000rpm
0–60MPH (96KM/H): 7.6 seconds
TOP SPEED: 237km/h (147mph)
PRODUCTION TOTAL: 150

MONTEVERDI SIERRA

SWITZERLAND 1977–84

By far the most conventional car that Peter Monteverdi ever made, the Sierra was a luxury saloon car that, much like the 375 and Hai models before it, was produced purely for Monteverdi's personal use, although he was happy to build them for customers if required. The Sierra was a three-box saloon based on the platform of the US Plymouth Volare, and used the same 5.2-litre (318cu in) Chrysler V8 engine and Torqueflite three-speed automatic transmission.

The large slab-sided panels were simple, but somehow still managed to look alluring, giving the car the appearance of an oversized Fiat 130 Coupé. The car was first shown at the 1977 Geneva Motor Show, and at least three cars were made between 1977 and 1984, as Monteverdi was seen driving three different ones himself. No records were kept of any other vehicles, so the final production total is unclear – although the high list price would have certainly limited the Sierra's appeal.

ENGINE: 5210cc (318cu in), eight-cylinder
POWER: 180bhp (134kW)
0–60MPH (96KM/H): n/a
TOP SPEED: 210km/h (130mph)
PRODUCTION TOTAL: n/a

ALFA ROMEO GIULIETTA

ITALY 1977–85

Built to complement rather than replace the Alfetta, the smaller Giulietta revived a famous name from the past. Under the skin, it used a truncated Alfetta platform, complete with the same unusual but effective rear transaxle and de Dion suspension set-up, which more than made up for its dull looks with impressive handling.

Two engines were plucked from the rest of the Alfa range in both 1.3-litre (78cu in) and 1.8-litre (110cu in) form. Each delivered willing performance, but it was the smaller engined car that was the more rewarding to drive, as its twin-cam powerplant was so free-revving and eager that it encouraged a committed driving style.

A face-lift in 1981 removed some of the Giulietta's angular appearance and made it more attractive, drawing attention to its unusual kicked-up rear end. Popular in southern Europe, the Giulietta failed to penetrate many other markets, but was still a successful model for Alfa Romeo.

ENGINE: 1570cc (96cu in), four-cylinder
POWER: 109bhp (81kW)
0–60MPH (96KM/H): 10.5 seconds
TOP SPEED: 168km/h (105mph)
PRODUCTION TOTAL: 379,689

Thanks to its clever rear transaxle, the Giulietta's handling benefited from excellent weight distribution.

CHRYSLER HORIZON

UK/FRANCE 1977–85

Although it looked very similar to the smaller Sunbeam, the Chrysler Horizon was completely new under the skin and was based on the floorpan of the French Simca 1100. It was an aged design, but the Simca had tidy handling and was a fun car to drive.

The Horizon replaced the 1100 and rear-engined Simca 1000 on its launch, but Chrysler also drew on a number of elements of the larger Alpine for the new hatchback, including its engine range. This meant the same 1.1-litre (67cu in), 1.3-litre (79cu in) and 1.5-litre

(91cu in) overhead-valve engines, as well as torsion bar suspension.

The Horizon also had similar refinements to the Alpine in the form of electric windows and velour trim. Inside, the cabin was well trimmed and spacious, with a generous load area and better standard equipment than many of its rivals, but it was never especially innovative and there were no performance models on offer.

Like all Chrysler models, the name was changed to Talbot after Peugeot took over Chrysler's European operation in the late 1970s, although Chrysler retained the rights to the design, and the company built the car as both a Plymouth Horizon and a Dodge Omni for sale in the United States.

ENGINE: 1118cc (68cu in), four-cylinder
POWER: 59/68bhp (44/51kW)
0–60MPH (96KM/H): 15 seconds
TOP SPEED: 152km/h (95mph)
PRODUCTION TOTAL: 50,000, plus 51,320 Talbots

PORSCHE 928

GERMANY 1977–86

Porsche originally intended for the 928 to be a replacement for the 911, but the demand for the iconic original model was such that it remained in production unabated. Instead, Porsche touted the 928 as a luxury grand tourer, and the flagship of its range.

Underneath the cleanly styled if somewhat rounded lines was an all-new 4.7-litre (285cu in) water-cooled V8 engine, which offered exceptionally smooth and flexible performance, while unusual features included odd-looking revolving headlights and trapezoid side windows, plus a rounded rump with separate housings for each of the rear lights.

The majority of 928s came with four-speed automatic gearboxes, as the prodigious torque output made the optional manual gearbox somewhat baulky to operate, although the manual option was taken up by a more traditional breed of Porsche buyer.

The 928's power was increased to 310bhp (231kW) in 1979, when the car received a slight face-lift, while a 5.0-litre (305cu in) 928S model was to become the range's flagship in 1988. In 1995, at the end of an impressive 17-year career, a limited-run 5.4-litre (330cu in) model was introduced that produced 350bhp (261kW). Today, it is the most prized of all the 928 variants.

ENGINE: 4664cc (285cu in), V8-cylinder
POWER: 310bhp (231kW)
0–60MPH (96KM/H): 6.3 seconds
TOP SPEED: 250km/h (155mph)
PRODUCTION TOTAL: 39,210

Porsche's first V8, water-cooled engined car, the 28, successfully combined performance and luxury.

MASERATI QUATTROPORTE III

ITALY 1977–90

Given some of the striking designs produced under the auspices of Citroën, Maserati's new models under Alejandro De Tomaso started to appear uninspiring. The Quattroporte was very luxurious, but bland.

Alejandro de Tomaso's second project at the helm of Maserati was to revive the Quattroporte name and apply it to a big but keenly priced luxury saloon aimed at broadening the Maserati's appeal.

The Quattroporte III was developed on a tight budget, so underneath the new car's angular Giugiaro-styled bodywork sat the platform and 5.0-litre (306cu in) Ford V8 engine as fitted to the de Tomaso Deauville. After the first handful of cars was built, Maserati reverted to its 4.1-litre (252cu in) and 4.9-litre (301cu in) units.

Despite its humble origins, the Quattroporte III was quite a composed car to drive and acquired a small but steady following over the years. The smaller engine was dropped in 1985, and, in 1989, the car was renamed the Royale, as Maserati was planning an all-new Quattroporte, based on the BiTurbo, which had debuted in 1981.

The most unusual versions of the Quattroporte III were hand-built by Italian company SD Coachbuilding, which offered a stretched version with hand-trimmed ostrich leather interior and a privacy divider between the cabin's front and rear.

ENGINE: 4930cc (301cu in), eight-cylinder
POWER: 288bhp (215kW) at 5600rpm
0–60MPH (96KM/H): 9.3 seconds
TOP SPEED: 198km/h (123mph)
PRODUCTION TOTAL: n/a

TVR 3000S

UNITED KINGDOM 1978–79

TVR's shortest-lived model, although you would be hard pressed to tell it apart from any later cars, the 3000S was sold for one year only between 1978 and 1979. Never officially known as the 3000S (a name retrospectively applied by students of the TVR marque), the car was officially sold as the TVR Convertible. It was a drophead version of the 3000M, shorter than the Taimar, but with an otherwise identical front from the windscreen pillars forwards.

The rear end was redesigned to allow for a flat rear boot (trunk) and space to stow the hood, while the cabin was especially cramped by virtue of the need to house the gearbox bellhousing and TVR's trademark steel backbone chassis. This remained unchanged from the original Grantura, but still blessed the car with impeccable handling and a firm but sporting ride.

Like the Taimar, and countless other TVRs old and new, power came from Ford's 3.0-litre (183cu in) 'Essex' V6 engine, although a handful of Convertibles were offered with a turbo conversion, boosting the power output to 230bhp (171kW). The 3000S was dropped in 1979 in readiness for the all new wedge-shaped Taimar, but its basic shape would reappear in 1986 in the new TVR S series.

ENGINE: 2994cc (183cu in), six-cylinder
POWER: 138bhp (103kW)
0–60MPH (96KM/H): 7.7 seconds
TOP SPEED: 200km/h (125mph)
PRODUCTION TOTAL: 258

DATSUN 280ZX

JAPAN 1978–83

If the 260Z had been evidence that there was little wrong with the original 240Z concept, then the 280ZX was categorical proof. Unlike its predecessor, the newcomer evolved the 240Z's original concept a step too far, putting on weight, growing in length and girth, and pandering to the needs of new safety and emissions legislation, which saw it sprout ugly plastic impact bumpers and a catalytic converter in the US market, where it was expected the bulk of sales would be.

Although a competent GT, with enough power from its 2753cc (168cu in) straight-six engine to sound quite healthy on paper at 140bhp(104kW), the 280ZX was dreadfully slow. It took 11 seconds to reach 60mph (96km/h) from rest and had a top speed of only 180km/h (112mph). The car's cabin was also ruined, with new soft plastics on the dashboard, velour trim and the option of automatic transmission.

To try to add a little excitement to the range, Datsun decided to offer a T-Top removable roof, and, in 1981, a turbocharged model was introduced to try to give performance a boost. A wide range of body and styling kits were also available to try to disguise the gruesome bumpers.

Although the 280ZX could not be considered a sales disaster by any means, in terms of the Datsun Z car range, it certainly epitomized the slow and steady decay of the character that had defined the original 240Z model.

ENGINE: 2753cc (168cu in), six-cylinder
POWER: 140bhp (104kW)
0–60MPH (96KM/H): 11 seconds
TOP SPEED: 180km/h (112mph)
PRODUCTION TOTAL: 414,358

A good seller, but not a good Z-car. The 280ZX was an emaciated, underpowered and poorly finished pretender to the 240Z's throne. Slow and sluggish it marked a major step back.

MATRA RANCHO

FRANCE 1978–84

A car ahead of its times in many ways, the Matra Rancho was an unusual car that tried in vain to carve a niche for itself. A niche that, ironically, is today one of the most lucrative areas of the new car market. In the Rancho's day, however, it certainly was not.

Mechanically, the car was a 1442cc (88cu in) version of the Simca 1100 saloon and shared the French car's front bodywork, but from the doors backwards it was entirely new, with a tall rear end, large glass area and chunky black body mouldings which gave the car the appearance of an off-roader, even though it was just a two-wheel drive Simca underneath. Immensely practical with its split tailgate, huge load bay and excellent rear passenger space, the Rancho still failed to reach its peak. It was decent to drive, reliable and surprisingly durable, but buyers failed to cotton on to the car's appeal. In 1984, it was quietly dropped, just ahead of the quiet revolution that was slowly forming in the pseudo-SUV market.

If the Rancho was not a success, at least it was a car that started a massively successful trend.

ENGINE: 1442cc (88cu in), four-cylinder
POWER: 78bhp (58kW)
0–60MPH (96KM/H): 12 seconds
TOP SPEED: 144km/h (90mph)
PRODUCTION TOTAL: 56,700

JEEP CJ-7

Jeep's CJ model was previously marketed as a military vehicle only, but the company realized the vehicle's commercial appeal in the late 1970s and introduced a civilian variant. To all intents and purposes the same as the military vehicle, the CJ-7 had a few additional creature comforts and concessions to its new retail environment.

The CJ's simple separate chassis and basic bodywork remained, complete with trademark seven-slat radiator grille, while underneath it retained twin live axles and selectable four-wheel drive. The car was usually driven by its rear wheels only, but a separate lever in the cabin could be used to engage drive to the front axle when the going got slippery.

Inside, the car's seats and dashboard were made more user-friendly for civilian purposes, while the 4.2-litre (258cu in) or 5.0-litre (304cu in) engines were offered in a higher state of tune for on-road use.

Jeep was taken over by American Motors in 1980 and again by Chrysler in 1987, during which time the CJ-7 remained in production. In 1988, the CJ was replaced by the Wrangler, which was effectively the same vehicle but with new, square headlights and a newer drivetrain. It remains in production to date, with no signs of demand abating.

ENGINE: 4235cc (258cu in),
V8-cylinder
POWER: 110bhp (82kW)
0–60MPH (96KM/H): 14.1 seconds
TOP SPEED: 149km/h (93mph)
PRODUCTION TOTAL: n/a

Originally built for military use, the Jeep soon found itself plying its trade as a civilian fashion accessory.

MAZDA RX-7

Mazda's persistence with rotary power finally paid off with their rival to the Porsche 924, the RX-7, a car that sold successfully in both Europe and America despite its unusual engine type.

Mazda revisited the rotary engine theme with its Porsche 924 rival, the RX-7, launched in 1978. The RX-7 was by far the most successful commercial application of the rotary engine until Mazda's RX-8 debuted in 2002, and not without good reason. For a start, the twin rotary Wankel engine was truly reliable for the first time, with none of the rotor seal tip wear that had blighted earlier cars.

More than that, however, the RX-7 was a great sports car.

The car's engine provided good performance and incredibly smooth acceleration, albeit at the expense of fuel economy, while the car's light weight made for agile and responsive handling. A power boost came in 1981, lifting the power from 105bhp (78kW) to 115bhp (86kW). In 1983, Mazda unleashed a lively turbocharged

variant, with 165bhp (123kW), boosting performance yet further.

The car's neat looks remained unchanged until 1987, when a new RX-7 was launched using the same platform. With rounder front and rear styling and the option of a convertible body, the new car still had plenty of appeal . It also came with a new generation of rotary engine, producing 148bhp (110kW), along with independent

rear suspension. The RX-7 was a great car that deserved to sell the half a million units it managed over a 14-year production life.

ENGINE: 573cc (35cu in),
twin-rotor Wankel
POWER: 105bhp (78kW)
0–60MPH (96KM/H): 8.4 seconds
TOP SPEED: 181km/h (113mph)
PRODUCTION TOTAL: 474,565

OPEL MONZA

ENGINE: 2968cc (181cu in),
six-cylinder
POWER: 180bhp (134kW)
0–60MPH (96KM/H): 8.5 seconds
TOP SPEED: 215km/h (133mph)
PRODUCTION TOTAL: 43,500

With the Commodore coupé advancing in years and no sign of a drop in demand for big GTs in the German market, Opel decided to build an all-new car on the platform of the 3.0-litre (181cu in) Senator saloon. Called the Monza, the cleanly styled car made its debut in 1978 and was truly huge, with an incredibly spacious cabin and plenty of luggage space in its cleverly designed hatchback rear end.

The Monza's size, and resultant weight, did not detract from the car's performance aspirations in any way because the 3.0-litre

Although based on the platform of a luxury saloon car, the Monza was an exciting car to drive, with good performance, and self-assured handling.

powerplant had so much torque that you simply did not notice. Acceleration and outright top speed were impressive, whether fed to the rear wheels through a manual or automatic gearbox.

For 1983, the Monza was given a face-lift that ushered in a new, rounder front end and fuel injection, increasing performance further and extending the production run as far as 1986, by which time the

big coupé market across Europe had dwindled considerably. As a footnote, the car was also sold in the United Kingdom as the Vauxhall Royale – a car that differed from the Monza by badge alone.

RENAULT 5 TURBO

Not to be confused with the later front-wheel drive 5 Turbo, the first of the breed was a mid-engined special built specifically for rally homologation.

Surprisingly, it kept the standard 5's 1.4-litre (89cu in) engine, but significantly modified and turbocharged to produce a mighty 160bhp (119kW), although the engine was mounted directly in the middle of the car to ensure perfect weight distribution. Power was fed to the rear wheels through a close-ratio five-speed gearbox,

As chic as a normal Renault 5 to look at, but significantly more aggressive to drive, the early rear-wheel drive 5 Turbo was a fabulous road car as well as a rallying success.

and weight was kept to a minimum, thanks to aluminium doors, bonnet (hood) and tailgate panels.

Although it was immediately recognizable as a Renault 5, the Turbo differed by being much wider, with bulbous front rear wheelarches and fattened-out rear wings (fenders), These incorporated huge air scoops to suck cool air into the engine.

If you could forgive the cramped and hot cockpit, the 5 Turbo was incredibly easy to drive, unlike most rally-derived cars. Such was demand for the car from the public that, in 1983, a Turbo 2 version was introduced, even though the 5's rally career was at an end. The Turbo 2 differed from the original because the panels were all steel. Also, the cabin was more comfortable, as it was no longer a homologation special.

ENGINE: 1397cc (85cu in), four-cylinder
POWER: 160bhp (119kW)
0–60MPH (96KM/H): 7.7 seconds
TOP SPEED: 218km/h (135mph)
PRODUCTION TOTAL: 5007

RENAULT 18 TURBO

FRANCE 1978–87

On the back of its reputation for effective turbocharging, led largely by the success of the 5 Turbo in rallying, Renault decided to offer this technology to the masses in the humble 18 saloon.

The standard 18 was not an especially interesting car, offered as a conventional, comfortable and fairly pleasant family saloon or estate (station wagon). It was certainly never a machine to set the pulse racing. A sporty model at the top of the range was just what Renault needed to add some spice to the 18's sales recipe, and the end result was interesting, to say the least.

Externally, the car differed little from a standard 18, save for its Turbo side graphics, black rubber boot (trunk) spoiler and unusual slatted alloy wheels, but under the bonnet (hood) lived a much-modified version of the standard car's 1.6-litre (97cu in) engine.

The powerplant was beefed up with the aid of a Garrett T3 turbocharger, which upped its output to 125bhp (93kW). That may not sound a lot in modern terms, but the effect on the lightweight 18 was dramatic, giving it a 0–60mph (96km/h) sprint time of less than 10 seconds. It was the way the power was delivered that was most surprising, with huge turbo lag at first, followed by squealing tyres, torque steer and a rather brutal amount of thrust. Not refined by any stretch of the imagination, the 18 was a precursor of the many turbocharged family cars on the market today.

ENGINE: 1565cc (96cu in), four-cylinder
POWER: 125bhp (93kW)
0–60MPH (96KM/H): 9.9 seconds
TOP SPEED: 195km/h (121mph)
PRODUCTION TOTAL: n/a

SAAB 900

SWEDEN 1979–93

Safety, unusual styling, turbocharged power and all-round innovation were what people had come to expect from Saab, so its no surprise to learn that all of these elements were encompassed in the 900 saloon, designed to offer a more luxurious alternative to the compact 99.

The 900 was based on the 99's floorpan, but with a lengthened platform and wheelbase, and even longer bodywork to allow the Saab to incorporate crumple zones and energy-absorbing safety bumpers.

Four bodystyles were offered – two- and four-door saloons, and three- and five-door hatchbacks, making the 900 one of the most versatile cars in its class.

It was also one of the best to drive, with surefooted handling, ample performance and exceptional comfort, although some of Saab's styling cues, such as the doors that wrapped round over the sills and the floor-mounted ignition lock barrel, were just plain weird.

The best-known and highest regarded 900 is the Turbo model, introduced in 1981, which accounted for more than half of 900 sales overall. There was also an exceptionally pretty cabriolet, introduced in 1986, which remained on price lists as late as 1995.

ENGINE: 1985cc (121cu in), four-cylinder
POWER: 100bhp (75kW)
0–60MPH (96KM/H): 13.3 seconds
TOP SPEED: 161km/h (100mph)
PRODUCTION TOTAL: 908,810

Replacing cars wasn't something Saab did very often, which meant the 900 remained on sale for 16 years, although it was fundamentally based on the Saab 99, which dated back a further decade. It featured the usual Saab characteristics of safety, unusual styling and turbocharged power.

MIDAS BRONZE

In styling terms at least, the Midas Bronze was a revival of the ill-fated Mini-Marcos, reviving all of the car's body panels and built on similar principles with a BMC A-Series engine and Mini subframes.

It was a weird car to look at, but the Midas was a hoot to drive, thanks to its Mini-based powertrain and underpinnings.

Despite the similarities, the two cars were significantly different to drive. Engineered by McLaren racing product manager Harold McDermott, with the help of Gordon Murray, who went on to design the sensational McLaren F1 supercar, the Midas Bronze was brilliantly conceived. The car had excellent steering, limpet-like grip and sensational handling, much of which was down to some incredibly clever

Formula One–derived under-car aerodynamics, which were not immediately visible, but gave considerably more downforce than you would have been able to get from an original Mini-Marcos.

Enthusiasts could easily forgive the ungainly looks and flimsy-feeling construction because of the incredible driving characteristics, especially when the last-of-the-line models were fitted with a 100bhp

(74kW) engine from the MG Metro Turbo, giving the Bronze enough power to embarrass many a more potent sports car on the right road.

ENGINE: 1275cc (78cu in), four-cylinder
POWER: 76bhp (57kW)
0–60MPH (96KM/H): 11 seconds
TOP SPEED: 161km/h (100mph)
PRODUCTION TOTAL: n/a

BMW M1

Originally planned to race in endurance racing, although the idea never came to fruition, the BMW M1 was nevertheless a great car of its era. As an alternative to more exotic machinery, such as

the Ferrari 308 or Lamborghini Uracco, the M1 was a bold-looking and imposing two-door coupé, featuring a mid-mounted engine, angular Giugiaro-designed bodywork and the exceptional

build quality for which BMW had become regarded.

The engine was a turbocharged 3.5-litre (211cu in) straight-six, developing 277bhp (206kW), which would later go on to power other

BMW road cars, including the M535i and 635CSi coupé. The M1 was also the first M-badged BMW, so that it created a legend of its own, which even today is worn proudly by the German firm's top-performing models across its model range.

The M1 was great to drive and had awesome performance, but it did not have the easiest start in life. The company's own plants were geared up for mass production, so a low-volume supercar was not something that was easily integrated into the production schedules. This meant that most of them were assembled by coachbuilders Baur, with parts built and developed by Italian suppliers, including Lamborghini.

ENGINE: 3453cc (211cu in), six-cylinder
POWER: 277bhp (206kW)
0–60MPH (96KM/H): 5.5 seconds
TOP SPEED: 260km/h (161mph)
PRODUCTION TOTAL: 456

A huge and costly diversion for BMW, the M1 never enjoyed the motorsport success expected of it, although it became a hugely desirable road car.

BMW M535I

If the M1 was the first BMW M-car, then it was the M535i that would set the precedent for all future versions of the M line-up. Based on the E28 5-Series saloon, the M535i was a subtle-looking but no less

A cracking drive and the first of the M-Power saloon car series, it's surprising that enthusiasm for the M535i isn't greater.

exciting version, using a 218bhp (162kW) version of the M1's 3.5-litre (211cu in) engine.

The car's power was fed to the rear wheels via a five-speed manual gearbox, which used a dog-leg arrangement for the first ratio, in the style of many contemporary supercars. Uprated brakes and a unique suspension system that was developed for BMW by damper manufacturers

Bilstein added further to the M535's capabilities.

Much of the M535i's appeal came from its stealth; externally, the car looked little different from a standard 5-Series, despite its monumental performance and incredible handling agility. The only differences were a small chin spoiler, wider alloy wheels and an optional rear spoiler. Inside were sports front seats and a replica M1

steering wheel. The M535i was one of the most competent BMW M-Cars and was certainly the most subtle of the lot.

ENGINE: 3453cc (211cu in), six-cylinder
POWER: 218bhp (162kW)
0–60MPH (96KM/H): 7.1 seconds
TOP SPEED: 224km/h (139mph)
PRODUCTION TOTAL: 1650

TRIUMPH TR8

Heavily criticized for not making the TR7 butch enough to be a true TR sports car, Triumph developed the TR8 in order to try to make the car appeal to those who felt the current range offered nothing to suit them.

Effectively a TR7 that was reengineered to accommodate the 3.5-litre (215cu in) Rover V8 engine, the TR8 took four years to bring to market and was initially planned to be sold in the United States only, although several right-hand drive models slipped through the net and were sold unofficially in the United Kingdom.

But Triumph, it seemed, just could not win. When it finally announced the TR8 in 1979, it was

If only Triumph had fitted the V8 engine from the start, the TR7 project could have been a greater success.

on the cusp of another energy crisis, when demand for large-engined cars was again in freefall.

This was a real shame because the TR8 unleashed the latent potential of the TR7. Thanks to stiffened suspension and sharper steering, the TR8 was a lively and exciting car to drive, although the nose-heavy weight distribution did make the back end a little twitchy in the wet.

Sadly, however, the TR8's days were already numbered, and, in 1981, production stopped after fewer than 2500 cars were built. Today, several more TR8s exist than were officially built, largely due to enthusiasts adapting standard TR7s to V8 power – an easy and popular conversion.

ENGINE: 3528cc (215cu in), V8-cylinder
POWER: 137bhp (102kW) at 5000rpm
0–96KM/H (60MPH): 8.4 seconds
TOP SPEED: 193km/h (120mph)
PRODUCTION TOTAL: 2497

SUZUKI SC100 WHIZZKID

JAPAN 1978–82

Suzuki's smallest model, and by far one of its most interesting, the SC100 debuted at the 1971 Tokyo Motor Show as a Giugiaro styling concept. It would take another seven years before the car would go into production, powered by a 574cc (35cu in) rear-mounted engine for its domestic market. Suzuki realized that, to bring the car to Europe, the SC100, or Whizzkid, as it became affectionately known, needed more performance, so it was modified to accept a 970cc (59cu in) all-alloy four-cylinder unit developing 47bhp (35kW), which gave the car enough power to reach a top speed of 131km/h (81mph).

The unusual looks did little for practicality, with a cramped cockpit, limited front luggage space and a tiny fuel tank, but this failed to put people off. Certainly the 2000 cars a year imported into the United Kingdom were quickly snapped up.

Much of the car's appeal came from it's engine layout – with rear-wheel drive and the powerplant mounted aft of the rear axle, it had handling characteristics that resembled those of a Porsche 911, but could be driven at much safer speeds. Sadly for fans of the model, Suzuki replaced it in 1982 with the utterly conventional Alto hatchback – a car with no redeeming features whatsoever, and not a worthy successor.

ENGINE: 970cc (59cu in),
four-cylinder
POWER: 47bhp (35kW)
0–60MPH (96KM/H): 17.3 seconds
TOP SPEED: 131km/h (81mph)
PRODUCTION TOTAL: 894,000
(all models)

AC 3000 ME

UNITED KINGDOM 1979–84

The thinking behind AC's 3000 ME was good enough – a mid-engined, Ford-powered affordable sports car clad in a smart glassfibre body, and assembled by one of the most established and evocative names in the business. It was first shown in prototype form at the 1973 London Motor Show as the Diablo Concept, but it would be six years before the ME was finally ready for production. Initially, it was planned that the car would sell for between £3000 and £4000, and would be on sale within a year.

Constantly changing legislation, AC's financial troubles and a generally slow development process kept knocking the car back and pushing the development cost up. By the time it appeared, the car cost £13,000. Even factoring in the meteoric inflation rises of the era, that was a massive sum more than AC originally planned. Buyers were not exactly forthcoming.

Added to that, the 3000 was by now out of date, while road testers criticized its poor ride, average performance and lack of handling composure when compared to contemporary rivals from TVR and Lotus. In 1973, production ceased prematurely, when AC fell into receivership. While the company returned, the car never did.

ENGINE: 2994cc (183cu in),
six-cylinder
POWER: 138bhp (103kW)
0–60MPH (96KM/H): 8.5 seconds
TOP SPEED: 202km/h (125mph)
PRODUCTION TOTAL: 82

After spending far too much time in gestation, the 3000ME nearly bankrupted AC. It also ended up costing significantly more to buy than the British firm had originally intended. But the intentions behind it – a Ford-powered, affordable, glassfibre-bodied sports car – was sound enough.

ALFA ROMEO SIX

With rivals such as BMW and Mercedes running away with the executive-car market, Alfa Romeo tried to react with the Six, a large, well-appointed saloon with a big V6 engine, automatic transmission and leather trim.

The styling came from Bertone, but was not especially dynamic, favouring a traditional three-box layout. Also, Alfa Romeo could never get the large chassis to handle properly – it was prone to understeer and had a bouncy, rather uncomfortable ride.

The Six's only saving grace was the V6 engine, borrowed from the GTV6 and just as wonderful here as anywhere else, although the other options – a 2.0-litre (122cu in) four-pot and a turbodiesel – did little to increase the car's appeal in an increasingly demanding market.

Only a handful more than 12,000 Sixes were made between 1979 and 1987. At this point, the car was replaced by the infinitely more desirable and far more successful 164 range.

ENGINE: 2492cc (152cu in), six-cylinder
POWER: 158bhp (118kW)
0–60MPH (96KM/H): 11.4 seconds
TOP SPEED: 194km/h (121mph)
PRODUCTION TOTAL: 12,288

MITSUBISHI COLT LANCER 2000 TURBO

Most cars that begin a trend end up being hero-worshipped by those who adore their successes. In the case of the Mitsubishi Colt Lancer 2000 Turbo, this is not that car. In fact, today the car is largely forgotten – yet its influence on motoring was immense.

The 2000 Turbo was the seminal hot Mitsubishi Lancer – the original forebear of the incredibly successful Evo models for which the company became famous both in showrooms and across rally circuits during the 1990s and early twenty-first century. It was not as technically advanced as its modern-day successors, using a fairly ordinary 2.0-litre (122cu in) overhead-cam engine, onto which Mitsubishi attached a turbocharger of its own design. The end result was an astonishing 168bhp (125kW). As long as you could cope with the immense turbo lag and torque steer, you could propel the Lancer from a standstill to 60mph (96km/h) more quickly than a Jaguar XJS, and on to a top speed of more than 210km/h (130mph) – remarkable for its day.

The 2000 Turbo was Mitsubishi's first real performance car, as well as its first to compete successfully in rallying. It sowed the seeds for a bold future and is one of the most significant sports saloons of its era.

ENGINE: 1997cc (122cu in), four-cylinder
POWER: 168bhp (125kW)
0–60MPH (96KM/H): 8.6 seconds
TOP SPEED: 205km/h (127mph)
PRODUCTION TOTAL: n/a

The forefather of today's breed of Japanese super-saloons, the Lancer Turbo was very much the equivalent in its day of the company's fabled Evo models today. The car is largely forgotten today, but its influence has been immense.

FERRARI 400I

Replacing the 400GT, but looking almost identical, the 400i appeared in 1979 and used a new Bosch K-Jetronic fuel injection system, which actually reduced power of this already unpopular model by 30bhp (10kW) to 310bhp (231kW). In a further move towards comfort, Ferrari dropped the manual gearbox option from the GT and revised the car's suspension, offering a self-levelling rear set-up and making it the softest sprung Ferrari model ever.

The car's cabin was made more luxurious, too, with big leather seats, split-level air conditioning, electrically adjustable seats, electric windows and a larger boot (trunk), plus increased rear legroom.

Not Ferrari's finest hour, the 400 GT was a car with an identity crisis: a grand tourer that tried too hard to be a sports car.

Power steering and standard ABS brakes went a stage further to reduce driver input – an unusual move from a manufacturer that built its reputation on sports, racing and supercars.

Naturally, Ferrari's traditional fans were horrified that their beloved marque had created a car that was so obviously built for comfort and

not for speed, but there was plenty of method behind Ferrari's apparent madness. After all, the 400 GT was an awkward compromise – performance enthusiasts thought it too bulky and sloppy to drive, and those looking for a big luxury GT thought it was too cramped and compromised. It was a formula that evidently worked, for more

than five times as many 400is were sold as 400 GTs.

ENGINE: 4942cc (302cu in), 12-cylinder
POWER: 340bhp (253kW)
0–60MPH (96KM/H): 6.7 seconds
TOP SPEED: 249km/h (155mph)
PRODUCTION TOTAL: 2558

RENAULT FUEGO

Launched as Renault's answer to the Ford Capri and Opel Manta, the Renault Fuego was styled by ex-Citroën designer Robert Opron, which may explain why its glass 'clamshell' rear hatch was similar to that of the legendary Citroën SM.

Built on the Renault 18 floorpan, it was not especially dynamic to drive, but it was pretty to look at, was reliable and was well equipped.

Even the basic models came with remote control central locking – a world first on a production car.

Like its key rivals, the Fuego was available with a wider range of engines, from a basic 1.4-litre (85cu in) unit up to a flagship 2.0-litre (122cu in) powerplant, which was introduced in 1981. One of the more intriguing variants was the Fuego Turbo, which used the

1565cc (96cu in) engine from the 18 Turbo and had even faster acceleration (plus even more violent turbo lag), and a top speed in excess of 210km/h (130mph).

Bizarrely, the Fuego was one of Renault's most successful exports. It was sold in the United States under the AMC brand, and, after French production ceased in 1984, tooling was shipped to Argentina,

where the Fuego not only lasted until the mid-1990s, but also was the country's best-selling car.

ENGINE: 1647cc (100cu in), four-cylinder
POWER: 64bhp (40kW)
0–60MPH (96KM/H): 11.2 seconds
TOP SPEED: 172km/h (107mph)
PRODUCTION TOTAL: 265,257

MATRA MURENA

Based on the Bagheera and sharing most of its unusual body panels, the Matra Murena incorporated few aerodynamic changes that reduced its drag coefficient to just 032cd, making it one of the most air-efficient cars of its generation. This did not improve performance, however, because the car's body was now made out of steel rather than

glassfibre, which increased the weight considerably.

Other changes included new coil-sprung front suspension to replace the original torsion bars and a new 2.2-litre (132cu in) Chrysler-sourced engine, which produced 118bhp (88kW) and offered greater fuel economy. The unusual three-abreast seating layout remained, however, and the

car's distinctive profile was as it always had been.

The car was also sold in some markets as a Talbot, as Matra had been absorbed by the PSA Peugeot-Citroën-Talbot conglomerate in the late 1970s. The Murena went out of production in 1984, though, when Matra was bought from PSA by Renault and supplies of the engine stopped, as Matra focused

itself on developing the all-new and much more profitable Renault Espace people-carrier.

ENGINE: 1592cc (97cu in), four-cylinder
POWER: 118bhp (88kW)
0–60MPH (96KM/H): 9.3 seconds
TOP SPEED: 194km/h (121mph)
PRODUCTION TOTAL: 10,613

Effectively an updated version of the original Bagheera, the Murena was Matra's last stab at a sports car of its own, although it did later build the Alpine A610 for Renault. Sold in some markets as a Talbot, as in the late 70s Matra had been absorbed by Peugeot-Citroën-Talbot.

BRISTOL BEAUFIGHTER

UNITED KINGDOM 1980–90

Despite the many criticisms levelled at the slab-sided 412 when it appeared in 1975, Bristol decided to persist with the basic shape as it entered the 1980s, and commissioned the Beaufighter as an updated version. Named after the company's legendary World War II aircraft, the Beaufighter used all of Bristol's traditional design cues, including its archaic ladder frame chassis, alloy panelled body and traditional Chrysler V8 engine.

There were also some new developments. The V8 engine was turbocharged, giving plenty more horsepower – although nobody knows quite how much because, like Rolls-Royce, Bristol had by this point stopped releasing outputs and stated that the Beaufighter simply had 'enough' power. It certainly felt quick from behind the wheel, albeit in a slightly unnerving softly sprung way.

Other changes included a new four-headlight front end, replacing the old Ford Granada lights with those from a Toyota Celica. A glass lift-out roof panel also meant that the Beaufighter could be enjoyed as either a coupé or a convertible.

ENGINE: 5900cc (360cu in), V8-cylinder
POWER: n/a
0–60MPH (96KM/H): 5.9 seconds
TOP SPEED: 242km/h (150mph)
PRODUCTION TOTAL: n/a

TVR TASMIN

UNITED KINGDOM 1980–90

ENGINE: 2792cc (170cu in), six-cylinder
POWER: 160bhp (119kW)
0–60MPH (96KM/H): 7.7 seconds
TOP SPEED: 201km/h (125mph)
PRODUCTION TOTAL: 2563

After sticking with essentially the same body shape for more than 20 years, TVR decided to do something dramatically different for the 1980s. Enter the Tasmin – a distinctively pointy, wedge-shaped machine with pop-up headlights, a low-slung front end and a choice of oddball coupé or far prettier convertible bodystyles.

The newcomer was fairly compact and used TVR's traditional steel

At last, a new look for TVR. The Tasmin was so different from the firm's previous models that it was difficult to relate them.

backbone chassis – a platform that could trace its roots back to the late 1950s, but was not the worse for it, with its exceptional grip and agility. The Ford 'Essex' V6 engine found in most TVRs of the 1970s

was supplanted by the fuel-injected 2.8-litre (170cu in) 'Cologne' V6, but its source (the range-topping Ford Capri) was still the same.

In 1981, a 2+2 variant joined the range and was surprisingly

spacious, if you could clamber through the tiny gap to access the back seats. The following year a 2.0-litre (122cu in) variant called the Tasmin 2000 was introduced, using a Ford Pinto engine and

bringing the car into the range of some less wealthy owners. The final development of the model came in 1983, with the addition of the 3.5-litre (215cu in) Rover V8, in a new version called the 350i.

BENTLEY MULSANNE

UNITED KINGDOM 1980–92

ENGINE: 6750cc (412cu in),
  eight-cylinder
POWER: n/a
0–60MPH (96KM/H): 6.8 seconds
TOP SPEED: 207km/h (128mph)
PRODUCTION TOTAL: 2039

Although still badge-engineered, Bentley's replacement for the T-Series was somewhat different to the Rolls-Royce variant of the same car, as the maker identified the need for greater differentiation between the two. Named after the famous start-finish straight at Le Mans 24-Hour racing circuit, the Mulsanne recalled Bentley's past glories. That did not mean it was an especially sporting machine – at least not when it was new.

The bodywork was identical to that of the Rolls-Royce Silver Spirit, but, as the model aged, the two grew further apart. The Bentley gained a matt black radiator insert, sports alloy wheels, figure-hugging front seats and a less fussy dashboard. The theory was that a Rolls-Royce was bought by an owner who liked to be driven, but a Bentley was chosen by someone

who preferred to drive themselves. The ultimate version was the Mulsanne Turbo, introduced in 1982, which had a significant performance advantage over the normally aspirated model and the

Rolls-Royce, accelerating from rest to 96km/h (60mph) in less than seven seconds. The chassis was also revised to cope with the extra performance, giving a firmer ride and sharper steering.

Seen here on the banking at the Brooklands race circuit, the Mulsanne is at the scene of many an emphatic victory for Bentleys of yore, such as that in the background.

ROLLS-ROYCE SILVER SPIRIT

UNITED KINGDOM 1980–97

Replacing the successful Silver Shadow presented Rolls-Royce with a challenge, especially as it did not have the necessary finances to introduce a completely new car. Instead, the Silver Spirit was a heavily reworked Shadow for the 1980s, with new, more angular bodywork and a revised air suspension set-up. The engine and platform were identical, although neither was deficient in either performance or refinement.

The Spirit was true to traditional Rolls-Royce virtues, with a whisper-quiet cabin, supreme comfort and every conceivable creature comfort in the sumptuously trimmed cabin, although some of the marque's more traditional buyers balked at the rectangular headlights, which were not in keeping with Rolls-Royce's heritage.

The Silver Shadow-based chassis was over 15 years old at launch, but the Silver Spirit did a good job of appearing modern.

Unlike the Bentley Mulsanne, the Silver Spirit was softly sprung and had over-assisted power steering, which made it difficult to handle at speed, although the ride quality was exceptional. For the majority of owners, who travelled in the rear, that was all that mattered. A long wheelbase version, called the

Silver Spur, was also offered, while all models from 1984 onwards were fitted with fuel injection.

Although it was never as prevalent as the other car, the Silver Spirit actually enjoyed a longer production life than the Silver Shadow. The Silver Spirit remained in price lists until 1997,

when it was replaced by the BMW-powered Silver Seraph.

ENGINE: 6750cc (412cu in), eight-cylinder
POWER: n/a
0–60MPH (96KM/H): 9.5 seconds
TOP SPEED: 215km/h (133mph)
PRODUCTION TOTAL: n/a

CHAPTER FIVE

THE MODERN MOTOR CAR

1981 TO THE PRESENT DAY

From the early 1980s onwards, the car industry developed at an incredible pace – although to drive a car from 1980 compared to one launched 20 years later, you wouldn't instantly notice too many differences.

For the past 30 years, the main focus of the world's car makers has been to make its cars safer, more efficient, better value and more comfortable than ever before, while the scale and quality of competition means that new innovations were constantly sought as manufacturers did battle with each other in a market that grew ever more competitive.

As well as some of the most thrilling supercars ever made, from the doomed De Lorean DMC-12 through to the incredible Bugatti Veyron, the period from 1981 to date has seen some truly innovative cars. The humble Peugeot 205, for example, was an excellent example of a European supermini, which in GTI form evolved into a performance car legend, while the era also saw the birth and death of Group B Rallying, which saw some truly incredible machines doing battle in the forests and deserts of the world, including the fire-breathing Audi Quattro and Ford RS200, through to the unusual yet beguiling MG Metro 6R4.

The latest models, such as the Lamborghini Murcielago and Bentley Continental GT, show that despite the constant environmental pressures and economic challenges faced by the motor industry, there is still some seriously desirable machinery out there. A tribute, indeed, to the early pioneers, and proof that the motor industry is still in enthusiastically good health.

Cars got faster, bigger and more technologically advanced through the 1980s and 1990s. Love it or hate it, the imposing Ferrari Testarossa was certainly a bold styling statement, and it was a regular star of Hollywood movies.

DELOREAN DMC-12

Best known for its role in the movie *Back to the Future*, the DeLorean DMC-12 was nowhere near as exotic as its unusual looks and silver screen pedigree might suggest.

The brainchild of former Pontiac boss John Z. DeLorean, the car was developed jointly in the United States and the United Kingdom; the UK government invested a huge amount of money in the project as part of a plan to regenerate areas of Northern Ireland, where the DMC-12 would be assembled. It certainly looked unique, with unusual brushed-alloy bodywork and lift-up gullwing doors, but the unusual choice of a rear-mounted Renault V6 engine and gearbox from the Renault 30 executive saloon meant that the DeLorean never lived up to the performance that its looks promised.

It was never great in handling terms either. The stainless panels were stretched over glassfibre for ease of build, but this added to the car's weight. As a result, it felt heavy and unwieldy if driven at speed.

With a high purchase cost and dubious build quality from the car's Belfast factory, the DeLorean's sales were slow. Things were made even worse when DeLorean himself was indicted on fraud charges, causing the company to collapse and take a lot of British taxpayers' money with it.

ENGINE: 2849cc (174cu in), six-cylinder
POWER: 132bhp (98kW)
0–60MPH (96KM/H): 10.2 seconds
TOP SPEED: 194km/h (121mph)
PRODUCTION TOTAL: 8583

Fondly remembered only for its role in the hit film *Back to the Future*, the Anglo-American De Lorean was an unmitigated disaster in sales terms.

BITTER SC

Based on the Opel Monza, the Bitter SC was an incredibly attractive new car to replace the ageing CD, styled by Michelotti. Despite its obvious charm, the car was not without its initial problems. Erich Bitter originally planned the

Erich Bitter's last car before he lost interest, the handbuilt SC was based on the platform of the Opel Monza.

car in the early 1970s. With no financial backing from other investors, he was forced to raise the development money himself.

He also had trouble finding a coachbuilder to create the car, so set up a separate company called Bitter Italia, which used Turin-based OCRA to make the bodyshells, before transporting them to Bitter's works in Schwelm, Germany, for final assembly. The arrangement would have worked well, but

OCRA used cheap recycled steel in the first cars, and this led to dreadful corrosion problems – an issue that did little for a company whose initial reputation was built on its engineering integrity.

Production of the bodies was moved after only 79 cars were built, to a new coachbuilder, Maggiore, which did a far better job. For the next four years, Bitters were built in coupé, convertible and saloon bodystyles and earned

an excellent reputation. But Erich Bitter's other business interests, plus rising costs, caused him to cease building them in 1985, when production was wound down.

ENGINE: 3848cc (235cu in), six-cylinder
POWER: 210bhp (156kW)
0–60MPH (96KM/H): 9 seconds
TOP SPEED: 210km/h (130mph)
PRODUCTION TOTAL: 450

LOTUS ESPRIT SE

To prepare the long-serving Esprit for the 1990s, Lotus looked to its in-house design team to modernize the existing design. There was no need at this stage to alter the Esprit mechanically, as, even after 11 years on sale it was still a sharp and exciting car to drive, so the steering, suspension and 2.2-litre (133cu in) engine were left well alone.

A new look was essential, however, and the design team was charged with creating a car that not only looked sensational, but also added to the aerodynamic efficiency of the original design. The styling was the work of Lotus design chief Peter Stevens, who neatly rounded off the edges of the original car and added a front spoiler, smart side skirts and a large boot (trunk) spoiler, along with a new range of alloy wheels, black mirrors and door handles. The result was a superb attempt, giving the Esprit a new lease of life that saw it remaining on sale with almost the same styling until 2003.

But big changes were to come in 1990, with larger, more powerful engines (eventually including a V8), aggressive body kits and more luxurious cabins. The 1990 model year was the last for the 2.2-litre (133cu in) all-alloy engine.

ENGINE: 2174cc (133cu in), four-cylinder
POWER: 172bhp (128kW)
0–60MPH (96KM/H): 6.5 seconds
TOP SPEED: 221km/h (138mph)
PRODUCTION TOTAL: 385

LAMBORGHINI JALPA

ENGINE: 3485cc (213cu in), eight-cylinder
POWER: 255bhp (190kW)
0–60MPH (96KM/H): 6.5 seconds
TOP SPEED: 233km/h (145mph)
PRODUCTION TOTAL: n/a

Lamborghini went back to naming its cars after bulls with the Jalpa (pronounced 'hal-pha') of 1981. With its name taken from a famous Spanish breed of fighting bull, the car was a development of the earlier Silhouette, but was much more successful, with 419 cars sold over a seven-year period.

The Jalpa was intended to fulfil the role of a more affordable Lamborghini, being much cheaper than the Countach. Instead of the big car's V12 engine, it was fitted with a transversely mounted 3.5-litre (202cu in) V8 that developed 255bhp (158kW). The bodywork was designed and built by Bertone, updating the style of the Silhouette but retaining its basic profile.

Compared to the Countach, the Jalpa was much easier to drive. It had better visibility and was far less temperamental in heavy traffic or at slow speeds. Originally, the plastic bumpers, air intakes and engine cover were moulded in black, and the rectangular taillights came from the Silhouette. In 1984, a face-lift gave the Jalpa a fresher look, with body-coloured plastic mouldings and new rear lights.

Hardly bargain basement, but the Jalpa (a Spanish breed of fighting bull) was the least expensive way into Lamborghini ownership and that meant it enjoyed reasonable sales success, especially in the USA.

MASERATI BITURBO

Criticized by fans of the marque, but nonetheless a successful sales prospect for Maserati, the Biturbo marked the essence of the company's new design direction. Much smaller than most of the company's previous cars, far less sporting and much cheaper to buy, the Biturbo was essentially a two-door saloon car, styled in-house and almost a little too nondescript to comfortably wear the company's evocative trident badge.

It was quick, though. The car had two turbochargers fitted to its quad-cam 2.0-litre (122cu in) V6 engine, giving it impressive performance and ironing out much of the turbo lag that affected many of its single-turbo rivals. Later on, the engine size was increased to 2.5 litres (152cu in) and again to 2.8 litres (171cu in), while a 4.3-litre (261cu in) V8 joined the range at the end of the 1980s.

A four-door saloon, called Quattroporte in deference to the company's past, appeared three years after the launch, joined in 1984 by a Zagato-built Biturbo Spyder convertible. The range had a face-lift in 1987 and again in 1996, before being replaced entirely by the new-look Quattroporte in 1996. By this time Maserati had been taken over by Ferrari, and some much-needed character was injected back into the range.

ENGINE: 2491cc (152cu in), V6-cylinder
POWER: 185bhp (138kW) at 5500rpm
0–60MPH (96KM/H): 7.2 seconds
TOP SPEED: 201km/h (125mph)
PRODUCTION TOTAL: n/a

The P-registration plate marks this out as one of the very last BiTurbos. The British registration number dates from August 1996, two months after the car had officially been taken out of production.

FERRARI 328 GTB/GTS

It was very much a case of evolution rather than revolution when Ferrari pulled the covers off its new 328 at the 1981 Geneva Motor Show, for only the most ardent of fans was able to tell it

It's a case of spot the difference with the 328, which looks almost identical to the 308, save for the radiator grille and door mirrors.

apart from its sanctified predecessor. The steel-bodied 328 differed only in so far as it had bigger, colour-matched bumpers, a broader air intake and a new design of alloy wheels, while the range-topping GTS model had a pop-out roof panel.

The big news was the addition of a new engine. Ferrari had bored and stroked the original 2926cc (179cu in) unit (which it always

claimed was a 3.0-litre unit despite being closer to 2.9) and increased its capacity by a very impressive 269cc (16cu in) to 3195cc (195cu in), giving a useful 15bhp (9kW) more power in the process.

As in previous models, the engine was located transversely behind the two seats and had excellent performance, coupled to a fine-handling chassis. ABS brakes were available for the last two years

of production, but some Ferrari fans decried this safety feature because they claimed it took away some of the driver involvement.

ENGINE: 3195cc (195cu in), V8-cylinder
POWER: 270bhp (201kW)
0–60MPH (96KM/H): 6.4 seconds
TOP SPEED: 262km/h (163mph)
PRODUCTION TOTAL: 7412

MITSUBISHI COLT STARION

Mitsubishi was a latecomer to the lucrative coupé market, but that did not stop its two-door Starion being one of the better Japanese sports coupés of the 1980s. Its angular styling looked quite impressive, especially with the optional chrome alloy wheels, while performance from the 2.0-litre (122cu in) turbocharged engine was incredible. The car was not especially refined, however,

with immense turbo lag and a very twitchy rear-wheel drive chassis, although to some enthusiasts this actually made the Starion more interesting to drive. It also brought it not inconsiderable success on the tarmac rally circuit in the hands of Finnish driver Pentti Airikalla.

For the final two years of production, Mitsubishi tried to address the prodigious turbo lag problem by increasing the stroke

of the engine. The new 2.6-litre (159cu in) unit gave more torque and slightly less power, making the new EX-badged models more obedient to drive, albeit with less of the drama associated with earlier cars. These later cars were better equipped, though, with leather trim and more comprehensive equipment levels.

Interestingly, the name 'Starion' allegedly came from a mixed-up

telephone call with Mitsubishi in Japan and its Japanese importer, who suggested that the car be called the 'Stallion' …

ENGINE: 1997cc (122cu in), four-cylinder
POWER: 177bhp (132kW)
0–60MPH (96KM/H): 6.9 seconds
TOP SPEED: 215km/h (133mph)
PRODUCTION TOTAL: n/a

LOTUS EXCEL

ENGINE: 2174cc (133cu in), four-cylinder
POWER: 160bhp (119kW)
0–60MPH (96KM/H): 6.8 seconds
TOP SPEED: 211km/h (131mph)
PRODUCTION TOTAL: 1327

The Lotus Elite was dropped in 1981 due to a decline in the market, but the Eclat continued, morphing into a more modern incarnation. Initially called the Eclat Excel to remind people which model of Lotus the car was

replacing, the model became known as simply Excel from 1984 onwards. The gradual name change also helped Lotus to avoid having to go through the time-consuming and costly process of approving an entirely new car.

The Excel at first used the same engine and chassis as found in the outgoing Eclat, but with sleeker, more round-edged bodywork and a more upmarket cabin. The car came with a new Toyota-sourced gearbox and final drive unit, as

Based on the Eclat, the Lotus Excel had rounder styling and a more modern interior. Later models, such as this one, came with a Toyota-sourced engine. Lotus's last front-engined car.

well as the ventilated disc brakes from a Toyota Celica Supra.

In 1986, the Excel underwent a midlife face-lift. The result was an even rounder look for the body, which was styled by Peter Stevens

as a precursor to the revised Esprit, while a more steeply raked windscreen and lower roof improved the aerodynamics. The new SE models also received a power boost of up to 180bhp

(134kW) over the 160bhp (119kW) of earlier cars.

Production of the Excel ceased in 1982, and it was to become the last front-engined car that was produced by Lotus.

BRISTOL BRITANNIA

ENGINE: 5900cc (360cu in), eight-cylinder
POWER: n/a
0–60MPH (96KM/H): 7.2 seconds
TOP SPEED: 226km/h (140mph)
PRODUCTION TOTAL: n/a

Like the Beaufighter, which was based on the old 412, the Britannia was essentially a rebadged and updated version of the 603, again with a name inspired by one of Bristol's old fighter planes.

As was tradition, the newcomer was not hugely different from the car it replaced. The main visual differences were a squarer front

It was hard to tell the Britannia apart from the Bristol 603, the major visual difference being rectangular headlamp lenses.

end with rectangular headlights and new rear light lenses taken from a Renault 4 van, further proving the eccentricity of Bristol design ethics.

The external modifications were matched by a new vinyl-coated

dashboard inside, and the use of Jaguar steel sports wheels with larger tyres to improve the ride.

Otherwise, there were very few surprises in store. The Britannia had the same 5900cc (360cu in)

Chrysler V8 engine as the 603 and the same separate steel chassis, so there was very little difference in the way that the cars drove – in other words, performance was ample, but handling left a lot to be desired.

BRISTOL BRIGAND

Less than a year after the appearance of the Britannia, the Bristol Brigand made its debut and, surprise, surprise, looked exactly the same as the older 603. Under the bonnet (hood), it was a different story. Bristol had taken the potent turbocharged V8 engine from the Beaufighter and transplanted it into the Britannia's shell, in the process creating a car

with near supercar performance. Yet while the performance was on a par with the latest generation of hi-tech sports models, the chassis was still as archaic as ever.

Able to trace its roots back to the 1940s and completely lacking in sophistication, the chassis did give the car a certain rudimentary charm, as driving the Brigand quickly was certainly not an

experience for the faint-hearted. Bizarrely, given its fairly basic nature, the Brigand was, for a short time, Britain's most expensive car. The appeal of buying one came not from the car's ability, nor its build quality, but from the sheer experience of owning a Bristol.

The company's charismatic owner, Tony Crook, would consult with each customer, and the way a

potential Bristol buyer was treated often made them feel special enough to buy the car regardless.

ENGINE: 5900cc (360cu in), eight-cylinder
POWER: n/a
0–60MPH (96KM/H): 5.9 seconds
TOP SPEED: 242km/h (150mph)
PRODUCTION TOTAL: n/a

PORSCHE 944

Buyers had taken a while to get used to the notion of a front-engined water-cooled Porsche, but the steady sales success of the 924 led Porsche to take the idea forwards and introduce a faster, more exciting vision of the concept.

Not wanting to risk investing too much money in the project, the German firm very cleverly developed the car off the existing 924 bodyshell – a move that not only proved cost-effective, but actually turned the 944 into its most profitable model line as well, thanks partly to its popularity and its ease of build. Externally, the car differed from the 924 by growing wider, fatter wings (fender) in the style of the 924 Turbo, as well as larger wheels, low-profile tyres, lower suspension and a smart boot (trunk) spoiler that clamped around the back window.

An all-new engine appeared and was effectively half a bank of the V8 unit fitted to the 928. The 2.5-litre (151cu in) unit delivered 163bhp (121kW), although the power output gradually increased throughout the car's life.

Initially available with a five-speed manual gearbox only, the 944 was praised by contemporary road testers because of its tenacious grip and excellent handling, although it quickly became apparent that cars without the optional power steering were unpleasant to use in towns and could be difficult to park. Overall, though, the car was exceptionally well received, and even many of the purists, who believed that Porsches should have air-cooled engines behind the rear axle, had to admit that the essential DNA of the marque was apparent in the way that the car accelerated, steered and went round corners.

A hot Turbo model joined the 944 range in 1984, complete with a more bluntly styled front end and huge bonnet (hood) bump to accommodate the turbocharger. Built specifically for rally homologation purposes, it could spring from 0–60mph (96km/h) in less than six seconds and was blisteringly quick, albeit with rather alarming turbo lag.

From 1986 onwards, the standard 944 had its engine size upped from 2.5 litres (151cu in) to 2.7 litres (165cu in), when a new twin-cam 16-valve head was introduced and the engine given greater torque and power. Further changes came in 1988, when a 3.0-litre (183cu in) powerplant was introduced, along with the long-awaited 944 convertible.

The 3.0-litre models also saw the range receive a minor face-lift to take it into the 1990s, with bigger front and rear bumpers, a new range of alloy wheels and a revised chassis. The new chassis maintained the original car's impressive handling capabilities but improved the ride, which was the one area of the original car that was often criticized at the time of its launch.

Wider and more powerful than the 924 on which it was based, the Porsche 944 was, as a result, a much more popular choice with enthusiasts.

The 944 range was eventually replaced in 1993 by the 968, although its successor was, in fact, little more than a thorough rework of the existing car, with a revised chassis and a new 928-style nose.

Despite being much more modern and advanced, the 968 did not have the appeal of the 944 and was more expensive, meaning that numbers sold only ever reached a fraction of the 110,000 944s sold in the car's 12-year life.

ENGINE: 2479cc (151cu in), four-cylinder
POWER: 190bhp (142kW)
0–60MPH (96KM/H): 6.7 seconds
TOP SPEED: 226km/h (140mph)
PRODUCTION TOTAL: 112,550

BENTLEY TURBO R

It may have looked essentially the same as the Rolls-Royce Silver Spirit on which it was based, but the Bentley Turbo R was a totally different beast and was aimed far more at owners who preferred to drive themselves than be driven.

The chassis was completely reworked, and had a much firmer ride than the Silver Spirit, while the steering and brakes were also upgraded. The standard-issue 6750cc (412cu in) engine was fitted, but with a turbocharger equipped to give it a significant power boost. No official figure was published, but output is estimated to be around 320bhp (238kW). This gave the car rather dramatic acceleration and earned it quite a following among enthusiastic drivers in society's higher echelons.

Throughout its life, the Turbo R's top speed was limited to 218km/h (135mph), not because the car was unsafe above this speed, but because Bentley could not find a company that manufactured tall-profile tyres strong enough to cope with the car's immense performance. Unrestricted versions, with low-profile rubber, were tested at speeds in excess of 270km/h (170mph), proving that the turbocharger turned the already potent engine into a powerhouse.

ENGINE: 6750cc (412cu in), V8-cylinder
POWER: 320bhp (238kW)
0–60MPH (96KM/H): 6.6 seconds
TOP SPEED: 218km/h (135mph)
PRODUCTION TOTAL: 4815

TVR 350I

TVR was up to its old tricks again with the 350i – it looked identical to the car it replaced, and when you looked under the skin you were hard pushed to find differences, either.

Originally part of the Tasmin range, the V8-engined model outlived the rest of the range to become a TVR model in its own right. Called the 350i, it differed from the Tasmin by gaining side skirts, front and rear spoilers, and different rear lights, along with a new range of alloy wheels and a revised interior.

Power came from the 3.5-litre (215cu in) Rover V8 engine, which gave the 350i healthy acceleration and a compelling exhaust note, although feeding the powerplant's prodigious torque through the rear wheels made for some interesting handling characteristics in wet conditions. Affordable, sharp-looking and blisteringly quick, the appearance of the V8 engine made all other Tasmin models look superfluous. As demand tailed off completely, the 350i was left as the sole model in the line-up. It was offered as both a two-door coupé and a convertible, although the open-top model accounted for well above 90 per cent of total sales, making the coupé a rare but no more desirable version today.

Also rare, but again with no additional value, is the handful of automatic models – the Rover V8 engine was usually found attached to an automatic transmission in large saloon cars, but TVR fans generally favoured the five-speed manual option.

ENGINE: 3528cc (215cu in), eight-cylinder
POWER: 190bhp (142kW)
0–60MPH (96KM/H): 6.6 seconds
TOP SPEED: 218km/h (136mph)
PRODUCTION TOTAL: 955

AUDI QUATTRO

Using the coupé version of the Audi 80, coupled to an all-new five-cylinder engine and four-wheel drive chassis, Audi managed to create one of the most legendary cars of the late twentieth century.

Built specifically to compete in the World Rally Championship and increase Audi's profile among the motorsport fraternity, adding much needed excitement to the brand, the Quattro's engine was a development of the five-cylinder unit found in the 200 saloon. The 2.1-litre (131cu in) powerplant used a Triple-K turbocharger and Bosch fuel injection, giving it an impressive power output of 200bhp (149kW), but it was the way in which the car attacked corners with incredible grip that made it especially exciting.

The Audi Quattro was undeniably a rally car for the road – and it was reflected in the direct way in which it drove.

The four-wheel drive system offered tenacious cornering ability, while the brilliantly precise steering meant that the Quattro could be driven with plenty of gusto, regardless of surface or weather conditions. Naturally, this made it a huge success on the rally circuits, and Audi even developed a short-wheelbase version, called the Quattro Sport, to make the car more agile when driven hard through narrow forest stages.

Four WRC championships later, the Quattro had rightfully become a legend in its own lifetime, and the model remained on sale until 1991, with the later 20-valve models being the fastest and most impressive road cars.

ENGINE: 2144cc (131cu in), five-cylinder
POWER: 200bhp (149kW)
0–60MPH (96KM/H): 6.5 seconds
TOP SPEED: 222km/h (138mph)
PRODUCTION TOTAL: 11,560

FERRARI 288 GTO

Developed as a homologation special for Group B racing, the 288 GTO became one of Ferrari's all-time greats almost by accident. Based on the 308, the 288 had a smaller engine to allow it to fit into Group B's sub-3.0-litre (183cu in) regulations; however, its 2855cc (174cu in) engine certainly was not lacking in power. A shortened version of the 308 engine, it came with twin IHI turbochargers and Behr intercoolers to provide it with an enormous power output of 400bhp (298kW) and an incredible top speed of 306km/h (190mph).

The 288's engine was located in a slightly different position to that of the 308 and was mounted longitudinally, which meant that Ferrari had to stretch the car's chassis by 11cm (4.3in), and the mechanical layout also included an extended front and rear track.

This meant that the body needed a mild redesign, without losing the profile of the 308 on which it was based. Pininfarina

skilfully carried out the restyle, which managed to widen the rear end and alter the car's roofline to cunningly disguise the engineering changes. Weight was kept to a minimum by using Kevlar and Nomex on certain panels.

Sadly for Ferrari, the Group B racing formula for which the car was developed never came to pass, meaning that the huge development cost injected into the project was largely wasted – although, in the process, the 288 GTO did become one of the finest Ferrari road cars of all time.

ENGINE: 2855cc (174cu in),
  eight-cylinder
POWER: 400bhp (298kW)
0–60MPH (96KM/H): 4 seconds
TOP SPEED: 306km/h (190mph)
PRODUCTION TOTAL: 273

It never had the chance to achieve the racing success it deserved, but the 288 GTO was one of the best Ferrari road cars.

FIAT STRADA 130TC

ITALY 1984–87

Although the family hatchback on which it was based was never a great car, the Fiat Strada 130TC was one of the seminal hot hatches. Tuned by Abarth, the 130TC (also sold as the Ritmo) was an incredibly lively car that was truly thrilling to drive.

Power came from a 1995cc (121cu in) twin-cam engine with twin DCOE 40 carburettors helping

it develop a healthy 130bhp (95kW), but the car's excellent torque and sweet, free-revving nature were far more important than its actual power output.

The power was fed to the front wheels via a close-ratio five-speed gearbox, which was a delight to use. A sports exhaust system ensured that the 130TC had the aural appeal to match its performance. It also

enjoyed great handling due to the firm suspension, excellent brakes and brilliant steering. Even inside the 130TC felt special, with smart Recaro sports seats and a three-spoke steering wheel featuring Abarth's Scorpion logo.

A left-field choice in a market saturated with VW Golf GTis, Ford Escort XR3s and difficult-to-control Renault turbos, the Strada was the

bunch. If you can find one that has not rotted away, it makes a great cheap classic.

ENGINE: 1995cc (122cu in),
  four-cylinder
POWER: 130bhp (97kW)
0–60MPH (96KM/H): 7.9 seconds
TOP SPEED: 188km/h (117mph)
PRODUCTION TOTAL: n/a

TOYOTA MR2 MK 1

JAPAN 1984–89

ENGINE: 1588cc (97cu in),
  four-cylinder
POWER: 91kW (122bhp)
0–60MPH96KM/H (): 7.7 seconds
TOP SPEED: 193km/h (120mph)
PRODUCTION TOTAL: 166,104

Spotting a gap in the market, Toyota used the 1983 Tokyo Motor Show to gauge public reaction to its idea of a two-seater mid-engined sports car priced at the same level as the average small hatchback. The concept, called SV-3, received such great acclaim that, immediately after the Tokyo show closed, Toyota commissioned a production version. Less than a year later, it

The first generation MR2 was a sensation – a fine handling sports car that surpassed most critics' expectations.

was ready to pull the wraps off its angular new model.

The mid-engined MR2 was rear-wheel drive and had near-perfect weight distribution. A choice of 1453c (89cu in) or 1588cc

(97cu in) engines was on offer. While not especially powerful, they were effective, thanks to the MR2's incredibly light weight of just 1050kg (2300lb). Both engines could rev incredibly freely up to

7500 revs, making the power delivery both smooth and lively, while the handling was superb thanks to the car's great balance, MacPherson strut suspension and all-round disc brakes.

The car also shared Toyota's enviable reputation for being thoroughly reliable, making it an especially appealing prospect when compared to fragile rivals such as the Fiat X1/9 and Reliant SS1.

BMW M635 CSI

GERMANY 1984–89

BMW's replacement for the incredibly popular CS models was the slightly squarer 'shark-nose' 6-Series, which had been part of the German firm's range since 1977. Dynamically, the 6-Series was excellent, sharing much of its running gear with the highly praised 7-Series saloon and blessed with a range of refined and responsive six-cylinder engines.

Still, the big coupé lacked the excitement of its predecessor – the car that had spawned the legendary 3.0 CSL 'Batmobile'.

To give the 6-Series a boost, BMW enrolled the services of its recently created M-Division, which had transformed the 5-Series range with the introduction of the M535i. The highly tuned 3.5-litre (211cu in) straight-six engine was

taken more or less directly from the M535i, but with power increased to 286bhp (213kW), which was fed to the back wheels through a close-ratio five-speed gearbox.

Visually, the 635 CSi could be identified by its M-Technic body kit, sports seats and body-coloured mirrors, but was overall fairly understated – a facet that arguably was very much part of its appeal.

Unlike the brutish Batmobile, the 635 CSi was a subtle-looking car, but no less of a performance icon.

ENGINE: 3453cc (211cu in), six-cylinder
POWER: 286bhp (213kW)
0–60MPH (96KM/H): 6 seconds
TOP SPEED: 242km/h (150mph)
PRODUCTION TOTAL: 5803

PEUGEOT 205 GTI

FRANCE 1984–94

If the VW Golf GTi was the performance icon of the 1970s, then it was a car with the same three letters after its name that defined the hot hatch market in the 1980s. Small, light and incredibly agile, the 205 GTi was

It wasn't the first car to wear the hallowed GTi badge, but the Peugeot 205 was still one of the finest cars of its generation.

an incredible car, helped no doubt by the standard 205's pretty styling. GTi models had sports seats, red carpets, a three-spoke steering wheel and red print on the dials to make them feel special from the inside. On the outside, the three-door-only GTi had front fog lamps, alloy wheels, red inserts in the rubbing strips and tinted glass.

It was initially available with an underpowered 1.6-litre (98cu in) engine developing just 105bhp

(78kW), but this changed from 1986 onwards. For the new model year, the 1.6-litre engine had its power upped to 115bhp (86kW), while a new 1.9-litre (116cu in) unit was introduced in top models, identifiable by their larger wheels. The 1.9 models were faster, with 130bhp (97kW) available, but fans of the model generally preferred the 1.6-litre cars. These were easier to tune and had better handling balance – the nose-heavy 1.9-litre

cars tended to be very twitchy at the rear, especially if you lifted off the accelerator mid-bend.

The 205 GTi was a great car, one that pretty much defined its era.

ENGINE: 1905cc (116cu in), four-cylinder
POWER: 130bhp (97kW)
0–60MPH (96KM/H): 7.8 seconds
TOP SPEED: 195km/h (121mph)
PRODUCTION TOTAL: n/a

RELIANT SS1

UNITED KINGDOM 1984–90

Its unfortunate name aside, the Reliant SS1 did not have the greatest start in life. The car's styling was initially the work of Italian stylist Giovanni Michelotti; however, Michelotti died before

the styling project was complete, and the work was finished off by Reliant's own engineers, with the unfortunate result that the car always possessed a slightly disharmonious appearance.

The wedge-shaped two-seater was planned to fill the gap that had been left by the demise of cars such as the MG Midget and Triumph Spitfire, which disappeared at the start of the 1980s. In the

end, there were many expectant buyers who were disappointed by the car that Reliant finally produced. As well as the styling problems, there was a major engineering oversight in the form of the engine bay. Reliant had intended to use the fuel-injected Ford Escort XR3i powerplant, but, when it came to install the engine in the car, it found that it was too tall for the car's profile. Reliant had a choice of either adding an unsightly lump to the bonnet (hood) or using the far less powerful 1.6-litre (97cu in) carburettor-fed engine from the standard Escort hatchback, which was the eventual solution.

Initial road tests criticized the SS1's oddball looks and poor performance. Things did improve with the addition of a Nissan-sourced 1.8-litre (110cu in) engine from the Silvia Turbo, which provided a much-needed dose of excitement, but nonetheless the car was never a success.

ENGINE: 1809cc (110cu in), four-cylinder
POWER: 135bhp (101kW)
0–60MPH (96KM/H): 6.9 seconds
TOP SPEED: 203km/h (126mph)
PRODUCTION TOTAL: n/a

BENTLEY EIGHT

UNITED KINGDOM 1984–92

Although the majority of Bentley customers preferred the more luxurious and faster Mulsanne, Rolls-Royce introduced an entry-level car with the Bentley badge for 1984 to appeal to customers who thought the Rolls-Royce badge a little too old-fashioned.

Essentially a rebadged Rolls-Royce Silver Spirit, the Bentley Eight was a handsome car, with twin round headlights to replace the Spirit's rectangular ones, a mesh-style Bentley grille, front spoiler and alloy wheels. The Bentley colour palette also differed from the Rolls-Royce one, with brighter, more vibrant hues. The luxury and refinement were as you would expect from the marque, while the Eight's ride quality was a little softer and smoother than that possessed by the more sports-oriented Mulsanne.

Although never a brilliant seller, the Eight was successful enough to introduce a new generation of buyers to the Bentley brand, and the model was to account for one in ten of all orders that were placed to Rolls-Royce during its eight-year production cycle.

ENGINE: 6750cc (412cu in), V8-cylinder
POWER: n/a
0–60MPH (96KM/H): 9.6 seconds
TOP SPEED: 207km/h (128mph)
PRODUCTION TOTAL: 1734

FERRARI TESTAROSSA

ITALY 1984–92

Built to replace the 512 BB, the wide and angular Testarossa made a huge impact at the Paris Motor Show in 1984. The styling by Pininfarina was dominated by the massive side intakes that supposedly directed air to the rear-mounted radiators, but were also

It's impossible to mistake the Testarossa for anything else, but whether you like the bodywork is a matter of personal taste.

there as very much a design feature that reflected the excesses of wealth in the 1980s.

The chassis was a stretched and much modified version of the 512's, with the same basic double wishbone suspension, but featuring twin coil-over units at the rear to cope with the increased weight created by the car's immense bulk.

Power came from a new four-valve-per-cylinder version of the 4943cc (302cu in) engine from the 512 BB, with Bosch K-Jetronic fuel injection, Marelli electronic ignition and a healthy power output of 390bhp (291kW). This gave the car furious performance, with the ability to exceed 290km/h (180mph) and sprint to 60mph (96km/h) in less than six seconds.

The brash bodywork was remarkable, much copied, and admired by those who bought a Testarossa to get noticed. As well as the large air intakes, a black slatted grille covered the rear lights, while a black band covered the lower part of the sills and front air dam. The drag coefficient of 0.36 seemed disappointingly high, but was partly justified because the shape was primarily designed for maximum downforce.

ENGINE: 4942cc (302cu in), 12-cylinder
POWER: 390bhp (291kW)
0–60MPH (96KM/H): 5.8 seconds
TOP SPEED: 291km/h (181mph)
PRODUCTION TOTAL: 7177

LANCIA THEMA 8.32

ITALY 1984–94

Lancia's 'Car for Europe', the Thema, was developed in conjunction with Saab, Fiat and Alfa Romeo as part of a cost-saving manufacturing agreement between the four brands. Sharing its underpinnings with the Saab 9000, Alfa Romeo 164 and Fiat Croma, the Thema was given a more edgy appearance and sports-tuned chassis to distinguish it from its more ordinary brethren.

Even with these changes, the car perhaps did not have the spirit of previous Lancias, so to counter this the Italian maker approached

Ferrari to give the car a much-needed injection character.

The result was the 8.32, so called because it had an eight-cylinder engine and 32 valves. The powerplant itself came from the Ferrari 308, much to the horror of overprotective Ferrari purists who scorned their beloved engine being used in a saloon car. For Lancia enthusiasts, things were very different – the Thema was manna from heaven alongside more mundane cars in the range.

Despite prodigious performance, the 8.32 was fairly bland to look at, with no excessive sporty modifications and only a small boot (trunk) spoiler, which itself popped up only if manually operated.

ENGINE: 2927cc (178cu in),
   V8-cylinder
POWER: 215bhp (160kW) at 6750rpm
0–60MPH (96KM/H): 7.2 seconds
TOP SPEED: 225km/h (140mph)
PRODUCTION TOTAL: 2370

Okay, so it doesn't look all that special, but under the bonnet Lancia's top of the range Thema was powered by a Ferrari V8 engine. Lancia enthusiasts loved it, while some precious Ferrari purists were horrified.

FORD UK RS200

UNITED KINGDOM 1985–86

The Ford RS200 received its name because of the 200 cars built for rallying homologation. It was a bespoke rally car built to thrash its way round forest tracks and compete with the likes of the all-conquering Lancia Delta S4 and Peugeot 205 Turbo 16 on the world's rally circuits.

Although it shared some parts with previous and current Ford models, the RS200 was effectively built from scratch on a spaceframe chassis, with a mid-mounted four-cylinder 1802cc (110cu in) engine. The powerplant was a derivative of that designed for the ill-fated Escort RS1700T, which had never made it through to full-blown competition. The bore and stroke were increased, however, and a

Ford lost masses of money on the RS200 project, as Group B rallying was banned before the car ever competed. A shame, because it was a fabulous car.

Garrett turbocharger to force air into the engine.

The RS200's four-wheel drive chassis was developed by FF Developments on Ford's behalf and was built from Kevlar and carbonfibre to keep weight to a minimum. The suspension was fully adjustable to suit either tarmac or rough forest events.

Campaigned successfully as a prototype in the 1986 season, the RS200 was not fully homologated until the following year, by which time the FIA had banned Group B cars following the death of Peugeot driver Henri Toivonen, and the RS200 was never properly campaigned in homologated form. But, by this stage, 200 road cars

had been completed, and were eagerly snapped up by collectors.

ENGINE: 1802cc (110cu in),
   four-cylinder
POWER: 250bhp (186kW)
0–60MPH (96KM/H): 6 seconds
TOP SPEED: 225km/h (140mph)
PRODUCTION TOTAL: 200

RENAULT GTA

FRANCE 1985–91

Effectively a modernized version of the Alpine A310, the Renault GTA was a hugely appealing car of the 1980s, thanks in part to its alluring styling, but more because of its exceptional price tag.

Almost as quick as a genuine supercar, and just as striking to look at, the GTA was built for Renault by Matra at the same factory in Dieppe, France, as the Espace people-carrier was produced. The

only thing the GTA had in common with the Espace, however, was the use of glassfibre for some of its body panels, as in all other respects the car was a lot more dynamic and appealing.

Behind the seats was mounted either a normally aspirated 2.8-litre (171cu in) engine or, in later models, a 2.5-litre (150cu in) turbocharged V6, both of which offered excellent performance.

Despite a weight bias to the rear and rear-wheel drive, the GTA demonstrated tenacious grip from its chassis, which caused many commentators to compare it to the Porsche 911 in both concept and handling characteristics. Indeed, the only thing that really went against the GTA was its name – in a market where the badge on the keyring often meant more than the qualities of the car itself, the

Renault moniker simply did not have the same wine bar appeal as the German marque. Nonetheless, it was a truly great sports car.

ENGINE: 2458cc (150cu in),
   V6-cylinder
POWER: 200bhp (149kW)
0–60MPH (96KM/H): 5.7 seconds
TOP SPEED: 266km/h (165mph)
PRODUCTION TOTAL: 17,450

LANCIA DELTA HF TURBO

Subtle looks disguise the HF's impressive performance – the car was very much the precursor to the later Integrale and Evolution models that stormed the world rally championship in the 1990s.

Following the success of the Delta S4 on the Group B rally scene, Lancia decided to take its motorsport appeal into the showrooms with the introduction of the Delta HF Turbo. Available with optional 'Martini stripes' to match those of the rally cars, the HF was four-wheel drive and came with a turbocharger, making it an incredibly hot hatch as well as a desirable rally-bred road car, despite what was initially an extremely steep purchase price.

Visually, there was very little to distinguish the HF Turbo from ordinary Delta models, with only some subtle alloy wheels and discreet 'Turbo' badges on the car's side skirts suggesting that the HF was anything more than an ordinary family hatch. Yet the car was stunningly quick and had superb roadholding, setting the precedent for a whole generation of hot Deltas.

With changes to rally regulations forcing Group B cars into early retirement for 1987, Lancia developed a 'Group A' showroom rally car using the HF Turbo as a base. Called the Integrale, the new car evolved through six different generations as a rally car and as a road car, in the process scoring three world championships and several showroom successes. Still, it is with the original, far more subtle HF that the phenomenon started.

ENGINE: 1995cc (122cu in), four-cylinder turbo
POWER: 165bhp (123kW) at 5250rpm
0–60MPH (96KM/H): 6.6 seconds
TOP SPEED: 209km/h (130mph)
PRODUCTION TOTAL: n/a

MG METRO 6R4

Making a group B rally car out of a Mini Metro may seem an unusual idea, but that is exactly what Austin-Rover decided to do when it went into top-level competition. In all honesty, though the 6R4 had very little in common with the supermini on which it was based, sharing only its headlights, doors and dashboard. The '6' part of the name stood for the car's V6 engine, the 'R' for 'rally car' and the '4' for four-wheel drive. Under the vaguely Metro-shaped bodywork, there was a bespoke tubular spaceframe chassis developed by motorsport engineering company TWR.

The 3.0-litre (183cu in) V6 powerplant was also built for Austin-Rover by TWR and broke from group B tradition by not being turbocharged. Instead, the normally aspirated engine was designed to develop huge amounts of torque, giving it phenomenal acceleration without the need for any assistance. The bodywork was made out of glass-reinforced plastic to keep weight to a minimum, while the car had permanent four-wheel drive, thanks to a separate driveshaft to each wheel.

After showing early promise in competition, finishing third on its debut outing, the 6R4 was developed further. Its life was cut short, however, when group B rallying was banned for safety reasons in 1987. The incredible engine would reappear in 1989, however, under the bonnet (hood) of the Jaguar XJ200 supercar.

ENGINE: 2991cc (183cu in), six-cylinder
POWER: 250bhp (190kW) at 6250rpm
0–60MPH (96KM/H): 4.8 seconds
TOP SPEED: 225km/h (140mph)
PRODUCTION TOTAL: 220

Yes, it looks like a Metro, but under the skin the 6R4 was a bespoke rally machine, built on a handmade tubular spaceframe chassis and fitted with permanent four-wheel-drive.

ASTON MARTIN V8 ZAGATO

With no new models in the pipeline and criticism from certain quarters that its cars were too old-fashioned and traditional-looking, Aston Martin enrolled the services of Italian design house Zagato to give the AM V8 a more modern and dynamic look.

Built on a shortened AM V8 chassis and designed to be built in strictly limited numbers, following the success of limited-edition specials such as the Ferrari 288 GTO and Porsche Carrera RS models, the V8 Zagato was an odd-looking beast, with flush-fitted

The Zagato was Aston Martin's attempt to shake off its overly traditional reputation with a modern, streamlines shape – but it enjoyed only limited success.

revised engine and chassis gave it greater appeal among the supercar fraternity, especially when it was revealed that the breathed-on 5.3-litre (326cu in) V8 engine had a power output of 423bhp (315kW), enough to give it the ability to top 240km/h (150mph) and sprint from 0–60mph (96km/h) in around five seconds.

ENGINE: 5340cc (326cu in), eight-cylinders
POWER: 423bhp (315kW)
0–60MPH (96KM/H): 5 seconds
TOP SPEED: 241km/h (150mph)
PRODUCTION TOTAL: 83

glass, a tall, bulbous roofline and a new, rounded front end that, although few realized it at the time, pointed the way to the company's new face, which would

be seen 'officially' for the first time two years later on the Virage.

The Zagato was first seen at the 1985 Frankfurt Motor Show and went into production shortly after,

with Aston Martin increasing its original estimate of 50 cars to 83 to satisfy greater demand than it expected for the model. Despite its awkward looks, the V8 Zagato's

---

TVR 450 SEAC

ENGINE: 4441cc (271cu in), eight-cylinder
POWER: 324bhp (241kW)
0–60MPH (96KM/H): 4.7 seconds
TOP SPEED: 265km/h (165mph)
PRODUCTION TOTAL: 18

The ultimate version of the car that started life as the TVR Tasmin, the 450 SEAC was an especially wild roadster derivative of the wedge-shaped sports car. The 'SE' part of the name stood for 'Special Equipment', while the 'AC' part meant 'Aramid Composite' – a more technical way of saying that the car's body panels were made of lightweight Kevlar instead of glassfibre, making it stiffer and stronger as a result.

The engine was based on Rover's 3.5-litre (215cu in) V8, but was bored out to 4441cc (271cu in) and had a strengthened block, bigger valves, gas-flowed cylinder heads and an uprated camshaft. The upshot of this was a massive boost in power, from 190bhp (142kW) in

the standard 350i on which it was based to 324bhp (241kW).

This gave the SEAC incredible performance and supercar-rivalling acceleration, but the expensive materials also led the car to be

very costly – almost twice the price of the 350i. Blisteringly quick and incredibly tricky to drive, the SEAC was very much a specialist model, and only 18 cars were completed over a two-year period.

Once again, TVR launched another car that looked exactly the same as the one before, but this time with a larger engine. The 450 SEAC's engine was based on the Rover 3.5-litre V8.

BMW M3

The smallest of BMW M-cars and also the most legendary, the E30 M3 appeared in 1986 as a lightweight four-cylinder saloon, partly to become an iconic flagship for the popular 3-Series range, but more as a homologation special for saloon-car racing. This is what led to the decision to use a compact four-cylinder engine instead of one of BMW's trademark sixes.

Visually, the M3 differed from a standard 3-Series with a deep front

spoiler, rear wing (fender) on the boot (trunk) lid and smart side skirts, plus dark grey multi-spoke alloy wheels and widened wings and wheelarches. The changes were not only cosmetic, as BMW's engineers also changed the rake angle of the car's rear window to improve downforce, while the raised height of the M3's boot lid added further to aerodynamic efficiency.

Power came from a 2302cc (140cu in) straight-four, which

was, quite literally, the six-cylinder engine from the M1 supercar with one bank of cylinders chopped off to reduce its capacity. Despite the loss of two cylinders, the M3 was still blisteringly quick, with 200bhp (149kW) fed through the rear wheels via a Getrag five-speed gearbox with a dogleg first gear.

The M3's handling was sensational, its rear-drive chassis being perfectly balanced for optimum power delivery, coupled

to superbly communicative steering. A huge success, both in showrooms and on the racetrack, the M3 is remembered as a performance-car legend.

ENGINE: 2302cc (140cu in), four-cylinder
POWER: 200bhp (149kW)
0–60MPH (96KM/H): 7.1 seconds
TOP SPEED: 226km/h (140mph)
PRODUCTION TOTAL: 17,184

BMW Z1

The car that never was – the BMW Z1 was never intended to pass the prototype stage, but its handling was too good to ignore.

door roadster layout that would become the Z1, complete with unusual doors that slid down into the car's sills to facilitate entry.

The car was tentatively shown to the public to gauge reaction; such was the demand for the Z1 to be put into production that BMW decided to build a limited run of 8000 cars, powered by the 2494cc (153cu in) six-cylinder engine fitted to the BMW 325i. The punchy engine and well-honed chassis were a promising combination, but the Z1 never really delivered on that promise from behind the wheel. Even so, its curious styling and rarity value make it an interesting choice of modern classic.

ENGINE: 2494cc (153cu in), four-cylinder
POWER: 170bhp (127kW)
0–60MPH (96KM/H): 7.9 seconds
TOP SPEED: 226km/h (140mph)
PRODUCTION TOTAL: 8000

Amazingly, the BMW Z1 was never earmarked for production. It came into existence by accident, while BMW was developing a new rear suspension system known as the Z-Axle, which would be fitted

to its E36 3-Series model from 1991 onwards. With no obvious testbed for the new suspension, BMW's engineers built a handful of development 'mules', and it soon became apparent that these short

wheelbase prototypes were impressive enough to evolve into a production car in their own right.

BMW experimented with clothing the car in a variety of bodystyles and eventually settled on the two-

FORD UK SIERRA COSWORTH

One of the most successful circuit and rally cars of the 1980s, the Ford Sierra was not originally intended to have a career in motorsport. Ford had invested huge amounts of money developing the RS200 for Group B rallying while the sport was at its peak, but new, more stringent safety regulations led to the dismissal of group B cars, and Ford reassessed its motorsport programme as a result. The rear-

drive Sierra was by far the easiest car in its range to tune, and it appeared to have more potential in circuit racing than rallying, so this is where Ford refocused its motorsport investment. Sierras did go rallying, but it is on the racetracks of Europe where the Cosworth is best remembered.

Based on the three-door XR3i, the Sierra Cosworth initially appeared in 1986, as a limited edition for homologation purposes. The engine

was a 2-litre (122cu in) twin-cam 'Pinto', redeveloped by Cosworth engineering and turbocharged to develop 200bhp (149kW); the unit could easily achieve 300bhp (224kW) in racing tune.

The car was so popular that its special-edition status was soon removed, and it became a standard addition to the range. A special model called the RS500 (with 224bhp/167kW) was introduced in 1987, tuned and trimmed by Aston

Martin Tickford. The four-door Sierra Sapphire bodyshell was used from 1988, followed by a four-wheel drive version, developed more for rallying, in 1990.

ENGINE: 1993cc (122cu in), four-cylinder
POWER: 204bhp (152kW)
0–60MPH (96KM/H): 8 seconds
TOP SPEED: 233km/h (145mph)
PRODUCTION TOTAL: 5000

MARCOS MANTULA

ENGINE: 4600cc (280 cu in), eight-cylinder
POWER: 190bhp (138kW)
0–60MPH (96KM/H): 6.0 seconds
TOP SPEED: 223km/h (139mph)
PRODUCTION TOTAL: n/a

A revived Marcos company appeared in 1981, building cars that looked very similar to the Dennis Adams–designed originals

Available as a convertible and a coupé, the Marcos Mantula was a bold-looking design that echoed the styling of the 1960s original Marcos GT. On early models the nose lifted at high speed.

and powered by the same 3.0-litre (183cu in) Ford V6 engines. But big changes were afoot for 1984, with the Mantula's introduction. The newcomer came with the famous 3.5-litre (215cu in) Rover V8 engine, which developed 185bhp (138kW) and gave the lightweight car tremendous performance.

The downside of this was the car's aerodynamics, which were far from perfect and caused the nose to lift at high speed, with alarming consequences. As a result, all but the earliest cars were fitted with a revised nosecone that featured a big air dam, along with subtle side skirts along the side of the car.

Two bodystyles were on offer – a traditional two-door coupé or a two-door convertible – both of which retained the rather unusual teardrop shape that was an easily distinguished feature of Marcos.

Cars built from 1989 onwards came with a larger 3.9-litre (241cu in) engine derived from

that fitted to the Range Rover and were even more powerful, but this served only to highlight the car's handling deficiencies even more.

Despite a spate of financial problems and a car that was, essentially, completely out of date, Marcos still kept the Mantula in production until 2000.

PORSCHE 959

ENGINE: 2994cc (183cu in), six-cylinder
POWER: 405bhp (302kW)
0–60MPH (96KM/H): 3.7 seconds
TOP SPEED: 318km/h (197mph)
PRODUCTION TOTAL: 200

keep weight down, the 959 had aluminium doors, bonnet (hood) and boot (trunk) panels, which were attached to a strong plastic monocoque usually reserved for aircraft fuselages.

The 959 was sensational to drive. Twin turbos gave it phenomenal acceleration and very little turbo lag, and the chassis was agile in a way that only a Porsche's can be. The top speed was just shy of

Porsche's 322km/h (200mph) target at 318km/h (197mph). Unlike most supercars, it was also pleasantly easy to drive, with light controls, a smooth six-speed gearbox and a comfortable cabin.

Porsche proved the 959's capabilities before the car even went on sale, with a prototype model reigning victorious in the gruelling 1986 Paris–Dakar Rally.

Based on the 911, the 959 was developed with only one purpose in mind – to become the world's fastest production car. It was something that Porsche achieved and a record it held for two years, until a sulking Ferrari developed the F40, rejected the design four times in the process until it was faster than the Porsche.

The 959 retained the 911's rear-engined layout, with a traditional flat-six positioned adrift of the back axle, while the handling was sharpened up using a four-wheel drive system that would later go on to appear in the Carrera 4. To

Terrifically fast, refined and exceptionally well made, the 959 was a comfortable and actually easy to drive supercar.

FERRARI F40

Incensed that Porsche had built the fastest car in the world, Ferrari set out to build a very special vehicle to mark its fortieth anniversary, as well as knock the 959 off its pedestal by cracking the 322km/h (200mph) barrier.

Revealed in the summer of 1987, although production would not begin until the following year, the F40 was very much a racing car for the road, and was designed with sheer speed in mind above any kind of driver comfort or efficiency, unlike the comfortable and user-friendly Porsche.

But this was a market where the performance figures counted above all else, to Ferrari at least, so the car was developed with only one target in mind.

The engine and chassis were loosely based on those of the 288

GTO. The engine was a 2936cc (179cu in) development of its V8, still with four valves per cylinder, but with twin IHI turbos and Behr intercoolers, which increased efficiency and helped generate a huge 478bhp (356kW) of power.

The compression ratio was on paper a modest 7.8:1, but the turbo boost pressure used was an exceptional 16psi. The engine itself was quite an exotic creation, made from a composite material called Silumin, with shrink-fitted alloy liners in the block itself. On top were twin belt-driven

In an attempt to challenge the Porsche 959, the Ferrari F40 was was cramped, hot and tricky to handle, but at least it beat the Porsche on top speed.

camshafts for each bank of cylinders. Best of all, this work of engineering art was clearly visible through the louvred plastic engine cover in the middle of F40. If all that power were not enough for some buyers, there was a factory upgrade kit available with larger turbochargers and revised camshafts that could add another 200bhp (149kW).

The chassis retained the wheelbase and basic suspension arrangement of the GTO, but featured wider tracks front and rear. The wheels were huge 43cm (17in) diameter Cromodara items, 33cm (13in) wide at the rear and fitted with 335/35 Pirelli P-Zero tyres. At the front, the wheels were 20cm (8in) wide, with 245/40 tyres.

Due to the low ground clearance, some cars featured suspension height control and could be manually raised for traversing less than glass-smooth surfaces – all part of the quest to reach 322km/h (200mph) despite the fact that the Porsche 959's aerodynamic efficiency meant that it could travel nearly this fast with more than three inches (7.5cm) of ground clearance.

The bodywork, which clothed a tubular steel spaceframe, was a completely new design, although, in Ferrari tradition, it was once again styled by Pininfarina. Using carbonfibre, Kevlar and aluminium components, it was aerodynamic, functional and above all incredibly lightweight. The F40 weighed just

1089kg (2400lb), although the optional opening windows added 10kg (22lb) and were fitted to almost every roadgoing F40, as the standard fixed Perspex items made the car very unpleasant otherwise.

The huge air ducts on the side were an incredibly clever piece of design, feeding air to the turbos and the rear brakes, while at the same time giving more aerodynamic downforce to the back of the car.

As extravagant and eye-catching as the F40 was on the outside, inside there were no luxurious touches. Lots of Kevlar was visible, but no carpet – this was a stripped-out racer.

Ferrari achieved its goal – the F40 was the world's fastest production car, with a top speed of

323km/h (201mph), but it would not stay there for long, with the Jaguar XJ220, Lamborghini Diablo and McLaren F1 all appearing shortly afterwards to knock the F40 from its perch.

Despite being especially crude and unpleasant to drive, the cachet of its performance made the F40 surprisingly popular, and Ferrari's initial plan to build just 450 was scuppered; total orders eventually reached 1315.

ENGINE: 2936cc (179cu in), eight-cylinder
POWER: 478bhp (356kW)
0–60MPH (96KM/H): 3.9 seconds
TOP SPEED: 323km/h (201mph)
PRODUCTION TOTAL: 1315

LANCIA DELTA INTEGRALE

ITALY 1987–94

Following on from the subtle yet highly competent HF turbo, the Integrale marked Lancia's assault on the Group A rally scene.

The word 'integrale' is Italian for 'complete' and was chosen because the hottest ever Delta was intended to be very much the complete rally car, as well as being just about as exciting a road car as money could buy. Developed from the HF turbo, initially as a 5000-

only homologation run, later abandoned due to demand, the car featured modified bodywork, with more bulbous wheelarches and front and rear wings (fenders), big air scoops in the bonnet (hood) and a rear boot (trunk) spoiler, which served to enhance rather than detract from Giugiaro's handsome original lines.

The car delivered electrifying performance and superb handling,

which made it an immense success on the rally circuits, while, as a road car, it simply grew better year after year. In 1990, a 16-valve version was introduced which had greater torque and smoother power delivery, followed in 1991 by the Integrale Evoluzione, with more power, faster steering, sharper suspension and an even beefier body kit. This was a legendary rally car and, at the

same time, a great performance car on the road. It is little wonder, then, that the Integrale has developed such a cult following.

ENGINE: 1995cc (122cu in), four-cylinder turbo
POWER: 185bhp (138kW) at 5300rpm
0–60MPH (96KM/H): 6.4 seconds
TOP SPEED: 209km/h (130mph)
PRODUCTION TOTAL: n/a

TVR S

UNITED KINGDOM 1987–PRESENT

With the appearance of the wedge-shaped Tasmin cars in the early 1980s, TVRs became expensive cars to buy and run, leading to some criticism from traditional exponents of the marque. To address this, TVR

launched the convertible-only TVR S to appeal to those who had previously owned M-series or Taimar-derived models.

Based on the 3000S, the S came with the Ford V6 engine from the Capri 2.8 Injection special. The

2792cc (191cu in) unit developed 160bhp (119kW), which provided impressive performance when coupled to the car's lightweight bodyshell and steel backbone chassis. The S was almost impossible to distinguish from the

earlier 3000S, as it used exactly the same body panels and interior layout, but the car still proved popular. An S2 version with a bigger 2.9-litre (177cu in) variant came out in 1988, followed by the face-lifted (spot the difference ...) S3 cars in 1990.

The final variant of the S came out in 1991 and used a 3.9-litre (238cu in) Rover V8 engine, which made it incredibly quick and lairy. But this version defeated the object of the original S by being an expensive car to buy, and, by this time, there were more modern and desirable cars in the TVR range and in other sectors of the sports-car market, meaning that it was always a slow seller.

ENGINE: 2792cc (170cu in), V6-cylinder (S1)
POWER: 160bhp (119kW)
0–60MPH (96KM/H): 7.6 seconds
TOP SPEED: 205km/h (128mph)
PRODUCTION TOTAL: 2600

For those who didn't admire the wedge-shaped lines of the Tasmin, TVR reintroduced its classically shaped models in the late 1980s.

VOLKSWAGEN CORRADO

GERMANY 1988–96

The Karmann-built Scirocco was a huge success for Volkswagen for more than 14 years, but by the late 1980s it was starting to both look and feel its age. There was still strong demand for the model, however, so Volkswagen decided to introduce an all-new model based on the platform of the very able Mk 2 VW Golf GTi.

The Corrado appeared in 1988 and was instantly praised for its smart looks and fine handling. Two versions were available initially – a normally aspirated 1.8-litre (110cu in) version and a supercharged variant using the same basic powerplant, called the G60.

In 1992, a pair of new engines was introduced – a 2.0-litre (122cu in) four-cylinder to replace the original 1.8 and a 2.8-litre (178cu in) V6, which was fitted to a model called the VR6 – a variant that today is regarded as the most desirable of the Corrado range.

VR6 and G60 models featured an electronic rear spoiler that would automatically raise when the car passed 60mph (96km/h) to add further downforce to the already agile-handling chassis.

The Corrado was a superb car, and fans went into mourning when it was withdrawn in 1995. Demand at the time was still high, but, as it was based on the floorpan of the old Golf Mk 2, which had long since gone out of production, it was not viable to keep the Corrado on sale. The last models were limited editions called 'Storm'. All had the VR6 engine, discreet Storm badges and full leather trim.

ENGINE: 1781cc (110cu in), four-cylinder
POWER: 160bhp (118kW)
0–60MPH (96KM/H): 8.1 seconds
TOP SPEED: 226km/h (140mph)
PRODUCTION TOTAL: 102,444

GINETTA G32

UNITED KINGDOM 1988–92

The G32 marked an all-new look for Ginetta, with the original curvaceous bodywork replaced by new, square-edged looks for the 1980s, which were not dissimilar to those of the Toyota MR2 Mk 1.

Underneath the angular new panels lurked technology that was very familiar to fans of the Ginetta marque. It had the same box-section steel chassis as its predecessors; double wishbone and coil springs at the front, coupled to Ford Fiesta rear struts, gave the car tremendously agile handling.

The powerplant came from the Ford Fiesta XR2i and delivered a modest power output of 110bhp (82kW), but this was enough to provide the lightweight Ginetta with surprisingly lively acceleration, while the mid-engined layout gave excellent weight distribution. Inside, the car was a little more luxurious than previous Ginettas, with the dashboard borrowed from the Ford Fiesta and comfortable, supportive sports seats.

An open-top version appeared in 1990, bringing more diversity to the range. Production continued until 1992, when the car was replaced by the similar-looking G33.

ENGINE: 1597cc (97cu in), four-cylinder
POWER: 110bhp (82kW)
0–60MPH (96KM/H): 8.2 seconds
TOP SPEED: 192km/h (120mph)
PRODUCTION TOTAL: n/a

ASTON MARTIN VIRAGE

UNITED KINGDOM 1988–2002

By the time the Virage appeared, Aston Martin was desperate for a new model. With the exception of the short-lived V8 Zagato, the company had relied on the AM V8 as its only model for well over a decade. By the late 1980s, it was

After 15 years, Aston Martin launched an all-new model in the shape of the Virage, but it kept the 5.3-litre engine of the AM V8.

looking dated and vulgar. But Aston Martin did not have huge reserves of cash, so the AM V8's replacement had to be developed at a minimum cost.

Its new body was designed by Ken Greenley and John Hefferman, who were both tutors at the Royal College of Art in London, and the panels were all handmade from rolled alloy, as with the previous V8. Under the skin, the Virage was little different from the car it replaced. Finances meant that many of the components were carried over, including the proven 5.3-litre (326cu in) V8 engine, although this was shipped out to Callaway engineering in the United States to be reworked. It came back with a catalytic converter to meet new emissions legislation, and a new four-valves-per-cylinder head, along with a power boost to 310bhp (231kW). The Virage was a heavy car, though, so, unless you

bought the even more potent 330bhp (246kW) Vantage version, the performance difference was negligible. A convertible Volante appeared in 1993 and the Virage soldiered on until 2002.

ENGINE: 5340cc (326cu in), eight-cylinder
POWER: 330bhp (246kW)
0–60MPH (96KM/H): 6.8 seconds
TOP SPEED: 253km/h (157mph)
PRODUCTION TOTAL: n/a

ALFA ROMEO SZ

ITALY 1989

Although not conventionally pretty, the Alfa Romeo SZ is certainly a distinctive and imposing car. First seen at the 1989 Geneva Motor Show, the SZ was based on a shortened version of the Alfa Romeo 75 saloon

Long after its debut, the Alfa Romeo SZ remains the only mainstream production car to have featured six headlights.

platform, complete with rear transaxle and lively 3.0-litre (183cu in) V6 engine.

Styled by Zagato, the car had six headlights and a distinctive Alfa Romeo shield built into the frontal styling, while a large glass area and unusual mixed angles all over the side bodywork tended to polarize opinion. Under the skin, the 75's suspension was modified by Giorgio Pianta, who was manager of the successful Lancia

rally team, while all models had a hydraulically adjustable ride height.

The SZ name stood for Stile Zagato, and all of the cars were finished in the same colour – bright red. This was because the thermoplastic body panels were injection-moulded in colour, and only one alternative was produced – a black car owned by Andrea Zagato himself.

The SZ was joined by a soft-top RZ model (for Roadster Zagato) in

1993, which was available in red, yellow or black to add more diversity to the colour range. Over a four-year period, 1000 SZs were made and 800 RZs.

ENGINE: 2959cc (183cu in), six-cylinder
POWER: 210bhp (157kW) at 6300rpm
0–60MPH (96KM/H): 6.9 seconds
TOP SPEED: 247km/h (153mph)
PRODUCTION TOTAL: 1800

CITROËN XM

FRANCE 1989–2000

Voted European Car of the Year at its launch, the Citroën XM was an intriguing and typical French interpretation of a luxury car. Styled by Bertone, the XM had a distinctive wedge-shaped profile, with a sharply drooping nose and an exceptionally comfortable cabin. The car had immense rear legroom and a clever glass divider in the rear, which kept the back-seat occupants snug while the tailgate was open.

The XM shared its floorpan with the much duller Peugeot 605, but, rather than stick with the Peugeot's standard suspension, Citroën fitted the XM with its famous hydraulic system, which settled to the ground when the engine was switched off and lifted the car up when running so that it drove around on a cushion of air – a combination that delivered a great ride and surefooted handling. Engine choices were a 2.0-litre (122cu in) four-cylinder

petrol, a 2.1-litre (129cu in) turbo diesel and a range-topping 3.0-litre (183cu in) V6 unit, which was incredibly smooth, but also had a thirst for fuel.

A truly massive XM estate (station wagon) appeared in 1992 and had a greater payload than many car-derived panel vans, making it very much a multipurpose vehicle. From 1994, face-lifted 'Phase 2' cars had softer frontal styling and a more conventional dashboard. Although

criticized when new for (often trivial) reliability problems, the XM today has a cult following and is regarded by many as the last truly mad, individualist big Citroën.

ENGINE: 1998cc (122cu in), four-cylinder
POWER: 135bhp (100kW) at 5500rpm
0–60MPH (96KM/H): 9.1 seconds
TOP SPEED: 205km/h (127mph)
PRODUCTION TOTAL: 330,000

PANTHER SOLO

UNITED KINGDOM 1989–90

Styled by Ken Greenley, who was responsible for the Aston Martin Virage, the Panther Solo was touted as a great British supercar

when it debuted at the 1989 London Motorfair. Built from a combination of aluminium and composite glassfibre, the Solo was

a striking-looking two-door sports car. It was built on a tubular steel chassis and powered by the 204bhp (152kW) engine from the

Ford Sierra Sapphire Cosworth, with its power fed through a Ferguson Formula four-wheel drive set-up.

The car received a positive response from the motoring media, who may have criticized its lack of top-end performance and refinement, but certainly had no qualms about its tenacious grip, superb handling balance and thrilling acceleration. But the car's promise was stunted almost as soon as it had appeared.

Even from the outset, Panther had said it would build only 100 cars, primarily to prove what it was capable of and mark the way forwards for future development. Extortionate development costs led the company into financial difficulties, however, and Panther went into receivership after only 12 cars had been completed, never to appear again.

ENGINE: 1993cc (123cu in), four-cylinder
POWER: 204bhp (152kW)
0–60MPH (96KM/H): 6.8 seconds
TOP SPEED: 232km/h (144mph)
PRODUCTION TOTAL: 12

FERRARI MONDIAL T

ITALY 1989–93

Ferrari's cheapest model was an almost cynical attempt to cash in on the strength of its name, by reviving an old model and equipping it with the mechanical parts of a newer version in order to appeal to those who could not afford the more expensive, better looking 348.

Based on the old 308 GT4, the Mondial T had subtle side strakes, a rounded front end and twin circular taillights, along with a longitudinal mid-mounted V8 engine. The unit was a detuned version of that in the 348 and had a displacement of 3405cc (208cu in), producing 300bhp (224kW). Coupé and convertible versions of the Mondial T were offered, but, despite the fairly high-power output, performance was swift rather than mind-blowing.

Purists derided the Mondial T, claiming that its ABS brakes, power steering and relatively low price tag made it a soft, diluted alternative to a true Ferrari, but in reality it was quite a desirable car, made all the more attractive by its relatively affordable tag. It was also one of the company's most user-friendly models. In other words, the Mondial T was a very rare beast – a Ferrari you could live with on a day-to-day basis without making any major compromises.

ENGINE: 3405cc (208cu in), eight-cylinder
POWER: 300bhp (224kW)
0–60MPH (96KM/H): 6.3 seconds
TOP SPEED: 254km/h (158mph)
PRODUCTION TOTAL: n/a

VAUXHALL LOTUS CARLTON

UNITED KINGDOM 1989–93

Few cars have caused quite as much media controversy as the Vauxhall Lotus Carlton. When it was launched, the car was the fastest saloon car ever made. Its official top speed of 285km/h (177mph) was colossally quick, and the fact that the vehicle on which it was based was a family car caused outrage from some of the more conservative sectors of the media. This did not deter Vauxhall – the more exposure the car received, the greater the interest from true motoring enthusiasts.

The Lotus Carlton's engine was hand-built, using the 3.0-litre straight-six unit from the standard Carlton 3000GSi as a base, but with an increased bore and stroke, and a Lotus-developed 24-valve cylinder head. The turbocharged engine was incredible, delivering masses of torque and supercar-like acceleration. A number of cars tested at much higher speeds than the official figure, suggesting that this was a conservative estimate. It is a good thing, then, that Lotus thoroughly sorted the already decent Carlton chassis, with its superb steering and incredible grip.

ENGINE: 3615cc (221cu in), six-cylinder
POWER: 377bhp (281kW)
0–60MPH (96KM/H): 5.1 seconds
TOP SPEED: 283km/h (177mph)
PRODUCTION TOTAL: 440

LOTUS ELAN FWD

UNITED KINGDOM 1989–94

The decision to revive the Elan name was greeted with enthusiasm by fans of Lotus, but treated with some suspicion when Lotus announced that the car would be its first front-wheel drive model.

It revived an old name, but the new, luxurious, front-wheel drive Elan had little in common with its predecessor.

They need not have worried. The Elan was a fabulous car to drive, with superb steering, immense grip and perfect weight distribution, thanks to its lightweight 1588cc (97cu in) engine. The powerplant itself was an Isuzu unit, which Lotus had secured use of as part of a deal it did with the Japanese company when it worked on the chassis of the Isuzu Piazza Turbo.

The Elan was styled by Peter Stevens and shared the company's familiar face, with a rounded, low nose and pop-up headlights, along with a gently sloped rear that echoed that of the bigger Esprit.

Initially, the Elan was a great success, but shortly after the car's launch it fell victim to a recession in Britain, forcing Lotus to drop the car in 1991. Lotus was taken over by Bugatti in 1993 (and later again by Proton) and the car was briefly revived, but was dropped in 1994 in readiness for the Elise's launch.

ENGINE: 1588cc (97cu in), four-cylinder
POWER: 165bhp (123kW)
0--60MPH (96KM/H): 6.6 seconds
TOP SPEED: 220km/h (137mph)
PRODUCTION TOTAL: 4657

MAZDA MX-5

Was it coincidence that the MX-5 appeared in the same year as the new Lotus Elan? After all, it was the Mazda that was closer in concept to Lotus's original 1960s model.

While Lotus was busy reviving the Elan's name, Mazda was busy reinventing its spirit in the form of the MX-5 – a simple, easy-to-maintain and basically engineered two-door sports car with a sharp rear-drive chassis, stubby gearchange and compact cabin that brought back completely the concept of open-top motoring on a relatively low budget.

The MX-5 was so true to the concept of the original Elan that it even managed to look like the little Lotus, causing obvious comparisons in the motoring press. It was also sensational to drive. Power outputs were modest at best, but this did little to put people off because power really was not important. The little Mazda's agile chassis and wonderful steering were more than enough to put a smile on the face of any keen driver, while the MX-5 had the added advantage of proven Japanese engineering, which made it infinitely more reliable than the

old British sports cars on which many of its buyers had previously cut their teeth.

Two engine choices were offered, a 1.6-litre (97cu in) and a 1.8-litre (110cu in), both of which had five-speed manual gearboxes, although a six-speed was an option on later models.

A second-generation MX-5 appeared in 1998, when newly introduced US safety legislation outlawed the original car's incredibly pretty pop-up headlights, forcing the MX-5 to develop a new and arguably less pretty front end. It was still a great car to drive, however, and remained incredibly popular right up until production ceased in 2005.

ENGINE: 1839cc (112cu in), four-cylinder
POWER: 140bhp (104kW)
0–60MPH (96KM/H): 8 seconds
TOP SPEED: 203km/h (127mph)
PRODUCTION TOTAL: n/a

ROVER 800 COUPÉ

A coupé version of the Rover 800 was on the drawing board as early as 1982, a whole four years before the company's new luxury flagship actually appeared. The car was considered essential if Rover was serious about returning to the US market, where the

Introduced too late and tarnished by the reputation of the other models in the same range, the Rover 800 Coupé was quite a different beast. Partially handbuilt, exquisitely trimmed and well made, it was curiously different from the norm.

popularity of 'personal coupés' had seen a boom in recent years. Rover's chief designer Roy Axe had already created a concept car, known as the 'XX', for evaluation.

Austin-Rover management decided to to delay the launch of the coupé until after the 800, which was badged 'Sterling' in the United States, had established itself in the US market. The Sterling brand appeared in the United States in the late 1980s, and dealers were crying out for the coupé straight away, forcing Rover to sign the car off for production. But the US business struggled, and Rover

pulled out of the US market in 1991. By this time, the Coupé was so far down the line that there was no point canning the project, so it was restyled along with the rest of the 800 range and sold in Europe, where, despite not having any obvious rivals, it sold fairly well.

This was partly because the coupé styling was so much more elegant than the 800 saloon and also because it was exceptionally well equipped, with hand-finished panels and a leather-trimmed cabin. Rover actually lost a lot of money on the 800 coupé project, but in the process produced one of its most intriguing and unusually desirable models of the 1990s.

ENGINE: 2675cc (163cu in), six-cylinder
POWER: 177bhp (132kW) at 6000rpm
0–60MPH (96KM/H): 8.0 seconds
TOP SPEED: 221km/h (137mph)
PRODUCTION TOTAL: about 10,500

JAGUAR XK8

Launched concurrently with the Aston Martin DB7, which shared its chassis, the XK8 was Jaguar's first eight-cylinder production car, using an all-new 4.0-litre (244cu in) powerplant called the AJ-V8.

Styled by Scottish designer Ian Callum, who headed up Jaguar's design team for over a decade, the XK was based on a heavily modified XJ-S platform and was available as

either a two-door coupé or as a convertible. In standard V8 form, the XK8 was swift enough, developing 290bhp (213kW) of power, but, for true performance fans, there was the supercharged XK8, which delivered an awesome 390bhp (287kW) and could out-accelerate some more focused supercars, albeit without quite the same handling agility.

Indeed, it was the XK8's chassis that was its most criticized aspect. Some road testers loved it for its tail-happy characteristics, but it lacked refinement and it was very difficult to recover if it stepped out of line. Cars built from 2003 on had a much better chassis set-up.

The XKR 100 was the ultimate derivative of the XK8, introduced in 2002 to mark Jaguar's centenary. It

had a unique Anthracite paint finish, 51cm (20in) polished alloy wheels and a cream leather interior.

ENGINE: 4.0-litre (244cu in), eight-cylinder
POWER: 390bhp (287kW) at 5500rpm
0–60MPH (96KM/H): 5.9 seconds
TOP SPEED: 250km/h (155mph)
PRODUCTION TOTAL: 86,000

After more than 20 years, Jaguar finally replaced the XJ-S with a car that was instantly desirable. The XK8 was a huge hit, and was sold as both a coupé and a convertible. It shared the chassis of the Aston Martin DB7.

PEUGEOT 406 PININFARINA COUPÉ

FRANCE 1996–2004

Peugeot's 406 saloon was a fairly competent and handsome family car, but not an especially exciting one. From its launch, however, development of a coupé version had been mooted.

Expectations were not especially high, even when Peugeot announced that the car would be designed and built on its behalf by Italian design house Pininfarina –

but, when the covers came off the car at the 1996 Paris Motor Show, the critics were silenced instantly. Put simply, the 406 coupé was stunning, its lithe two-door body, slimline headlights, narrow nose and flared rear end gave it the appearance of a scaled-down Ferrari 456GT. It really did not matter that the 406 coupé was no better to drive than the 406 saloon,

nor did it make a huge difference that only the 3.0-litre (180cu in) V6-engined variant had any kind of performance appeal, because the coupé was such a good-looking car. It accounted for at least one in ten of all 406s built and even spawned a diesel-engine variant to make it popular with company car drivers. When it went out of production in 2004 to make way

for the Peugeot 407, dealers reported a flurry of orders from customers who knew they would never have a chance to buy another.

ENGINE: 2946cc (180cu in), six-cylinder
POWER: 210bhp (157kW) at 6000rpm
0–60MPH (96KM/H): 7.9 seconds
TOP SPEED: 235km/h (146mph)
PRODUCTION TOTAL: n/a

FERRARI F50

ITALY 1996–97

Launched to mark Ferrrari's fiftieth anniversary, the F50 was first seen in 1995, but production did not start until the following year. Available only as a two-door two-seat convertible, the car was built on an aluminium spaceframe chassis and was powered by a mid-mounted 4.7-litre (287cu in) V12 engine with five valves per

cylinder, making it the world's first 60-valve production engine. The powerplant was a road-tuned version of that used in Ferrari's Formula One racing car, as raced by Michael Schumacher, which made quite a selling point.

Performance was phenomenal, with an incredible power output of 513bhp (383kW). It could easily

reach 325km/h (202mph) and accelerate almost as quickly as the Formula One car with which it shared its mechanical components.

Only 349 cars were ever made – Ferrari had estimated it could sell 350, so deliberately built one fewer than the market demand to ensure that the car would always remain sought after by collectors,

a theory borne out by the fact that even today prices regularly reach seven figures. Although only ever sold as a convertible, there was one coupé version of the F50 built. Called the Bolide, the car was commissioned by the Sultan of Brunei, who said an open-topped version would not suit the conditions in which he drove. The Bolide was never an official model and was completely reengineered to accept the new bodywork, which the sultan himself paid for to be commissioned and built in-house at Ferrari's Maranello factory.

ENGINE: 4698cc (287cu in), 12-cylinder
POWER: 513bhp (383kW) at 8000rpm
0–60MPH (96KM/H): 3.7 seconds
TOP SPEED: 325km/h (202mph)
PRODUCTION TOTAL: 349

As close as you can get to a road going race car? The F50 was powered by Ferrari's Formula One racing engine.

BMW Z8

Known internally as the E52, the BMW Z8 was designed to recall the look of the original 507 Cabriolet of 1956–59, a car globally regarded today as stunningly beautiful and highly collectable.

It was first seen at the Z07 prototype at the 1997 Tokyo Motor Show, where BMW announced that

the car would go into production and would be built at BMW's US factory in South Carolina.

When it debuted in 1998, the Z8 was almost unchanged from the Z07 concept, although the windscreen had to be slightly higher to meet crash safety regulations, and the front air dam

was made larger to aid cooling of the tightly packed V8 engine.

Inside, the car featured a very retro-styled cabin, with ivory-coloured dials and switches, and red leather trim. Beneath the styling, however, the Z8 was every inch a modern car, with all-alloy monocoque construction and the

same gutsy V8 engine as fitted to the M5 saloon.

The car received a good reception when it was launched, although road testers observed that it was very much a cruising car rather than a real sports model, thanks largely to its harsh ride and lack of real dynamics. Despite this, BMW managed to sell every single car it planned to build over a three-year production cycle, and the Z8 developed a cult following. It also starred on the silver screen in the James Bond movie *The World Is Not Enough*, which was released in 1999.

Engine: 4941cc (302cu in), eight-cylinder
Power: 394bhp (294kW) at 6600rpm
0–60mph (96km/h): 4.7 seconds
Top speed: 250km.h (155mph)
Production total: 2307

Stunning retro-styling and a lusty V8 engine happily disguised any of the Z8's dynamic shortcomings – it sold out instantly.

ASTON MARTIN VANQUISH

The Vanquish, or V12 Vanquish, to give it its proper title, was designed by Scotsman Ian Callum and saw a welcome return for James Bond to driving an Aston Martin, it being the official Bond car in the 2002 film *Die Another Day*. The Vanquish had been around long before that, as Ian Callum's original design was signed off in 1995. With the Virage order books still full, however, and the new DB7 on sale, Aston Martin decided to wait to bring the car to market, and at the same time develop an all-new engine.

The 5935cc (366cu in) engine was derived from Ford's 3.0-litre (183cu in) Duratec unit, and is effectively a pair of Duratec units fixed together. The incredible performance and prodigious torque that the unit produces show that this clearly is not a problem. In standard form, the Vanquish developed 460bhp (343kW), but

those wanting even more power could opt for the sportier Vanquish S, which developed 520bhp (388kW) and could reach 322km/h (200mph).

A convertible Volante model was added to the range in 2004 to give it even greater appeal, while the S had chassis and brake upgrades the same year to distinguish it further from the standard model.

The car was not without its faults, and much criticism was levelled at the amount of Ford switchgear that appeared in the cabin. Nonetheless, the Vanquish proved a great return to form for Aston Martin and a highly desirable supercar.

Engine: 5935cc (366cu in), 12-cylinder
Power: 520bhp (388kW) at 7000rpm
0–60mph (96km/h): 4.6 seconds
Top speed: 322km/h (200mph)
Production total: n/a

It was the car that saw James Bond ditch BMW and get back behind the wheel of an Aston Martin – the Vanquish had its first public unveiling in the movie *Die Another Day*.

JENSEN SV-8

Another of motoring's great might-have-beens, the Jensen SV-8 was an attempt at the start of the twenty-first century to revive one of the glorious names of the past. Launched at the 1998 Earls Court Motor Show in London, although it would take another

three years before it finally went on sale, the Jensen SV-8 was to be built in an all-new factory in Liverpool, England, where Jensen's new owners said 600 cars a year would be built. The company even held a factory open day to show journalists how it had invested in

state-of-the art paint rooms and production-line technology to bring the car to market.

Power would come from the popular 4.6-litre (281cu in) Ford Cobra V8 engine, as used in top versions of the Mustang, and would be installed in an all-steel

monocoque chassis, upon which was mounted an all-alloy body.

But it appeared that Jensen had perhaps invested too much in its new factory and its new staff. Despite having a full order book, the company went bankrupt in 2002, after only the first 20 cars had been built. A further 12 were assembled by SV Automotive Limited from the remaining spare parts, but most of those who ordered a Jensen never received their car, and the name appears to have now disappeared for good.

ENGINE: 4601cc (281cu in), eight-cylinder
POWER: 325bhp (242kW) at 6000rpm
0–60MPH (96KM/H): 4.8 seconds
TOP SPEED: 250km/h (155mph)
PRODUCTION TOTAL: 30

If only it had been given more time, the Jensen SV-8 might have been a success. But it never reached full-scale production.

LAMBORGHINI MURCIÉLAGO

ITALY 2002–PRESENT

Styled by eccentric Dutch designer Luc Donckerwolke, the Murciélago was the first all-new Lamborghini to be introduced with the VW Group in charge of the company. Its brief was simple: to create a car with all the presence of the Countach back in the mid-1970s and possessing blistering performance, and to equip it in finest Lamborghini tradition with a modernized version of the legendary V12 engine which had previously powered the Diablo and Countach.

The car made its debut in 2002 to universal acclaim – although not exactly pretty, the Murciélago has an enormous presence, and in true Lamborghini tradition it also took its name from a bull. Murciélago was a fighting animal that survived a record 24 sword strokes at a bullfight in Cordoba, Spain, in 1879, and has been a part of Spanish folklore ever since.

As well as the striking coupé, there is a roadster version of the

Murciélago, although owners are advised to remove the roof if they intend to travel over 225km/h (160mph), as otherwise it could simply be sucked off by the car's aerodynamic forces.

The most extreme version of the Murciélago is the LP640, which takes the V12 to a new extreme with 640bhp (471kW) and a colossal 660Nm (487lb/ft) of torque, along with an all-new six-speed 'paddle-shift' gearbox.

ENGINE: 6192cc (378cu in), 12-cylinder
POWER: 580bhp (433kW) at 7500rpm
0–60MPH (96KM/H): 3.8 seconds
TOP SPEED: 330km/h (205mph)
PRODUCTION TOTAL (n/a)

As wild and wacky as the Countach was back in the mid-1970s, the Murciélago marked a terrific return to form.

BENTLEY CONTINENTAL GT

UNITED KINGDOM 2002–PRESENT

First seen testing as early as 1999, the Bentley Continental GT arrived on the market after a long wait. The first Bentley to be entirely designed and developed by the VW Group, the newcomer had an incredible heritage to live up to, so VW had to get it right – and they did, with a new model that certainly caused a stir.

Designed by Dirk Van Braeckel, the Continental GT had flowing coupé bodywork that is difficult to

The first Bentley to be designed entirely under Volkswagen's stewardship, the Continental GT retains many of the marque's quintessential values.

appreciate the size of unless you see it in the metal, while inside it was pure Bentley, with thick pile carpets, the finest grain leather and a beautifully ornate burr walnut veneer dashboard.

The Continental GT was also the first production car to use a W12

engine, with four banks of three cylinders rather than two banks of six as you would find in a V12. The 5998cc (366cu in) unit delivered incredible torque and performance. Despite initial concerns about its technology being untried, it has proven thoroughly reliable.

A convertible model, called the GTC, was added to the range in 2005 to further broaden its appeal, although the enormous price tag meant that this car was always going to have limited appeal among the few who could afford to own it.

ENGINE: 5998cc (366cu in),
12-cylinder
POWER: 550bhp (411kW)
0–60MPH (96KM/H): 4.7 seconds
TOP SPEED: 312km/h (198mph)
PRODUCTION TOTAL: n/a

MORGAN AERO 8
UNITED KINGDOM 2002–PRESENT

Introduced in 2002, the Aero 8 was Morgan's first entirely new design since the Plus 8 appeared 34 years earlier. Unlike previous Morgans, which used a wooden frame bolted to a steel chassis, the Aero 8 has a computer-designed all-alloy chassis, although the wood frame for the car's internal box sections remains, just as Morgan's traditional customers would like it.

The subject of some controversy at the car's launch was Morgan's decision to use a BMW V8 engine, as traditionally the company's engines had always been sourced from British manufacturers. With the knowledge that the dependable Rover V8 that had powered several generations of Morgan was due to cease production, however, the company decided that it had to source a power unit roughly the

same size and weight as the Rover engine it had originally planned to use, and the BMW unit was the closest in concept.

The unusual looks also received some criticism, although the Aero 8 is nothing if not different, with its retro-styled body, inward-facing headlights and fluted taillights.

Like all of the company's models, the Aero 8 is assembled by hand in a small workshop in

the Cotswolds, and within a year of the Aero 8 going on sale there was already a two-year waiting list for a new one.

ENGINE: 4398cc (268cu in),
eight-cylinder
POWER: 325bhp (242kW) at 6100rpm
0–60MPH (96KM/H): 5.0 seconds
TOP SPEED: 258km/h (160mph)
PRODUCTION TOTAL: n/a

MCLAREN-MERCEDES SLR
UNITED KINGDOM 2003–PRESENT

ENGINE: 5439cc (332cu in),
eight-cylinder
POWER: 626bhp (467kW) at 6500rpm
0–60MPH (96KM/H): 3.6 seconds
TOP SPEED: 334km/h (210mph)
PRODUCTION TOTAL: n/a

An incredible machine matched only by its equally incredible price tag, the McLaren-Mercedes SLR is not so much a supercar as a 'Super GT'. Launched in 2003, the SLR recalls the glory of the original Mercedes 300SL Gullwing and even has similar-style openings for the doors. Rather than being a stripped-out race car for the road, it is a genuinely comfortable high-speed cruiser, with air conditioning, a multi-CD changer system, leather trim and electric seats.

Despite these concessions to comfort, the SLR is still remarkably quick. The V8 engine is derived from that of the McLaren Formula One racing car and is capable of 334km/h (210mph), making it the fastest production car ever at the time of its launch. Much of this was down to the lightweight materials used in the SLR's construction, with Kevlar panels, ceramic brakes, and a tubular alloy chassis. The car is assembled not by Mercedes, but by the McLaren racing team in England.

The ultimate version of the SLR is the 722 edition, named after Stirling Moss's racing number in the 1955 Mille Miglia race, which he won. The 722 produces a startling 650bhp (485kW) and has a top

speed of 337km/h (212mph). Since the introduction of the incredible Bugatti Veyron, it will have to go some way, however, to become once again the world's fastest production car.

Mercedes's fastest ever car owes its existence to the McLaren F1 racing team, which uses Mercedes engines. Between them, the two companies developed the fastest car of its day.

FORD GT
UNITED STATES 2003–2005

Launched to celebrate Ford's centenary in 2003, the GT made its debut at the 2002 Paris Motor Show and caused quite a stir. Designed by Ford's extrovert chief designer J. Mays, the car did not

so much draw inspiration from the legendary GT40 Le Mans 24-Hour winning cars as completely and honestly re-create them. The design is so similar to the original that it is easy to mistake them for each other.

In reality, the 2003 GT is slightly taller and a little longer than the original GT40, as well as being much more comfortable and easier to drive – although it has to be said that this is relative. Compared

to most cars of the same era as the new GT, it was very cramped, uncomfortable and impractical.

Not that this mattered, as Ford had achieved exactly what it desired to do. The company had created a car that sold out instantly and almost instantly became as much of a legend as the car which it re-created in spirit.

A limited production run was always on the cards, with only a handful of GTs allocated to each of Ford's markets. All examples were sold before the first car had even come off the production line. Among the GT's famous owners are Britain's most notorious motoring journalist *Top Gear* presenter Jeremy Clarkson and US chat show host Jay Leno.

ENGINE: 5409cc (330cu in),
  eight-cylinder
POWER: 550bhp (410kW)
0–60MPH (96KM/H): 3.5 seconds
TOP SPEED: 330km/h (205mph)
PRODUCTION TOTAL: 4302

Launched in 2003 to much acclaim, the Ford GT is a faithful reproduction of the all-conquering GT40 racing cars of the 1960s. All examples were sold before the first car had even come off the production line.

MG SV-R

ENGINE: 4996cc (305cu in),
  eight-cylinder
POWER: 400bhp (298kW) at 6000rpm
0–60MPH (96KM/H): 4.9 seconds
TOP SPEED: 284km/h (176mph)
PRODUCTION TOTAL: 78

Produced by MG Sports and Racing after it acquired the rights to the Italian Qvale Mangusta supercar, the MG XPower SV was an unusual launch from a company that was suffering from well-documented financial problems.

The SV was based on a tubular steel chassis with carbonfibre bodywork, and was powered by a 4.6-litre (281cu in) Ford Mustang V8, while the range-topping SV-R version, designed for motorsport homologation purposes, came with a 5.0-litre (305cu in) powerplant

developing 400bhp (298kW). All cars were built in the former de Tomaso plant in Modena, Italy, and were fine-tuned at MG's Sports and Racing headquarters in Birmingham, United Kingdom.

The car was first seen in 2003 as the X80 concept car. It was designed by Peter Stevens, who was formerly of Lotus fame, but had been employed by MG Rover since the mid-1990s as its chief stylist. When the SV debuted at the British Motor Show the next year, it looked even more aggressive, with huge cooling fins on the side and a dramatic-looking body kit.

The SV possessed incredible performance and was well received, although the rear-drive chassis could prove tricky to handle in damp or greasy conditions, and there were some initial concerns about build quality. These paled

into insignificance compared to concerns over MG Rover's future. SV production stopped abruptly in 2005, after only 78 cars had been completed, when the company called in the receivers.

Powered by a Ford Mustang engine and developed by De Tomaso, the MG SV-R was an interesting project, but was doomed by parent company MG Rover's financial woes.

BUGATTI VEYRON

The fastest car ever made, the Veyron is quite an engineering achievement. Named after legendary Bugatti racing driver Pierre Veyron, it was finally launched in 2005 after a six-year gestation period, during which time VW's engineers set themselves the task of building an engine that could produce in excess of 1000bhp (745.7kW). That engine was the world's first and only W16 powerplant, with four banks of four cylinders.

The engine is so powerful that it can transmit its power to the road only via a sequential automatic 'DSG' gearbox; if a conventional manual shift were used, the clutch would wear out every time the car was driven away from a standing start, such is the prodigious power

and torque output. Remarkably engineered and undeniably fast, the car is also reported as being fairly difficult to handle. The immense power makes the rear wheels spin even on a gentle throttle, while the bodywork is so low that on anything other than a super-smooth surface it is at risk of bottoming out.

Regardless, there is no question at all that the Bugatti Veyron will be remembered as one of the all-time greats of motoring.

ENGINE: 7993cc (488cu in), 16-cylinder
POWER: 1006bhp (750kW)
0–60MPH (96KM/H): 2.5 seconds
TOP SPEED: 408km/h (254mph)
PRODUCTION TOTAL: n/a

The world's fastest ever car by quite some margin, the sensational Bugatti Veyron produces in excess of 1000bhp from the world's first and only W16 powerplant, with four banks of four cylinders.

INDEX

PICTURE CREDITS